THE MONSTER BOOK

BY CHRISTOPHER GOLDEN,

STEPHEN R. BISSETTE, AND THOMAS E. SNIEGOSKI

SIMON PULSE

New York London Toronto Sydney Singapore

Special thanks to the following people:

Debbie Olshan and Caroline Kallas

Nancy Pines, Patricia MacDonald, Kara Welsh, Donna O'Neill,
Gina DiMarco, John Vairo Jr., Penny Haynes, Brian Blatz, Lisa Feuer,
Linda Dingler, Twisne Fan, Rodger Weinfeld, Kathryn Briggs-Gordon,
Margaret Clark, Ian Jackman, Marjorie Hanlon,
Rebecca Springer, and Jennifer Robinson

Editor: Lisa A. Clancy
Editorial Team: Elizabeth Shiflett and Micol Ostow
First Simon Pulse edition July 2002
First Pocket Books trade paperback printing August 2000

Simon Pulse
An imprint of Simon & Schuster
Children's Publishing Division
1230 Avenue of the Americas, New York, NY 10020-1586

DESIGNED BY: Lili Schwartz

Printed in the U.S.A.
ISBN: 0-671-04259-9

4 6 8 10 9 7 5

DEDICATIONS

For Lisa Clancy,
Caroline Kallas, and
Debbie Olshan.
Blood from a stone.
Heh heh.
—C. G.

To Rick, Kathie,
Maia Rose, and Daniel...
(Brother, Sister,
Daughter, Son)
... for the Blood is the Life.
—S. R. B.

For LeeAnne.
Without her love, patience,
and hard work, this book
would never have been
completed.
—T. E. S.

ACKNOWLEDGMENTS

CHRISTOPHER GOLDEN would like to thank: Connie, for her infinite patience and support; the Boston Bronzers (actual and honorary), for their enthusiasm and concern; Little Willow for help beyond the call of duty; Lori Perkins; Micol Ostow; Liz Shiflett; and Beth Gwinn. Special thanks to Joss Whedon, David Greenwalt, Marti Noxon, Jane Espenson, David Fury, Doug Petrie, Todd McIntosh, Dean Batali, and Rob Des Hotel for their time. Thanks also to Jamie, for watching all those *Creature Features* with me, and my mother, Roberta, for allowing us to be both frightened and inspired.

STEPHEN R. BISSETTE wishes to thank: Marjory Bleier, first and foremost, along with: Maia Rose and Daniel Bissette, whose considerable help with the Bogeymen chapter proved I've raised 'em right; David Holzapfel and Marlboro Elementary School; Alan Goldstein, April Stage, and everyone at First Run Video; Donna Frank and Pete Powers at WEQX-FM in Manchester, Vermont; Karen and Gary at Austin's Antiquarian Books; Rob at the late, lamented Mystery/Trek; Del at Dark Delicacies; G. Michael Dobbs; Chris Stewart at protoncharging.com; Michael Bleier; Noah Kitty; Jean-Marc and Randy Lofficier; Michael H. Price; Marlene O'Connor; John Morrow and Jon B. Cooke; Kim Newman; Stephen Jones; Don Markstein; Scott Shaw!; Rick Bradford; Jim Hanley; Tad Stones; Rich Morrissey; Gene Phillips; John Green; Chris Medellin; John Dorrian; Eric Hess; and Rick Veitch, Steve Conley, "Mute," "Blinky," "Heckboy," "Hugo," "YDunc," and "Sir Jon" for help via comicon.com; Mom and Dad for indulging this lifelong obsession with (gulp) monsters; and, of course, Lori, and Lisa, for everything.

THOMAS E. SNIEGOSKI would like to thank: Mom and Dad; Mom and Dad Fogg; the guys at Cole's Comics; Dave Krause; Lori Perkins; Lisa Clancy; and a special thanks to Susan Parsons for her invaluable assistance and for showing me that there was a light at the end of the tunnel.

CONTENTS

v INTRODUCTION

1 DEMONS

89 VAMPIRES

161 MAGIC USERS

211 PRIMALS

257 GHOSTS

289 THE WALKING DEAD

329 BOGEYMEN

347 INVISIBLE PEOPLE

359 FAITH AND THE HUMAN MONSTER

INTRODUCTION

The Mythology

BUFFY THE VAMPIRE SLAYER debuted on the WB television network on March 10, 1997. As captivatingly played by Sarah Michelle Gellar, Buffy Summers is a young woman who is not at all thrilled that she has been chosen by "The Powers That Be" to receive special abilities and become a warrior against the forces of darkness.

With its balance of humor and drama—and perhaps most important, the way it used monsters as metaphor for the real social and emotional problems faced by teens—the series struck a nerve and became an instant hit for the burgeoning network. By the beginning of its fourth season in the fall of 1999, it had spun off a second series revolving around Angel, the charismatic "good" vampire who had become Buffy's one true love.

Monsters are not merely metaphor, however. *Buffy the Vampire Slayer* has brought horror, the supernatural, and all their trappings back into popular culture with an enthusiasm unmatched in recent memory. Vampires, werewolves, zombies, witches, ghosts, demons, and so many more . . . they're all on *Buffy*. Consequently, they're all in *here*.

The Monster Book catalogs every major supernatural creature to have crawled across the TV screen in the series' first four seasons. It explores the *Buffy* mythology, revealing heretofore unknown information about the nature of vampires, demons, and other monsters on the series. In these pages, you'll find interviews with the writers and producers of the show, as well as its creator, **Joss Whedon,** in which they discuss the monsters on the series, the mythology, and the influences and inspirations that are always with them when working on the show.

But *The Monster Book* is more than that. In addition to all the material on the universe of *Buffy the Vampire Slayer*, this volume includes an exhaustively researched history of monsters in folklore and popular culture, providing an enormous reference text, a tale of the way frightening myths have developed into entertainment, and the evolution of monsters in the consciousness of Western civilization that contributed to the creation of *Buffy the Vampire Slayer*.

So, what do you need to know?

At Hemery High School in Los Angeles, popular sixteen-year-old **Buffy Summers** discovered that she had been mystically chosen to fight the forces of darkness. The **Council of Watchers**—an international group based in London that has trained and guided Slayers for centuries—sent a Watcher named **Merrick** to aid her. After training her, he was killed. During a battle against vampires at Hemery, she was forced to burn down the gymnasium, and was subsequently expelled.

Her parents, **Hank** and **Joyce Summers,** then divorced, and the Slayer moved with her mother to **Sunnydale,** California, about two hours away on the southern California seacoast. Though she had hoped to abandon the responsibilities of the **Chosen One,**

Buffy soon discovered that her relocation to Sunnydale had been no accident of fate. Rather, the Powers That Be had somehow influenced her life and that of her mother so that they would settle there.

Sunnydale is located on a **Hellmouth,** a place where the barrier that separates Earth from the multitude of demon dimensions is worn thin. Another Watcher, **Rupert Giles,** was sent to continue her training and guidance. Along with Giles and her closest friends—**Willow Rosenberg** and **Xander Harris**—Buffy has continued the battle against vampires, demons, and other monsters through high school and into college. She wishes for a normal life, but Buffy takes her duties as the Slayer very seriously.

Shortly after her arrival in Sunnydale, Buffy met a vampire named **Angel,** unique in that he was—as far as we know—the only vampire in the world to also have a human soul (see Vampires: Angel). After he had made a name for himself as Angelus, the cruelest vampire in existence, he was cursed with the return of his soul, which allowed him to feel the guilt of all that he had done. By the time Buffy met him, Angel was seeking redemption for the horrors he once perpetrated.

Their relationship was filled with tribulation. When they made love—Buffy's first time—a new part of the curse was set in motion and Angel became a murdering, savage monster again. The curse was cast a second time, and his human soul returned. Despite their love for each other, it became clear that their relationship could not work. Angel was immortal and would not age. Buffy could not marry or have children with Angel and would grow old, whereas he would stay ever young. He eventually left Sunnydale for Los Angeles (and his own series, *Angel*).

Buffy experienced other tragedies as well. During her sophomore year she was attacked by the vampire known as the **Master,** who drained some of her blood and left her to drown. She died, but Xander used CPR to revive her. That brief death activated a second Slayer named **Kendra,** who later came to Sunnydale, only to be murdered herself by the vampire **Drusilla.** In Kendra's wake came **Faith,** a Slayer who became Buffy's friend, only to switch sides and ally herself with the evil mayor of Sunnydale (see Faith and the Human Monster).

The Council fired Giles as Buffy's Watcher during her senior year, and replaced him with **Wesley Wyndam-Pryce.** At the end of her senior year, just before the chaos that would erupt at her graduation, Buffy told Wesley she would no longer take orders from the Council. She quit. Presently, as a student at the University of California at Sunnydale, she unofficially continues with the duties of the Slayer, to fight the forces of darkness wherever they arise.

As noted, monsters frequently are metaphors on Buffy, most often representing some of life's unpleasant truths. It is a story of mythic proportions, about a hero and her journey of self-discovery. But it is also the story of one American teenager, with all the hopes and fears that implies.

"The show is designed to . . . work on the mythic structure of a hero's journey. Just to reframe that as the growth of an adolescent girl," Joss Whedon told National Public Radio. "The things she has to go through—losing her virginity, dying and coming back to life—are meant to be mythic, and yet they're meant to be extremely personal."

As such, there is a great deal more to Buffy's story. (See *Buffy the Vampire Slayer: The Watcher's Guide*, volumes 1 and 2.) But *The Monster Book* is, of course, about the monsters.

Joss Whedon and his staff love monsters, but their interest goes deeper than that, particularly Whedon's.

"As a child, I was afraid of a lot of stuff. I've always been attracted to horror," he told Michael Silverberg of NPR. "There is an element of being a child within it that I can't get away from. Grown-up horror is different. That's something I'm just learning about as I gradually and all too slowly *become* a grown-up. There's something about the way a child experiences pure horror—the innocence and yet the almost unseemly attraction children have to that—that is, to me, the most primal and interesting. Where there's horror, I tend to find youth and growth.

"I think there's a lot of people out there who say we must not have horror in any form, we must not say scary things to children because it will make them evil and disturbed. . . . That offends me deeply, because the world is a scary and horrifying place, and everyone's going to get old and die, if they're that lucky. To set children up to think that everything is sunshine and roses is doing them a great disservice. Children need horror because there are things they don't understand. It helps them to codify it if it is mythologized, if it's put into the context of a story, whether the story has a happy ending or not. If it scares them and shows them a little bit of the dark side of the world that is there and always will be, it's helping them out when they have to face it as adults."

The Influences

WITHOUT A DOUBT, Joss Whedon has his own very unique frame of reference. Everyone does, and yet those frames of reference, those influences and inspirations, seem to have more power in the minds of creative individuals.

When it came to working on *Buffy*—both his script for the 1992 film version and the TV series he has shepherded from Day One—Whedon was able to draw on his own frame of reference to create a singular vision. Though inspired by films, comic books, books, myths, and television, Whedon crafted something wholly original with *Buffy the Vampire Slayer*.

In order to get a peek into the creator's mind and the minds of the writers working on the show day by day, we spoke with them about their "monster memories," the pop-culture images and stories that have stayed with them over the years.

Whedon fondly recalls director George A. Romero's *Living Dead* trilogy, also noting that "there are influences on the show like *The Lost Boys*, the remake of *The Blob,* and *Night of the Comet*." But he makes it clear that the monsters on the series are not based on any one template.

"In terms of the monsters, there is no one absolute." For instance, he notes that "we refer to Ted [from the episode of the same name] as *The Stepfather-Terminator-Collector*," revealing only three of the films that contributed to the frame of reference for a single character.

When explaining an idea or atmosphere to his staff, he often makes movie references. But the frame of reference is not made up entirely of science fiction and horror. "Sometimes it's like, 'Watch *Dracula*, watch *Day of the Dead*, watch *Places in the Heart*,'" he explains.

Interestingly, Whedon has also found inspiration in a more recent motion picture release. "For me," he says, "all movies should be *The Matrix. The Matrix* is the beginning and end of all films."

David Greenwalt, the executive producer of *Angel* and consulting producer of *Buffy*, who has written many episodes for both series, also recalls the impact certain films have made on him.

"The movie that was the most life-changing for me was Alfred Hitchcock's *Psycho*," Greenwalt says. "I went to see a movie by the guy who made that charming *North by Northwest* the year before, and had the living bejesus scared out of me. I realized that films could touch you so deeply and scare you on such a deep level."

Until he began to work with Joss Whedon on *Buffy the Vampire Slayer*, Greenwalt notes, he was not "a gigantic horror genre or comic-book fan. I didn't realize the power of myth—and how demons and myth can collide to create powerful metaphors—until I learned the ways of the high-school-as-hell metaphor from Joss."

Just as Joss Whedon creates monsters to reflect real-world concerns, Greenwalt reinforces the notion that on this series, the supernatural is not nearly as important as the all-too-real.

"I generally don't just think, 'Ooh, what's scary,' but 'What's your deepest fear?' The first episode I ever wrote was 'Teacher's Pet.' This is a deep fear of mine: that the beautiful woman you love is actually a gigantic bug who wants to eat your head. So I think the metaphor there is fairly obvious. In 'Nightmares,' which Joss and I wrote together, what was frightening to me was someone you love—like a parental figure—telling you something terrible about yourself, which you believe in your heart of hearts is true, though it isn't really true at all. There's the scene where Buffy's father says, 'Your mother and I split up because of you, it's all your fault.'"

Writer and supervising producer **Marti Noxon** has her own disturbing movie memories.

"One of the first things I remember getting terrified about was *The Exorcist*, and I didn't even see the movie. I was too young," she recalls. "But I remember my mother going out on dates and stuff—she was single at that time—and I would stand at the door as she left and say 'Don't see *The Exorcist!*' I was so afraid of just the idea that she would see it and get really scared. I was afraid of the movie and the ideas in the movie, and I was afraid that I would get possessed."

The movies weren't the only source of anxiety for Noxon, however.

"*Planet of the Apes* was on television. I had a TV in my room and I was a total insomniac. I stayed up watching TV, and I caught either the movie or the TV show. I was really little, and for months I thought there were apes in the house.

"The macabre played a huge part in my mythology and childhood. I had a lot of rituals and games that I'd play to keep the monsters away. My family situation was pretty rough. My dad left when I was eight, and there were a lot of problems in my family and I felt really alone in the world. Trying to explain things was really important to me, but I couldn't put a name to my dread, this feeling of being afraid all the time. So monsters became a really big thing. They were my way of saying 'I'm scared.'"

As an adult, Noxon brought all those concepts and lessons to her work on television. Many of her pop-culture inspirations and influences have stayed with her as well. "I love *The Twilight Zone* and *The Outer Limits* in reruns," she says, then adds the movies "*Futureworld, Westworld, Logan's Run*. The one that scared the crap out of me was *Soylent Green*."

Writer and executive story editor **Douglas Petrie** has come at *Buffy* from another angle: he shares Joss Whedon's passion for comic books.

"Growing up, I was an enormous fan of Marvel Comics. In the seventies, that was everything I lived for," Petrie recalls fondly. "*Spider-Man* and *Fantastic Four* were huge. When John Byrne and Chris Claremont took over *X-Men*, I was just addicted to it. Everything that Marvel Comics did, from 1975 to Frank Miller's run on *Daredevil*, I absorbed completely and that's become a huge part of my vocabulary.

The writers of *Buffy:* (from left) Marti Noxon (seated), David Fury, Tracey Forbes, Jane Espenson, Doug Petrie, Joss Whedon (seated), and David Greenwalt (not pictured)

"Anything Frank Miller has done has crept so far into what we do here. For inspiration for Faith, I read [Miller's graphic novel] *Elektra Lives Again* about a hundred times. In a different, teen, punkier context, Faith is so much like Elektra.

"I loved Gene Colan's art. *Tomb of Dracula* was interesting because it genuinely scared me. That was the comic you'd read on a rainy Sunday. It was actually creepy and dark, and it seemed so grown-up.

"It was tough for me to follow *Dr. Strange* a little, in that his powers were so broad and never really clearly defined. I loved the character, I loved his cool New York City apartment. But like Joss is always saying, 'Iron Man, I get it. A guy with a bad heart who fights evil in an iron suit.' Dr. Strange was always so much more amorphous than that, but I did love it."

Co-producer and writer **Jane Espenson** reveals that she was "drawn to *Buffy* because of the comedy. I started out in sitcoms. However, I recently wrote *Texas Chainsaw Massacre 5*, because they wanted to have a *Buffy* kind of feel to it, and I wrote it, as much as I could, as a comedy. I think what makes *Buffy* special, what makes it work, is the perfect balance between the two. If you concentrate too much on the horror, you're missing something."

As a teen, she notes, Espenson was not very interested in horror films. "But I read the original novels of *Dracula* and *Frankenstein*. I enjoyed the way they made the monsters real; you could get inside their heads. I liked the idea that the bad guys were as well-motivated as the good guys."

Writer/producer **David Fury,** who grew up on Long Island in New York, recalls, "There were two shows opposite each other on Saturday nights when I was a kid, *Creature Feature* and *Chiller Theatre*. This was before VCRs of course. They were great old B-movies, sometimes C, very rarely A. Some of my favorite memories were watching those. I was very into the classic Universal monster movies. Including *Creature from the Black Lagoon*, which led into my very first *Buffy* episode, 'Go Fish.'"

"I didn't get to read a lot. I saw the occasional *Tales from the Crypt* comic book. When I was younger, horror was such a visual, visceral thing, it didn't occur to me that I could read and get scared quite as well as I could watching little brain monsters or something crawling around."

Little brain monsters haven't shown up on *Buffy* yet, but anything is possible, as evidenced by the menagerie of creatures that have already appeared on the series. Although all of the major monster archetypes have been touched on to some degree or other—vampires, werewolves, mummies, zombies, Frankenstein's monster, the Creature from the Black Lagoon, invisible people, ghosts, bogeymen, demons—they have all been explored in new ways by the inventive writers behind this series. Demons and vampires in particular have been redefined for the twenty-first century by Joss Whedon.

So, what specifically will you find herein? Well, monsters of course. But the definition of the word *monster* is a pliable one (something we'll address in more depth in our final chapter, Faith and the Human Monster). For the most part, we have determined a monster to be anything that is more or less than human, with powers or abilities usually of supernatural origin. Though a large majority of the "monsters" on *Buffy the Vampire Slayer* are evil, they certainly cannot all be categorized that way. Willow Rosenberg, for instance, is a witch. In truth, with this widest of definitions, Buffy herself could be considered a monster. So we narrowed our parameters a bit more than that.

In the following chapters, you will find examinations of the major categories of monsters from the series—demons, vampires, magic users, primals, ghosts, the walking dead, bogeymen, invisible people—with entries detailing the introduction, activities, and current status of every significant individual monster that has appeared in the first four seasons of *Buffy the Vampire Slayer.* (All right, three and three-quarters. We're already past deadline, so we might miss a few from the last episodes of the fourth season.)

Some monsters were left out of the book because they were simply too insignificant to include. Vampire henchman #27, for instance, didn't make the cut. On the

other hand, **the Bezoar**, from season two's "Bad Eggs," didn't make it in because there was simply no logical way to categorize them. They were not demons, but rather some sort of prehuman race, more a previously unknown animal than anything else. For the most part, though, you'll find them all right here.

Through original interviews with Joss Whedon and many members of the series' writing staff, we'll cover most of the major influences on the series, in the writers' own words.

Believe it or not, that's only half the story. For the other half of each chapter is an in-depth folklore and pop-culture history of each variety of monster. Monsters are fascinating, true, but equally interesting is the history behind each one. Why do we fear bogeymen? Where did belief in witchcraft originate? Each chapter features an extensive background on the monster and archetypes in question, following them through myth and fairy tales right on up to books, comic books, TV, and movies. For research, reference, or simple curiosity, we have created a comprehensive chronicle of the monsters on *Buffy*, and all of the centuries of storytelling that laid the foundations for one of the most popular TV series today.

You might expect a book about the monsters on *Buffy the Vampire Slayer* to start with vampires. But let's not forget, the vampires of Joss Whedon's creation are demons first and foremost. So that's where we'll start. With Demons . . .

Buffy the Vampire Slayer

DEMONS

"THEY'RE JUST ANIMALS, MAN. PLAIN AND SIMPLE. GRANTED, A LITTLE RARER THAN THE ONES YOU GREW UP WITH ON THAT LITTLE FARM IN SMALLVILLE—"

—FORREST, EXPLAINING HIS THEORY ABOUT DEMONS TO RILEY—JUST BEFORE ONE BREAKS FREE AND CHOKES HIM IN "DOOMED"

THE CONCEPT OF DEMONS is as old as humanity. In the earliest ages of man's sentience, our ancestors believed that their lives were guided and manipulated by supernatural beings, gods, and goddesses, some of whom were of malicious intent. In some cultures, those cruel deities had evil servants who were called demons. In others, the malevolent gods evolved over time into demons.

When creating *Buffy the Vampire Slayer*, Joss Whedon made an interesting choice. Most of the monsters on the series are demons of one sort or another, but despite the proliferation of and emphasis on Christian demons in Western pop culture (or perhaps because of it), the demons on *Buffy* have very few ties to that belief system.

In essence, the demons on *Buffy* are a variety of ancient, prehuman races who originally lived on earth. This approach is unusual, but not without precedent. Perhaps the best known and most influential precursor was the works of horror grandmaster H. P. Lovecraft. Lovecraft invented a new definition for demons or, as he called them, the Elder Gods (aka the Great Old Ones, a term Whedon has used on *Buffy*, via the Master's dialogue).

Like Lovecraft, Joss Whedon has put his own twist on demon lore, crafting a brand-new mythology for *Buffy the Vampire Slayer*.

"Demons, in their pure state, roamed the earth in evil fashion," Whedon explains. "When mammals, humans, and whatnot started to evolve, the demons got pushed out. Some of them fled. Some of them stayed but evolved into a more human form. Those are all lesser demons."

So where did the demons flee to?

"We don't think of it as hell, exactly," he elaborates. "It's a demon dimension, and we talk about more than one. The place Buffy went to [in the third season opener, "Anne"] was a demon dimension that [certain characters] referred to as hell because that was their belief system. Lily thought she was in hell because that was where she thought she deserved to go. The demon Ken was just playing off that. It wasn't a Christian hell, per se. It was just a really, really shitty place."

LILY: "I always knew I would come here...sooner or later...I knew I belonged here...."
BUFFY: "Where?"
LILY: "Hell."
BUFFY: "This isn't hell."
KEN: "Isn't it? What is hell, but the total absence of hope? The substance, the tactile proof of despair? You're right, Lily. This is where you've been heading all your life. You come from nothing, to become nothing." —**"ANNE"**

Rather than hell, in the Buffyverse there are multiple "demon dimensions," where the various evil, monstrous denizens of prehuman Earth now make their residence.

These are parallel worlds existing side by side with our own, in which the various races of demons wait for an opportunity to prey on humanity. There are, by all accounts, a great many demons and a great many such dimensions.

However, nearly all of the demons seen on the series are, according to Whedon, "lesser demons": those who are part human. Most of the full-blooded demons usually cannot make it across into this world.

"There are almost no pure demons left on earth," Whedon states. "But in the demon dimensions, there are bundles, just waiting to get out. We're beginning to see that there are some who are purer than others. They war amongst themselves; they look down upon each other. Some of them are actually okay. Some have integrated themselves into human society. There's definitely a hierarchy here, or at least, there are different races, and racism."

ANYA: "You've never seen a demon."
BUFFY: "Excuse me, killing them professionally for four years running…"
ANYA: "All the demons that walk the earth are tainted, human hybrids, like vampires. The Ascension means a human becomes *pure* demon. They're different."
BUFFY: "How?"
ANYA: "Well, for one thing, they're bigger." —**"GRADUATION DAY, PART ONE"**

In Sunnydale, of course, there is a Hellmouth. As previously described, it is a vulnerable place that is a constant target for malevolent forces on the earthly plane who wish to let the demons in, a kind of supernatural magnet drawing all manner of horrible creatures to Sunnydale.

> **"Dig a bit into the history of this town and I think you'll find there've been a steady stream of fairly odd occurrences. I believe this area is a center of mystical energy. Things gravitate toward it that you might not find elsewhere."**
> —**GILES, IN "WELCOME TO THE HELLMOUTH"**

When asked if there is more than one Hellmouth, Whedon answers simply enough: "Yes."

As for ever seeing another one on the series, he says that the producers "just don't have the money. We might address it, but again, the thing with *Buffy* is that we don't tend to get into the broader scope of the more fantastical issues unless it services a very personal story. It's not built like many fantasy shows. There are a hundred cool concepts and great twists and fun ideas and intense milieus that we'll never use because they don't relate to the personal experience of growing up and going to college. It's not designed like most fantasy shows. A lot of avenues we're just not going to take, even though we spend our own time talking about what does this mean and how does this work and isn't this cool."

Though most of the series's demons do not have any element of religious significance at all, there are exceptions. Vampires are also demons [see Vampires], and many of them fear the symbols of religious faith. Also, season three's Christmas-themed episode, "Amends," seems to come the closest to using a Christian template with the demon known only as the First.

Whedon confirms that this creature was the very first evil on earth, though he maintains that it should not be interpreted to be the Christian Satan.

"The concept of the First, along with the concept of whatever redemptive power saved Angel [in "Amends"]—which we refer to on *Angel* a lot as the Powers That Be—is being broached more and more. If [the First] does show up again, it will probably be on *Angel*. Just because that show deals with the more fantastical, Gothic themes of good and evil, and *Buffy* tends to deal more with the here and now and the everyday.

"I would not say the Powers That Be is God, but I would say that some people would interpret it as God. That's just as valid as whatever interpretation they can come up with. We keep it vague for a reason. If people want to believe it's God, we're not going to say it's not any more than we're going to say it is."

The Influences

THE WRITERS OF *BUFFY THE VAMPIRE SLAYER* all have their own thoughts about demons, many of which spring from influential or inspirational images or scenes from pop culture, as well as from religion. Executive story editor Douglas Petrie, for instance, has a unique thought process when it comes to approaching the creation of a new demonic monster for the show.

"With demons, I'm always thinking medieval," Petrie remarks. "Or something like Genghis Khan. Lagos, the demon from [the episode] 'Revelations,' is a really good embodiment of that. [He looks like] a soldier, a part of Lucifer's army. As a kid in Catholic school, they would tell us about the war of the angels. Lucifer took his guys and challenged God and the angels had this big fight. How cool is this? As a kid, my brother had the soundtrack to the James Bond movie *Thunderball*, and on the album cover they had a picture of five hundred guys from Specter fighting five hundred British secret service guys, all in their wet suits. I always figured that's what the war of the angels looked like."

Petrie also has certain artistic abilities that come into play during his brainstorming. When he first came on staff on the series, he began work on the ideas for the episode that eventually became "Revelations."

"Joss said he wanted a glove," Petrie recalls. "Originally, we had an idea we were really excited with; it was like a demonic falconer's glove. When you put it on and raised your arm, this huge, dark cloud would burst through the ceiling and take the form of a bird that spits fire. We went nuts when we thought of it.

"It was one of my first weeks here, and I was so proud that I came up with something that I really liked. Then David Greenwalt said it was completely unfeasible. We cannot possibly afford that. Joss said if we could get it down to six shots, we could afford it. I spent a long weekend doing storyboards. I'm something of a cartoonist. I went crazy. I drew twenty-five pages of storyboards, which cut it down to six shots of the cloud bursting through the skylight, taking the form of the bird, landing on her arm, shooting out fire, and roasting people. Then at the end it turns on her, grabs her in its talons, and flies through the window.

"They said, 'Yeah, we can do it.' We held on to it for a really long time. But I'd see the producers in the hallway and they'd go, 'Yeah, what's your name again? Yeah, you wrote the unfilmable one.' Eventually, Joss said, 'We might want to think about some alternatives,' and I knew that it was over. I was actually really happy with the way it turned out, though. I thought it was a cool ending."

Petrie did not give up the demon bird story, however. The creature appeared in a *Buffy* graphic novel he wrote for Dark Horse Comics. One of Petrie's disappointments, however, has to do with an aspect of demon imagery that is rarely seen on television because it is difficult to do convincingly, and expensive even to try.

"The one thing that's really hard to do in terms of demons that we'd like to do is winged creatures," he elaborates. "It would be great to do flying creatures. I think they're really scary. They're so primal, with medieval imagery. That's what we think of when we think of hell—these huge, bat-winged things. When I saw *Jurassic Park*, I was kind of bummed that they didn't have pterodactyls. We may still have winged creatures on the show.

"But that's where all that came from. We went back and forth about a million times as to whether Mrs. Post was human. Originally she wasn't. Eventually she was human, but she'd gone bad. I like doing demons who are like Whistler. They're completely human looking, but they say, 'You know what, if you saw my real form or heard my real language, you'd go blind and insane. So I'm just presenting this form to you because it's palatable to humans.'"

On the subject of traditional demon imagery most familiar to Westerners from the film *The Exorcist*, former *Buffy* staff writers **Rob Des Hotel** and **Dean Batali** have surprisingly differing opinions, considering how long they've worked as a team.

"I believe very specific things about demons, and what they're dealing with on *Buffy* are not demons by traditional definition," Batali asserts. "Joss always refers to them as demons, and I refer to them as monsters. To me, demons are the things that possess people in *The Exorcist*. I subscribe to a more biblical view of what demons are. In *Buffy* lingo, demons and monsters seem interchangeable.

"With any of the ones Rob and I created, I always felt there was carte blanche, and there was no spiritual connection to anything. Eyghon [from "The Dark Age"] was one of the most literal demons that we used. My viewpoint is that demons have to be invited [into a person's life]. That's where I differ a lot from Joss' theology, if we can call it that. We did that with Eyghon and Giles, but Jenny didn't invite Eyghon in. That's probably why I don't fear them, because they have to be invited in."

Des Hotel sees the pop-culture representation of demons from another angle.

"I think *Buffy* has used demons wisely and somehow made them more tangible than they have been in other films or shows," he says. "*The Omen* works because it's a kid. *The Exorcist* works because it's a kid. There's a demon at work, but it's personified. [Otherwise,] there's just an ethereal quality to them. I don't know if Eyghon was that successful. He wasn't really a factor until he possessed Jenny. There were flashbacks, but we weren't really invested in what was going on until he possessed Jenny.

"Demons, to me, are like little brothers who pester and bother you and then run away. We did some *Buffy* episodes where there were demons and Willow would be in her bedroom a mile away, casting a cyber-spell to get rid of the demon. With Eyghon, we had the demon that jumped from body to body, and there's just such an agitating quality to them that makes them lose their threat. If I were a demon, why wouldn't I kill Buffy?

"Sometimes demons just aren't as threatening as if you have a werewolf running around. You can't sit in a room and light a candle and cast a spell to get the werewolf out of there. You have to go after it because it's going to eat some kids. You have to go and attack and take it on. There's sort of a chicken quality to demons that kind of renders them nonthreatening. They don't seem to ever fulfill the evil that they promise."

For makeup supervisor **Todd McIntosh,** it is difficult not to approach the subject of demons from two perspectives, one a practical standpoint having to do with creating the makeup, and the other a creative use of his own inspirations and influences. Actually coming up with the creatures' designs, McIntosh reminds, "is a synthesis between the producers and [makeup SFX company] Optic Nerve. Even the coloring and the presentation of the character are sort of taken out of my hands. It's my art ability that makes it all come together, but it's Joss and [Optic Nerve honcho] **John Vulich's** vision as to what demons look like. Vulich has a propensity toward alligators. You'll notice a lot of lizard influence in the demons. That's his vision."

When it comes time to do makeup over the sculpted pieces designed by Optic Nerve, or to create a less complicated demon with makeup alone, McIntosh brings his own influences to bear.

"To me, when we start getting into the rather nebulous area of demons, it brings up the whole pantheon of creatures that work for Satan. Each has a specific role to play. For example, the greed demon, or the lust demon. That's where I go. What is the function of this creature? I try to have that show [in its appearance]."

The Monsters

IF YOU'RE LOOKING FOR racial diversity, you won't find a better example than the demons of *Buffy the Vampire Slayer*. By human perception, most of them are fairly hideous, but beyond that, they have little in common. The series has a demon for almost every occasion, each one of them different from the last. Interestingly, not all demons are evil; most of them have a human somewhere in their family tree, or once were human themselves, and they don't always *stay* demons. You will find them all below, in order of appearance.

MOLOCH THE CORRUPTOR

GILES: "I need your help. But before that, I need you to believe something you may not want to. Something has gotten into...inside....There's a demon in the Internet."
JENNY: "I know." —"I ROBOT, YOU JANE"

EPISODE: "I Robot, You Jane," season one

KEY RELATIONSHIPS: When Moloch awoke in modern times he gathered human acolytes around him, including Sunnydale students Dave and Fritz. He also used the Internet to begin a relationship with Willow Rosenberg.

UNIQUE ATTRIBUTES: After being bound into a book, Moloch had no physical form. In modern times he escaped into the Internet, living in cyberspace. He forced his acolytes to build him a nasty-looking, horned demon robot body.

MOST MONSTROUS MOMENT: Despite Fritz's loyalty, Moloch snapped his neck on a whim.

CURRENT STATUS: Trapped within his robotic body, Moloch was apparently destroyed when it was short-circuited and then blown up.

In medieval Italy, the horned demon Moloch surrounded himself with a group of human acolytes who worshiped him despite his savage, tyrannical ways. He promised to fulfill their wildest dreams in return

(if they survived his mood swings). Eventually, however, a group of monks led by **Brother Thelonious** magically trapped him inside a leather-bound book.

> "There are certain books that are not meant to be read. Ever. They have things trapped within them....In the Dark Ages, demons' souls were sometimes trapped in certain volumes. The demon would remain in the volume, harmless, unless the book was read aloud." —GILES, IN DIALOGUE CUT FROM THE FINAL BROADCAST OF "I ROBOT, YOU JANE" DUE TO LENGTH

Moloch remained trapped for centuries. The book arrived in a shipment of arcane texts for Giles just as Willow and computer science teacher Jenny Calendar were aiding him with a project in which they were scanning his books into the computer for easier research and access. When that particular tome was scanned in, Moloch escaped into the computer, and from there to the Web beyond.

Though Moloch had been out of action for ages, it did not take him long to adjust. He began reaching out to impressionable young people online. Under the alias **Malcolm Black**, he became an e-mail pal for Willow, who had never had a boyfriend and was flattered by the attention.

Moloch recruited **Fritz** and **Dave**, a pair of Sunnydale High computer nerds, as his modern-day acolytes, and commanded them to kill Buffy. Fritz was willing, but Dave gave the Slayer a timely warning and Moloch killed him for it. Along with several scientists who were also under Moloch's influence, Fritz co-opted the facilities of an abandoned computer company and built the demon a robotic body, only to have Moloch kill him as well.

The demon's desire for a body was his undoing, however. With the help of Jenny Calendar—who had turned out to be a technopagan, a mystic and scholar who used the Internet to learn about the occult and communicate with like-minded individuals—Giles performed a spell that should have drained Moloch from the Net and put him back into the book. The demon's only choice was to leave cyberspace and concentrate himself fully within the robot body. Once he was out of the Net and into a single form, he was vulnerable. Buffy fought the demon robot, electrocuting him and causing him to short-circuit and then explode.

THE BROTHERHOOD OF SEVEN

"Every seven years these demons need human organs—a heart and a brain—to maintain their humanity. Otherwise they revert back to their original form, which is slightly less appealing."

—GILES, IN "THE PUPPET SHOW"

EPISODE: "The Puppet Show," season one

UNIQUE ATTRIBUTES: The Brotherhood of Seven (or just "the Seven") took the form of young humans, but could only maintain those forms if they ate a fresh human heart and brain every seven years.

MOST MONSTROUS MOMENT: They ate hearts and brains. What, that's not enough?

CURRENT STATUS: Over the years, demon-hunter Sid tracked and killed all seven of them in order to free himself from his curse.

Though this band of demons (or rather, their last surviving member) was not the focal point of the season-one episode "The Puppet Show," co-writer Dean Batali considers their creation "some of the deeper mythology Rob [Des Hotel] and I created. We had to give more thought to the Seven, to their logic, what they were doing and why."

As a result, the seven demons had been preying on humans for eternity, magically disguised as young people. Every seven years they had to harvest the organs from two separate "donors" in order to maintain their human form.

When the last surviving member of the Brotherhood arrived in Sunnydale—perhaps drawn by the evil aura emanating from the Hellmouth—it drew the attention of Buffy and her cohorts by killing **Emily**, a dancer in the school talent show, and literally stealing her heart.

Buffy and her friends began to investigate. At first they believed that the killer was a demon, but soon their attention began to focus more on **Morgan Shay**, who had a ventriloquism act in the show. Morgan was an oddball who had frequent headaches and seemed to have a very strange relationship with his dummy, Sid.

Things took a surprising turn when Morgan was murdered and his brain harvested by the demon. Buffy found herself in battle with the dummy, Sid, whom she assumed must be a demon. Sid, however, thought the same of Buffy. It turned out that they were both hunting for the last of the Seven.

> **"On rare occasions, inanimate objects of human quality such as dolls and mannequins, already mystically possessed of consciousness, have acted upon their desire to be human by harvesting organs."** —WILLOW, IN "THE PUPPET SHOW"

To the astonishment of all involved, it was discovered that Sid was a demon-hunter who had been systematically killing the members of the Seven for years. Once he had been human, but a run-in with the Brotherhood had ended with Sid's human body destroyed and his spirit cursed to reside within the dummy until he could kill all of the demons responsible.

Buffy, Giles, and Sid all agreed that the demon was likely to be someone participating in the talent show, given the targets it had chosen. Now that it had the organs it needed, it would probably move on. At the next rehearsal, however, all of the participants were in attendance. The gang was baffled until they discovered that Morgan had had a brain tumor, which made his brain unacceptable. The demon would have to find another one, and it would likely go after the most intelligent person available. Since they assumed the demon would seek a youthful "donor," they determined to protect Willow, not realizing that Giles was actually the one in danger.

The demon was masquerading as **Marc,** the student magician, who lured Giles to place his neck onto a guillotine that was supposed to be a part of his magic act. In reality, he intended to behead Giles and harvest his brain. Buffy and Sid arrived just in time, and a fight broke out. During the conflict, Buffy held back so that Sid could dispatch the last of the Seven. After the demon's death, Sid's spirit left the dummy, presumably going on to whatever afterlife awaited him. (Also see Ghosts: Sid)

HELLMOUTH SPAWN

WILLOW: "And if [the Hellmouth] opens?"

BUFFY: "Remember that demon that almost got out the night I died?"

WILLOW: "Every nightmare I have that doesn't revolve around academic failure or public nudity is about that thing. In fact, one time I dreamed that it attacked me while I was late for a test and naked."

BUFFY: "It'll be the first to come out."   —**"THE ZEPPO"**

FIRST APPEARANCE: "Prophecy Girl," season one

OTHER EPISODES: season three: "The Zeppo"

UNIQUE ATTRIBUTES: As pure demons from other dimensions, they are far more powerful—not to mention uglier and slimier—than the average earthbound demons.

MOST MONSTROUS MOMENT: In both episodes the demons on the other side of the Hellmouth attempted to break through.

CURRENT STATUS: Beaten back . . . but waiting.

As Joss Whedon has established, beyond our dimension there exist multiple demon dimensions. The Hellmouth is a place in Sunnydale—located beneath what is now the ruins of Sunnydale High School, specifically under the old school library—where the dimensional barrier is quite thin. Beyond that barrier, unimaginably horrible full-blooded demons await with their minions to cross over and take back the world they were forced out of eons ago.

In the season one finale, "Prophecy Girl," and the season three episode "The Zeppo," the Hellmouth was briefly opened, and viewers were given a glimpse of the monstrosities that exist on the other side, their dark, horrible tentacles tearing into our world, trying to burst through. In "Prophecy Girl," the Hellmouth closed when Buffy killed the Master, who had been the one responsible for its opening in the first place. In "The Zeppo," whatever demon tried to come through the Hellmouth was also horrible and tentacled, but seen only in small glimpses and cuts. It seemed to have come farther into our world in that episode before Giles and Willow used a binding spell from **Hebron's Almanac** to send it back.

In season four's "Doomed," an effort was made to open the Hellmouth for a third time, but Buffy and the gang managed to close it before anything slipped out.

MACHIDA

"Some guy's attacking Buffy with a sword! Also, there's a really big snake."
—WILLOW, IN "REPTILE BOY"

EPISODE: "Reptile Boy," season two

KEY RELATIONSHIPS: Machida was worshiped by the fraternity brothers at Crestwood College's Delta Zeta Kappa for decades.

UNIQUE ATTRIBUTES: "Machida is half man, half snake. He has a muscular body (from the waist up) and the enlarged and frightening head of a man with the fangs and horrible eyes of a snake. His skin has the diamond pattern of a snake — thus the diamond carvings on his 'people.' From the waist down, he is all snake — and a big 'un too, his snake body trails behind him into the depths of the pit. God knows how long this guy is."

—PRODUCTION NOTE FROM THE "REPTILE BOY"
SCRIPT BY DAVID GREENWALT

MOST MONSTROUS MOMENT: Machida ate human females offered as sacrifice by his worshipers.

CURRENT STATUS: Though Buffy chopped Machida in half at the end of "Reptile Boy," investigators never found his body. It is possible that he managed to survive and still lives somewhere beneath Sunnydale.

Persuaded by **Cordelia Chase** to attend a Delta Zeta Kappa fraternity party at local Crestwood College, Buffy discovered that the rich frat boys who resided in the house were keeping up a century-old family tradition. They, and their fathers and grandfathers before them, were in a deal-with-the-devil sort of pact, worshiping and offering sacrifices to a demon in the fraternity house's basement in exchange for wealth and power. The frat brothers/cult members had an altar in the basement where they branded themselves with diamond-shaped scars in honor of their demon benefactor.

Buffy's and Cordelia's dates, **Tom Warner** and **Richard Anderson**, drugged them and chained them in the basement to await the demon's arrival. When they woke, they discovered that they were chained alongside a girl named **Callie** who had also been abducted.

Earlier in the episode, Buffy had discovered a bloody bracelet not far from the Delta Zeta Kappa house. At the library, Giles and Willow used the clue of the bracelet to connect it to the missing Callie, and discovered that at least two other girls had disappeared on the same date a year before. Given where Buffy had found the bracelet, they realized that it was possible the fraternity brothers had been abducting the girls. With Angel in tow, they raced to the frat house, where Xander was trying to crash the party.

In the basement, the cult members, dressed in robes with hoods that hid their faces, intoned a ritual calling the demon to rise and take the girls as offerings. The leader, Tom, dropped three stones into the pit by the altar, and they splashed into water far below. One stone for each offering, each girl. The snakelike Machida emerged from a pit in the basement floor that led to a subterranean lair, his body covered with diamond-shaped markings like those the frat brothers branded themselves with.

Even as Giles, Willow, Angel, and Xander broke into the frat house and fought with some of the cult members, Buffy tore her chains out of the wall, freeing herself, and then cut Machida in two with a sword. The Delta Zeta Kappa brothers were handed over to the police and charged with murder. Investigators found bones of the missing girls in a huge cavern beneath the frat house and other bones dating back fifty years. Machida's body was never found.

As initially conceived, Machida was intended to survive Buffy's attack. Greenwalt, who also directed the episode, notes that there was not enough time in the production schedule to shoot the final sequence, so Machida remained dead. Had time allowed, however, things would have ended quite differently. This is the section of the shooting script that was cut to make this adjustment.

(from scene 86)

Tom comes to near the altar. And, unbeknownst to any of our heroes, the snake body begins slowly moving. Until it joins up with the torso. A squooshy sound of flesh and protoplasm meeting and the two halves re-join!

CORDELIA (cont'd) (to Tom) And you, you're going to jail for about fifteen thousand years.
Oh god, it's over...it's really...
That's when Machida, re-joined, suddenly pops up again. Angel takes a threatening step forward next to Buffy, growls. Machida towers over Tom:
MACHIDA For a hundred years I have given your forbears wealth and power. And this is how you repay me? From this day forth you are alone in the world.
Machida slides back down. Cordelia is afraid to breathe. With good reason. Machida pops back up, grabs Tom.
MACHIDA (cont'd) Li'l somethin' for the road.
Machida disappears into the pit with Tom. We hear Tom's screams, a quick couple of chomps, and then silence.

Like many *Buffy* episodes, "Reptile Boy" is a sort of cautionary tale. David Greenwalt puts it in very direct terms:

"How do the young and rich stay young and rich?" he asks. "That group you desire to be part of? You should dig a little deeper."

EYGHON THE SLEEPWALKER

"You're like a woman, Ripper, you cry at every funeral. You never had the strength for me, you don't deserve me. But guess what, you've got me—*under the skin!*"

—EYGHON, IN "THE DARK AGE"

FIRST APPEARANCE: "The Dark Age," season two

KEY RELATIONSHIPS: Eyghon was called up by Rupert Giles, Ethan Rayne, and a group of their friends some two decades ago. In order to return him to his dimension, one of their number lost his life. However, they were branded with his mark, making them all targets when he managed to return to this plane, as well as vessels whom it was apparently easier for him to occupy.

UNIQUE ATTRIBUTES: Eyghon, once called from his dimension, could occupy the bodies of dead or sleeping humans. If he used a dead body as host, energy would be leached from it and it would eventually disintegrate, becoming a pool of strange, mercurial fluid. Eyghon could also track anyone with his mark on their flesh. His true appearance is unknown, but given the transformation of Jenny Calendar when the demon possessed her, it can be presumed that Eyghon's true countenance is scaly and somewhat reptilian.

MOST MONSTROUS MOMENT: He murdered Giles's old acquaintance Philip Henry, among others.

CURRENT STATUS: Forced out of Jenny Calendar's body, Eyghon attempted to possess Angel, only to find the vampire's body already crowded with a human and a demon soul. Eyghon struggled to get control, but was defeated. It is unknown if Eyghon was destroyed or merely dispatched in his weakened state back to his original dimension.

Giles's father and grandmother had been members of the Council of Watchers. It was therefore presumed that he would follow in their footsteps and become a Watcher himself. At some point he rebelled against that expectation. In his early twenties, he and a circle of friends (including Ethan Rayne) became involved in the occult, dabbling in magic, and eventually performed a complicated ritual to invite the ancient Etruscan demon Eyghon to earth. That ritual involved all of the members of the group being tattooed with a symbol called the Mark of Eyghon. One of the group would go to sleep and the others would call "the Sleepwalker" to inhabit the sleeper. During that initial contact, Eyghon was driven from the earthly plane, but doing so cost the life of one of the group, **Thomas Sutcliffe**. Eventually, Giles decided to take up the destiny that his family had wished for him. The forces of darkness, he had learned, were not something that should be treated lightly.

However, in "The Dark Age," a much more serious sequence of events came to pass. Since all of the members of the circle had been tattooed with the Mark of Eyghon, the demon had apparently waited for one of them to die in order to inhabit her corpse and then kill the others. The first to die was **Deirdre Page**.

> "Eyghon, the Sleepwalker, can only exist in this reality by possessing an unconscious host. Temporary possession imbues the host with a euphoric feeling of power...unless the proper rituals are observed, the possession is permanent, and Eyghon will be born from within the host...Once called, Eyghon can also take possession of the dead, but its demonic energy soon disintegrates the host and it must jump to the nearest dead or unconscious person to continue living." —WILLOW, IN "THE DARK AGE"

Deirdre/Eyghon killed **Philip Henry,** another old friend, and Eyghon possessed his corpse so that he could continue hunting for a more permanent home. He was able to use the tattoos to track the others—namely Giles and Ethan. When the form of Philip Henry began to deteriorate, Eyghon jumped into the nearest sleeper—Giles's girlfriend, Jenny Calendar, whom Philip had knocked unconscious in a final demonic attack.

In battling Eyghon/Jenny, Buffy and the others knew they had to be careful not to harm her, but they also needed to force the demon out before she was permanently transformed into it. Pretending to strangle Jenny (in a chilling foreshadowing of her eventual murder), Angel induced Eyghon into fleeing her body and attempting to possess him.

BUFFY: (to Willow) "You knew that if the demon was in danger it would jump into the nearest dead guy."
(Willow nods, even smiles.)
ANGEL: "I put it in danger."
WILLOW: "And it jumped."
ANGEL: "But I've had a demon inside me for a couple hundred years just waiting for a good fight."
BUFFY: "Winner and still champion." —"THE DARK AGE"

The demon entered Angel, and there was a battle within him between Eyghon and Angel's own demon soul. Angel's features altered between his human face, his vampiric countenance, and the demonic visage of Eyghon before he drove it out. The demon within him either destroyed Eyghon completely or weakened it so much that it was forced to retreat to its own dimension.

NORMAN PfISTER

BUFFY: "You and bug people, Xander. What's up with that?"
XANDER: "But this dude was different than the praying mantis lady. He was a man *of* bugs. Not a man who *was* a bug."
WILLOW: "Okay. (beat) Huh?" —**"WHAT'S MY LINE? PART TWO"**

EPISODES: "What's My Line? Parts One and Two," season two.

KEY RELATIONSHIPS: Mr. Pfister was a member of the Order of Taraka, a guild of supernatural assassins who were hired by Spike to kill the Slayer.

UNIQUE ATTRIBUTES: Mr. Pfister completely comprised of maggotlike bugs and grubs, but could appear to be human when those organisms were joined together.

MOST MONSTROUS MOMENT: Hello? Maggots? (Or door-to-door salesman?)

CURRENT STATUS: Disassembled into his bug form, Pfister was stomped to death by Cordelia and Xander.

In the second-season two-parter "What's My Line?" it was never firmly established if Mr. Pfister was a demon or something else entirely. However, until proven otherwise, we have included him in this section.

An assassin sent to kill the Slayer, Pfister somehow managed to maintain a human appearance, despite the fact that his body was made up entirely of maggots and worms. The creature was one of the most disturbing monsters ever invented for the show. That sentiment was best expressed by Xander in a line from the original script.

> **"You know, just when you think you've seen it all, along comes a worm guy."**
> —XANDER, IN A SCENE CUT FOR LENGTH FROM THE BROADCAST OF "WHAT'S MY LINE?"

Pfister disguised himself as a door-to-door salesman for Blush Beautiful Skin Care and Cosmetics. He used that masquerade to take one of the Summers' neighbors by surprise and kill her, so that he could surveil Buffy's house. He used the salesman ruse to gain entrance into Buffy's house, though only Cordelia and Xander were there looking for

Buffy. Pfister offered Cordelia free samples of his products to get her to let him in.

Norman Pfister was a member of the Order of Taraka, a collective of assassins that includes all manner of supernatural creatures and, apparently, humans as well. Giles called them "a society of deadly assassins dating back to King Solomon."

> "Their credo is to sow discord and kill the unwary. . . . They're a breed apart. . . . Unlike vampires, they have no earthly desires except to collect their bounty. They find their target and eliminate it. You can kill as many of them as you like. It won't make any difference — where there is one, there will be another. And another. They won't stop coming until the job is done. Each one of them works alone. His own way. Some of them are human. Some are not. We won't know who they are . . . until they strike."
> —GILES, IN "WHAT'S MY LINE? PART ONE"

The Order's members all wear a certain ring that identifies them as Tarakan assassins. In "What's My Line?" the vampire Spike engaged their services to eliminate Buffy, but the three assassins sent by the order all failed and were killed. The first two were brought down in physical combat, but one of Giles's arcane books revealed that due to his composite nature, Pfister could only be destroyed when he was in his disassembled state. In order to kill him, Xander and Cordelia mocked him, and then took refuge behind a door so he could reach them only by breaking apart and swarming under the door in his maggot/worm form. When the bugs emerged, they were trapped in a mess of paint Xander and Cordy had splashed there, and were stomped to death.

Marti Noxon, writer of the episode, notes that "Mr. Pfister and all of the monsters in 'What's My Line?' were pretty much all Joss pitches. We were trying to think of something supercool. There was so much happening with the characters that we weren't feeling a lot of pressure to make the monsters metaphors [this time]. They were more than just good and creepy. We had bug tests for Pfister. Worm auditions. We met a lot of worms until we found the right kind. They had worm wranglers, and every time you have a living creature [on a show] you have to have a rep from the ASPCA."

OCTARUS

ANGEL (examining the defeated Octarus's ring): "You're in danger. You know what the ring means?"

BUFFY: "I just killed a Super Bowl champ?"   —**"WHAT'S MY LINE? PART ONE"**

EPISODE: "What's My Line? Part One," season two

KEY RELATIONSHIPS: Octarus was a member of the Order of Taraka.

UNIQUE ATTRIBUTES: Aside from being hideous, at nearly eight feet tall Octarus was a giant. Part of his face was ruined, and he had only one good eye.

MOST MONSTROUS MOMENT: He attempted to kill Buffy at an ice skating rink where she had gone to relax with Angel.

CURRENT STATUS: Buffy cut his throat with the blade of one of her skates.

As another member of the Order of Taraka, Octarus was among those hired by Spike and his vampire girlfriend, Drusilla, to kill Buffy (in the second-season two-parter "What's My Line?").

DALTON: "The Order of Taraka? I mean, isn't that overkill?"
SPIKE: "No. I think it's just enough kill."   —**"WHAT'S MY LINE? PART ONE"**

In spite of his status as a member of the Order of Taraka, Octarus's behavior did not mark him as particularly smart. Buffy cut Octarus's throat with one of her ice skates. (It should be noted that in the next episode, "Ted," it was revealed that the contract had been called off.)

The original script described Octarus as "a giant. Seven feet tall in boots, and a hard four hundred pounds. A thick milky cataract covers one eye. His other eye is set deep in the fleshy mask of assorted scars and carbuncles he calls a face." Fortunately, the Octarus that reached the final version of the episode was just as horrifying.

THE JUDGE

"It's a legend. Way before my time. Of a demon brought forth to rid the earth of the plague of humanity. To separate the righteous from the wicked...and burn the righteous down. They called him the Judge."   —ANGEL, IN "SURPRISE"

FIRST APPEARANCE: "Surprise," season two

OTHER EPISODES: "Innocence," season two

KEY RELATIONSHIPS: Though he had once been hacked into pieces and his body parts spread around the world, Spike and Drusilla managed to gather them and put him back together again. He was allied with them during this brief resurrection.

UNIQUE ATTRIBUTES: With bright blue skin, the Judge was certainly one of the most colorful demons ever seen on *Buffy*. He could not be killed by any weapon forged by man. Also, his touch could burn all the goodness and humanity out of any being he laid hands on.

MOST MONSTROUS MOMENT: He used his burning touch on Dalton, a vampire lackey of Spike's, simply because the poor fellow liked to read.

CURRENT STATUS: Buffy blew up the Judge with a rocket launcher in "Innocence." His remaining parts, from big to very tiny, were then scattered to prevent him from being revived once more.

In ancient days, the blue-skinned demon known as the Judge was brought forth from some demon dimension to eradicate humanity from Earth, presumably to make it habitable once more for the demons driven out when man first rose to prominence.

During the Judge's first attempt, it seemed very much as though he would succeed. Part of his demonic strength was that he could not be killed by any weapon forged by human hands. It took an army to subdue him; they hacked him to pieces, sent his dismembered parts around the world, and buried them all separately.

In "Surprise," it was revealed that Spike had been gathering the parts of the Judge as a gift for Drusilla, who was gleeful about the possibility of reassembling him and thus bringing about Armageddon. Despite the efforts of Buffy, Angel, and the others to keep the final pieces from falling into Spike's hands, the horned, armor-clad Judge was reassembled.

The Judge began immediately to seek out righteousness and goodness to destroy. In fact, his first instinct upon his revival was to burn Spike and Dru. Revolted by their affection for one another, he told them that they "stink of humanity." Instead, he turned his attention to nerdy vampire Dalton, whose love of knowledge and books gave him human qualities that caused him to burn to smoldering ashes upon the Judge's touch.

At the end of "Surprise," Buffy and Angel made love. Due to the gypsy curse upon him, that moment of bliss caused Angel's human soul to be torn from him. In the following episode, "Innocence," the now-evil Angel went to Spike and Drusilla, who did not believe he was one of them again until the Judge touched Angel . . . with no reaction.

The Judge would not always have to touch his victims to burn them, however. The centuries he spent dismembered took their toll, and he was weak upon his revival. With each life he took, his strength began to grow and he promised Spike that eventually he would not need direct contact at all to perform his duties.

SPIKE: "What's Big Blue up to, anyway? He just sits there."
THE JUDGE: "I am preparing."
SPIKE: "Yeah, it's interesting to me that preparing looks a great bit like sitting on your arse. When do we destroy the world already?"
THE JUDGE: "My strength grows. And every life I take will increase it further."
SPIKE: "So let's take some! I'm bored!"
THE JUDGE: "I fought an army. They hacked me to pieces. For six hundred years my living head lay in a box buried in the ground. I've learned to be patient."
—"INNOCENCE" (BOLDFACED TEXT WAS CUT FROM THE SCRIPT FOR LENGTH)

Only the fact that he had not yet gained his full strength kept the Judge's touch from killing Buffy before she escaped him in "Surprise." In the end, it was Xander who made the necessary connection for the gang to realize how the Judge could be killed. No weapon "forged" could destroy him. But modern weaponry was not forged. Certainly a rocket launcher would do the job.

And it did.

THE JUDGE: "You are a fool. No weapon forged can stop me."
BUFFY: "That was then. (hoists the rocket launcher Xander has procured for her) This is now."
—"INNOCENCE"

The pieces of the Judge—blown apart by the rocket launcher—were retrieved and kept separated to prevent the demon from being brought to life once more.

CORDELIA: "Pieces? We're getting pieces? Our job sucks!"
OZ (finding one): "Arm."
—"INNOCENCE"

Other than the fin-headed Kulak ("Homecoming"), the Judge was perhaps Buffy's most colorful adversary. "Yeah, he'll be blue, that'll be good," reflects Marti Noxon, who wrote "Surprise." "The Judge ended up looking like a Smurf with a bad attitude. Blue [is] just not that menacing."

WHISTLER

BUFFY: "What are you, some immortal demon sent down to even the score between good and evil?"
WHISTLER: "Wow, Good guess."   —"BECOMING, PART TWO"

EPISODES: "Becoming, Parts One and Two," season two

KEY RELATIONSHIPS: Though he is a demon, Whistler apparently works for certain cosmic entities responsible for maintaining the balance between good and evil in the universe. He was briefly a mentor to Angel and, in fact, was the one who brought Buffy to Angel's attention.

UNIQUE ATTRIBUTES: Whistler looked human, but was not.

MOST MONSTROUS MOMENT: Every morning while choosing his wardrobe.

CURRENT STATUS: Whistler was last seen in Sunnydale in "Becoming, Part Two." His current whereabouts are unknown.

According to *Buffy* creator Joss Whedon, Whistler "was our introduction to the concept of a good demon." In his first appearance, in part one of the season two finale, "Becoming," Whistler explained his purpose.

> "A demon, technically. But I'm not a bad guy—not all demons are dedicated to the destruction of all life. Someone has to maintain balance, you know. Good and evil can't exist without each other, blah blah blah. I'm not like a good fairy or anything. I'm just trying to make it all balance—do I come off defensive?"
>
> —WHISTLER, IN "BECOMING, PART ONE"

His age is unknown, but in 1996, Whistler located Angel in New York City, where the vampire was living on the streets, still tortured with guilt after having had his soul returned to him almost a century before. In his mission to keep a balance between good and evil, it was up to Whistler to give Angel a purpose so that he would become a warrior for the Powers That Be. Previously, Angel had been living as a homeless person subsisting on the blood of rats.

> "You could become an even more useless rodent than you are right now, or you could become...someone. A person. Someone to be counted."
> —WHISTLER TO ANGEL IN "BECOMING, PART ONE"

Whistler took Angel to Los Angeles so that the cursed vampire could see Buffy for the first time. He told Angel about the evil the Slayer would have to face, and Angel was filled with the desire to help her.

> "She's gonna have it tough, that Slayer. She's just a kid. And the world is full of big bad things."
> —WHISTLER, IN "BECOMING, PART ONE"

In "Becoming, Part Two" Whistler and Buffy met for the first time. It fell to the demon to prod her to do what had to be done in order to stop the evil Angel.

> **BUFFY:** "Why don't you try getting off your immortal ass and **fighting** evil once in a while? 'Cause I'm tired of doing this by myself."
> **WHISTLER:** "In the end, you're always by yourself. You're all you got. That's the point."
> **BUFFY:** "Spare me." —"BECOMING, PART TWO"

Subsequent to that episode, Whistler disappeared and has not been seen since. And according to Joss Whedon, "We probably won't see him. We could, if we think of a cool story involving him. But at this point we don't have any big plans in that direction."

Whedon confirms, however, that Whistler continues to work to keep the balance between good and evil in the Buffyverse.

ACATHLA

> "The demon universe exists in a dimension separate from our own. With one breath Acathla will create a vortex, a kind of whirlpool that will pull everything on earth into that dimension, where any non-demon life will suffer horrible, eternal torment."
> —GILES, IN "BECOMING, PART ONE"

FIRST APPEARANCE: "Becoming, Parts One and Two," season two

UNIQUE ATTRIBUTES: Acathla was capable of creating a vortex that would suck all the living things on Earth into the demon dimensions. Centuries ago, he was thwarted by a knight who ran him through. The demon was turned to stone.

MOST MONSTROUS MOMENT: That whole vortex thing.

CURRENT STATUS: Though Acathla once again turned to stone at the end of the second season, the current whereabouts of his stone form are unknown.

Before the Gypsy curse that restored his soul, Angel was renowned the world over as one of the most evil vampires who had ever lived, not to mention one of the most savage. When he became evil again in season two's "Surprise," he exhibited many of the sadistic tendencies audiences had come to expect from what had already been revealed of his past life. But in the two-part season finale, "Becoming," the depths of Angel's evil were revealed.

Construction workers digging foundations for high-rise buildings outside Sunnydale discovered the enormous stone tomb that held Acathla.

> **"Acathla, the demon, came forth to swallow the world. It was killed by a virtuous knight who pierced the demon's heart before it could draw breath to perform the act. Acathla turned to stone, as demons sometimes do, and was buried where neither man nor demon would be wont to look. Unless of course they're putting up low-rent housing."**
> **—ANGEL, IN "BECOMING, PART ONE"**

Angelus and his henchmen stole the entombed demon and brought it back to the mansion Angel shared with Spike and Drusilla. The tomb was opened, revealing the hideous demon—turned to stone—resting inside with a sword protruding from its chest.

SPIKE: "Let me guess. Someone pulls out the sword—"
DRUSILLA: "Someone worthy—"
SPIKE: "...the demon wakes up and wackiness ensues—"
DRUSILLA: "He will swallow the world."
ANGEL: "And every creature living on this planet will go to hell. My friends, we're about to make history...end."
—**"BECOMING, PART ONE"**

After making several errors in performing a ritual to open the vortex, Angel tortured Giles into revealing the key—the vampire's own blood was the element missing from the ritual. In the climactic battle of the second season, Buffy and Angel battled with swords in front of Acathla, whose mouth had already opened, the vortex forming. Just as Angel's blood had been required to open the portal, Buffy was forced to reverse it with

the same ingredient. She ran Angel through with the sword, and then shoved him into the vortex, which closed once he was on the other side.

KEN

"Welcome to my world. I hope you like it. You're never leaving."   —KEN, IN "ANNE"

EPISODE: "Anne," season three

KEY RELATIONSHIPS: Ken lured young runaways to a shelter, but rather than help them, he transported them through a dimensional gate to a hellish world where they were made slaves.

UNIQUE ATTRIBUTES: Ken wore a false human face over his true demonic visage.

MOST MONSTROUS MOMENT: Ken not only worked the slaves until they were old and withered before returning them to our world, but he and his guards spent those years breaking them down and stealing away their individuality, driving them insane.

CURRENT STATUS: Buffy wounded Ken in battle. When she had led all the captives back through the portal, it closed on Ken's legs, whereupon Buffy decapitated him.

Known only by the name "Ken," and wearing a human face glued over his demonic countenance, this creature set up a clever demon scam in Los Angeles that Buffy uncovered in the third-season opener, "Anne." With the help of a human lackey who worked for a local blood bank—where runaways would sometimes go to

donate blood for money—Ken found healthy runaway teens and transported them through a gateway into his own demon dimension.

"This isn't a good place for a kid to be," Ken said of Los Angeles. "You grow up way too fast here." Obviously he had a gift for irony, given what he was doing with the runaways he abducted.

The kids were taken to become slave laborers. While there, Ken and his demon guards drummed into the slaves' heads that they were no one and nothing, they had no identity other than the work. When they became too old or infirm to work, they were returned to Earth, having long since been driven insane by the constant labor and the demon guards' insistence that they did not matter, that they were no one.

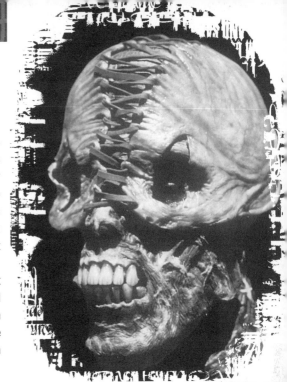

> "Time here moves more quickly than in your dimension. A hundred long years will pass here—on Earth, just a day." —KEN, IN "ANNE"

A girl named **Lily** (**Chanterelle** from season two's "Lie to Me") recognized the runaway Buffy, who was working as a waitress under the name Anne (her middle name). When Lily's boyfriend turned up missing, and then Lily herself was abducted, the trail led Buffy to Ken and to the alternate demon dimension. Ken was the dominant demon there, but there were many others under his command.

To Ken's horror and outrage ("Humans don't fight back! That's not how this works!"), Buffy led the slaves to revolt. After suffering brutality from both Buffy and Lily, Ken was killed. Everyone escaped, and the portal to the demon dimension closed.

OVU MOBANI

See the "Dead Man's Party" entry in The Walking Dead.

KULAK of THE MIQUOT CLAN

> "We all feel the desire to win, whether we're human...vampire...or...whatever the hell you are, my brother, got spiny looking head things, I never seen that."
> —MR. TRICK TO KULAK, IN "HOMECOMING"

EPISODE: "Homecoming," season three

UNIQUE ATTRIBUTES: With his bright yellow skin and the fin on his head, Kulak was one of the most unique-looking demons ever to appear on *Buffy*. He also was able to produce organic blades from his arms, which he used in battle.

MOST MONSTROUS MOMENT: Kulak was among those assassins who took part in Slayerfest '98, paying for the privilege of participating in that contest to see who could kill Buffy and Faith.

CURRENT STATUS: Kulak was accidentally blown up in a cabin in Miller's Woods.

Though little is known of the fascinating Kulak, it is obvious in speaking with Joss Whedon and the show's writers that he is a favorite among them.

"He was fun," Whedon recalls. "I designed him, too. That reptile spine on the head for a Mohawk was cool. We wanted specifically [for him to be part of] a clan, because we talked about him as a warrior, a brave. 'I hunt with my knives. Yes, they come out of my fore-arm.' He's more of a traditional fellow. He was a lot of fun."

In his debut appearance, the Mayor of Sunnydale had assigned Mr. Trick to dispose of both Buffy and Faith. The erstwhile vampire henchman organized "Slayerfest '98," in which he invited various monsters and assassins to come to town and to pay to participate in a murderous competition whose goal was . . . well, to kill the Slayers, of course.

Kulak was able to produce organic blades from his arms and used them in battle. He attempted to kill Buffy and Cordelia (who had been mistaken for Faith) in a cabin in Miller's Woods, where they had taken refuge. During the fight, another assassin tossed an explosive device into the cabin. Though Buffy and Cordelia escaped, Kulak did not.

A second Miquot was shown in captivity at the Initiative headquarters in the fourth-season episode "The Initiative."

THE MAYOR

"[Here] we are. Journey's end. And what is a journey? Is it just distance traveled? Time spent? No. It's what happens on the way, it's the things that shape you. At the end of the journey, you're not the same. Today is about change. Graduation doesn't just mean your circumstances change, it means you do. You ascend to a higher level. Nothing will ever be the same. Nothing. So as we look back on…on the events that have brought us to this day…we….We must all….AHH. It has begun. My destiny. Little sooner than I expected—I had a whole section about civic pride, but—I guess we'll just get to the big finish." —THE MAYOR, AS THE ASCENSION BEGINS, IN "GRADUATION DAY, PART TWO"

FIRST APPEARANCE: "Homecoming," season three

OTHER EPISODES: season three: "Band Candy," "Lover's Walk," "Gingerbread," "Bad Girls," "Consequences," "Doppelgangland," "Enemies," "Choices," "Graduation Day, Parts One and Two," season four: "This Year's Girl"

KEY RELATIONSHIPS: The Mayor was married to Edna Mae in 1903. She later died. He employed Mr. Trick and, through Trick, also employed Ethan Rayne and others at various times.

His most significant relationship of the last few years of his life was with Faith, the renegade Slayer to whom he became a kind of father figure. He cared for her deeply, which was ironic for a being bent on becoming a pure demon and bringing darkness down upon the world.

UNIQUE ATTRIBUTES: Quirky and germophobic, the Mayor had an antiquated sense of propriety, despite his demon worship and evil aspirations. Thanks to a ritual the Mayor was completely invulnerable for the last hundred days before his Ascension—the moment at which he became a pure demon, something he had been working toward for a century. As a pure demon he was an enormous snakelike creature.

MOST MONSTROUS MOMENT: There are many to choose from, considering his intentions. When he became a pure demon, for instance, he ate Principal Snyder, who despite being annoying had been a loyal lackey.

CURRENT STATUS: Snake jerky.

Throughout *Buffy*'s second season, a conspiracy began to reveal itself. The chief of police, the city council, and Sunnydale High School's **Principal Snyder**—who was frequently on the phone to the Mayor about the Slayer—were all involved in some way. The Mayor of Sunnydale, it seemed, knew that Buffy Summers was the Slayer and was doing his best to thwart her. He did not, at that point, make any move to kill her, however, apparently preferring not to draw attention to himself until he had become more powerful.

Richard Wilkins III first appeared in season three's "Homecoming." He wanted Buffy out of the way; that much was clear. To do that, he would employ anyone or anything, from Mr. Trick to Ethan Rayne (in "Band Candy"). Still, never was there a happier evildoer than the mayor of Sunnydale. He had an obsession with cleanliness and enjoyed reading comics.

> **MAYOR:** "I just love *The Family Circus*. That P.J.'s getting to be quite a handful."
> **MR. TRICK:** "I like *Marmaduke*."
> **MAYOR:** "Oh! He's always on the furniture. Unsanitary."   **—"BAD GIRLS"**

He also frowned upon bad language among his supernatural lackeys.

In "Bad Girls," the Mayor performed a ritual that made him invulnerable to harm for 100 days, and we learned that it was a major step toward what he called his "Ascension." Over the course of the next few episodes, the Mayor's plan was revealed. He had started out, once upon a time, as a human being who worshiped the forces of

darkness. In 1899 he founded Sunnydale, and magically kept himself young ever since, apparently taking on the identity of his own son, grandson, and so on over the years. He married a woman named **Edna Mae** in 1903 and remained with her until she died, presumably of natural causes.

Through a series of carefully planned rituals and other events—such as eating the demonic spiders from the Box of Gavrok Faith retrieved for him in "Choices" the Mayor would have his wish: to become a full-fledged, pure demon.

In the first half of the two-part third season finale "Graduation Day," Anya (a former demon herself) revealed that she had once witnessed an Ascension.

> "About eight hundred years ago, in the Koskov Valley, above the Urals, there was a sorcerer there who achieved Ascension. Became the embodiment of the demon Lohesh . . . it decimated the village. Within hours. Maybe three people got out."
>
> —ANYA, IN "GRADUATION DAY, PART 1"

This demon was far more of a threat than the average demon of the Slayer's experience.

As previously quoted on page three, Anya explained the demon's Buffy battled daily were really hybrids, "tained" by walking the earth. Pure demons arrive here through specific rituals, such as the Ascension, and are therefore bigger, stronger, in esssence more evil.

One interesting facet of the Mayor's character was his relationship with the Slayer Faith. She became disillusioned with the Good Fight (see Faith and the Human Monster) and enlisted in his service, after which they developed a dark and twisted father-daughter relationship. Faith was the child he had never had, and he was the doting father she had always longed for.

Despite the horrible devastation he planned to wreak upon the earth, it was clear that the Mayor loved Faith, in his way. When Buffy and Faith battled, and Faith was badly injured and fell into a coma, the Mayor was heartbroken and furious with Buffy.

Given the massive threat posed by the Mayor's impending Ascension, Buffy did something previously unthinkable. She recruited the rest of the senior class to help her against him. Everyone had been keeping up a pretense that they were unaware of what really went on in Sunnydale, and that Buffy was battling those evil forces, though the facade of ignorance had slipped somewhat in "The Prom," when the senior class gave Buffy an award to thank her for being "Class Protector." Then, in

"Graduation Day, Part Two," at their graduation, the class came together under Buffy's leadership to fight the Mayor and his minions (the vampires were able to fight during the day thanks to an eclipse) with flamethrowers, stakes, and other weapons.

Upon his Ascension, the Mayor was transformed into a sixty-foot serpentine demon. It ate Principal Snyder, among others. However, Buffy, Giles, and the others were aware that at the time of the Mayor's Ascension, he lost the invulnerability he had previously achieved for one hundred days. During the battle, Buffy, playing on the Mayor's grief over the injured Faith—led the demon-snake on a wild chase through the school and into the library, where it became stuck . . . only to realize that Buffy and her friends had filled the school with explosives. The Slayer escaped out the window, and the school exploded, destroying the no-longer-invulnerable demon that the Mayor had become.

The Mayor made a brief appearance in Faith's dream before she woke up from her coma in season four's "This Year's Girl."

LURCONIS

"'Lurconis dwells beneath the city, filth to filth.' . . .'Lurconis,' it means 'glutton,' and…it'll be in the sewers." —GILES, IN "BAND CANDY"

EPISODE: "Band Candy," season three.

KEY RELATIONSHIPS: Lurconis was an enormous eel-like demon that resided in the sewers under Sunnydale. As a human hoping to ascend to true demonhood one day, the Mayor worshipped him and offered a tribute every thirty years.

UNIQUE ATTRIBUTES: Despite its size, Lurconis was lightning-fast.

MOST MONSTROUS MOMENT: It ate human babies given to it in tribute.

CURRENT STATUS: Buffy burned Lurconis to death.

In the *Buffy* universe, Lurconis is inextricably tied to the mayor of Sunnydale, Richard Wilkins III. In his hundred-year quest to become a pure demon himself, the mayor worshipped many demons. Among them was Lurconis, to whom a tribute had to be paid every thirty years.

Lurconis—a huge, swift, eel-like demon—lived in the sewers beneath Sunnydale. The tribute? Live human babies for the demon to devour.

In the season three episode "Band Candy," the Mayor decided that in order to get the babies without anyone noticing, he needed a major diversion. His henchman Mr. Trick hired the sorcerer Ethan Rayne to create that diversion—chocolate bars that made every adult in town psychologically regress to their irresponsible teenage years.

The Slayer was, of course, already a teenager. Buffy figured out the Mayor's plan, stopped Ethan and Trick, and destroyed Lurconis by burning it to death.

Jane Espenson, who wrote the episode, notes that "Lurconis is the Latin word for glutton. The root of the episode, obviously, is the horror of seeing your parents as children. They're the symbol of a loss of control. There's a primal fear of losing control of yourself, losing your parents, and the primal fear of snakes.

"They seem to have no obvious method of locomotion. If I lie on the floor and ripple my muscles, I'm not going to scoot along like a snake. So snakes seem kind of magical in how they move. They look wet, but they're not wet when you touch them. They shed their skin, which is very alarming.

"Lurconis appeared as a snake, primarily because if you imagine something else, like a giant sewer rat, in order to suggest size, all you could do is a big paw and the tip of its nose. But with a huge snake, being long and skinny, you can see a portion of it but suggest that it extends forever."

LAGOS

BUFFY: "I'm gonna vent a little hormonal angst by going out there and killing a Lagos, whatever that is."

ANGEL: "Lagos?"

BUFFY: "Yeah, he's some kind of demon looking for an all-powerful thingimibob and I've got to stop him before holy havoc's unleashed and it's another Tuesday night in Sunnydale."   —**"REVELATIONS"**

EPISODE: "Revelations," season three

UNIQUE ATTRIBUTES: A tall, warriorlike demon, Lagos wielded an ax and dressed in battle armor.

CURRENT STATUS: Buffy decapitated Lagos.

A seven-foot demon dressed in ancient battle gear and wielding an ax, Lagos appeared in the season three episode "Revelations." Gwendolyn Post had come to town pretending to be Faith's new Watcher, and she quickly marshaled both Slayers in an attempt to prevent Lagos from retrieving a powerful ancient weapon called the **Glove of Myhnegon.**

Mrs. Post wanted the Glove for herself, though Buffy managed to thwart her in that effort.

Giles discovered that the Glove was housed in the Von Hauptman family crypt in Restfield cemetery. Later, Buffy fought Lagos near the crypt, and beheaded him with his own ax.

ANYA (ANYANKA)

XANDER: "Hey, it's demon Anya, punisher of evil males. Still haven't got your powers back?"

ANYA: "No. I will, though, it's just a matter of time. You can laugh, but I have witnessed a millennium of treachery and oppression from the males of the species. I have nothing but contempt for the whole libidinous lot of them."

XANDER: "Then why are you talking to me?"

ANYA: "I don't have a date for the prom."

XANDER: "And gosh, I wonder why not. Can't possibly have anything to do with your sales pitch…"

ANYA: "Men are evil. Will you go with me?"

XANDER: "One of us is very confused, and I honestly don't know which."   —**"THE PROM"**

FIRST APPEARANCE: "The Wish," season three

OTHER EPISODES: season three: "Doppelgangland," "The Prom," "Graduation Day, Part One." season four: "The Harsh Light of Day," "Fear Itself," "Pangs," "Something Blue," "Hush," "A New Man," "The I in Team," "Goodbye, Iowa," "Who Are You," "Superstar," "Where the Wild Things Are," "New Moon Rising," "The Yoko Factor," "Primevil," "Restless"

KEY RELATIONSHIPS: The demon D'Hoffryn transformed Anya into a vengeance demon many centuries ago. When the amulet that held her power was destroyed, she became a human again. As a human, she is the girlfriend of Xander Harris.

UNIQUE ATTRIBUTES: As a demon, and now as a human, Anya has the ability to imagine horribly agonizing and creative methods of death and torture for the males of the species. As a demon, she could appear to be human but also had a monstrous visage.

MOST MONSTROUS MOMENT: In "The Wish," Anya gave Cordelia Chase her wish—that Buffy Summers had never come to Sunnydale. The town transformed into an alternate reality where vampires ruled. When the amulet that held Anyanka's power was destroyed, all reverted to normal.

CURRENT STATUS: Anya is fully human, involved with Xander, and a bit skittish around the members of the Initiative, as she is uncertain how they feel about *ex*-demons.

Eleven hundred and twenty years ago, a human girl named Anyanka became involved in the occult, specifically with a demon named D'Hoffryn.

> "Anyanka raised a demon to ruin her unfaithful lover. The demon did her bidding—but then cursed her and turned her into a sort of patron saint for scorned women. Apparently, the cry of a wronged woman is like a siren's call to Anyanka . . . she grants wishes." —GILES, IN "THE WISH"

In the season-three episode "The Wish" (which also gave us, albeit briefly, a nasty **"mucus-y demon"** that Buffy quickly dispatched), Anyanka was drawn to Sunnydale by the despair of Cordelia Chase. Cordy had caught her boyfriend, Xander Harris, kissing Willow Rosenberg. Anyanka let Cordelia hold an amulet that contained the focus of her wish-granting ability. Without realizing the power in her hands, Cordelia wished that Buffy—whom she blamed for all her woes—had never come to Sunnydale.

That wish altered reality. Cordelia found herself in a very different Sunnydale, a dark and frightening place where vampires ruled the night—including vampiric versions of Xander and Willow—and no human went out after dark. The Master was running this vampire kingdom and had created a machine that would drain the blood from humans, a vampire assembly line, so to speak. In that dark world Willow kept Angel as her pet, torturing him at her leisure, and she and Xander were the Master's pride and joy.

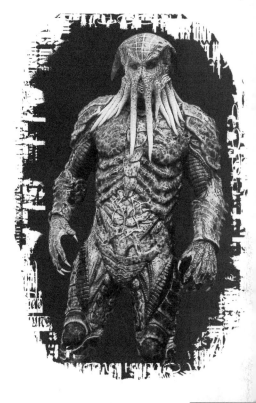

Cordelia knew what had gone wrong, what had changed, and tried to explain what had happened, but she was quickly killed by Xander and Willow. Fortunately, her words and the amulet, which she still had, inspired Rupert Giles and his group of vampire hunters to research Anyanka. Giles realized that Cordelia's claims of another reality might be true, and that destroying Anyanka's amulet might return things to normal. He took a huge leap of faith and smashed it. All was returned to the way it had been before, though not before Oz had staked the vampire version of Willow, and Buffy—never having been trained by Giles—was killed by the Master.

There was one major consequence of those events that remained in this reality: with her amulet destroyed, Anyanka, also known as Anya, lost all of her demonic power. In the episode "Doppelgangland," she appealed to D'Hoffryn to restore her power.

> **"For a thousand years I wielded the power of the wish. I brought ruin upon the heads of unfaithful men; I offered destruction and chaos for the pleasure of the lower beings. I was feared and worshiped across the mortal globe and now I'm stuck at Sunnydale High. A mortal! A child! And I'm flunking math."**
>
> **—ANYA, IN "DOPPELGANGLAND"**

Anya pleaded with D'Hoffryn to create a fold in time so that she could change the events that had taken place. D'Hoffryn refused, telling her that her time had passed. Anya then went to witch-in-training Willow and asked for her help to create the fold in order to retrieve something very special to her. Not yet aware of Anya's true nature, Willow agreed to help.

WILLOW: "Okay, that's a little blacker than I like my arts."
ANYA: "Oh, don't be such a wimp."

WILLOW: "That wasn't just a temporal fold, that was some weird hell place. I don't think you're telling me everything."

ANYA: "I swear, I'm just trying to find my necklace."

WILLOW: "Did you try looking inside the sofa in *hell?*"

—"DOPPELGANGLAND"

The spell failed. Partially. They were not able to retrieve Anya's amulet before it was destroyed. Instead, however, the vampiric version of Willow was drawn into *Buffy*'s reality. Eventually, she was sent back (just in time to be dusted; see Vampires: Vamp Willow). Thereafter, Anya had to come to grips with the truth of her situation. The millennium-old demon was merely a girl again, subject to raging hormones, the whims of high school teachers, and unable even to order a drink in a bar.

Now fully human for the first time in a thousand years, Anya had to learn to deal with the life of an eighteen-year-old girl. One facet of her new life that distracted her endlessly, and disturbed her deeply, was the relationship between females and males. Anya found herself drawn to Xander, and had an overwhelming urge to ask him to the prom.

She offered very helpful information to Buffy and the others when they went up against the Mayor in the two-part season three finale "Graduation Day," though she fled town rather than face the Mayor.

In the fourth season Anya was back, and quickly became more deeply involved with Xander. Though her age and her experiences as a demon give her a very strange perspective on almost everything—and her former demon status sometimes complicates their relationship—the couple have become boyfriend and girlfriend.

"We never intended for her to be a running character," notes "The Wish" writer Marti Noxon. "But [Emma Caulfield is] such a good actress. And it's fun having this disgruntled ex-demon around . . . who's sort of assimilating. We also needed a Cordelialike character around who would tell it like it is, who doesn't suffer fools gladly and is very opinionated. And that's Anya."

> "I'm not a demon, little girl. I'm something you can't conceive. The first evil. Beyond sin, beyond death . . . I am the thing the darkness fears. You will never see me, but I am everywhere. Every being, every thought, every drop of hate—"
>
> —THE FIRST, IN "AMENDS"

EPISODE: "Amends," season three.

KEY RELATIONSHIPS: The First is literally the first evil to have existed on earth, the precursor to all subsequent forces for darkness in the world.

UNIQUE ATTRIBUTES: While it is unknown if the First has any tangible form, it can manifest itself as pure energy and is capable of, if not reading minds, at least plucking images and emotions out of one's thoughts. The First can also create illusions including simulacrums of human beings. The limits of its power have not yet been explored.

MOST MONSTROUS MOMENT: The First attempted to drive Angel to madness so that he would murder Buffy.

CURRENT STATUS: When its plan was revealed, the First withdrew from Sunnydale. Its current whereabouts are unknown.

Technically, the First is not a demon. As previously noted, the First is the chaotic or evil entity that opposes the orderly goodness of the Powers That Be; it is the darkness that is in constant combat against the light. "Demon" is too simple a term, but other than giving it its own category, it seems logical to include it here. So what is it?

> "Evil. Absolute evil, older than man, than demons—very few have heard of it, fewer believe in it. But it is a force that transcends all realities, all dimensions, and if focused, could have had the power to bring Angel back." —GILES, IN "AMENDS"

At the beginning of season three, Angel returned from the hellish demon dimension that had sucked him in at the end of the previous season. How and why Angel returned were questions that went unanswered for a very long time. In that season's "Amends," however, we began to get an inkling of the purpose behind his return. Or, at least, we were given affirmation that there was a purpose.

Initially Giles suspected that the First was responsible for Angel's return. However it was revealed that the **Bringers**, eyeless high priests of the First, were drawing on its power to conjure false manifestations of those Angel had killed in the past in order to haunt him, to drive him either to madness or to evil. The primary manifestation created by the First was in the image of Jenny Calendar, an ally of Buffy's whom the evil Angel had killed. Through Jenny and others, the First attempted to convince Angel that he had been brought back to embrace his evil destiny and murder Buffy.

In his research, Giles found a reference to indicate that "nothing shall grow above or below" them, which prompted Buffy to recall a patch of mysteriously dead vegetation at a Christmas tree farm she and her mother had been to.

GILES: "They're known as the Bringers, or the Harbingers…. High priests of the First. They can conjure spirit manifestations of the power, set them on people. Influence them, haunt them…"

BUFFY: "These are the guys working the mojo on Angel."

XANDER: "We gotta stop 'em."

GILES: "You can't fight the First, Buffy. It's not a physical being."

BUFFY: "But I can fight these priest guys."

—"AMENDS"

Buffy defeated the Bringers, only to come face-to-face with a manifestation of the First.

The First warned Buffy that Angel would be dead by sunrise and then departed. For his part, Angel had been driven so far over the edge that he planned to let the sun of Christmas morning destroy him. Buffy tried to convince him otherwise, and they were still arguing about it when it began to snow, preventing the sun from killing him.

It was clear that this was some sort of miraculous intervention by a higher power. It was possible at that time to interpret Angel's return—from a demon dimension at the beginning of the season—in two ways. Either the First had brought him back in order to drive him mad and use him as a weapon, or some other power had brought him back, and the First considered him a threat.

The First remains a significant threat not merely to Buffy and Angel but, apparently, to the whole world.

"They've never been seen alive, just dead. A lot."   —BUFFY, IN "GINGERBREAD"

EPISODE: "Gingerbread," season three

KEY RELATIONSHIPS: Though actually a single being (see "unique attributes" below), this vengeance demon was apparently the inspiration for the Hansel and Gretel story.

UNIQUE ATTRIBUTES: Hans and Greta were actually two parts of a single vengeance demon that could separate itself and take on the appearance of two young children. It could manipulate and influence human minds.

MOST MONSTROUS MOMENT: The demon spent centuries moving from village to town and whipping up anti-witch hysteria that led to a multitude of executions over the years.

CURRENT STATUS: Buffy impaled the combined demon with the very post upon which—thanks to evil influence—she was nearly burned at the stake for witchcraft.

A boy and girl appeared in Sunnydale at the beginning of the season three episode "Gingerbread." They had apparently been murdered in some sort of ritual, signified by certain markings found at the crime scene. Their deaths caused the entire community to rise up against witchcraft and magic, and to strike out at those young people who were believed to dabble in such things. At first, this was only in a relatively normal parental manner, as the parents joined together in a group called **Mothers Opposed to the Occult** (or, MOO).

With demonic influence, and the encouragement of seemingly ghostly apparitions of the dead children, the parents' furor over witchcraft soon turned into mob madness. Willow Rosenberg, Amy Madison (see Magic Users), and Buffy herself were tied to stakes. The town's adult population, led by Buffy's and Willow's mothers, planned to burn them to death for witchcraft.

By that time, however, the gang had already figured out that the dead children were neither normal children nor were they actually dead. Every fifty years, dating back to Germany in 1649, a similar crime occurred—with a similar response from the community. The first record was the 1649 report by "a cleric from a village near the

Black Forest. He found the bodies himself. Two children . . . Greta Strauss, age six. Hans Strauss, eight."

That discovery led to a startling hypothesis:

GILES: "There's a fringe theory held by a few folklorists that some regional stories have actual, very literal antecedents. . . ."

BUFFY: "And in some language that's English?"

OZ: "Fairy tales are real."

BUFFY: "Hans and Greta. Hansel and Gretel."

GILES: "There are demons that thrive on fostering persecution and hatred among the mortal animals. Not on destroying men, but on watching them destroy each other. They feed us our darkest fear, and turn peaceful communities into vigilantes."

BUFFY: "Hansel and Gretel go home and tell on the mean old witch. . . ."

GILES: "And she and probably dozens of others are punished by a righteous mob. It's happened throughout history. It happened in Salem, not surprisingly." **—"GINGERBREAD"**

Thus, there were never children by the name of Hansel and Gretel, only a **chaos demon** (capable of splitting itself into two forms) that enjoyed fomenting such violence and hatred among humans. The people of Sunnydale were under the influence of "Hansel and Gretel." Giles used magic to free the townspeople from the demon's influence and to drop the illusion it used to disguise its true appearance. It merged back into its one, true form, and Buffy ran it through.

Buffy co-producer Jane Espenson penned the final "Gingerbread" script. "Much of 'Gingerbread' is not mine," she says. "It was largely based on someone else's pitch and then was rewritten after I was done with it. But the one aspect of it that was mine all the way through was Hansel and Gretel. I was very proud of that.

"As I set out to write this, I was thinking, we have two little kids who are evil, who were little kids forever, and are going to foment this anti-witch sentiment. I was thinking, two little kids who hate witches, why is this resonating? It occurred to me that I knew two little kids who hate witches and they were young and cute and blond, which was what we wanted. In that myth, our heroes, the little kids, push the old lady into the oven, and kill her. They cook her. These are our good guys. Why are they the good guys? Even in self-defense, to push someone into an oven and cook them seems extreme.

"I thought, let's turn that myth around and say that they were the bad guys, that she was a helpless old lady, and that they've been cooking witches for many years. We have had the human monstrousness of burning women suspected of witchcraft for a very long time, and doesn't it kind of make sense that there was some agency, some force behind it? I like the idea of demons that use the appearance of youth and innocence to create fear and killing.

"One of my original problems with the story was that people die in Sunnydale all the time, so why are they getting so upset now? It has to do with the fact that these were little kids. The fact that they were young and cute and Hansel-and-Gretel-y is what gives them power. It's power out of the appearance of weakness. That's a common trick. If you meet the helpless old lady in the forest and she asks for a bite of your food, chances are she's a big powerful witch and if you don't give it to her, you're in trouble. The idea of smallness as a lure is really interesting because we're so susceptible to it.

"Also, the fact that they turned into one demon at the end was something that I had been toying with. They were two entities to all appearances, but they seemed to act on a single impulse. I had them finishing each other's sentences and speaking in unison a lot in my draft. It seemed to me that they were acting as one thing. I thought about making them one demon, but I didn't have an okay to do that. So I wrote it as two. Then we were talking about it, and Joss said, 'Shoot, we're going to have to get two costumes made.' And I said, 'Well, I have this other notion. What if they became one demon?' And he said, 'Great, do that!'

"Also, I specifically tried to make the demon look German, because Hansel and Gretel were German. It was supposed to have a kind of Wagnerian aspect to it. That's why Giles comes in at the end screaming like Hitler. He's chanting in German.

"I think we called it a chaos demon, which we've mentioned in the series before. Human beings love order. The world is full of disorder. Human beings are constantly trying to bring it into some semblance of order, and the world always fights back. Disorder became demonized, as if it were an actual entity against which we struggle. Entropy as demon. I think that's why so many of our demons have that function. They just want to get in and mess things up.

"The Hansel and Gretel demons thrive on a very specific kind of disorder; they thrive on persecution, a human failing. This is a way, historically, for people to divorce themselves from human weaknesses. 'I wasn't really persecuting, I was possessed by a demon of persecution.' When people speak of their failings as 'personal demons,' they're trying to dissociate themselves from them. Something from outside is influencing me and making me do these bad things. It's a way to protect our notions of ourselves and the goodness at our core. That's why it is natural to speak of a persecution demon, it means there's no human responsibility."

THE SISTERHOOD OF JHE

"The Sisterhood of Jhe is an apocalypse cult. They exist solely to bring about world destruction. And we've not seen the last of them. More will follow."

—GILES, IN "THE ZEPPO"

EPISODE: "The Zeppo," season three

UNIQUE ATTRIBUTES: Hideous she-demons, the Sisterhood is an apocalypse cult, dedicated to world destruction.

MOST MONSTROUS MOMENT: They opened the Hellmouth.

CURRENT STATUS: Several members of the Sisterhood of Jhe were slain in "The Zeppo." It is not known if others of their number still survive.

Beyond what Giles related about them in "The Zeppo," little is known about the Sisterhood of Jhe. They came to Sunnydale to perpetuate their apocalyptic agenda by opening the Hellmouth and shattering the barrier separating Earth from the demon dimensions. Buffy, Faith, Giles, Willow, and Xander battled them at the opening of the episode, during which they were revealed to be huge, hideous, and obviously female demons.

Later in the episode Faith battled one of the demons herself. It gave her quite a bit of trouble, and when Xander rammed it with a car, it was only momentarily stunned. Faith got into the car with Xander and they left the scene, presumably because Faith realized that stopping the approaching apocalypse was more important than defeating a single member of the Sisterhood.

Though they never appeared again in the episode, it was clear that the Sisterhood achieved their goal of opening the Hellmouth, albeit briefly. While Buffy, Angel, and Faith battled the massive demons that attempted to escape into our dimension, Giles and Willow cast a binding spell to close the Hellmouth up again. The fate of the Sisterhood of Jhe was not revealed and their current whereabouts, if they indeed survive, are unknown.

BALTHAZAR

> "Okay. We got ten, maybe twelve bad guys and one big demon in desperate need of a Stair-Master." —BUFFY, IN "BAD GIRLS"

EPISODE: "Bad Girls," season three

KEY RELATIONSHIPS: Balthazar had once wielded influence in Sunnydale before being driven out in 1899 by Richard Wilkins (later the town's mayor). He employed El Eliminati, a sect of Italian vampire swordsmen.

UNIQUE ATTRIBUTES: Balthazar was extraordinarily obese and pale, and his skin was so dry that it had to be constantly moistened by servants. He had the magical ability to move objects and people by the sheer force of his will.

MOST MONSTROUS MOMENT: Making his servants bathe his blubbery back.

CURRENT STATUS: Balthazar was elotrocuted by Buffy at the climax of "Bad Girls."

A group of Italian vampire swordsmen called **El Eliminati** had appeared in Sunnydale, and the newly arrived Watcher, Wesley Wyndam-Pryce, was familiar with them.

> "Fifteenth-century duelist cult. Deadly in their day, their numbers dwindled in later centuries due to an increase in anti-vampire activity and a lot of pointless dueling. They eventually became the acolytes of a demon called Balthazar, who brought them to the new world. Specifically, here. . . . They were driven out a hundred years ago. Balthazar was, happily, killed." —WESLEY, IN "BAD GIRLS"

Rumors of Balthazar's death had, as they saying goes, been greatly exaggerated. It turned out that he was still alive and that El Eliminati were still in his employ. Balthazar was back in Sunnydale in search of an amulet he had left behind when he had been driven out a century earlier. Later revelations indicate Balthazar knows of the Mayor's plan to Ascend (Given the dates involved it's possible Balthazar was driven out by the Mayor one hundred years ago).

In 1999 Balthazar was in a greatly weakened state and his acolytes were attempting to find his amulet in order to restore his power. It had once belonged to him and was buried in one of the tombs in Sunnydale.

When first shown onscreen, Balthazar is revealed to be absolutely repulsive in appearance. "A horrible, five-hundred-pound demon," according to the script. "Pale, pasty-white skin. A vampire ladles water onto his enormous expanse of a back, keeping him wet."

So . . . gross.

The demon also had a kind of magical telekinesis, the ability to move objects by merely willing it. Though Giles and Wesley were briefly captured by El Eliminati, Buffy, Giles, and Angel killed most of the sword cult, and Buffy herself electrocuted Balthazar. He gave her a final warning before gasping his last, however. "When he rises," the demon wheezed, "you'll wish I had killed you all." An obvious reference to the Mayor, though the gang did not know that at the time.

Executive story editor Douglas Petrie, who scripted "Bad Girls," is quick to point out the inspiration for the demon's repulsive appearance.

"Balthazar is directly linked to Marvel Comics," Petrie says. "I've always wanted to do a character who was like [the Marvel Comics' villain] the Kingpin, especially Frank Miller's version. For a lot of reasons, there was never a place for that. There was an issue of Miller's *Daredevil* where he gets flushed down into the sewers of New York and he runs into this doppelganger of the Kingpin. [The doppelganger is] pale white, and he has this club and he's horrible and he's the king of this underground world. I thought that was great. I wanted to do a grotesquely obese villain who was completely unhealthy, really pale white, and scary. I would draw sketches but no one ever saw them. I would doodle this guy.

"Joss and I, over Thanksgiving vacation last year, came up with [Balthazar]. Then the art department just went nuts creating this huge suit. The actor did a great job finding the humor in it without undercutting the menace. It was so gross. I wanted it to be disgusting and they took it so much further than I envisioned. It's hard to watch, but it's hilarious."

D'HOFFRYN

"D'Hoffryn is one of the lower beings. He made me a demon eleven hundred and twenty years ago."
—ANYA, IN "SOMETHING BLUE

FIRST APPEARANCE: "Doppelgangland," season three

OTHER EPISODES: "Something Blue," season four

KEY RELATIONSHIPS: D'Hoffryn is part of a council of demons who can bestow power and immortality upon humans by making them vengeance demons. He once did so for Anya, and in "Something Blue," offered to do so for Willow, who refused.

UNIQUE ATTRIBUTES: D'Hoffryn apparently has extraordinary powers of magical observation, able to watch earthly goings-on from his own dimension, to and from which he can also transport people.

MOST MONSTROUS MOMENT: Offering to turn Willow ino a vengeance demon.

CURRENT STATUS: D'Hoffryn is believed to still be in his home dimension, monitoring the progress of the vengeance demons he has created in the past, and possible candidates for the future.

D'Hoffryn is part of a sort of demon council whose purpose is to offer human beings with a gift for malice and mischief the chance to become full-fledged, immortal, vengeance demons. Anya (Anyanka) received her demon upgrade from him. D'Hoffryn first appeared in "Doppelgangland," when Anya appealed to him to restore her demonic power and aspect, which had been taken away when Giles destroyed her amulet in "The Wish."

> **"I'd been dumped, I was miserable. Doing a few vengeance spells—boils on the penis, nothing fancy—the lower beings got wind of me, they offered to elevate me. They made me a demon."** —ANYA, IN "SOMETHING BLUE"

D'Hoffryn returned in season four's "Something Blue."

Grieving after Oz's departure from Sunnydale, Willow cast a spell in an effort to force him to love her again. The result of the spell, however, was that anything she said would come true. Chaos ensued. D'Hoffryn was so impressed—for he thought Willow had done that on purpose—that he brought her to a demon dimension and offered to make her a vengeance demon as he had done with Anya.

> **"The pain and suffering you brought upon those you love has been inspired. You are ready to join us."** —D'HOFFRYN, IN "SOMETHING BLUE"

Willow declined, of course, and was returned to her own dimension. D'Hoffryn, however, gave her a talisman she could use to contact the lower beings just in case. "You change your mind, give us a chant."

SKYLER

SKYLER: "Check 'em out. That's quality merchandise. Worth five grand, easy."
FAITH: "Books of Ascension?"
SKYLER: "Original editions and everything. Great condition: a little worn on one spine, slight foxing, otherwise perfect. Now the five grand is, you know, negotiable."
FAITH (stabbing him): "I don't like to haggle." —"ENEMIES"

EPISODE: "Enemies," season three

UNIQUE ATTRIBUTES: A sniveling coward, Skyler dressed like a middle-aged tourist.

CURRENT STATUS: Murdered by Faith.

A sniveling but enterprising demon black-marketeer with small horns, pointed ears, and a horrible fashion sense, Skyler nervously approached Buffy and Faith with an offer to sell them the Books of Ascension in season three's "Enemies." At that point, Buffy, Giles, and the others were still quite in the dark about the Mayor's plans. No doubt the books would have come in handy. Unfortunately for them, and for Skyler, Faith had already begun to work for the Mayor. While the others worked out if and how to pay the demon, Faith went to the place where Skyler was staying, killed him, and took the books to the Mayor for safekeeping.

TELEPATHS

WILLOW: "Scabby Demon got away?"

BUFFY: "Scabby Demon number two got away. Scabby Demon number one, big check in the 'Slay' column."

WILLOW: "I don't like this 'no mouth' thing. It's disquieting."

BUFFY: "Well, no mouth means no teeth—unless they have them somewhere else...."

—**"EARSHOT"**

EPISODE: "Earshot," season three

KEY RELATIONSHIPS: With one another.

UNIQUE ATTRIBUTES: These demons have no mouths and communicated with one another telepathically.

MOST MONSTROUS MOMENT: When Buffy killed one of the demons and it bled on her, she was infected with its telepathic power until the blood of the second was used to cure her.

CURRENT STATUS: Buffy killed the first, and Angel later killed the second in order to use its blood for Buffy's cure.

Though they are never given a species name, the pair of telepathic **"scabby demons"** in season three's "Earshot" episode were fascinating. When Buffy killed the first one, it bled on her, with dire results. As Giles later explained, she was thus tainted by "an aspect of the demon."

Buffy found that she had been infected with uncontrollable telepathy. She could hear the thoughts of those around her, which she found pretty cool at first, but the cacophony of mental voices began to drive her mad. Once the source of her ailment was revealed, Angel killed the surviving mouthless demon so that Giles could make an antidote, and Buffy was cured.

The episode is a favorite of its writer, series co-producer Jane Espenson. "The story was pitched originally as psychic cheating, so we needed a method to get somebody psychic," she recalls. "As like breeds like, a psychic demon seemed like a good place to start. It was just my whimsy that a psychic demon wouldn't need a mouth.

"The fact that you're a Slayer means you associate with demons. Therefore, infection through demon contact is sort of a professional hazard. Like cops and criminals. Cops hang out with cops and criminals. I've heard it said that sometimes when cops go over the edge and become bad cops and take money and stuff, it's because this is the world that they're immersed in. Buffy has special nonhuman powers; there's a hint of the demon world in her. This is an episode in which you got to explore the idea of Buffy having powers beyond human. Willow even *thinks,* 'She's hardly even human anymore.' So I think this is an episode where we take Buffy to the point of being a monster. The notion of balance, that you need the good and the evil—which Whistler articulates, and then Doyle articulates in the pilot of *Angel*—has certainly been a part of mythology and theology in our actual world for a very long time. You need these two opposing forces, and Buffy is the captain of one of them, but her job would be meaningless without the other."

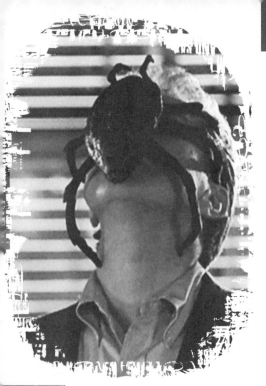

GAVROK SPIDERS

> "I wouldn't leave that open…."
> —THE MAYOR, REFERRING TO THE BOX OF GAVROK,
> CONTAINING THE GAVROK SPIDERS, IN "CHOICES"

EPISODE: "Choices," season three

KEY RELATIONSHIPS: There were billions of these creatures in the Box of Gavrok. The Mayor ate a number of them as part of his preparations for his Ascension.

UNIQUE ATTRIBUTES: The creatures from the Box of Gavrok are not truly spiders but enormous mutant insectoids whose appearance is reminiscent of giant spiders. They kill by tearing off a human's face though it seems likely that there is also some form of venom or suffocation at work as well.

MOST MONSTROUS MOMENT: See "tearing off people's faces."

CURRENT STATUS: It is unknown how many spiders remain in the Box of Gavrok, or what the current location of the box is.

Though not necessarily demons, the creatures within the Box of Gavrok are most certainly evil. They are savage, mindless, insectoid creatures, and the box purportedly contains billions of them. In "Choices," the Mayor acquired the box as part of his preparation for Ascension. It was briefly in Buffy's possession, but when the Mayor took Willow captive, they were forced to trade it back to him in exchange for her freedom.

Some of the spiders escaped during this exchange, and one of them killed a Sunnydale High security guard by ravaging his face and literally tearing it off. One of the escaped spiders was crushed to death by Buffy and the other was killed by Faith with a knife (The Mayor—still invulnerable for one hundred days—was impervious to their attack.)

The Mayor needed to eat some of the Gavrok Spiders. How many he ate and how many remain in the box are as much of a mystery as the current whereabouts of the box itself.

According to series producer David Fury, who wrote the episode, "You can credit Marti Noxon with the spiders. The Box of Gavrok was pretty much your basic MacGuffin. We knew it was something the Mayor wanted for part of his Ascension. When it came time to decide what it was going to be, it was 'what scares you, Marti?' Marti's very scared of spiders. We talked about a lot of different things. We have limited resources to pull off a lot of great effects. I don't know if you noticed, but they're six-legged spiders. Right away, they look more like evil ticks. So we called them spiders, but they have this bulbous body with six legs. I'd love to tell you that it was some genius behind it, but it was almost arbitrary. What can we do that's in the box that will be creepy and Buffy can fight?"

HELLHOUNDS

"My three fiercest babies are on their way to the dance right now. You think formal wear makes them crazy? Wait till they see the mirror ball."

—TUCKER, IN "THE PROM"

EPISODE: "The Prom," season three

KEY RELATIONSHIPS: Trained by Tucker Wells.

UNIQUE ATTRIBUTES: Demonic foot soldiers who have the appearance of large savage hounds.

MOST MONSTROUS MOMENT: They eat brains. Enough said.

CURRENT STATUS: Buffy killed the four Hellhounds in "The Prom," but others likely exist.

Mindless demonic beasts, the Hellhounds were raised by **Tucker Wells**, a Sunnydale High student with a gripe ("The Prom"). Tucker trained four of them to attack anyone dressed in typical formal wear, (using videos of *Carrie, Pretty in Pink,* and others to get them to recognize the trappings of a prom) so that he could ruin the Sunnydale High prom and kill many of the students there.

"Particularly vicious foe. It's a type of demon foot soldier, bred during the Mahkash wars. Trained solely to kill, they feed on the brains of their foes."   —GILES, IN "THE PROM"

Buffy managed to kill the Hellhounds—by stabbing, shooting with an arrow, and snapping a neck— before they could ruin the prom.

KATHY NEWMAN AND TAPPARICH

"It wasn't enough for her to take my sweater, now she has to horn in on my dreams! She's the most ever mooch—oh! And I haven't even gotten to the floss."

—BUFFY, IN "LIVING CONDITIONS"

FIRST APPEARANCE (KATHY): "The Freshman," season four

OTHER EPISODES (AND FIRST APPEARANCE OF TAPPARICH): "Living Conditions," season four

KEY RELATIONSHIPS: Kathy fled her demon dimension to escape her controlling father, Tapparich. Disguised as a human, she enrolled at UC Sunnydale, and was briefly Buffy Summers's roommate.

UNIQUE ATTRIBUTES: A self-involved, obsessively neat demon, she has a fondness for bubble-gum pop music.

MOST MONSTROUS MOMENT: In "Living Conditions," Kathy performed a ritual that drew all the goodness out of Buffy and into herself in hopes that the demons her father sent to bring her home would mistakenly take Buffy instead. (Oh, and she borrowed Buffy's favorite sweater without asking and then spilled ketchup on it!)

CURRENT STATUS: Tapparich came to Earth and took Kathy back home with him.

When the fourth season opened, Buffy was enrolled at the University of California at Sunnydale. By the second episode, "Living Conditions," it became obvious that she was—like many college students—having trouble getting along with her new roommate, Kathy. She seemed amiable enough, but her personality—everything from her love of bland pop music to her borrowing Buffy's sweater without asking—clashed with Buffy's at every possible turn.

The two encountered a demon on the campus, and Buffy saved Kathy without her roommate even becoming aware of the danger she was in (apparently). The tension between them, however, only continued to grow.

> "Argggh! She's even affecting my work now! She's the *Titanic!* She's a crawling black cancer!"
> —BUFFY, ON KATHY, IN "LIVING CONDITIONS"

Despite the obvious conflict, Buffy's severely hostile response seemed an overreaction, even to her friends. Add to that a certain amount of anxiety over dreams she had been having—dreams in which a grotesque figure chanted in a guttural voice while pouring blood into her mouth, placed a scorpion on her belly, then sucked a kind of ectoplasmic light out of her mouth—well, she was a bit on edge.

> "Kathy's evil. I'm an evil-fighter. It's simple. I have to kill her."
> —BUFFY, IN "LIVING CONDITIONS"

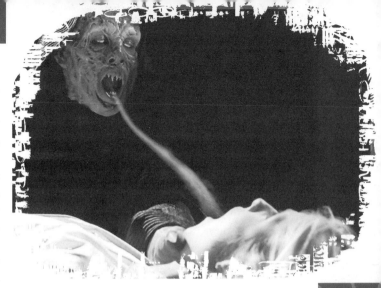

This new, paranoid, obsessed Buffy collected her roommate's toenail clippings and measured them. She believed that they were still growing, and that this indicated that Kathy was a demon, making her fair game for slaying. Giles and Buffy's other friends—convinced Buffy was not in her right mind, perhaps possessed by the demon she had met on campus earlier in the episode—held her captive so that they might help her.

In a murderous rage, Buffy escaped and returned to her dorm room, where she finally faced off against Kathy. In the initial moments of their physical conflict, Kathy's "human" face was ripped off, revealing Kathy as a demon from the same dimension as those Buffy had fought on campus. She had fled from the controlling attitudes of her father—the demon Tapparich—and taken up life in false human guise. Buffy's dreams were part of an elaborate ritual that Kathy was performing each night; a ritual that would make her pursuers take Buffy rather than her.

> "Look, I'm sorry, okay? I left my dimension to go to college and they sent these guys after me. They don't know what shape I took as a human, but they can always sense a creature without a soul, which I don't have. So I'm borrowing yours. . . ."
> —KATHY, IN "LIVING CONDITIONS"

Just as with the sweater, Kathy was borrowing without asking. Each night, she had taken a piece of Buffy's soul. When Giles examined the toenail clippings Buffy had given him earlier, he discovered that Buffy was indeed correct. He and Willow quickly performed a spell to reverse Kathy's soul-sucking ritual. Just in time, too, as Tapparich appeared moments later to reclaim his daughter.

TAPPARICH: "There you are. Do you have any idea how much trouble you're in young lady?"
KATHY: "I'm not going back!"
TAPPARICH: "Don't take that tone with me."
KATHY: "I'm three thousand years old! When are you going to stop treating me like I'm nine hundred?"
TAPPARICH: "When you stop acting that way. I can't tell you how much you've upset your mother."

KATHY: "You never let me do anything."

TAPARRICH: "Enough. You're coming home."

—TRANSLATED FROM THE DEMON DIALOGUE IN "LIVING CONDITIONS"

Kathy's demon father drew her through a portal back to the demon dimension of her birth. It is presumed that she still resides there, and that she spends a good deal of her time sulking about it.

Marti Noxon, who wrote the episode, notes that she "went through a lot of ideas about that character. At one point I asked Joss, 'Do you think they get television in hell? Cause maybe she's been watching reruns of *The Paper Chase* or something?' The idea was that she runs away to join the human race. We had played with making her a more sympathetic character, but that didn't really work. She was a runaway who just wanted to be like the other kids, but had the misfortune of trying to steal the soul of the Slayer."

GACHNAR

Fig. 237 GACHNAR - FIR MEIT

XANDER: (baby talk): "Who's a little fear demon? C'mon, who's a little fear demon?"

GILES: "Don't taunt the fear demon."

XANDER: "Why? Can he hurt me?"

GILES: "No, it's just…tacky."   —"FEAR, ITSELF"

EPISODE: "Fear, Itself," season four

KEY RELATIONSHIPS: Gachnar is a Fear Demon.

UNIQUE ATTRIBUTES: Though hideous and fearsome looking, Gachnar is in reality only a few inches tall. He is capable, however, of rooting through the human psyche for a person's innermost fears and making them manifest in terrifying ways. He is also capable of altering the physical surroundings of an area in which he has been summoned.

MOST MONSTROUS MOMENT: All of the Halloween decorations at the fraternity party during which Gachnar was summoned were suddenly made real by his power. The peeled grapes meant to look like eyeballs? Yep, them too.

CURRENT STATUS: Buffy stomped this tiny demon, literally. However it seems that this was only a single manifestation of Gachnar, and that the Fear Demon is now in his own dimension, continuing to fulfill his evil function.

In the fourth episode of the fourth season, *Buffy* presented its second Halloween-themed show. David Fury, the episode's writer, notes that "it was a very big deal to do this on Halloween, because the first *Buffy* Halloween episode was a classic. It was hard to come up with an idea that didn't play off of costumes. Trying to get to the root of Halloween, which is fear."

Given the previously established bit of lore that prescribed very little supernatural activity on Halloween night, Buffy felt free to attend a Halloween masquerade party with her friends at a UC Sunnydale fraternity house. Unbeknownst to our stalwart Scooby Gang, however, a frat brother had used chalk to draw an occult symbol on the floor. Copying it from a book, the student was unaware that the symbol was a real one . . . with real power. In this case, it had the power to call upon Gachnar, a Fear Demon, if a splash of blood was added to the symbol. Oz cut his hand, and the final ingredient for the chaotic recipe was in place.

The result of the calling of Gachnar was twofold, apparently reflecting the demon's specific powers. First, the more general fears of humanity represented by the many Halloween decorations were exacerbated when the decorations became real. Tarantulas and skeletons came to life, fake eyeballs in a bowl were no longer mere tasty treats. More particularly, however, the individual fears of those within the house were also brought to life. Oz could no longer predict his change into a werewolf, as it was suddenly out of synch with the phases of the moon. Xander became invisible to his friends. Willow could not control her magic, and she lost Oz.

"These characters have seen every horrible thing imaginable," says David Fury. "We dealt with their more hidden fears in the episode 'Nightmares' in the first season. This could be seen as a companion piece to that. We toyed with the idea of some of those fears and nightmares rearing their heads and [the characters now] reacting to them differently. We grow. The things that scared us two years ago are not the same things we fear now. That's why the fears are personalized: Oz fears hurting Willow, Willow fears her magic getting the better of her, Xander fears getting left behind by his friends and ceasing to exist for them now that he's a townie and they go to college. It was sort of taking the 'Nightmares' idea and looking at our characters two years later and seeing where they're at."

Gachnar also tried to prey on the fear of desertion that had festered in Buffy since her parents' divorce and grown to epic proportions in the wake of Angel's departure, but she was much too strong a person for the demon to overwhelm. She managed to ignore its influence and bring her friends back to their right minds as well. Thereafter, Willow discovered the book the student had copied the occult symbol from in the first place, and they identified the symbol on the floor as the Mark of Gachnar.

WILLOW: "The icon's called the Mark of Gachnar. I think this is a summoning spell for something called . . ."
XANDER: "Gachnar?"
WILLOW: "Yes! Somehow the beginning of the spell was accidentally triggered. Gachnar's trying to manifest itself. To come into being."

BUFFY: "How?"
WILLOW: "It feeds on . . . fear."
BUFFY: "Our fears are manifesting. We're feeding it. We have to stop."　　**—"FEAR, ITSELF"**

Soon enough, Giles and Anya managed to break into the house. The Watcher immediately realized the situation, and knew that they had to prevent Gachnar from manifesting. Giles found a passage in the spell book and began to read: "The summoning spell for Gachnar can be shut down in one of two ways. Destroying the Mark of Gachnar . . ."

Buffy instantly did precisely that, shattering the floor where the mark was inscribed . . . only to have Giles continue to read, greatly annoyed. ". . . is *not* one of them, and will, in fact, immediately bring forth the Fear Demon, itself."

Uh-oh. But not so much, actually. When Gachnar immediately manifested, it was revealed to be a very tiny demon, inspiring chuckles from those gathered.

"Gachnar is a tiny, two-inch demon because that's what your fear is," says David Fury. "It doesn't amount to much. We make much more of our fears than what they are. There had been talk about a big-ass fight at the end with Buffy. It seemed funnier if there was no fight. All this stuff they're dealing with doesn't really amount to much."

BUFFY: "This . . . is Gachnar?"
XANDER: "Big overture. Little show."
GACHNAR: "I am the Dark Lord of nightmares, the bringer of terror . . . Tremble before me! Fear me!"
WILLOW: "He's so cute."　　**—"FEAR, ITSELF"**

Buffy stomped the demon with one foot, and the tiny threat was averted. The crisis had passed. However, it must not be assumed that simply because Gachnar's manifestation was destroyed that the demon himself does not still exist.

"They destroyed that manifestation of Gachnar, but that doesn't mean he's dead," Fury assures us. "A lot of these demons, you can't really kill. He's been summoned, and you could summon him again."

VAHRALL DEMONS

WILLOW: "An ancient ritual—it uses the blood of a man, the bones of a child, and…and something called the Word of Valios. It's all part of a sacrifice. 'The Sacrifice of Three.'"

BUFFY: "Let me guess. It ends the world."

—"DOOMED"

EPISODE: "Doomed," season four

UNIQUE ATTRIBUTES: Vahrall demons are large, silent creatures with long talons and enormous strength. They carve their symbol, a stylized eye, upon the flesh of their victims.

MOST MONSTROUS MOMENT: After collecting the blood of a man (through murder), the bones of a child (through grave robbing) and the Word of Valios (a talisman they brutalized Giles to acquire), the Vahrall demons attempted to use those items to perform a ritual that would open the Hellmouth.

CURRENT STATUS: After one of the demons managed to leap into the breached Hellmouth, and a second was thrown into it by Spike, Buffy managed to go in and bring back the third, and then killed it. By doing so, she prevented their ritual from being completed, and the Hellmouth remained closed.

At the beginning of season four's "Doomed," Sunnydale was rocked by its latest earthquake. Given that the last time there was a quake in town (in season one's "Prophecy Girl") Buffy was killed by the Master and brought back to life, she was concerned that the latest seismic activity might have signaled the approach of the apocalypse. A reasonable suspicion, given Sunnydale's history, save for the fact that Southern California is commonly afflicted with earthquakes. Giles was more concerned about discovering the truth about the **Initiative** (a truth Buffy, who had fallen for Initiative member Riley, was not ready to share with him at the time), and so initially disregarded her fears.

At a fraternity party, an enormous creature called a Vahrall demon killed a student and drained him of blood. The Vahrall demon carved an eye symbol on the chest of its victim. Giles quickly realized his error—the apocalypse was at hand after all.

GILES: "The end of the world."

XANDER/WILLOW: "Again?"

GILES: "The earthquake, this symbol—"

BUFFY: "I told you! Giles, I said 'end of the world,' and you're all like . . . pooh pooh, Southern California pooh pooh—"

GILES: "I'm so very sorry. My contrition completely dwarfs the impending apocalypse."

WILLOW: "No. No. It just can't be. We did this already."

XANDER: "It is losing its impact a little."

GILES: "End of the world. Divisions break down, hell itself flows into our lives like a sea of fire. Loss, tears and heart-rending pain without end for every human man, woman, and child on this Earth. Death ten times over. For each of you and everyone you love."

XANDER: "Hmm. Feeling the impact again." —**"DOOMED"**

When Buffy came upon one of the Vahrall demons stealing the bones of a child from a mausoleum, Giles and Willow were able to determine what the demons' plan was—to open the Hellmouth. The Vahrall species themselves are huge, vicious demons, described differently by Giles's research and the Initiative's methodical agent, Riley Finn.

GILES (reads): "'Slick like gall, and gird in moonlight, father of portents and brother to blight . . .'"

BUFFY (taking over): "'Limbs with talons, eyes like knives. Bane to the blameless, thief of lives.'" —**"DOOMED"**

" . . . three meters tall, approximately one hundred to one-twenty kilograms, based on my visual analysis . . . Here's one for the good guys. Thing's got a pheromone signature a mile wide." —**RILEY, IN "DOOMED"**

The ritual the Vahrall demons were planning to perform was part of "the sacrifice of three." It required the blood of a man, the bones of a child, and "something called the Word of Valios." Buffy, Giles, and the others knew that if they could keep the Word of Valios from the demons, all would be well. In the midst of researching that very thing, Giles discovered that he had it in his possession all along. It was an amulet, a talisman. Just after he dug it out of an old trunk, however, he was attacked by three Vahrall demons. They took it and beat him before departing.

"It was in a lot I purchased at a sorcerer's real estate sale. I really only glanced at it once, thought it was a knockoff." —**GILES, IN "DOOMED"**

With Giles injured, Buffy had to proceed to the ruins of Sunnydale High School—which had been blown up in the previous season's finale—the site of the Hellmouth. Along with her friends and Spike, she battled the demons to keep them from completing their ritual sacrifice and opening the Hellmouth. The sacrifice of three turned out to be a sacrifice of the demons' own lives. Though all three of the demons entered the crack in the dimensional barrier with their respective tributes, Buffy—with Riley anchoring her—dove into the gap in the barrier to retrieve the third one. She dragged it back up and broke its neck, preventing the Hellmouth from being opened.

At least one, possibly two, of the Vahrall demons survived, but given that they are now stuck on the other side of the Hellmouth, it seems unlikely that Buffy will encounter them again. On the other hand, they are part of a species, which indicates that there likely are more roaming around on Earth.

RUPERT GILES (AS A DEMON)

SPIKE: "Why the hell are you suddenly a Fyarl demon? 'Cause I like to think I'm pretty observant, and I never saw a sign of it, I swear."
GILES: "It's a funny story. If funny meant horrific."

—"A NEW MAN"

EPISODE (AS A DEMON): "A New Man," season four

KEY RELATIONSHIPS (AS A DEMON): Giles's old friend (and current enemy), the sorcerer Ethan Rayne, used a spell to transform him into a Fyarl demon. During this period, he was unable to speak English and was hunted by those closest to him. Spike, fortunately, was able to speak Fyarl, but Giles had to *pay* him for assistance.

UNIQUE ATTRIBUTES (AS A DEMON): As a Fyarl, Giles was incredibly strong and had the ability to shoot jets of paralyzing mucus from his nostrils. He had enormous curling horns and yellow-tinged skin.

MOST MONSTROUS MOMENT (AS A DEMON): While in demon form, Giles used his new appearance to frighten Maggie Walsh, just for laughs (okay, maybe not *so* monstrous).

CURRENT STATUS: When Buffy realized the Fyarl demon was Giles, they forced Ethan to return Giles to his human form.

In the fourth season's hysterical "A New Man," the former Watcher, Rupert Giles, was briefly turned into a **Fyarl demon**, with two enormous, down-turned curving horns, yellowish skin, and sharp ridges on his chest and back. Ethan Rayne, a chaos worshipper who had once been a friend of Giles's, cast a spell on him in hopes that Buffy would eventually kill him without realizing who he was, because Giles could only speak in the language of the Fyarl. Giles frightened Xander, Maggie Walsh, and others, but finally received some help when he realized that Spike was able to understand the language. (Spike made him pay in cash for the assistance, however.) Spike had once employed two Fyarl demons, and informed Giles that they were quite strong and could shoot jets of paralyzing mucus out of their noses. He also told Giles that the longer he remained a Fyarl, the more the demonic nature would dominate his human nature.

Unfortunately, when Giles finally came into contact with Buffy, Spike was not around to explain the situation. She nearly killed him, but in the last possible moment she saw something in his eyes that she recognized as Giles. Realizing the truth, Buffy forced Ethan to return Giles to normal. Ethan was then turned over to the custody of the Initiative.

POLGARA DEMONS

"This is your objective: Sub-T-67119 demon-class, Polgara species. Though visual confirmation has not yet been made, we're confident of the target's approximate position as it leaves behind a distinct protein marker. Dr. Angleman will brief you on its defenses."
—MAGGIE, IN "THE I IN TEAM"

EPISODE: "The I in Team," season four

UNIQUE ATTRIBUTES: The towering demon had a huge, distorted cranium. Like all those of its species, it had long bone skewers that jutted from its forearms during battle.

CURRENT STATUS: The Initiative captured the Polgara alive in "The I in Team." However, Maggie Walsh and Dr. Angleman (of the Initiative) killed it so they could cut off one of its arms to attach to their pet project, the patchwork monster called Adam.

By the time season four's "The I in Team" came around, Buffy had become part of the Initiative. Already, though, she was suspicious of **Maggie Walsh,** the program's director, and of what Maggie might be doing in the heavily guarded Room 314. Maggie claimed it was a special research project, and she was not lying (see Walking Dead: Adam).

In that episode, Buffy joined her boyfriend Riley and the other Initiative commandos to hunt a Polgara demon, described by Maggie as a "Sub-T-67119 demon-class, Polgara species." Sub-T was likely shorthand for Hostile Sub-Terrestrial, also known as an HST. (The use of the name Polgara is of particular note here, as it has been confirmed that writer David Fury named that particular species of demon in honor of a *Buffy the Vampire Slayer* fan who often posted messages using that name on the show's official posting board, the Bronze.)

The Initiative's **Dr. Angleman** (also named after a Bronze-based fan) explained that the demon was capable of projecting skewers from its forearms during battle. He also warned the team not to damage the arms while attempting to capture it. Buffy challenged that order:

> "Why exactly can't we damage this Polka thing's arms? Not that I want to. Just, in my experience, when you're fighting for your life, body parts get damaged. And better its bits than mine."
> —BUFFY, IN "THE I IN TEAM"

However, her inquiry was ignored.

Buffy, Riley, and the Initiative commandos used tasers and nets to capture the Polgara demon, a greenish-yellow, scaly creature with a large, oddly configured cranial structure. It was later killed by Maggie and Dr. Angleman while in captivity. The two cut off one of its arms and attached it to their secret project, a patchwork-Frankenstein type monster called Adam.

Demons, Devils, and Satan Himself

EACH CULTURE AND RELIGION on earth has its own diverse pantheon of demons. The ever-hungry pop-cultural palate has at one time or another plundered them all. Were we to attempt to examine every demonic presence in folklore and popular culture, it would have required many hundreds, perhaps thousands of pages. Thus, we have chosen to concentrate largely on the most influential demon pantheon—that of Christian religions—with only a few necessary detours.

The belief in evil spirits is among mankind's oldest legacies. Seeking external causes for otherwise inexplicable disasters or accidents, or handy scapegoats for base human behavior, such evil spirits have taken countless forms. Dread of the possible or suspected influence of the dead informs many such beliefs. Natural elements and forces, such as lightning, storms, extreme heat or cold, floods, or other conditions beyond human control such as madness, famine, diseases, and so on were thought to be manifestations of evil spirits and demons. All religions and cultures have their respective notions of evil and the beings associated with evil. (The related subject of witches, warlocks, and demon-worshippers is discussed in our chapter on Magic Users.)

Our analysis of demon legend and lore will chart five distinctive routes. The first traces the evolution of the classical image of Satan, as embodied in the Bible, Dante's *Inferno*, Milton's *Paradise Lost*, and all that followed. This section will also cover minor demons from those detailed in Christian mythology and medieval religious art to more contemporary examples such as *The Prophecy* film series, Jack Kirby's comic book *The Demon,* and Todd McFarlane's media phenomenon *Spawn.*

The second path chronicles the venerable "pact with the devil" archetype, beginning with Marlowe's *Dr. Faustus* and Goethe's *Faust*. Though Marlowe and Goethe's immortal creations were hardly the first of their kind, no previous works had so compellingly explored or embodied the theme. The allure of the premise, the endless ways in which mortals tried to wriggle their way out of the consequences of their contracts, and the ingenious ways the devil (almost) always collected on his debts provided fodder for countless plays, songs, stories, novels, films, and comic books.

The third strand covers the mythic and pop-cultural genre concerned with the birth of the Antichrist and the fourth route plunges into the murky waters of demonic possession so memorably explored and exploited in William Peter Blatty's *The Exorcist*.

Finally, we will briefly explore the wholly invented, non-Christian notion of "elder" demons and gods who once possessed the earthly realm and seek to reclaim our world as their own, a concept proposed by pulp author H. P. Lovecraft and popularized by countless others in the seventy-five years since the first Lovecraft Cthulhu Mythos stories were published. This is where we will also touch upon the occasional spillover from other world religions and cultures into Western legend, lore, fiction, and pop culture. It is also the facet of demonology most pertinent to the development of demons on *Buffy the Vampire Slayer*.

satan, ı presume?

THE WORD *DEMON* is derived from the Greek *daimon*, meaning both "dealer of fate" and "teacher," and understood in Greek myth as a benevolent go-between linking gods and mankind. In Greece, evil spirits were known as *kakodaimones*, source of the evil demons we know and fear today. The Greek word *diaballos*, meaning "accuser" or "deceiver," provided the basis for our concept of Satan: the Accuser, the Deceiver, the ruler of hell. But the Greeks and Romans did not have a devil, a singular personification of evil in their myths, though the occasional behavior of some figures (like the Roman Saturnus) suggested future incarnations. In Oriental religions, there are no single supreme demons like Satan, but countless demons and devils of equal rank who plague mankind.

Among all the elements associated with evil spirits and demons, fire remains the most pervasive and powerful. Fire is linked with the beginning of civilization as we understand it. It is necessary to warmth and life, and yet destructive as well. In many religions and in science, the world began in fire; and in many religions and myths, the world ended (to be reborn), or will end, in fire.

The being in Nordic myth who most resembled our classical image of Satan was Surtur, who dwelled in the realm of Muspelheim, wielded a powerful Flaming Sword, and would eventually join the giants in their fight against the gods. It was Loki, however, whose behavior and role in Nordic myth foreshadowed and laid some of the groundwork for the image of Satan in myth. The evil Loki forever conspired against Odin the Father, and Loki's demonic children included Hela, who ruled over the land of the dead (see Walking Dead). The conflict between Odin and Loki culminated in Ragnarok, the apocalypse.

In Judeo-Christian belief, Adam and Eve were the first man and woman, created by God in his own likeness, and they were placed in the idyllic Garden of Eden to dwell in peace. The popular Christian understanding is that when Satan came to Eve in the guise of a serpent to tempt her with the forbidden fruit of the Tree of Knowledge, he was the catalyst for Adam and Eve's subsequent banishment and thus the source for many of mankind's woes. Thereafter, Satan and his angels were punished for having deceived the whole world by being thrown down from the heavens by the archangel Michael and his angels (Revelations 12:7).

But we are getting ahead of ourselves.

What is this "devil"?

Who is Satan?

In Christianity, Satan—aka Belial, the devil, or the Accuser—is the personal head of the forces of evil. The concept of Satan was a late development in post-Judaic religions. As noted in the biblical Book of Isaiah, God identified himself as creating both good and evil: "I form the light, and create darkness; I make peace, and create evil: I, the Lord, do all these things." To this day, Judaism does not acknowledge the existence of Satan, or any separate figure fulfilling his function (though there is a being known as Satan in the Judaic tradition: an angel in the service of God who brought great misery upon Job in the Bible).

As Christianity emerged from a fusion of Jewish and Hellenistic traditions, the concept of Satan as a being coalesced. By the time of the writing of the biblical Book of Revelations, Satan

was personified as the archenemy of God, leader of a band of angels who had rebelled against God and been cast out of heaven for their affront.

The contemporary image of Satan was formalized for Christian belief during the Fourth Lateran Council, which was convened in Rome in A.D. 1215 by Pope Innocent III. This effort to unify the Christian world firmly defined some of the basic tenets of Roman Catholicism for the first time. Thereafter Satan was forever understood to be the ruler of hell, an empire of fallen angels. His fallen angel minions are demons, the evil beings and pagan deities of primitive lore and religion capable of possessing human beings, appearing during seances or rituals, and occasionally appearing in our realm to do mischief.

Lutheran students catalogued these demons first, and their results were published in the mid-sixteenth century in Feyerabend's *Theatrum Diabolum*, divulging the "fact" that there were at that time 2,665,866,746,664 demons extant. A different set of figures was published in Dr. Johann Weier's *De Prestigiis Daemonum* (1568), offering a census of 72 princes and 7,405,926 devils in hell, with 1,111 legions comprised of 6,666 demons in each and six categories of their kind (igneous, aerial, terrestrial, aquatic, subterranean, and lucifugous).

Satan was also known as Lucifer, Mephistopheles, or Beelzebub, "The Lord of the Flies." The names are used interchangeably today, but historically these were at times three distinctive beings. Milton's Lucifer in *Paradise Lost* was referred to as "the day star," reflecting both the name's Latin meaning ("light bearer") and the Latin translation of the Hebrew term meaning "shining one," from Isaiah 14:12, which refers to the fallen angel as "O shining one, son of morning." Beelzebub was the prince of demons identified with (not as) Satan by Jesus in The New Testament. The Philistines once worshipped this figure as "Baalzebub," the name itself perhaps derived from the Assyrian term "bel-dababi" ("adversary in court" or "enemy"). Mephistopheles was the name given the devil in German lore and literature, particularly those associated with Faust (see below), wherein he was an evil spirit who was an agent of Satan rather than Satan incarnate.

Early in his existence, when the Greek ideal of beauty held sway, artists depicted Satan as a handsome if sinister figure. This image revolted later Christian practitioners, and the Church sanctioned only the most monstrous of Satan's guises. He was usually pictured in the Middle Ages as a hideous horned, split-hooved, bat-winged, barb-tailed being comprised of various animal and human anatomical parts.

Many of these artists were inspired by Dante Alighieri's epic poem *Divina Commedia* (*The Divine Comedy*, 1308–21), particularly the first of its three books, *Inferno*, popularly known as *Dante's Inferno*.

In that narrative, led (on Good Friday) by the Roman poet Virgil into the depths of the underworld, Dante made himself the cartographer of hell, traveling through eight distinctive circles to arrive at the ninth and lowest circle of the Inferno. That was where Satan himself dwelled, trapped in the ice of Tartary, a multi-eyed, multi-mawed, all-devouring monster: "In each mouth he crushed a sinner with his teeth as with a heckle and thus he kept three of them in pain." These three sinners were Judas, Cassius, and Brutus, history's most notorious traitors.

By the fifteenth and sixteenth centuries, the bountiful demonic imagery of Italian religious art had spread north into much of Europe, culminating in the celebrated visionary works of painters like Hieronymus Bosch and Bruegel the Elder. Bosch's delirious interpretations of demons, the devil, the damned, and hell remain among the most well-known of this period, to this day adorning record and CD covers, movie credits, etc., and pirated by contemporary illustrators. Martin Schongauer's horde of demons bedeviling St. Anthony, Sandro Botticelli's illustrations for Dante's *Divina Commedia*, Albrecht Durer's *Apocalypse*, and Jean Duvet's apocalyptic delineations of the *Book of Revelations* extended this tradition with feverish clarity and frightening invention. With the seventeenth-century Renaissance, the imaginative element in representing images of demons became more playful, losing the tactile reality that had become the norm in the previous three centuries, reverting to a broader range of interpretations not unlike those found in pre-fourteenth-century renderings.

Though he forever seduced, tempted, and fooled men in his mission to turn mortals away from God and hence acquire their souls, the devil was oten portrayed in medieval lore as one capable of being outwitted by wily mortals. This strain of Satan literature culminated in its classic execution in Christopher Marlowe's *The Tragical History of Dr. Faustus* (1588) and Johann Wolfgang Goethe's *Faust* (1808, 1832). The narrative of these works (see below) established a specific theme for most literature and fiction dealing with man's relationship with Satan (see Deals with the Devil, below), but they also validated a less medieval image of Satan, eschewing the bestial monsters of previous centuries' religious art to portray the devil as a beguiling man of the world.

Though still the tempter, the accuser, the harvester of souls, Marlowe and Goethe's Mephistopheles was a deceptively handsome, amiable gentleman, able to move among society with ease due to his razor wit and affable manner. This concept of the devil dominated countless subsequent works, only a few of which we will be able to discuss here as there are far, far too many from which to choose.

The other definitive literary portrait of the devil to have a profound influence on all that followed was that of Satan in English poet John Milton's epic *Paradise Lost* (1667, revised in 1674), an exquisite, expansive blank verse twelve-book poem that stands as one of English literature's greatest works. Wishing to (in his own words) "justify the ways of God to man," Milton's masterpiece related the incidents of Genesis against the canvas of Satan's rebellion against God, and his subsequent fall from grace. Milton also wrote *Paradise Regained* (1671), a four-book portrait, drawn from the Gospels, of Satan's vain attempts to tempt Jesus Christ.

In some literature and theater, Satan the tempter took female form, as in Jacques Cazotte's *Le Diable Amoreux* (*The Devil in Love*, 1772) and Matthew Lewis's classic supernatural novel *The Monk* (1796). The devil assumed human form to foment murder and suicide in James Hoggs's *The Private Memoirs and Confessions of a Justified Sinner* (1824) or to lord over a clan of witches, demanding human sacrifices to ensure his protection in *The Lancashire Witches* (1848).

By the nineteenth and early twentieth centuries, the concept of Satan as a literal being had become an embarrassment to most strains of Christianity, though his prominent role in art and imaginative fiction never waned. With the archetype established, there came many satiric turns, as in Edgar Allan Poe's "Bon-Bon" (1832), portraying the devil as a braggart savoring the souls he has claimed throughout the years, or Theophile Gautier's "Two Actors for One Role" (1843), in which Satan played himself in a stage production. Even as devoted a Christian author as C. S. Lewis embraced satire as a means of exploring the nature of man and evil in the witty novel *The Screwtape Letters* (1942), in which an elder devil passed his knowledge and insights on to a young upstart devil.

While literature pursued such potentially blasphemous avenues, the new medium of cinema plundered older, safer archetypes. French magician and cinema pioneer Georges Méliès (see Magic Users) was there first, directing and starring as a Gothic devil in *The Devil's Castle* (1896; also see Vampires), and in a second film by the same title (produced in 1898). Those were only the first of many, with the lead devils usually played by Méliès himself in trick shorts like *The Laboratory of Mephistopheles* (1897), *The Gigantic Devil* (1902), *Satan in Prison* (1907), and others (see Deals with the Devil, below).

Actor George Arliss popularized the suave, urbane, top-hatted Satan with his star performance in the turn-of-the-century play *The Devil*. Thomas Ince cast Edward Connelly in the role for his 1915 film version, while Arliss reclaimed the role in the 1921 remake. Edison and Biograph produced two unrelated films titled *The Devil* in 1908, with D. W. Griffith helming the Biograph production.

Satan visited New England to bring a scarecrow to life in Nathaniel Hawthorne's story "Feathertop" (1837). Once again, the devil took the theater-to-cinema route when Peter MacKaye's play version *The Scarecrow* was filmed as *Puritan Passions* (1923).

Vivid glimpses of hell (often hand-tinted red) and its denizens tormenting the souls of the damned spiced *The Warning* (1915), and *The Devil's Darling* (1915), and Cerberus—the three-headed guard dog of hell—made an appearance in *The Devil's Assistant* (1917).

Of course, Dante's *Inferno* inspired many cinematic sojourns. The Italians produced *L'Inferno* (1909 and 1910) and *Dante e Beatrice* (1912), while the British *Dante's Purgatorio* (aka *Purgatory*, 1911 or 1913) and American *Too Much Champagne* (1908) and *Dante's Progress and Experiences Through Paradise* (1912) covered similar infernal ground. Henry Otto directed *Dante's Inferno* (1924) for Fox, crafting a truly hellish nightmare sequence to scare its jazz-age millionaire into cleaning up his act amid a conventional contemporary morality play that owed more to Cecil B. DeMille than Dante. Twentieth Century Fox's sound-era remake, *Dante's Inferno* (1935), starred Spencer Tracy.

One of the most atmospheric sequences involving the conjuring of demons graced Paul Wegener's remake of *The Golem* (1920; see Walking Dead).

Gentle devils and demons inhabited John Collier's novel *The Devil and All* (1934). The pulp magazine *Weird Tales* featured its share of demon tales, including Manly Wade Wellman's "Coven," Seabury Quinn's "Is the Devil a Gentleman?" (both from the July 1942 issue), and Paul Ernst's adventures of the faux-devil antihero Doctor Satan, "The World's Weirdest Criminal," beginning in the August 1935 issue and continuing until the August-September 1936 issue. One of *Weird Tales'* finest satanic stories was Robert Bloch's classic "Hell on Earth," the cover story (art by Hannes Bok) of the March 1942 issue.

Satan subsequently starred in a string of 1940s fantasy films, an era peppered with comedies featuring angels, ghosts, witches, and Death itself. The devil was played by Laird Cregar in

Heaven Can Wait (1943), Claude Rains in *Angel on My Shoulder* (1946), Ray Milland in *Alias Nick Beal* (1949), and others. Olsen and Johnson's satiric 1938 stage revue *Hellzapoppin* was adapted for the big screen in 1941, including a lively opening with a finger-popping musical number set in Hades.

The oddest devil film of the era was producer Hal Roach's *The Devil with Hitler* (1942), which opened with the assembly of hell voting Satan (Alan Mowbray) out of office to recruit Adolf Hitler (Bobby Watson, who also played the role in *Hitler—Dead or Alive*, 1942) as his replacement.

The most vivid of the era's Satans was Bill Tytla's memorably animated taloned, bat-winged, horned Chernabog, which dominated the "Night on Bald Mountain" episode of Walt Disney's *Fantasia* (1941). Disney had already consigned Mickey Mouse's dog Pluto to an imaginary feline hell on *Pluto's Judgement Day* (1935). Other cartoon devils (there are far too many to detail further) included Frank Tashlin's *Wholly Smoke* (1938), featuring an anti-smoking demon named Nick O'Teen.

The devil was also a staple of the early superhero and horror comics. During World War II, the Axis powers (including Hitler himself) were often drawn as literal demons in the propogandistic superhero titles. *Mystic Comics* #4 (August 1940) introduced the Black Widow (not the later Marvel Comics character), whose origin was the first to depend on a trip to hell. Another female emissary from hell named Madam Satan harvested the souls of the wicked *and* the righteous in *Pep Comics* #16–20 (June–October, 1941).

Devils dominated the horror comics scene from its birth. Mr. Lucifer appeared in the first one-shot horror anthology titled *Eerie* #1 (1947). Devils crashed through the walls of a mine trespassing too close to hell's territory in *Adventures into Darkness* #12 (Standard, 1952). Devils, demons, and the fires of hell were a constant threat in the 1950s, as in Fiction House's *Ghost Comics*, Superior's *Journey into Fear,* and even in tamer National Periodical (DC Comics) titles like *House of Mystery*.

Also in the 1950s, the irrational nature of religion, myth, horror fiction, and belief in the devil was subjected to the piercing, rational scrutiny of science fiction. In Arthur C. Clarke's landmark novel *Childhood's End* (1953), the next step in the evolution of mankind was initiated by a race of alien beings who ironically looked like demons and returned to Earth to guide our species to its necessary next level.

Nigel Kneale's BBC teleplay *Quatermass and the Pit* (originally broadcast 1958) explored a similar path, in which construction of an underground train system in London uncovers a ship, interred in soil millions of years old along with fossils of mutated ancient man. Within the ship are the rotting remains of man-size insectlike creatures: the pilots. Professor Bernard Quatermass (André Morell) explores the possibility that these creatures were from Mars, and orchestrated the evolving of manlike creatures to attempt a colonization of earth.

FIVE MILLION YEARS TO EARTH

Scrutinizing one of the insects, Quatermass's associate Dr. Matthew Roney (Cec Linder) says, "You know, I think these are old friends we haven't seen for a long time"—the devil as a racial memory of prehistoric extraterrestrial visitors. In the apocalyptic finale, Roney and Quatermass plunder ancient beliefs in the devil to save London from disaster. Hammer Films mounted a concise color feature-length remake of *Quatermass and the Pit* (U.S. title: *Five Million Years to Earth*, 1967).

John Carpenter echoed the essentials of Kneale's scientific metaphysics for *Prince of Darkness* (1987), in which the devil was depicted as a vial of psychoplasmic ooze capable of manifesting a plethora of horrors.

With science fiction claiming Satan as its own, there were precious few devils left to go around. Edward Wood Jr.'s bizarre transvestite soap opera *Glen or Glenda* (1953) sported a devil, and Vincent Price's Satan brightened Irwin Allen's star-vehicle historical fantasy *The Story of Mankind* (1957). Richard Devon starred as the Devil in B-movie king Roger Corman's first horror film, an odd past-life regression medieval witchcraft curio titled *The Undead* (1957).

The Japanese *Jigoku* (*Hell*, 1960; remade in 1981) was a grave theological horror masterpiece in which two murderers, who were themselves dying, experience a Dante-esque journey through a Buddhist hell.

The devil made a comeback in the 1960s. The most visible pop-culture demon of the era was Harvey Comics' *Hot Stuff, The Little Devil* (1957–91), who shared the newsstand with other Harvey kids' titles like *Wendy the Good Little Witch* and the ever-popular *Casper the Friendly Ghost*. Hot Stuff proved popular enough to earn a spin-off series, *Devil Kids Starring Hot Stuff* (1962–81).

More serious hot stuff began to surface as the horror comics revival began; comics like publisher James Warren's black-and-white horror magazines *Creepy*, *Eerie*, and *Vampirella*. In 1960 Charles Beaumont's "The Howling Man" was anthologized (in Beaumont's *Night Ride and Other Journeys*) and adapted as an episode of Rod Serling's *The Twilight Zone* (1960). Manly Wade Wellman's tales of invented Appalachian folk hero Silver John (1946–62) were finally collected as *Who Fears the Devil?* (1963). A decade later, TV horror pioneer John Newland directed a film adaptation of Wellman's tales as *The Ballad of Hillbilly John* (1973).

Lon Chaney Jr. was Satan in *The Devil's Messenger* (1961), a compilation from an unsold TV series produced in Sweden under the title *No. 13 Demon Street*. Chaney made a far more persuasive devil than faux-psychic Criswell did in the Ed Wood Jr.–scripted *Orgy of the Dead* (1965). Better still was Burgess Meredith as the framing-story carny who revealed his true satanic nature to the damned souls whose horrible deaths provided the episodes for the Amicus anthology film *Torture Garden* (1967).

Hammer Films' excellent adaptation of Dennis Wheatley's *The Devil Rides Out* (aka *The Devil's Bride*, Twentieth Century Fox, 1968) pitted a regal Duc de Richleau (Christopher Lee) against the Aleister Crowley–inspired warlock Mocata (Charles Gray; see Magic Users). Christopher Lee also played Satan in the comedy *Poor Devil* (1973). *The Devil Rides Out* was significant not only for the quality of its production, Richard Matheson's script, and Terence Fisher's controlled direction, but also for its matter-of-fact depiction of evil and the devil as absolute realities that must be reckoned with.

A number of unique independent films also left their mark on the genre. *Dark Intruder* (1965) played theaters though it was originally produced as a pilot for an unsold series titled *Black Cloak*. The film introduced Leslie Nielsen as an occult sleuth working San Francisco of the 1890s in search of a clawed murderer.

Leslie Stevens's *Incubus* (1965) remains the only film dialogued completely in Esperanto, relegating it forever to obscurity (a single print was rescued at the end of the 1990s) and obscuring its accomplished, atmospheric tale of female succubi (sexual demons) claiming the souls of men. When one of them (Allyson Ames) fell in love with a mortal (William Shatner), her kin conjured a male incubus to rape and kill the mortal's sister.

THE DEVIL'S BRIDE

Satan often found his way into popular music as well, perhaps most prominently with the title of the Rolling Stones' album *Their Satanic Majesties Request* (1967) and especially their song "Sympathy for the Devil" (from the album *Beggar's Banquet*, 1968). French director Jean-Luc Godard constructed a feature film around the recording of the song for *Sympathy for the Devil* (1968), aka *One Plus One*.

Violence and murder plagued the Rolling Stones's appearance onstage during the notorious Altamont, California, free concert of December 6, 1969, only four months after the historic Woodstock concert's weekend of peace, love, and music. During the performance of "Sympathy for the Devil," the biker gang Hell's Angels (who had been hired as security) kicked and beat a fan onstage. During the tune "Love in Vain," an eighteen-year-old black man named Meredith Hunter was savagely beaten and stabbed to death by the Angels, who believed the young man had pointed a gun at Jagger. The tune remains prominent in the Stones' repertoire. The most recent use of the song in a film accompanied the closing credits of Neil Jordan's 1994 adaptation of Anne Rice's *Interview with the Vampire* (see Vampires).

Thanks to the 1970 relaxation of the self-regulatory Comics Code Authority (see Vampires), mainstream comic books were able to explore horrific themes with more freedom. Marvel Comics actually included Satan as a character in their self-contained Marvel Universe though, appropriately enough, he went by many names. Prior to Satan's appearance (by name) in Gary Friedrich and Mike Ploog's *Ghost Rider* story in *Marvel Spotlight* #6 (1972), there were only surrogate Satans in the Marvel Universe. Those included Dr. Strange's nemesis Dormammu (introduced in *Strange Tales* #126, 1964), Satannish (whose visage was not shown in his first appearance in *Dr. Strange* #174, 1968), and Mephisto (*Silver Surfer* #3, 1968) and his various offspring.

In the wake of the enormous popularity of the novel and movie adaptation of *The Exorcist* (1973; see below), however, Satan took a leading role in *Ghost Rider*, and spawned the misadventures of *Son of Satan* (*Marvel Spotlight* #12–24, 1973–75, and in his own series, 1975–77) and *Satana, The Devil's Daughter* (*Marvel Premiere* #27, 1974, etc.).

Jack Kirby's *The Demon* (DC Comics, 1972–74) was based on paganism and witchcraft. Its nominal hero was indeed a demon, Etrigan, spawned by Merlin's magic in defense of Camelot and living on into the twentieth century with an awakening awareness of his own human alter ego, Jason Blood. Eschewing any religious content to instead revamp comfortable genre staples, Kirby's *Demon* paled alongside the comparative boldness of Marvel's devilish contemporaries. But in later years, the Demon returned as a feature in *World's Finest Comics* and a guest star in titles like *Saga of the Swamp Thing* and others, earning his own short-lived series in the late 1980s and early 1990s and a guest spot on the *Batman* animated TV series (with Kirby villain Klarion the Witch Boy and his familiar, Teekl the cat).

Kirby's *The Demon* paved the way for later demonic antiheroes like Pat Mills, Kevin O'Neill, Bryan Talbot, and Jesus Redondo's *Nemesis the Warlock* (serialized in the British weekly *2000 A.D.*,1983–85) and Todd McFarlane's multimedia phenomenon *Spawn* (Image, 1992–present). Like *The Spectre*, *Deadman*, and *The Crow* (see Ghosts and Walking Dead), *Spawn* was another superhero whose death was only the beginning. Returning from hell as a vigilante demon, *Spawn* became a volatile marketing machine in quick order, spawning a 1997 live-action CGI-enhanced feature film, an animated series on HBO (1998–present), and a cutting-edge action-figure toy line that established new standards for the toy industry.

As the 1970s horror and monster comics flourished, the era of the British horror film came to a close. Among the most notable of the last gasps was Piers Haggard's evocative *The Blood on Satan's Claw* (1971), which depicted the eerily convincing manifestation of a demon in the British countryside of the seventeenth century.

Made-for-television movies also embraced demonic themes. They include one of the first American-broadcast made-for-TV features *Fear No Evil* (NBC, 1969); *Gargoyles* (CBS, 1972); *Horror at 37,000 Feet* (CBS, 1972), in which William Shatner was among the plane passengers threatened by an ancient sarcophagus containing a demonic force; and *Cruise into Terror* (ABC, 1978). *Star Trek* creator-producer Gene Roddenberry's failed pilot *Spectre* (NBC, 1977) was also of interest, featuring Robert Culp and Gig Young as demonologists struggling to curb the efforts of demon-incarnate sorcerer John Hurt.

On the big screen, Ernest Borgnine's gap-toothed grinning western devil threatened William Shatner and Eddie Albert in *The Devil's Rain* (1975), leading a coven and claiming the souls of eyeless shills Ida Lupino, a barely glimpsed John Travolta (in his first screen role), and others. The imaginative production boasted Anton LaVey, self-proclaimed High Priest of the Church of Satan, as its technical advisor. Victor Buono was the dapper cream-suited devil in the basement orchestrating the haunted-house antics of *The Evil* (New World, 1978).

Director Michael Winner's adaptation of Jeffrey Konvitz's debut novel *The Sentinel* (1974; movie version from Universal, 1977) boasted some jarring Dick Smith makeup effects in its wild tale of a suicidal fashion model (Cristina Raines) who moved into a Brooklyn apartment building that actually harbored the gates of hell. *The Sentinel* had an all-star cast, including Burgess Meredith and John Carradine as a blind priest. The film also offered an offensive caricature of lesbian lifestyles (they are demons) and use of genuine human oddities (appearing as the demons at the gate). It was successful enough to prompt Konvitz to write a follow-up novel, *The Guardian* (1979), and inspire an even grosser succession of Italian variations on the "gates of hell" theme, including Lucio Fulci's *Gates of Hell* (1980) and *The Beyond* (1981).

The gates of hell were also relevant to friendlier, mass-market fare such as *The Gate* (1987). While *The Gate II* (1990) had a harsher edge, the film still ended happily; it was, after all, a family horror film.

Horror also merged with fantasy at times, as when makeup artist Rob Bottin transformed actor Tim Curry into the most visually striking cinematic Prince of Darkness ever seen for Ridley Scott's lavish fairy tale, *Legend* (1985), and earned an Academy Award nomination for best makeup.

The past twenty years have spawned their share of animated demons and devils as well, including Homer Simpson's neighbor Ned Flanders on one of the celebrated Halloween episodes of *The Simpsons*, which also found Homer visiting hell more than once. Satan greeted Ren when he whizzed on the electric fence in the classic "Sven Hoek" episode of *The Ren and Stimpy Show* (1991), and the perennial "Red Guy" is forever bedeviling Cartoon Network's *Cow and Chicken* (1997–present). Satan was a sympathetic gay character in Trey Parker and Matt Stone's hilarious *South Park: Bigger, Longer, and Uncut* (1999), tormented by his cruel lover Saddam Hussein and performing a Disney-parody showstopping tune.

While Satan may be the showstopper, his minions appear almost as commonly. Stephen King's short story "Sometimes They Come Back" (1974) became a TV movie (CBS, 1991) starring Tim Matheson as a schoolteacher confronted during his first teaching gig by the ghosts of a gang of punks who had killed his brother twenty-seven years before. King's wedding of devil and ghost themes became increasingly demonic in the first direct-to-video sequel *Sometimes They Come Back...Again* (1996) and the sequel-in-name-only *Sometimes They Come Back...for More* (1999).

Not all representations of the Devil and his minions are so grave, however. Hell's denizens were set up for pratfalls and laughs in Neil Gaiman and Terry Pratchett's apocalyptic fantasy-comedy *Good Omens* (1990), subtitled *The Nice and Accurate Prophecies of Agnes Nutter, Witch*, setting the somewhat fey, precious tone of their delightful satire.

Gaiman's comic-book series *The Sandman* (1989–97; see Bogeymen) presented a nightmarish alternative in which hell was ruled by a trio of demons, the most powerful of whom was Lucifer Morningstar, a version of the fallen angel of Christian lore. *The Sandman* was published by DC's "mature readers" imprint, Vertigo, which also presented groundbreaking, horrifying takes on hell, the devil, and demons in such titles as *Swamp Thing* (1982–96) and its spin-off, *Hellblazer* (1988–present), a series that has also used the deal-with-the-devil theme to great effect more than once.

Another successful 1990s comics series more specifically focused on demons was artist-writer Mike Mignola's stylish *Hellboy*. Unfolding over the course of many miniseries and single-issue stories from 1994, *Hellboy* is the tale of a demon-human half-breed brought to Earth by Nazi sorcerers during World War II who goes on to work with the Allies. He becomes the world's leading paranormal investigator—a job for which he is uniquely suited. As of this writing, *Hellboy* is in development as a feature film at Universal.

American filmmaker Kevin Smith offered his own idiosyncratic reinterpretation of the Catholic hierarchy of angels and devils in *Dogma* (1999), starring Ben Affleck and Matt Damon. Smith's bad-boy angels may have owed a debt to the Costra Nostra archangels of *The Prophecy* (1995). Viggo Mortensen made a striking Satan in that film's final act. Writer-director Gregory Widen's conceit of angels as God's hit men (his original title was indeed *God's Army*) still duking it out amongst themselves benefited enormously from the presence of Christopher Walken as the archangel Gabriel, intent upon reclaiming God's favor.

With Walken stalking the scenery, there was no need for Satan to make a return appearance in the direct-to-video *The Prophecy II: Ashtown* (1998), in which Gabriel fought to prevent the post-Apocalyptic coupling of angel (Russell Wong) and mortal woman (Jennifer Beals) or slay their savior offspring. The year 1999 brought *The Prophecy III: The Ascent.*

Chris Carter's *Millennium* series also flirted with the theme, particularly in *X-Files* writer Darin Morgan's episode "Somehow, Satan Got Behind Me" (1998), in which a clutch of demons meet in a coffee shop to casually discuss their place in the contemporary world, a thorough and often hilarious dissection of the theme; it remains one of the best hours of television of the 1990s.

Deals with the Devil

MANY FOLK TALES CONCERN MORTALS whose desire for gold, earthly pleasures, or love prompt them to make deals with the devil or his minions. Those have spawned countless plays, novels, and short stories. A number of anthologies collect the best of the short stories, such as *Deals with the Devil* (1953), edited by Basil Davenport. Many famous stories hinge on implicit pacts, with Oscar Wilde's classic *The Picture of Dorian Gray* (1891) providing the best example. Wilde never spelled out the supernatural agency that made it possible for Gray to remain young and unravaged by his hedonistic lifestyle while his hidden portrait aged and corrupted accordingly, but the results and consequences were Faustian, indeed.

Cultural reinterpretations of the archetype cut across genre lines: Seymour's (Jonathan Haze) fatal dependence on the carnivorous plant Audrey II in Roger Corman's *The Little Shop of Horrors* (1960) was in its way another deal with the devil, just as Charlie Sheen's Faustian relationship with Michael Douglas's reptilian high-powered broker in Oliver Stone's *Wall Street* (1987) evoked the venerable legend. Our focus here, however, will remain with the explicit pacts made with the devil and his demons.

The classic version of this theme was the tale of Faust, which can be traced to an actual Georgius Faust (1480–1540?), a sixteenth-century mountebank, magician, and physician of dubious repute who shamelessly promoted his traveling magic act and quack medicines by claiming to have sold his soul to the devil in exchange for his skillful sorcery. Faust's ballyhoo was accepted at face value, and he quickly became the focal point for many oral folk tales and chapbooks describing his pact with the devil in exchange for twenty-four years of empowerment, his marvels and misdeeds, and his death at the hands of the devil, who claimed his soul.

The anonymous *The History of Johann Faust* (1587) was among those early chronicles; it was translated by P. F. Gent and published as *The History of the Damnable Life, and Deserved Death of Doctor John Faustus* (1592). All of the previous versions were promptly eclipsed by Christopher Marlowe's play *The Tragical History of Dr. Faustus* (believed to have been written in 1592 or 1593).

Marlowe retained the narrative and many of the particulars of the folk tale, though he emphasized the tragedy of Faust's situation by making him a devoted man of science instead of a charlatan. Johann Wolfgang von Goethe's verse *Faust* (1808, 1832) extended Marlowe's metaphor, making Faust the embodiment of Western civilized aspiration and progress, who lays his soul on the line bartering for forbidden knowledge. Faust broke the contract and saved his soul, leaving Mephistopheles the loser in Goethe's version. Indeed, his dealings with the once-noble doctor actually improved mankind's lot, doubly cheating the devil of his due.

The tale of Faust and Mephistopheles inspired Nikolaus Lenau's epic *Faust* (1835) the ballad "Faust"(1851) by Heinrich Heine, and was also set to music in Nerval's *Faust* (1825), Hector Berlioz's *Faust Scenes* (first performed in 1828) and later oratorio "The Damnation of Faust," and Charles Gounod's opera *Faust* (1859). Franz Liszt's "The Mephisto Waltz" (1861) followed, personifying the devil as the virtuoso violinist Paganini, associated with Liszt's impressive body of musical work derived from the Faust theme that culminated in the *Faust Symphonie* (1861).

There were also Richard Wagner's overture, Robert Schumann's musical impressions of scenes from Goethe's *Faust*, and Arrigo Boito's opera *Mefistofele* (1868, revised 1875). More than a century later, singer-songwriter Randy Newman would stage and record his own production of *Faust* (1995).

Charles Robert Maturin's Gothic classic *Melmoth the Wanderer* (1820) concerned a seventeenth-century Irishman who contracted with the devil to extend his life and gain omnipotent power, becoming a kind of devil himself. Intent on transferring the contract to another hapless mortal, Melmoth's quest for an individual desperate or foolish enough to save his soul encompassed six narrative arcs involving doomed characters who, in each case, refused damnation, sentencing the antihero Melmoth to continue his search.

Melmoth the Wanderer garnered a vocal following that included the poet Charles Baudelaire and the novelists Victor Hugo and Honoré de Balzac. Balzac composed a sequel to *Melmoth the Wanderer* entitled *Melmoth Reconciled* (1830), detailing the consequences when Melmoth finds a mortal willing to accept his damning contract, and Hugo scribed his own variation, *Dr. Basilius* (1870).

Baudelaire and Balzac also revered (and translated into French) the works of Edgar Allan Poe, which included the brutal satire "Never Bet the Devil Your Head" (1841). Federico Fellini directed a hallucinogenic elaboration of Poe's story under the title "Toby Dammit," the final episode of the omnibus film *Spirits of the Dead* (1968). Fellini's devil was a pale, blond little girl playing with a ball . . . and later claiming Toby's (Terence Stamp) severed head.

Celebrated American writer Washington Irving had already presented a more traditional approach to the pact-with-the-devil theme with his short story "The Devil and Tom Walker" (1824). There, the devil popped up in Massachusetts and carried himself as a pragmatic businessman, answering to the name "Old Scratch." William Makepeace Thackeray's "The Painter's Bargain" (1834) treated its contract with the devil as an amusing dream fantasy.

By the turn of the century, many novels and short stories had been drawn from the Faustian theme, including Frederick Perkins's satiric "Devil Puzzlers" (1877), Robert Louis Stevenson's "The Bottle Imp" (1893), and others. In Marie Corelli's *The Sorrows of Satan* (1895), the devil incarnate was Mr. Lucio Rimanez, who tempted London authors with guaranteed positive critical reviews in exchange for pawning their souls. Queen Victoria herself was said to be a fan of the novel, which D. W. Griffith adapted to the screen in 1926.

Another writer's vanity was indulged by a devilish pact in Max Beerbohm's "Enoch Soames" (1919), which hurled the titular Mr. Soames a hundred years into the future to spread his fame to the next century. A craftier old sea dog outwitted Satan in "The Devil and the Old Man" (1913), wriggling out of his contract with his arcane knowledge of the sea—and killing the devil in the bargain.

Georges Méliès adapted the *Faust* theme to many of his formative special effects showcases, including *Faust and Marguerite* (1897), his first adaptation from a literary work. *The Damnation of Faust* (1898, remade in 1903) and *Faust* (1904) followed, the latter designed to be shown in conjunction with its 1903 precedent and in synchronization with an orchestral musical passage from the opera by Gounod. British magician George Albert Smith also filmed his own adaptation of *Faust and Mephistopheles* (1898). Across the Atlantic, Edwin S. Porter mounted his own *Faust and Marguerite* (1900). J. Stuart Blackton's *The Devil and the Gambler* (1908) was typical of the period, too, with the devil bargaining for a gambler's soul until the fool's wife brandished a cross, anticipating the tomfoolery of *Bill Bumper's Bargain* (1911) and others.

Three German films titled *The Student of Prague* (1913, 1926, and 1935) owed a debt to Edgar Allan Poe's classic doppelganger tale "William Wilson" (1839), altering Poe's narrative to link a pact with the devil with the presence of a man's mirror-image double. Some sources also cite E. T. A. Hoffmann's "The Sand Merchant," while others credit a poem by Alfred de Musset, though screenwriter Hanns Heinz Ewers told essentially the same tale as Poe's.

The Student of Prague launched the influential Teutonic silent horror cycle. The standout image of the 1926 version (one of many) was of the black-garbed, umbrella-toting Dr. Scapinelli (Werner Krauss)—the devil—standing against the gnarled stump of a tree, holding his stovepipe hat against the fierce winds; he remains among the cinema's most striking incarnations of the devil.

German director F. W. Murnau cast Emil Jannings as Mephistopheles in his visually inspired adaptation of Goethe's *Faust* (1926). The opening image of night settling over a village as the black cloak of a cosmically outsized devil was unforgettable. With the coming of sound, other versions of *Faust* followed from around the world, including *Faust Fantasy* (1935) from the United Kingdom, *Pan Tvardovski* (1937) from Poland, *Le Leggenda di Faust* (1948) from Italy, *La Beauté du Diable* (1949) from France, and more.

Also quite influential was Pulitzer Prize–winning author Stephen Vincent Benét's story "The Devil and Daniel Webster" (1937), which pit New England's renowned attorney against the devil to save the soul of a foolish New Hampshire farmer. Hollywood snapped up the rights to Benét's popular story, casting Walter Huston as the wiliest devil ever to grace the screen in *All That Money Can Buy* (aka *The Devil and Daniel Webster*, RKO, 1941).

Huston's grizzled devil was assisted by the demoness Simone Simon (who went on to star in Val Lewton's *The Cat People* the following year; see Primals), who seduced the desperate farmer (James Craig) until Daniel Webster (Edward Arnold) came to the rescue.

As the golden age of television drama anthologies came to a close, Edward G. Robinson

accepted one of his few television roles to play Daniel Webster against David Wayne's Scratch in *Breck Golden Showcase*'s eerie adaptation of Benét's story. Few impressionable children who caught the broadcast would ever forget the death's-head moth crying with a damned soul's voice before Scratch scooped it into his pocket. The services of a lawyer weren't needed in Robert Arthur's sly contemporary of Benét's tale, "Satan and Sam Shay" (1942). Thomas Mann's novel *Doctor Faustus* (1948) based its Faust surrogate Adrian Leverkuhn on a rumor that composer Arnold Schoenberg had bartered with Satan for his soul. Mann's novel was filmed in 1982, one year after the filming of his son Klaus Mann's novel *Mephisto*, which abandoned the fantasy elements completely to tell the tale of a German actor (Klaus Maria Brandauer) who figuratively lost his soul dealing with the Nazi Third Reich. Klaus Mann had based his novel on the life of German theater performer Gustaf Grundgens, who had himself had a part in a German film version of *Faust* (1960).

M. R. James's clever story "Casting the Runes" (1911) was adapted to film as *Curse of the Demon* (1957). The off-screen pact was implicit to the film adaptation's building sense of dread as the magician Karswell (Niall MacGinnis) passed arcane runes that would lure a murderous demon to the latest of his foes, an American scientist (Dana Andrews).

Still, Faustian pacts with dapper demons (rather than bestial monsters) held the popular imagination. Ray Milland's sinister contemporary Satan wore a fashionable slouch hat and corrupted an honest politician (Thomas Mitchell) in *Alias Nick Beal* (1949), with the seductive aid of Audrey Totter. Lola (Gwen Verdon) was the saucy temptress in the employ of the devilish Mr. Applegate (Ray Walston) in the popular Broadway musical *Damn Yankees!* (1955), conniving a winning season for the Washington Senators baseball team when an aging fan offers his soul in exchange, becoming their star player in the bargain. Walston, Verdon, and other cast members made the leap to the big screen for the 1958 film adaptation. The TV anthology program *Robert Montgomery Presents* offered "Faust '57" (1957), while France produced *Marguerite de la Nuit* (1955); *Faustina* (1956) and *El Extrano Caso del Dr. Fausto* (1969) beckoned from Spain, and Romania offered *Faust XX* (1966).

On the comic-book racks, *Classics Illustrated* finally got around to adapting *Faust* (Gilberton, 1962). The cinema followed suit as Richard Burton's *Doctor Faustus* (1968) returned to the text of the Marlowe play, a worthy production that seemed anachronistic in the wake of Peter Cook's mod '60s model of Satan in *Bedazzled* (1967). Burton was back as Mephisto, reincarnated in an insane asylum in *Hammersmith Is Out* (1972).

Rumors that musicians, from classical composers to rock stars, had made pacts with the devil were not uncommon. Primary among these artists was blues legend Robert Johnson (1911–38), whose stunning guitar work and lyrics referring to demons and the devil fed into the creation of such rumors. Johnson's classic songs, such as "Cross Road Blues," "Me and the Devil," and "Hellhounds on My Trail" fueled speculation that Johnson had indeed acquired his potent musical powers via a pact with Satan. Johnson died before the age of thirty, poisoned outside Greenwood, Mississippi, by a jealous husband.

Such associations led to any deviation from spirituals or religious music being commonly referred to as "the devil's music." This lore later inspired Walter Hill's feature film *Crossroads* (1986), in which a young, white, Juilliard-trained classical and blues guitar player (Ralph

Macchio) accompanied an elderly bluesman (Joe Seneca) to the legendary crossroads, and saved their souls by outplaying the devil's reigning guitar acolyte (Steve Vai, in a great cameo role). A similar, though entirely fictional, theme ran through the 1979 Charlie Daniels Band song "The Devil Went Down to Georgia."

The first and best of the cinematic rock 'n' roll Fausts was Brian DePalma's *Phantom of the Paradise* (1974), an inventive wedding of Gaston Leroux's *Phantom of the Opera*, Marlowe's *Faust*, and the ongoing "shock rock" vein of showmanship. Later rock 'n' roll demons tempted teenage faux Fausts such as Marc Price in *Trick or Treat* (1986), Stephen Geoffreys in *976-EVIL* (1988), Stephen Quadros in *Shock 'Em Dead* (1991), and Edward Furlong in the virtual-reality computer game update *Brainscan* (1994).

Clive Barker's first novel *The Damnation Game* (1985) offered a fresh spin on the archetype, as did Barker's novella *The Hellbound Heart* (1986), which Barker parlayed into his directorial debut for the bracing adaptation *Hellraiser* (1987). Barker's wholly invented demonology was truly unlike anything audiences had seen before. *Hellraiser* introduced the sadomasochistic Cenobites, flayed, splayed, and bondaged demons who savored the pleasures inherent in pain and claimed the bodies and souls of any mortals clever and foolish enough to solve the infernal Chinese-puzzle-like Lament Configuration.

The Cenobites were genuinely exotic devils, alluring yet frightening exaggerations of the agonies of damnation and sainthood, catching (and fanning) the flames of an emerging "modern primitive" subculture dedicated to body piercing, tattoos, and cosmetic surgery. The lead Cenobite, Pinhead (played by veteran Barker associate Douglas Bradley), became the post–Freddie Krueger pop monster of choice, earning Barker and his producers the horror franchise they desired.

Hellbound: Hellraiser II (1988) and its sequels did not have the benefit of the writer-director's hands-on involvement. *Hellbound: Hellraiser II* featured Pinhead and an acolyte (Kenneth Cranham), who ended up transformed into a new Cenobite before paying the inevitable price for his hubris. *Hellraiser III: Hell on Earth* (1992) trotted out a fresh pack of Pinhead companions, including a Cenobite incorporating compact discs into his anatomy and arsenal. *Hellraiser IV: Bloodline* (1996) brought the series to its current closure, but *Hellraiser V* is in postproduction as of this writing. The *Hellraiser* comics series (Marvel/Epic, 1990–93) explored concepts left untouched by the later films, and introduced a staggering array of new Cenobites and demons.

In the wake of Barker's revival, many Faustian novels followed, including Emma Tennant's *Faustine* (1992), Christopher Fowler's *Spanky* (1994), Kim Newman's *The Quorum* (1994), Alan Judd's *The Devil's Own Work* (1995), and others. Oscar Zarate's graphic-novel adaptation of

He's been maimed and framed, beaten, robbed and mutilated. But they still can't keep him from the woman he loves.

PHANTOM OF THE PARADISE

THE MOST HIGHLY ACCLAIMED HORROR PHANTASY OF OUR TIME

Marlowe's *Faust* (1986) also followed, a stylized, politicized update of the sixteenth-century play that altered the context (to the twentieth-century arena) but not the substance of the original text. Faust made a movie comeback, too, popping up in the Italian *Mefisto Funk* (1986) and Czech animator Jan Svankmajer's *Faust* (1994), an enigmatic meditation on all incarnations of the legend from the medieval puppet plays to the present.

CLIVE BARKER

PHOTO BY BETH GWINN

In the 1980s and 1990s, every major male star seemed to take a stab at playing Satan in a procession of high-budget Faustian revamps. Robert DeNiro was Louis Cyphre, using voodoo to claim Mickey Rourke's soul in New Orleans in Alan Parker's *Angel Heart* (1987, based on William Hjortsberg's novel *Falling Angel*); Jack Nicholson was Daryl Van Horne in George Miller's *The Witches of Eastwick* (1987; based on the John Updike novel, see Magic Users); and Al Pacino was John Milton, seducing hotshot young attorney Kevin Lomax (Keanu Reeves) into joining his affluent Manhattan law firm (and so much more) in Taylor Hackford's *The Devil's Advocate* (1997).

In late 1995 and early 1996, DC Comics presented *Underworld Unleashed*, a massive story-line that ran throughout most DC titles at that time. The story was a very successful effort to revitalize many of the villains in the DC stable. Neron, a Satan-like figure new to the DC superhero universe, offered a plethora of four-color bad guys a traditional deal with the devil: In exchange for their souls, he would overhaul their bodies and powers, making them new and improved versions of themselves.

As we enter the twenty-first century there is little doubt that the deal-with-the-devil theme will continue to echo through our popular culture.

The Antichrist

BELIEF IN THE ANTICHRIST presupposes the divinity of Jesus Christ and the existence of the devil, who will sire or incarnate the false messiah, the Antichrist. The prophecies warning of the Antichrist's impending arrival instruct that all Heaven and Earth will become a war zone in the battle between good and evil with the coming of Armageddon, the apocalypse.

Stories of the Antichrist, the false messiah, date from a body of apocalyptic literature in Judaism that lies between the two testaments of the Bible, written prior to the founding of the Christian Church. The concept of a final war between good and evil was evident in many religions (Persian, Babylonian, and Judaism) and myths (Nordic and others) before the emerging Christian ideology embraced the theme.

The term Antichrist appeared only in the First and Second Epistles of John. However, Revelations and passages of Daniel remain the primary sources for contemporary belief in the

Antichrist (where he was referred to only as "the Beast," denoting an incarnation of Satan), the Mark of the Beast, the Second Coming and Battle of Armageddon, and the Last Judgment. The idea of the Mark of the Beast is rooted in Revelations 14:9–19: "If any man worship the Beast and his image, and receive his mark in his forehead, or in his hand... He shall be tormented with fire and brimstone in the presence of the holy angels."

The Christian belief in the Antichrist began to take a very specific form early in the church's history. In *Christian Mythology*, Brother George Every cites "an influential sermon ascribed to St. Ephrem, who died about [A.D.] 373... What is most interesting is his description of the attractiveness of anti-Christ, who would not be an incarnation of Satan but his organ, exquisitely formed in the womb of a young girl whose morals would be distinctly loose." According to this sermon, this handsome being would fool all men with his kindness and righteousness, until securing power as a ruler and devastating the earth in the process of conquering his foes. According to the saint, the Antichrist's "power would last for three years and a half before the end of the world and the coming of Christ."

This sermon informed William Bousset's *The Anti-Christ Legend* (1895), religious philosopher Vladimir Soloviev's *War, Progress, and the End of History* (1899), and almost every Christian apocalyptic interpretation, analysis, prophecy, or fantasy since, including all the pop-culture entries discussed below.

Ira Levin's novel *Rosemary's Baby* (1967; also see Magic Users) midwifed the modern pop-cultural concept of the Antichrist and, inadvertently, all the possession novels and films that followed in its wake. Thus, before beginning this section's chronological study, we must pause to consider Levin's novel and the brilliant, popular film adaptation by director Roman Polanski (1968).

Polanski remained absolutely faithful to Levin's novel, vividly capturing Rosemary Woodhouse's (Mia Farrow) growing conviction that her husband, Guy (John Cassavetes), and their elderly neighbors, the Castevets (Ruth Gordon and Sidney Blackmer), were members of a satanic cult who had conspired to impregnate her with the Antichrist. Rosemary's vague impressions of the child's conception after Guy and the Castevets apparently drugged her included a glimpse of a demonic being atop her, inhuman yellow eyes blazing.

Confronting the coven after being told her child was stillborn, Rosemary met her reptilian-eyed infant. "He has his father's eyes," Mr. Castevet told her. Thus, the screen's first Antichrist was introduced.

Rooting its narrative in biblical prophecy, *The Omen* (1976) chronicled the birth (born of a jackal), adoption, and early years of the Antichrist Damien's childhood. He was raised in the pampered custody of a government ambassador (Gregory Peck) and his wife (Lee Remick). *The Omen* was conceived by writer David Seltzer and producer Harvey Berhard as a trilogy tracing the Antichrist's life to adulthood.

Director Richard Donner (later of *Lethal Weapon* fame) helmed *The Omen* with polished efficiency, mounting jaw-dropper set pieces like the slow-motion decapitation of a photographer (David Warner). *The Omen* made a fortune and a new cycle of demonic children inevitably followed. In the midst of the knockoffs, the planned Damien trilogy was completed to ever-diminishing box-office returns.

Ever ready to surf the pop-cultural wave, the Italians scored with Alberto De Martino's *Holocaust 2000* (U.S. title: *The Chosen*, AIP, 1978). Kirk Douglas discovers his full-grown son Angel (Simon Ward) is the Antichrist, and the seven-spired nuclear-power plant he has designed is actually the seven-headed beast prophesied in the Book of Revelations.

Gregory Peck's death at the climax of *The Omen* while trying to kill adopted-son Damien with a clutch of sacred daggers, set the stage for *Damien: Omen II* (1978). The sequel detailed the orphan's teenage years as the ward of his rich uncle (William Holden), who packed Damien (Jonathan Scott-Taylor) off to military school, where carefully positioned servants of the devil (including Lance Henriksen) prepared the boy for his rise to ultimate power. In hindsight, *Damien* was the most chilling of the series, despite its shortcomings. The follow-up, *The Final Conflict* (1981), brought the trilogy to a tired conclusion. An unnecessary TV-movie extension, *The Omen IV: The Awakening* (1991), featured Damien's daughter, Delia (Asia Viera).

ABC-TV's *Look What's Happened to Rosemary's Baby* (aka *Rosemary's Baby II*, 1976) was another tepid follow-up to a groundbreaking original. Frank LaLoggia's directorial debut feature *Fear No Evil* (1981) extended the biblical battle between the archangels and Satan's fallen angels into the arena of an upper New York high school where the teenage Antichrist (Stefan Arngrim) and angel Gabriel (Kathleen Row McAllen) have a showdown. All in all, *Fear No Evil* stands as a fascinating precursor to *Buffy the Vampire Slayer*, in which the battle for good and evil plays itself out in high school and college campus settings. LaLoggia went on to fulfill his promise with one of the finest recent ghost films, *The Lady in White* (1988).

Antichrist and demonic-children novels still sold on the paperback racks, led by Gordon McGill's *Omen* sequels, *Omen IV: Armageddon 2000* and *Abomination: Omen V*. Neither could hold a candle to Marv Wolfman and Gene Colan's *Tomb of Dracula* comic-book series run with Dracula's son as the Antichrist or Rick Veitch's satiric, secular revamp of the Second Coming and Antichrist prophecies, *The One* (Marvel/Epic Comics, 1985–86; collected in graphic novel form by King Hell Press, 1989).

Canadian cartoonist Rob Walton, an animator and former theological student, has been the most adventurous comic-book creator since Rick Veitch in exploring the theme. Walton's *Blood Lines* (1987–88) involved the apocalyptic battle of divine and demonic forces through gang warfare in a blighted urban landscape. Walton returned to his apocalyptic premise in the satiric *Ragmop* (1993–98), a dizzying revamp of the Christian prophecies of the Second Coming, the Antichrist, and Armageddon.

Low-budget religious films and comics, along with the growing number of evangelical-horror bestsellers specifically written and published for the growing Christian bookstore market (including Frank E. Peretti's *This Present Darkness*, 1987, and Dave Hunt's *The Archon Conspiracy*, 1989), paved the way for far more polished works focusing more specifically on Armageddon as a facet of this milieu. Jerry B. Jenkins and Tim

DAMIEN: OMEN II

LaHaye's popular post-Rapture Left Behind novel series has spawned a juvenile series, *Left Behind: The Kids,* and an upcoming film adaptation. Christian filmmakers mounted a fresh slate of Armageddon-inspired feature films, including Peter and Paul Lalonde's ambitious trilogy *Apocalypse* (1997), *Revelation* (1998), and *Tribulation* (2000). Unlike prior efforts, these films were produced with million-dollar budgets. *The Omega Code* (1999) was similar in specifics and tone to Alberto De Martino's *Holocaust 2000*, as hero Casper Van Dien discovered that proper decoding of biblical passages from the books of Daniel and Revelations revealed that his affluent mentor (Michael York) was the Antichrist.

Featuring a top-drawer Hollywood cast and produced for a budget ($7.2 million) far beyond the means of road-show predecessors, *The Omega Code* earned considerable box-office success (claiming the Number 10 spot in October 1999 weekend theatrical earnings) and attention from the mainstream press. Apocalyptic Christian action video games have begun to carve out a niche for themselves too. Valusoft's *The War in Heaven* (1999) was among the first, allowing the player to engage with the game as either a divine angel or a fallen angel.

Perhaps in response to this growing Christian market, Hollywood edged many later *Omen*-inspired religious horror films into more devotional territory with W. W. Wicket and Carl Schultz's *The Seventh Sign* (1988), Michael Tolkin's *The Rapture* (1991), and others. Apocalyptic scenarios in these films evolved into parables about redemption rather than damnation, even as the narrative setups echoed horror movie conventions.

Alex de la Iglesia's *Day of the Beast* (1996) took an irreverent attitude toward Armageddon and the Antichrist, culminating in a lively confrontation with the goatlike Satan atop a Spanish skyscraper. Peter Hyams's Arnold Schwarzenegger vehicle *End of Days* (1999) resembled nothing more or less than a big-budget action-movie revamp of Dennis Wheatley's *To the Devil . . . A Daughter*—despite Gabriel Byrne's persuasive performance as the devil, once again foiled in his bid to breed a son via mortal woman. *End of Days* is an example of the remarkable persistence of the Antichrist theme.

Demons and Demonic Possession

DEMONIC POSSESSION makes an individual's body a battlefield between the forces of good and evil. The belief in exorcism presupposes the existence of the devil as a reality, exerting his evil influence over mortal lives. Lesser devils and demons take the driver's seat in legends, songs, stories, films, and comics dealing with demonic possession. Though the devil and his minions forever tempt mortals, provoking a person to lie, steal, murder, or commit other crimes, they may take more aggressive action and actually dominate an individual by seizing control of the body. When a devil or evil spirit controls the will or bodily actions of an individual, the individual is possessed and likely to manifest the demonic presence within him with seizures, superhuman strength, physical deformities, or by uttering curses or speaking in tongues.

Possession is difficult to identify or verify, as its apparent symptoms may actually be due to a physical condition, disease, mental illness, or emotional imbalance. Many symptoms of what are now referred to as multiple personality disorders resemble those historically associated with possession. However, such medical diagnoses do not explain the movement of objects in the vicinity of the possessed person that may also occur, or that the evil spirit may jump from one individual to another, or into an object. Some Christian denominations and other religions (including Judaism) have rituals designed to drive out such possessing spirits. In some cases, there must be another vessel for the demon to move into, such as an animal.

More often than not, the demons are never seen or shown per se in tales of possession, manifesting themselves only in the deformities, voices, and behavioral extremes that plague their chosen human vessels. The possessing demon may be Satan himself, but it is more often one of his lesser demons. The possession subgenre is particularly inviting to low-budget film producers, who find foul language, vomit, scar tissue, sexual deviance, and the occasional outburst of telekinetic energy much cheaper to believably depict onscreen than the most modest inhuman demon.

Russell Hope Robbins's *Encyclopedia of Witchcraft and Demonology* chronicled thirty-three documented cases of demonic possession (1491–1816) in nuns and children. Aldous Huxley's *The Devils of Loudon* (1952) detailed the seventeenth-century atrocities in the fortified French village of Loudon precipitated by the apparent possession of the local convent's nuns. Huxley depicted their possession as a case of mass hysteria, brought on by their attraction to their confessor, Father Urbain Grandier, and the pent-up association of their sexual arousal with the power of Satan. Grandier was tortured, convicted, and burned alive at the stake. Huxley's novel was later adapted to the stage by John Whiting, as an avant-garde musical by Krzysztof Penderecki (1969), and filmed by British director Ken Russell as *The Devils* (1971). A similar story unfolded in Chelsea Quinn Yarbro's 1984 novel *A Mortal Glamour*.

The Roman Catholic Church has its own exorcism rites, a ritual involving the use of holy relics, oils, tools, the sacrament of baptism, and the recitation of certain prayers over the possessed individual, casting out the demon in the name of Jesus Christ. Around A.D. 200, the Church formally established a position for priests trained to perform exorcisms. The Exorcist retains this office, but can only perform the ritual as deemed necessary by a bishop.

Jewish belief includes the belief in possession of a person by devils or a restless spirit, as in the rare film *The Dybbuk* (1937), based on the play by S. Ansky (first translated and performed on the U.S. stage in 1925). In *The Dybbuk*, a young bride was possessed by a deceased relative's spirit. As the rabbi performed the Judaic rites of exorcism, the furniture moved about. Similar possessions by restless or angry spirits of the dead occurred in more recent films such as *The Possession of Joel Delaney* (1972), *J.D.'s Revenge* (1976), *Ruby* (1977), and *Retribution* (1988). *Audrey Rose* (1977, from the 1976 novel by Frank De Felitta), and *All of Me* (1984) linked the theme with the belief in reincarnation (also see Ghosts).

ROBERT BLOCH

PHOTO BY BETH GWINN

The traditional occult mode of demonic possession informed many short stories, including G. G. Pendarves's "The Sin Eater" (from *Weird Tales*, December 1938). Robert Bloch's "Yours Truly, Jack the Ripper" (1943), held that the mysterious Ripper was an immortal sorcerer surviving into the present day via blood sacrifices to the evil demons he worshiped. Bloch's conceit immediately captured the public imagination, becoming the author's most-reprinted tale and earning radio, TV, and comic-book adaptations, and it continues to inform Ripper-related fiction. Bloch adapted the premise to the distant future in his script for the *Star Trek* episode "Wolf in the Fold" (1967), introducing the concept of the Ripper as a mobile spirit capable of possessing others. The premise has been carried on in many works from Hammer Films' excellent *Hands of the Ripper* (1971) to Alan Moore's and Eddie Campbell's remarkable graphic novel *From Hell* (1989–99).

Demonic possession began to creep into the cinema with the partially 3-D gimmick horror film *The Mask* (aka *The Eyes of Hell*, 1961) and especially Reginald LeBorg's effective *Diary of a Madman* (1963), in which Vincent Price commits murder under the influence of an invisible evil spirit called the Horla. The screenplay was drawn from the Guy de Maupassant story "The Horla" (1887), which did not overtly embrace possession in its narrative. This was among the first films to involve demonic possession as such. Thereafter, made-for-TV movies picked up the theme: demonic possession threatened Darrin McGavin's family in Steven Spielberg's early TV directorial effort *Something Evil* (CBS, 1972).

According to some sources, a thirteen-year-old Maryland boy exhibited increasingly bizarre, self-destructive behavior beginning in January 1949. The condition eluded any medical diagnosis or treatment, and apparent poltergeist and telekinetic activity accompanied this change, which also coincided with the death of a beloved aunt. The boy's parents called upon their local Lutheran reverend, Miles Schulze, who personally observed similar symptoms and subsequently referred the family to Mt. Rainier's St. James Roman Catholic Church.

Father E. Albert Hughes performed the Catholic ritual of exorcism on the boy in Georgetown University Hospital; Hughes was injured, and the ritual terminated. In March, the family moved in with relatives in St. Louis, Missouri, where a "successful" exorcism was reportedly completed in St. Louis' Alexian Brothers' Hospital. Contemporary accounts related the manifestation of scratches, writing, spitting, blasphemous language, ongoing telekinetic displays, and even images of the devil "drawn" into the boy's flesh. In his article in *The Washington Post*, reporter Bill Brinkley declared the incident "perhaps one of the most remarkable experiences of its kind in recent religious history" ("Ritual of Exorcism Repeated: Priest Frees Mt. Rainier Boy Reported Held in Devil's Grip," *The Washington Post*, August 20, 1949).

The case was later detailed in Thomas B. Allen's book *Possessed: The True Story of an Exorcism* (1993) and dramatized for Charles Vanderpool's Discovery Channel documentary *In the Grip of Evil* (1997). Journalist Mark Opsasnick investigated the account, tracing and speaking to the now adult "possessed boy" and his friends and family. In his articles for *Strange Magazine* (#20, 1998) and *The Fortean Times* (#123, July 1999), Opsasnick concluded that, though the boy actually did suffer a prolonged emotional event that was untreated by doctors and dealt with via exorcism by church officials, "there is not one shred of hard evidence to support the notion of demonic possession" (*The Fortean Times* #123). Still, the legacy lingers.

Author William Peter Blatty was an undergraduate at Georgetown University when the case was reported in the newspapers. Blatty subsequently researched the case of possession and exorcism and wrote *The Exorcist* (1971). The novel was a fictionalized account of the Maryland case, changing the gender of the child. It explored the core issues of philosophy and religious belief that fascinated Blatty, a former theological student. The novel immediately rocketed up the bestseller list and the screen rights were snapped up by Warner Brothers. The studio agreed to the condition that Blatty himself craft the script and produce the adaptation, working with director William Friedkin.

Bringing on makeup master Dick Smith and veteran actress Mercedes McCambridge (providing the voice of the demon), the filmmakers crafted a vision of demonic possession that absolutely captivated and terrified audiences with its graphic horrors. The transformation of young Regan (Linda Blair) into a hideously scarred, golden-eyed demon child indulging in blasphemous language and behavior, projectile vomiting, bone-crunching 360-degree head-spinning, and more was unlike anything ever seen before. The horrors were tactile, almost palpable, and rendered with utter conviction. Friedkin also employed a nerve-jangling audio mix and occasional "subliminal" images (including single frames of a demonic face intercut with closeups of young Regan) to orchestrate a startlingly fresh modern horror epic.

The film version of *The Exorcist* debuted on December 26, 1973, playing to capacity audiences. There were reports of audience members vomiting, fleeing, or fainting, which only attracted larger crowds, as did the lurid press and studio publicity concerning mysterious events that had plagued the supposedly cursed production. The curse apparently did not extend to its earnings, as *The Exorcist* broke international box-office records and became one of the highest grossing films in history (save in the U.K., where the British Board of Film Classification banned the feature from the video market for fifteen years).

As Blatty had hoped, the film also prompted a broad cultural debate about the existence of the devil, demons, and fundamentals of religious faith.

The phenomenal success of *The Exorcist* prompted immediate imitation, none of which held a candle to Blatty and Friedkin's innovative blockbuster. Warner Brothers took legal action against the "blaxploitation" revamp *Abby* (AIP, December 25, 1974), with *Blacula* star William Marshall as the exorcist. One year later, the courts settled in Warner Brothers' favor, preventing any subsequent exhibition of *Abby* or sequels sans their permission.

Be that as it may, the floodgates had already burst. *Abby* arrived late to the party: Italian producers had already popped their own knockoff, *Che Sei?* (literally, "Who Are You?," a line from *The Exorcist*) into theaters in November 1974, beating another lurid Italian variation *L'Anticristo* (U.S. title: *The Tempter*, Avco Embassy, 1978) by a month and millions of *lire* in box office. *Che Sei?* opened in the United States as *Beyond the Door* (Film Ventures, 1975), and broke records again, becoming the most profitable Italian import up to that time.

Marvel Comics jumped on the bandwagon with their black-and-white magazine line, which never required the sanction of the Comics Code. *The Haunt of Horror* #2 (1974) ballyhooed itself as a "Special Issue on Satanism, Introducing: The Man Called Gabriel, Devil-Hunter" amid a brief flurry of *Exorcist*-inspired tales of demonic possession and exorcism.

Across the globe in 1974, movie producers were rushing their *Exorcist* rip-offs into every available market. In Spain, horror star Paul Naschy (see Primals) was rushing his *Exorcism* into theaters neck-and-neck with *The Possessed* from director Amando De Ossorio (creator of the *Blind Dead* series; see Walking Dead). The Germans offered the possessed nymphomaniac *Magdalena, Von Teufel Besessen* (U.S. title: *Beyond the Darkness*, aka *The Devil's Female*, 1976), upping the sexual content. The Italians followed suit with *L'Ossessa* (*The Tormented*, 1978, aka *The Eerie Midnight Horror Show*, 1980), *Il Medaglione Insanguinato* (U.S.: *Night Child*, Film Ventures, 1976), *Cries and Shadows*, and others.

Britain almost missed the boat, casting Joan Collins (in her pre-*Dynasty* days) in *The Devil Within Her* (AIP, 1976). In a last-ditch effort to rescue their failing studio, Hammer Films turned to another Dennis Wheatley novel, *To the Devil...a Daughter* (1953) and mounted their final theatrical horror feature in 1976, using Wheatley's title.

Mario Bava's evocative parable *Lisa and the Devil* (1973) starred Elke Sommer as an innocent caught in a time loop where a century-old series of murders were re-created in an ancient villa under the ministrations of an enigmatic devil (a playful Telly Savalas, complete with *Kojak* lollipop). Unable to sell the film, Italian producer Alfred Leone gutted Bava's masterwork, financing recuts and new footage. The lively mishmash was retitled *The House of Exorcism* (Peppercorn-Wormser, 1976) to secure playdates.

Bava's original version was restored and released on video in 1998. Alas, Bava's final masterpiece, the gripping ghost story *Shock* (1977), was misrepresented to U.S. audiences as a sequel to *Beyond the Door*, exploiting the tale's weird little boy (who sees and is occasionally possessed by his dead father's spirit) to play as *Beyond the Door 2* (Film Ventures, 1978); it was, at least, uncut.

Graham Masterton's novel *The Manitou* (1975) proposed the rebirth of four-hundred-year-old Native American shaman Misquamancus through the vessel of an urban white woman's body. The 1978 film adaptation, *The Manitou,* had the title character emerging out of Susan Strasberg's spine. Ignoring the film's failure, Masterton continued Misquamancus's saga in *Revenge of the Manitou* (1979) and *Burial* (1992).

Made-for-TV features timidly tiptoed onto the bandwagon with *Exorcist* knockoffs like *Can Ellen Be Saved?* (ABC, 1974), Richard Matheson's feminist-backlash curio *The Strange Possession of Mrs. Oliver* (NBC, 1977), *The Possessed* (NBC, 1977), *Good Against Evil* (ABC, 1977), and others.

Coming at the end of such frantic exploitation and endless variations was Warner Brothers' long-awaited *Exorcist II: The Heretic* (1977). Irish director John Boorman (*Point Blank*, 1967; *Deliverance*, 1972; *Zardoz*, 1973) tried to take the high ground, eschewing the sensationalism he reportedly felt had characterized the original (and certainly dominated its many imitations) in order to intellectualize its morality play, and provide a mythic context for the possession.

Tormented by residual memories of the possession and exorcism, now-teenage Regan (Linda Blair), her therapist (Louise Fletcher), and a priest (Richard Burton) uncovered the African origins and true nature of the Assyrian demon Pazuzu that had possessed her. Boorman mounted some dazzling sequences but the coda—with Burton and Blair emerging from the wreckage to proselytize on the need to fight evil—unfortunately undercut the film's good points. It made for a talky religious melodrama rather than the thrilling horror sequel audiences anticipated, and Warner's wide release of the sequel was an immediate critical and commercial failure.

The initial June 17, 1977, weekend earnings for *The Exorcist II: The Heretic* were the highest the corporation had ever enjoyed, but bad reviews and negative word of mouth prompted an emergency re-edit of the final reels by director Boorman that resolved nothing. The re-edit of the film never played theatrically in the United States, opening instead in the rest of the world as the preferred version. Both versions have been released to video domestically, though they were not differentiated.

Low-budget "Linda-come-lately" possession entries like *Beyond Evil* (1980), *Teenage Exorcist* (1990), *The Antichrist* (1991), and imports like *Guardian of Hell* (aka *The Other Hell*, 1979/1985), and *Beyond the Door III* (1989) were relegated to obscurity. Even Linda Blair later parodied her star-making role in *Repossessed* (1990).

Blatty rewrote his own unproduced screenplay follow-up to *The Exorcist* and published it as the novel *Legion* (1983), which he eventually directed himself as *The Exorcist 3: Legion* (1990).

Blatty drew the title and premise for his sequel from a passage in the book of Mark in the New Testament, in which Jesus Christ exorcised a possessed man in the country of Gerasenes, casting his demons into a herd of swine, which then threw themselves into the sea. The brief dialogue between Christ and the demon was chilling: "For he said unto him, come forth, thou unclean spirit, out of the man. And he asked him, What is thy name? And he saith unto him, My name is Legion: for we are many" (Mark 5: 8–10).

THE EXORCIST 3: LEGION

Legion took place fifteen years after the events detailed in *The Exorcist*. While investigating a horrific series of serial murders resembling those committed by a killer executed the night of Regan's exorcism, Detective Kinderman (George C. Scott, re-creating the role originally played by Lee J. Cobb) uncovers their supernatural source in a patient at a local asylum. He was Legion, committing murders by selective, multiple-choice possession of different hosts.

Blatty's involving narrative eloquently expanded upon the themes of redemption he feared had been subsumed by the film version of his original novel, and despite refilming and re-edits of the final act (inserting a new character, a priest played by Nicol Williamson), *Exorcist 3: Legion* remains an effective shocker.

Though he has received little credit for the innovation, Blatty's conceit of a demon opportunistically leapfrogging from one human vessel to another as needed became the choice plot device of the decade's demonic fiction and films. Robert Resnikoff's *The First Power* (1989) beat Blatty's film adaptation of *Legion* to the screen by a full year, and its demonic serial killer set the stage for much of what followed, spawning many descendants up through the recent *Fallen* (1998). Sadly, many critics dismissed Blatty's fine film adaptation of *Legion* as just another permutation of this cycle, rather than its seminal text.

Jack Sholder's *The Hidden* (1987) had already made its mark with a science-fiction variation, a homicidal insectlike alien possessing its hosts. It returned in *The Hidden 2* (1994). There were high-tech variations, like Wes Craven's *Shocker* (1989), *Ghost in the Machine* (1993), *Virtuosity* (1995), and others blending vague mysticism with hardware gadgetry.

A further externalization of this shift in pop consciousness involves the wedding of the Christian belief in possession and exorcism with the Christian belief in stigmata, inexplicable manifestations of Jesus Christ's crucifixion wounds in the hands, feet, and body of devout mortals. *The X-Files* episode "Revelations" (1995) rallied Agents Mulder and Scully to the defense of a stigmatic young boy being stalked by a killer, probing Scully's own faith and religious beliefs. In a surprisingly anti–Roman Catholic narrative, Patricia Arquette was the mortal vessel of the film *Stigmata* (1999), possessed not by a demon or Jesus Christ but the spirit of a deceased priest whose outrage at the Vatican's suppression of a secret gospel text could not be silenced by death.

Janusz Kaminski's *Lost Souls* (2000) opened with a harrowing sequence of possession and exorcism gone wrong, subsequently tracing the event's devastating impact on a young schoolteacher (Winona Ryder) whose faith was shaken by the incident, and her attempt to rescue a writer (Ben Chaplin) from the devil's schemes. *The X-Files* has had its share of supernatural demonic possession episodes, the most well-crafted being "Grotesque" (1996) and the extraordinary "Terms of Endearment" (1999), in which a bigamist demon (Bruce Campbell) left a wake of aborted, buried fetuses behind him in his attempts to sire an offspring. In the surprising final act, he met his mate and match in a prospective mother (Lisa Jane Persky) with her own agenda.

Stephen King's *Storm of the Century* (ABC, 1999) capped the decade with a compelling variation on the theme that also touched upon the bogeyman archetype so central to King's body of work (see Bogeymen). King's potent parable of an isolated Maine island community visited by a demonic stranger named Linoge (Colm Feore) during a winter storm of frightening intensity culminated in Linoge's demand of a sacrificial "lamb" in exchange for the entire community's survival: a village child for the demon to claim and raise as his own (possibly to take his place, recalling *Melmoth the Wanderer*). The son of local sheriff Michael Anderson (Tim Daly) was chosen. In the chilling coda, Anderson glimpsed Linoge and his now-teenage son on the streets of San Francisco just long enough to see that the boy had acquired Linoge's demonic attributes.

The precise nature of shape-shifting Linoge's origins or mythic demon lineage were never disclosed, evoking both the bogeyman archetype and that of Satan and the Antichrist, claiming a son to succeed him, though King's mini-apocalypse was strictly a localized phenomenon. At one point, however, the tale's heroes realized that "Linoge" was an anagram for "Legion," harkening back to the biblical reference.

An episode of the *Buffy* spinoff series *Angel*, "I've Got You Under My Skin" (2000), featured a riveting twist on the demonic possession theme. A cruel, evil young boy tormenting his family was revealed to be possessed by a demon. But when the demon was exorcised from the child, Angel discovered that the infernal creature was terrified and had been trapped within the boy—that the boy himself was far more evil than the demon possessing him.

THE MASTER

"Priorities. Really, if I had the power of the black mass I'd set my sights a little higher than making the pep squad."
— GILES, "WITCH"

BUFFY and ANGEL

DARLA

MOLOCH

"So this is the Slayer. You're prettier
than the last one."
— THE MASTER, "NIGHTMARES"

"Buffy killed a vampire last night." — WILLOW, "WHEN SHE WAS BAD"

DARYL EPPS

THE ANOINTED ONE

> "From now on we're gonna have a little less ritual and a little more fun around here."
> — SPIKE, "SCHOOL HARD"

SPIKE

DRUSILLA

AMPATA

"Some guy's attacking Buffy with a sword!
Also there's a really big snake."
—WILLOW, "REPTILE BOY"

MACHIDA

ETHAN RAYNE

"They don't know who they are, everyone's become a monster, it's a whole big thing. How are you?"
—CORDELIA, "HALLOWEEN"

Jenny Calendar possessed by Eyghon

BUFFY and KENDRA

MR. PFISTER,
ORDER OF TARAKA ASSASSIN

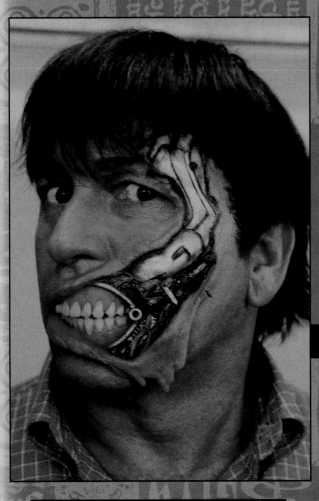

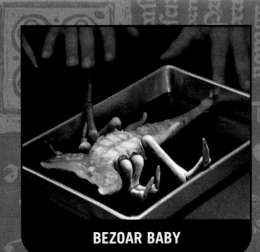

BEZOAR BABY

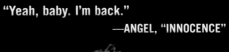

TED

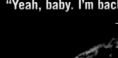

THE JUDGE

"Yeah, baby. I'm back."
—ANGEL, "INNOCENCE"

Oz, on a full moon

Amy Madison, a powerful witch

DER KINDESTOD

A former member of the Sunnydale Swim Team

James Stanley and Grace Newman

Ending the ritual of Acathla

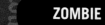

ZOMBIE

KEN

KAKISTOS

MR. TRICK

"Only a person with tremendous will and character could survive that and retain any semblence of self."
—GILES, "BEAUTY AND THE BEASTS"

PETE

LURCONIS

GWENDOLYN POST

ANYANKA

VAMP WILLOW and VAMP XANDER

"I need to...I need to know why I'm here."
—ANGEL, "AMENDS"

HARBINGER

Demon from "Gingerbread"

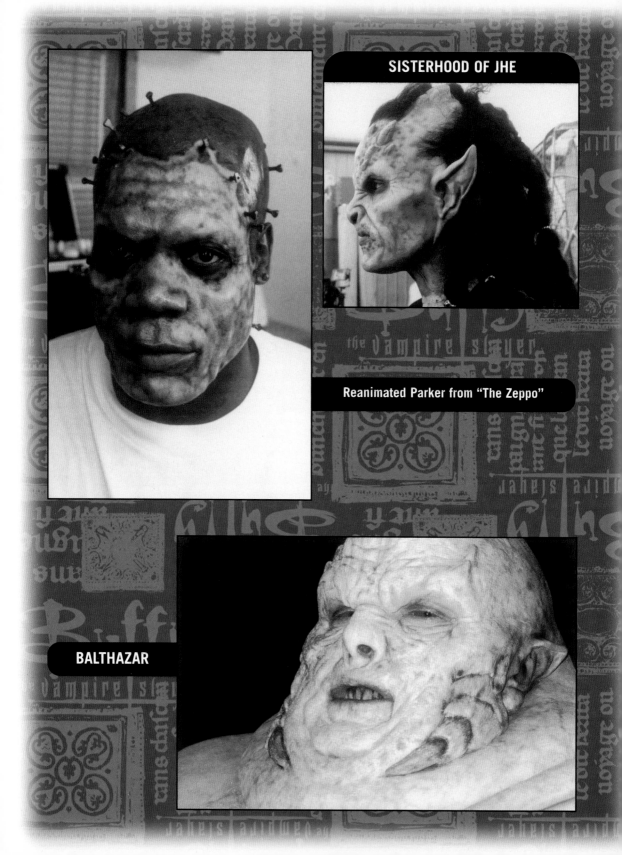

SISTERHOOD OF JHE

Reanimated Parker from "The Zeppo"

BALTHAZAR

One of the many cases of contemporary exorcism reported in the wake of *The Exorcist* was dramatized in a TV movie as *The Demon Murder Case* (NBC, 1983). The February 16, 1981, arrest of Arne Cheyenne Johnson for the murder of Alan Bono in Brookfield, Connecticut, was followed by accounts of demonic possession (including that of an eleven-year-old boy) as the possible cause of the crime.

Judge Robert Callahan refused to permit the presentation of a "possession defense," and Johnson was convicted in November 1981 of manslaughter in the first degree. The involvement of paranormal investigators Ed and Lorraine Warren led to a book, Gerald Brittle's *The Devil in Connecticut* (1983). The TV-movie "docudrama" fictionalization, *The Demon Murder Case*, starred Kevin Bacon as Kenny Miller (pseudonym for Arne Johnson) and Harvey Fierstein as the demon's voice.

Whereas popular culture continues to weave fictions around exorcism and possession, supposedly real cases continue to be reported. Archbishop Emmanuel Milingo of the Pontifical Council in Vatican City is a modern-day exorcist who has purportedly cast out many devils. Scientists, psychologists, psychiatrists, parapsychologists, theologians, and Church scholars still debate the realities of such cases, forever questioning whether they represent earthly incarnations of the forces of evil or extreme physical manifestations of psychological afflictions.

Elder Gods and Demons

AS THE LITERAL BELIEF IN SATAN and his minions diminished at the close of the nineteenth century, imaginative fiction began to manifest a wholly invented demonology that implied the earth as we know it had once belonged to an elder race of monstrous beings. If nothing else, this mythos was Darwinian in nature: Victorian and Edwardian culture had elevated mankind (and the British Empire) to the ranks of God's Chosen above all of God's other creations, only to have their conceit dashed by Darwin's *Origin of Species* (see Primals).

Defensive but humbled, and with Satan no longer a literal reality in civilized circles, invented mythologies like the Cthulhu lore of author H. P. Lovecraft evoked a cosmic sense of awe and terror Christianity had lost for many.

Those invented beings—referred to as both gods and demons—predated language, recorded history, and all known religion, be it mythic, pagan, or Judeo-Christian. They were timeless, immortal, and impossibly gigantic, their forms almost incomprehensible to our senses, their intelligence and designs on our world beyond imagining. They waited in some netherworld—beneath the earth or seas, in the depth of space, or in another dimension—to reclaim what was once theirs. Knowledge of their existence unhinged the mind, the mere sight of them drove men mad. Legendary tomes associated with their existence, or worship of these ancient beings, were forbidden texts. Primary among these was the *Necronomicon*, a moniker that has become part of our vocabulary to the point where many believe such a book exists or once existed outside the parameters of H. P. Lovecraft's pulp fiction (it does not).

At the most primal level, such beings placed mankind at the base of a very ancient food chain. Mankind was beneath notice, unless these Elder Gods had some use for our mortal coils;

at the most, humans served as birthing vessels (as in the short story "The Dunwich Horror," 1929), or provided sustenance of some kind, physically (as meat), emotionally (fear-as-food), or metaphysically (life-force-as-food).

Lovecraft wrote about this aspect of the mythos in a letter dated July 5, 1927, noting that his short stories were "based on the fundamental premise that common human laws and interests and emotions have no validity or significance in the vast cosmos-at-large." Referring specifically to his story "The Call of Cthulhu" (1926), Lovecraft concluded, "To achieve the essence of real externality, whether of time or space or dimension, one must forget that such things as organic life, good and evil, love and hate, and all such local attributes of a negligible and temporary race called mankind, have any existence at all."

The prehuman Elder Gods or "Great Old Ones" of Lovecraftian fiction set the stage for the demons on *Buffy the Vampire Slayer*, who were here before humanity and now reside in various alternate demon dimensions awaiting their chance to return.

H. P. Lovecraft's early fiction occasionally evoked this imaginary realm in stories like "Dagon" (1917, featuring a sea god who later became a minor being in the Cthulhu pantheon), "The Nameless City" (1921; published in 1938), "The Hound" (1924), and "The Festival" (1925). The fictional author of the *Necronomicon*, "the mad Arab Abdul Alhazred," was mentioned in "The Nameless City," along with a passage of text by Alhazred that Lovecraft would later (in "The Hound") attribute to the as-yet-unnamed *Necronomicon*: "That is not dead which can eternal lie/ And with strange aeons even death may die."

It was "The Call of Cthulhu" in *Weird Tales* (February 1928) that overtly introduced Lovecraft's unique universe of ancient demonic gods to the genre. As a story, "The Call of Cthulhu" was fairly shapeless: an unnamed narrator inherited an archaeological artifact bearing a relief-carving of a hideous monstrosity and discovered a worldwide cult dedicated to worshiping the thing in the carving—Cthulhu—culminating in the appearance of a previously submerged island harboring ancient temples and Cthulhu itself. In the telling of the tale, Lovecraft evoked other mysterious names such as the demon R'lyeh and referred to the "Great Old Ones," laying the bedrock for what came to be known as the Cthulhu Mythos.

In time, the gallery of Lovecraft's invented gods became impressive indeed. The author shunned particulars, offering tantalizing, fragmentary descriptions of these monstrous beings, allowing the readers' imaginations to give form to their dread names and reputations. Along with Cthulhu, there were: Nyarlathotep, the devil-god; Yog-Sothoth, the guardian of the gate; Azathoth, the progenitor of the Great Old Ones; Shub-Niggurath, Yuggoth, the dark planet (Pluto); Sarnath the Doomed; and invented New England locales like the witch-plagued village of Arkham, Massachusetts, and the Miskatonic University Library, where one of the only remaining copies of the *Necronomicon* was kept. Though Lovecraft himself never referred to his work as such, by the early 1930s fans of his writings coined the phrase "Cthulhu Mythos," giving definite shape to a specific selection from Lovecraft's oeuvre.

"The Dunwich Horror" (from *Weird Tales*, April 1929) offered Lovecraft's first hybrid offspring sired by the Great Old Ones, Wilbur Whateley, a repugnant backwoods child prodigy whose research into the *Necronomicon* and other forbidden texts invites disaster. With his death, Wilbur was revealed to be a half-human monstrosity, leading the townspeople to the eventual discovery of Wilbur's even more monstrous imprisoned sibling: *"It was his twin brother, but it looked more like the father than he did,"* Lovecraft concluded (italics were his).

Another important element in the development of the mythos was the growing circle of fellow authors with whom Lovecraft corresponded: Frank Belknap Long, Clark Ashton Smith, and two aspiring young Wisconsin authors, August Derleth and Robert Bloch, among others. Working through the mail, Lovecraft would often edit or revise the work of other writers, and in short order this circle of authors began to slip references to each other's invented universes into their own stories. Thus, the Cthulhu Mythos quickly spread beyond the parameters of Lovecraft's fiction alone.

Lovecraft's own contributions included "The Shadow over Innsmouth" (1936; see Primals: Snake Women and Fish Men), which expanded on the import of Dagon with its amphibious half-human beings, The Deep Ones, the descendants of "Father Dagon and Mother Hydra," and introduced the Shoggoths. The Shoggoths returned in his novella *At the Mountains of Madness* (1936), an epic, nightmarish sojourn into arctic regions where hints are found of prehuman races whose extraterrestrial origins predate the evolution of primal man.

In March 1937 Lovecraft succumbed to the ravages of intestinal cancer and Bright's disease, leaving forever this "negligible and temporary race called mankind." But his work and imaginative universe outlived him.

In subsequent years, Lovecraft's circle of writing associates continued to expand the mythos by writing new fiction involving Lovecraft's and their communal creations. As they did so, new writers joined the procession, including Ramsey Campbell, Henry Kuttner, Colin Wilson, Lin Carter, and others. August Derleth founded Arkham House, a publishing firm initially dedicated to collecting and reprinting Lovecraft's work. Not surprisingly, Derleth was one of the primary participants in popularizing the mythos with his own creative contributions, including a clutch of posthumous "collaborations" with Lovecraft.

Lin Carter (with *Lovecraft: A Look Behind the "Cthulhu Mythos,"* 1972) and L. Sprague De Camp (author of *Lovecraft: A Biography*, 1975) dedicated their efforts in part toward documenting Lovecraft's life, work, and fictional offspring; a legacy scholar and author S. T. Joshi has continued admirably to the present. In recent years, prominent practitioners like Stephen King (with "Jerusalem's Lot," 1967; published in 1978), Karl Edward Wagner ("Sticks," 1974), and many others have carried on the proud tradition. Anthologies such as *Tales of the Cthulhu Mythos* (1990) are still published, and Arkham House carries on the legacy of its founding father August Derleth and its godfather, H. P. Lovecraft.

It is almost impossible to chart the ever-proliferating pop-culture items and artifacts that owe a debt to Lovecraft's works in the space we have here. Narrowing the focus only to those works involving Lovecraft's imaginary demonology simplifies the task somewhat, since Lovecraft adaptations like *Re-Animator* (1984; see Walking Dead) and *Lurking Fear* (1994) fall outside of the Mythos.

Lucio Fulci's zombie epic films like *Gates of Hell* and *The Beyond* (see Walking Dead) evoked Lovecraft's imaginary New England settings by pirating the name of Dunwich and featuring an imagined forbidden book, but those bloodbaths were hardly Lovecraftian efforts. Films like J. Piquer Simon's *Cthulhu Mansion* (1991) borrowed the name without incorporating any of Lovecraft or the Mythos.

The first comics adaptation of Lovecraft was "The Thing at Chugamung Cove" in *Amazing Mysteries* #32 (May 1949; the first Marvel horror comic), an uncredited revamp of "The Shadow over Innsmouth." Author and comics scholar Will Murray also excavated a series of "Red Dragon" backup stories in *Super-Magician Comics* #8–10 (1946) featuring an interdimensional villain named "Chthtlu" [sic]. Murray also cited stories from the earlier horror comics era that featured ersatz *Necronomicon* tomes, such as *Weird Fantasy* #14 (1950), and *Hand of Fate* #21 and *The Thing!* #11 (both 1953).

The *Necronomicon* was appropriated by a wizard to fight the Justice League of America in a two-part adventure scripted by Gardner Fox (in *Justice League of America* #10–11, 1962).

The first cinematic appearance of the Great Old Ones was in Roger Corman's *The Haunted Palace* (1963) starring Vincent Price, a reasonably faithful adaptation of Lovecraft's non-Mythos novel *The Case of Charles Dexter Ward* (1927) that was falsely peddled as another entry in Corman and Price's Edgar Allan Poe series. Dan O'Bannon mounted a remake in 1991 titled *The Resurrected*, sans the overt Cthulhu references.

Daniel Haller, designer of *The Haunted Palace*'s very impressive sets, directed *Die, Monster, Die!* (1965), an adaptation of Lovecraft's science fiction tale "The Colour Out of Space" (1927). The film featured one overt reference to the mythos when its brash American hero (Nick Adams) found a book entitled *Cult of the Outer Ones*, though the real threat turned out to be accelerated radiation poisoning from an extraterrestrial meteor. Dell Comics published a comic book adaptation, and the story was later remade as *The Curse* (1987), sans any Mythos touchstones.

Haller assumed the helm one more time for *The Dunwich Horror* (1969), which updated Lovecraft's original story by imposing a *Rosemary's Baby*–inspired plot thread with Sandra Dee facing imminent demonic impregnation, and by downplaying the demon-human hybrid nature of occultist Wilbur Whateley (Dean Stockwell) in order to play up his Charles Manson–like lunacy. However, the particulars (including the *Necronomicon*, Miskatonic University, and the Whateley legacy) hewed close to the Lovecraft text, concluding with a ritual to conjure Yog-Sothoth and a startling point-of-view rampage by Wilbur's barely visible, hydralike "big brother."

By the 1970s, comic books had begun to embrace Lovecraft's pantheon of demons. *Swamp Thing*, *Doctor Strange*, *Conan the Barbarian* (via Robert E. Howard's own pulp-era contributions to the Mythos), and other four-color mainstream comics featured Mythos-inspired menaces. *Doctor Strange* had always featured Lovecraftian beings and demons with evocative names like Raggador, Dormammu, Cyttorak, and others. By 1972 entities like N'Gabthoth and Shuma-Gorath (from Robert E. Howard's mythos entries) had plagued the good doctor, and writer Roy Thomas had even scripted a pastiche of "The Shadow over Innsmouth" under the title "The Spawn of Sligguth." Marvel Comics adapted a number of Lovecraft stories, including *Journey into Mystery*'s illustrated versions of the Mythos' one-two punch of Robert Bloch's "The Shambler from the Stars" (in #3, February 1973) and Lovecraft's follow-up "The Haunter of the Dark" (#4, April 1973).

Swedish artist extraordinaire H. R. Giger packaged an eye-popping collection of his paintings under the title *Necronomicon* (1977), around the same time that French comics artist Philippe Druillet illustrated his own arcane *Necronomicon* simulacrum.

The most Lovecraftian of all films was, surprisingly enough, *Ghostbusters* (1984; see Ghosts). Dan Aykroyd and Harold Ramis's screenplay was peppered with overt references to Lovecraft and his circle of associates. The hellhounds recalled Frank Belknap Long's story "The Hounds of Tindalos" (1929) and may later have themselves inspired the Hellhounds in the *Buffy* episode "The Prom." The film's references to the evil spirits possessing their human hosts as "The Keymaster" and "The Gatekeeper" (with the expected sexual innuendo fulfilled) and the opening of a dimensional portal through which an ancient demigod named Gozer manifests itself echoed the Mythos.

The subsequent *The Real Ghostbusters* cartoon series (see Ghosts) featured "The Collect Call of Cthulhu," in which a cult theft of the *Necronomicon* leads to the cult's attempt to raise Cthulhu from the Coney Island surf; the Cthulhu cult returned in the episode "Russian About."

Though producer Brian Yuzna and director Stuart Gordon's *Re-Animator* wasn't a mythos entry, their semi-sequel *From Beyond* (1986) adapted Lovecraft's 1920 short story. Yuzna later produced the anthology feature *Necronomicon* (1993), featuring three segments from three different directors, France's Christopher Gans, Japan's Shu Kaneko, and Yuzna himself. Only the last episode touched on the Mythos, to little effect. Jean-Paul Ouellette directed *The Unnameable* (1988) and *The Unnameable 2: The Statement of Randolph Carter* (1992), which featured the *Necronomicon* and a startling pair of female albino monsters with wings, horns, talons, and hooves (played by Katrin Alexander and Julie Strain).

Japanese horror anime (animated) features and direct-to-video series have often involved Lovecraftian demons seeking to reclaim the earth as their own. Anime have embraced every conceivable genre, and horror anime break all imaginable taboos. They are filled with invented devil lore and arcane demonology, rendered with ruthless abandon. Go Nagai's *Devilman* (comic book 1971–73, anime version 1987) introduced the genre, and soon demons were a fixture of medieval Japan horror adventures such as *Curse of the Undead—Yoma* (1989) and *Ninja Scroll* (1993).

Wicked City (1987), based on the manga (comic book) novel by Hideyuki Kikuchi, popularized the fusion of futuristic hard-boiled film noir, science fiction, and sex with its tale of an elite police squad dedicated to maintaining the peace between our earthly realm and the demonic netherworld. When a cult of the shape-shifting demons ignored the pact between the worlds, all hell literally broke loose. There was no looking back: *Demon Beast Invasion 1* and *2* (1990), *Demon City Shinjuku* (1991), *Doomed Megalopolis* (1991), and many others pushed the envelope further with every episode.

Anime director Hideki Takayama brought Toshio Maeda's horror manga epic *Urotsukidoji* (1987–89) to the screen with all its outrageous sex and violence intact, incorporating visual elements from American horror films like *The Evil Dead* (see Walking Dead) and John Carpenter's *The Thing* (see Primals) with its unique demon mythos. The narrative began like a standard college coming-of-age romance typical of anime, but quickly erupted into a nastier breed when a pushy female gym coach metamorphed into a multitentacled male demon that ravaged the ingenue heroine: the first evidence of the demon invasion into the mortal realm.

To Western audiences, the apocalyptic horror, explicit sex, and kinetic violence were unlike anything ever seen before. More Lovecraftian demons invaded high schools in graphic anime entries like *Angel of Darkness 1* and *2* (1994–95).

The feature-length edited version of the *Urotsukidoji* serial played urban "midnight shows" as *Legend of the Overfiend* (1989), chopping down the series' four-hour running time to a barely coherent 108 minutes, retaining enough of its rapist demons, splashy gore, and global destruction to shock the most jaded U.S. viewers. The uncut anime series became a breakthrough success in the Japanese and, eventually, the U.S. video market. Live-action horror films have yet to approach the transgressive imagery of these films, or the inventive demonic menagerie that inhabits them.

The made-for-cable TV movie *Cast a Deadly Spell* (1991) reveled in a satiric turnabout on the Lovecraft myth, in which H. P. Lovecraft (Fred Ward) was a down-and-out private investigator in an alternate-reality Los Angeles in which magic and the occult were aspects of everyday life. In the end, an impressively mountainous Lovecraftian deity materialized to gulp the villain down like a bonbon. The sequel, *Witch Hunt* (1994), brought Dennis Hopper in to play Lovecraft, but the black magic storyline had nothing to do with the Mythos.

Lovecraft's Cthulhu Mythos has forever changed contemporary imaginative demonology. New stories and novels are written every year that touch upon, incorporate, or expand elements of Lovecraft's imaginary pantheon of the Great Old Ones. Recent examples of particular note include Peter Straub's wonderful 1999 novel *Mr. X*, in which a young man with strange abilities reads Lovecraft's work and becomes convinced that it is all true, offering himself as an acolyte to the Great Old Ones. Also notable from 1999 was comics artist-writer Daniel Brereton's *Giantkiller* (DC Comics), in which a portal to a hellish dimension opens—pouring out a wonderful catalog of Lovecraftian demons—and Earth scientists are forced to genetically engineer a monster-man capable of killing them.

With the virtually endless possibilities CGI technology offers for bringing such creatures to cinematic life, the coming millennium only promises a more dazzling and disgusting array of Lovecraftian beings.

Buffy
the vampire slayer

VAMPiRES

"It's the weirdest thing. He's got two little holes in his neck and all the blood's been drained. Isn't that bizarre? Aren't you just going, 'Ooooh'?"
—BUFFY, TO GILES, IN "WELCOME TO THE HELLMOUTH"

THOUGH SHE HAS put an end to a wide array of monsters, Buffy Summers is, by job description at least, a *vampire* Slayer. Before the creation of this series (as you will see in the sections that follow) there were really only two major schools of thought on vampires: the traditional, as founded by Bram Stoker and continued by masters such as Stephen King (in *'Salem's Lot*), and the modern, as perhaps most uniquely exemplified in the works of Anne Rice.

Joss Whedon's creations, then, could well be considered postmodern. Like nearly all effective tellers of vampire tales in the latter half of the twentieth century, Whedon reinvented the wheel to fit his own purposes. In *Buffy the Vampire Slayer*, the transformation from human to creature of the night is quite different from that in other such tales. Rather than human beings turned into undead monsters, Whedon's vampires are human corpses inhabited by otherwise bodiless demons. Though there are ancient precedents for such a concept, Whedon has said in an interview that he was unaware of them when creating his dark universe.

That bit of lore was probably the only one he was not aware of, however, as Joss Whedon has an encyclopedic knowledge of monsters on film (and films in general, actually) and elsewhere. His love of comic books is well known, and his love for the seminal vampire comic-book series *The Tomb of Dracula*, well documented.

Still, *Buffy* is a unique creation, distilled from the remnants of everything in Whedon's frame of reference and then forged anew with his own inimitable imagination.

There's an entire world here, and, of course, he has it all in his head. Joss Whedon has created not only a new vampire, but an entirely new mythology.

"The mythology expands with every show we write," he says. "With *Angel*, it's expanding a lot."

Beyond what has already been stated, we know this about Whedon's vampires:

✦ **When "killed" a vampire turns to ash.** (The exception was the Master.)

✦ **They can be killed by fire.** Buffy noted in season one's "Welcome to the Hellmouth" that she had burned down her previous high school's gymnasium to kill the vampires she had trapped inside.

✦ **They are burned by direct sunlight** ("Earshot," many others) and will be immolated and explode into ash if exposed to prolonged sunlight ("Becoming, Part 1"). In "Amends," Angel attempts suicide by simply waiting ouside for the dawn to arrive. In most recently created vampire mythologies, daylight will destroy a vampire. But in *Buffy* (and *Angel*), as in *Dracula*, it must be *direct* sunlight, rather than merely daylight. A heavily overcast day or some other kind of covering is sufficient to keep the creature alive for a period of time.

+ **They can be killed by decapitation,** as in "The Harvest," when Buffy lops off a vampire's head with a cymbal from a drum set.

+ **They can be killed by the penetration of the heart,** but only with wood.

+ In season three's "Helpless," Buffy killed the vampire Zachary Kralik by tricking him into **drinking holy water,** which burned him from within, and destroyed him.

+ Unlike vampires in other mythologies, **they cannot transform into bats, or change their shapes at all,** for that matter, as established in "The Harvest." In that episode, when Xander asks if vampires can fly, Buffy says, with great emphasis, "They can *drive.*"

+ Unlike traditional vampires of myth, **they do not have any problems with running water,** as seen in "Surprise."

+ Also unlike traditional vampires, **they do not need to sleep in a bed of their native earth.** As Angel notes in the *Angel* episode "Parting Gifts," "Vampires don't sleep in coffins. It's a misconception made popular by hack writers and an ignorant media. In fact, we can and do move around during the day, as long as we avoid direct sunlight."

+ Though **they cast no reflection** (as Giles notes in "Out of Mind, Out of Sight" upon first meeting Angel), **vampires *do* cast shadows,** as viewers can see in many episodes. Traditional vampires have neither shadow nor reflection.

+ **Vampires can be photographed** ("Helpless"), **and they *can* be filmed or videotaped** ("Halloween").

+ While **they do not actually need to breathe**—at least not in the sense that humans do, with the intake of oxygen—vampires can simulate breathing in order to smoke cigarettes or to help them create the illusion that they are human. In "Prophecy Girl," when Buffy had drowned and needed CPR, Angel could not help her. "I have no breath," he told Xander.

+ The vampire Drusilla has **certain psychic abilities,** including limited hypnosis, but they appear to be natural abilities unrelated to her status as a vampire. In "Becoming, Part One," in a flashback to London in 1860, Drusilla revealed her prescient power to Angel (who was posing as a priest) *before* he made her a vampire.

+ Like Stoker's vampires, Whedon's vampires **cannot enter the private residence of a human being without an invitation.** We have seen evidence of this in many episodes, but the rule has been clarified in the *Angel* spinoff. In that series' episode "Somnambulist," Wesley and Angel broke into a vampire's apartment. "I invite you in," Wesley said ceremoniously. "Relax," Angel told him. "That's only for humans. Breaking and entering another vampire's lair isn't a problem." It should also be noted that if the human owner or resident of a domicile has died, vampires have no trouble entering (*Angel*, "Lonely Hearts").

✦ **Once a vampire has been invited into a home, he can return at any time.** However, there is a spell that may revoke that invitation. Buffy performed the spell with Willow to keep Angel out of her house in "Passion." "Sorry, Angel," she told him, "I've changed the locks."

✦ The traditional vampire cannot enter houses of worship or tread on hallowed ground, and they fear religious symbols, particularly the Christian cross. Whedon's creations **are capable of entering a church**—as Angel does in the *Angel* episode "I've Got You Under My Skin"—**but touching actual consecrated earth causes them great suffering** ("When She Was Bad"), and **most do fear—and are burned by direct contact with—the cross** (*Angel*, "I've Got You Under My Skin" and various episodes of *Buffy*).

✦ Though the process of doing so has yet to be revealed, **vampires can be scientifically rendered incapable of harming human beings.** In season four's "The Initiative," the titular group of American government scientists were revealed to have implanted a device in Spike's brain that prevented him from attacking humans. It did not, however, stop him from perpetrating violence upon other demons.

The origin

"This world is older than any of you know, and contrary to popular mythology, it did not begin as a paradise. For untold eons, demons walked the earth, made it their home, their hell. In time, they lost their purchase on this reality, and the way was made for mortal animals. For man. What remains of the Old Ones are vestiges: certain magicks, certain creatures . . .

"The books tell that the last demon to leave this reality fed off a human, mixed their blood. He was a human form possessed—infected—by the demon's soul. He bit another, and another . . . and so they walk the earth, feeding. Killing some, mixing their blood with others to make more of their kind. Waiting for the animals to die out, and the Old Ones to return."
—GILES, IN "THE HARVEST"

That's just scratching the surface, however. Whedon has a great deal more back story for his vampires that he hasn't yet shared with his millions of viewers.

What, then, is the origin of vampires in Buffy's world?

"Demons, in their pure state, roamed the earth in evil fashion. When mammals, humans, and whatnot started to evolve, the demons got pushed out. Some of them fled. Some of them stayed but evolved into a more human form. Those are all lesser demons," Whedon explains.

"Vampires were created when a demon fed off a human and possessed him. More than any other demon, they're sort of the half-breeds. They need a human host to live in. Plus, there are burrowing demons that live in human shells. But vampires are half demon and half human, which makes them sort of the losers of the demon set.

"As far as how many vampires there are, I have no idea. They're working as busboys in the demon restaurant."

Which brings into focus one of the primary questions regarding vampires. With their terrible power and savagery, and their ability to reproduce so quickly and decisively, it would seem a simple thing for them to dominate the human world. That, however, would require an organization and hierarchy that such selfish, evil creatures simply do not have.

"They do form attachments and groups and even communities in a human way," Whedon notes. "But we tend to think of them as backward and sort of feudal. They could never actually build an entire city. They're too selfish and strange. They could never actually be a real working community. They exist in these little pockets."

However, the show's creator does acknowledge that there is enough of a vampire community that they keep tabs on one another—a vampire grapevine if you will. And the series' established Mythology indicates that while the majority of vampires are relatively savage, instinctive creatures, they are easily swayed by more dominant vampires, such as Angel, Spike, and the Master.

Given Whedon's history of vampires, and the manner in which the first vampire was created, one is forced to wonder if the very first vampire ever created is still alive.

"Good question," he responds. "I'm not ruling it out."

The Look

WHICH BEGS THE QUESTION OF JUST HOW EVIL—and ugly—such a creature would be. According to producer-writer-director David Greenwalt, the passage of years has a cumulative effect on vampires.

"Really ancient and really evil vampires, such as the Master—and to a smaller degree Kakistos—become more demonic as time goes by. They remain vampires, but they become more demonic and hideous. After a few hundred years or a thousand years, they become more of what they are."

Over time, Greenwalt observes, the outer human shell of the vampire begins to

reflect more of the demon that's inside, such as Kakistos's development of hooves. This is not aging in any way, only a gradual revelation of the demonic nature within.

As for the "look" of vampires in the *Buffy* universe, according to Buffy makeup supervisor Todd McIntosh, that is simply another part of Joss Whedon's vision for the series.

"Joss originally told Tom and Barry Berman, who designed the makeup for the presentation [a kind of mini-pilot used to pitch the show to networks]—and I was in the room at the time so I was witness to this—that it should have the feeling of *The Lost Boys*, but meaner. So the concept of having these pronounced batlike foreheads came from Joss, and from his vision."

From there, the team at Optic Nerve created prosthetics that could be applied to an actor's face, over which McIntosh would use makeup to fulfill the look that Whedon had envisioned.

"We started making them pale from the very first episode. Very white with lots of dark around the eyes," McIntosh recalls. "But we found that in the lighting, it didn't achieve what we wanted it to. It looked clownlike. And in any kind of white lighting it was like having a white piece of paper with white light off [reflecting] of it. It had no definition and it was just glaring. So our hands were tied by film stock and lighting, which forced us to try come up with a [different] color scheme that would look right on film.

"I think if we were ever to have the luxury to do a feature, we might be able to adjust back to something more of what [was initially imagined] in skin color and little details. You have the time to make sure that the details are right. Television forces you into decisions and forces you onto a path that can be very creative, but not necessarily where you intended to go."

The Influences

AS NOTED ABOVE, Joss Whedon has seen and read it all. When it comes to vampires, he points to the original *Nosferatu* and the '80s teen-vamp flick *The Lost Boys* as particular favorites. But it is interesting to observe that each of the show's key writers has her or his own thoughts about vampires and the formative influences they recall.

"This is so cheesy, but my [earliest] influence is Frank Langella [in the 1979 film version of *Dracula*]," recalls producer and frequent writer Marti Noxon. "Besides the classic black and white [with Bela Lugosi], that was one of the first vampire movies I saw. We got somebody to buy us tickets and sneak us in. I just remember thinking it was one of the sexiest things I'd ever seen in my life."

Noxon, despite her early influences, is not really a traditionalist.

"The influences that I prefer are the great romantic tortured souls, like Armand in the Anne Rice books," she notes. "I just love the romantic notion of someone who gets what we all think we want, which is eternal life, and then has to live with the loneliness and isolation, as they watch people come and go, not being able to be part of the real world. [Eternal life is] such a wish ful-fillment—the idea of being able to make someone your mate forever. For me it's more a romantic, sexual fantasy. That's why I love working on *Angel* so much. For me, he is that guy. We will continue to tell sexy stories about Buffy, but she and Angel had that classic vampire-human romance thing."

For staff writer Douglas Petrie, the appeal of vampires is bound up in his love for history.

"Vampires can be any age you want them to be; they can come from any age in history you want them to," Petrie says. When developing a new vampire character, "I usually start visually. What's the coolest place they could come from for that particular story? In 'Bad Girls,' Balthazar had a bunch of vampires working for him. It had been a while since we had done a sword fight. It got a little bit lost in the shuffle by the time the show hit the air, but the original idea for those guys was that they were a corps of Italian swordsmen, and they had the old thirties-movie sword and dagger fighting style. The show climaxed with Giles saving Wesley in a big sword fight.

"For those characters, it was fun to start with this visual, Marvel Comics–style imagery. I'm always trying to put in a vampire who was part of Genghis Khan's army, some guy who's just been around forever. I recently wrote an *Angel* episode where there's a torture expert named Marcus, who's a vampire, and he learned his skills with the Romans. You can pick and choose whatever you want from history and use it to suit your needs. What's great is that they're still alive now. If this guy was a Roman, but he's still alive now, how would he dress, how would he think, how would he talk? Would he speak like a Roman or a modern man? You get to combine old and new. For me, that's the basic approach."

Obviously, Petrie thinks visually. But there are parameters that guide his thoughts in a particular direction when dealing with vampires in the *Buffy* universe.

"I think of street gangs," Petrie reveals. "*The Lost Boys* was a big visual influence. Dracula is so iconic that he kind of spoils the game for us. You can't do Dracula—he's the lord of vampires."

Staff writer David Fury's earliest influences when it comes to the idea of vampires were old movies.

"*Count Yorga, Vampire* is one I remember from a long time ago," he remembers. "There was *The Night Stalker* [TV movie, which became the series *Kolchak: The Night Stalker*]. There are so many vampire myths, but the ones I find the most interesting are when the characters are less glib and have more quiet menace. As interesting as Stephen King's take was with '*Salem's Lot*, which I discovered when it was a TV movie, that was a little late to inspire me."

Fury also shares a primary influence with *Buffy* creator Whedon. "There's something otherworldly and creepy about *Nosferatu*," he says.

Rob Des Hotel, a former staff writer on the show, draws a line right down the middle of what we've termed "traditional" vampire stories, in this case, between *Nosferatu* and *Dracula*, connecting the latter more with modern vampire tales.

"I like the vile type of vampires, perverse *Nosferatu* characters. I've never connected with the sexy, dark, seductive Dracula. It may just be that I haven't bought it in the movies I've seen. I could never really—pardon the pun, I'm sorry—sink my teeth into a book like *Interview with the Vampire*. To me it's not sexy and cool, it's sad and depressing and evil and dark.

"Part of my problem at the beginning of working on *Buffy* was that I wanted to have a discussion between Buffy and Giles about, y'know, these used to be people, and I'm killing them. I think in our first script, we had a short discussion, but Joss didn't want that in there, and I think rightly so. They're not people; they're monsters now. The people were killed half an hour ago. But I was always thinking about the people's families. Your poor wife became a vampire and now Buffy's killed her.

"Being a vampire is just sad to me, but you can't dwell on that. You have to get on with the series, because her job is to kill vampires."

The show's makeup supervisor, Todd McIntosh, is something of an expert on vampires in popular culture. For him, it all began with another TV program that featured vampires, witches, and werewolves.

"The whole reason I got into makeup was *Dark Shadows*," McIntosh says. "I was maybe five or six when I was first watching it. Someone on the show had remarked about the two holes in the neck. Somehow, in my mind, I had a hole on either side of the neck, and I couldn't quite figure it out. I remember asking my stepmother 'How does that work? How do they bite like that?'

"So really Dan Curtis's vision—the mythology of *Dark Shadows*—was the starting point for my interest. After *Dark Shadows*, I tried to figure it all out. The best way of doing that is to go back to the source. So I read Bram Stoker's novel. From there, it launched a real interest in the books and I just devoured vampire novels from the age of ten on."

McIntosh readily admits to being a traditionalist when it comes to vampire tales and a purist when it comes to the original pop-culture vampire story. As such, there were things about Francis Ford Coppola's 1992 version of *Dracula* (released as *Bram Stoker's Dracula*) that bothered him.

"Though it definitely has its flaws, I think Coppola's *Dracula* is really close to being a brilliant movie. But I don't understand how anyone can expect us to watch this creature who feeds on babies, throws babies to his brides and cackles over it, and then halfway through the movie becomes a romantic love interest.

"A lot of my ideas come from my very traditional background with monsters. I act as a little conscience [on the set of *Buffy*] every once in a while, and say, 'Do you realize that he's standing in the daylight?'

"When Jenny Calendar gets her neck snapped, they're standing in front of a big arched window, and you can see out into the night. Because the background is black, you can see their reflections. I went up to the director and said, 'We just made a whole point about Angel not having a reflection, and here he is reflected in this glass.' They moved the camera and the light, but if I hadn't been there, no one would have caught it.

"In that context, Joss's vision is the vision that guides this show. We're guided by that. But I will get crew members coming up to me and saying, 'You know about vampires. Why is this happening?' As though there's one explanation. I keep saying to them, it's all about the writer's universe. Anne Rice's vampires behave completely differently from Bram Stoker's vampires or Joss's vampires. *Necroscope* has big slugs living inside people."

As to his favorite vampire movies, McIntosh finds it hard to choose one.

"Almost every vampire movie falls a little bit short from where I would like them to go," he says. "Though there are some that I really love for different reasons. *Curse of the Undead* is great. It's a black-and-white cheapie Western that they threw a vampire plot into. Really interesting. You never see fangs or a lot of blood, but the vampire element was so integrated into the plot that it really worked. And, of course, you can't fault Hammer's Dracula films."

the vampires

JUST AS THERE ARE A MULTITUDE of variations on the formation of vampire images and frames of reference among the series' writers, so are there a multitude of variations on the vampire in *Buffy the Vampire Slayer*. They're all Joss Whedon's particular brand of vampires, but each of the major vamps has had his or her own identity.

ANGEL

BUFFY: "What, some great honking evil takes credit for bringing you back and you buy it?"
ANGEL: "It told me to kill you....It told me to lose my soul in you and become a monster again."
BUFFY: "I know what it told you to do. Why does it matter?"
ANGEL: "Because I wanted to! Because I want you so badly, I want to take comfort in you and I know it'll cost me my soul and a part of me doesn't care. I'm weak. I've never been anything else. It's not the demon in me that needs killing, Buffy. It's the man."　　**—"AMENDS"**

FIRST APPEARANCE: "Welcome to the Hellmouth," season one

OTHER EPISODES: season one: "The Harvest," "Teacher's Pet," "Never Kill a Boy on the First Date," "Angel," "Out of Mind, Out of Sight," "Prophecy Girl"; all season two and season three episodes; season four: "Pangs," "The Yoko Factor"

KEY RELATIONSHIPS: Sired by Darla (herself sired by the Master). Formerly part of the Order of Aurelius. Sired Drusilla (who sired Spike). Has been boyfriend and lover of Buffy Summers, the vampire Slayer, though that relationship has ended. Currently a warrior for the mysterious Powers That Be, a force for good and order in the universe.

UNIQUE ATTRIBUTES: Angel is the only vampire known to still have his human soul (in addition to the demon within him). Any moment of true bliss (such as sex with someone he loves) will remove it again, reverting him to evil form. Certain drugs that produce a blissful state can also bring forth the evil Angel, but the effects are temporary

MOST MONSTROUS MOMENT: Angel murdered his entire family, their friends, and their friends' children. Among his many other victims was Giles' girlfriend, Jenny Calendar (in "Passion").

CURRENT STATUS: Angel resides in Los Angeles, California, where, with the help of Cordelia Chase and Wesley Wyndam-Pryce (a former Watcher), he runs a private investigation service, through which he combats evil.

Before he took his quest for redemption to Los Angeles and his own eponymous television series, Angel spent almost three years in Sunnydale, finding a reason to live. That reason, of course, was Buffy herself.

Our earliest knowledge of Angel (whose real name was **Liam**), was presented in "Becoming, Part One," at the end of the second season. A great deal of his past was revealed in one short scene.

Irish by birth, Liam was the son of a family of some means. But he was a drunk and a scoundrel, irresponsible to a fault. One night in 1753, in Galway, Ireland, Liam planned to steal the silver from his family home to pay a prostitute for her services. Before he could do so, however, he was drawn away into a dark alleyway by a beautiful blond woman named **Darla.**

A vampire.

ANGEL: "Nver been anywhere, myself. Always wanted to see the world, but . . ."
DARLA: "I could show you."
ANGEL: "Could you, then?"
DARLA: "Things you've never seen. Never even heard of."
ANGEL: "Sounds exciting."
DARLA: "It is. And frightening."
ANGEL: "I'm not afraid. Show me. Show me your world."
DARLA: "Close your eyes."   —"BECOMING, PART ONE"

The results of this meeting are no less than catastrophic. Darla "sired" Angel or Angelus, killing the human man Liam and making way for his body to be usurped by the nameless, bodiless demon that would take the place of his human soul. Once there the demon retained the knowledge, memories, and some of the personality of its host form.

Darla had been sired by **Heinrich Joseph Nest**, known by his followers as the Master. Thus, the vampire Angelus became part of the Master's "family," known as the **Order of Aurelius.** He also became "the scourge of Europe."

"Angelus leaves Ireland, wreaks havoc in Europe for several decades. Then, about eighty years ago, a most curious thing happens . . . he comes to America, where he shuns other vampires and lives alone. There's no record of him hunting here. . . ."
—GILES, IN "ANGEL"

The ancient Master himself once referred to Angelus as "the most vicious creature I ever met. . . He was to have sat on my right, come the day," the Master said with regret ("Angel").

Liam had never gotten along with his father. As a vampire, he returned home. His little sister invited him in, and perhaps gave him his new name.

He murdered his sister, parents, extended relations, and a great many others over the ensuing thirteen decades or so. Among his most hideous deeds was the vicious, malicious manipulation of Drusilla, a young English girl plagued by visions.

In London in 1860, Angelus murdered a priest inside the confessional, only to find himself suddenly the confessor of a girl searching for understanding. Drusilla's mother had told her that her clairvoyance was the devil's work, and she had fled to the only place she knew she could find the answers—the church—not realizing that the "devil" had already compromised her sanctuary.

> **DRUSILLA:** "My mum says I'm cursed. My seeing things is an affront to the Lord. That only He's supposed to see anything before it happens. But I don't mean to, Father, I swear. I try to be pure in His sight and do my penance. I don't want to be a thing of evil."
>
> **ANGEL:** "Hush, child. The Lord has a plan for all creatures. Even a devil child like you."
>
> **DRUSILLA:** [mortified] "A devil..."
>
> **ANGEL:** "Yes, you're a spawn of Satan, all the Hail Marys in the world aren't going to help. The Lord will use you and then smite you down, He's like that."
>
> **DRUSILLA:** "What can I do?"
>
> **ANGEL:** "Fulfill His plan for you, child. Be evil. Perform evil works. Attack the less fortunate. You can start small: laugh at a cripple. You'll feel better. Just give in..."
>
> **DRUSILLA:** "No...I want to be good...I want to be pure..."
>
> **ANGEL:** "We all do, at first. World doesn't work that way."
>
> **DRUSILLA:** "Father, I beg you...help me."
>
> **ANGEL:** "Very well. Uh, ten Our Fathers and an Act of Contrition. Does that sound good?"
>
> **DRUSILLA:** "Yes, Father, thank you."
>
> **ANGEL:** "The pleasure was mine." [She starts to go.] "Oh, and my child?"
>
> **DRUSILLA:** "Yes?"
>
> **ANGEL:** "God is watching you."   —"BECOMING, PART ONE"

This was only the beginning. Subsequent to that meeting, Angelus made a kind of mission of Drusilla, slaughtering each of her loved ones in turn and driving her insane. Desperate to escape, Drusilla fled to a convent, hoping once again to find some respite and clarity in the presence of God. On the day she would have taken her vows and become a nun, Angel took her at last and made her a vampire.

This horror, and so many others, were perpetrated by Angelus, as he said, "with a song in my heart" ("Angel").

Angelus and Darla created chaos and slaughtered humans across Europe for more than a century. Angel sired Drusilla, and later, when he tired of her, brought her a vicious young murderer whose nicknames—**William the Bloody,** or Spike—spoke volumes about him. Drusilla sired Spike, attempting to fill the void Angel had left in her life.

Darla and Angelus, Angelus and Drusilla, Drusilla and Spike . . . a more bizarre, more incestuous family can barely be imagined. Little is known of the depravations this group perpetrated together, save for insinuations. In Budapest, Angelus and Darla plucked human beings "like fruit off the vine" ("Angel"). He delighted in torturing both animals and people, as he later revealed while torturing Giles:

> "I want to torture you. I used to love it, and it's been a long time. I mean, the last time I tortured someone they didn't even have chain saws."
>
> —ANGEL, IN "BECOMING, PART TWO"

This savage career would likely have continued indefinitely were it not for one fatal night in 1898. As an expression of her affection, Darla brought Angelus a young, beautiful Gypsy girl to feed on (as first revealed in "Angel"). It was a mistake that would change everything. For this particular clan of Romani, the **Kalderash,** had access to certain magics. For revenge, they placed a spell on Angelus—one that would have far-reaching impact. First, his human soul was returned to his body and now shared that corporeal form with the demon/vampire thing inhabiting it. Thus, his curse was to have done such hideous things and to have a full memory of them, and the human anguish and guilt over having done them.

> "When you become a vampire, the demon takes your body. But it doesn't get your soul. That's gone. No conscience, no remorse...it's an easy way to live. You have no idea what it's like to have done the things I've done, and to care."—ANGEL, IN "ANGEL"

But there was more to the curse, a caveat Angel was not to discover for some time.

Once he had been "re-souled," Angel was nearly driven mad. He spent a century wandering the earth, living in alleys and feeding off rats (revealed in the two-part "Becoming").

By 1996 (again as revealed in "Becoming") he had retreated to living as a homeless person, taking blood from vermin, and simply trying to forget. The demon Whistler, a messenger in the employ of the Powers That Be—a mysterious force for good and order in the universe—tracked him down there, and challenged him to shake off his guilt and try to make a difference, to find redemption for the outrages against humanity he had committed.

Whistler took Angel to Los Angeles, where they observed Buffy Summers as she was confronted, for the first time, with the news that she was the Slayer. Angel fell in love with her instantly and wanted desperately to help her. But he also saw Buffy as perhaps the key to finding the redemption he so desired.

WHISTLER: "She's gonna have it tough, that Slayer. She's just a kid. And the world is full of big bad things."

ANGEL: "I want to help her. I want to . . . I want to become someone. I want to help."

—**"BECOMING, PART ONE"**

Though he did not aid her (as far as we know) during the brief time Buffy spent in Los Angeles after becoming the Slayer, Angel did come into her life once she had relocated with her mother to Sunnydale. At first, he attempted to keep his distance, not trusting himself to stay objective. He tried to help her behind the scenes, and with whatever information he could provide. But it soon proved impossible for him not to take a more active role. He loved Buffy, and soon enough, she loved him as well.

Angel became a part of Buffy's circle, the group of friends who aided her in combating the forces of darkness. It was not long before Buffy and her friends learned the truth about Angel. Not only was he a vampire, but he was perhaps the most notorious vampire who had ever lived. He had been sired by Darla, who was now in Sunnydale, and he was of the lineage of the Master, an ancient vampire who was trapped beneath the town and ran the vampire operations of Sunnydale from there.

Still, Angel proved his loyalty time and again, and he was accepted by Buffy's friends. Later Drusilla arrived in Sunnydale with Spike ("School Hard"), and the two of them made things more difficult, both in their efforts to kill the Slayer and because they were vivid reminders of the era when Angel was the most feared creature in all of Europe.

Despite Spike and Drusilla's presence, the Slayer and the soulful vampire grew more and more deeply in love. Finally, on Buffy's birthday, they made love for the first time ("Surprise").

Their lovemaking had catastrophic results. The Romani curse upon Angel had a second facet of which Angel was unaware. Should he ever achieve even a single moment of perfect bliss—such as the rapture of making love to a woman who had captured his heart—his human soul would leave him once again.

And it did. When Buffy woke the next day, it was to a world completely turned upside down. Angel was truly evil again, completely the Angelus creature who had terrified and feasted upon Europe.

Almost immediately, the newly restored Angelus fed upon a human—something he had not done in a century—and then sought out Drusilla and Spike to reassert his dominance over them. At first, preoccupied with the demon war machine they'd resurrected—the Judge—Spike and Dru did not realize what had happened:

> THE JUDGE [urged by Spike to burn all the goodness out of Angel] "This one cannot be burned. He is clean."
> SPIKE: "Clean? You mean he's —"
> THE JUDGE: "There's no humanity in him."
> DRUSILLA: "Angel?"
> ANGEL: "Yeah, baby, I'm back." —"INNOCENCE"

Without hesitation, Angelus set about establishing himself as the patriarch of the "family" that consisted of Drusilla, Spike, and himself. During this period, Spike was confined to a wheelchair, and Angelus tortured him relentlessly about his infirmity. He also went to great lengths to inspire jealousy in Spike, flirting with Drusilla, perhaps doing more than flirting (as specifically implied in "Passion," "Bewitched, Bothered and Bewildered," and "I Only Have Eyes for You"). Drusilla, having been sired by Angel, was connected to him so strongly that she could not resist him.

But toying with his "family" was only a distraction. Angelus's priority was the emotional torture of the Slayer. He hated Buffy because she had made him feel love, and he feared her for her power. Thus, Angel tormented Buffy and her friends for weeks.

> **"She made me feel like a human being. That's not the kind of thing you just forgive."**
> **—ANGEL, IN "INNOCENCE"**

He turned a local girl named **Theresa Klusmeyer** into a vampire just so the newly risen creature could remind Buffy he was around (in "Phases"; Theresa was dusted in the same episode). He sneaked into Buffy's room at night and left sketches of her sleeping, as though to prove how easy it would be for him to kill her ("Passion"). He attempted to murder Willow, threatened Buffy's mother, and then purposely revealed to Joyce Summers that he had slept with her daughter—with the same unrelenting cruelty that he once used on the hapless Drusilla.

> DRUSILLA: "You don't want to kill her, do you? You just want to hurt her. Just like you hurt me."
> ANGEL: "Nobody knows me like you do, Dru."
> SPIKE: "She'd better not get in our way."
> ANGEL: "Don't worry about it."

SPIKE: "I do."

ANGEL: "Spike, my boy. You really don't get it, do you. You've tried to kill her and you couldn't. Look at you. You're a wreck....Force won't get it done. You gotta work from the inside. To kill this girl...you have to love her." **—"INNOCENCE"**

This series of brutal perversions culminated in Angel's most terrible act of this period, the callous murder of Jenny Calendar ("Passion").

Jenny's story is strange in itself. She appeared in the lives of Buffy and her friends first as a computer science teacher and technopagan ("I Robot, You Jane"), and later fell in love with Giles, Buffy's Watcher. But Jenny hid a terrible secret. She was part of the Kalderash clan, sent there to watch Angel. When he became evil once more, Jenny felt a terrible burden of guilt.

GYPSY MAN: "Angel was meant to suffer. Not to live as a human. One moment of true happiness, of contentment...one moment where his soul that we restored does not plague his thoughts—and that soul is taken from him."

JENNY: "Then, if somehow he has...if it's happened, then Angelus is back. Uncle, this is insanity." **—"INNOCENCE"**

Her love for Giles and concern for Buffy and her friends overrode her loyalty to her people, and she worked to find a way to return Angel's soul to him once more, to repeat the curse her people had placed upon him. Eventually Jenny did find the answer.

But Angel snapped her neck before she could implement it. Then he laid her body out on Giles's bed, littering the floor and stairs of his place with rose petals to make it seem as though Jenny were waiting for Giles in bed. It was twisted and sadistic, but only one example of what the evil Angelus was like.

Not long thereafter, Angelus changed course entirely. He was through wasting his time with the Slayer. Instead, he acquired the remains of the demon Acathla, with the intention of resurrecting it.

If Acathla was awakened, he would open his mouth and a channel into the demon dimensions would be created (see Demons: Acathla).

DRUSILLA: "He will swallow the world."

ANGEL: "And every creature living on this planet will go to Hell." **—"BECOMING, PART ONE"**

Though Willow had discovered Jenny's notes about restoring Angel's soul and was working feverishly to re-create the original curse, Buffy did not have time to wait. She went to find Angel and faced him in battle ("Becoming, Part Two"). Willow managed to complete the curse, but not before the gateway to the demon dimensions began to open. Though Angel had his soul back, Whistler had already told Buffy what she must do.

> "Angel's the key. His blood will open the door to hell. Acathla opens his big mouth, creates the vortex, then only Angel's blood'll close it. One blow. Send 'em both back to hell. But I strongly suggest you get there before that happens."
> —WHISTLER, IN "BECOMING, PART TWO"

Buffy knew that the only way to close the portal was to make Angel bleed and then thrust him through the portal, and she did so.

Subsequently, Angel spent some months in the demon dimensions. However, time passes differently in those dimensions, and for him, many years of suffering went by.

GILES: "Time in demon worlds moves quite different than here—"
BUFFY: "Yeah. I remember . . . .So—Angel would have been there for like a hundred years?"
GILES: "Yes."
BUFFY: "Of torture."   —"BEAUTY AND THE BEASTS"

When he was returned to the world—by mysterious intervention—he was like an animal, mindless and savage ("Beauty and the Beasts"). Realizing how her friends would react to Angel's return, Buffy kept it secret for some time. Their love resumed, but it was forever tainted by the knowledge that it was impossible.

GILES: "To hide this—to take into your own hands . . ."
BUFFY: "I was going to tell you! But I didn't know why he was back or anything. I wanted to wait—"
XANDER: "For what? For Angel to go psycho again the next time you give him a happy?"
BUFFY: "I'm not going to . . . We're not together like that!"
OZ: "But you were kissing him."
BUFFY: (to Xander): "You were spying on me? What gives you the right?"
CORDELIA: "What gives you the right to suck face with your demon lover again?"
BUFFY: "It—it was an accident."
XANDER: "What? You tripped and fell on his lips?"
BUFFY: "It was wrong. It can't happen again. But I—I'd never put you guys in danger. If I thought Angel was going to hurt anyone—"   —"REVELATIONS"

Angel and Buffy could never make love again, or the curse would remove his human soul once more. Simply being together was absolute torture for the two, and their doomed passion began to wear on both of them.

In the Christmas episode, "Amends," Angel was seemingly haunted by the ghosts of those he had slain. It was revealed that these were merely manifestations of an ancient evil called the First that wanted to drive Angel to madness in hopes that he would kill Buffy. It nearly worked. Instead, however, Angel briefly became suicidal. He waited for the sun to rise, hoping it would burn him to death, but in a miraculous turn of events, it began to snow in Sunnydale. The Powers That Be had intervened on his behalf, sending him a clear message that he had been brought back from hell for a greater purpose.

During that third season, the Slayer Faith had arrived in Sunnydale. Eventually, Faith became a traitor, allied with the demonic Mayor, and the two attempted to sway Angel to their cause. Faith hoped to seduce Angel, and pointed out how hopeless his love for Buffy was. In order to fully reveal Faith's duplicity, Angel pretended to have become evil once more. Seeing him in this way only made Buffy feel even more uncertain, an emotional state that others, particularly the Mayor, attempted to use to their advantage.

> "You're immortal, she's not. It's not easy. I married my Edna Mae in aught three and I was with her right until the end. Not a pretty scene. Wrinkled and senile and cursing me for my youth, it wasn't our happiest time. And let's forget the fact that any moment of true happiness will turn you evil. What kind of life can you offer her? I don't see a lot of Sunday picnics in the offing. Skulking in the shadows, hiding from the sun—she's a blossoming young girl! You want to keep her from the life she should have till it's passed her by and by God I think that's a little selfish. Is that what you came back from hell for? Is that your greater purpose?"
>
> —THE MAYOR, IN "CHOICES"

Finally, Buffy's mother confronted Angel with the hard truth about his relationship with her daughter ("The Prom"). It was doomed. Everyone knew it. He could not offer her anything but pain, as she grew old and died and he remained the same.

JOYCE: "I don't have to tell you that you and Buffy come from different worlds."
ANGEL: "No, you don't."
JOYCE: "Good. Because when it comes to you, Angel, Buffy's not a Slayer. She's just like any other young woman in love. You're all she can see of tomorrow. But I think we both know there's gonna be some hard choices ahead. If she can't make them, you're going to have to. I know you care about her. I just hope you care enough."   —"THE PROM"

Thus, Angel decided that after the Mayor was destroyed, he would leave Sunnydale.

Before the Mayor's Ascension to true demonhood was scheduled to come about, however, Angel was poisoned by Faith. The poison was powerful, and the one thing that could save Angel was the blood of a Slayer. Buffy fought Faith, hoping to use her blood to save Angel, but merely succeeded in wounding her before Faith escaped. Realizing it was the only way to save him, Buffy forced Angel to drink of her, to take her blood, and he nearly killed her.

They both survived, however, and the Mayor was defeated (see Demons: The Mayor).

In the aftermath of the battle against the Mayor, Angel left Sunnydale for Los Angeles, where he is a sort of supernatural private detective (*Angel,* "City Of") running Angel Investigations with the help of pre-stardom Cordelia Chase. It has also been revealed that he and Buffy are both Warriors for the Powers That Be (*Angel,* "I Will Remember You"). Angel has come into contact with Buffy several times since his move to L.A., but now realizes that, thanks to their separate natures and obligations, they are fated never to be together.

SPIKE

> "Innit a fantastic day? Birds singing, squirrels making lots of rotten little squirrels. Sun beaming down in a nice, nonfatal way. It's very exciting. I can't wait to see if I freckle." —SPIKE, HAVING RECOVERED THE GEM OF AMARRA, IN "THE HARSH LIGHT OF DAY"

FIRST APPEARANCE: "School Hard," season two

OTHER EPISODES: season two: "Halloween," "Lie to Me," "What's My Line? Parts One and Two," "Surprise," "Innocence," "Bewitched, Bothered, and Bewildered," "Passion," and "Becoming, Parts One and Two"; season three: "Lover's Walk"; season four: "The Harsh Light of Day," "Wild at Heart," and all thereafter

KEY RELATIONSHIPS: Sired by Drusilla (herself sired by Angel). Formerly boyfriend and lover of Drusilla, and later Harmony Kendall.

UNIQUE ATTRIBUTES: The paramilitary antimonster U.S. government operation called the Initiative implanted a control chip in Spike's brain that currently prevents him from harming humans.

MOST MONSTROUS MOMENT: Spike killed two Slayers, one during the Boxer Rebellion in China in 1900, the other sometime later.

CURRENT STATUS: Since he cannot—at present—harm humans, Spike often exercises his bloodlust and violent tendencies by working with Buffy Summers and her friends to combat demons.

No villainous character has been more welcomed by *Buffy* fans than Spike. Whether as part of the gruesome twosome made up of himself and his lady love, the mad-vampiress Drusilla, or as a solo act, Spike is the devilish rogue of the series, the "Big Bad," as he sometimes refers to himself. No proof is needed beyond this: as with certain comic-book villains who become fan favorites (the *X-Men's* Sabretooth, *Spider-Man's* Venom), the fourth season found Spike unable to harm humans and thus allied with his enemies, though quite unhappily so.

But Spike isn't just a favorite among fans. He and his counterpart, the lovely and psychotic Drusilla, are favorites among the writers as well.

"We always said the inspiration was Sid and Nancy," notes Marti Noxon. "What if Sid and Nancy were vampires?"

As to their appeal, David Greenwalt has an explanation:

"Villains having fun is always good," he says. "They're up to no good, but they're having a great time. They really love each other, and in their own twisted world, that makes perfect sense. Like the Bizarro World: they're the opposite of what normal people should be. They're happier than people who have to suffer the pangs of normal humanity. They don't feel guilt or remorse. They're psychos, but they also have a kind of deep, twisted love, and have a great take on things. They're able to observe humans and the silly slings and arrows of outrageous fortune that humans suffer."

Jane Espenson agrees.

"I like the idea of a character without remorse," she notes. "I like positive people, who really believe in what they're doing and are happy doing it. Vampires, other than Angel, seem happy in their work. As do Ethan and Trick and the Mayor and Ted. This makes evil scarier. If evil's having a good time, then it's much scarier. If evil is happy, that's creepy. It's aware of what it's doing and it likes it.

"Look at the Joker versus Batman. The tortured, unhappy guy is the good guy. The happy guy is the bad guy. Look at the difference between bad Angel and good Angel—which of those boys is happy? There's something nice about being able to put the joy in the bad guy and suggesting that evil is more fun. That probably comes from a Puritan ethic that doing good can't be fun. That if you're having fun you're doing evil. It makes Buffy being on the good side all the more heroic. Faith was weak and went for the fun. But Buffy's heroic and strong."

Unfortunately, after season two, Spike has been without Drusilla. It was a turn of events that concerned fans and Buffy's writers and producers alike, but no more:

"I always thought Spike was missing something without Drusilla, but when you first see him in season four, with Harmony, he's terrific," Greenwalt says. "Still a formidable presence. When he made his return onscreen, we all knew it was coming, but we all gasped."

Spike, also known as "William the Bloody," made his first appearance in the episode "School Hard." He drove his car into the "Welcome to Sunnydale" sign on his way into town. With Drusilla flitting around as though she was on an acid trip, Spike quickly took charge of the local vampire contingent, the remnants of the Master's Order of Aurelius. In the wake of the Master's death, the Order was led by the child-vampire called the Anointed One. The vampires were disorganized, lacking an effective leader.

Until Spike arrived.

A pair of vampires, referred to in the script only as **Big Ugly** and **Lean Boy**, are arguing when Spike enters the factory wherein the Anointed One has set up shop.

> **BIG UGLY:** "This weekend, the Night of St. Vigeous, our power shall be at its peak! When I kill her [the Slayer], it'll be the greatest event since the crucifixion. And I should know, I was there."
>
> **SPIKE:** "You were there? Oh, please. If every vampire who said he was at the crucifixion was actually there, it would have been like Woodstock."
>
> **BIG UGLY:** "I ought to rip your throat out."
>
> **SPIKE:** "I was actually at Woodstock. That was a weird gig. Fed off a flower person and I spent the next six hours watching my hands move. . . . So, who do you kill for fun around here?"   **—"SCHOOL HARD"**

Spike also revealed that he had killed two Slayers in his life, one of them during the Boxer Rebellion in China, which lasted the entire summer of 1900. Subsequent to that bit of résumé-brandishing, Spike introduced Drusilla to "the gang," making it instantly apparent that his world revolved around her.

DRUSILLA: "Spike, I'm cold."
SPIKE: "I've got you."
DRUSILLA: "I'm a princess."
SPIKE: "That's what you are." —"SCHOOL HARD"

Then, to put the cap on his introduction to a new town, he vowed to kill the Slayer. Spike began immediately to manipulate things to his own benefit. Big Ugly, who had challenged him upon his arrival, was set up as bait for Buffy. Spike urged him to draw Buffy out, fully expecting the other vampire to die, mainly so that he might observe her fighting style.

It was revealed not long thereafter that Angel knew Spike from his dark past. "Once he starts something, he doesn't stop until everything in his path is dead," Angel explained. Later, Giles found references to Spike in the Watcher diaries.

"Our new friend, Spike. 'Known as William the Bloody, earned his nickname by torturing his victims with railroad spikes. . .' Ah, but here's some good news, he's barely two hundred, not even as old as Angel.'" —GILES, IN "SCHOOL HARD"

Though Spike referred to Angel as his "sire," creator Joss Whedon insists that the character was using the word only in terms of Angel having been Spike's mentor. For, though Angel sired Drusilla, it was Drusilla herself who made Spike into a vampire. Though the circumstances of this are unclear, it has been implied that Angel had grown tired of Drusilla and brought Spike to her almost as he would have a puppy, to entertain her so that Angel himself would no longer have to.

As for the how-to of being a vampire, however, it seems clear that Angel taught Spike all he knows. He does, after all, refer to Angel as his "Yoda" (in "School Hard"), a reference to the wizened alien Jedi master of the *Star Wars* films who taught Luke Skywalker how to be a Jedi.

When Spike failed to kill Buffy in "School Hard," the Anointed One grew angry. Spike, frustrated and appalled at the thought of taking orders from the child-vampire, killed the Anointed One, declaring that: "From now on we're gonna have a little less ritual and a little more fun around here."

Among those Spike made into a vampire was **Sheila Martini**, a Sunnydale High School student (in "School Hard"); Sheila is apparently still at large, her current whereabouts are unknown.

Spike made other attempts on Buffy's life, but in the two-part "What's My Line?," he was crippled. (Ironically, this happened just after a ceremony during which he had been attempting to return Drusilla to health.) It was a twist of fate that sent the vampire into a bout of severe depression. His new weakness crippled him in more than one sense, so that he took a backseat to the restored Drusilla, whom he still adored.

However, when Angel made love to Buffy and his curse was lifted, reverting him to the evil Angelus, Spike was snapped out of his despondency by jealousy. Angelus joined them, reminding them all of old times. He flirted with Drusilla, much to her delight, and taunted Spike mercilessly. The situation quickly became so untenable, with Drusilla more and more obviously turning her attentions to Angel, that Spike was forced to act.

> **DRUSILLA:** "My Angel! Where have you been? The sun is almost up and it can be so hurtful. We were worried."
> **SPIKE:** "No, we weren't."
> **DRUSILLA:** "You must forgive Spike. He's just a bit testy. Doesn't get out much anymore."
> —"PASSION"

Though he had regained the use of his legs, he allowed Angelus and Drusilla to believe he was still crippled. Later, in the second-season finale ("Becoming, Part Two"), he allied himself with Buffy. Angelus had a plan to end the world with Acathla, and aside from wanting to be rid of Angelus as a romantic rival, Spike had determined that he sort of liked the world the way it was. In exchange for Buffy's promise not to slay Drusilla, Spike agreed to help her stop Angel and vowed that he and Dru would leave Sunnydale forever.

> "We like to talk big, vampires do. 'I'm gonna destroy the world'—just tough guy talk, strutting around with your friends over a pint of blood. Truth is, I like this world. You got dog racing, Manchester United, *Love Boat,* and you got people. Billions of people walking around like Happy Meals with legs. It's all right here. But then someone comes along with a vision. A real passion for destruction. Angel could pull it off. Good-bye Picadilly, farewell Leicester bloody Square, you see what I'm saying?"
> —SPIKE, IN "BECOMING, PART TWO "

In the chaos of the second-season finale, Spike managed to knock Drusilla unconscious and get her into his car. Its windows blacked out to protect them from the sun, Spike drove Drusilla out of town, supposedly never to return.

That promise was broken quickly enough. In "Lover's Walk," the eighth episode of season three, it was a pitiful, drunken Spike who returned to Sunnydale—without Drusilla, whom he had caught canoodling with a chaos demon.

Brokenhearted, Spike attempted to force Willow Rosenberg to create a love spell that would bring Drusilla back to him. When his plan went awry, however, Spike wasn't as disappointed as one might expect. He had become so disgusted with Buffy and Angel's moping about their own doomed love that he realized the only way for him to get Drusilla back was to return to his old ways, to be the old Spike.

When he left town for the second time, it was on a quest to win back the psychotic Drusilla's love. However, when he returned in "The Harsh Light of Day," the third episode of season four, it was revealed that his quest had only been temporarily successful. He had reunited with Drusilla only to find her once again in the arms of another, this time a fungus demon.

Back in Sunnydale, Spike acquired a new girlfriend in Harmony Kendall, a former friend and classmate of Cordelia Chase's who had been turned into a vampire in the previous season's finale. Soon—with the help of a vampire engineer named **Brian**, who is still on the loose—he came into possession of the **Gem of Amarra** (the only reason he'd returned to Sunnydale, a place he despises), which made its wearer invulnerable to harm, a property that would allow a vampire to go about during the day without danger, among many other things.

Unfortunately for Spike, Buffy managed to get the ring away from him and sent it to Los Angeles as a gift to Angel. Though Spike followed Oz, who delivered the ring, he was not able to get the ring back. Angel eventually destroyed the ring (in *Angel*, "In the Dark").

In yet another attempt at vengeance toward Buffy, Spike appeared on the UC Sunnydale campus (at the opening of "Wild at Heart"), only to be taken captive by mysterious commandos. The following episode, "The Initiative," revealed those commandos to be employed by a group of U.S. military scientists who study supernatural beings.

Though Spike managed to escape—with the help of another captive vampire named **Tom**, whom he promptly betrayed and left in the Initiative's clutches—he had been first implanted with a neural inhibitor that causes him great pain any time he attempts to harm a living human. The Initiative had found a way to do the seemingly impossible: to use scientific, nonmagical methods to control the behavior of supernatural creatures.

Desperate for blood, Spike eventually found himself relying on the goodwill of his former archenemies, who protected him while trying to learn as much as possible about the Initiative.

Finally, in "Doomed," Spike discovered that he could fight and kill evil creatures without the usual pain. He has since become a very willing participant in the fight against his own kind.

> "What's this? Just sitting about watching the telly when there's evil afoot? Not very industrious of you. I say we get out there and kick a little demon ass! Can't go without your Buffy, is that it? Too chicken? She is the Chosen One after all. Come on! Vampires, grrrr—nasty! Let's annihilate 'em! For justice! And . . . and for the safety of puppies . . . and Christmas, right? Let's fight that evil! Let's kill something! Oh, come on . . ."
>
> —SPIKE, IN "DOOMED"

Once again, Spike exhibited what is perhaps his strongest character trait: self-interest. That self-interest became even more intimately tied to the Slayer at the end of "Goodbye, Iowa" when Spike was attacked by a demon angry that he had been working with Buffy.

DEMON: "What did you expect, Spike? A welcome party? Word's out—you've been making war on the demon world."

SPIKE: "War?"

DEMON: "With the Slayer. You kill other demons, and the rest of us don't hold with that. Still, if I see you around here again I'll be inclined to break that code."

—"GOODBYE, IOWA"

In the closing episodes of season four, Spike allied himself with the patchwork monster Adam (see Walking Dead: Adam) after the latter promised to remove the chip in Spike's brain that prevented him from killing humans. At Adam's request, in "The Yoko Factor," Spike purposely exacerbated already bruised feelings and egos among the Scooby Gang in an attempt to drive them apart and force Buffy to act on her own. The gang figured out what was happening just in time, however, and quite fortunately, as it was only through a spell that merged the life energies of Giles, Willow, and Xander with Buffy that the Slayer was able to defeat and kill Adam. Though Spike had done his bidding, Adam never removed the chip from the vampire's brain. Despite his betrayal, the final moments of the episode "Primevil" have Spike fighting beside the gang once again.

DRUSILLA

> "Ah, I was dreaming. We were in Paris. You had a branding iron. . . and there were worms in my baguette."
>
> —"WHAT'S MY LINE? PART TWO"

FIRST APPEARANCE: "School Hard," season two

OTHER EPISODES: season two: "Halloween," "Lie to Me," "What's My Line? Parts One and Two," "Surprise," "Innocence," "Bewitched, Bothered and Bewildered," "Passion," and "Becoming, Parts One and Two"

KEY RELATIONSHIPS: Sired by Angel. Drusilla sired Spike. Formerly girlfriend and lover of first Angel and later Spike. Left the latter for a chaos demon and a fungus demon.

UNIQUE ATTRIBUTES: Has both prescient visions and some facility with hypnosis. Not quite sane. Prone to hallucinations.

MOST MONSTROUS MOMENT: Drusilla murdered a Slayer named Kendra (in "What's My Line? Part Two").

CURRENT STATUS: Drusilla's current whereabouts are unknown.

The other half of the Sid and Nancy of vampires. Though for some time she was just as important to the mythos as Spike—and she remains eminently popular among fans—the fact that Drusilla's appearances are confined to the second season of *Buffy* has shifted the fans' focus more toward Spike.

When she first appeared, in "School Hard," Drusilla was not unlike certain female characters in classic operas such as *La Traviata*, who suffer from such ailments as consumption and flit madly about the stage like blind, dying butterflies. Needless to say, she was the oddest of characters. Upon her introduction, it was quite obvious that Drusilla was insane. Sickly and weak, her every need or desire was attended to by Spike despite her obvious madness as she babbled nonsense, discussed her bizarre prophetic visions, and had tea parties with her blindfolded dolls.

> "Do you like daisies? I plant them, but they always die. Everything I put in the ground withers and dies."
> —DRUSILLA, IN "SCHOOL HARD"

> "Miss Edith speaks out of turn. She's a bad example and will have no cakes today."
> —DRUSILLA, ABOUT HER FAVORITE DOLL, IN "SCHOOL HARD"

> "You know what I miss? Leeches."
> —DRUSILLA, IN "HALLOWEEN"

Drusilla's prophetic visions are an odd counterpoint to the prescient dreams that Buffy, as the Slayer, sometimes has.

> "I met an old man. I didn't like him. He got stuck in my teeth. And then the moon started whispering to me. All sorts of dreadful things."
> —DRUSILLA, IN "BECOMING, PART ONE"

In a rare moment of clarity, Drusilla recalled the wonderful times she had in Prague, though Spike is quick to point out that she was nearly killed by a mob in that city. When not wandering about in a daze, tormenting her dolls, or having visions,

Drusilla would go out at night from time to time. During one of these nocturnal journeys, in "Lie to Me," she ran into Angel, who later discussed her with Buffy.

> **ANGEL:** "I did a lot of unconscionable things when I became a vampire. Drusilla was the worst. She was . . . an obsession of mine. She was pure and sweet and chaste."
>
> **BUFFY:** "You made her a vampire."
>
> **ANGEL:** "First I made her insane. Killed everyone she loved, visited every torture on her I could devise. She eventually fled to a convent, and the day she took her Holy Orders, I turned her into a demon."   **—"LIE TO ME"**

Despite her own evil, Drusilla was clearly still haunted by the horrors Angel had visited upon her and her family. They were, after all, the things that had driven her insane in the first place. Perversely, she also loved him very much.

> **DRUSILLA:** "My mummy ate lemons. Raw. She said she loved the way they made her mouth tingle. Little Anne, her favorite was custard . . . brandied pears . . ."
>
> **ANGEL:** "Dru . . . "
>
> **DRUSILLA:** "Ssshhhh. And pomegranates. They used to make her face and fingers all red. Remember little fingers? Little hands? Do you?"
>
> **ANGEL:** "If I could, I . . ."
>
> **DRUSILLA:** "Bite your tongue! They used to eat. Cake. And eggs. And honey. Until you came and ripped their throats out."   **—"WHAT'S MY LINE? PART TWO"**

Drusilla's weakness and overall poor health dogged her, and she kept after Spike to cure her. Eventually, in the two-parter "What's My Line?" he managed to do just that. In order to do so, however, he needed the blood of her sire, Angel. Though Dru was restored to health with the **du Lac ritual,** Spike was crippled in the same episode. For a brief time thereafter, Drusilla became the de facto leader of the group of vampires they had surrounded themselves with.

When Angel reverted to the evil Angelus upon the removal of his human soul, Drusilla happily welcomed him back. Though she claimed to love Spike, she seemed to either not care or not notice his anger and jealousy at Angel's behavior and her own flirtations with their returned patriarch.

It is strongly implied in subsequent episodes that Drusilla and Angel became physically involved once again. The tension continued to rise, even as it was revealed that Spike had recovered the ability to walk and not shared that information.

Then, in the two-part second-season finale, "Becoming," everything changed. As previously quoted in Vampires: Angel, the audience learned a bit more about Drusilla's past in a flashback to her first encounter with Angel in London in the year 1860.

Also in that two-parter, Drusilla hypnotized and then murdered Kendra—another Slayer who had been called to action when Buffy "died" at the Master's hands ("Prophecy Girl")—by slashing her throat. Later, she used hypnosis to make Giles believe that she was Jenny Calendar to induce him into revealing some information Angel needed to wake the demon Acathla and destroy the world.

As Angel attempted to do just that, however, the final battle arrived. Drusilla was no help at all to Angel, as Spike—allied with Buffy in order to save Dru for himself—overwhelmed her and removed her from the fight. At the end of season two's finale, Drusilla was taken from Sunnydale by Spike, who had promised Buffy that neither of them would ever return.

When Spike did return in seasons three and four without Drusilla, he revealed that she had left him in Brazil, having flirted with chaos demons and fungus demons. Apparently, they later reconciled, but only briefly.

Her current whereabouts are unknown.

THE MASTER

"Vampires! Undeniably, we are the world's superior race. Yet we have always been too parochial. Too bound by the mindless routine of the predator. Hunt and kill . . . hunt and kill . . . Titillating? Yes. Practical? Hardly. . . . Meanwhile, the humans, with their plebeian minds, have brought us a truly demonic concept: *mass production*. . . . The days of compromise, of living alongside the humans, are over. It's time to take them out."
—THE MASTER, IN "THE WISH"

FIRST APPEARANCE: "Welcome to the Hellmouth," season one

OTHER EPISODES: season one: "The Harvest," "Never Kill a Boy on the First Date," "Angel," "Nightmares," "Prophecy Girl"; season two: "When She Was Bad"; season three: "The Wish"

KEY RELATIONSHIPS: Sire of Darla. Leader of the Order of Aurelius. Grandsire to Angel. Great-grandsire to Drusilla. Great-great-grandsire to Spike.

UNIQUE ATTRIBUTES: So powerful that when staked, his bones did not turn to dust with the rest of his body.

MOST MONSTROUS MOMENT: The Master is the only vampire to have actually killed Buffy Summers. (She got better.)

CURRENT STATUS: The Master was killed by Buffy in "Prophecy Girl," and she smashed his bones to dust in "When She Was Bad."

For some people, the vampiric image that lingers upon the mind is that of Bela Lugosi descending a staircase. For others, it is the glaring red eyes (or contact lenses) of Christopher Lee. Both are relatively human, though sinister. There is a third image, however, one far more nightmarish; an image taken from nightmares and the grimmest of fairy tales. Bald and pale, with pointed ears and an animal's fangs, and with the long, tapered talons of a savage beast, Nosferatu (in both film versions, see below) was truly a monster. Not cruel and intimate and sexual like Lugosi and Lee but otherworldly and evil in a way the others could not match. In the mold of Nosferatu, only Barlow, the main vampire from Stephen King's novel 'Salem's Lot (and the eponymous TV miniseries) lingers in the memory.

Until the Master.

Only with the Master—the chief villain of Buffy the Vampire Slayer's first season—we're given a postmodern version, a Nosferatu who had seen Clive Barker's Hellraiser, perhaps.

Though most vampires in Joss Whedon's cosmology are solitary creatures, too selfish to ever belong to an organized group, the Master was powerful enough to gather around him a great many vampires as members of a sect called the Order of Aurelius.

Though the Master's real name and history have never been revealed in the series, Joss Whedon wrote in his script of the pilot that the Master's real name is Heinrich Joseph Nest. Whedon judged his age at roughly six hundred years.

Sometime in the 1930s, the Master brought the Order to Sunnydale, California, in search of the legendary Hellmouth, a portal between the world of our heroes and the demon dimensions. The Master hoped to open the Hellmouth and release those he worshiped, referred to as "the Old Ones"—a term reminiscent of the Cthulhu Mythos created by horror forefather H. P. Lovecraft (see Demons).

Upon his arrival, the Master went about preparing to open the Hellmouth, and he might very well have succeeded if not for the intervention of fate, or plain bad luck. In 1937 Sunnydale, was struck by an earthquake that literally swallowed "about half the town." The submerged sections of town included the old church where the Master had begun to open the Hellmouth. The earthquake disrupted the process, not only preventing the Hellmouth from opening, but trapping the Master between worlds.

> "Opening dimensional portals is tricky business. Odds are he got himself stuck, like a cork in a bottle."
> —GILES, IN "WELCOME TO THE HELLMOUTH"

Sunnydale High School was built on the shattered earth near the sunken church. The Hellmouth was located directly below the school. For sixty years, until 1997, the

Master was stuck between worlds. Over the first half of that year, he tried several times to free himself with the aid of the vampire followers he gathered around him, including Luke, Darla, the Three, **Lucien**, Thomas, and the Anointed One. All save the last died in his service. For a very brief time (in the episode "Nightmares") the Master was freed by the reality-warping powers of a young boy named **Billy Palmer,** but when reality was restored the Master was returned to his domain.

Then, in the first season's final episode, "Prophecy Girl," the Master was freed from his purgatory. The prophetic *Pergamum Codex* had predicted that the Slayer would face the Master and the Slayer would die. Buffy reluctantly went to confront the Master in his lair—the underground church. By doing so, Buffy herself made the prophecy reality, by putting herself within reach of the ancient vampire.

The Master bit Buffy and drained some of her blood, which gave him the power to escape his imprisonment. Then he dropped Buffy in a pool of water, where she drowned. The *Codex* had predicted her death but not specified its manner. For all intents and purposes, she was dead, until Xander Harris found her and performed CPR to revive her.

Upon the Master's release, the Hellmouth was opened. The Old Ones began to emerge. Only Buffy's defeat of the Master was able to stop it, closing the portal again. The Master was impaled upon some shattered furniture in the school library and quickly decomposed, leaving only his bones behind. It was an odd death for a vampire given that every other of that hellish species we had previously seen killed had exploded in a cloud of dust.

After her triumph in that episode, Buffy went to Los Angeles to spend the summer with her father. During that time, Giles, Willow, and Xander buried the Master's bones, sanctifying the ground.

In the second-season premiere, "When She Was Bad," the Order of Aurelius—under the direction of Absalom and the Anointed One—dug up the Master's bones and attempted to resurrect him. Buffy intervened again, of course, and destroyed the Master's bones with a sledgehammer to prevent them from ever attempting to raise him again.

> "We could grind our enemies into talcum powder with a sledgehammer, but, gosh, we did that last night."
> —XANDER, IN "WHEN SHE WAS BAD"

Though the Master was destroyed at last, it was not the final time we were to see him. In season three's "The Wish," the vengeance demon Anyanka granted Cordelia Chase a single wish. Cordy blamed Buffy for all her woes, so she wished that the Slayer had never come to Sunnydale. When the wish came true, we were given a vision of what life would have been like in that town without Buffy Summers.

That alternate reality included the Master, of course.

> "It's time to treat humans like . . . well, let's not mince words here . . . like the cattle they are!"
> —THE MASTER, IN "THE WISH"

Fortunately for Buffy and the rest of the world, that alternate reality version of the Master was destroyed when Giles shattered Anyanka's amulet. Although, if the evil vampire version of Willow could be plucked from that alternate reality . . .

DARLA

> "Is there anything better than a natural disaster: the panic, the people lost in the streets, like picking fruit off the vine."
> —"ANGEL"

FIRST APPEARANCE: "Welcome to the Hellmouth," season one

OTHER EPISODES: season one: "The Harvest," "Angel"; season two: "Becoming, Parts One and Two"

KEY RELATIONSHIPS: Sired by the Master. Darla was Angel's sire, and therefore Drusilla's grandsire and Spike's great-grandsire. She was a member of the Order of Aurelius.

UNIQUE ATTRIBUTES: In 1898, brought Angel the Gypsy girl he killed, whose family placed the curse on him that restored his soul.

MOST MONSTROUS MOMENT: After Angel turned into a vampire in 1753, he killed his entire family as a final act of rebellion against his father . . . and Darla, who had encouraged this, mocked him, telling him that the memory of his father's disapproval would haunt him forever (*Angel,* "The Prodigal").

CURRENT STATUS: Darla was dispatched by Angel in "Angel," but was resurrected in *Angel's* first-season finale.

Darla has the distinction of being the very first vampire ever seen on *Buffy the Vampire Slayer*. In the teaser for the pilot, "Welcome to the Hellmouth," she fed upon a high school dropout after they broke into Sunnydale High together after dark.

This intro might well have led the viewer to believe Darla was just another vampire, but that possibility was quickly dispelled. Not only was she a member of the

Order of Aurelius, she was the first vampire in Sunnydale to meet the Slayer in combat when Buffy chased her into a crypt to rescue Xander and Willow, and she survived the experience (with Luke's help).

In addition, after her death the Master specifically said that Darla was his favorite "for four hundred years." That status gave her the ability to say things to the Master with impunity that would have gotten other vampires killed. Upon Luke's death at the end of the second half of the two-hour series premiere ("The Harvest"), Darla became the Master's second-in-command. In "Angel," when the trio of vampire assassins known only as the Three failed to murder the Slayer as the Master had commanded, he allowed Darla the pleasure of killing them. She then hatched a plan to make Angel abandon his human soul, to kill again, and to come back to the Order of Aurelius to be with her.

THE MASTER: "Do I sense a plan, Darla? Share."
DARLA: "Angel kills [Buffy] and comes back to the fold."
THE MASTER: "Why would he kill her if he feels for her?"
DARLA: "To keep her from killing him."   **—"ANGEL"**

Darla craftily orchestrated a conflict between Buffy and Angel by biting the Slayer's mother, Joyce Summers, and framing Angel for the deed. Her scheme failed, however.

In "Angel," the nature of Darla's relationship to Angel was revealed in detail.

BUFFY: "So you guys were . . . involved?"
DARLA: "For several generations."
BUFFY: "Well, you're going to pile up a few exes when you've been around since Columbus. You are older than him, right? One gal to another, you look a little worn around the eyes."
DARLA: "I made him. And I brought him that Gypsy girl. . . . There was a time when we shared everything. Wasn't there, Angelus?"   **—FROM "ANGEL"**

The two were once romantically involved and Darla still loved him. She wanted Angel back in the fold with her, as part of the Order.

Darla had unwittingly been responsible for choosing the girl whose murder led to Angel's curse, the return of his soul. In 1753, in Galway, Ireland, Darla had spotted him in a pub and set her sights on luring him to her life, on making him a vampire. After turning him, she manipulated him into slaughtering his family, specifically his father, whose approval he'd yearned for (*Angel,* "The Prodigal").

ANGEL: "He always said I would come to nothing. But in the moment before his death, I proved him wrong."

DARLA: (laughing) "Your victory over him took but moments. But his defeat of you will last lifetimes."

ANGEL: "What are you talking about? He can't defeat me now."

DARLA: "He already has. You've seen to that—He can never approve of you now—can he? And yet he'll be with you, always. The ghost you've made will haunt you forever."

—*ANGEL*, "THE PRODIGAL"

At the end of "Angel," Darla was dusted by Angel himself, only to be resurrected in the first-season finale of *Angel*.

LUKE

"The sleeper will awaken. And the world will bleed."

—LUKE, IN "WELCOME TO THE HELLMOUTH"

FIRST APPEARANCE: "Welcome to the Hellmouth," season one

OTHER EPISODES: season one: "The Harvest"

KEY RELATIONSHIPS: The Master's right hand. Meant to be the Vessel in the 1997 ritual that would have allowed the Master to escape his Hellmouth prison.

UNIQUE ATTRIBUTES: Pre-Buffy, he was undefeated in battle for more than a century and a half.

MOST MONSTROUS MOMENT: As the brutal and ruthless leader of the attack on the Bronze in "The Harvest."

CURRENT STATUS: Buffy staked him on the stage at the Bronze at the end of "The Harvest."

In the two-hour *Buffy* pilot, comprised of "Welcome to the Hellmouth" and "The Harvest," Luke was the Master's lieutenant, or second-in-command. A member of the Order of Aurelius, he was quite a powerful vampire.

THE MASTER: "A Slayer . . . have you any proof?"
LUKE: "Only that she fought me and yet lives."
THE MASTER: "Very nearly proof enough. I can't remember the last time that happened."
LUKE: "1843. Madrid. He caught me sleeping."

—"THE HARVEST"

151

In "The Harvest," Luke performed a ritual that made him a supernatural conduit through which the power he received from feeding on humans would be transferred to his captive Master. It was hoped that there would be enough power for the Master to free himself when Luke and the rest of the Order attacked the Bronze and started slaughtering people. In that attack on the Bronze, however, Luke was slain by Buffy, and thus, the conduit destroyed. Therefore, the Master remained imprisoned.

JESSE (AS A VAMPIRE)

"Oh, right! Put me out of my misery! You don't have the g—"

—JESSE, IN "THE HARVEST"

FIRST APPEARANCE: "Welcome to the Hellmouth," season one

OTHER EPISODES: season one: "The Harvest"

KEY RELATIONSHIPS: One of Xander Harris's best friends (as a human). A servant of the Master (as a vampire).

MOST MONSTROUS MOMENT: Jesse led his friends to the Master's lair and attempted to kill them.

CURRENT STATUS: Jesse was "accidentally" staked by Xander at the end of "The Harvest."

Jesse was a Sunnydale High School student, and a close friend of Xander Harris and Willow Rosenberg. He was among the group Buffy Summers became friendly with when she first arrived in Sunnydale. Unfortunately, the Master made him into a vampire, and he then betrayed his friends. In a chaotic battle in the Bronze (at the end of "The Harvest"), he attempted to kill Xander. Though Xander had a stake and threatened to dust Jesse, the newborn vampire did not believe Xander would do it. In the chaos, a woman accidentally bumped Jesse from behind, impaling him on Xander's stake.

THOMAS

"Okay, first of all, what's with this outfit? Live in the now, okay? You look like DeBarge. Now we can do this the hard way, or . . . well, actually, there's just the hard way."
—BUFFY TO THOMAS, IN "WELCOME TO THE HELLMOUTH"

EPISODE: "Welcome to the Hellmouth," season one

KEY RELATIONSHIPS: A member of the Order of Aurelius, the followers of the Master.

MOST MONSTROUS MOMENT: Thomas attempted to kill Willow, but Buffy stopped him.

CURRENT STATUS: Buffy dusted Thomas in a graveyard crypt.

Thomas is notable mainly as the first vampire Buffy spotted in Sunnydale, in the pilot episode, "Welcome to the Hellmouth." Amid the teens at The Bronze, Thomas was dressed in eighties fashions, and it was his lack of fashion sense that tipped Buffy off to his vampiric nature, a fact that irked Giles, who had been attempting to teach her to sense a vampire by instinct.

"A Slayer should be able to see them anyway. Without looking, without thinking. Can you tell me if there's a vampire in this building? . . . You should know! Even through this din you should be able to sense them. Try. Reach out with your mind. You have to hone your senses, focus until the energy washes over you. . . ."   —GILES, IN "WELCOME TO THE HELLMOUTH"

That Buffy was able to discern that Thomas was a vampire from his clothes, rather than the manner in which Giles was attempting to instruct her, was an excellent example of the way in which their divergent approaches would come together to make them a formidable team.

At The Bronze, Thomas flirted with the shy, virginal Willow and asked her to get an ice cream with him. Instead, he led her into the cemetery, to a large crypt that was an entrance to the Master's underground lair. Thanks to his bad luck in choosing Willow as a potential victim, Thomas also had the distinction of being the first vampire in the series killed by the Slayer. Buffy followed them, and dusted Thomas when he revealed his true nature.

CLAW

BUFFY: "So I'm an undead monster who can shave with his hand—How many things am I afraid of?"

GILES: "Not many, and not substitute teachers, as a rule."

—DISCUSSING A SIGHTING OF "FORK-GUY," IN "TEACHER'S PET"

EPISODE: "Teacher's Pet," season one

KEY RELATIONSHIPS: A former member of the Order of Aurelius.

UNIQUE ATTRIBUTES: Had a claw in place of a hand he had cut off.

MOST MONSTROUS MOMENT: The guy cut off his own hand!

CURRENT STATUS: Buffy exterminated Claw in "Teacher's Pet."

Claw, aka "fork-guy," was once a member of the Order of Aurelius, the Master's followers. According to Giles, he "displeased the Master and cut off his [own] hand for penance." Claw then replaced the severed hand with a kind of metal substitute. Previous to the events in season one's "Teacher's Pet," Claw apparently battled Angel, wounding him, but both of them survived the encounter. Angel told Buffy, "Don't give him a moment's mercy, he'll rip your throat out."

In "Teacher's Pet," Buffy caught up to Claw while he was stalking people in Weatherly Park, but he fled from her. Buffy followed and watched him stalk substitute biology teacher Miss French, who turned out to be the She-Mantis. It was Claw's fear of her seemingly human form that tipped Buffy off to Miss French's true nature. Later, when Xander and **Blayne Mall** were abducted by Miss French, Buffy tracked Claw again and used his fear of the She-Mantis to turn him into a kind of vampiric bloodhound, only to dust him easily when he had served his purpose.

THE ANOINTED ONE

"There will be a time of crisis, of worlds hanging in the balance. And in this time shall
come the Anointed, the Master's great warrior. The Slayer will not know him, will
not stop him. And he will lead her to hell.

"As it is written, so shall it be.

"Five will die, and from their ashes the Anointed One shall rise. The Order of Aurelius
shall greet him, and usher him to his immortal destiny.

"As it is written, so shall it be." —THE MASTER, READING FROM THE WRITINGS
OF AURELIUS IN "NEVER KILL A BOY ON THE FIRST DATE"

FIRST APPEARANCE: "Never Kill a Boy on the First Date," season one

OTHER EPISODES: season one: "Angel," "Nightmares," "Prophecy Girl"; season two: "When
She Was Bad," "School Hard"

KEY RELATIONSHIPS: Destined to be the Master's greatest warrior.

UNIQUE ATTRIBUTES: Well . . . he *is* the Anointed One.

MOST MONSTROUS MOMENT: Led Buffy to her death in the Master's lair in "Prophecy
Girl."

CURRENT STATUS: The Anointed One was killed by Spike in "School Hard"

The funny thing about the passage above is the last line. "As it is written, so shall
it be." And yet, according to Rob Des Hotel and Dean Batali, the writers of "Never Kill
a Boy on the First Date," it was written and rewritten
a multitude of times. Seven shall die, seven shall
rise. Budgetary concerns lowered it to five. The num-
bers jumped around quite a bit, but eventually, Joss
Whedon settled it all.

The Anointed One was to be a child.

"Most of the plot things happen by freak accident," Batali observes. "Our initial draft had a big
fight with seven vampires. At that time, I don't think
the one who rose was a child. I don't remember there
being anything about the Anointed One. But then
Joss said there should be a kid, because people
wouldn't expect it."

The kid was **Collin,** a small boy who ended up
being the Anointed One, prophesied to do great
things, including being the Master's heir. He was on
an airport bus that was attacked by vampires who

killed the driver and the four passengers on board, including Collin. Two of the passengers—a man named **Andrew Borba,** who was wanted by local police for questioning in relation to two murders—and Collin, were turned into vampires. Nothing more was known of Collin, save that the last words he was heard to speak were "I went on an airplane."

Giles uncovered a prophecy indicating that "from the ashes of five, one shall rise." When he read the newspaper coverage of the five deaths—reported as a bus crash—he suspected that the prophecy was coming true. It was natural for them to believe that Borba was to be the Anointed One and, indeed, when they went to the morgue to check, he *was* a vampire. But not the Anointed One. That fate was left to the boy, Collin.

Though Batali and Des Hotel didn't write Collin after that initial episode, they were part of the staff that worked out the stories. The Anointed One was a classic "evil child" story, a perennial favorite in supernatural pop culture.

"The evil-child thing had been done so well before with *The Exorcist* and *The Omen* that we didn't really think about it much," Des Hotel recalls. "It was our first episode, and we wanted to get Buffy and Giles and the gang all down. The child, at that point, was really a device, though he became important later."

Yet, despite the promise of the character's introduction, the Anointed One never really amounted to much. When Darla—who had been in the Master's service—was killed, the Master was distraught. In the confident, flat tones of the demon within the child's youthful innocence, he promised to bring the Slayer to his Master.

> **THE MASTER:** "Darla . . ."
> **THE ANOINTED ONE:** "Forget her."
> **THE MASTER:** "How dare you! She was my favorite! For four hundred years . . ."
> **THE ANOINTED ONE:** "She was weak. We don't need her. I will bring you the Slayer."
> —"ANGEL"

It was a promise he fulfilled in "Prophecy Girl," guiding a knowing Buffy to the underground lair.

After the Master's destruction, the Anointed One was the titular head of the Order of Aurelius, though by the beginning of season two, a new vampire, Absalom, had come to town to act as a sort of regent for him. Together, they attempted to resurrect the Master in "When She Was Bad," during which Absalom was killed. Three episodes later, in "School Hard," Spike and Drusilla arrived on the scene. Spike dispatched the Anointed One almost dismissively, by throwing him into a cage and hauling him up into direct sunlight.

The Anointed One's coming was prophesied in the twelfth century by **Aurelius** himself, the founder of the Order. Interestingly (and commonly, in *Buffy*), the prophecy itself came true, but Buffy still found a way to work around it.

THE THREE

FAITH: "What about you? What was your toughest kill?"

BUFFY: (thinking of Angel) "They're all tough in different ways, I guess . . oh, but do you guys remember the Three? Or, you never met the Three . . . . But anyway—"

—BUFFY, CUT OFF, IN "FAITH, HOPE, AND TRICK"

EPISODE: "Angel," season one

KEY RELATIONSHIPS: Engaged by the Master to kill Buffy.

UNIQUE ATTRIBUTES: The Three were so obsessed with their honor and their reputation that when they failed to kill Buffy, they offered the Master their lives.

CURRENT STATUS: The Three were executed by Darla for their failure.

Summoned by the Master in his war against Buffy (in "Angel"), The Three were battle-scarred, armor-clad, warrior vampires. When Buffy teamed with Angel—in a fight that led to the pair growing closer, and eventually to Buffy's discovery that Angel was a vampire—the two of them barely managed to survive the encounter. Their attack on Buffy provided her with one of the most difficult battles of her life, as she noted when talking to Faith in "Faith, Hope, and Trick."

Having failed, the Three offered their lives to the Master, who gave the pleasurable duty of dispatching them to Darla. She staked them one at a time as they bowed to the Master.

ABSALOM

"We have been put down, my kinsmen. We have lost our way, and we have lost the night. But despair is for the living. Where they are weak, we will be strong. Where they weep, we rejoice. Where they bleed, we drink. Within these three days a new hope shall arise. We shall put our faith in *him* . . . and he will show us the way." **—ABSALOM, IN "WHEN SHE WAS BAD"**

EPISODE: "When She Was Bad," season two

KEY RELATIONSHIPS: Absalom functioned as a regent for the Anointed One, helping him to rule what remained of the Master's followers.

MOST MONSTROUS MOMENT: Despite his eloquence, when entering into battle with Buffy, Absalom became just as brutal as the average vampire.

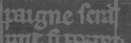

CURRENT STATUS: Buffy burned Absalom to death.

Absalom arrived in Sunnydale sometime during the summer between first and second season. He managed to set himself up as a guardian-protector for the Anointed One. It is entirely possible, even probable, that Absalom was already a member of the Order of Aurelius, but had been doing the Master's bidding elsewhere at the time of the Master's destruction at Buffy's hands.

Whatever the case, by the time he first appeared in the second-season opener, "When She Was Bad," Absalom had risen to a position of some power in the Order. He was the chief organizer of the effort to resurrect the Master.

> **ABSALOM:** "Your day is done, girl. I'll grind you into a sticky paste. And I'll hear you beg before I smash in your face."
> **BUFFY:** "So, are you gonna kill me? Or are you just making small talk?"
>
> —**"WHEN SHE WAS BAD"**

At the conclusion of "When She Was Bad," Buffy burned Absalom to cinders.

ST. VIGEOUS

"This weekend, the Night of St. Vigeous, our power shall be at its peak!"

—**BIG UGLY, IN "SCHOOL HARD"**

EPISODE: None; discussed in "School Hard"

UNIQUE ATTRIBUTES: Patron saint of vampires.

MOST MONSTROUS MOMENT: Led an ancient vampiric crusade.

CURRENT STATUS: Unknown.

According to the lore Giles discovered (in "School Hard"), St. Vigeous was a sort of patron saint of vampires. In ancient times, he led a vampiric crusade which swept through "Edessa, Harran, and points east," destroying everything in its path.

The Feast of St. Vigeous is a time when the power of the vampire is at its peak.

"For three nights, the unholy ones scourge themselves into a fury, culminating in a savage attack on the Night of St. Vigeous."   —**GILES, IN "SCHOOL HARD"**

In a bit of dialogue expurgated from the final broadcast due to length, Jenny Calendar referred to it as "a Holy Night of Attack."

DALTON

FIRST APPEARANCE: "What's My Line? Part One," season two

OTHER EPISODES: season two: "Surprise"

KEY RELATIONSHIPS: Dalton was a lackey of Spike and Drusilla.

UNIQUE ATTRIBUTES: An academic— a rarity among vampires.

CURRENT STATUS: Dalton was burned by the Judge.

The quiet, bookish vampire Dalton first appeared in the second season's "What's My Line? Part One," where he attempted to translate the manuscript Spike hoped would cure Drusilla.

> **DALTON:** "I'm not sure . . . it could be . . . *Deprimere ille bubula linter.*"
> **SPIKE:** "Debase the beef . . . canoe. (beat) Why does that strike me as not right?"
> 　　　　　　　　　　　　　　　—"WHAT'S MY LINE? PART ONE"

Later, in "Surprise," Dalton was part of the effort to rebuild the Judge, but he made the mistake of annoying Drusilla. She wanted to kill him, but, uncharacteristically, Spike came to his defense.

> "Dru, sweet. You might give him a chance to find your lost treasure. He's a wanker, but he's the only one we've got with half a brain. If he fails—you can eat his eyes out of the sockets for all I care."　　　　　　—SPIKE, IN "SURPRISE"

Due to his intellect and his interest in books, there was some good in Dalton. That element of his personality led to his death at the hands of the Judge in "Surprise." The Judge had the ability to burn goodness out of any being, and when he did precisely that to Dalton, the vampire expired.

LYLE, CANDY, AND TECTOR GORCH

GILES: "Your new playmate is a fellow of some repute, it seems. Lyle Gorch. The other one is his brother, Tector. They're from Abilene. Made their reputation massacring a Mexican village in 1886."

BUFFY: "Friendly little demons."

GILES: "No, that was before they became vampires."   —**"BAD EGGS"**

FIRST APPEARANCE (Lyle and Tector only): "Bad Eggs," season two

OTHER EPISODES (Lyle and Candy only): season three: "Homecoming"

KEY RELATIONSHIPS: Lyle and Tector were brothers. Lyle later married Candy (also a vampire).

UNIQUE ATTRIBUTES: Lyle has a cowardly streak; twice, he fled from the Slayer rather than fight to the death.

MOST MONSTROUS MOMENT: Before becoming vampires, the brothers slaughtered the entire populace of a village in Mexico.

CURRENT STATUS: Tector was killed by the ancient beast called the Bezoar (in "Bad Eggs"). Candy was staked by Cordelia (in "Homecoming"). Lyle's current whereabouts are unknown.

The Gorch brothers have a fascinating origin, in that they are a nod to one of the great American film directors and one of the great Western films ever made.

"They came from *The Wild Bunch*," Marti Noxon confirms. "There are a pair of brothers in that movie named the Gorch brothers. [*The Wild Bunch*] was what we were going for. That was what we were drawing from."

In the second-season episode "Bad Eggs," Lyle and Tector showed up in Sunnydale, apparently drawn there simply because, as the town with the Hellmouth, it was the place to go for vampires. Lyle was the first to fight Buffy after she stopped him from killing a girl at the Sunnydale Mall. He barely escaped. Later, itching for a rematch, he brought brother Tector with him.

The murderous Gorches did end up attacking Buffy together, during her attempt to stop the Bezoar threat. The Bezoar killed Tector, and though Lyle fled the scene, he blamed her for his brother's death.

Later (in season three's "Homecoming"), Lyle and his wife, Candy Gorch, were two of the killers who participated in Mr. Trick's "Slayerfest '98" (see Vampires: Mr. Trick).

> **"Me and Candy's blowing our whole honeymoon stash on this game."**
> —LYLE GORCH, IN "HOMECOMING"

Though Candy was dusted—by Cordelia!—with a spatula!—Lyle turned tail and ran for the second time.

Lyle Gorch is still at large. His whereabouts are unknown.

ANDREW HOELICH

XANDER: "What was with the acrobatics? How did that happen?"
OZ: "Wasn't Andrew Hoelich on the gymnastics team?"
XANDER: "That's right, he was! Cheater!"   —ON THE ONE THAT GOT AWAY, IN "ANNE"

EPISODE: "Anne," season three

UNIQUE ATTRIBUTES: In life, Hoelich was an excellent gymast, a skill that carried over into his life as a vampire.

CURRENT STATUS: Xander dusted Hoelich in "Anne."

A Sunnydale High School student and member of the gymnastics team, Andrew Hoelich was killed by a vampire in 1998 at the age of seventeen. While Buffy Summers, the Slayer, was in Los Angeles trying to figure out her life, her friends back in Sunnydale contended with the town's vampires as best they could. Among those was Andrew, who gave them a difficult time mainly due to his gymnastic ability.

Xander, Willow, Oz, and Cordelia realized he might return to Hammersmith Park, where he had spent a lot of time as a human. They went there and used Cordelia as bait. While Xander and Cordelia argued, Hoelich attacked Willow. The gymnastic vampire was staked by Xander.

KAKISTOS

BUFFY: "Oh, the [vampire] who nearly bit me said something about 'kissing toast,' he lived for kissing toast."

GILES (alarmed): "You mean Kakistos?"

BUFFY: "Is that bad?"

GILES: "Kakistos is Greek, it means the worst of the worst. It's also the name of a vampire, so old his hands and feet are cloven."   —**"FAITH, HOPE, AND TRICK"**

EPISODE: "Faith, Hope, and Trick," season three

KEY RELATIONSHIPS: Employed Mr. Trick.

UNIQUE ATTRIBUTES: Cloven hooves and hands. Had a large scar on his face.

MOST MONSTROUS MOMENT: Murdered Faith's first Watcher.

CURRENT STATUS: Faith killed Kakistos in "Faith, Hope, and Trick."

"Faith, Hope, and Trick," the third episode of season three, introduced all three of the title characters: **Scott Hope,** briefly a love interest of Buffy's, the vampire Mr. Trick, and Faith, the Slayer who was called upon Kendra's death, along with a vampire called Kakistos.

Kakistos had lived a very long time prior to his arrival in Sunnydale. As David Greenwalt, who wrote this episode, has pointed out, vampires' external appearance changes over time to more accurately reflect the demon soul within. This has been evident in the series with the Master and Kakistos.

Prior to his arrival in Sunnydale with his henchman, Mr. Trick, Kakistos was apparently preying on a community in Missouri. There, he kept alligators as pets and eventually came into conflict with Faith. In fact, it was in pursuit of Faith that Kakistos ended up in Sunnydale. The circumstances of their earlier conflict were not fully revealed, but it is clear that Faith grievously wounded him, apparently with an ax to the face. Kakistos, for his part, killed Faith's Watcher in a particularly nasty fashion, leaving that Slayer terrified of him.

In the end, however, with Buffy's help Faith rose above her fear and dusted Kakistos.

MR. TRICK

"Sunnydale. Town's got quaint, and the people: he called me sir, don't you miss that? Admittedly, not a haven for the brothers—strictly the Caucasian persuasion in the Dale—but you gotta stand up and salute their death rate. I ran a statistical analysis and Hello, Darkness—makes D.C. look like Mayberry. And nobody sayin' boo about it. We could fit right in here. Have some fun." —MR. TRICK, IN "FAITH, HOPE, AND TRICK"

FIRST APPEARANCE: "Faith, Hope, and Trick," season three

OTHER EPISODES: season three: "Homecoming," "Band Candy," "Bad Girls," "Consequences"

KEY RELATIONSHIPS: Employed by Kakistos, and later by the Mayor of Sunnydale.

UNIQUE ATTRIBUTES: Has a taste for the employees of fast-food restaurants.

MOST MONSTROUS MOMENT: Organized "Slayerfest '98."

CURRENT STATUS: Faith dusted Trick in "Consequences."

Mr. Trick's history is shrouded in mystery. He first appeared in "Faith, Hope, and Trick" as a lackey of the vampire Kakistos. Right away, Trick showed a love of fast food (pizza delivery boys, takeout window employees) and a gift for self-preservation. When Buffy and Faith had Kakistos on the ropes, Trick wisely retreated.

Shortly thereafter, with his former employer dead, Trick entered the employ of the Mayor of Sunnydale, Richard Wilkins III, a demon worshiper who aspired to become a true demon himself. On the Mayor's behalf, Trick planned "Slayerfest '98" (in "Homecoming") in which various assassins—human, demon, and vampire—competed in a contest to kill both Buffy and Faith (though they mistook Cordelia Chase for Faith). The effort obviously failed. Also on the Mayor's behalf, Trick hired Ethan Rayne (in "Band Candy") to whip up some chaos to distract the Slayer and friends from the Mayor's plans.

Though Trick was a loyal employee, the rest of his tenure was rather uneventful, save for the fact that his efforts helped the Mayor achieve the 100 days of invulnerability he sought on the way to his Ascension to true demonhood. Trick was dusted by Faith in "Consequences."

ZACHARY KRALIK

"I can be sealed in a box for six years, give or take, and not care. Because I know I won't be alone much longer. I'll have your daughter. I won't kill her . . . I'll make her like me. Different. She'll go to sleep and when she wakes up . . . your face will be the first thing she eats."
—ZACHARY KRALIK TO JOYCE SUMMERS, IN "HELPLESS"

EPISODE: "Helpless," season three

KEY RELATIONSHIPS: His psychotic behavior could be directly linked to his abusive mother.

UNIQUE ATTRIBUTES: A homicidal maniac—even by vampire standards—Kralik was obsessed with mothers.

MOST MONSTROUS MOMENT: Kralik killed his own mother.

CURRENT STATUS: Buffy killed Kralik by tricking him into drinking holy water.

In the third season's "Helpless," on her eighteenth birthday, Buffy was given a severe test by the Council of Watchers called the **Tento di Cruciamentum:** a serum was injected into her body that removed her Slayer gifts, and the Council intended to send her against a vampire under controlled circumstances.

Soon enough, however, circumstances spun out of control, mainly because the vampire in question was Zachary Kralik. Kralik, a psychotic vampire with mother issues, was named by writer David Fury after his own four-year-old nephew.

"I tried to make him different," Fury says of the character. "He had a kind of Hannibal Lecter thing going that made him a lot of fun to write. Other vampires are somewhat goofy followers—they need the leadership of Mr. Trick or Spike and Drusilla. Kralik was a guy who operated more or less on his own.

"He also had decidedly more issues than a lot of vampires do, which made him interesting to write. He was a guy who had cannibalized several people before he became a vampire. And the mother issues played into his capture of Buffy's mother. But he doesn't have any clear agenda, whereas the more villainous leader vampires have ruling the world as their agenda. He just wants to create mayhem in a completely twisted way. He's not really patterned after vampires so much as he's patterned after serial killers."

The Council of Watchers apparently kept Kralik in a box for six years before using him as part of Buffy's test. He was psychotic, and was kept on drugs that apparently were intended to keep him sedated and stable. Kralik later continued to take the pills after he was free, if an agonizing fit of pain overcame him. This would seem to indicate the possibility that vampires can be addicted, in addition to the fact that human mental illness can carry over to their demonic selves after they have become vampires.

Kralik escaped, as noted above, and killed a pair of Council members named **Hobson** and **Blair** (the latter of which Kralik made a vampire, but who did not survive an encounter with Buffy). Kralik's issues with his own mother led him to kidnap Joyce Summers, mother of the Slayer.

> **"My mother was a person with no self-respect of her own, so she tried to take mine, ten years old and she had the scissors. You wouldn't believe what she took with those. She's dead to me now. Mostly because I killed and ate her. But also because Time's been a healing salve. I'm shunned by my kind. . . . I'm aware of that. . . . I have a problem with mothers. I'm aware of that."** —ZACHARY KRALIK, IN "HELPLESS"

Kralik nearly killed Buffy before she dusted him by substituting holy water for the water with which he took his psychosis medicine.

VAMP WILLOW

CORDELIA: "Okay, it wasn't even like I was that attracted to Xander, it was more just that we kept being in these life or death situations and that's always sexy and stuff. I mean I more or less knew he was a loser but that doesn't make it okay for you to come around and—what? Do I have something on my neck?"

VAMP WILL: "Not yet..."

—CORDELIA AND VAMP WILLOW, DISCUSSING THE ETHICS OF BOYFRIEND STEALING, IN "DOPPELGANGLAND"

FIRST APPEARANCE: "The Wish," season three

OTHER EPISODES: season three: "Doppelgangland"

KEY RELATIONSHIPS: Employed by the Master. Girlfriend and lover of Vamp Xander.

UNIQUE ATTRIBUTES: Apparently bisexual. Wears a lot of leather. Keeps Angel as a pet.

MOST MONSTROUS MOMENT: Tortured Angel in "The Wish."

CURRENT STATUS: Vamp Willow was killed by the alternate-reality version of Oz in "The Wish," and that moment was replicated in "Doppelgangland."

In season three's "The Wish," we had a glimpse into an alternate reality. Heartbroken and furious after discovering Xander and Willow kissing in the previous episode, Cordelia was approached by a new girl at school named Anya, also known as Anyanka, a vengeance demon. It was within her power to grant Cordelia a wish of vengeance, and Cordy wished that Buffy had never come to Sunnydale.

> "You know what I've been asking myself a lot this last week? Why me? Why do I get bitten by snakes? Why do I fall for incredible losers? And I think I've finally figured it out. What my problem is. It's *Buffy Summers*." —CORDELIA, IN "THE WISH"

Poof. Before she ever came to Sunnydale, Buffy was drawn into the war against darkness elsewhere and never made it to Sunnydale, never met up with Giles for her training. Thanks to her absence, not only was the Master still alive, but he had escaped the Hellmouth and begun to build a kind of vampire kingdom in Sunnydale. No one went out after dark. Vampires caught any stray humans and herded them into machines that leached them of their blood. The Age of Industry had finally caught up to vampirism.

Giles had made it to Sunnydale to wait for Buffy, but she never arrived. Instead he did his best to battle the Master with a handful of volunteer vampire hunters, including the alternate-reality versions of Oz, **Larry**, and another student named **Nancy**. In that alternate reality, Willow and Xander had both been turned into vampires and were gleefully evil. The Master had captured Angel, and Willow liked to torture the vampire-with-a-soul, calling him her "puppy."

Nancy was killed. In a stunning twist, Vamp Willow and **Vamp Xander** also murdered Cordelia, whose wish had caused the reality shift in the first place. Buffy eventually found her way to Sunnydale. In the final battle, most of the vampires were dusted. Vamp Willow, ironically, was staked by the alternate-reality version of Oz—her boyfriend in the regular continuity. Anya's talisman of power was destroyed by Giles, leaving her a normal human with all the memories of having been a demon.

Seven episodes later ("Doppelgangland"), Anya was revealed to be trying to figure out a way to get her power back. (It didn't hurt that fans loved the sexy, evil vampire Willow, and wanted to see her again.) Anya asked Willow to help with the spell, secretly intending to grab her talisman from that alternate reality. They believed that the spell had failed . . . until they realized that the vampire Willow from that alternate reality had been brought over from the moment before her dusting and now existed alongside her counterpart.

It caused a great deal of confusion, of course, with Buffy and friends at first believing that the Willow they knew and loved had been turned into a vampire. It also monumentally freaked out the real Willow to see herself evil, and also to be the object of lust from her own evil self, evidently a bisexual vampire.

"I'm so evil and skanky," a horrified Willow told Buffy, "and I think I'm kinda gay."

Vamp Willow enlisted the aid of a group of vampires led by a bloodsucker named **Alphonse**. They were defeated, of course, and Vamp Willow was returned to her own reality, only an instant before being dusted once more by that alternate reality's Oz.

SUNDAY

> "I have to say, you've really got me now. This is a diabolical plan. Throw yourself at my feet with a broken arm and no weapons of any kind, how am I ever gonna get out of this one?"
> —SUNDAY, TO BUFFY, IN "THE FRESHMAN"

EPISODE: "The Freshman," season four

KEY RELATIONSHIPS: Leader of a pack of none-too-bright vampires at the University of California, Sunnydale.

UNIQUE ATTRIBUTES: A sharp wit and the ability to intimidate Buffy Summers.

MOST MONSTROUS MOMENT: She "vampirized" Buffy's new college friend, Eddie.

CURRENT STATUS: Buffy dusted Sunday and her followers at the end of "The Freshman."

Of the truly minor (single episode) characters in Buffy's four seasons, few have elicited the reaction Sunday received from Internet-based fans of the series when she appeared in the fourth-season opener, "The Freshman."

Sunday was the leader of a band of vampires who had set up their lair in an abandoned frat house on the UC Sunnydale campus. It was a cynically savage operation, in which they found lonely, floundering freshmen, killed them, removed their belongings, and then faked notes indicating that the students had dropped out and gone home.

The band of vampires consisted of Sunday, **Dav**, a stoner vampire known only as **"the rookie,"** and **Eddie**, who had briefly been a friendly acquaintance of Buffy's at UC Sunnydale. Sunday wasn't exactly pleased with their performance. As she said: "I need better lackeys."

SUNDAY: "Freshmen, man, they're so predictable."
ROOKIE: "And you can never eat just one." —"THE FRESHMAN"

When Sunday discovered the Slayer was on campus, not only was she not impressed, she also gave the floundering Buffy a severe thrashing in their first fight.

> "The Slayer? Wow, I heard you might be coming here. This is—well, I mean, what a challenge. A Slayer . . . I'm Sunday. I'll be killing you in a minute or so . . . .Don't take this the wrong way, but you fight like a girl."
>
> —SUNDAY, IN "THE FRESHMAN"

Later, however, once Buffy had regained her confidence, Sunday and her entire group were dusted.

It is interesting to note that her name has inspired a certain amount of speculation among die-hard Internet *Buffy* fans—particularly those at the posting board The Bronze—as to whether Sunday might actually have been one of a group of vampire septuplets, which would mean that Monday, Tuesday, Wednesday, Thursday, Friday, and Saturday might be out there, looking for revenge.

HARMONY KENDALL (AS A VAMPIRE)

> "Hey, I don't have a pulse. Cool. Can we eat a doctor and get a stethoscope so I can hear my heart not beating?" —HARMONY, "THE HARSH LIGHT OF DAY"

FIRST APPEARANCE: "The Harsh Light of Day," season four

OTHER EPISODES: season four: "The Initiative," "Pangs"

KEY RELATIONSHIPS: Was briefly Spike's girlfriend.

UNIQUE ATTRIBUTES: Even though she's a vampire, she still fights by slapping and pulling hair.

MOST MONSTROUS MOMENT: Whines a lot.

CURRENT STATUS: Living as a vampire somewhere in Sunnydale.

Along with Buffy and friends, Harmony was a member of the Sunnydale High Class of 1999. Once, she was quite close with Cordelia, but when Cordelia began to date Xander, Harmony essentially usurped her position as most popular girl in school (and the title of "richest, snobbiest, most shallow girl" as well).

At graduation, however, Harmony took part—as did the entire class—in the effort to defeat the Mayor and prevent his Ascension to true demonhood. Unfortunately, Harmony was fed upon by one of the Mayor's vampire henchmen, and, as season four revealed, became a vampire herself.

> "Harmony's a vampire? She must be dying without a reflection."
> —BUFFY, IN "THE HARSH LIGHT OF DAY"

As of season four, Harmony has had an on-again, off-again relationship with Spike, who has used her for his own ends and otherwise ignored her.

The ancient world

THOUGH MOST OF US PROBABLY NEVER THINK ABOUT IT, vampires are a part of our lives. Stories about vampires have existed in one form or another in nearly all cultures since the dawn of time. Likely arising from man's natural fear of death and the unknown, vampires have evolved from a means of explaining the inexplicable and controlling social behavior to pop icon status and inspiration for certain alternative lifestyles.

Originally described as demons, spirits, and living corpses, vampires were to be avoided and feared. Now, in our technologically and scientifically advanced society, vampires have become romantic and even tragic figures, sometimes inspiring terror, sometimes merely awe.

Several early cultures presented the vampires of myth as female, with the legends seeming to grow from difficulties with childbirth, particularly stillborn children. The Greek legends about the vampiric creature the *lamia* portray the creature as attacking babies and very young children; scholars believe that those attributions provided an explanation for the otherwise inexplicable deaths of mothers in labor or their newborn children.

These *lamiai* were said to be descendents of Lamia, a queen with whom Zeus fell in love. A jealous Hera, enraged by Zeus' infidelity, stole Lamia's children. The grief-stricken Lamia hid in a cave and took revenge on human children, eventually being transformed by the act into a hideous beast. The *lamiai* were said to be ugly women with deformed lower bodies who could turn themselves into beautiful maidens to attack unsuspecting men.

The *lamiai* were only one form of vampire, however. Ancient myths and legends contain hundreds of varieties. Some scholars point to Lilith as the very first vampire of myth. According to Hebrew folklore, Lilith was Adam's first wife. After an argument over sexual domination, she fled to the Red Sea, which at the time was home to a variety of demons. There she mated with several demons, and produced thousands of children (incubi and succubi) that preyed on infants (especially those from illicit encounters) and men, and caused all kinds of complications with childbirth. Children who were heard laughing in their sleep were said to be playing with Lilith as she stole away their souls.

In Malaysian folklore, similar spirits are known as *langsuyar.* Here, once more, we see the pattern of the stillborn child, as the original *langsuyar* was said to be a woman whose child was stillborn. Women who died in childbirth or during the forty days following were at risk of becoming *langsuyar,* and elaborate steps were taken during the preparation of the body for burial to prevent such an occurrence.

Whereas all of these entities were known to suck blood, they were phantasms, not corporeal, and almost always killed their victims rather than pass their curse along to the victim. The idea of vampires as revivified corpses seems to be more prevalent in the ancient folklore of the Slavic regions, although references can be found in other areas such as ancient Greece, China, and Scotland.

The vampire of ancient Greek folklore, known as a *vyrkolakas,* was at first a benign entity, usually a family member returning from the dead to attend to unfinished business. Occasionally a *vyrkolakas* would reclaim its position in the family. On rare occasions, it would move to another village and start a new life. Although it was something to be avoided, and could occasionally be quite annoying, the *vyrkolakas* was not necessarily feared. If a *vyrkolakas* was violent, it was always for a reason, such as exacting revenge for a murder.

The formation of the familiar myth

AS THE EASTERN ORTHODOX CHURCH gained footholds in the Slavic regions of Europe early in the eleventh century, ancient legends and regional folklore intermingled. Today, the Eastern European notion of the vampire provides the basis for the most prevalent of our modern-day images and concepts regarding vampires. In fact, there were several instances of supposed vampire contact in the region we now call Serbia, which stimulated Western interest in vampires and may even have sparked the growth of a fascination with horror in Western culture.

Eastern European folklore presented the vampire as the risen corpse of a human being, whose bite—and appetite for blood—could transform others into vampires as well. These vampires were eternally suspended at the age they were upon their death. Commonly, they were described as wearing their burial clothes or shrouds. These vampires had the ability to pass through small areas, command such animals as rats, moths, foxes and wolves, and transfix their victims with hypnotic powers. They were not usually harmed by daylight but preferred a nocturnal existence. They could transform themselves into animals, usually wolves and sometimes rats. Always driven by hunger, the vampire tended to claim its victims slowly, usually beginning with its own living family members.

The various ways in which a person could be made a vampire were strange and quite numerous. In Eastern European folklore, virtually anyone suffering a violent or unexpected death could return as a vampire to seek vengeance on those who may have caused that death. Gypsies actually viewed any death that could have been caused by the influence of evil as unnatural, although those who suffered untimely deaths were at an even greater risk to become undead. Anyone who died under a curse, or—more important as the Greek Orthodox Church exerted more influence over the lives of the Eastern Europeans—anyone who was excommunicated or who was not buried according to Church tradition, could become a vampire.

In some areas, including China and Macedonia, a cat jumping over a dead body could lead to vampirism. Anyone who was born on days of religious observation, or born "different" (red hair, blue eyes, harelip), was believed to have vampiric tendencies and was in danger of becoming a vampire after death. In Poland, those born with a caul—a thin membrane that sometimes covers a newborn's face at birth—or with two teeth were destined to become vampires. A most definite clue in many cultures was a red face and hyperactivity.

Great pains were taken with the burial preparations of those at risk. The most common precaution was to place objects in the coffins that were believed to prevent the vampire from leaving its resting place. Religious articles were often used, but occasionally a branch of hawthorn or ash or a piece of iron was added to the grave.

Some cultures also believed that vampires had a fascination with counting, and as such a potential vampire might be buried with seeds or grains of sand so they would be prevented from roaming the world of the living by the almost endless work of counting. Sometimes a net was thrown over the body in the belief that the vampire would have to untie the knots before being able to leave the grave. In more extreme cases, the clothing of the corpse would be nailed to the inside of the coffin or a stake of ash or iron would be driven through the body to keep it in place. In some areas, boiling hot water would be poured over the grave after burial or a stake driven into the ground to prevent the vampire from rising.

In areas of Russia and Germany, the bodies of potential vampires were thrown into rivers under the assumption that the earth could not hold a vampire. Occasionally, water used in the preparation of the body for burial was poured on the road leading from grave to home as a barrier to prevent a suspected vampire's return.

In spite of these precautions, however, folklore tells us that a vampire would occasionally escape the grave. Any unusual occurrences such as widespread destruction of property, unusual noises in the night, unexplained deaths of livestock, or sightings of a recently deceased member of the village would signal its presence.

Once it was determined that a vampire was on the loose, the local populace gathered and a search got under way. Anyone who had died within forty days of the outbreak of vampiric activity was suspect.

Vampire detection methods varied. Cemeteries were searched for graves with small holes in them. Sometimes a white stallion that had never gone to stud and never stumbled would be set free in a cemetery in the belief that it would not step over a vampire's grave. Bodies were exhumed upon the logic that vampires' corpses did not decompose, and their hair and nails continued to grow after death. The vampire's body might have blood around the mouth and would bleed when pierced, long after a normal corpse could be expected to be bloodless.

When a corpse believed to be a vampire was found, the threat was usually eliminated by simply driving a stake (made of ash, juniper, hawthorn or iron) through the heart and then reburying the corpse with religious rites. In more extreme cases, the corpse would be decapitated; less often, burned.

The incidences of whole villages finding and destroying a suspected vampire were fairly rare. The late 1600s to early 1700s saw the bulk of these outbreaks, largely among the southern Slavs (especially in Serbia). The most famous of these, the Arnold Paole case, sparked a renewed Western interest in vampire lore.

In 1727, after serving in the Serbian army in Turkey, Arnold Paole returned to his village north of Belgrade, where he eventually settled down to farming and became engaged. He was respected by the villagers as an honest, pleasant man, but they all noted a strange sense of unhappiness about him. Paole finally admitted to his fiancée that he had been attacked by a vampire during his tenure in the army. Although he had killed the vampire and cleansed his wounds in its blood, he was still afraid that he might be tainted. A week later, Paole was killed in an accident and buried immediately.

Three weeks after his death, there were several sightings of Paole. When three of the men who had made these reports died, panic began to spread through the village. Paole's body was exhumed and found to have a layer of new skin under the dead layer. The fingernails had also continued to grow, and the body bled when pierced. His body was staked, decapitated, and burned. The bodies of Paole's supposed victims were also treated in a similar manner.

Several years passed. Then, in the same area, several people died mysteriously, vampirism being the suspected cause. When a young girl reported being attacked by a recently deceased neighbor, the neighbor's body was exhumed and found to be in the same state as Arnold Paole's. It was determined that, years earlier, Arnold Paole had attacked and infected several cows, some of which the now vampiric neighbor had fed on. As a result, forty more graves were opened and another seventeen supposed vampires were found. All were staked and burned.

The printing of this story in two British magazines in 1732 sparked a great intellectual controversy in the West. (In fact, the English word *vampire* can trace its origin to the Serbian word vampir, first used in these lurid stories.) Several ecclesiastical and secular papers were written on the subject. The most famous was written by Dom Augustine Calmet, a Benedictine abbot and well-known biblical scholar who condemned the desecration of graves and set forth some rational explanations such as normal bodily changes after death and premature burial. He did not entirely rule out the possibility of supernatural involvement. His 1746 "Treatise on the Vampires of Hungary and the Surrounding Regions" enjoyed great success, but it also triggered some of the most heated debates about vampires and vampirism, and much criticism was heaped upon Calmet by church and state officials.

The latter half of the eighteenth century essentially brought an end to the debates, as more and more laws were enacted against the desecration of graves and the mutilation of corpses.

Although the general consensus remained that vampires do not actually exist, belief in them can be found even to this day in some remote areas, such as in the Philippine Islands, Malaysia, rural Mexico, Serbia, and among the Kashubs in northern Canada. Belief is especially strong in those areas where burial preparations continue to be the responsibility of family and friends rather than professional undertakers.

"Real" vampires

VAMPIRES ENJOY A HEALTHY EXISTENCE in folklore and popular culture. The power of the vampire archetype has sometimes carried over into human behavior. Perhaps the most infamous "real-life" vampire was Countess Elizabeth Bathory, born in 1560 in what is now the Slovak Republic. Though she comported herself with the utmost propriety in public, the countess was a monster in private. She captured women from the countryside and used her teeth to tear into their flesh so that she could drink their blood. The Countess believed that this practice kept her young. It is believed that Elizabeth Bathory killed more than six hundred girls in this manner.

In 1611 she was sentenced to life imprisonment in solitary confinement for her crimes. She was placed in a room in her castle with no doors or windows and only small slits for access to air and food. There she died three years later.

Post–World War I Germany's serial killer Fritz Haarmann—aka the Hanover Vampire—tore out the throats of some of his victims with his teeth. Haarmann was also a cannibal and sold portions of his victims to local butchers as sausage meat. He was tried in 1924 and executed for murder. His case was filmed as *The Tenderness of the Wolves* in 1973.

Peter Kurten, known as the Vampire of Düsseldorf, first killed at the age of nine, when he murdered two playmates. Kurten often drank the blood of his victims, continuing even after it made him sick. In 1929 he went on a murder spree that led to his arrest the following year and his execution in 1931. Kurten's story was filmed as *M* in 1931, and the film was remade by Columbia Pictures in 1951.

There are far too many such cases to explore them all. In addition, however, it should be noted that there is a rather large subculture in Western society of people who believe themselves to be vampires, or simply believe in the restorative properties of human blood. These are not killers like Bathory or Haarman, but seemingly average stockbrokers and engineers and musicians. Katherine Ramsland examines this phenomenon in her extraordinary book *Piercing the Darkness: Undercover with Vampires in America Today*.

from Myth to fiction

WHILE THE NINETEENTH CENTURY brought the end of widespread belief in vampires with the Age of Enlightenment and increased secularization, it heralded the beginning of the role of the vampire in popular culture. Beginning with the 1897 publication of Bram Stoker's *Dracula*, vampires have enjoyed incredible success as pop icons though there were a number of vampire-related works preceding that classic novel.

The appearance of the modern literary vampire seems to have been first explored in the short German poem "Der Vampir" by August Ossenfelder in 1748. Goethe's 1797 poem, "The Bride of Corinth," featured a young woman returning from the dead to be with her intended. Goethe's poem was based on a story from the third century A.D. by Philostratus. Keats's influential 1820 poem "The Lamia" had the same source.

The vampire theme was introduced into British poetry through Samuel Taylor Coleridge's haunting poem "Christabel." But it wasn't until 1819 that the first work of prose fiction about vampires was written in English.

John Polidori, the traveling companion of Lord Byron, was staying with Byron and some of his friends at the Villa Diodati outside Geneva. At Byron's urgings, each guest (including Mary Shelley of *Frankenstein* fame) concocted a supernatural story for their entertainment. In Polidori's short story "The Vampyre," about the mysterious Lord Ruthven, a vampire was portrayed as a thinking character as opposed to a mindless, bloodthirsty monster. Polidori's short story inspired plays and other creative works about vampires throughout Europe during the nineteenth century.

Aleksei Tolstoi introduced the vampire to Russian literature with his 1841 novella "Vampire," set in contemporary Russian society. In 1847 he wrote *The Family of the Vourdalak*, a tale distinctly influenced by the Arnold Paole case.

During the second half of the nineteenth century, various incarnations of the vampire myth were turned into stories by such legendary writers as Alexandre Dumas, Ambrose Bierce, Nathaniel Hawthorne, Guy de Maupassant, and Baudelaire, but none had the impact or staying power of Bram Stoker's *Dracula*.

Some of those works may have had an effect on Stoker's imagination, including *Varney the Vampire*, which was written by James Malcolm Rymer in the mid-1840s and was the first full-length vampire novel in English, and the short story "Carmilla" by Joseph Sheridan Le Fanu. "Carmilla" (1872) is remarkable as the first piece to attach more erotic themes to the vampire tale, emphasizing the unearthly, sexual bond that forms between the vampire and its victim. "Carmilla" also introduced an overt lesbian theme to the genre, which would later be embraced in many vampire films.

Stoker's *Dracula* quickly became the most influential of all vampire works, setting the stage for the modern vampire tale. Stoker created the ultimate supernatural villain, borrowing elements from vampire literature, European folklore, and real life to create one of the most recognized literary creations in the world. Many traits now associated with vampires actually had very little to do with folklore and more to do with Stoker's imagination. Some of these characteristics created by Stoker include the need to rest in a coffin filled with one's native earth, the inability to enter a dwelling without an invitation, the lack of a reflection, and the inability to cross running water.

Although the success of *Dracula* generated a renewed interest in vampire lore, few novels of any genuine worth were written immediately after its publication. No vampire novel has ever surpassed the popularity of *Dracula*, which has never been out of print and has inspired a string of stage and screen productions almost from the moment of its initial publication.

Vampires continued to be popular subject matter, particularly for pulp magazines, well into the early part of the twentieth century. *Weird Tales*, first published in 1923, was one of the many pulps that featured short stories by such notable horror and fantasy writers as Robert Bloch (*Psycho*) and Robert E. Howard (*Conan*). But the greatest influence on the general public's perception of vampires at this time came from motion pictures.

The 1896 feature *The Haunted Castle* first introduced elements of vampire mythology to the movies. The very first vampire film was *The Secrets of House Number 5,* a Russian-made detective story that featured vampires, ghosts, and ghouls, though little else is known about the 1912 production.

The first film adaptations of Stoker's novel were a 1920 Russian production titled *Dracula* and a 1921 Hungarian film, *Drakula*. No copies of either film are known to exist.

Perhaps the most resounding early vampire film is the 1922 *Nosferatu* by German director F. W. Murnau, one of the most influential post–World War I German horror films, along with *The Cabinet of Dr. Caligari* (1919) and *The Golem* (1920). All three films are available today on video.

The first full-length American movie about a vampire was MGM's *London after Midnight* (1927). Lon Chaney starred as a police inspector who impersonates a vampire in order to trick a suspected murderer into revealing himself. Although more mystery than horror, the makeup designed by Chaney himself was considered one of the more disturbing visual interpretations of a vampire ever captured on film. Tragically, *London After Midnight* is a lost film, as not a single copy is known to exist.

NOSFERATU (1979)

Carl Dreyer's *Vampyr*—which was released in Europe in 1931 but did not reach American shores until the following year—was a dreamlike adaptation of "Carmilla," and is considered an international classic.

What is believed by many to be the definitive movie version of *Dracula* hit the screens on February 13, 1931. Surprising in hindsight, *Dracula*, starring Bela Lugosi, was not an immediate success. Some reviewers dismissed the film as little more than a freak show. However, the film obviously struck a nerve with Depression-era audiences looking for something other than the glitzy Busby Berkeley musicals and Prohibition-obsessed gangster films of the period. Through word of mouth, the film slowly grew in popularity to become Universal's biggest moneymaker that year. Lugosi's interpretation of the immortal Count, dressed in tuxedo and tails, long opera cape flowing behind him, would become the standard for all movie vampires that followed.

It's interesting to note that even though Lugosi was not Universal's first choice for the movie version, he became so identified with the role of Dracula that it was difficult for him to find non-villain roles. Lugosi continued to play various vampires, mad doctors, and evil henchmen throughout his career, including the faux vampire of *Mark of the Vampire* (1935, a remake of *London after Midnight*) and the mad creator of a giant vampire bat in *The Devil Bat* (1940). He donned his trademark cape to play Count Armand Tesla in *Return of the Vampire* (1943), which notably placed its vampire in a very contemporary setting, resurrected from his London grave by a bomb during the Nazi blitz. The film climaxed with the first graphic onscreen vampire disintegration as the sun's rays melted Lugosi's features from his skull. Lugosi finally returned to the role of Count Dracula in Universal's 1948 horror comedy farce, *Abbott and Costello Meet Frankenstein* (1948).

Lugosi's final role was as a vampire in Ed Wood's *Plan 9 from Outer Space* (American Releasing Corporation, 1958). *Dracula*'s parent studio, Universal, also produced a sequel, *Dracula's Daughter* (1936), starring Gloria Holden as the count's daughter, whose overt lesbian desire for a female victim laid the groundwork for the lesbian vampire films of the 1970s.

Universal found other actors to replace Lugosi for its procession of screen Draculas: Lon Chaney Jr. was Count Alucard in *Son of Dracula* (1943), and John Carradine was the first to sport the mustache worn by the vampire of Stoker's novel for *House of Frankenstein* (1944) and *House of Dracula* (1945). Other fresh variations on the theme included Humphrey Bogart's turn as the first medical vampire (dependent on transfusions instead of fangs) in Warner Brothers' *The Return of Dr. X* (1939), producer Val Lewton's use of the Greek *vyrkolaka* legend in the atmospheric *Isle of the Dead* (RKO, 1945), and the screen's first vampire dog (walking through walls and supping on blood) in Monogram's *The Face of Marble* (1946).

It wasn't until 1935 that the vampire made his first appearance in a comic book. *New Fun Comics* #6, published by National Periodical Publications (DC), featured a story titled "Dr. Occult Vs. The Vampire Master," written and drawn by Jerry Siegel and Joe Shuster—the creators of Superman.

Batman, the Dark Knight Detective, had his first run-in with a vampire back in 1939. *Detective Comics* #31 and #32 featured a red-robed vampire villain called the Monk who became interested in millionaire Bruce Wayne's (Batman's) then girlfriend.

Writers in the 1940s continued to play with the vampire Mythos. Science fiction writer A. E. Van Vogt was the first to combine elements of horror and science fiction with his 1942 short story,

"Asylum." The story gave us vampires not from Eastern Europe but from the stars. Those space travelers fed on the various life-forms of other planets before finally reaching Earth.

But, even as vampires were beginning to change in novels and short stories, more traditional vampires were flourishing in comic books. A *Nosferatu*-like vampire appeared on the cover of the first horror anthology comic, the Avon one-shot *Eerie* #1 (1947). American Comic Group introduced the first successful comic-book horror title, *Adventures into the Unknown*, which remains the longest-lived horror comic ever, running for 174 issues between 1948 and 1967. This series nearly always featured at least one vampire story, as well as other lurid tales of terror. *Adventures into the Unknown* was so successful that other comic-book publishers began springing up to try and grab a piece of the pie.

In 1950, Educational Comics (EC) published its first horror title, *Crypt of Terror*, which would later become *Tales from the Crypt*. This title was so successful that EC launched two other titles the same year, to meet the growing demand for horror comics. *Haunt of Fear* and *Vault of Horror*, All three titles frequently featured vampires in their monthly tales of terror. In 1953, the periodical version of *Eerie*, published by Avon Periodicals, featured the first comic-book adaptation of *Dracula*, indicating that Stoker's tale was still looked to as the primary archetype.

It was not until 1954 that another vampire novel was able to have any lasting literary impact. Richard Matheson took the traditional concepts of vampires and vampirism and mixed them with elements of science fiction in his masterpiece, *I Am Legend*. The book told the tale of a biological dis-

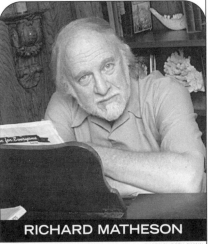

RICHARD MATHESON

PHOTO BY BETH GWINN

ease that transformed people into vampires as well as of the one man immune to that plague. The novel successfully altered the traditional setting. *I Am Legend* took the vampire out of its archetypal old-world environment and placed the horror in a realistic urban setting. The novel was reportedly the inspiration for the influential 1968 Image Ten horror film *Night of the Living Dead*.

Even as the literary representation of vampires explored new horizons, 1954 saw the end of horror comics. Child psychologists had begun to grow alarmed by the popularity of horror comics. One psychologist in particular, Dr. Frederick Wertham, believed the sex and violence he was finding in horror comics such as *Vault of Horror* and *Tales from the Crypt* was somehow responsible for the increase in juvenile delinquency in the United States. (His claim sounds chillingly familiar in light of recent violent events in the United States, and the political climate surrounding them.)

Wertham's 1953 book, *The Seduction of the Innocent,* demanded that such comic books no longer be published. Comic-book publishers, chastised by the 1954 Senate Subcommittee investigation and hearings led by Senator Estes Kefauver, skirted possible government censorship by forming a self-regulatory group called the Comic Magazine Association of America (CMAA) in hopes of keeping the government out of their business. CMAA in turn created the Comics Code, an attempt to control the glamorization of crime and the portrayal of graphic violence in comics.

Of course, the horror comic was targeted. The Comics Code called for the discontinuance of the words *horror* and *terror* in comic books and subjects like the walking dead, torture, werewolves, ghouls, cannibals, and vampires were forbidden.

As the comics industry was driving a stake into the heart of the vampire, the movie industry was about to breathe new life into the undead. The Turkish adaptation of Stoker's novel, *Drakula Istanbulda* (1953), is important for having introduced the real-life, historical Dracula, Vlad Tepes, to the tradition, incorporating elements from Ali Riza Seyfi's novel *The Impaling Voivode*.

The American science fiction and monster movie boom of the 1950s quickly found ways to incorporate vampire themes into their atom-age scenarios. The fleetingly glimpsed extraterrestrial invader of *The Thing from Another World* (RKO/Winchester Pictures, 1951) proved to be a vanguard for the alien and space-age vampires that appeared in *Not of This Earth* (Allied Artists, 1957), *It, The Terror from Beyond Space* (Vogue/United Artists, 1958), *The First Man into Space* (Amalgamated/MGM, 1958), and Lugosi's cameo in *Plan 9 from Outer Space*.

Pharmaceuticals turned scientist John Beal into *The Vampire* (United Artists, 1957), while the teen monster craze spawned the girls' school vampiress of *Blood of Dracula* (American International Pictures, 1957), the successor to the popular *I Was a Teenage Werewolf* (American International Pictures, 1957).

The giant monster craze created by America's post-Hiroshima fears of atomic disaster invited the *Attack of the Giant Leeches* (Sinister Cinema, 1959), and ongoing popularity of the 1950s Westerns led to the inevitable hybrid, the first gunslinger vampire (Michael Pate), in *Curse of the Undead* (Universal, 1959). As the sci-fi monster boom fizzled out, the Gothic tradition reasserted itself in the underrated *The Return of Dracula* (Gramercy/United Artists, 1957) and the Italian *The Devil's Commandment* (1956), which was photographed by Italian cinematographer Mario Bava.

The Hammer horror film was born in 1958. Hammer Films was a British studio that had gained notice for bringing a new dimension to classic horror stories. Universal Pictures, which owned the movie rights to both *Frankenstein* and *Dracula,* was no longer interested in producing horror films. The owners of Universal worked out a deal that allowed Hammer to make new pictures based on their classic monster properties.

Hammer's first production under this deal was *The Curse of Frankenstein* (1957), a Technicolor version of Mary Shelley's classic tale of a man-made monster. Audiences, used to the black-and-white subtleties of the old Universal productions, were shocked by the film's graphic violence and bloodshed.

Hammer immediately launched into their interpretation of the next Universal property, *Dracula*. The film was called *The Horror of Dracula* (1958), and it brought an entirely new atmosphere to the vampire film. Based loosely on Universal's *Dracula* and Stoker's novel, *The Horror of Dracula* gave audiences a much more intense interpretation of the classic story. For the first time, dripping red blood flowed freely and razor-sharp fangs protruded menacingly from the mouths of the vampires.

The Hammer film also introduced a far more overt sexuality to the character. One explanation for this is the actor who portrayed Dracula, Christopher Lee. A tall, dark, charismatic actor who lent a certain animal magnetism to the role, Lee's Dracula was savage and athletic, bounding around rooms doing battle with his nemesis, Professor Van Helsing, as portrayed by the great British actor Sir Peter Cushing.

The Horror of Dracula was an enormous success. Christopher Lee became an international star and Hammer films the most successful British film studio since World War II. Hammer mounted a worthy sequel, *The Brides of Dracula* (1960), pitting Peter Cushing's Van Helsing against the blond Baron Meinster (David Peel), who turns his mother into a vampire and preys on a nearby girls' school. Lee returned to play the resilient vampire in six more films, *Dracula Prince of Darkness* (1965), *Dracula Has Risen from the Grave* (1968), *Taste the Blood of Dracula* (1969), *Scars of Dracula* (1970), *Dracula A.D. 1972* (1972) and, finally, *The Satanic Rites of Dracula*, also released as *Count Dracula and His Vampire Brides* (1973). Lee also appeared in his Dracula apparel in the Italian horror comedy *Uncle Was a Vampire* (Embassy, 1959), *The Magic Christian* (1969), and the French spoof *Dracula and Son* (Quartet Films, 1976), and played Count Karnstein in the Italian "Carmilla" adaptation, *Terror in the Crypt* (1963).

Thanks to the success of the Hammer Dracula series, the Gothic vampire film enjoyed an international renaissance. The most striking Hammer contemporaries heralded from Italy, which offered *The Vampire and the Ballerina* (Consorzio Italiano, 1960), *Goliath and the Vampires* (Ambrosiana Cinematografica/AIP, 1961), and Mario Bava's rich efforts. Bava's first complete directorial outing, *Black Sunday* (American-International, 1960), made Barbara Steele a genre icon in her dual role as the two-hundred-year-old vampire witch Asa and her innocent descendant, and established Bava's lush visual style with this, the last great black-and-white Gothic horror film.

Bava went on to cast Christopher Lee as the vampirelike ruler of Hades in *Hercules in the Haunted World* (Omnia S.P.A. Cinematografica, 1961). Bava returned to vampiric themes in the third story of the anthology film *Black Sabbath* (Galatea/Emmepil/Cinematografica/AIP, 1963), featuring Boris Karloff in his only vampire role as the blood-drinking *vourdalak* derived from Aleksei Tolstoi's novella, and the colorful vampires-in-space romp *Planet of the Vampires* (1965).

Former underground filmmaker Curtis Harrington offered his own breed of extraterrestrial vampire in *Queen of Blood* (American International, 1966), starring the exotic Florence Marley as a mute, green-blooded hemophiliac vampiress. A decade later, this science-fiction detour culminated in Colin Wilson's novel *The Space Vampires* (Random House, 1976), which proposed extraterrestrial origins for our planet's vampire legends. Tobe Hooper filmed Wilson's novel as *Lifeforce* (Cannon/Tri-Star, 1985).

In all media, the vampire was increasingly sexualized in taboo-breaking narratives. In Theodore Sturgeon's novel *Some of Your Blood* (1961), vampirism is a purely psychosexual disorder. One of Hammer's best non-Dracula vampire films, *Kiss of the Vampire* (1962), inspired Roman Polanski's black comedy *The Fearless Vampire Killers* (Cadre and Filmways, 1967), a sly satire that introduced the first Jewish vampire (unfazed by the crucifix), the first gay male vampire, and the first twist ending in which the vampires were triumphant—another taboo broken.

The 1960s vampire films were book-ended with adaptations of Le Fanu's "Carmilla" emphasizing bisexual and lesbian elements, beginning with Roger Vadim's stylish *Blood and Roses* (EGE Films/Documento Films, 1960), and closing with Hammer's *The Vampire Lovers* (1970), in which Ingrid Pitt flaunted her charms with unprecedented enthusiasm. Spurred by the film's worldwide success, Hammer followed with Pitt as the notorious Elizabeth Bathory in *Countess Dracula* (1971), and the fresh blood of *Vampire Circus* (1971), *Twins of Evil* (1972), *Captain Kronos, Vampire Hunter* (1973), and a more explicitly sexual "Carmilla" variation, *Lust for a Vampire* (1971).

Continuing a trend toward more creative twists on vampire lore, Spain offered Paul Naschy's film *Count Dracula's Great Love* (Janus/Eva, 1972) and the tragic end-of-the-dynasty *The Dracula Saga* (1972), memorable for its vampire baby, the final heir to the name. The German *Jonathan* (Iduna/New Yorker, 1970) adapted Stoker's novel as a political metaphor for Hitler and the Nazi party's rise to power.

Increasingly marginalized by the more explicit modern horror film extremes and a changing marketplace, Hammer made a last-ditch attempt to regain its claim on the genre. Among these efforts was a fascinating but misbegotten attempt to mix horror with the martial arts Kung Fu film trend, *Legend of the Seven Golden Vampires*.

By 1962, compliance with the Comics Code was taking its toll. The Code tolerated a Draculalike character that popped up in comedy-star DC comics like *Bob Hope* and *The Adventures of Jerry Lewis*, but that was all. Publishers were not allowed to profit from the renewed popularity of the horror genre. Aurora Model Kits launched a profitable series of plastic model kits depicting the Universal Monsters—including Dracula, second in the series and among its most popular. Ironically, these model kits were advertised in Code-approved comics that were forbidden to feature vampires, werewolves, or the walking dead in their stories.

However, three publishers—Gilberton Publications, Dell, and Gold Key—had never signed with the Comics Code Authority. Having firmly established a reputation for publishing wholesome comics and a strong newsstand presence prior to the Code's existence, they alone were free to exploit the early 1960s horror "boom." Gilberton Publications rushed its *Classics Illustrated* adaptations of *Frankenstein* and *Dr. Jekyll and Mr. Hyde* into multiple printings with new painted covers, and Dell topped it by licensing the Universal Monsters from its parent studio. *Dracula* hit the comic racks in 1962, and it was one of the best in the series, loosely adapting the 1931 film and gleefully detailing atrocities that had been barred from the newsstand for almost a decade: giant bats carrying off screaming victims, premature burials, and more.

With the success of two horror-based comedy shows on TV, *The Munsters* and *The Addams Family*, the comics publisher Gold Key, known for its media tie-ins, licensed the rights to both series. Both shows featured vampirelike characters—Morticia on *The Addams Family* and Grandpa and Lily on *The Munsters*—who should not have been allowed to appear in comic books. Despite that obvious conflict, however, *The Munsters* comic was published in 1965.

Dell and Gold Key also licensed more horrific fare: Dell's *The Twilight Zone* was very popular, and was eventually picked up by Gold Key to continue in the 1980s, occasionally featuring vampires. Gold Key also licensed Boris Karloff's *Thriller*, which was changed to *Boris Karloff's Tales of Mystery* and continued into the 1970s, as did *Ripley's Believe It or Not True Ghost Stories*, many of which had their share of tame bloodsuckers.

Famous Monsters of Filmland publisher James Warren circumvented the Code with magazine-format publications (magazines were exempt from the Code). *Famous Monsters* proved so successful during the early 1960s horror boom that Warren launched a sister title, *Monster World*, which began to run tightly written and drawn "monster comics" in every issue, beginning with an adaptation of Hammer's *Horror of Dracula.* Those led to a trio of one-shot photo-fumetti comic magazines, horror movie adaptations in comic format using stills, frame blow-ups, and word balloons to tell the stories. The third, and most successful, of these adapted the Hammer double feature *Curse of*

Frankenstein and *Horror of Dracula*, and featured a shot of Dracula's final decomposition that had been cut from the U.S. version of the film.

Warren subsequently launched his horror comics, *Creepy* (1964) and *Eerie* (1965), as black-and-white magazines, racked apart from the comics and therefore still exempt from Code regulation. Editor/writer Archie Goodwin had been a great fan of the EC comics, and he crafted a series of excellent scripts for many EC veteran artists. *Creepy* was hosted by the cadaverous Uncle Creepy and *Eerie* by his corpulent Cousin Eerie. In the tradition of EC Comics, the magazines contained stories about all manner of monsters: ghouls, goblins, ghosts, animated corpses, zombies, ax murderers, genetic mutations—and, of course, vampires.

On ABC television in 1967 a daytime soap opera called *Dark Shadows* was not performing well in the ratings. Its creator, Dan Curtis, added a brooding, tortured vampire by the name of Barnabas Collins to the show. Reportedly, the idea was to introduce the vampire and then get rid of him when the ratings improved. However, the show became a hit and Barnabas Collins a household name. The character even starred in the 1970 film *House of Dark Shadows*. Once again the dark allure of the vampire had captured the imagination of the general public.

In 1969, thanks in large part to the success of Warren Publishing's *Creepy* and *Eerie* and a revitalized interest in horror on television, pressure was on the rise from color comic-book publishers to revise the Comics Code. Yet again, Gold Key led the challenge when it produced the comic-book version of *Dark Shadows*. It was the first serious color comic-book title to feature a vampire as its main character since the introduction of the Code.

Meanwhile, Warren Publishing was riding high, producing its third black-and-white horror magazine, *Vampirella,* created to cash in on the success of the 1968 Jane Fonda science fiction film *Barbarella: Queen of the Galaxy* (Paramount). Inspired in part by character co-creator (and editor of *Famous Monsters*) Forrest J. Ackerman's affection for the American International film *Queen of Blood* (in which he had a cameo, displaying the female vampire's eggs), *Vampirella* featured a scantily clad female vampire from outer space and quickly became a hit.

By the time it ceased publication in 1983, *Vampirella* had become one of the longest running and most popular vampire comics in the history of the medium. In 1991 Harris Comics obtained the rights to the character and began publishing monthly comic books. As of this writing, *Vampirella* is still being published.

A bracingly contemporary, street-smart urbanity lent an edge to the vampire films of the 1970s, anticipating the savvier generation of *Buffy the Vampire Slayer* viewers who have seen the key vampire films and have at least rudimentary knowledge of the lore. A planned sex film titled *The Lovers of Count Iorga* was softened to *Count Yorga, Vampire* (Erica/American International, 1970), starring Robert Quarry as the suave vampire guru who finds a comfy niche in post–Charles Manson Los Angeles, feeding on hippies and fringe freaks until the nifty twist ending echoing Polanski's *Fearless Vampire Killers*.

Quarry was back in the upscale remake *The Return of Count Yorga* (American International/Peppertree, 1971) and as a more Manson-like *Deathmaster* (AIP, 1972). Hippie and redneck vampires also populated the eerie, underrated *Let's Scare Jessica to Death* (Jessica Co., 1971).

William Marshall starred as *Blacula* (American International, 1972), an African prince cursed by the bite of slavemaster Dracula, who finds true love in modern-day Harlem; he was back, seeking a cure from voodoo priestess Pam Grier in *Scream, Blacula, Scream!* (American International, 1973). Black filmmaker Bill Gunn made *Ganja & Hess* (1972), rooting its arty vampire tale in indigenous African myth and emphasizing the culture clash with Christian beliefs and artifacts.

Michael Pataki played a vampire in *Grave of the Vampire* (Entertainment Pyramid/Millennium, 1972), which is of particular interest for the notion that vampirism is hereditary.

The best of the lot came out of Pittsburgh, home of George Romero's *Martin* (Laurel Group/Libra, 1976), the downbeat chronicle of a misfit teenage orphan who may or may not be an eighty-year-old vampire. Forced to live with a strict, suspicious Old-World relative eager to end the boy's "Nosferatu" ways, fangless Martin has no supernatural powers and uses razor blades and hypos to feed. He is plagued with guilt over his twisted sexuality, his victims, and an affair with an unhappy older woman, the first "normal" sexual encounter of his life, and seeks comfort in confessing all to a late-night radio talk show host who laughingly called him "the Count." Alas, there is no comfort—this is, after all, a George Romero movie—and teenage vampires would never be the same.

Andy Warhol had already put out his NYC underground take on *Batman Dracula* (Filmmaker's Cooperative, 1964), but Warhol's frequent director/collaborator Paul Morrissey topped them all with the X-rated *Andy Warhol's Dracula* (aka *Blood for Dracula*, Bryanton Pictures, 1973), in which Udo Keir's sullen count scours the countryside for "wirgin's" blood and vomits gore when he sips on unpure blood. The film's cult stature cannot be underestimated: Keir, whose allure blends the exotic accent and sex appeal of Lugosi with the self-deprecating humor and bulging eyes of Peter Lorre, has become an iconic participant in many 1990s vampire films, including *Blade* (New Line, 1998) and *Modern Vampires* (1999).

Bowing to the tenor of the times, and embarrassed by the considerable success of a Spider-Man antidrug story that Marvel Comics published without the Code seal of approval, the Comics Code was finally revised in 1971. Though the Code still discouraged the depiction of gore, torture, and sadistic acts, its stand on creatures of the supernatural, including vampires, was reversed. Vampires, ghouls, and werewolves could now appear in comic books, provided they were portrayed as they were in classic literature. With only that restriction, monsters were on their way back into the four-color world of comics.

With the revision, Marvel Comics jumped on the horror bandwagon in 1971 with *Tomb of Dracula*. Considered by many to be the finest vampire comic ever produced, *Tomb of Dracula* resurrected the count and set his new adventures in the 1970s U.S.A. This Dracula was a complex, multilayered character with a range of emotions and feelings about his place in the world. The series also boasted a strong supporting cast made up of descendants from the characters of Stoker's novel who had joined together to combat the newly resurrected evil of Dracula. *Tomb of Dracula* also introduced readers to Blade, the vampire slayer, made ever more popular by the hit 1998 New Line movie of the same name, starring Wesley Snipes.

Dracula was also integrated into the Marvel Universe of superhero figures, eventually mingling with such characters as the Silver Surfer, Thor, and even the X-Men.

Suddenly vampires were all the rage at Marvel. In 1971 *The Amazing Spider-Man* introduced one of the arachnid hero's strangest villains. Michael Morbius was a brilliant scientist transformed into the Marvel Universe's first science-based vampire. Morbius, the living vampire, would continue to appear in Spider-Man's various titles as well as headlining *Adventure into Fear*. He received his own series in 1992. It ran for twenty-five issues.

The revision of the Comics Code also made way for the slow rise of vampire themes in juvenile literature that culminated with an explosion of vampire stories for all ages in the late '80s. The Hardy Boys mystery series was the first to use a vampire theme, in book #50, *Danger on the Vampire Trail*, published in 1971. The popular children's PBS series *Sesame Street* introduced Count von Count, a Bela Lugosi–type character whose specialty was counting. In 1979, Deborah and James Howe introduced the lovable vegetarian rabbit, *Bunnicula*. Bunnicula was found in a theater during a screening of *Dracula* by Pete and Toby Monroe, who took him home. Bunnicula was a strange rabbit with fangs rather than the usual bunny buckteeth. He also slept all day and raided the refrigerator at night. The popular story spawned a series of books throughout the 1980s beginning with *The Celery Stalks at Midnight* in 1983 and was filmed as an animated children's movie in 1987. The 1980s and '90s proved ripe for young people's horror fiction. Some of the more popular series that favored vampire stories included *The Fifth Grade Monsters* by Mel Gilden, *Goosebumps* by R. L. Stine, and, specifically for high schoolers, *The Vampire Diaries* by L. J. Smith.

Vampires were hotter than ever. Embracing the street-smart edge of its big-screen contemporaries, television producer Dan Curtis, who had brought Barnabas Collins to the world, would again be responsible for introducing one of the genre's most influential characters. *The Night Stalker*, which aired in 1972 on ABC during its Movie of the Week slot, is easily one of the best vampire films ever produced.

The Night Stalker, about a vampire loose in Las Vegas and the reporter who pursues him, was based on a story by writer Jeff Rice and produced by Curtis, with a screenplay by Richard Matheson (*I Am Legend*). *The Night Stalker* introduces us to Carl Kolchak, one of the most unique characters in TV history. As played by Darren McGavin, Kolchak is a typical down-on-his-luck reporter looking for that next big story, poking his nose into areas where it doesn't belong and stumbling onto things best left undiscovered.

The movie did so well that Kolchak soon returned in another telefilm, *The Night Strangler*, also produced by Curtis with a script by Matheson. The second movie performed as well as the first and prompted ABC to give Kolchak his own series, retitled *Kolchak: The Night Stalker*. It lasted only one season but proved to be extremely influential for many future television creators. In fact, *X-Files* creator Chris Carter often cites *The Night Stalker* as a source of inspiration for his hit television series. There are even rumors circulating that Carl Kolchak may return in the foreseeable future on the big screen as well as in books and comic books.

In 1972 vampires became a little more real thanks to the publication of *In Search of Dracula*, by Raymond T. McNally and Radu Florescu, which was the first book about the real man thought to have served as partial inspiration for Stoker's *Dracula*. McNally and Florescu told the story of the fifteenth-century Romanian prince Vlad, whose cruelty and ruthlessness earned him the nickname "the Impaler." Although his reign was brief, only six years, Vlad the Impaler is thought to have been responsible for the deaths of some forty thousand people. A highly popular and critically acclaimed book, *In Search of Dracula* sparked a renewed interest in vampire lore by adding a historical dimension to the previously superficially treated character. A documentary feature film version played theaters the same year, and Richard Matheson's TV movie adaptation of *Dracula* (1974) for producer Dan Curtis meshed the historical Vlad the Impaler into its compelling portrayal of the count (Jack Palance).

In 1973 Marvel Comics threw itself headlong into the monster craze, unleashing its own line of black-and-white horror magazines, including *Dracula Lives* and *Vampire Tales*, both of which featured recurring characters and short, self-contained horror stories. *Dracula Lives* featured the count as seen in the color *Tomb of Dracula* series, but in much more violent, adult story lines. *Vampire Tales* also contained more mature story lines, but focused on Morbius the Living Vampire as a regular character.

Tomb of Dracula inspired a fresh vein of vampire media when it was adapted to animation by Toei Animation for broadcast on Japanese television in 1979. A variety of anime blood drinkers, prominent among them *Vampire Hunter D* (Epic/Sony/Streamline Pictures, 1985), followed soon thereafter.

There was little innovation in the vampire novel from Matheson's *I Am Legend* and Sturgeon's *Some of Your Blood* until Stephen King's novel *'Salem's Lot* (1975), in which the author managed to put a new spin on the classic vampire archetype. *'Salem's Lot* recasts the basic structure of *Dracula* in small-town America, giving the classic tale a modern perspective and creating of it something wholly new.

Originally entitled *Second Coming*, *'Salem's Lot* involves a small town in Maine being slowly infested with the evil of vampirism. The mysterious European nobleman who is in fact a bloodthirsty, supernatural monster; the horrific creature attempting to spread its evil in a new land; the stalwart band of heroes who discover the threat and attempt to thwart the monster's plans—King took all the characteristics we had come to associate with the traditional vampire novel or film and portrayed them in a contemporary way that made them seem not only fresh, but intimate and familiar, and all the more frightening for that.

The novel was adapted to television for a CBS-TV miniseries in 1979. Writer-director Larry Cohen produced a direct-to-video sequel, *A Return to 'Salem's Lot*, in 1987.

Following on the heels of *'Salem's Lot* was Anne Rice's novel *Interview with the Vampire,* published in 1976. Since then, the novel and its many sequels have dramatically altered pop-culture perception of the vampire. *Interview* is the story of Louis—a man transformed into a vampire centuries ago—as told to a young reporter. The novel gave perhaps the first intimate peek into what it might be like to become a vampire—to *be* a vampire.

Interview with the Vampire also introduces Lestat de Lioncourt, the vampire responsible for changing Louis. Through these two characters the reader experiences their strange, alternative lifestyle, and mainstream popular culture is presented with the amorphous sexuality of the vampire in a manner that could not be ignored. Lestat has since become a major figure in contemporary vampire fiction, returning in numerous Anne Rice novels including *The Vampire Lestat* (1985), *The Queen of the Damned* (1988), *The Tale of the Body Thief* (1992), and *Memnoch the Devil* (1995), among many others.

In her books, Rice eliminates many of the myths we had come to associate with vampires subsequent to Stoker's novel. Her vampires are not affected by religious artifacts, cannot turn into animals, and need not rest in a coffin filled with their native soil. Although they do sometimes sleep in coffins, Rice's vampires seem just as comfortable burrowed beneath the earth for their daily rest. Rice's vampires are nearly immortal, but can be killed by exposure to sunlight. By removing many of the restrictions legend and folklore had placed on vampires, Rice managed to at least partially humanize them, and yet they are even more horrifying for all of that.

While Anne Rice was giving us sympathetic vampires, Fred Saberhagen, Les Daniels, and Chelsea Quinn Yarbro introduced us to the concept of vampires as heroes. In 1975 Saberhagen wrote *The Dracula Tapes*, a retelling of Stoker's *Dracula,* which recast the count not as a monster but as a good guy of sorts. Saberhagen continued to portray Dracula as hero with six more works; *The Holmes Dracula File* (1978), *An Old Friend of the Family* (1979), *Thorn* (1980), *Dominion* (1982), *A Matter of Taste* (1990), and *A Question of Time* (1992).

In 1978 Les Daniels's *Black Castle* introduced his gentleman vampire, Don Sebastian de Villanueva, an honorable monster living among despicable examples of humanity. Don Sebastian would return in four other installments; *The Silver Skull* (1979), *Citizen Vampire* (1981), *Yellow Fog* (1988), and *No Blood Spilled* (1991).

Also in 1978, in the novel *Hotel Transylvania*, Chelsea Quinn Yarbro introduced us to her character, the Count de Saint Germain. Based on a mysterious alchemist who appears in various eras of history, the fictional Saint Germain is a romantic figure who happens also to be a vampire. In the no less than fifteen volumes in the Saint Germain series (including the short-story collection *The Saint Germain Chronicles* (1983) and the three volumes dedicated to Saint Germain's vampire lover, Atta Olivia Clemens), the count interacts with historical figures over a three-thousand-year span. Subsequent books in the series include *The Palace* (1979), *Blood Games* (1980), *Path of the Eclipse* (1981), *Tempting Fate* (1982), *Out of the House of Life* (1990), *Better in the Dark* (1993), *Darker Jewels* (1993), *Mansions of Darkness* (1996), *Writ in Blood* (1997), *Blood Roses* (1998), and *Communion Blood* (1999).

In the late 1970s and early '80s, the horror comic was beginning to experience a decline. The cancellation of *Tomb of Dracula* came in 1979 after seventy issues and *Vampirella* followed in 1983. Marvel tried to renew interest in its failing black-and-white comic magazine line with a new *Tomb of Dracula* title, but that was canceled after only six issues.

While interest in the count was flagging in comics, it was thriving in film and onstage. In 1977 the BBC and American Public Television produced a version of Stoker's *Dracula* for public television. *Count Dracula* starred Louis Jourdan in the title role. The longest of the *Dracula* adaptations, coming in at 135 minutes, it is also the most faithful version of Stoker's book, retaining all of the characters from the novel. Jourdan brings a cool, European manner to the role of Dracula, yet an intense savagery seethes beneath his stare.

In 1978 Frank Langella assumed the role of Dracula in a new Broadway production of the Hamilton Deane/John Bladerston version of *Dracula*. Langella portrayed a very sexual, sensual creature. This was a Dracula that audiences could connect with—not a monster, but a thinking, feeling being. The play received two Tony awards and Langella was asked to reprise his role in Universal's 1979 big screen version.

The 1980s and '90s brought an incredible surge in vampire literature and films. In 1981, despite the decline of horror in comics, DC Comics successfully introduced a new feature in its *House of Mystery* series called "I. . .Vampire." Running for three years, "I. . .Vampire" told the story of Lord Andrew Bennet, a war hero who was bitten and transformed into a vampire.

Two more novels that took the literary vampire in interesting directions were published in 1981. The first, *They Thirst* by Robert McCammon, tells the epic story of a vampire plague overrunning

Los Angeles. *They Thirst* abandons the then-popular themes of vampires as sexy, tormented beings and brings us back to basics. The vampires of this novel are foul, savage monsters with distending fangs like rattlesnakes. There is nothing even remotely sensual about McCammon's interpretation of the undead.

The second novel of note in 1981 was Whitley Strieber's *The Hunger*, which introduces the fascinating character of Miriam Blaylock and the concept that vampires are a separate species of life upon the planet. Miriam has the ability to transform humans into vampires, but they are not immortal and over time experience accelerated aging while the consciousness continues to survive. The book tells the story of Miriam's search for a cure for this condition so her current lover will not suffer the same horrible fate as others she has turned throughout the centuries. Strieber does a wonderful job of emphasizing the loneliness Miriam feels as the last immortal of her kind. Tony Scott's theatrical feature adaptation, *The Hunger* (MGM/UA, 1983), emphasized stylish confection.

In 1983 Dracula was again proving to be a threat to the Marvel Universe. In *Doctor Strange* #62, Dracula faces off against the Sorcerer Supreme in an epic battle to the death. At the climax, Strange performs a magical ritual called the Montesi Formula that supposedly destroys all the vampires in the Marvel Universe. This story was reportedly the result of an editorial edict that claimed there were too many vampires in the Marvel Universe and it was time to clean house.

Although fewer vampire stories were being published, there was no danger that fascination with them would ever really die. At DC a two-part story in the series *Saga of the Swamp Thing* gave us one of the more interesting takes on the vampire to appear in quite some time. That 1985 storyline introduced a race of vampires that evolved under water after their vampire-infested town had flooded years earlier.

Also in 1985, Columbia Pictures released the film *Fright Night,* in which a teenage boy is convinced that his new next-door neighbor is a vampire but can't get anyone to believe him. Desperate for help, the teenager seeks the aid of a washed-out horror-movie actor and host of a local *Creature Feature*–type program. Of course the neighbor really is a vampire and the two unlikely heroes must enter the home of the monster and vanquish him. Part comedy, part thriller, *Fright Night* combined elements of the classic horror film with modern special effects to make it one of the best big-screen vampire efforts in years.

In 1986 the evolution of the modern vampire took another turn, with the publication of John Skipp and Craig Spector's *The Light at the End*, a novel greatly influenced by the punk rock movement that swept the United Kingdom and much of the United States in the early 1980s.

With this novel, Skipp and Spector reminded its readers that there are still quite a few scary things to be said about vampires. The vampire fiction that followed in its wake would also be informed by the very real dread of a new, modern, blood-linked plague, HIV, the virus that causes AIDS. One notable example is Tim Lucas' stream-of-consciousness 1994 novel *Throat Sprockets*.

Also in 1986, the American comic-book industry was beginning to expand and advances in printing technology were making it easier for smaller, independent publishers to produce quality comics. The new publishers were looking for something more exciting than the standard superhero fare currently dominating the marketplace at that time. Warp Comics gave us the first of several new vampire titles, *Blood of the Innocent*. Another young company, Apple Comics, produced its own title featuring the immortal count, *Blood of Dracula*. Soon thereafter, Eternity Comics, yet another new publisher, produced an adaptation of Stoker's *Dracula* and another series that pitted Count Dracula against Sherlock Holmes, called *Scarlet in Gaslight*.

A pair of films released in 1987 brought a freshness to the movie vampire. What Skipp and Spector's *The Light at the End* did for vampire novels, director Kathryn Bigelow's *Near Dark* did for vampire movies. *Near Dark* is the tale of a Texas teen transformed by the bite of a sexy vampire and forced to join a gang of the nastiest redneck bloodsuckers one will ever see on screen. The movie completely dispenses with any Gothic trappings, feeling more like a modern western than traditional vampire fare. *Near Dark* is widely considered to be one of the best vampire pictures ever produced.

The second film, *The Lost Boys,* is part *Near Dark* and part *Peter Pan* as it tells the story of a youthful gang of punk vampires who stalk the boardwalk of a sleepy California coastal town. Not as intense as *Near Dark*, *The Lost Boys* still delivers cheap chills, laughs, and some interesting makeup effects in the look of the vampires.

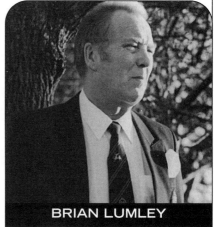

BRIAN LUMLEY

PHOTO BY BETH GWINN

British author **Brian Lumley** brought a wild twist to the vampire Mythos with his novel, *Necroscope*, published in 1986. Harry Keogh is a man who has the ability to communicate with the dead—a Necroscope. Keogh's unique powers push him into the world of espionage, where he is pitted against a Russian necromancer who has powerful connections to an ancient vampire, Thibor Frenczy. Lumley's take on vampires steers clear of Anne Rice territory and gives us vampires as vicious, shapeshifting monsters. There's nothing tragic about these guys.

Necroscope spawned no fewer than a dozen sequels: *Vamphyri!* (1988*), The Source* (1989), *Deadspeak* (1990), *Deadspawn* (1991), *Blood Brothers* (1992), *The Last Aerie* (1993), *Bloodwars* (1994), *The Lost Years* (1995), *Resurgence* (1996), *Invaders* (1999), and two others unreleased as of this writing. In 1992 the Necroscope novels were adapted into comic book form by Malibu Comics Entertainment and later by Caliber Comics in 1997.

In 1989, and throughout the following decade, the theme of vampire as hero or protagonist became more popular than ever. Nancy A. Collins introduced us to Sonja Blue, a vampire that kills other vampires, in her 1989 novel *Sunglasses After Dark* and multiple sequels, including *In the Blood* (1992) and *Paint It Black* (1995). In 1990, P. N. Elrod released the first novel in her longrunning Vampire Files series featuring Jack Fleming, an investigative reporter transformed into a vampire who becomes a private eye.

Vampires were not only showing up as the good guys in book form, but also on film. *To Die For* (Skouras, 1989) and *To Die For II: Son of Darkness* (Arrowhead Entertainment, 1991) features a heroic Vlad Tepish in conflict with others of his ilk who are intent on making the world their feeding ground. A female vampire who only feeds on bad guys in the mob was the central character of *Innocent Blood* (Warner Brothers, 1992).

Television was also giving us the vampire hero with the 1989 ABC made-for-TV movie, *Nick*

Knight, featuring a vampire police detective fighting crime as well as the forces of evil. The movie spawned the popular syndicated series *Forever Knight*.

Author Dan Simmons took an interesting and original approach in his 1989 novel, *Carrion Comfort*, in which he introduced vampires that feed not on blood, but on the life energies of others—psychic vampires who secretly control the world. An equally inventive new take on vampires was present in Tim Powers's 1989 novel *The Stress of Her Regard*, in which the poets Byron, Keats, and Shelley struggle with their muses—erotic, serpentine, vampire women.

Vampires also made an enormous comeback in the comic-book industry beginning with Innovation Comics twelve-issue adaptation of Anne Rice's *The Vampire Lestat* in 1990. Following that success other companies jumped on the bandwagon and began doing comic adaptations of classic vampire works. Eclipse Comics translated Matheson's *I Am Legend* into a completely faithful four-issue black-and-white miniseries in 1991.

DC Comics put an interesting spin on its Batman character by doing a series of stories taking place on an alternate world where Batman had to face the threat of Dracula. *Batman and Dracula: Red Rain*, originally done as a fully illustrated hardcover, ended with Batman defeating Dracula, but not before being bitten and transformed. This vampiric take on one of comics' most popular characters led to two sequels, *Batman: Bloodstorm* (1994) and *Batman: Crimson Mist* (1999).

Meanwhile, Marvel Comics realized they had to reintroduce the creatures to their universe after having completely destroyed them in 1983. *Doctor Strange: Sorcerer Supreme* #14 announced the return of vampires to the Marvel Universe in the guise of Morbius, the living vampire. Morbius had been cured of his vampirism by Doctor Strange's Montesi Formula in 1983, but he was changed back following an encounter with the voodoo witch Marie Laveau. Morbius proved such an interesting character that Marvel awarded him his own series in 1992.

In the early '90s vampires also began invading the world of role-playing games, or RPGs. An RPG is a game played almost entirely in the imagination and usually centered on an another world, usually a fantasy or supernatural realm. In the '90s, vampires had become a topic of great interest. One of the most popular vampire role-playing games is *Vampire: The Masquerade*. Created and distributed by White Wolf Games, players create a character within the imaginary vampire communities and enact the almost infinite number of situations and stories that could possibly occur in a world where vampires walk among us.

Interestingly, author Nancy A. Collins published the novel *A Dozen Black Roses* in 1997, which incorporated her creation Sonja Blue into the world of *Vampire: The Masquerade*.

Thanks to Francis Ford Coppola, Dracula returned to the big screen in 1992 in yet another successful adaptation of Stoker's classic. *Bram Stoker's Dracula* was hailed as one of the most faithful adaptations of the novel but deviates in its attempt to make Dracula a more sympathetic character. Though often spectacular to look at and occasionally chilling, that adaptation does not compare to the BBC and American Public Broadcasting version.

Also on the big screen in 1992 was the movie version of *Buffy the Vampire Slayer* from Twentieth Century Fox. Starring Kristy Swanson as Buffy, and featuring Luke Perry, Donald Sutherland, Rutger Hauer, and Paul "Pee-Wee Herman" Reubens, the film was based on Joss Whedon's original screenplay, but with an added level of kitsch and silliness that defused the ominous elements of the story. Whedon wasn't really happy with the result, but his dissatisfaction would soon lead to a major turning point in vampire popularity in America.

Bolstered by the success of Coppola's take on *Dracula*, DC Comics gave vampires another try with the 1993 series *Scarlett* and a 1994 miniseries under DC's more adult Vertigo line called *Vamps*. *Scarlett* did not capture the audience it needed to run beyond twelve issues. *Vamps*, however, which focused on the bizarre concept of vampire biker chicks and their adventures on the road, was so successful it spawned two sequels, *Vamps: Hollywood in Vein* (1996) and *Vamps: Pumpkin Time* (1998).

Kim Newman's brilliant vampire novel *Anno Dracula* appeared in 1993. The book posited a world where Dracula had suborned English rule, and vampires were taking over. It was also an extraordinary catalog of cameos and in-jokes featuring vampires and vampire-hunters from throughout folklore and popular culture. There have been two sequels, *The Bloody Red Baron* (1995) and *Judgment of Tears: Anno Dracula 1959* (1998).

One of the most popular literary vampire series of the 1990s was born when the first novel in **Laurell K. Hamilton**'s Anita Blake, Vampire Hunter series was published in 1994. *The Laughing Corpse* introduced Blake and an alternate-reality world where vampirism is legal, lycanthropy is a well-known condition, and other supernatural creatures are almost com-

LAURELL K. HAMILTON

PHOTO BY BETH GWINN

mon. The successful series continued through nine more books to date, including *Guilty Pleasures* (1995), *The Circus of the Damned* (1995), *Obsidian Butterfly* (2000), and *Kiss of Shadows* (2000).

Also in 1994 the long delayed film version of Anne Rice's *Interview with the Vampire* was finally brought to the screen by Geffen/Warner Brothers. It starred movie heartthrob Tom Cruise as the vampire Lestat and equally hunky Brad Pitt as the tortured Louis. Despite the trepidation of some, the film proved to be one of the most intriguing vampire films ever made. Both Cruise and Pitt turned in strong performances as the vampire leads, but the young Kirsten Dunst as the forever-young vampire child, Claudia, stole the film.

Over at Marvel Comics, Blade, the vampire hunter who had first appeared in the classic *Tomb of Dracula*, was awarded his own series in 1994. Marvel had only recently canceled *Nightstalkers*, another action-horror series that featured Blade. Hopes that a film version, then in production, would bring a new and larger audience to the character did not materialize, and the series lasted only ten issues. In 1998 Marvel tried *Blade* one more time, following the release of the movie, but the comic failed again.

Despite the travails of Blade, however, vampires continue to have quite a presence as different pop-culture mediums search for a new slant to the old story. In 1996 a recently resurrected vampire warrior, Vladimir Giurescu, proved to be a thorn in the side of comic-book creator Mike Mignola's paranormal investigator, Hellboy. And at DC's Vertigo imprint, a rogue Irish vampire by the name of Cassidy is a regular cast member of the hit series *Preacher*. *Crimson*, a regular monthly series from DC/Wildstorm Comics, tells the story of a teenage boy coming to grips with the fact that not only has he been transformed into a vampire, but he may also be some kind of vampire equivalent to the Messiah. In *Astro City*, also from DC/Wildstorm, a mysterious crime fighter by the name of the Confessor has been revealed to be one of the undead.

Even Anne Rice, who continued her vampire series with *The Vampire Armand* in 1999, has re-entered the comic-book arena, joining with new publisher Sicilian Dragon Comics to produce an adaptation of her *Tale of the Body Thief*.

Hollywood is also looking for that fresh approach to an old subject matter. Owing a clear debt to George Romero's *Martin*, a new trend developed, anticipated by NYC indie filmmaker Buddy Giovinazzo's *Jonathan of the Night* and the rap music–influenced horror comedy *Def by Temptation* (Bonded Enterprises/Orpheus Picture/Troma, 1990). In *Nadja* (Kino Link, 1995), *The Addiction* (Fast, 1995), (2000 AD, 1987) and *Habit* (Glass Eye, 1997), a trio of New York City–based independent filmmakers explored a downbeat urban approach linking the craving for blood with drug addiction and the street life in the age of AIDS.

Blade, featuring Marvel's vampire slayer, was a major late-summer hit for New Line Pictures in 1998. Just as entertaining was *John Carpenter's Vampires* (Storm King/Largo/Film Office), a movie adaptation of John Steakley's novel, *Vampires,* about vampire hunters working for the Vatican. Carpenter gave us an interesting mixture indeed, paying homage to classic horror films as well as the Sergio Leone western.

John Carpenter's Vampires and *Blade* showed that the vampire has not worn out its welcome on the silver screen. Not even a well-placed stake could forever destroy the overwhelming presence of the vampire that has become such a major ingredient of our popular culture.

Network television in the 1990s found vampires scarce, possibly due to the failure of the attempted revival of *Dark Shadows* and the goth-opera vampire series *Kindred: The Embraced*. An episode of *The X-Files* offered one of the few well-received presentations of vampires during this period.

All of that changed on March 10, 1997, with the television debut of *Buffy the Vampire Slayer*, which has had perhaps the most significant impact on the presence of vampires in present-day popular culture. Unlike the campy tone of the film, the TV show offers humor that comes from the characters themselves, in a dark and dangerous supernatural setting. With its girl-power themes, and the manner in which it combines the heroic yet brooding modern vampire (Angel) with more traditional evil bloodsuckers, *Buffy* may well be the first postmodern vampire story.

In the fall of 1999, the vampire-with-a-soul from *Buffy the Vampire Slayer* received his own spin-off series, *Angel*, to excellent ratings and critical reception, putting the vampire more in the limelight of American pop culture than it had been in years.

In this new series, Angel works as an unlicensed private investigator operating out of an office in Los Angeles. Together with his girl Friday, *Buffy*'s Cordelia Chase, he helps people whose lives are endangered by supernatural forces. On *Angel*, the main character has now been revealed to be a warrior for the Powers That Be, a benevolent force in the universe. *Angel*'s debut episode actually beat Buffy's fourth season bow in the ratings, making him the most popular television vampire since Barnabas Collins. Of course, Angel doesn't have a musical theater production yet, but give him time. After all, Barnabas apparently sings. In January 2000 *Dark Shadows* producer Dan Curtis announced he was developing a stage musical version of the series.

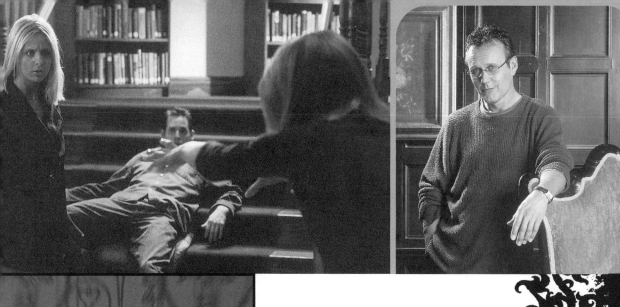

Buffy the Vampire Slayer

Magic Users

OLIVIA: "All that time you used to talk about witchcraft and darkness and the like...I just thought you were being pretentious."

GILES: "Oh, I was. But I was also right."

OLIVIA: "So everything you told me was true?"

GILES: "Well, no, I wasn't actually one of the original members of Pink Floyd." —"HUSH"

WIZARDS, SORCERERS, AND WITCHES. Those words bring to mind so many different images. Fundamental to the universe of *Buffy the Vampire Slayer* is the fact of magic's existence. It is real. It can be used and accessed and manipulated, much like other forms of energy. "Magicians," human or otherwise, can access magical energy through the utilization of knowledge. They might study ancient texts, commit spells to memory, come into possession of talismans or arcane artifacts that have power of their own, but in all such cases, they are merely channeling magical energy. They have no such power of their own. Though they might be called wizards or witches, they would be better categorized by the words *spellcaster* or *magician*. For the moment let us settle upon the term *magician* for anyone, human or supernatural, who utilizes magic but has no innate magical power of his or her own.

We have seen a great many magicians on *Buffy the Vampire Slayer*. In truth, most of our major characters have taken part in one spell or another and might then be called magicians if the definition stretched to its finest point. There are also a great many characters who are not so easily defined, however, and that brings us to our second category. For the sake of clarity, we will call them *sorcerers*. (Note: These "categories" are not meant as definitions that would carry over to the series, nor have they been used on the series. Rather, we are attempting to explain the three major types of magic user thus far presented on the show.)

If a magician is a being who utilizes or only channels outside magical forces, we might say a sorcerer is a being who becomes invested with magical abilities given him by an outside force. It is not *his* power, but it has now become a part of him; it can also be taken away. Humans willing to serve or worship magical beings can gain access to that power for their own ends. For instance, Ethan Rayne, who has appeared in multiple episodes, including "Halloween" and "Band Candy," serves the forces of chaos. Though there is no conclusive evidence to elevate Ethan from the level of magician to that of sorcerer, it seems reasonable to believe that he has *received* certain power for his servitude.

> **ETHAN:** "The natural order. It's being tampered with."
> **GILES:** "Natural order, my ass. You worship chaos."
> **ETHAN:** "Don't be so literal. I believe chaos *is* the natural order."
> **GILES:** "Please, let's not go down that road. 'Chaos is beautiful, chaos is healthy.' Chaos is a big bloody mess, that's what it is." —**"A NEW MAN"**

That leads directly to our third type of magic user, those born with the innate power of magic. Often such beings still require training in spellcasting, but they have within them, from birth, the power to control magic and influence their surroundings in a way that others are simply incapable of. This might also be considered to be an affinity for the use of magic rather than any actual power. Either way, they have a greater capacity for the use of magic than most other creatures. For the purposes of our discussion only (and setting aside the political implications of the word examined below), we can refer to them as *witches*. When asked if she was a witch, series character Jenny Calendar replied that she did not "have that kind of power." Proof enough that to become a witch requires more than training and intention.

> **WILLOW:** "I mean, I'm not a full-fledged witch. That takes years. I just did a couple of pagan blessings and a teeny glamour to hide a zit."
>
> **BUFFY:** "It doesn't scare you?"
>
> **WILLOW:** "It has. I tried to communicate with the spirit world and I so wasn't ready for that. It was like being pulled apart inside. Plus I blew the power out for the whole block."
> —"DEAD MAN'S PARTY"

Witchcraft, then, takes on a new meaning. In the universe of *Buffy the Vampire Slayer*, it seems, one can *practice* witchcraft without actually being a witch.

For the most part, we can merely offer conjecture about whether a given character is a magician, sorcerer, or witch. In the case of elder gods, Lords of Chaos, and other ancient supernatural beings, it seems obvious to say that they have power of their own. But it should be noted that demons in the *Buffy* universe (see Demons) are seemingly definable in the same manner as humans. Some have innate magical power of their own while others merely wield it.

In the first four seasons of *Buffy*, we have seen both humans and demons utilize magic, but most of them are merely magicians, accessing that mystical energy and the powers both natural and unnatural that control our world. It appears that, according to the mythology of the series, almost anyone can do this, but not without endangering himself. Even a person who has been trained in its use, such as Buffy's friend and former Watcher, Rupert Giles, is always vigilant and cautious while using magic.

witchcraft as truth, fiction, and metaphor

ON *BUFFY THE VAMPIRE SLAYER*, nearly every supernatural element is really a metaphor for something else. In the case of witches, as Marti Noxon explains, the metaphor is both very powerful and very subtle.

"Witches are very much a cultural metaphor for women's power," Noxon states. "Women have a kind of mystery and a connection to the universe that can make people afraid. I think that women have felt in their own hearts and minds that there's a whole part of them that's untapped because of our position in society. Until very recently, we haven't been allowed to live up to our full potential.

"I've always felt like the idea of a witch is what would happen if all our [women's] power was unleashed. When that idea is demonized, I think it's people's fear—particularly men's fear—of what would happen if they didn't keep the oppressed oppressed. I think the reason witchcraft has become politically correct is that women are being more integrated into society, and women tapping into their power turns out not to be scary but empowering."

Willow, it should be noted, is a believer in Wicca, the modern religion based on ancient paganism and the natural powers of nature. Wicca is also known as witchcraft, though the stigma attached to the pop-culture imagery surrounding witchcraft frequently causes confusion.

The writers and producers of *Buffy* have undertaken a difficult task by walking the line between the religious beliefs of Wiccans and the legends and pop culture about witches. Although they have not focused in great detail on defining what Wicca means to the witches on the series, they have attempted to infuse those characters with many of the essential ideals of Wicca.

"Someone who doesn't know snowboarding might call a snowboarder a skier, figuring it's all the same thing," notes series co-producer Jane Espenson. "But once you get into it, you realize the term for that is snowboarding. Someone who seriously began engaging in witchcraft as a commitment would do the research and find out that they're referred to now as Wiccans."

While Wiccans believe in magic—the power to access the energy of the world around us to effect change upon it—they also believe that once a spell is cast, it reflects back upon the caster with three times the energy. Thus a benevolent spell will bring good things to the one who cast it, but a malicious spell will return that malice threefold upon its originator.

Though this philosophy has never been explained within the context of the show, its implementation is obvious in the fortunes of Catherine Madison—Amy's cruel mother—and even in Willow's life, during those times when she has tried to cast spells with tainted motivations.

BUFFY: "Honey, we have to talk about the [wedding] invitations. Do you want to be 'William the Bloody,' or, like, just 'Spike,' 'cause either way it's gonna look majorly weird."

SPIKE: "Whereas the name 'Buffy' gives it that classic touch of elegance."

BUFFY: "What's wrong with Buffy?"

GILES: "Such a good question."

—FOLLOWING A SPELL OF WILLOW'S GONE HORRIBLY AWRY, IN "SOMETHING BLUE"

In the fourth-season episode "Hush," when Willow first meets Tara, another powerful spellcaster to whom she finds herself quite attracted, a distinction is very clearly made between Wicca and the magic power accessible to certain individuals, including Willow. When the subject of spells comes up, the so-called Wiccans in her university group don't even take her seriously, thus staking out a separate territory for Willow, Tara, and characters like Amy Madison.

WILLOW: "Talk! All talk: blah blah Gaia blah blah moon, menstrual lifeforce power. . . I thought after a few sessions we'd get into something real but..."

BUFFY: "No actual witches in your witch group."

WILLOW: "Buncha wannablessedbe's. It's just a fad. Nowadays every girl with a henna tattoo and a spice rack thinks she's a sister to the dark ones."   —"HUSH"

Still, telling such stories involves a large gray area that can be misinterpreted. *Buffy* makeup supervisor Todd McIntosh—a longtime aficionado of horror films—has established good relationships with Laura Parker and Lysette Anthony, who played witches on the original *Dark Shadows* TV series and its 1991 incarnation, respectively. Such characters, who were entirely supernatural, don't raise red flags. But once Wicca is brought into the mix, as it has been on *Buffy*, McIntosh points out that it invites some people to examine the series more closely for potential offense, in much the same way a zombie episode using voodoo trappings would draw scrutiny.

"The one thing you have to understand is that Wicca is an established and legitimate religion," he says. "To keep throwing demons into it . . . there is no devil in witchcraft. They do not believe in it. They do not believe in demons or the Christian mythology of devils."

McIntosh notes the importance of looking beyond such trappings and recognizing the message the series and creator Joss Whedon are attempting to send.

"I like what Joss is trying to say there: that it is possible that we can manipulate our environment. That is the essence of what's happening with Willow. As she's growing, she's discovering that we can alter things for good or evil, but we should not use negativity to make that happen. Willow has done some things out of spite or anger. Witches believe that if you do anything bad it comes back at you three times. We've seen that; we've *seen* her make a spell and have its effect come back to her and make everything worse. On the other hand, let's *say* [that that is a basic tenet of Wicca]. Let's actually put those words in there so that the people who follow this religion are a little bit mollified.

"There was a young man in one episode who was Wiccan, and he was referred to as a warlock. The origin of the word *warlock* is teller of lies. No real witch would ever refer to himself as a warlock."

Marti Noxon takes the issue of political correctness in reference to witchcraft one step further:

"The whole idea of [witches being evil] isn't just politically incorrect, it simply isn't true," she notes. "There are good people and bad people. Good women and bad women. On *Buffy*, we play with the idea of witchcraft or magic, and it's always about the intention of the person who uses it. Magic per se is not a bad thing. What they do with it is either going to be good or bad."

"Everyone's first encounter with witches is probably *The Wizard of Oz*," Jane Espenson points out. "You have that picture that there are good witches and bad witches and they can do wonderful things. It's interesting that everyone pictures the pointy hat, because at the very same time that you meet the Wicked Witch, you meet Glinda. Yet Glinda has not become part of our prototype for witches, because the Wicked Witch makes a much stronger impression. Glinda just seems like a nursery school teacher. The witches on our show are more like those kids in school who had a special skill. They seem to have some focus. They weren't always around because they went to gymnastic competitions. These are kids with an extracurricular activity."

Espenson wrote the season three episode "Gingerbread," which concerns, among other things, local parents getting up in arms about their children becoming involved with witchcraft, no matter how benevolent—in the form of Wicca—it may be.

"Most of our episodes are driven by a metaphor," she observes. "In the case of 'Gingerbread,' witches are a metaphor for kids who get in trouble for the stuff you find in their locker. They're counterculture kids reconceptualized as witches."

MRS. ROSENBERG: "Sit down, honey."
WILLOW: "Principal Snyder talked to you."
MRS. ROSENBERG: "Yes. He's quite concerned."
WILLOW: "Mom. I know what it looks like, but I can totally—"
MRS. ROSENBERG: "You don't have to explain, honey. This isn't exactly a surprise."
WILLOW: "Why not?"
MRS. ROSENBERG: "Identification with mythical icons is perfectly typical of your age group. It's a classic adolescent response to the pressure of incipient adulthood."
WILLOW: "Oh. Is that what it is?"
MRS. ROSENBERG: "Of course, I could have wished you would identify with something a little less icky, but developmentally speaking—"
WILLOW: "Mom, I'm not an age group. I'm me. Willow group."   —"GINGERBREAD"

"Witches are one place where we are not drawing on myth at all," Espenson says with emphasis. "We are drawing much more on our experience of being in high school. Witch is just another way to say outcast."

Still, despite the witch-as-every-kid attitude of some episodes, and the spells, incantations, symbols, and ideas from Wicca that have permeated the themes of *Buffy the Vampire Slayer*, it is a series steeped in the trappings of traditional horror stories. Those stories include a very different kind of magic user, one whose intentions are not benevolent at all. More often than not, such ideas are represented on the series not by witches, but by other sorts of magic users—sorcerers and chaos worshipers such as Ethan Rayne.

The Magic Users

> **GILES:** "Remember that time? We were at the pub with Deirdre and…what was her name? Stupid name."
>
> **ETHAN:** "Carlotta. Little skinny thing, figure like Twiggy."
>
> **GILES:** "You did something…"
>
> **ETHAN:** "Oh, right, the transparent sweaters! One of my first big magics. Still a winner at parties."
>
> **GILES:** "My God, is that really how it all started? A way to get birds?"
>
> **ETHAN:** "Nothing wrong with that." —**"A NEW MAN"**

The most important thing to note at the outset of this section is this: not all magic users are monsters. What, then, do we mean by the term *monster?* In this case, we have extended it to include all those who, through supernatural means, are significantly more than mere humans. By that definition, of course, our "monsters" are not necessarily evil. It also means that Slayers would be considered monsters, at least to a certain extent. In this section, however, we concern ourselves mainly with witches and sorcerers.

WILLOW ROSENBERG

> "Mom! I'm not acting out—I'm a *witch.* I make pencils float. I summon the four elements! Well—two elements—but four soon. And I'm dating a musician!"
> —**WILLOW, IN "GINGERBREAD"**

FIRST APPEARANCE: "Welcome to the Hellmouth," season one

OTHER EPISODES: all other episodes

KEY RELATIONSHIPS: Willow is a core member of the "Scooby Gang," best friend to the Slayer, Buffy Summers, and to Xander Harris. Xander was her first love, Oz was her first boyfriend, and she is currently involved in a relationship with Tara. Rupert Giles, the Watcher, was her mentor in her earliest efforts at learning magic.

UNIQUE ATTRIBUTES: Willow is a spellcaster and witch. She has an innate affinity for magic.

MOST MONSTROUS MOMENT: In "Something Blue," she cast a spell that caused her every word to become reality. This led to a great deal of chaos and to her being offered demonic immortality by D'Hoffryn. (She refused.)

CURRENT STATUS: Willow attends the University of California at Sunnydale, where she remains a vital part of the life of the Slayer.

A native of Sunnydale, California, Willow spent her early years like most of that town's residents—completely ignorant of the horrible, supernatural evils that existed in the world around her. Her parents, **Ira** and **Sheila Rosenberg,** were conservative about Willow's upbringing. Sheila, a scholar, seemed incapable of understanding her daughter on a personal level, instead applying what she knew academically of the average teen to their relationship.

Willow's life changed during her sophomore year of high school when a new girl—Buffy Summers—joined her class. Though Buffy had once been among the "popular crowd" at her old school in Los Angeles, she had been alienated by that crowd and could now relate to the shy and bookish Willow. It wasn't long before the two girls became friends.

Shortly after Buffy's arrival in Sunnydale, Willow found herself threatened by a vampire named Thomas, only to be rescued by Buffy. Ever since learning of Buffy's mission to combat vampires, demons, and the forces of darkness, Willow has dedicated herself to aiding her friend. A small group of teens willing to put their lives on the line to help began to gather around Buffy and her Watcher, Rupert Giles. That group included Willow, her best friend Xander Harris, a reluctant Cordelia Chase—the too-popular, shallow girl Xander and Willow had both hated since first grade—and later Oz, a musician (and also a werewolf) who became Willow's boyfriend.

Though at first Willow was mostly helpful due to her research and computer skills, it wasn't long before she began to develop an interest in magic and spellcasting. This may have partially resulted from her association with Amy Madison, a classmate who was a witch (as was Amy's mother, though the Madison women were on opposite ends of the spectrum as far as intentions were concerned). As a Watcher, Giles had been trained in the use of magic and was able to do certain spells with preparation. For a time, he was aided in that respect by Jenny Calendar, a technopagan, whose beliefs were apparently similar to those of the Wiccan religion, but focused on the use of technology to further those beliefs.

When Jenny was brutally murdered, Willow—who had admired her—substituted as the computer teacher for the balance of that school year. During that time, she also became interested in both the earth-worship aspects of Wicca and the spellcasting elements of witchcraft.

In the two-part second-season finale, "Becoming," Willow cast her first major spell. Though Angelus had tried to kill her, Willow put her own life in jeopardy in order to cast the spell that would restore his soul and transform him once again into the noble Angel, eradicating the evil Angelus.

> **WILLOW:** "The curse. We never got to finish it. Maybe we *can* restore Angel's soul."
>
> **XANDER:** "I don't like it. You're talking about messing with powerful magic, and you're weak."
>
> **WILLOW:** "I'm okay."
>
> **XANDER:** "You don't look okay. Does she?"
>
> **CORDELIA:** "Listen to him. The hair is *so* flat, and do you even *use* base?"
>
> **WILLOW:** "There's no use arguing with me. Do you see my resolve face? You've seen it before, and you know what it means. Just help me cast the spell and you can give me a complete makeover."
>
> **CORDELIA:** "You're not just saying that?"   **—"BECOMING, PART TWO"**

Willow proved to have an affinity for magic, an innate power that sets her apart from the average spellcaster or magician. Subsequent to her first spells she learned to levitate small objects and has cast several other spells.

Willow is a vital part of *Buffy the Vampire Slayer*. As the Slayer's best friend, a case might be argued that she is the most important of the series' supporting characters. Whereas Buffy's relationship to her mother, her Watcher, or a boyfriend might change, Willow remains the one true constant in her life. Perhaps the best evidence of that was Buffy's relief (in season three's "Choices") when Willow revealed that she had decided to forgo more prestigious colleges to attend the University of California at Sunnydale with her best friend.

Though she puts the lie to all the negative stereotypes about witches, Willow has been forced to combat them. When a demon influenced the population of Sunnydale (in season three's "Gingerbread"), fomenting antiwitch hatred, her own mother turned against her. Willow had been practicing spells with Amy Madison and another classmate, a boy named Michael Czajak.

Though Sheila Rosenberg attempted an academic approach to the revelation that her daughter was involved with witchcraft, the demon's influence led her to take part in a plan to burn the town's suspected witches at the stake. Thus Willow—along with Buffy and Amy Madison—were nearly murdered by "concerned parents," including Buffy's and Willow's own mothers.

After the demon was destroyed, it remained unclear whether those it had influenced retained their memories of the events in question. Still there is no doubt that those events caused Willow to evolve somewhat, to come to grips with her impending adulthood and with her interest in magic.

During "Gingerbread," Amy Madison attempted to cast a spell to turn the maddened parents into rats, only to have the spell backfire so that she transformed herself instead. Since that time, Willow kept Amy in a cage in her room at home, and later at college, in hopes that she would be able to find the spell—and summon the power—to turn Amy human again.

Willow is loyal to a fault, but there have been many times when those she depended on let her down. Throughout most of her youth she was in love with Xander Harris, only to have Xander fall in love first with Buffy and then Cordelia, and then he had sex for the first time with the Slayer Faith (in "The Zeppo"). Though Buffy is her best friend, there have been times when she has felt left behind, as when (in the third season) Buffy began to do Slayer patrols with Faith, and (in the fourth season) when Buffy's burgeoning relationship with Riley Finn took precedence over her friendship with Willow.

Despite her usual loyalty, the young witch had a taste of what it was like to be on the other side of that coin when Oz and Cordelia discovered her kissing Xander (in season three's "Lover's Walk"). This was highly unusual behavior for a character so persistently noble, but it proved that even Willow was fallible. Oz eventually forgave her, but their relationship was doomed.

In season four's "Wild at Heart," Oz's animal attraction to Veruca, the singer from another band performing at the Bronze, was finally revealed to be driven by the fact that Veruca was also a werewolf. The beast inside Oz could not deny the attraction, no matter what his human mind and heart desired. Though Oz killed Veruca to save Willow's life, he left Sunnydale so that he might have time to consider the relationship of beast to man within him. Willow was shattered by his departure.

Though she became more proficient with magic, any spells Willow cast without the purest of intentions have backfired on her, most notably in season four's "Something Blue." In that episode, grieving because Oz had left, she attempted to use magic to make him return to her, to force her will upon the world, with disastrous results.

> **D'HOFFRYN:** "You have much anger and pain. Your magic is strong, but your pain…. It's like a scream that pierces dimensional walls. We heard your call."
> **WILLOW:** "I'm sorry. I'll try for a quiet rage." ——**"SOMETHING BLUE"**

However, in season four a great many things began to change in Willow's life. She had begun her college career, lost her boyfriend, and become Buffy's roommate. But in "Hush," she discovered that the college's Wicca group didn't even believe in magic. They were more concerned with gossip and fund-raising, and their comments implied that their interest in Wicca was more a cool, alternative lifestyle statement than any actual belief. However, in that same group, she met one person who believed as she did, a witch named Tara. In a life-threatening situation, Willow and Tara found that, when they pooled their magical strength, the whole was far greater than the sum of the two parts.

They also found a great attraction for one another. While initially their mutual interest in and affinity for magic brought them together, their relationship eventually became a romantic one. (The open nature of Willow's sexual identity was hinted at in season three's "Doppelgangland" when an evil, vampire version of Willow—who was very obviously bisexual—was brought to our more familiar reality through magical means.) By the time Oz returned for one episode in season four ("New Moon Rising"), Willow was already involved with Tara.

At the time of that development, Joss Whedon addressed the issue on the *Buffy*-related Internet posting board, the Bronze. "Willow and Tara's relationship is definitely romantic," Whedon said, confirming speculation. "Thorny subject; the writers and I have had long [talks] about how to deal with the subject responsibly, without writing a story that sounds like people spent a long time discussing how to deal with it responsibly. To me it feels just right. All the relationships on the show are sort of romantic (hence the [Bring Your Own] Subtext principle) and this feels like the natural next step for [Willow]. . . . We're not going to do an *Ally [McBeal]* or *Party of Five* in which we promote the hell out of a same-sex relationship for exploitation value that we take back by the end of the [episode]. . . . I just know there's a sweet story there, that would become very complicated if Oz were to show up again." Which, as noted, he did. It remains to be seen how the relationship between Willow and Tara will develop.

RUPERT GILES

"In the world of international sorcery, things get…complicated. It's not all pointy hats and purple cloaks, as I'm sure you well know."
—GILES, IN DIALOGUE CUT FROM THE FINAL BROADCAST OF "WHO ARE YOU?" DUE TO LENGTH

FIRST APPEARANCE: "Welcome to the Hellmouth," season one

OTHER EPISODES: all other episodes

KEY RELATIONSHIPS: Giles was Buffy's Watcher in Sunnydale until he was fired from that position by the Council of Watchers. He was in a relationship with Jenny Calendar until she was murdered. Now he has a relationship with a woman from out of town named Olivia.

UNIQUE ATTRIBUTES: Trained as a Watcher, Giles has vast knowledge of the supernatural. He also has certain skills involving the use of magic.

MOST MONSTROUS MOMENT: In season three's "Helpless," Giles participated in a secret test of Buffy's abilities that was standard for the Council. In doing so, he betrayed her trust and put her life in danger.

CURRENT STATUS: No longer Buffy's Watcher, Giles remains in Sunnydale as friend and mentor to the Slayer and her gang.

Rupert Giles was first exposed to magic and the supernatural when his father revealed to the ten-year-old Rupert that the family had long been involved with the Watchers Council. Both his father and grandmother had been Watchers in their time. Giles was expected to follow the same path. It was his destiny. He was greatly disappointed, even at that age, for he wanted to be either "a fighter pilot or a grocer" (as revealed in "Never Kill a Boy on the First Date").

As he grew up, it is reasonable to presume that Giles received some education in the ways of the supernatural and the forces of darkness. However, while in London, he fell in with a group of other students with an interest in the occult, including Philip Henry, Deirdre Page, and the troublemaker of the lot, Ethan Rayne. Together they dabbled in the occult, going so far as to call up a demon known as Eyghon the Sleepwalker, who would inhabit one of them while they were sleeping (see Demons: Eyghon). The friend who became inhabited by Eyghon died in their efforts to return the demon to whence it had come.

Subsequent to those horrors, he returned to the path his father had set out for him years before and rejoined the Watchers Council. He presumably studied a great deal more about the occult, and eventually he became a Watcher. Giles was a member of the Council for many years, during which time he was also a curator at the British Museum. Later, he was given the Council's most significant assignment, to be the Watcher for the Chosen One, the current and active Slayer, Buffy Summers.

Buffy had already begun her tenure as Slayer, when her first Watcher—a man named Merrick—was killed. After the situation in Los Angeles became untenable for her family and her parents decided to divorce, Buffy's mother, Joyce, moved the two of them to Sunnydale, California. By the time Buffy and her mother arrived in town, Giles was already ensconced in an occupation that would pay him a salary and allow him to keep close watch on the Slayer—he was the librarian for Sunnydale High School.

Though Buffy was at first very reluctant, not to mention put off by what she perceived as a certain British stuffiness about Giles, she soon realized—just as Giles had done years before—that she could not escape her destiny. In short order he became her friend, mentor, and trainer. Though he did not approve, Buffy soon brought several friends into her confidence. Xander Harris and Willow Rosenberg formed, with Buffy, the nucleus of what Xander would eventually label "the Scooby Gang."

In addition to his duties as Watcher—which included Buffy's training as well as the lion's share of the research regarding any given supernatural subject—Giles was the resident spellcaster and magic user of the group. Soon enough (in season one's "Witch") he proved that, though he was by no means a sorcerer or witch, his magical facility was enough that he could perform such complicated spells as were required to revert two spirits whose bodies had been switched back to their original forms. He also showed his abilities in such episodes as season one's "I Robot, You Jane," and season two's "Bewitched, Bothered, and Bewildered." In the latter he was called upon to reverse a love spell gone awry and to restore Buffy—who had been turned into a rat—to human form.

As time went on, however, Willow began to prove herself not only interested in magic, but to have a natural affinity for it. Giles took on the role of her mentor in order to be certain she did not go so fast as to lose control over the spells she was weaving.

When Sunnydale was plagued by a demon (in season three's "Gingerbread") Giles took a more active role, coming to the rescue with a spell in German that revealed the demon's true form and freed the townspeople from magical mind control. When an evil alternate-reality version of Willow was brought to Sunnydale (in season three's "Doppelgangland") Giles was again instrumental in sending her back.

Giles, it seemed, was often being called upon to reverse some awful spell. Though he was always stalwart in his work as the Watcher, as mentor to both Buffy and, to a lesser degree, Willow, and figurehead to the entire Scooby Gang, he went through a great deal of change himself. Upon first arriving in Sunnydale, he was precisely the stiff-upper-lip Brit his father and the Council likely hoped he would be. Over time, probably influenced by his relationship with Buffy and the revelation of his rebellious past, he began to loosen up, which made him a more effective Watcher, but got him in hot water with the Council.

Matters both pleasant and unpleasant contributed to those changes. On Halloween (in the episode of the same name), his old friend Ethan Rayne came to town to wreak havoc and create chaos (he was a chaos worshiper, after all). Seeing Ethan, and furious that the man might have endangered Buffy and was treading on his territory, Giles experienced a rage that belied his calm exterior. Ethan's dialogue revealed that in their university days, Rupert Giles had gone by the nickname "Ripper." In "Halloween," he gave Ethan a beating that made the name seem appropriate.

When Ethan returned in "The Dark Age," and menaced Jenny Calendar—whom Giles had been briefly dating (since "Some Assembly Required") and fallen in love with—Giles reverted to "Ripper" a bit more, desperately trying to save Jenny, who had been possessed by Eyghon.

Thereafter came a string of horrible experiences for the Watcher. Jenny was first revealed to be conspiring against Buffy and Angel (in "Surprise") and then was murdered by Angel (in "Passion"). Angel then abducted and tortured Giles (in "Becoming"). A second Slayer, Kendra, implicitly also under his watch, was murdered.

When Angel returned from a demon dimension, no longer evil, Buffy hid his return from Giles, testing their friendship and mutual respect. Giles eventually rose above his misgivings. Over time he had developed what Council member **Quentin Travers** (in "Helpless") called paternal feelings for her, of which the Council did not approve.

Ethan Rayne returned (in "Band Candy") and reverted Giles and the other adults in Sunnydale to teenage behavior, during which time Giles had sex with Buffy's mother, an experience that would cause some consternation on the part of the Slayer (in "Earshot").

Council tradition forced Giles to conduct a test on Buffy on her eighteenth birthday, which betrayed her trust in him and put her—and Joyce—in danger from the mad vampire Zachary Kralik (in "Helpless"). He broke Council rules and aided her, but as a result and citing Giles's obvious fatherlike affection for Buffy, the Council sent a new Watcher, Wesley Wyndam-Pryce, to Sunnydale, and Giles was officially relieved of his duties as Watcher (in "Bad Girls"). Faith, the Slayer who replaced Kendra, switched sides and began working for the evil mayor of Sunnydale. At Buffy's graduation ("Graduation Day, Parts One and Two"), the Mayor became a true demon and a lot of people died before he was destroyed.

In the aftermath of that high school graduation and the summer that followed, Giles's life was altered significantly. After the string of horrors he had experienced, he began to relax a little. Buffy was off to college, no longer working for the Council, just as Giles was not. She had come into her own, and though she still needed his counsel and knowledge and friendship, she no longer needed him as trainer or Watcher. He became more a part of the group rather than its figurehead. As revealed in "Hush," he also rekindled an on-again off-again relationship with an old friend from England named **Olivia,** who has made several visits from there and only recently became aware of Giles' background and supernatural activities.

When Ethan Rayne returned once more (in season four's "A New Man"), Giles had begun to be depressed by Buffy's independence. Ethan took advantage of that

to distract Giles with nostalgia and catch him off guard, casting a spell on him that transformed him, briefly, into a Fyarl demon. Ethan's hope was that Buffy would kill Giles, not realizing who he was. Those hopes were dashed when the Slayer recognized Giles by his eyes. Ethan was forced to return him to normal (see Demons: Giles).

With Willow coming more into her own as a witch, Giles has been called upon less and less for his skills with magic. What his place in Buffy's life will be in the future, we can only guess.

AMY MADISON

AMY: "All right! You want to fry a witch! I'll give you a *witch*! Goddess Hecate, work thy will..."

BUFFY: "Uh-oh."　　　　　**—AS AMY TURNS HERSELF INTO A RAT, IN "GINGERBREAD"**

FIRST APPEARANCE: "Witch," season one

OTHER EPISODES: season two: "Bewitched, Bothered, and Bewildered"; season three: "Gingerbread"; season four: "Something Blue"

KEY RELATIONSHIPS: Amy's mother, Catherine Madison, was also a witch.

UNIQUE ATTRIBUTES: Though Amy seems to have a great deal of innate magical power (likely inherited from her mother), she never really had the proper training. That lack of training contributed to her accidentally turning herself into a rat.

MOST MONSTROUS MOMENT: Amy turned Buffy into a rat (in "Bewitched, Bothered, and Bewildered.")

CURRENT STATUS: As a rat, she lives in a cage in Willow and Buffy's dormitory room.

First introduced in season one's "Witch," Amy Madison has not had it easy. Overweight in junior high, she was also subjected to constant pressure from her divorced mother, Catherine, who had been the cheerleading queen of Sunnydale High in her day. Catherine missed her former glory and was insanely jealous of her daughter's youth. She was also a witch.

Catherine used magic to switch her body for Amy's, trapping her poor daughter in her own corporeal form while she trained, slimmed down, and tried out for the cheerleading squad in Amy's body. Eventually, with Buffy and Giles's help, Amy was returned to her own body and Catherine's spirit was trapped inside a cheerleading trophy.

> **"The cheerleader trophy. It's like its eyes follow you wherever you go. I like it."**
> —OZ, IN "PHASES"

At the end of that episode Amy went to live with her father, apparently without any interest in witchcraft. However, in season two's "Bewitched, Bothered, and Bewildered," Xander Harris spotted her using magic to convince a teacher she had handed in homework that she didn't have.

XANDER: "Amy! Good to see you! You're a witch!"
AMY: "No I'm not! That was my mom, remember?"
XANDER: "I'm thinking it runs in the family. I saw you working that mojo on Miss Beakman. Maybe I should tell someone about that."
AMY: "That's not even—I never—that's so mean!"
XANDER: "Blackmail is such an ugly word."
AMY: "I didn't say blackmail."
XANDER: "Yeah, well, I'm about to blackmail you so I thought I'd bring it up."
—"BEWITCHED, BOTHERED, AND BEWILDERED"

He convinced Amy to cast a love spell for him that went horribly awry, forcing every woman in Sunnydale to love him (Amy included) except for Cordelia—who had been the object of the spell!

In that same episode, delusional from the love spell, Amy briefly turned Buffy Summers, whom she saw as a contender for Xander's affections, into a rat.

In the third season's "Gingerbread," a demon fomented local hatred for witches, and Amy was one of those young magic users who was persecuted, along with her friends Willow Rosenberg and Michael Czajak. The townspeople attempted to burn her at the stake, and when she tried to use magic to turn them all into rats, she ended up turning herself into a rat by accident.

Since that time, Amy has remained a rat, in the care of Buffy and Willow. She currently resides in a cage in their dormitory room at the University of California at Sunnydale. In the fourth season's "Something Blue"—thanks to a spell Willow cast that made everything she said come true—Amy was transformed into a human again, but only for mere seconds—and unseen by Willow—before she found herself a rat once more.

CATHERINE MADISON

GILES: "Your daughter is up to something very dangerous. Are you aware of that?"

CATHERINE: "You have to go. She's gonna be home soon."

GILES: "The girl is very sick. You will shut up and you will listen to me. Your daughter has access to some very powerful magics. Somehow your obsession with cheerleading has made her—"

CATHERINE: "I don't care about cheerleading! It's not my fault she's doing stuff. She's out of her mind. Ever since Dad—her dad left. I can't control her."

BUFFY: "Amy? Are you Amy?"

GILES: "I don't understand…."

BUFFY: "She switched you, didn't she? She switched your bodies. She wanted to relive her glory days. Catherine the Great."

CATHERINE: "She said I was wasting my youth…so she took it."   —"WITCH"

FIRST APPEARANCE: "Witch," season one

OTHER EPISODES: None. (Unless you count the cheerleader trophy, which we see at the beginning of "Phases.")

KEY RELATIONSHIPS: Amy Madison's mother.

UNIQUE ATTRIBUTES: Catherine was a powerful witch.

MOST MONSTROUS MOMENT: She switched bodies with her daughter so that she could relive her glory days as a high school cheerleader.

CURRENT STATUS: Catherine's mind remains trapped inside a cheerleading trophy.

Amy Madison's mother, Catherine, has appeared in the flesh in only one episode, the first season's "Witch." She was the first magic user to appear on the series. As a teenager, Catherine had been homecoming queen and the star cheerleader of Sunnydale High. Now divorced, and with a teenage daughter, she was appalled at her own daughter's lack of interest in such things. Catherine used witchcraft to switch bodies with her daughter so that she could revisit her former glory as a cheerleading star, but when she only made the alternate squad, she began using magic to sideline all those ahead of her on the waiting list with mysterious injuries and accidents.

In the final magical battle, Rupert Giles cast a spell that forced Catherine back into her own body. When she attempted to use her own magic against Buffy, the Slayer put a mirror between them, deflecting the witch's magic back upon her. Catherine's own spell trapped her spirit inside a cheerleading trophy in a display case at Sunnydale High. When subsequently seen (at the beginning of season two's "Phases") its eyes looked eerily alive. Though it has not been seen since the destruction of Sunnydale High (in the third-season finale), the script for season four's "Doomed" included a specific notation that the statue remains in the ruins of the school.

It should also be noted that Catherine Madison had a black cat who guarded her book of spells, which would indicate that in the Buffyverse some witches can develop ways to communicate and bond with certain animals, called *familiars*.

JENNY CALENDAR

ANGEL: "What do you want?

JENNY: "I want to die in bed, surrounded by fat grand-children, but I guess that's off the menu." —**"AMENDS"**

FIRST APPEARANCE: "I Robot, You Jane," season one

OTHER EPISODES: season one: "Prophecy Girl"; season two: "When She Was Bad," "Some Assembly Required," "School Hard," "Lie to Me," "The Dark Age," "Ted," "Surprise," "Innocence," "Bewitched, Bothered, and Bewildered," "Passion," "Becoming, Part Two"; season three: "Amends"

KEY RELATIONSHIPS: Jenny's real name was Janna, and she was a member of the Kalderash tribe of Romani Gypsies who had once cursed Angel. Her uncle **Enyos** had sent her to spy on Angel. She was Giles's girlfriend until Angel murdered her.

UNIQUE ATTRIBUTES: Jenny was a technopagan, a dabbler in magic who used the Internet to investigate and share information about her pagan beliefs and her interest in the supernatural.

MOST MONSTROUS MOMENT: Despite her love for Giles, Jenny hid the fact that she had been sent to Sunnydale to spy on Angel.

CURRENT STATUS: Angel snapped Jenny's neck (in season two's "Passion").

Jenny's is a tragic tale. When first introduced in "I Robot, You Jane" (season one), she was presented as an edgy, hip, funny, and charming computer science teacher. By the end of the episode it was revealed that Jenny was also a technopagan—she practiced a form of worship similar to Wicca in that it was earth-based, was also interested in magic, and pursued the two interests using computers and the Internet.

Soon thereafter, she began a flirtation with Rupert Giles and they had their first date in season two's "Some Assembly Required." They fell in love, and their mutual interest blossomed into a relationship. Though Giles despised most technology, which was Jenny's other great love, they did have one major interest in common: magic and the occult. Giles was a Watcher, and Jenny was a technopagan and sometime spellcaster who helped Buffy and her friends when she could.

Their romance hit its first snag (in "The Dark Age") when—due to events in Giles's past—Jenny was briefly possessed by the demon Eyghon. Though the demon was forced from her, she found it difficult not to blame Giles for that experience. Over time, however, they repaired their relationship.

It was not to last. In the second season's "Innocence," it was revealed that Jenny was more than what she appeared to be. She did love Giles, and she did want to help, but those feelings were in direct conflict with her heritage. One hundred years earlier, the vampire Angel had killed a young woman of the Kalderash Gypsy tribe in Romania. In vengeance, they cursed him by restoring his soul so that he might feel all the guilt for what he had done. But the curse had a second element. If Angel should ever find a moment of true happiness in spite of his guilt, he would become evil once more.

When the Kalderash became concerned that Angel's move to Sunnydale might mean that his guilt could be fading, they sent one of their American-educated children to observe him. Her name was **Janna Kalderash.**

Jenny Calendar.

In "Innocence," the unthinkable happened. In the previous episode, Angel and Buffy had sex, and he lost his human soul for the second time. Jenny revealed the truth to Giles, and he and the others spurned her for it. Though they would barely speak to her—and her own people would condemn her for it—she worked to try to find a way to restore the curse, and Angel's soul, as an effort to make up for what she had done. Her betrayal drove a wedge between Giles and Buffy, though the friction between them did not last.

Meanwhile, the evil Angel/Angelus tormented Buffy as often as he was able. As part of that torment, in the episode "Passion," he brutally murdered Jenny before she could change him back. (Something Willow eventually managed at the end of that season.)

ANGEL: "The Orb of Thesula. If memory serves, this is supposed to summon a person's soul from the ether, store it until it can be transferred. You know what I hate most about these things? (hurls it against the wall, shattering it) They're so damned fragile. Must be that shoddy Gypsy craftsmanship. (looking down at the computer monitor) I never cease to be amazed at how much the world has changed in just two and a half centuries. It's a miracle to me. You put the secret to restoring my soul in here (swipes the computer and monitor to the floor where they crash, begin to spark and smoke. He turns back to the printer, which holds the pages) …and it comes out here. (takes the pages from the printer, scans them and smiles). The Ritual of Restoration. Wow, this brings back memories (starts to tear the pages)."

JENNY: "Angel, wait!…That's your—"

ANGEL: "My what? My 'cure?' No, thanks. Been there, done that. And déjà vu just isn't what it used to be. Well, isn't this my lucky day. The computer *and* the pages. Looks like I get to kill *two* birds with one stone. (goes vamp face) And teacher makes three."

—**"PASSION"**

Angel snapped her neck and then, quite sadistically, transported her body to Giles's apartment, where he left flowers strewn on the stairs to guide the Watcher up to his loft bedroom. Upon the bed, laid out in a pose that resembled sleep, was Jenny's corpse.

Ironically, she probably could have prevented Angel from becoming evil again by merely sharing information about the "one perfect moment of happiness" clause, but out of loyalty to her clan, she kept silent. Had she spoken up, she would likely still be alive today.

Jenny was at least partially redeemed in that just before her murder she had finally completed a translation of the spell that would restore Angel. It was on a disk that fell beneath her desk, to be found later by Willow. In subsequent episodes both Drusilla (in "Becoming") and the First (in "Amends") appeared as Jenny to influence Giles and Angel, respectively.

ETHAN RAYNE

"Look, a box full of farm-fresh chicken."
—BUFFY, UPON FINDING ETHAN HIDING IN A BOX, IN "BAND CANDY"

FIRST APPEARANCE: "Halloween," season two

OTHER EPISODES: season two: "The Dark Age"; season three: "Band Candy"; season four: "A New Man"

KEY RELATIONSHIPS: In college, Ethan was part of a group of young magic users who called up the demon Eyghon. Among those magic users was Rupert Giles. His current relationship with

Giles is a mixture of hatred and nostalgic fondness. Ethan has hired out his services in the past, in particular to the Mayor of Sunnydale in "Band Candy."

UNIQUE ATTRIBUTES: Ethan worships and serves chaos. His magic usually has no purpose other than to appease his master by creating chaos.

MOST MONSTROUS MOMENT: Ethan turned Giles into a demon in "A New Man," hoping that, unable to speak in a human tongue, he would be killed by the Slayer.

CURRENT STATUS: When last seen, Ethan was in the custody of the Initiative, an American government operation that researches the supernatural.

As a young man in London, Ethan Rayne fell in with the wrong crowd. He dabbled in black magic and demon worship, along with a group of friends at his university, including Rupert Giles. Giles, of course, changed his ways and went on to become Buffy's Watcher. Ethan went the other way entirely, evolving from dabbler to chaos-worshipping magician.

He first appeared in season two's "Halloween," during which he cast a spell over Sunnydale that turned anyone who bought their costume at his store into whatever they were dressed as.

> **ETHAN:** "What? No hug? Aren't you pleased to see your old mate, Rupert?"
> **GILES:** "I'm surprised I didn't guess it was you. This Halloween stunt stinks of Ethan Rayne."
> **ETHAN** (proud): "Yes, it does, doesn't it? Don't want to blow my own horn, but—it's genius. The very embodiment of 'be careful what you wish for.'" **—"HALLOWEEN"**

Later that season he returned for "The Dark Age," fleeing from Eyghon, the very same demon he, Giles, and some friends had raised in London in their youth.

> **BUFFY:** "I know you, you ran that costume shop."
> **ETHAN:** "I'm pleased you remember."
> **BUFFY:** "You sold me that dress for Halloween and nearly got us all killed."
> **ETHAN:** "But you looked great." **—"THE DARK AGE"**

The demon was destroyed, of course, but no thanks to Ethan, who slipped away.

The would-be sorcerer returned in "Band Candy" during season three, when the demonic Mayor of Sunnydale engaged him to wreak a little havoc as a feint, to distract

Buffy and the others from his own plans. Ethan used cursed chocolate bars to cause all the adults in Sunnydale to behave like teenagers, with hilarious results.

"I don't get this. The candy's supposed to make you all immature and stuff, but I ate a ton and I don't feel any diff—never mind."   **—XANDER, IN "BAND CANDY"**

This seemed to imply that not only was Ethan a known commodity in the supernatural community, but that he had at least some history hiring his services out. In the end, Buffy caught up to Ethan.

BUFFY: "So, Ethan. What are we playing? You're pretty much in a talk or bleed situation. Your call."
ETHAN: "I would like to point out that this wasn't my idea."
BUFFY: "Meaning?"
ETHAN: "I'm subcontracting. It's Trick you want. I'm just helping him collect a tribute. For a demon."
GILES: "He's lying. Hit him!"
BUFFY: "I don't think he is. And shut up."
GILES: "You're *my* Slayer. Knock those capped teeth down his throat!"   **—"BAND CANDY"**

After she had given Ethan a sound thrashing, however, her attention was diverted and he managed to escape.

In the fourth-season episode "A New Man," Ethan returned to create chaos in Sunnydale once again (as well he should, given that he was finally revealed in this episode to be a chaos worshiper) by turning Giles into a Fyarl demon. Despite their hatred for one another, Ethan was able to use nostalgia to play on Giles's insecurities, so that the Watcher let his guard down and Ethan was able to work that spell.

According to co-producer Jane Espenson, "Ethan Rayne is mostly just a bad guy who's using every trick at his disposal. He's a man who will find the book that will teach him what he's had in his mind to do. He does these things for personal gain, but also because he worships chaos, literally. He is the closest thing we have to a Trickster character from myth. He does it for the joy of chaos."

"I've got to learn to just do the damage and leave town. It's the stay-'n'-gloat that gets me every time."   **—ETHAN, IN "A NEW MAN"**

"Yes, there's personal gain to be had; he's a very selfish person," Espenson says. "'What will make me happy? What will get me out of trouble?' He's very much id, but he's not an id monster, he's an id person. He's a little human guy with a few tricks. 'Sorcerer' makes him sound too important. 'Warlock' makes him sound like he's got a philosophy. He's a pest with some spells. Things never work out for him. If Giles had never grown up . . . Ethan is sort of Ripper continued."

> **GILES:** (drunk) "It's all over. No job. No Slayer. Replaced by a snotty professor and demon-catching technology that I can't begin to understand. The toothy-boy was right. I am retired. I was Ripper. And then I was Giles. And now I'm…someone else I don't even know. 'S pretty pathetic, 's what it is."
>
> **ETHAN:** (suddenly sober) "You don't have to worry about all that anymore, mate. I slipped poison in your drink, you'll be dead in an hour. (Giles stares at him). Nah. Kidding."
>
> **GILES:** "Christ, I'm gonna feel like hell in the morning."
>
> **ETHAN:** (ominous) "Yes, you will. (then, drunk again) Kidding again. Relax. Stop thinking so much and enjoy the night. We're sorcerers and as long as there is such a thing, night is our time."
> —**"A NEW MAN"**

Though his main focus is on serving chaos, it is clear that Ethan harbors certain resentments toward Giles and will likely continue to plague him.

But at the end of season four, it is believed that Ethan Rayne is in the custody of the United States government, specifically that of the arm of the government that originally sponsored the Initiative project.

GWENDOLYN POST

> **MRS. POST:** "Mr. Giles—where do you keep the rest of your library?"
>
> **GILES:** "I'm sorry, the…rest?"
>
> **MRS. POST:** "Yes, the actual library. "
>
> **GILES:** "I assure you, Mrs. Post, this is the finest occult reference collection…"
>
> **MRS. POST:** "This side of the Atlantic, I'm sure."
> —**"REVELATIONS"**

EPISODE: "Revelations," season three

KEY RELATIONSHIPS: Formerly a member of the Watchers Council (she was kicked out), Mrs. Post pretended to be Faith's new Watcher until she revealed her true intentions.

MOST MONSTROUS MOMENT: Mrs. Post manipulated everyone, particularly Faith, and her betrayal was among the many catalysts that drove Faith to the dark side.

CURRENT STATUS: Buffy severed Mrs. Post's arm—upon which was the powerful Glove of Myhnegon. The false Watcher was then struck by lightning and incinerated.

Gwendolyn Post was a member of the Council of Watchers for an indeterminate period of time. Long enough, however, for her to learn a great deal about Rupert Giles and Buffy Summers, and for her to somehow get access to information about Faith. Mrs. Post was not cut out for the Council, however.

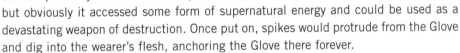

"She was kicked out of the Council two years ago for misuses of dark power. They swear there was a memo . . . ."
—GILES, IN "REVELATIONS"

Unfortunately, Giles never received a memo. Mrs. Post arrived in Sunnydale and pretended to be a new Watcher assigned to Faith, to work in tandem with Giles and Buffy. In reality, she was using them all to locate the Glove of Myhnegon, and to keep it out of the hands of a demon named Lagos. It was unclear precisely what the Glove's power was, but obviously it accessed some form of supernatural energy and could be used as a devastating weapon of destruction. Once put on, spikes would protrude from the Glove and dig into the wearer's flesh, anchoring the Glove there forever.

Mrs. Post put the Glove on, betraying Faith's trust—and that of everyone else— and tried to kill them all. Buffy used a large shard of glass like a discus and severed the faux Watcher's arm from her body, separating her from the Glove's power. However, Buffy did so after Mrs. Post had called on the power the Glove would have channeled. When that power went into Mrs. Post sans the Glove, it struck her as lightning and she was incinerated on the spot.

MICHAEL CZAJAK

CORDELIA: "You're going to be one busy little Slayer, baby-sitting for [Amy and Michael]."
BUFFY: "I doubt they'll have more trouble."
CORDELIA: "I doubt your doubt. Everyone knows witches killed those kids. Amy is a witch. And Michael is whatever the boy of "witch" is, besides being the poster child for yuck. If you hang with them, expect badness, because that's what you get for hanging with freaks and losers. Believe me, I know. . . .That was a pointed comment about me hanging out with you guys."   —"GINGERBREAD"

EPISODE: "Gingerbread," season three

KEY RELATIONSHIPS: Michael was involved with a Wicca group that included Willow Rosenberg and Amy Madison.

CURRENT STATUS: It is presumed that Michael graduated from Sunnydale High School. His present whereabouts are unknown.

Michael was a Sunnydale High classmate of Buffy's who favored a dark, Goth look. His sole appearance on the show was in the third-season episode "Gingerbread," during which a demon influenced local parents into an antiwitchcraft frenzy. Since Michael was a practicing witch—had indeed been meeting with Willow Rosenberg and Amy Madison to attempt certain spells—he was one of those targeted, though not singled out to be burned at the stake with Amy, Willow, and Buffy.

TARA

WILLOW: "I'm sorry you're feeling blechy. But we'll get together with Buffy another time, sometime soon. I really think you'll like her—"
TARA: "She's not your friend."
WILLOW: "I may have overestimated the 'you liking her' factor. But I wish you'd give her a chance; she's very important to me."
TARA: "No, I mean…I don't think she's…her…. A person's energy has a flow, a unity. Buffy's was fragmented; it grated, like something forced in where it doesn't belong. Plus she was kinda mean."
　　　—TARA, CLUING WILLOW INTO THE BUFFY-FAITH BODY SWITCH, IN "WHO ARE YOU?"

FIRST APPEARANCE: "Hush," season four

OTHER EPISODES: season four: "A New Man," and all thereafter

KEY RELATIONSHIPS: Tara is romantically involved with Willow Rosenberg, with whom she also practices her skills at magic. She also has a cat.

UNIQUE ATTRIBUTES: Tara has a strong natural affinity for magic, and her family used magic as well.

CURRENT STATUS: Tara attends the University of California at Sunnydale.

Tara first appeared in the fourth season's landmark "silent" episode, "Hush," as a painfully shy member of Willow's on-campus Wicca group. Though Tara was not nearly as outspoken as Willow about it, both were unfulfilled by the group, whose other members were not only uninterested in spellcasting, but didn't actually believe in it at all. Tara told Willow she had grown up with witchcraft in her family and had hoped to find others she could talk to about it.

Fortunately she found Willow. During "Hush," demonic beings known as the Gentlemen stole the voices of everyone in Sunnydale. Thinking that she and Willow might be able to locate a counterspell, Tara went to her room, only to be set upon by the Gentlemen and their lackeys. She did manage to evade them and find

Willow, however, and when the two of them connected, they found that together, their magic was much more powerful than either of them was capable of on her own. Though Tara told Willow that she did not think she was as powerful as her new friend, it seemed likely that she had at least as much magical power as Willow.

They practiced spellcasting a bit in "A New Man," two episodes later. But in season four's "The I in Team," the nature of their relationship was brought under the spotlight. Throughout her initial appearances, Tara and Willow seemed to be developing a romantic relationship, and in "The I in Team," it was strongly implied that that relationship was sexual. Joss Whedon confirmed that fact (see "Willow" above) on the Internet the week before "The I in Team" was scheduled to air.

Later (in "Goodbye, Iowa"), for an unknown reason, Tara purposely  fouled up a spell that Willow was casting that would have revealed the location of all supernatural creatures in Sunnydale. Her reason for doing so has not yet been made apparent.

Tara continued to become a more significant part of the lives of the Scooby Gang as the fourth season came to a close. Buffy and Xander discovered that Willow's relationship with the other witch was a romantic one. When Buffy and Faith switched bodies (in "This Year's Girl" and "Who Are You?") Tara was the first to realize that Buffy was not herself, and helped Willow not only to discover how that had happened, but to conjure a magical mechanism that would reverse the process.

In the fourth-season finale, "Restless," when Giles, Willow, Xander, and Buffy are menaced in their dreams by the primal energy of the very first Slayer, they are aided and advised within that dream state by Tara. It is unclear whether or not this was a sort of dream projection of Tara's consciousness, or merely part of their individual dreams.

which witch?

STORYTELLERS FROM the Brothers Grimm to L. Frank Baum, from Walt Disney to the creators of Looney Tunes, have wrought within the collective consciousness of Western popular culture an image of the wicked witch: a green-skinned hag with a long, warty nose and stringy gray hair. Although presented in fairy tales and fictions—including *The Wizard of Oz* and *Snow White* in their various incarnations—as profoundly evil and hideously ugly, modern culture has seen the term *witch* splintered by several different meanings. There is, of course, the traditional witch we have just described, as well as those adept women who wield magic for good, including everyone from Glinda the Good Witch of Oz to Mary Poppins to the sisters of television's *Charmed* and, of course, Willow Rosenberg on *Buffy the Vampire Slayer*.

Those are all fictional witches.

Unlike the other "monsters" in this book, however, witches have a real life counterpart: practitioners of an established modern-day religion called Wicca. This earth-worshiping collective is, in fact, a fast-growing religion, and there's nothing diabolical about it. Wicca can trace its origin to ancient pagan religions with its roots in nature and its goal to be in harmony with the universe.

It should be made perfectly clear, however, that when we discuss witches or witchcraft in the following section, unless otherwise noted we are talking about creatures of myth or fiction that are wholly different from practicing Wiccans. No connection between the two is intended here.

While the words *witchcraft* and *sorcery* are frequently used interchangeably, upon examination of folklore and legend they are found to be slightly different. Sorcery has been described by many as the lowest form of magic, a technical craft involving the use of rituals, herbs, and charms in order to produce a desired result. According to legend, witches use sorcery but are also able to call upon their own inner powers to affect an outcome. What truly separates the two, however, seems to be nothing more than public perception. Historically, the practice of sorcery (the purported practice, to be accurate) has been largely tolerated in most cultures throughout the ages, whereas alleged witches have nearly always been looked upon with fear and dread.

The formation of the familiar myth

THE INQUISITION BEGAN in the thirteenth century as an effort by the Roman Catholic Church to root out heretics, those who opposed the Church's teachings or taught against them. All manner of perverse behavior was attributed to heretics, including raucous sexual orgies, communion with the devil, and the eating of babies. Such assertions were made to set the populace against heretics and force people to adhere more closely to the teachings of the Church. Those accused as heretics would be interrogated, often tortured, until they either died or confessed. In the fifteenth century, a man named Flavio Biondo—who was then the apostolic secretary to Pope Nicholas V—wrote about accused heretics in his book *Italia Illustrata.*

"They were very thoroughly investigated," he wrote. "And as they obstinately refused to come to their senses, were burned, as they deserved."

Throughout the fifteenth, sixteenth, and seventeenth centuries, any person of authority who desired to be rid of an individual or a group would need to do little more than accuse them of witchcraft, and the persecution, torture, and execution would begin.

Wholesale slaughter ensued. The traditional image of the wicked witch was, therefore, partially an invention of the Inquisition. The idea of witches as servants of Satan is certainly a Christian notion.

However, belief in sorcerers and witches can be traced back to prehistoric times—as long as we've had a collective sense of events happening around us that couldn't be explained. Why are the crops failing? Why did that child die so young? Why did the storm destroy the village? Blaming hardships and bad weather on local spellcasters seemed logical, and if punishing that evildoer could remedy the situation, that was even more logical still.

The deepest roots of belief in sorcery can be traced back some twenty-five thousand years, growing out of early man's fear of the unexplainable, uncontrollable forces of nature. In that age, gods were responsible for every aspect of life, including weather, hunting, and fertility. Rituals were created to manipulate these forces and influence the gods in an attempt to exert some control over daily life. Although the importance of these gods and rituals varied from culture to culture, the basic premise remained the same, forever linking religion with magic.

Early cave paintings depicting rituals for successful hunts seem to indicate that even prehistoric man practiced some simple form of sorcery. However, as belief systems evolved, so too did the practice of sorcery. Many ancient civilizations had complex belief systems involving multiple gods, spirits, and demons. Sorcerers served a vital function by acting as a link to the netherworld—performing rituals to gain the favor of the gods, invoking spirits for protection, and exorcising demons. Sorcerers were welcomed when their magic was performed for the benefit of the community and considered evil when magic was performed for a fee or for individual benefit.

The greatest influences on European witchcraft came from the ancient Greeks, Romans, and Hebrews. The Greeks believed that sorcerers consulted spirits—at first considered neither good nor evil—to work their magic. "High magic" was that used publicly in religious ceremonies whereas "low magic" was used privately and considered a menace to the community at large. Over time, those beliefs evolved into the notion of gods and demons. Consulting a god was deemed merely wise, but consulting a demon was considered an evil act.

Many of the characteristics of the Greek and Roman demons and deities were eventually assigned to witches—such as the Roman *strega*. The Greek feast of Dionysus—with its riotous, indulgent behavior—became the blueprint for the European notion of the witches' sabbat.

In ancient Rome, sorcery was popular among the general public, but Roman officials were quite intolerant of it. Accusations of sorcery were made indiscriminately and punishment was harsh, a tactic later to be adopted by the Christian Inquisition.

Like those other ancient cultures, the Hebrews also practiced sorcery. The Old Testament calls for the execution of malevolent sorcerers in the Book of Exodus, though the translation has become muddied throughout the years. Exodus 22:18 states, "Thou shall not suffer a kashaph to live." *Kashaph* is Hebrew for diviner or sorcerer, but when the instruction was translated into Latin, the term *maleficus* was used. *Maleficus* was later adopted to refer to witches, and the Christians of the fifteenth, sixteenth, and seventeenth centuries were able to use this verse as justification for the cruelty of the Inquisition.

Christianity is a monotheistic culture. They believe in only one true God, but also in that entity's evil counterpart, Satan, also called Lucifer or simply the devil. The evil spirits of the Christian faith are demons under the leadership of Satan who fought to undermine God and the human race. Sorcerers could invoke spirits. It therefore followed (per early Christian thought) that sorcerers were in league with the devil. That dubious connection was the fundamental building block of the sinister image of witchcraft so prevalent in mid-second-millenium Europe.

Prior to the thirteenth century, there was a general belief that magic existed naturally. Alleged witches who used magic for evil purposes were punished by civil courts. Common wisdom held that sorcerers were more likely to use magic for good. Although they were still regarded with some suspicion, purported sorcerers were generally tolerated, and the term was frequently applied to learned men such as physicians or alchemists, for it was thought their knowledge came from supernatural forces.

In fact, though the early Catholic Church expressly forbade the use of witchcraft, no such provision was made against sorcery, and some of the first popes were actually suspected of practicing it. As Christianity began to evolve and the old pagan, polytheistic religions began to dissipate, the notion of natural magic gradually changed to the belief that no magic existed naturally and it must therefore be diabolical. If the power did not come from God, it must come from Satan. The distinction between witchcraft and sorcery disappeared. Both were considered heresy and were now ecclesiastical crimes.

evolution of the Inquisition

IN 1144 POPE LUCIUS II BEGAN the Inquisition by creating the first investigative board of bishops. The group looked into allegations that priests were not teaching Church doctrine appropriately, and it pursued those charges with the decree that the accused were guilty until proven innocent. During the next two hundred years a series of papal edicts increased the power of the Inquisitors and expounded upon the evils of witchcraft and sorcery.

In 1484 Pope Innocent VIII reinforced papal support for the Inquisition and increased the powers of two German Inquisitors, Heinrich Kramer and Jakob Sprenger. Under the auspices of Innocent VIII, Kramer and Sprenger wrote the *Malleus Maleficarum* in 1486. Inspired by Exodus 22:18, the *Malleus Maleficarum* discussed the evils of witchcraft; explained how witches cast their spells and how to break them; and described the legal procedures for obtaining confessions, presenting evidence and sentencing those found guilty. Despite its blatant sexism and many contradictions, the *Malleus Maleficarum* quickly became the guide by which Inquisitors and judges (both Catholic and Protestant) conducted themselves. The Inquisition began in earnest, and during the next two hundred and fifty years more than one hundred thousand people (a modest estimate) were tortured and executed as witches before the madness of the European witch hunts began to decline by the middle of the seventeenth century.

Though the last accused witch was executed in Europe in 1685, the madness that had so long reigned over the people of that continent seemed to infect the New World in 1692. The Massachusetts Bay colony in New England was founded by Puritans, a Christian religious sect to whom every facet of life was a product of God's benevolence or the devil's malevolence. For such a fanatical group, the idea that witches might be among them was all too easy to believe.

It began, ghastly as it was, with precocious, rebellious children who chafed against their puritanical upbringing. For whatever reason—modern scholars believe it may have been to escape punishment—they blamed their improper behavior on demons, spirits, servants of Satan . . . witches were the cause, they claimed. And then they began to point fingers.

By January 1693 the fever had spread, causing townspeople in what was then part of Salem, Massachusetts, and the surrounding environs to accuse hundreds of their neighbors. All were investigated, and thirty-one were condemned to die for witchcraft. Of those, nineteen were hanged, one was pressed to death, two died in jail, one escaped, one remained in jail for an undetermined period, and seven were eventually released. Contrary to popular belief, no one was burned at the stake.

It was not until the last of the laws against witchcraft were repealed in England in the 1950s that practitioners of modern witchcraft began to be open about their religion and Wicca started to gain popularity. A worldwide revival of interest in the occult during the 1960s and '70s saw the spread of Wicca to the United States and elsewhere.

Wiccans view themselves as healers and helpers. Their religion is a diverse extraction of ancient pagan beliefs, Western esoteric tradition, folk magic, and more recently, shamanism and tribal doctrine.

from myth to fiction

DESPITE THE EFFORTS of modern-day witches to change public perception, popular culture continues to promote the stereotype of the wicked witch. Rarely has the persecution of witches— during the European Inquisition or the witch trials of New England—been represented with any sympathy toward those persecuted.

Tales about mythical witches can be found in literature as far back as the ancient Greeks. In his epic *The Odyssey* (eighth century B.C.), Homer told of Circe, the daughter of Hecate, who has long been considered the patron goddess of witchcraft and magic.

Among legendary users of magic, Merlin the magician is perhaps the most well known and, not coincidentally, the most often translated to entertainment media. His first appearance in literature occurs in the Latin works of Geoffrey of Monmouth, a twelfth-century Welsh cleric. *The Prophecies of Merlin*, written in the early 1130s, is comprised of prophecies allegedly made by a man in the fifth century named Merlin, though many historians believe that much of the book was the product of Monmouth's imagination. In the *History of the Kings of Britain*, completed in 1135,

Monmouth lays the groundwork for the Arthurian legends, with the wizard Merlin coming into his own as a character. A magical child, born of a union between a mortal woman and a spirit, he was endowed with great powers of prophecy and magic.

One of the best known and most influential literary works featuring Merlin is the epic poem *Le Morte D'Arthur*, written by Sir Thomas Malory in 1485. The poem details Merlin's involvement in the illicit encounter leading to Arthur's conception and his path to the throne. It also tells of his own fate, as the wizard is brought down by his passion for the sorceress Nimue.

Additional books featuring the popular magician include Spenser's *The Faerie Queene* (1590), Alfred Lord Tennyson's *Idylls of the King* (1917), C. S. Lewis's *That Hideous Strength* (1946), Mark Twain's *A Connecticut Yankee in King Arthur's Court* (1889) and T. H. White's *The Once and Future King* (1937), the latter of which served as the basis for the hit musical *Camelot*.

Macbeth, first published in 1623 (although likely written several years earlier), is one of William Shakespeare's most famous tragedies. It presents the tale of Macbeth's dubious rise to the throne of Scotland and subsequent fall from grace. The play opens with three witches performing incantations around a black cauldron. *Macbeth* is likely the most influential literary work when it comes to the public perception of witches as old hags. In fact, theatrical lore about the supposed curse associated with productions of *Macbeth* (unexplained "accidents" have frequently plagued the play) might be directly related to Shakespeare's portrayal of witches and witchcraft.

Macbeth has been translated to the silver screen several times by directors with the most prestigious of pedigrees including the 1948 version written, directed by, and starring Orson Welles, and Roman Polanski's 1971 film starring Jon Finch and Francesca Annis.

Following *Macbeth*, the next significant portrayal of witchcraft was Thomas Middleton's 1627 play titled *The Witch*. The production concerns a wealthy young woman who seeks revenge on her husband after he forces her to drink a toast from a cup made out of her father's skull.

Another influential tale of witchcraft, "The Sleeping Beauty," was recorded in 1696 by the French storyteller Charles Perrault. It is the tale of seven fairies that appear at the baptism of a king's daughter. Six give their blessings to the baby but the seventh fairy withholds her good wishes. An evil old hag full of misplaced anger because she didn't get her invitation in the proper manner casts a spell upon the child, cursing her so that the princess will fatally prick herself with the needle of a spindle. Later the curse is amended with a counterspell from the seventh good fairy, so that instead the princess merely falls asleep for a hundred years, only to be awakened should she receive the kiss of a prince.

Although the king orders all spinning wheels in the kingdom destroyed, while exploring one day the princess comes upon an old hag at a spinning wheel she had hidden away. Curious, the princess reaches out and pricks her finger on a needle. As predicted, one hundred years pass before the prince arrives with the prophesied kiss. The story has been adapted to film and television many times, but the most memorable was Walt Disney Studios' 1959 animated classic.

It is impossible to discuss tales about witches without mentioning the Brothers Grimm. As children, we are all told the Grimms' stories, including "Hansel and Gretel," in which an evil hag lures the children into her oven so that she can eat them. In our collective consciousness, at our most impressionable age, the Grimms taught us our first prejudicial thoughts about witches.

The two hundred stories known as *Grimm's Fairy Tales* were published in 1812 by Jacob and Wilhelm Grimm, after the brothers had spent some thirteen years gathering them from German citizenry. The majority of the villains in the Grimms' tales were women. From cooks to stepmothers, women were represented most often as voracious cannibals.

Many of the women in these tales are experts in the art of weaving spells. They are the witches and enchantresses for whom uttering curses rather than eating children is the favored pastime. Upon consideration, it is curious, even startling, that those horrible figures continue to occupy so prominent a position in the tales told to children.

There were stories published based upon accounts of supposedly real witches as well. *The Lancashire Witches*, written by William Harrison Ainsworth in 1849, has the distinction of being the first English novel based on actual witch trials. Those trials took place in the Pendle Forest area of Lancaster County, England, in 1612, where an eighty-year-old woman was accused by a local rival of being a witch.

After being questioned by authorities, the old, blind woman confessed and then accused her two granddaughters as well. In all, twenty people were arrested, most related to the three accused witches, and ended up testifying against each other. Ten of the accused were eventually found guilty and hanged.

In 1851 Salem, Massachusetts, native Nathaniel Hawthorne, widely considered one of the great writers of early American fiction, authored *House of the Seven Gables*. This novel explores the moral concept of an individual paying for the sins of his forefathers and may have been written out of guilt over the actions of his distant relative, John Hathorne, a magistrate in the Salem witch trials.

The arrival of the twentieth century brought witches to the new entertainment medium, the motion picture. From its very roots, cinema owed a debt to magic and sorcery—particularly its male practitioners. As Erik Barnouw documented in his book *The Magician and the Cinema* (1981), popular stage magicians played a vital role in the evolution of the cinema itself, working as inventors, producers, and exhibitors at the end of the nineteenth century. At first, the use of projected moving images enhanced stage trickery, but soon film became a vehicle for the magicians themselves.

The most prominent and influential of these pioneers was French filmmaker Georges Méliès, who almost single-handedly laid the bedrock for all film special effects techniques and popularized fantasy and science fiction cinema. Méliès wrote, directed, and starred in most of his playfully inventive short films, often playing a magician or sorceror performing magic among dancing girls (echoes of the nearby Paris Folies Bèrgere).

In his first year of film production, Méliès starred as the *Conjuror Making Ten Hats in Sixty Seconds* (1896). Later productions included *The Bewitched Inn* and two separate productions adapted from *Faust*: *Black Magic* (1898) and *Fantastical Illusions* (1898). Witches figured prominently, too, in Méliès's shorts like *Beelzebub's Daughters, The Enchanted Well, The Witch's Revenge* (all 1903), *The Merry Frolics of Satan* (1906), and *The Witch* (1906).

In America, cinema pioneers such as Thomas Edison, J. Stuart Blackton, and stage magicians such as Harry Houdini were producing their own magic on-screen, while G. A. Smith and Walter

R. Booth broke similar ground in the U.K. Smith mounted the first film version of *Cinderella* (1898) in England, and Edison produced the first known adaptation of *Hansel and Gretel* (1909).

Another significant turn-of-the-century male magician was the notorious self-proclaimed practitioner of "magick" Aleister Crowley (1875–1947). He joined Britain's most prominent magic cult, the Hermetic Order of the Golden Dawn, in 1898, and thereafter studied in Egypt and founded his own magical order, the Argentinum Astrum. Occultist Crowley was also referred to as Frater Perdurabo, "The Beast 666," and "England's Worst Man," and his lifetime (and often public) exploration of "magick," hedonistic sex, drugs, religious cults, and more earned him a reputation as a murderer, a child-killer, and a cannibal.

Though Crowley was eventually banished from Italy (after the death of one of his followers) and other countries, none of those accusations led to a trial, much less being burned at the stake. He died penniless and obscure in 1947. He left behind him a number of books—including *Diary of a Drug Fiend* (1922), *The Moonchild* (1929), and *The Confessions of Aleister Crowley* (1930)—as well as the edict "Do what thou wilt shall be the whole of the law" and a legacy that outlived him.

Crowley inspired W. Somerset Maugham's novel *The Magician* (1923), which Rex Ingram filmed in 1926 with German horror star Paul Wegener in the title role. He was the model for a procession of evil, cinematic magic users (Boris Karloff in *The Black Cat*, 1934, among them) and dominating mesmerists and cult figures (John Barrymore as *Svengali* and *The Mad Genius*, both 1931). John Symonds's book *The Great Beast* (1951) reinvigorated the public fascination with Crowley. American underground filmmaker Kenneth Anger considered himself a disciple of Crowley, and his interest in "magick" and ritual informed many of his films, including *Inauguration of the Pleasure Dome* (1954) and *Invocation of My Demon Brother* (1969). Dennis Wheatley's novel *The Devil Rides Out* (1934) and others featured satanic cult leaders inspired by Crowley, an archetype embodied by actor Charles Gray in the Hammer Films' adaptation of *The Devil Rides Out* (aka *The Devil's Bride,* 1968). Crowley's influence continued until it was eclipsed in the late 1960s by that of cult leader and convicted murderer Charles Manson (see below).

In 1922, Swedish auteur Benjamin Christensen directed *Witchcraft Through the Ages*, still considered the most comprehensive film on witchcraft. Christensen carefully crafted "re-creations" of centuries-old pagan rites, black magic, and the inhumanities of the Inquisition. Its vivid horrors—including witches' orgies, the boiling of babies, nudity, and gore—were trimmed in many countries, and the film was banned in others. In 1966 William Burroughs recorded a narration for the film, earning a rerelease and renewed stature on the art house and college circuits.

Witchcraft and sorcery were common fodder for the sensationalist pulp magazines so common in America in the early twentieth century, including, naturally, *Witches' Tales*. Horror radio dramas featuring witches and witchcraft were also popular in the pre-television era.

In the comic-book medium, one of the oldest and most recognizable magic users was Mandrake the Magician. Created in 1934 by writer Lee Falk and artist Phil Davis, Mandrake didn't possess any magical powers at all. Rather, he was the world's foremost illusionist and hypnotist. Despite the natural explanation for his mysterious talents, Mandrake's adventures were often quite incredible, taking him to other dimensions and planets and pitting him against such strange creatures as ghosts, werewolves, and alien invaders. Mandrake's adventures can still be read in newspapers around the world.

Mandrake inspired his share of imitators, most notably Zatara the Master Magician. First appearing in *Action Comics* #1 in 1938, John Zatara was the grandson of the great stage magician Luigi Zatara and began his own professional career as a magician at nineteen. Zatara was killed in a 1980s storyline in DC Comics' *Swamp Thing* while battling the otherworldly Shadow Creature.

The year 1937 brought the classic fairy tale witch to the world with Walt Disney Studios' first full-length animated feature, *Snow White and the Seven Dwarfs*, based on the Brothers Grimm fairy tale.

In this now-familiar story, the vain witch-queen consults the spirit of the magic mirror and discovers that Snow White is more beautiful than she. The jealous queen orders a huntsman to take the girl into the forest and kill her, but at the last minute he relents and leaves her in the care of the seven dwarfs. When the queen learns Snow White is still alive, she disguises herself as an old hag and offers the girl a poisoned apple. Snow White falls into a deep coma until a handsome prince happens by and breaks the spell with a kiss. The wicked witch-queen is killed by lightning, and Snow White, the prince, and the seven dwarfs live happily ever after.

The character of the queen-witch, once described by Walt Disney himself as a cross between Lady Macbeth and the Big, Bad Wolf, was created by Art Babbitt and drawn by Norm Fergusson. They created a character who was haughty and beautiful, but who could also cast a spell to disguise herself as an ugly, contorted old woman dressed in a black robe with a pointed hood. The end result was a classic interpretation of the traditional evil witch. A live action and far more adult version of Snow White was broadcast on cable television in 1997. *Snow White: A Tale of Terror* is a dark retelling of the story.

In 1939, MGM cemented the traditional old hag image to witchcraft in *The Wizard of Oz*. Based on the 1900 novel by L. Frank Baum, the film grafted its wicked witch so indelibly onto the collective consciousness of twentieth-century society that the image of actress Margaret Hamilton—dressed all in black, cackling and green-faced as she rides atop her broom—is still the one that comes most quickly to mind for many when they hear the word *witch*. *The Wizard of Oz* presents a world in which there are good witches and wicked ones. The film's presentation of magic includes spells, familiars (flying monkeys, oh my!), crystal balls, and broomsticks, though of course the titular wizard turns out to be a fake. The following year Mickey Mouse appeared as the title character of "The Sorcerer's Apprentice," a segment of the animated film *Fantasia*.

Another major magical debut in 1940 was Dr. Fate, the most powerful sorcerer in the DC Comics universe. Dr. Fate first appeared in *More Fun Comics* #55, in which archaeologist Sven Nelson and his young son, Kent, were exploring an ancient temple in the Valley of Ur in Mesopotamia. Young Kent found the tomb of the wizard Nabu the Wise, who was actually just in a state of suspended animation. Nabu offered to teach the boy the ways of sorcery, magically transforming him into a man. Eventually Kent became an agent in the never-ending battle between order and chaos, and was presented with a golden helmet, cape, and amulet that would increase his magical powers. Dr. Fate was the first of the gaudily costumed, superhero magic users that would become such a staple in comic books. The concepts of order and chaos implicit here were tapped into much later by *Buffy the Vampire Slayer*'s representation of its sorcerer Ethan Rayne, a chaos worshiper.

Also making his first appearance in *More Fun Comics* #55 was Wotan, a mysterious and unearthly sorcerer who did battle with Nabu the Wise many millennia ago. Sporting a high-backed, red-collared, flowing green cape and a bizarre hairstyle, Wotan is one of the more interesting-looking villains to plague the heroes of the DC universe.

Yet another comic-book magician similar to Mandrake and Zatara was Sargon the Sorcerer. Making his first appearance in *All-American Comics* #26 in 1941, Sargon's alter ego was archeologist John Sargent, who gained amazing magical powers from the Ruby of Life. Sargent launched a career as the stage magician, Sargon the Sorcerer, so people would think the magical effects he created were merely stage tricks. He too became a master crime fighter and joined up with the All Star Squadron. Sargon the Sorcerer met a gruesome end alongside Zatara in DC Comics' *Swamp Thing*.

The 1940s were the golden age of Hollywood romantic comedies, and witchcraft was just as likely a subject as any other as a springboard for such films. One of the most popular classic romantic comedies was *I Married a Witch* (United Artists, 1942). Based on the novel *The Passionate Witch* by Thorne Smith, the film was directed by René Clair and starred Fredric March and Veronica Lake. Using Hollywood beauty Lake as a witch was a first step in shifting people's perceptions away from the belief that witches were evil, ugly old crones.

In 1943 legendary horror producer Val Lewton's *The Seventh Victim* was released by RKO. This offbeat, eerie production was directed by Mark Robson and starred Kim Hunter as an innocent stumbling into a New York City coven of devil worshipers. Its surprisingly sober presentation of a contemporary urban coven, and the almost palpable sense of despair that drives one of its characters to suicide, are still striking today. Republic Pictures produced a similarly understated, atmospheric contemporary witch tale, *The Woman Who Came Back* (1945).

The late 1940s and 1950s produced a great many versions of the by now familiar sinister figure of the haglike witch. One of the most memorable of these was the Old Witch, who hosted tales of terror in the EC Comics title *The Haunt of Fear*. The Old Witch would introduce each story, often hunched over a bubbling cauldron filled with all kinds of disgusting things.

The Chronicles of Narnia is a series of seven children's books written by C. S. Lewis and set in the mythical land of Narnia. Imbued with Christian values, the books were designed to stimulate young imaginations and contain all kinds of supernatural characters and kingdoms. Witches are the villains in three of the books.

In the first volume, *The Lion, the Witch, and the Wardrobe*, published in 1950, the White Witch casts a spell over Narnia, causing perpetual winter, and has the ability to turn people into statues with a wave of her magic wand. *The Magician's Nephew*, written as a prequel to the first book, tells the story of the birth of Narnia and the evil queen Jadis's journey to becoming the White Witch. In the series' sixth installment, *The Silver Chair*, Prince Rilian is bewitched by the Lady of the Green Kirtle (who also killed his mother) and must be rescued by two London schoolchildren.

The 1953 Fritz Leiber novel *Conjure Wife* (first published in the pulp magazine *Unknown* in 1943) brought the witch into modern society. It is the story of a professor who learns that his wife is a witch. He throws away all of her charms, herbs, and so on, only to discover that his wife is a good witch, who was furthering his career through magic and protecting him against the evil spells of other university wives.

The novel deftly plays on the male notion that women possess secret powers and use them to their advantage. *Conjure Wife* has been adapted to film three times. *Weird Woman* (Universal, 1944) starred Lon Chaney Jr. and was the second of the studio's Inner Sanctum series. *Burn, Witch, Burn!* was a 1961 British effort scripted by Charles Beaumont and Richard Matheson and directed by Sydney Hayers for American International Pictures (AIP). *Burn, Witch, Burn!* captured the contemporary edge of Leiber's novel and remains one of the best witchcraft films. The third and weakest film was *Witches' Brew* (Embassy, 1980), Hollywood legend Lana Turner's last film.

The year 1953 also saw the first production of Arthur Miller's classic play *The Crucible*, based on actual events in 1692 in Salem. Written at the height of the McCarthy hearings on un-American, communist activities, *The Crucible* serves as an intentional metaphor for the modern-day witch-hunt. Miller himself was cited for contempt of Congress for not naming suspected communists.

The Witches of Salem was the first adaptation of Miller's play to the screen. Filmed in Europe in 1957, *The Witches of Salem* boasted a screenplay by Jean-Paul Sartre. The most recent film version of *The Crucible* (Twentieth Century Fox, 1996) was also the first made in America. It starred Winona Ryder and Daniel Day-Lewis, with a screenplay by Miller himself. The basic themes of the story were turned on their head in the third-season *Buffy the Vampire Slayer* episode "Gingerbread," in which a parents' group organized a witch-hunt targeting their own children.

In 1954, in the pages of Harvey Publications' *Casper the Friendly Ghost* #16, the world was introduced to one of the most innocent interpretations of the legendary witch to date, Wendy the Good Little Witch. She proved to be so popular that she received her own backup feature in *Spooky* (Casper's nasty cousin) *and Harvey Hits*, and eventually starred in her own title in 1960. *Wendy the Good Little Witch* was canceled in 1964, but the character survives in other media, including the direct-to-video film *Casper Meets Wendy* (1999).

Over the course of the years 1954 and 1955, legendary fantasy author J. R. R. Tolkien's famed trilogy The Lord of the Rings was first published, though it did not begin to achieve the height of its popularity until the following decade. The series featured a powerful but bewildering wizard named Gandalf, who has since become perhaps the most famous practitioner of sorcery since Merlin. The character had first appeared in Tolkien's children's classic *The Hobbit*, a prelude to The Lord of the Rings, that was revised and rereleased in 1966.

A 1978 animated version of *The Lord of the Rings* (Fantasy), made by Ralph Bakshi, covered the first one and a half books in the J. R. R. Tolkien series. Bakshi also made *Fire and Ice* (PSO) in 1983. In that tale of good versus evil, Lord Neckron uses sorcery and black magic in an attempt to overthrow King Jarol. Currently, a live-action version of the Rings trilogy is in production in New Zealand, directed by Peter Jackson and starring Elijah Wood, Ethan Hawke, Christopher Lee, and Liv Tyler.

In 1968 author Peter S. Beagle's *The Last Unicorn* first saw print. The tale—revolving around a unicorn's search for others of its kind—also introduced Schmendrick, a wizard who, thanks to the book's popularity, laid the groundwork for many bumbling, well-meaning magicians in the years to come.

Western images of witches had long since begun to make their way around the world when filmmaking giant Akira Kurosawa directed *Throne of Blood* (Toho, aka *Kumonosu Jo*) in 1957, an adaptation of Shakespeare's *Macbeth*.

The presence of witches in popular culture had by that time split into two main veins, one that played the witchcraft for humor and romance and another that focused upon the more sinister elements of witchcraft, including its violent history.

Following on the legacy of *I Married a Witch*, James Stewart, Kim Novak, and Jack Lemmon starred in *Bell, Book, and Candle* (Phoenix/Columbia, 1958), based on a comic stage play by John Van Druten. That film was the perfect example of the more innocent representation of witches in pop culture. However, 1960 brought to the screen a pair of cult classic motion pictures that focused upon a frightening, depraved brand of witches.

Black Sunday (Filmfax, 1960) is an Italian horror film starring Barbara Steele. Mario Bava directed this highly stylized movie about an ancient witch who is accidentally brought back to life. After she raises her vampire slave from his rotting grave, the two go on a reign of terror in a production that proved to be cinematically ahead of its time. What this film may lack in plot it more than makes up for in its atmospheric sense of dread and danger. *Black Sunday* is widely acknowledged as a masterpiece of horror cinema.

The second 1960 film to play on the traditional evil-witch imagery was the British *Horror Hotel* (United, also known as *The City of the Dead*). The great Christopher Lee is a college professor who specializes in witchcraft and the occult and practices what he teaches. When he sends an innocent young student off to the home of his coven in New England to research her term paper, we find an eighteenth-century witch running a hotel and the suspense begins. Though a bit dated now, *Horror Hotel* remains a chilling classic. The film is known to have been an influence upon *Buffy the Vampire Slayer* creator Joss Whedon, and an uncredited clip from the film appeared in the "mockumentary" *Curse of the Blair Witch* (1999).

Also in 1960, Marvel Comics introduced Dr. Droom in *Strange Tales* #79, a sorcerous character who would become the prototype for one of the best known magical characters in comics history, master of the mystic arts Dr. Strange. After Strange had been introduced and developed as a separate character, Marvel creators would return to Droom and transform him into Dr. Druid.

Now called Dr. Druid, the character was reintroduced to the Marvel Universe in 1974 with a reprint of his first adventure in *Weird Wonder Tales* #19. He was a Harvard-educated psychiatrist who retired from his practice to pursue a growing interest in the supernatural. A dying Tibetan lama mystically opened the doctor's mind to its hidden power, teaching him control over certain mystic arts. Druid now possessed the racial memory of his Celtic ancestors and employed the skill and powers of the ancient Druid priests. Eventually Druid became a member of the Avengers but was killed in battle during a Dr. Druid miniseries in 1995.

By 1962 teenagers ruled the entertainment world. Hence the teens of Riverdale High in Archie Comics' various series had a new addition to their roster: the adorable Sabrina, the teenage witch.

Like Wendy the Good Little Witch, Sabrina also lived with her witch aunts, who, in the first comics, resembled the stereotypical hags of myth and folklore. Sabrina made her first appearance in *Archie's Madhouse* #22 in 1962 and proved to be so popular that she showed up as a regular character in the new *Archie's TV Laugh Out* #1 in 1969. The teenage witch's popularity continued to grow with her appearances on the animated Saturday morning show, *The Groovie Ghoulies,* and her own cartoon series, *Sabrina the Teenage Witch.*

Sabrina received her own monthly comic-book series in 1971. Sabrina played host to tales of supernatural terror in *Chilling Adventures in Sorcery as Told by Sabrina.* Sabrina's involvement with that title lasted only two issues, as it changed to more of a straight horror format with issue #3. Sabrina has gone on to gain even greater popularity with several made-for-TV movies, a successful network television series starring Melissa Joan Hart, a series of novels, a new cartoon show, and the return of her monthly comic book.

Marvel Comics' *Fantastic Four* #5 (1962) marked the first appearance of Dr. Doom, not to be confused with the onetime prototype character Dr. Droom. Though primarily a villain of high-tech means, Dr. Doom dabbled in the art of sorcery and black magic to save the soul of a loved one—his mother, who he believed was trapped in some hellish alternate reality. When a device he made to contact her exploded, Doom hid his now disfigured face behind a metal mask and a high-tech suit of armor and spent his time trying to conquer the world and destroy his most hated enemies, the Fantastic Four. In 1989, however, he joined forces with Dr. Strange in the graphic novel *Triumph and Torment* to free his mother's trapped soul from the hellish realm of the demonic Mephisto.

DC Comics had focused mainly on superheroes in the '50s. In 1962, however, DC introduced a new character, the villainous Felix Faust, in *Justice League of America* #10. With the help of conjured demons, Faust took control of the superhero team, the Justice League of America, in an attempt gain magical supremacy over the world. Though he was eventually defeated, Faust has returned several times to torment the Justice League. Recently his son entered the world of superheroes, more an antihero than a villain like his father.

In 1963 Marvel Comics finally went back to the inspiration that had led to the creation of Dr. Droom three years earlier. The master of the mystic arts (and later sorcerer supreme) of the earth dimension, Dr. Strange first appeared in *Strange Tales* #110. An egotistical, heartless surgeon whose hands were irreparably damaged in a car accident after a night of drinking, Stephen Strange sensed he might have a chance to regain the use of his hands and embarked on a journey to Tibet in search of the Ancient One. Strange became a more caring person and a disciple of a holy man whose life he saved, eventually acquiring the Ancient One's vast power and becoming Sorcerer Supreme of Earth. Dr. Strange has been in almost continuous publication in the ensuing decades, both in titles bearing his own name and in various incarnations of *Strange Tales* and *The Defenders.*

The original sorcerer archetype returned in 1963, when Disney's animated *Sword in the Stone* gave us a very traditional interpretation of Merlin the magician, right down to long white beard, flowing gown, and pointed wizard's cap.

In 1964, *X-Men* #4 introduced Wanda Maximoff, the Scarlet Witch, as a member of Magneto's Brotherhood of Evil Mutants. Not an actual witch in the classic sense but possessing the ability to affect probability fields, the Scarlet Witch is now a member of the Avengers. She also has some training in sorcery and witchcraft, enabling her to hone her natural mutant abilities and gain more control over her powers.

Hawkman #4 in 1964 introduced Zatanna, daughter of the Golden Age superhero magician Zatara, who married a member of a race of humans with innate magical abilities. Since 1964 Zatanna has made frequent guest appearances in such books as *The Atom*, *Green Lantern,* and *Batman* and was made a member of the Justice League of America in issue #161 of that series. What set Zatanna apart from the other female superheroic magic users was her unique and quite sexy costume, which consisted of top hat, tails, and fishnet stockings. She starred in her own one-shot special in 1987 and received her own four-issue miniseries in 1993. Most recently Zatanna used her magic to help save the world from a vast supernatural threat in the 1999 comic-book miniseries *Day of Judgement.*

Another interesting witchlike character, the Enchantress, first appeared in DC Comics' *Strange Adventures* #187 in 1965. June Moore, a freelance artist, was transformed into the black-haired, green-eyed Enchantress. Although the Enchantress started out a hero, she later became a villain. In the recent 1999 supernatural event, *Day of Judgement,* the Enchantress sacrificed her life in order to reignite the fires of hell, which had been frozen over.

In 1964 the lighthearted variety of witches was represented in the children's film *Mary Poppins*, an adaptation of the 1934 book by P. L. Travers, starring Julie Andrews in her Academy Award–winning film debut, and actor-comedian Dick Van Dyke. Mary Poppins is an enchantress but the source of her power is never revealed. Through "magic" she is able to reunite the children with their busy banker father and, in the end, flies away with her umbrella to help other needy children.

The Emmy-winning *Bewitched* enjoyed an eight-year run on ABC, from September 1964 to July 1972. Elizabeth Montgomery, a tremendously versatile actress, brought Samantha—a beautiful young witch married to a human male—to life with great humor and humanity.

Samantha's witch mother, Endora, the mother-in-law from hell, was played by the great character actress Agnes Moorehead, and the befuddled, absentminded witch was embodied in the character of Aunt Clara, played so memorably by Marion Lorne. Comedian Paul Lynde played Uncle Arthur, the wisecracking, practical-joking warlock. Dick York played Samantha's husband, Darrin Stephens, from 1964 until 1968, when Dick Sargent assumed the role until 1972. *Tabitha*, a 1977 spin-off of *Bewitched*, followed the adventures of Samantha and Darrin's daughter as an adult. The series lasted only one season.

Bewitched remains one of the most popular of the older series in TV syndication. If Margaret Hamilton's is the face of the wicked witch in the collective consciousness of American popular culture, then Elizabeth Montgomery's is the face of the good witch.

The Addams Family, based on characters created by cartoonist Charles Addams in 1935 for

The New Yorker magazine, found a home on the ABC schedule from 1964 to 1966. In Grandmama Addams, an old witch frequently seen in the dungeon-like kitchen mixing up a brew, the series managed to combine the lighthearted comedic witch with the sinister hag of folklore. An animated version of *The Addams Family* ran on NBC's Saturday morning cartoon lineup from 1973 to 1975.

NBC added *I Dream of Jeannie* to their schedule in the fall of 1965. Though legend indicates that genies or *djinni* are not human and thus should probably not be included in this chapter at all, it would have been impossible to include Elizabeth Montgomery's Samantha without also noting Barbara Eden's Jeannie.

In 1966 Warner Brothers and Hammer Films collaborated to produce *The Devil's Own* (also called *The Witches*). Adapted by Nigel Kneale *(Quatermass)* from the Peter Curtis novel of the same name, the film is the story of an English schoolteacher who uncovers witchcraft in her small rural community.

THE DEVIL'S OWN

That same year, the Gothic soap opera *Dark Shadows* not only made a pop-culture icon out of a vampire, but introduced witches to daytime television as well. In 1785 Barnabas Collins, the son of a prominent landowner, had a heated affair with a servant girl and witch, Angelique Bouchard. Unfortunately, he also fell in love with the plantation owner's daughter, Josette. Angelique used her powers to make Josette fall in love with Barnabas's brother, who was challenged to a duel and killed by the spurned Barnabas.

Barnabas turned on Angelique, who carried her bitter hatred for her former lover beyond the grave and was reincarnated in modern times as a woman named Cassandra, who married Barnabas's descendant, Roger Collins. A very popular character, Angelique continued to pursue Barnabas throughout the series and is featured as the major threat in the second *Dark Shadows* film, *Night of Dark Shadows* (MGM/UA, 1971) as well as the 1991 NBC prime-time revival of the series.

Lara Parker, so memorable as Angelique in the original *Dark Shadows* series, also played a witch in "The Trevi Collection," an episode of the 1975 ABC series *Kolchak: The Night Stalker*. Parker was featured as a model who used witchcraft to control a fashion designer and to eliminate her competition.

Ira Levin's novel—and the 1968 Paramount movie—*Rosemary's Baby* (see Demons) perpetuates all of the negative stereotypes about witches. Satan instructs a group of devil worshipers who call themselves witches to find him a mortal woman he can rape to create a son who will become the Antichrist. Rosemary Woodhouse's husband, Guy, seduced by the coven, offers her up in exchange for success in his acting career. Rosemary endures a difficult pregnancy, cared for by her neighbors (and coven members), who ply her with herbs and insist she wear an amulet filled with foul-smelling tanis root. Although told the child died at birth, Rosemary hears the infant's cry and seeks him out, finding him swaddled in black in a black bassinet and surrounded by the coven, which now includes her husband.

The Conqueror Worm (American International Pictures, 1968, aka Witchfinder General) starred Vincent Price in an excellent performance as Matthew Hopkins, a real-life figure during the Cromwell era in Britain. The literate script, based on a novel by Ronald Bassett, pitted Price's character, the witch hunter, against two sympathetic young lovers. This extremely violent bit of cinema was set in 1645 and directed by Michael Reeves.

Director Ken Russell's The Devils (Warner/Russo) was released in 1971 amid much controversy and condemnation. The film was Russell's unique vision of a play by John Whiting, based on Aldous Huxley's 1952 novel The Devils of Loudun, which concerned actual events that occurred in France in 1634 and centers around a group of nuns who were supposedly possessed by demons (see Demons).

The international notoriety and box office success of The Conqueror Worm and The Devils opened the floodgates for a number of increasingly violent witch-hunt exploitation films, which chronicled similar medieval horrors with reckless abandon and heavy doses of nudity, torture, and gore. The most infamous of these was Michael Armstrong's Mark of the Devil (Lightning, 1971), with its "The First Film Rated 'V' for Violence!" ballyhoo and savvy vomit-bag-for-every-customer salesmanship (the original vomit bags are highly prized collector's items today). The MPAA sued the distributors over the false rating, but the German producer and American distributor rushed an even grislier sequel, Mark of the Devil 2 (Lightning, 1969), into theaters.

Franco's Night of the Blood Monster (1972) and others followed, though evidently sated audiences stayed away. Hammer produced possibly the best of the witch-hunt follow-ups, the excellent Freudian horror film Demons of the Mind (1972), but it, too, failed at the box office.

Inspired by the success of Rosemary's Baby and the sensationalistic notoriety of the Manson cult murders, there followed a series of films whose plots revolved around magic users with demonic connections. Not surprisingly, given the time period, most of these were depicted as hedonist youths, drug-crazed long-haired hippies, and wild-eyed religious fanatics. Andrew Prine practiced sorcery in the sewers of Los Angeles as Simon, King of the Witches (1971). Troy Donahue led a "family"-like cult into New York City to commit The Love-Thrill Murders (aka Sweet Savior, Troma, 1971). Robert Quarry led the hippie-vampire cult of Deathmaster (AIP, 1972). And vicious hippie satanists were infected with rabies and battled equally rabid rednecks in the bloody drive-in classic I Drink Your Blood (Cinemation, 1971).

The Dunwich Horror (AIP, 1969), based on a story by H. P. Lovecraft, turned Lovecraft's deformed bastard child from the union between mortal woman and ancient Elder monster-god into a handsome New England warlock (Dean Stockwell). Sexy sorceress sisters in Nebraska had their way with a pack of motorcyclists en route to California in the offbeat witch-Western-biker-hippie movie Hex (Twentieth Century Fox, 1973). Devil-worshiping youths plagued the medieval British countryside in the wonderfully evocative The Blood on Satan's Claw (Paragon, 1971) and Cry of the Banshee (AIP, 1970), among others. There was also Virgin Witch (1972), Ted V. Mikels's lurid Blood Orgy of the She Devils (1972), and the low-budget Michigan independent The Demon Lover (1976). The made-in-the-Philippines Daughters of Satan (1972) had little to recommend it save that it featured popular film and television actor Tom Selleck in his first film role.

Not all the witches were youngsters. Orson Welles donned a putty nose and black robes to oversee *Necromancy* (1972), Patrick Magee led the loony religious sect that terrorized London in *Beware My Brethren* (aka *The Fiend*, Monterey, 1971), and dying occultist Curd Jürgens transferred his soul to young Alan Alda's body in *The Mephisto Waltz* (Twentieth Century Fox/QM, 1971). Talented character actor Strother Martin starred in *The Brotherhood of Satan* (RCA/Columbia, 1971), the tale of a witch's coven taking over a town.

In hindsight, perhaps the most interesting of this cycle of early 1970s witchcraft movies was George Romero's overlooked and underrated *Season of the Witch* (aka *Jack's Wife* or *Hungry Wives*, Vidamerica, 1972). Though the production and performances betrayed their meager resources, this tale of a middle-aged Pittsburgh housewife (Jan White) embracing the Wiccan lifestyle was a decidedly subversive feminist drama.

In 1970 Marvel Comics managed to merge the lighthearted, benevolent witch and the sinister old hag in Agatha Harkness, who made her first appearance in *Fantastic Four* #94. Living in an old mansion in the Adirondack Mountains, Harkness dressed in long, flowing Victorian clothes and had a mess of wild white hair. She even had a cat familiar named Ebony that had the ability to transform into a demonic black panther. She became governess and protector to Reed Richards and Sue Storm's young son, Franklin, in *Fantastic Four*. It was also Agatha Harkness who taught the Scarlet Witch the art of witchcraft. Harkness has since passed on, but she does occasionally make an appearance from beyond the grave as spiritual adviser to the Scarlet Witch, not unlike *Star Wars'* Obi-Wan Kenobi's continuing guidance to his protégé Luke Skywalker.

In 1971 Disney Studios produced the musical fantasy *Bedknobs and Broomsticks*, starring Angela Lansbury. In lieu of a broomstick, the witch and the children ride on a flying bed, hence the title.

In 1972 Marvel Comics' *Fear* #1 presented an interesting spin on the teen-skewed "young girl gifted with great power" theme, an idea that would culminate in recent pop-culture television sensations such as *Charmed*, *Sabrina the Teenage Witch*, *The Secret World of Alex Mack,* and, in particular, *Buffy the Vampire Slayer*. The comic introduced us to Jennifer Kale, a teenager with an interest in witchcraft, whose grandfather was leader of a cult that worshipped the Atlantean sorceress Zahred-Ra. Since becoming a sorceress, she has allied herself with such powerful Marvel characters as Spider-Man, the Ghost Rider, and Dr. Strange.

A masterfully crafted, shudder-inducing motion picture, the cult classic *The Wicker Man* (British Lion/Brut, 1973) starred Edward Woodward and Christopher Lee. In this absorbing thriller written by Anthony Shaffer, Woodward portrayed a Scottish police sergeant who arrives on a small island to investigate the disappearance of a child and finds a society of modern pagans. Filled with seemingly authentic local color and flavor this film is erotic and eerie, a must-see for any fan of subtle horror films.

In 1974 Marvel Comics introduced readers to a new kind of magic and magic user in *Strange Tales* #169. To avenge his brother's death from an evil sorcerer's spell, Jericho Drumm learned the ways of voodoo from the mysterious Papa John, and, known as Brother Voodoo, Drumm established himself as a champion of the land.

In 1975, Modred the Mystic made his first appearance in *Marvel Chillers* #1. Sometimes portrayed as a villain and other times as a brooding antihero, Modred was a sixth-century British sorcerer who gave his soul to the demon Chthon in exchange for vast supernatural power and knowledge. Inhabited by a demon, Modred's body is virtually immortal and indestructible. Although his first appearance was in 1975, he wasn't seen again until he showed up as a villain to create chaos for the Avengers and the Scarlet Witch in the mid-1980s. In 1992 he became a regular in the short-lived series *Darkhold: Pages from the Book of Sins* with issue #3.

The theme of witches in a secret sect in a small community that had worked so effectively in *The Wicker Man* continued to be popular. Genuine Satan-worshiper Anton Le Vey fostered media attention (including talk show appearances) and acted as a consultant on the offbeat *The Devil's Rain* (United, 1975), which featured a surprisingly star-filled cast including Ernest Borgnine, Ida Lupino, William Shatner, Tom Skerritt, and a young John Travolta in his feature film debut. More effective was the low-budget *Race with the Devil* (Twentieth Century Fox, 1975). Peter Fonda and Warren Oates starred in the story of two couples who witness a black mass while vacationing in their motor home and end up running for their lives from the Satan-worshiping witches trying to protect their secret society.

The great Italian horror director Dario Argento made the dreamlike classic *Suspiria* (Magnum) in 1977. In this supernatural tale, Jessica Harper plays an American student attending a European ballet school that turns out to be run by a witch's coven. Following on that theme was the 1978 made-for-television movie *The Dark Secret of Harvest Home* (NBC), based on the novel *Harvest Home* by Thomas Tryon. Witches, witchcraft, warlocks, and witch hunters had been a fixture of network TV movies for a decade. Louis Jourdan tangled with sorcery in *Fear No Evil* (NBC, 1969) and *Ritual of Evil* (NBC, 1969). Roy Thinnes was sacrificed by devil worshipers in the offbeat western *Black Noon* (CBS, 1971), but he led his own cult in *Satan's School for Girls* (ABC, 1973). The spirits of colonial victims of a witch hunt haunted *Crowhaven Farm* (ABC, 1970).

Exorcist star Linda Blair was the teenage protagonist threatened by a teen witch in the TV-movie adaptation of Lois Duncan's young adult bestseller *Summer of Fear* (aka *Stranger in Our House*, NBC, 1978, directed by horror-meister Wes Craven). Shelley Winters starred as a sorority house mother in the college-witch-coven movie *The Initiation of Sarah* (ABC, 1978). There were many, many others.

Television also offered a pair of short-lived shows featuring magicians or sorcerers. *The Magician*, starring Bill Bixby, ran on NBC from October 1973 through May 1974. Broadcast on CBS from October 1981 to August 1982, *Mr. Merlin* transported Merlin (Barnard Hughes) from Camelot to the twentieth century, where "Max Merlin" owned and operated a garage in San Francisco.

Peter Straub's phenomenal landmark novel *Shadowland* (1980) is the story of Tom Flannagan, a young stage magician who has yet to realize his true potential, his friend Del Nightengale, and Del's uncle, the master stage magician Coleman Collins.

Coleman lives in a creepy old house called Shadowland. He begins to recognize the power hidden in Tom Flannagan and realizes that the boy could be a threat to his position as master magician, or King of Cats, as Straub refers to it. To preserve his status as master, Coleman destroys his own nephew and attempts to kill Tom. In a climactic magical battle to the death, Flannagan vanquishes Coleman to become the new King of Cats.

Shadowland is a remarkable example of the merging of stage magic—or prestidigitation—with real magic in fiction, though it has been followed by other stories using that premise, including Clive Barker's film *Lord of Illusions* and Christopher Priest's award-winning 1995 novel, *The Prestige*.

In 1981 Merlin the magician returned once more in director John Boorman's gritty, realistic interpretation of the Arthurian legend *Excalibur* (Orion). As portrayed by Nicol Williamson, Merlin is a strange old man dressed in flowing rags who speaks in a singsong voice.

The early 1980s saw a plethora of live-action, medieval adventure pictures with strong elements of sorcery. One of the most notable takes on the classic combination of the wizened sorcerer and his apprentice was in 1981 with Paramount/Disney's *Dragonslayer*, a fantasy adventure about a sorcerer's apprentice who takes on the challenge of slaying a dragon after his master's unexpected death. That same year the DeLaurentis film version of novelist Robert E. Howard's famous *Conan the Barbarian* (starring Arnold Schwarzenegger) introduced Thulsa-Doom, the sorcerous high priest of a snake-worshiping cult.

In *The Beastmaster* (MGM/UA, 1982) a king's baby is stolen by a sorceress and is then rescued by a commoner who is unaware of the child's birthright. The child grows up to be a powerful warrior who has the unique ability to communicate with animals. The film spawned two sequels and a syndicated TV series. Also in 1982, Lee Horsley (TV's *Matt Houston*) starred in *The Sword and the Sorcerer* (Chase), about a young prince whose parents are slain and whose kingdom is taken away.

World-renowned novelist Stephen King, though best known as a writer of horror, has drifted into the world of magic and fantasy several times. In 1982 the first volume of his series The Dark Tower introduced a pair of wizards, Marten and Walter, while alluding to Maerlyn (or Merlin) himself. In the subsequent volumes of the series—*The Drawing of the Three* (1987), *The Wastelands* (1991), and *Wizard and Glass* (1997)—King added Randall Flagg, a powerful sorcerer who has become a recurrent villain in King's enormous fictional universe, also appearing in *The Stand* (1978) and *The Eyes of the Dragon* (1987).

STEPHEN KING
PHOTO BY BETH GWINN

In 1982 one of the numerous new independent comic-book companies, Pacific Comics, introduced *Ms. Mystic,* who brought an ecological spin to the concept of superhero sorceress. Ms. Mystic served Gaia, the goddess of the earth, and used her elemental powers in an attempt to prevent us from destroying the environment.

Another notable comic-book sorceress of the period is Magik (Illyana Rasputin), the sister to the X-Men's organically armored member Colossus. Although Magik made her first appearance as a child in *Giant-Size X-Men* #1 in 1975, she did not gain her magical abilities until her eponymous four-issue miniseries in 1983.

Also in 1983, Circe made her first appearance in *Wonder Woman* #305. This comic-book character was supposed to be the same mythological sorceress who made Odysseus's life difficult in

Homer's *The Odyssey*. Warned by an oracle that the daughter of Hippolyta (Wonder Woman's mother) would be her undoing, Circe has repeatedly attempted to destroy Wonder Woman to no avail. Having merged her powers with those of Hecate the Crone, Circe delights in using her powers to fan the flames of mistrust between the sexes.

In 1983, Marion Zimmer Bradley—a renowned fantasy novelist—introduced her own version of the Arthurian mythology in *The Mists of Avalon*. Rather than focus on Merlin's magic, Bradley tells the story of King Arthur from the viewpoint of the magical women around him. The novel contains many themes that resonate with modern Wicca, such as the worship of the earth goddess and the conflict between pagan rituals and Christianity.

The following year, John Updike's novel *The Witches of Eastwick* brought the witch into suburbia with humor and a dark edge. The book tells the story of three witches who lived in a small New England town in the late 1960s. But it also features many of the negative stereotypes earlier associated with the wicked witch, including the use of spells and familiars, flying naked at night, and witch's marks (each has a third teat). Despite those trappings, these witches do not seem sinister. It is only when they fall under the spell of the new man in town—dark, mysterious and wealthy Darryl Van Horne (who also bears a remarkable resemblance to the Devil)—that the real evil, mayhem, and murder begins. The 1987 Warner Bros. film by the same name, directed by George Miller and starring Jack Nicholson, Cher, Michelle Pfeiffer, and Susan Sarandon, was only loosely based on the novel.

Disney returned to the world of magic and sorcery in the 1985 animated production *The Black Cauldron*, the tale of a young boy who must find a powerful black cauldron before it falls into the hands of an evil sorcerer, the Horned King. A very dark film by Disney standards, it was not released on video until fourteen years later.

That year the use of magic also took a dark turn in comic books, as legendary comics writer Alan Moore introduced a new character in the DC series *Swamp Thing*. John Constantine is a working class con man and thief, former punk rocker, sorcerer, and quite often savior of mankind. What makes this character unique is he is very much the everyman and far more easy to relate to than many of the superheroic magic users. Constantine is as likely to use his cunning wits to solve a problem as he is to use sorcery. He proved so popular that he received his own series, *John Constantine, Hellblazer*, in 1988, and it is still in publication as of this writing a dozen years later.

In 1986 novelist Whitley Strieber (*The Wolfen, Communion*) released his novel *Cat Magic*, which focused on the earth-worship angle of witchcraft far more than most other fiction of the time. That year also saw the publication of the first in humorous fantasist Craig Shaw Gardner's six-volume Ebenezum book series, *A Malady of Magicks*. The series, which ended in 1989 with *A Disagreement with Death*, followed the adventures of Wuntvor, apprentice to the master wizard Ebenezum. Gardner also used wizards to great effect in his more serious Dragon Circle trilogy, which included *Dragon Sleeping* (1994), *Dragon Waking* (1995), and *Dragon Burning* (1997).

Though the novel upon which it was based, William Hjortsberg's *Falling Angel*, was published in 1978, it was only upon the 1987 release of the film *Angel Heart* (Carolco/Winkast-Union) that this story inspired by the tale of *Faust* received the attention it deserved (see Demons). Mickey Rourke's character descends deeper into the mysticism and witchcraft of New Orleans and into the depths of his own soul.

Another film that has developed a following over time is MGM/UA's 1988 *Pumpkinhead*. The movie—starring *Millennium's* Lance Henriksen—marked the directorial debut of special effects and makeup wizard Stan Winston. Henriksen is a rural store owner whose son is killed in an accident caused by careless city kids passing through town. Driven by grief, he makes his way deep in the mountains to the cabin of an old witch—the stereotypical old hag—to seek her assistance in exacting his revenge. The witch raises up a powerful demon, Pumpkinhead, to fulfill Henriksen's wish. *Pumpkinhead* spawned a sequel, *Pumpkinhead II: Blood Wings* in 1993.

In 1989 an interesting curiosity came to the screen in the form of *Warlock*. Directed by Steve Miner, the New World film featured Julian Sands (*A Room With a View*) as an evil magic user pursued by a witch hunter, played by Richard E. Grant, and a woman, played by Lori Singer of *Footloose* fame. The film was popular enough that two sequels have been made.

After *The Black Cauldron*, Disney tried animation again in 1989 and this time they scored big. *The Little Mermaid*, based on a story by Hans Christian Anderson, includes the character of Ursula, the Sea Witch, one of the nastiest of all the Disney villains, part-octopus, part-human, and blue-skinned, with a shock of white hair and bright red vampy lips.

Though it was not released in the United States until the mid-'90s, *Kiki's Delivery Service* first played in its native Japan in 1989. An extraordinarily well-crafted film, written, directed and produced by Hayao Miyazaki, *Kiki's Delivery Service* is among the best animated films available. It presaged the "girl power" movement of the 1990s by several years and helped to establish Miyazaki as an acknowledged master of the craft.

Also technically a children's story—though not at all for children—was *The Witches* (Lorimar/Henson, 1990). Directed by Nicolas Roeg, the live-action film adapted the 1983 Roald Dahl novel by the same name about a boy who uncovers a coven's plot to poison all the children of England. Anjelica Huston is marvelous as the leader of the witches' coven whose members hide their hideous deformities with rubber masks and wigs.

The Witches was the second of three children's books with a magic theme by the prolific Dahl. In 1967 he penned *The Magic Finger* about a young girl who lives next door to two men who love to hunt and shoot anything for fun. She puts the "magic finger" on them and the next day they wake up as birds, complete with wings.

Witches and magic have always figured prominently in juvenile fiction. The 1970s brought us the successful Worst Witch series by British author Jill Murphy. The Worst Witch was Mildred Hubble, a student at Miss Cackle's Academy for Witches who could never seem to get a spell right. Mildred's misadventures were filmed as a 1986 British TV movie and starred Fairuza Balk (who would later appear in *The Craft*, see below) in the title role. A new television series based on the novels and produced in the United Kingdom currently airs on HBO.

The Teen Witch series followed in the 1980s. Written by Megan Barnes, the books are about a girl who discovers her powers at sixteen and uses them to become the best-liked girl at school. The series spawned a 1989 Media Pictures film titled *Teen Witch* starring Robyn Lively and also featuring Dick "Darrin Stephens" Sargent. Even the popular Goosebumps series featured a few magical themes in the 1990s, including *Bad Hare Day* (#41) and *Chicken Chicken* (#53).

In adult fiction, Anne Rice—who had made her career on vampires—turned her attention to

witches. In the 1990s, she fashioned her own world of witchcraft in her series The Lives of the Mayfair Witches, which include *The Witching Hour* (1990), *Lasher* (1993) and *Taltos* (1994). The story centers around Rowan Mayfair, the witch queen of her family coven; Lasher, a demon spirit made flesh; Ashlar, a supernatural being of the Taltos race; and the mystic scholars of an organization called the Talamasca. The books trace the lives of the Mayfair witches and various other supernatural beings through several centuries into modern times.

In 1990 Stuart Gordon directed *The Pit and the Pendulum* (Paramount Pictures) starring Lance Henriksen. The film is loosely based on Edgar Allan Poe's short story by the same name about a man's suffering in and escape from the dungeons of the Inquisition. Unlike its 1961 American International counterpart directed by Roger Corman (and starring Vincent Price) this presentation added elements of witchcraft and heresy.

Disney continued the streak of hit animated films it had begun with *The Little Mermaid* with 1992's *Aladdin*. Though the over-the-top genie, voiced by the always kinetic Robin Williams, stole the film with his feats of magic, *Aladdin* is included here for its villain, the evil Jafar, a very powerful sorcerer voiced by Jonathan Freeman. *Aladdin* is loaded with admirable qualities, from its musical score and songs to the art, the voice performances by Williams, Gilbert Gottfried, and others. Even so, the film would not work half as well were it not for the dastardly mystical doings of Jafar, who returned in a 1994 direct-to-video sequel.

Another Disney film, *Hocus Pocus* (1993), was a live-action comedy that starred Bette Midler, Kathy Najimy, and Sarah Jessica Parker as a trio of witches conjured up by a lonely teenage boy in Salem, Massachusetts.

In 1995 MGM released *Lord of Illusions*, an odd melange of a film written and directed by horror-fantasy novelist Clive Barker. The movie starred Scott Bakula as Harry D'Amour, a detective who specializes in the occult. The nightmarish motion picture combines private-eye story conventions with the savagery of Barker's previous films (*Hellraiser, Nightbreed*) to relate a mystery set amid the world of stage magicians.

Gregory Maguire's wonderful novel *Wicked: The Life and Times of the Wicked Witch of the West* also came out in 1995. As the title suggests, Maguire's revisionist story takes the villain of *The Wizard of Oz* and relates her life story, turning the image of the old hag wicked witch on its head to fascinating effect.

The 1996 feature film *The Craft* (Columbia Pictures), a horror-drama directed by Andrew Fleming, starred Robin Tunney, Neve Campbell, and a wonderfully over-the-top Fairuza Balk. Four young women begin to dabble in witchcraft and, as their powers grow, they develop a sense of empowerment and unity, feelings previously unknown to them. The film is witty and hip and it lays the groundwork for some of the territory of postmodern girl empowerment issues that would later be covered by the Willow Rosenberg character in *Buffy the Vampire Slayer* and the Halliwell sisters of *Charmed*.

The best-known magic user in late 1990s popular culture must be Harry Potter. J. K. Rowling's delightful 1997 book, *Harry Potter and the Sorcerer's Stone,* introduces us to Harry, a ten-year-old boy sent to live with his obnoxious aunt and uncle after the mysterious death of his parents. Life for Harry is miserable until one day he learns that his parents were in fact a great wizard and a powerful witch killed by the evil dark lord, Voldemort. A new life starts for him as he arrives at Hogwarts School of Witchcraft and Wizardry. Rowling has said that there will be seven volumes of Harry's adventures. Thus far, three more have been published, *Harry Potter and the Chamber of Secrets* (1998), *Harry Potter and the Prisoner of Azakaban* (1999), and a fourth one in summer 2000.

Alice Hoffman's novel *Practical Magic* (Berkeley, 1995) was adapted to the screen by Warner Bros. in 1998. Directed by Griffin Dunne and starring Nicole Kidman and Sandra Bullock, the film follows the lives of the Owens sisters, the latest generation in a family of witches.

Merlin the magician received his most prominent recent exposure in the 1998 NBC-TV miniseries *Merlin*, which featured Sam Neill in the title role. In this inventive version, Merlin is portrayed as a kind of everyman burdened with the responsibility inherent in his vast, innate magical power. This take on the character of myth is fascinating because for the first time we are privy to the events that unfold throughout his life from childhood to old age.

Though it contains very little by way of traditional references to witchcraft—nor the appearance of anyone or anything resembling a witch—the pop-culture phenomenon that put the word *witch* on the lips of every American in 1999 was Artisan Entertainment's *The Blair Witch Project*. In the vein of another shot-on-video independent "mockumentary," *The Last Broadcast* (1998), the low-budget feature starred a cast of unknowns. The story focused on three Montgomery College students arriving in Burkittsville, Maryland, to make a documentary on the local legend of the Blair Witch.

The motion picture is presented as if it were actual, choppy, amateurish footage shot by the three and found a year after their disappearance in the woods outside Burkittsville. Through the raw footage, we see the college students as they mentally disintegrate under the relentless assault of what seems to be the legendary Blair Witch. By the story's end all three characters are apparently killed, either by the witch or someone influenced by the witch.

The filmmakers did such a good job of creating a history and mythology for the Blair Witch that since the film's release the real-life town of Burkittsville has been deluged with tourists hoping for a glimpse of the elusive (and entirely fictional) supernatural entity.

Also in 1999, Paramount Pictures released *Sleepy Hollow*, directed by Tim Burton. Loosely based on Washington Irving's classic novella "The Legend of Sleepy Hollow," the film's entire cinematic look seems a throwback to the Hammer horror films of the late '50s and early '60s.

In this version of Irving's tale, New York City constable Ichabod Crane is sent upstate to the small town of Sleepy Hollow to investigate a series of decapitation murders, believed by the townsfolk to be the doings of the ghostly Headless Horseman. Through strange and quite disturbing dream sequences, we soon learn the reason for Ichabod's aversion to the supernatural: his mother was a practicing witch who was tortured and eventually put to death for her sins by her own husband—Ichabod's father. Ichabod also comes in contact with an old crone living deep in the woods. The old witch channels some harrowingly frightening spirits, forcing Ichabod to realize that the supernatural does in fact exist.

The documentary *American Movie* (1999) won the Grand Jury Prize in its category at the renowned Sundance Film Festival, although it received only a very limited theatrical release. The film chronicles the difficulties amateur Wisconsin filmmaker Mark Borchardt faced in making his short film *Coven* (1997), a forty-minute black-and-white featurette in which an alcoholic writer (played by Borchardt) suspects the local self-help confessional support group are satanists.

Like *The Last Broadcast* and *The Blair Witch Project*, both *American Movie* and *Coven* represent a new generation of films that are produced, marketed, and distributed (sometimes by the filmmakers themselves, using the Internet) outside of the usual industry channels. As the success of *Blair Witch* proved, their impact and influence should not be underestimated.

On the WB network, the TV series *Charmed* (which debuted in 1998) tells the story of the three Halliwell sisters. Reunited after the death of their grandmother, the girls found themselves in possession of an ancient text found in the attic of their grandmother's Victorian mansion. The Book of Shadows is a volume of witchcraft that describes three witches (the Charmed Ones) who receive their magical powers on the night of the full moon. *Charmed* is an example of the way modern storytellers have begun to merge the lighthearted suburban witchcraft of *Bewitched* and its precursors with the more classic sinister presentation of witches.

Perhaps the best example of the most contemporary interpretation of witches, however, is found on the WB's *Buffy the Vampire Slayer*, which debuted in 1997. One of the program's main supporting characters, Willow Rosenberg (played by Alyson Hannigan) has slowly developed magical abilities, evolving from a shy but intelligent wallflower into a confident young woman, partially due to the independence she has found while exploring witchcraft. As already discussed in great detail, the series draws lines between Wicca (which Willow also practices), neo-paganism, and the use of actual magic, though they are all combined in the character of Willow.

"What are you going to do, B? Kill me—you become me. You and me, girlfriend... we're enemies."

—FAITH, "ENEMIES"

THE MAYOR

GAVROK SPIDERS

"I don't like this 'no mouth' thing. It's disquieting." —WILLOW, "EARSHOT"

HELLHOUND

The Mayor's demonic manifestation.

"I need better lackeys."
—SUNDAY, "THE FRESHMAN"

"You're saying Buffy's been doing a Linda Blair on us because Kathy's been sucking her soul?"
— XANDER, "LIVING CONDITIONS"

Kathy, the roommate from Hell

TAPPARICH

SPIKE and HARMONY

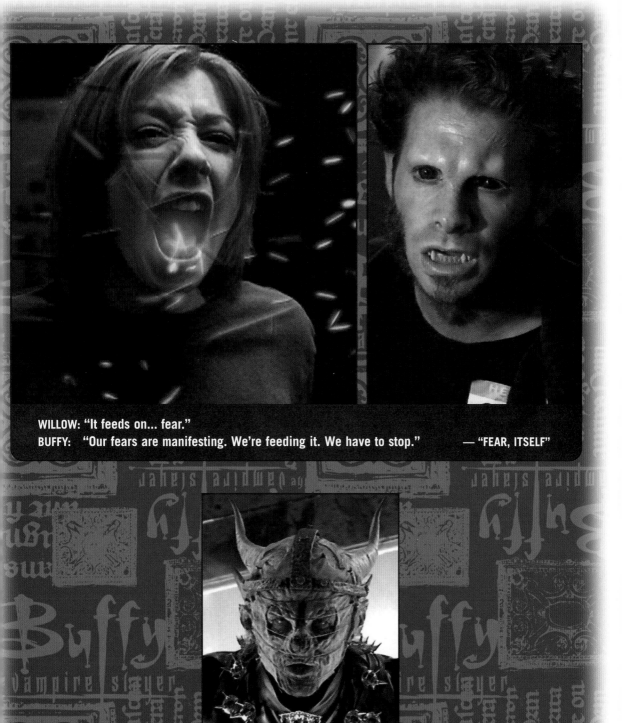

WILLOW: "It feeds on... fear."

BUFFY: "Our fears are manifesting. We're feeding it. We have to stop." — "FEAR, ITSELF"

GACHNAR

"I wanted you even before I saw you. I sensed you. Did you sense me?"
—VERUCA, "WILD AT HEART"

VERUCA

HUS

"Your magic is strong, but your pain....it's like a scream that pierces dimensional walls."
—D'HOFFRYN, "SOMETHING BLUE"

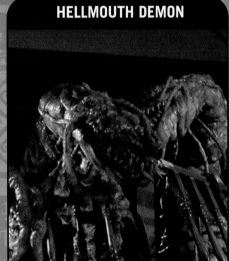

HELLMOUTH DEMON

THE GENTLEMEN

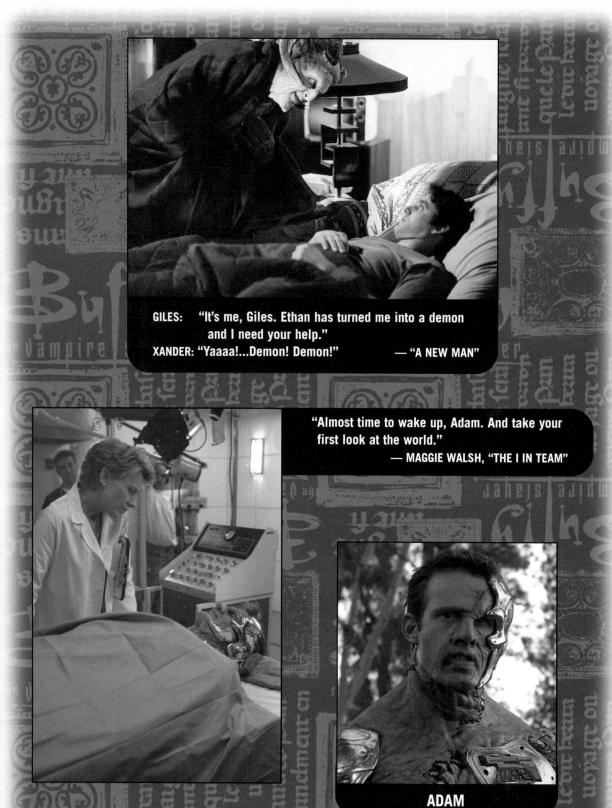

GILES: "It's me, Giles. Ethan has turned me into a demon and I need your help."
XANDER: "Yaaaa!...Demon! Demon!" — "A NEW MAN"

"Almost time to wake up, Adam. And take your first look at the world."
— MAGGIE WALSH, "THE I IN TEAM"

ADAM

"What'd you think? I'd wake up and we'd go for tea? You tried to gut me, blondie."
—FAITH, "THIS YEAR'S GIRL"

WILLOW and TARA

"So, what do you think? Where do you want to go?" —OZ, "NEW MOON RISING"

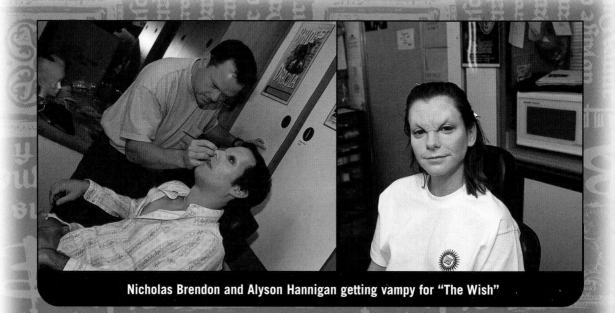

Nicholas Brendon and Alyson Hannigan getting vampy for "The Wish"

Todd McIntosh puts the finishing touches on Vamp Willow

DOPPELGANGERS

Anthony Stewart Head...

becomes a Fyarl demon.

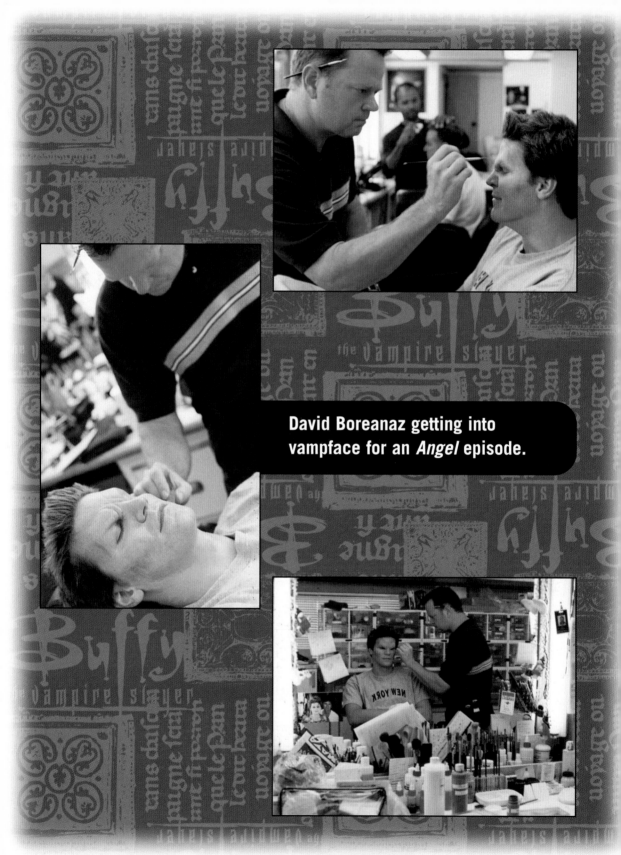

David Boreanaz getting into vampface for an *Angel* episode.

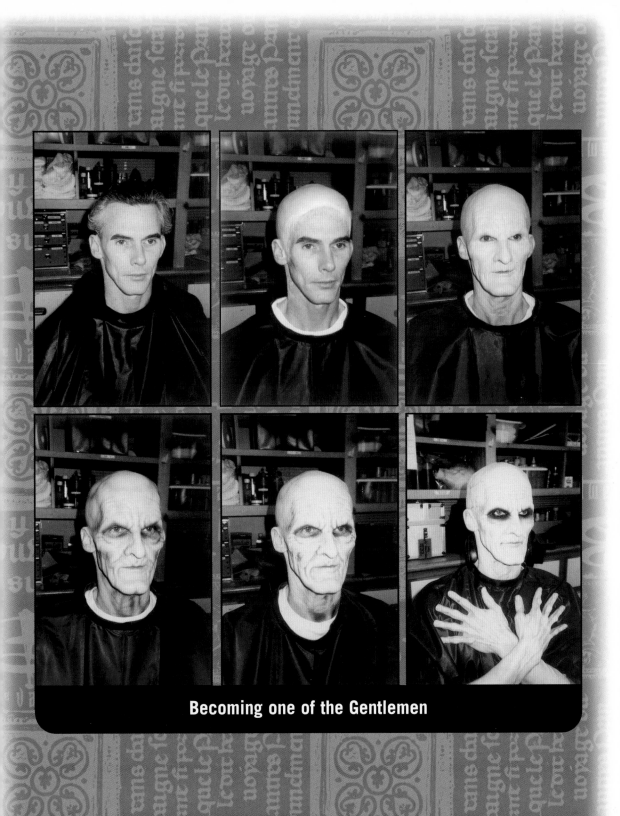

Becoming one of the Gentlemen

PRIMALS

WEREWOLVES, SHAPESHIFTERS, and ANIMAL-PEOPLE

VERUCA: "MAYBE YOU DON'T WANT TO ADMIT WHAT HAPPENED TO YOU. MAYBE YOU WANT TO PRETEND YOU'RE A REGULAR GUY..."

OZ: "I AM. I'M ONLY A WOLF THREE NIGHTS A MONTH."

VERUCA: "OR YOU'RE THE WOLF ALL THE TIME, AND YOUR HUMAN FACE IS JUST YOUR DISGUISE. EVER THINK OF THAT?"
—"WILD AT HEART"

HOW FAR REMOVED are humans from their animal cousins? The disturbing truth is that, no matter what we would like to believe, we are all still beasts at heart. No matter what laws or morals we introduce to govern the instincts that nature has instilled within us, people are animals.

Is it any wonder, then, that animal-based monsters—frequently humans succumbing to their baser, animal nature—are such a part of our folklore, our nightmares, and our popular culture? Even today, human killers have their behavior compared to the wild-blooded, savage nature of the wolf or to the cold-blooded, impassive brutality of the alligator.

Throughout history, myth and legend have explored such ideas and fears in the form of primal monsters, those that meld humanity with animals. Perhaps the best known of these is the werewolf, or lycanthrope. The werewolf, however, is only one form of shapeshifter in myth. There are legends and stories about humans who can transform into a wide variety of animals, from house pets to sea creatures. That alteration of the human form to something considered "less" than human and more bestial is the fundamental building block of all such mythical tales.

Just as Henry Jekyll did in *Dr. Jekyll and Mr. Hyde*, just as any of the werewolves or were-panthers or other were-creatures in folklore also felt, we feel, within us, the call of the wild, so to speak.

In the world of *Buffy the Vampire Slayer*, these ideas have been visited many times, most obviously in the case of Oz, one of our heroes, who also happens to be a werewolf.

> **"I must admit, I'm intrigued. A werewolf. It's one of the classics. I'm sure my books and I are in for a fascinating afternoon."** —GILES, IN "PHASES"

The show's writers and producers stuck quite faithfully to werewolf folklore—a bite from an existing werewolf causes a human to transform into a wolf beneath the full moon, the efficacy of silver bullets against werewolves, the lack of memory of the human who awakens after having been a wolf—but it comes as no surprise that Joss Whedon tinkered with the formula just a little bit. Instead of becoming a wolf only on the night when the moon is at its fullest, werewolves on *Buffy* also transform the night before and the night after the full moon.

> **GILES:** "My guess is that this werewolf will be back at next month's full moon."
> **WILLOW:** "What about *tonight's* full moon?"
> **GILES:** "Pardon?"
> **WILLOW:** "Last night was the night before the full moon. Traditionally known as…the night before the full moon." —"PHASES"

Those familiar with Whedon's penchant for horror comics, particularly those from the late '70s, might think this move inspired by the classic Marvel Comics series *Werewolf by Night*, which used the same time frame. The truth, however, is far more practical. Whedon didn't even remember that element of the old comic-book series. Instead, it all came down, as it often does on a series of *Buffy's* quality, to story-telling.

Dean Batali, a season-two staff writer and one half of the team that scripted "Phases," the episode in which Oz became a werewolf, explains:

"Of course, werewolves only come out on the full moon. But we knew if we did that, it would not work as a story. Otherwise the story would have had to take place all in one night, or over three months."

> **GILES:** "A werewolf is such a potent, extreme representation of our inborn, animalistic traits that it emerges for three consecutive nights — the full moon, and the two nights surrounding it."
>
> **WILLOW:** "Quite the party animal."
>
> **GILES:** "Quite. It acts on pure instinct, no conscience, predatory and aggressive." —**"PHASES"**

The simple solution: three nights instead of one. Which, when you think about it, gives the werewolves of *Buffy the Vampire Slayer* a lot more time for carnage. Beyond that change, however, the writers and producers have kept quite faithful to the traditional werewolf folklore.

The series has also explored the concept of primals in other, various and ingenious ways. In "The Pack," we were presented with animal spirits capable of possessing humans. "Teacher's Pet" introduced a giant praying mantis capable of taking on human form. In "Go Fish," we saw human/animal monsters created by science, a common theme in primal-based stories from pop culture.

Another episode that explored the Jekyll and Hyde theme was "Beauty and the Beasts," in which a student found a way to use a certain chemical formula to bring out the beast within.

"'Beauty and the Beasts' is the closest thing we've done to a 'very special episode,'" notes supervising producer Marti Noxon, who wrote the episode. That particular installment, she confirms, purposely addressed the fundamental theme of Robert Louis Stevenson's *The Strange Case of Dr. Jekyll and Mr. Hyde*: the two natures of man—human and animal. But the episode explored further.

"It also deals with the two natures of man in relation to young women," Noxon explains. "Young women have a tendency to be drawn to the darker side of man. To romanticize the bad boy. What is that about? And when does it become dangerous? When do you lose control?"

That question speaks to the way in which Buffy, Willow, and the others draw the line between werewolves and vampires. Werewolves are only monsters three nights out of a month. To kill the monster, you must also kill the human, something none of them was willing to do in Oz's case. Because he was inherently good, he fought the beast within. He was willing to be caged, to do whatever was necessary to control his curse. They even saved Oz from a werewolf hunter. But the line was more finely drawn later, when a second werewolf, Veruca, was introduced. Veruca embraced the beast within,

and so became a monster full time, rather than only when in wolf form.

Though not a werewolf, the "Beauty and the Beasts" character, Pete, embraced the monster just as Veruca would do later.

"Each woman in ["Beauty and the Beasts"] was trying to figure out where her man fell in that continuum," Marti Noxon says. "Oz is really bad three nights a month. Angel was really bad, but is he bad now? Which one of them is seeking out something destructive, and which of these relationships just have an element that is in all relationships? There is a side to men and to women that is more animal. People think it was our domestic-abuse episode. But it was more about women's attraction to the alpha dog and when relationships are just bad [as opposed to] when they're sick or dangerous.

"The episode where Oz leaves [season four's "Wild at Heart"] is a sister episode," Noxon adds. "What is our basic animal nature? How much of that should be fulfilled, and how much do we have to resist and say no, that's a dangerous impulse? Many of the problems we have between men and women are based on the fact that we deny a lot of these impulses and blame other things.

"The question of how much of me is animal and how much is man and how to control that is a big reason why Willow and Oz end up breaking up. At that age, kids are really wrestling with that. To stay faithful to one person from the time you're eighteen is a tall order. A lot of men will say, I can't help it, it's the dog in me. There is truth in that."

Thus, Oz departed. Despite the willingness of his friends to accept that as a werewolf he was two beings—human and animal—Veruca's influence had caused him to wonder if that were true, or if he was actually something in between. When Oz returned for a single episode ("New Moon Rising") viewers learned that a combination of herbs and meditation techniques had given him some control over his transformation. But Oz still struggles with his dual nature.

Once again, a subject of our nightmares, of our ancient folklore, and of art, literature, film and television: is our primal nature stronger than our human rationality?

Are we men and women . . . or are we monsters?

the influences

WE'VE ALREADY MENTIONED *Dr. Jekyll and Mr. Hyde*. Obviously, when one thinks of werewolves today, there are fresher, more brutal and visceral examples that spring to mind.

"I'm a big fan of *An American Werewolf in London*," notes Dean Batali. "I remember thinking that was a really funny movie, though I don't remember being scared at all. But we thought about that one a lot [while preparing to write 'Phases']. We didn't want a guy in a wolf suit—we wanted a wolf—partially because of *American Werewolf*."

His co-writer, Rob Des Hotel, agrees. "*American Werewolf, Wolfen,* and *The Howling* all came out during the same period," he notes. "I'm not even particularly a werewolf fan, but *American Werewolf* just made me want to do a werewolf story."

Seeing a pattern here? Ask Marti Noxon.

"I didn't watch a lot of werewolf movies," she confesses. "The only one I remember loving was *An American Werewolf in London*. That movie is really seminal, it's the one we draw on the most."

the monsters

YOUR FIRST RESPONSE here is likely to be "Hey, Oz isn't a monster. He's the sweetest guy in the world." On the other hand, would you want to be in that cage with him when the full moon rises?

Didn't think so.

OZ

OZ: (to Faith) "I'm wondering about your position on werewolves."
WILLOW: (proudly) "Oz is a werewolf."
BUFFY: "Long story."
OZ: "Got bit."
BUFFY: "Apparently not that long."
FAITH: "Hey, long as you don't go scratching at me or humpin' my leg, we're five by five."
OZ: "Fair enough." —**"FAITH, HOPE, AND TRICK"**

FIRST APPEARANCE: "Inca Mummy Girl," season two

OTHER EPISODES: season two: "Halloween," "What's My Line? Parts One and Two," "Surprise," "Innocence," "Phases," "Bewitched, Bothered, and Bewildered," "Becoming, Parts One and Two"; season three: all episodes; season four: "The Freshman," "Living Conditions," "The Harsh Light of Day," "Fear, Itself," "Beer Bad," "Wild at Heart," and "New Moon Rising," and "Restless."

KEY RELATIONSHIPS: Oz was Willow Rosenberg's boyfriend for nearly two years. He played

guitar for the Sunnydale rock band Dingoes Ate My Baby, and was a part of Buffy's "Scooby gang" for some time. He was very briefly involved with another werewolf named Veruca, whom he killed.

UNIQUE ATTRIBUTES: Oz is a werewolf. Three nights a month he transformed into his wolf form, during which time his human mind lost all control to the animal, though he has recently gained some measure of control over the transformation. As a human, however, he has a heightened sense of smell and is able to identify certain people by scent.

MOST MONSTROUS MOMENT: In "Phases," he might have killed Willow if he had not been tranquilized.

CURRENT STATUS: Oz has left Sunnydale (again). His current whereabouts are unknown.

Though his real name is **Daniel Osbourne,** viewers (and, it seemed, most of the characters on the show) were unaware that he had any other name but Oz. When first introduced in "Inca Mummy Girl" during season two, the laconic guitar player for Dingoes Ate My Baby—a live music staple at The Bronze—was mostly a background character.

In a collection of small moments in "Halloween" and other episodes, Oz became fascinated with Willow. The two finally met in season two's "What's My Line?" when, during Career Week, both were interviewed by a huge multinational software company.

An early defining moment for Oz as a character, that event revealed that in spite of his laid-back nature, his apparent lack of interest in school (which later resulted in his having to repeat his senior year), and the obvious fact that his only desire was to play with the band, Daniel Osbourne was a brilliant young man.

As he began to fall in love with Willow, however, Oz's life became significantly complicated by a minor run-in with his little cousin, **Jordy.** In the landmark episode "Phases," Oz discovered that he had become a werewolf.

"I think 'Phases' probably will end up as one of the top ten [*Buffy* episodes] when all is said and done," Dean Batali observes. "It's such a fun story. There's so much going on with it. I think it does come as a surprise that Oz, one of the major characters, is one of the monsters.

"Obviously there we had a certain legend to go by. For werewolves, we pretty much stuck with the classic structure. You get bitten, silver bullet, full moon. I remember thinking we were going to have to spend an entire act figuring out how he became a werewolf, maybe having a flashback, maybe even having Oz go to visit his uncle and trying to find out if Jordy is a werewolf. Then Joss said, 'How 'bout if he just calls and asks them if Jordy's a werewolf?' So that's what we did. And it worked perfectly."

> **"Is Jordy a werewolf? Uh-huh . . . and how long has that been going on? Uh-huh . . . no reason. Thanks. Love to Uncle Ken."**
> —OZ, ON THE PHONE, IN "PHASES"

Rob Des Hotel loves Oz as a character, too. "'Phases' is probably my favorite episode of the five we wrote," he says. "Oz just has an ability to pinpoint what's going on and make it sound absurd. I think there's a sweetness to him. In 'Phases,' Willow comes up to him and says 'Hi,' and Oz says, 'That's what I was gonna say.'"

During the episode—in which, as noted, Oz discovered that a bite from his cousin Jordy, also a werewolf, had given him that curse—he asked Willow out for the first time. In spite of his condition, Willow agreed, and that was the beginning of a relationship that would last nearly two years.

Also in "Phases," Oz was hunted by a werewolf trapper named **Gib Cain,** who wanted the supernatural beast for his hide. Of course, Buffy, Willow, Giles, and the gang came to his rescue.

> **"First they tell me I can't hunt an elephant for its ivory. Now I've got to deal with People for the Ethical Treatment of Werewolves."** —GIB CAIN, IN "PHASES"

For most of the next two years, Willow and her friends took turns "wolf-sitting"—keeping watch over a caged Oz during the nights of the full moon to make certain he would not escape and kill someone, or be killed himself. He escaped briefly during "Beauty and the Beasts," but in that case he was more help than danger, as he attacked the Mr. Hyde–type monster that one of the other students had become.

GILES: "Clearly we're looking for a depraved, sadistic animal."
OZ: "Present. (to Willow) I may be a cold-blooded jelly doughnut—but my timing's impeccable." —"BEAUTY AND THE BEASTS"

Later in the third season he escaped again, inadvertently catching the bad guy when he attacked Jack, the dead thug who tried to blow up the school in "The Zeppo."

In season four's "Fear, Itself," Oz found himself trapped along with his friends in a sort of haunted house where his biggest fear—that he might change unexpectedly and attack Willow—was exploited, though only in his mind.

OZ: "Something's happening."
WILLOW: (hopeful) "Something…good? (He turns his face into the light. Hair has sprouted all over his brow and face, his teeth have taken on a jagged quality.) Oh. Not good." —**"FEAR, ITSELF"**

During the following episode, "Beer Bad," everything began to change. A band called Shy was playing at The Bronze. Oz found himself powerfully, almost uncontrollably attracted to the lead singer, a girl named Veruca. As revealed in the next episode, "Wild at Heart," the explanation for this attraction was jarringly simple and disturbing: Veruca was also a werewolf.

Usually so completely in control of himself, Oz was forced to battle with the animal nature of the werewolf inside. He was forced to come to grips with the truth, that the werewolf was not really something hidden within, but that he, in fact, was the wolf, and could not always use his brilliant, rational human mind to overcome that primal nature. He'd mated with Veruca while in werewolf form, hidden the fact that the singer was another werewolf, and couldn't really explain himself. All of this, to no surprise, tore apart his relationship with Willow.

"Veruca was right about something. The wolf is inside me all the time. And I don't know where the line is anymore—between me and it. Until I figure out what that means, I shouldn't be around you—or anybody."
—OZ, IN "WILD AT HEART"

There is some evidence that he might have more control than he believes. He had previously seemed to "recognize" Willow when in wolf form, though it did not prevent him from attacking her. Yet in "Wild at Heart," when Veruca attempted to kill Willow, Oz attacked the other werewolf rather than the more likely prey of the human in the room.

Still, Oz determined that until he could

make sense of it all, could come to terms with what he had learned about his bestial nature, he needed to be on his own. He left Sunnydale in "Wild at Heart."

Oz returned for one episode later in the fourth season ("New Moon Rising") in which it was revealed that thanks to a combination of herbs and meditation techniques learned in Tibet, he now has some control over his transformation. The realization of Willow's relationship with Tara and a run-in with the Initiative showed Oz how tenuous that control is. He left Sunnydale again at the end of that episode. His current whereabouts are unknown.

THE SHE-MANTIS

"This type of creature, the Kleptes-Virgo or virgin-thief, appears in many cultures: the Greek Sirens, the Celtic sea-maidens who tore the living flesh from the bones of . . ."

—GILES, IN "TEACHER'S PET"

EPISODE: "Teacher's Pet," season one

KEY RELATIONSHIPS: The She-Mantis attempted to mate with Xander Harris and Blayne Mall, another Sunnydale student.

UNIQUE ATTRIBUTES: Though she can appear human, the She-Mantis is actually a giant praying mantis. Even in human form, however, she can turn her head one hundred and eighty degrees.

MOST MONSTROUS MOMENT: In order to search Sunnydale High for young prey, she murdered a biology teacher (by decapitation) and took on the identity of a substitute teacher.

CURRENT STATUS: Buffy destroyed the She-Mantis at the close of that episode. However, the creature did leave behind a single egg sac.

An ancient creature, the She-Mantis's origin, including whether or not it was the only one of its kind, is shrouded in mystery, though it is known that the creature frightens even vampires. Buffy came into contact with the creature during the season one episode "Teacher's Pet." The She-Mantis, which was able to take on the appearance of a human, replaced an aging substitute teacher named **Natalie French,** who had retired. How that alteration of appearance was accomplished has yet to be determined. The creature was either a "perception distorter" or was somehow able to alter its physical mass between a human form and its true form, that of a giant praying mantis.

BUFFY: "Dig this—'the praying mantis can rotate his head a hundred and eighty degrees while waiting for a meal to wander by…Hah! (off their looks) Well, come on, guys. Hah!"

WILLOW: "Well, Ms. French is sort of big. For a bug."

—**"TEACHER'S PET"**

The purpose of its ruse was to find a mate so that she could breed (and whom she would then *eat*). The She-Mantis had a taste for young male virgins, and the guise of a sexy schoolteacher was used to draw them in. In order to get close to such potential food, the creature killed Sunnydale High biology teacher **Dr. Gregory** so that the school would need the services of a substitute.

Like normal, insectoid mantises, the She-Mantis was a cannibal who ate her mate's head during the actual act of mating. She "lays her eggs and then finds a mate to fertilize them." She was capable of turning her head one hundred and eighty degrees, even in human form.

"No, no, I'm not saying she craned her neck. We are talking full-on *Exorcist* twist."

—**BUFFY, IN "TEACHER'S PET"**

During "Teacher's Pet," it was revealed that Giles's former associate, **Dr. Ferris Carlyle,** had "spent years transcribing a lost, pre-Germanic language" wherein he first read of the She-Mantis's existence. When several teenage boys were murdered, Carlyle went hunting for the creature.

After finally confronting the creature, yet managing to escape, Dr. Carlyle was committed to an insane asylum, where Giles contacted him. Carlyle advised that the creature be completely dismembered, and Buffy followed that advice. The difficulty was in getting close enough to the creature to do any damage. Buffy solved that problem herself, however. She first caused the creature pain and drove it back with a two-fisted dose of bug spray, then she used the recorded sounds of bat sonar to disrupt the creature's nervous system. Finally, she hacked it to bits with a machete.

The episode's final scene, however, revealed the existence of an extant egg sac. Thus it is quite possible that the offspring of the She-Mantis may one day appear.

HYENA PEOPLE

GILES: "Boys can be cruel. They tease, they prey on the weak, it's just a natural teen—"
BUFFY: "They prey on the weak. Xander started acting wiggy after the zoo. He and Kyle and those guys went into the hyena cage....God, that laugh..."
GILES: "Are you saying Xander's become a hyena?"
BUFFY: "Not just him, all of them."

—"THE PACK"

EPISODE: "The Pack," season one

UNIQUE ATTRIBUTES: Xander, Kyle, Rhonda, Tor, and Heidi, when possessed by the spirits of hyenas, behaved like animals, even to the extent that the Pack (excluding Xander) ate a human being.

MOST MONSTROUS MOMENT: "The Pack" ate Bob Flutie, principal of Sunnydale High School, as well as the school's porcine mascot, Herbert.

CURRENT STATUS: It is presumed that they graduated from Sunnydale High. Their subsequent whereabouts are unknown.

In the season-one episode "The Pack," we were presented with the theme of the two natures of man, familiar from *Dr. Jekyll and Mr. Hyde*, and other works. In this case, however, it very specifically involved the predatory nature of bullies. The episode also gave us a very different kind of primal—the possession of humans by the spirits of animals, in this case, hyenas.

Kyle, Tor, Rhonda, and Heidi were a group of Sunnydale High tough kids—bullies—dark and edgy teens on the periphery of the high school experience. During a trip to the Sunnydale Zoo, they chose as their latest target a studious boy named **Lance.** The four toughs terrorized Lance, then behaved as though they wanted to induct him into their gang, dragging him along on a tour of the zoo's Hyena House, which had been quarantined and was off-limits. Inside, the four joked about throwing Lance to the hyenas.

Outside, Xander, Buffy, and Willow had seen the kids' treatment of Lance. Xander followed them inside, planning to rescue Lance. As Xander went nose to nose with Kyle, about to have a fistfight, the hyenas' eyes began to glow yellow, as did the eyes of "the pack" of students and Xander. All five of them were possessed by hyena spirits.

Xander changed. He began to hang around with the pack and to behave just as aggressively and cruelly as they did. His friends were very concerned. Buffy asked Giles what could be wrong with him, but wasn't happy with his response:

GILES: "Xander's taken to teasing the less fortunate?"
BUFFY: "Uh-huh."
GILES: "There's been a noticeable change in both clothing and demeanor?"
BUFFY: "Yes."
GILES: "And otherwise all his spare time is spent lounging about with imbeciles?"
BUFFY: "It's bad?"
GILES: "It's devastating. He's turned into a sixteen-year-old boy! Of course, you'll have to kill him." —**"THE PACK"**

However, Giles realized he had dismissed Buffy's concerns too quickly when Xander and his new friends ate the school mascot, **Herbert the Razorback pig.** He recalled the story of a sect of animal worshipers called primals. Their goal was to become possessed by the spirits of the most predatory animals—hyenas, for example:

"The Masai of the Serengeti have spoken of animal possession for generations. I should have remembered that....They believe that humanity, consciousness, the soul—is a dilution of spirit. To them, the animal state is holy to them. They were able, through trans-possession, to pull the spirit of certain animals into themselves."
—**GILES, IN "THE PACK"**

Over time, the possessed would take on the characteristics of the animal that was possessing him or her, until they were little more than a savage beast. After Kyle, Tor, Rhonda, and Heidi ate the principal, while Xander attacked Buffy, Giles visited **the zookeeper** in charge of the hyenas, only to discover that the man was aware of the legend of the primals. He explained that the transference required a predatory act—the behavior of the pack toward Lance—and the presence of a totemic symbol, which Giles noticed had been drawn on the floor of the hyena house.

The zookeeper was revealed to be a believer in primals. When cornered, he threatened to cut Willow's throat, only to be attacked by Buffy. The rest of the pack, Xander now included, was also present. During that final confrontation, the zookeeper performed a spell that drew all the hyena spirits from the others and into himself. That had been his plan all along, to transform himself with the animal power of those spirits. However, during the ensuing fight, he fell into the pen where the hyenas were kept, and was eaten by them.

> "A Masai tribesman once told me that hyenas can understand human speech. They follow humans by day, learning their names. At night, when the campfire dies, they call out to a person. And once that person is separated...the pack *devours* him."
>
> —THE ZOOKEEPER, IN "THE PACK"

Though he tries to pretend otherwise, it has been implied that Xander remembers his actions during the time he was possessed. The current whereabouts of the members of the pack are unknown.

FISH MEN

WILLOW: "'Dodd McAlvy...torn tendon. Gage Petronzi...fractured wrist. . . . depression, headaches...'"
BUFFY: "It's all here in their school medical records."
WILLOW: "All symptomatic of steroid abuse."
XANDER: "But is steroid abuse usually linked with 'Hey, I'm a fish'?" —"GO FISH"

EPISODE: "Go Fish," season two

KEY RELATIONSHIPS: All of the "fish men" were members of the Sunnydale High School swim team.

UNIQUE ATTRIBUTES: Thanks to a bizarre chemical concoction introduced into the air in their steam room, they tore out of their human skin and became giant, horrible fish men.

MOST MONSTROUS MOMENT: They savaged and ate both the swim team coach and the school nurse.

CURRENT STATUS: The fish men were last seen swimming out into the Pacific Ocean.

Though it does concern men transforming into animals—in this case, fish—the season two episode "Go Fish" differs greatly from others of similar subject matter in one prominent way: The man-animal hybrids are created by science, not the supernatural. (The transformation of Pete in "Beauty and the Beasts" was also driven by science, but his transformation was impermanent, which is not the case here.)

During "Go Fish," several members of Sunnydale High's swim team were apparently murdered, only their torn and ravaged skins left behind. At first, Buffy and Giles believed that someone had cast a spell of some sort over the swim team. When Angel (reverted to evil Angelus form) tried to suck the blood of one of them and then spit it out, they realized something was wrong with the team members' blood, and they suspected steroid use. Xander even joined the team to help investigate. But it

took Buffy actually witnessing **Gage Petronzi** transforming to make them realize that the truth was more horrifying. The boys had been transformed into giant fish men.

The swim coach, **Mr. Marin,** with the complicity of the school athletic department's nurse, **Miss Greenleigh,** had been trying to give his team the advantage by exposing the swimmers to experimental steroids via the air of the steam room.

Dodd McAlvy, Gage Petronzi, Cameron Walker (with whom Buffy went on a date early in this episode), and at least one other swimmer, **Sean,** were transformed into human-fish hybrids.

The ill-fated nurse, Miss Greenleigh, tried to talk Coach Marin into abandoning the treatments. To protect himself and his experiment, the coach attacked her, and then fed her to the fish men, who tended to return to the sewers under the school. In the end, confronted by Buffy, the coach revealed the source of the mutations.

> **"After the fall of the Soviet Union, documents came to light detailing experiments with fish DNA on their Olympic swimmers. Tarpon, mako shark—but they never cracked it."**
> —COACH MARIN, IN "GO FISH"

During that confrontation, Marin managed to dump Buffy down into the grotto, where the fish men were waiting to be fed yet again. Buffy escaped and fought the coach, who ended up, quite fittingly, food for his team.

> **"Those boys really love their coach."**
> —BUFFY, WATCHING COACH MARIN BEING DEVOURED BY HIS "TEAM," IN "GO FISH"

During the episode, Xander was briefly exposed to the steam room "treatment," but he underwent plasma transfusions and showed no fishy developments later.

> **"I want you to know I still care for you, no matter what you look like. We can still date—or not date, but…I mean, I'll understand if you want to see other fish…and I'll try to make the quality of your life the best it can be, whether you need little bath toys or whatever…."**
> —CORDELIA, THINKING XANDER HAS BEEN TRANSFORMED INTO A FISH MAN, IN "GO FISH"

Buffy producer David Fury, who cowrote the episode, recalls his major influences in creating the fish men.

"I was very into the classic Universal monster movies. Including *Creature from the Black Lagoon*," he recalls. "As a freelancer [at the time], I knew I didn't want to do anything that involved the mythology of the series. I knew there would be things I was not privy to because I was not on staff at that time. So I wanted to get a nice stand-alone episode. I was racking my brain thinking of the type of monsters they hadn't done yet. They'd done an invisible girl. Inca Mummy Girl. Frankenstein. I went to the Creature.

"The Creature was something that scared me more than the others. The Creature was tall. I wasn't scared of things that were too big: Godzilla, Gorgo. I also wasn't scared of things that were human-sized. But when you get to eight-foot and nine-foot-tall monsters, that scared me somehow. Of course, the monsters in 'Go Fish' weren't that big, but the inspiration was there."

Fury notes that the inspiration for "Go Fish" was partly the Creature, and "partly an H. P. Lovecraft story called 'The Shadow Over Innsmouth,' which I read a long time ago and had a great effect on me. People turning into fish. Maybe it's because I'm Pisces or something.

"Another image that crossed my mind was Newt from *Aliens*. She's sitting in the water, waiting to be rescued. There's something very scary about being in waist-deep water and knowing something could be under there. The alien rises up behind Newt. In *Buffy*, the coach pushes her into the pit, and that's where that image comes from.

"In their transformation, these guys were supposed to become really fast swimmers. But the cumbersome nature of the costumes meant the actors couldn't move very well. It didn't quite have the effect we were hoping for. When Cordelia is standing at the swimming pool and the creature is swimming, I was imagining a creature zipping through the water very quickly. You can't really do that when it's an actor in a rubber suit and it's filling up with water and he's sinking. It was hard to get that effect. I think it was the most expensive episode up to that date.

"They're not demons," he adds emphatically. "It was one of the rare times when the fact that they were on the Hellmouth was almost irrelevant. There was nothing from Giles to explain what was going on. It was simply bad chemistry. They didn't really have an evil agenda, more of a biological one. I do think they're unique in the *Buffy* universe, that there aren't [any others of their kind]."

When last seen, the fish men were swimming out into the Pacific, apparently to find a home in the ocean. Their current whereabouts are unknown.

PETE

EPISODE: "Beauty and the Beasts," season three

KEY RELATIONSHIPS: Pete was dating a girl named Debbie.

UNIQUE ATTRIBUTES: Pete created a chemical formula to make himself more manly; it turned him into a brutal monster instead.

MOST MONSTROUS MOMENT: Pete murdered his girlfriend.

CURRENT STATUS: Angel killed Pete at the end of the episode.

First introduced as a friend of **Scott Hope**—whom Buffy briefly dated during season three—Pete turned out to be the series' answer to Dr. Jekyll. The fourth episode of that season, "Beauty and the Beasts," presented the twisted relationship Pete had with his unsuspecting girlfriend, **Debbie.**

Afraid that he wasn't macho enough to hang on to Debbie as his girlfriend, Pete used his advanced knowledge of science to create a chemical concoction that would increase his masculine nature. The problem, of course, was that what it really did was bring out the savage nature of the beast within, primal man. That beast, feeling threatened by virtually any man who paid attention to Debbie, became a killer, taking out Debbie's (and Buffy's) guidance counselor, and attacking Oz, a friend of Debbie's.

More importantly, the lines between Pete the human and Pete the monster became blurred. The bestial nature of the monster began to surface in Pete's everyday persona, and Pete developed the ability to change his form at will, no longer requiring the formula. This begs the question of whether Pete's formula altered him, or merely released what was already inside him.

Eventually Pete killed Debbie as well and was subsequently killed himself by Angel, who was only just beginning to regain control of his own animal nature after he had been driven to the brink of madness by a prolonged stay in a demon dimension.

Some might be tempted to draw a parallel between Pete and the students-turned-cavemen in the fourth season's "Beer Bad," in that all were apparently regressed to a primal state. But where the male characters in "Beer Bad" devolved, Pete's formula merely released his own internal beast, his other nature.

As noted above, Marti Noxon has made clear that the episode's most powerful metaphor has to do not merely with abuse, but with the way in which some women are attracted to the "Alpha dog," the bad boy. Indeed, despite Pete's behavioral changes, Debbie still loved him, even defending him to Buffy and the others, echoing the tragic and often fatal behavior of many a battered woman.

VERUCA

VERUCA: "I can help you, Oz. You're scared. I was, too. But now I accept it. The animal. And it's powerful . . . inside me all the time. Soon you'll feel sorry for other people. They only wish they could be as alive as we are. As free—"

OZ: "Free to kill people? I won't do that. And you shouldn't either."

VERUCA: "You don't understand. But you will. And you'll see that we belong together."

—"WILD AT HEART"

FIRST APPEARANCE: "Beer Bad," season four

OTHER EPISODES: season four: "Wild at Heart"

KEY RELATIONSHIPS: Veruca was the lead singer of the band Shy. She pursued Oz, both as a human and a werewolf.

UNIQUE ATTRIBUTES: Veruca was a werewolf.

MOST MONSTROUS MOMENT: Not only did she relish—as a human—the killing she did as a wolf, but Veruca also used the animal attraction between herself and Oz to drive a wedge between him and Willow.

CURRENT STATUS: Oz, as a werewolf, tore out Veruca's throat in "Wild at Heart."

Lead singer of the band Shy, Veruca was also a werewolf. Unlike Oz, she had gleefully adapted to her predatory nature and regularly killed during the full moon. After

passing each other on campus, she and Oz were drawn to each other on an instinctive level. In the episode "Wild at Heart," Veruca attempted to get Oz to join her on her hunts, to stop allowing himself to be caged and to embrace the primal urge of the wolf. Her mere presence, and the effect it had on his instincts, were enough to drive him into such a frenzy that he broke from his cage. In the morning, he awoke to find himself naked in Veruca's arms.

She taunted him about his situation, that he was so domesticated, and made it clear that she felt the powerful, instinctive sexual attraction between them. When Oz asked her to come see him at sundown that night and then locked her into the cage with him, he claimed that it was to protect others from her. Veruca believed that it was due to their mutual animal attraction. They began to kiss, and then to transform into wolves.

The next morning, Willow discovered them in the cage together. Oz felt terrible guilt and was torn between his human and animal sides. Still, it was clear that he loved Willow. When Veruca began to believe that Oz's love for Willow was keeping him from accepting his true nature—never taking into account his basic decency—Veruca became determined to kill Willow. She trapped Willow in a room as the sun set, but Oz, in werewolf form, got to Veruca first and killed her.

origins and definitions

WEREWOLVES, LYCANTHROPES, AND THERIOMORPHS (the politically correct term of the 1990s for animal people, shorn of its horrific baggage) are essentially shapeshifters. Contrary to current pop-cultural beliefs (codified by screenwriter Curt Siodmak's invented lore for the 1941 Universal classic *The Wolf Man*), shapeshifters of ancient myth, folklore, and "real life" have always been capable of changing at will. They also transform *completely* into their animal form, rather than the half-animal, half-human menagerie of popular horror literature, pulp fiction, horror comics, television, cartoons, and movies, which tend to literalize the Anglo-Saxon roots of the term *werewolf,* which indeed means "man-wolf."

Beings much like them—talking wolves and manlike beasts—frequently appeared in folk tales, Mother Goose rhymes, and the classical fairy tales transcribed by the Brothers Grimm and Charles Perrault, including popular fixtures like "Little Red Riding Hood" and "Beauty and the Beast."

In addition to mythology and legends, however, scholars, historians, and folklorists have gathered supposedly true tales of shapeshifters and werewolves for centuries. Among the most distinguished of these studies are Sabine Baring-Gould's *The Book of Werewolves* (1865), Elliot O'Donnell's *Werewolves* (1912), and Frank Hamel's *Human Animals, Werewolves, and Other Transformations* (1915), which covers all imaginable variations on worldwide beliefs in shapeshifters and animal-people. Famed occult researcher Reverend Montague Summers's exhaustive tome *The Werewolf* (1933) remains the definitive text, while Robert Eisler's *Man into Wolf* (1947) offered the first comprehensive modern anthropological and psychological study of the subject.

Lycanthropy is a term commonly used in two different ways, to refer to humans who actually alter their flesh-and-blood forms into those of animals (or vice versa), and also to describe humans who, through some psychological disorder, actually believe themselves to be animals.

Primal beings—beast-people who are not associated with shapeshifting or lycanthropy—have other forms, associations, and origins throughout history. Tales of ancient races, often tied to lost worlds like Atlantis and Mu or mythical "hollow earth" realms beneath our feet, were often populated by subhuman, amphibious, or bestial races. With few exceptions, these were *never* shapeshifters; their subhuman appearance and behavior was immutable, characteristic of their race or species. We will touch on a few of these relevant to lycanthropy, while steering clear of revived prehistoric men and the legendary Yeti and Sasquatch "missing links," as those are seen as human or animal, rather than both—the essential element of those creatures discussed herein.

With the publication of Charles Darwin's groundbreaking scientific thesis *The Origin of Species* (1859) and successors like *The Descent of Man* (1871), *primal* took on other connotations, firmly rooted in Darwin's theories about man's prehistoric origins. Thereafter, man's bestial side was more often associated with apes than wolves in all except supernatural fiction and the most superstitious cultures. The Victorian era's shocked reaction to Darwin's theories—to this day, the theory of evolution is branded as heresy by many Christian factions—meant there were still elements of the devil and the taint of evil associated with Darwinian primals in popular belief and pop culture. The emerging sciences of psychology, psychiatry, and psychoanalysis also had an impact.

The merger of these seemingly opposing perspectives—the supernatural primal of legend and lore, and the new scientific Darwinian and Freudian prototypes—was forged by Robert Louis Stevenson's classic *The Strange Case of Dr. Jekyll and Mr. Hyde*, which is discussed in this chapter. As a product of chemistry rooted in lycanthropic lore and a belief in man's simian primal self, Mr. Hyde was arguably the first scientific primal, ushering in a new era of shapeshifters, customized to more contemporary Western cultural beliefs. Though the cause of such throwbacks would vary from story to story—chemistry, surgery, brain or gland transplants, mutation, genetics—as would their nature, with some able to return to human form, whereas others were not—this was a new archetype in the popular imagination.

Hereafter, we will refer to bestial beings rooted in ancient races, lost worlds, and/or Darwinian science as primals, to distinguish them from lycanthropes, werewolves, and supernatural shapeshifters.

The Formation of the Familiar Myths

IN MOST EARLY WESTERN CULTURES, wolves were traditionally the animal guise assumed by witches or warlocks wishing to travel incognito, defend their turf, or attack and prey on mortals. They transformed themselves by donning the animal's skin, by drinking a vile potion (made from special herbs, human blood, and the fat of dead infants), or via a pact with Satan or his minions. Certain lore held that agents of the devil had double-sided skins: human on one side, lupine (wolflike) on the other.

In other lore, werewolves were the unfortunate victims of either a witch's curse or demonic possession—innocents doomed to involuntarily become predatory monsters by night and awaken tormented by the knowledge of their condition and crimes, longing for release or death. There were also overt connections between lycanthropy and vampirism, beyond the common bond of bloodthirst, or the vampire's ability to change into a wolf. In some cultures it was believed a person who was a werewolf in life was damned to return from the grave as a vampire. Thus death would provide no deliverance for the innocent cursed with the affliction.

The persistent association of lycanthropy with witchcraft throughout Europe led many presumably innocent victims of the notorious European witch hunts to be torched as "weir-wolves." In the sixteenth century, convicted werewolf Peter Stubbe confessed under torture to wearing a magic belt given to him by Satan allowing him to become a wolf, killing and partially devouring many children in and about Cologne, Germany, for twenty-five years. Stubbe, his daughter, and his sister were executed; the "magic belt" was never found.

Between 1520 and 1630, more than *thirty thousand* cases of lycanthropy were reported in central France. In Labourt, France, in 1619, appointed witch finders Pierre de l'Ancre and

Commissioner Espaignel ferreted out many "weir-wolves." Convicted "weir-wolves" were too dangerous to hang and then burn; they had to be burned alive and their ashes tossed to the winds.

Every corner of the globe has its indigenous lycanthropes. In England, witches were thought to change into cats thanks to magical ointments; in Mexico, witches metamorphosed into coyotes to drink children's blood; in India, women could change into dogs by slipping into canine skins; in Burma, vengeful married women changed into tigers by wearing tiger skin or could become venomous serpents (see the separate discussion of snake-people and primals below).

In Jamaica, twin brothers were said to be able to inhabit the bodies of rats at will, sneaking into the homes of their enemies to lick (numbing the skin) and nibble the soles of their feet away as they slept. Native American mythology posited the existence of "skin walkers," individuals who wore wolf skins and could shapeshift into evil, bestial forms and move at incredible speeds. In Germany, men became wolves by wearing a magic belt, while an equally magical strap worn on the head could change women into foxes. In China it was believed that foxes could assume human guise, much like the Celtic and Gaelic seal-people—the Roane of the Highlands, the Selkies of the Orkneys and Shetland, and the Merrows of Ireland.

The Leopard Men of West Africa were feared for centuries, just as the carnivorous Wendigo demon frightened Canada's Inuits, cursed polar bear–men terrified Norwegians, dangerous reindeer-people roamed Lapland, and Russians dreaded shapeshifting bear-men. Other corners of Russia and Scandinavia were haunted by their own local breeds of werewolves.

North America has its share of shapeshifter beliefs. In the Ozarks witches are believed to assume the form of wolves or giant cats for nocturnal visits to their lovers, or to travel. In *Ozark Superstitions* (1947), folklorist Vance Randolph tells the tale of "a drunken bravo in northwestern Arkansas" who fired at an enormous cat, blowing off its foot and causing a woman to scream nearby; the next morning, a woman in a neighboring cabin died, having bled to death from the loss of her foot in a rumored shooting accident.

Though the French word *loup-garou* has been popularly thought to refer to traditional werewolves, French-Canadian lore links *loup-garou* to sorcerers with the magical ability to torment their enemies by assuming the form of owls, bears, or wolves. Louisiana Cajun legends speak of the *loup-garou* as either cursed or willing lost souls, spiced with inventive variations unique to their culture: Cajun *loup-garou* gather to dance together on the Bayou Goula; control giant bats that carry them about, and some can change themselves into mules to work their land. To frighten them away, one has to throw a frog at them, or leave a sifter outside the home, as they are compelled to count every hole. If sprinkled with salt, they catch fire and dash out of their skins.

Many cultures indeed believed the condition to be communicable by either bite or exposure to a werewolf's saliva, and most cultures consider lycanthropy a curse (both elements are essential to the pop-cultural werewolf mythology). There are exceptions: Wiccan beliefs invite male devotees who sleep naked under the night sky to let the wolf spirit possess their bodies to dream of future events, while Amazonian tribal rituals summon the jaguar spirit to inhabit human form.

In each respective culture's lycanthrope lore, there are certain characteristics that might identify the damned in his or her mortal form. In many Christian cultures, it was believed that the unlucky few born on December twenty-fifth, the date of Christ's birth, were cursed to become werewolves. Certain physical deformities marked a lycanthrope: red hair, eyebrows that join over the bridge of the nose, hairs on the palm of the hands, hair growing under the skin, or index and middle fingers of the same length were sure signs of lycanthropy. (Nocturnal disappearances, an unnatural affinity for raw or bloody-rare meat, a proclivity toward sexual attacks, and a particular craving for human flesh were considered tip-offs, too.)

case Histories

COULD SUCH THINGS EXIST? Pioneer researcher of scientific anomalies and impossibilities Charles Fort (whose legacy outlived him, in part through the Fortean Society, dedicated to preserving and continuing Fort's efforts) wrote in his book *Wild Talents* (1932): "What is there that absolutely sets apart the story of a man who turned into an ape, or a hyena, from the story of a caterpillar that became a butterfly?"

Fort went on to document a 1918 account of a Nigerian village plagued by hyena attacks; when the tracks were followed, they gave way to human footprints. When the marauding hyena was finally shot in the jaw and disappeared, a villager was later found dead, his jaw shot away.

Fort also linked the mysterious anachronistic appearances of animals discovered far from their native habitat, sans any rational explanation—citing the case of a lemur, an animal unique to Madagascar, found dead in Lincoln, Nebraska, in November 1931—to beliefs in shapeshifting, evoking Darwinian science. "It is a matter of common belief that men have come from animals called 'lower,'" Fort continued, "not necessarily from apes, though the ape-theory seems to fit best, and is the most popular. Then why not that occasionally a human sloughs backward?"

Non-Forteans seek other explanations. There are many documented cases of feral children and adults, raised among or as animals, found naked, incapable of speech, or any of the niceties of "civilized" behavior. Lucien Malson's *Les Enfants Sauvages* documents more than fifty authenticated cases of feral children discovered since the mid-fourteenth century, reportedly raised by a variety of creatures, including wolves, panthers, leopards, various apes, and even ostriches. The most famous of these French savages was the Wild Boy of Aveyron, rescued by hunters in 1799 and subsequently studied and raised by Dr. Jean Itard. Though he never spoke, the boy (named Victor de l'Aveyron) was eventually taught to read, enjoy civilized comforts, and lived to the (approximated) ripe age of forty; François Truffaut played Itard in his film about the Wild Boy, *The Wild Child* (1970).

In *Wolf Child and Human Child* (1941), Dr. Arnold Gesell detailed the case of Kamala and Amala the feral brother and sister supposedly raised by wolves and discovered in Midnapore, India, by Reverend J. A. L. Singh in 1920.

In the netherworld between nineteenth-century spiritualism and the twentieth-century emergence of psychoanalysis, odd descriptions of lycanthropy and werewolves linger. In her book *Psychic Self-Defense,* occultist and early psychoanalysis advocate Dion Fortune described her experience with an ectoplasmic werewolf that manifested itself from her own ire toward a person who had angered her. She claimed the creature was linked to her by an ectoplasmic umbilical cord, through which she withdrew energy from the spectral brute. Her experience remains a fascinating bridge between ancient beliefs (she refers to having experienced visions of "Nordic" werewolf lore before the manifestation) and the modern scientific orientation to psychological lycanthropy.

Driven by the inexplicable reappearance of ancient symbols in the dreams of unrelated people with no waking experience that would provide such a link, Carl Jung proposed that archetypal subconscious memories of our common bestial origins survive in all of us. Jung argued that atavistic dreams or waking visions of such overwhelming primal power might break through into conscious behavior of some persons, prompting savagery and even lycanthropy.

Dr. Sigmund Freud's "The Case of the Wolf-Man: From the History of an Infantile Neurosis" (1915) was his classic analysis of such a disorder in a Russian immigrant. Freud refuted Jung's arguments, finding the roots of the condition in the unfortunate man's childhood. Remarkably, the "Wolf-Man" himself followed up on Freud's psychoanalysis with an autobiography, *The Memoirs of the Wolf-Man* (1952), and maintained contact with other psychoanalysts until his death in the 1970s. Drawing from this seminal case history, Freudian psychology links beliefs in lycanthropy and recorded cases of lycanthropic behavior disorders as expressions of usually repressed sadistic sexual instincts, leading in extreme cases to mutilation, blood drinking, and cannibalism.

Via either interpretation, modern psychologists recognize lycanthropy as a mental disorder, a condition in which the patient does not physically transform but certainly identifies unnaturally with primal animal behavior and, in extreme cases, lapses into canine stance (walking on all fours), diet, and aggressive attacks. Other psychologists argue that autistic behavior may account for many reported cases of lycanthropy, especially if the autism was extreme, manifesting in near-feral, nocturnal, and/or excessively violent behavior including biting and clawing.

Some physicians and historians argue that outbreaks of rabies or hydrophobia among either animal or human populations explain the persistent belief in lycanthropy. Other researchers argue that such beliefs can be traced to certain hallucinatory drugs, either self-administered (as with the witch's potions and ointments of lore) or accidental (i.e., fungal ergot poisoning of grain crops, now considered a common occurrence in the Middle Ages). The link with hallucinogenics is persuasive. Fortean researcher Joe McNally cites an archaic 1615 textbook (*De la lycanthropie, transformation, et extase des scorciers* by Nynauld) that lists the necessary ingredients for a transformative ointment, including belladonna root and nightshade, both poisonous.

Dissecting the famed Don Juan chronicles of author Carlos Casteneda, Neville Drury and Stephen Skinner's *The Search for Abraxas* (1971) suggest the hallucinogenic paste derived from datura root, the "devil's weed," may have been similar to the "witch's paste" of legend and lore that allowed them to fly and shapeshift (or, more accurately, to believe that they had).

More recently, doctors point to the blood disease porphyria as a possible source of such pervasive werewolf and vampire lore, a link publicized by Britain's Dr. Lee Illis in the early 1960s. The terrible toll of the disease includes ulcers that deform and destroy tissue, including the face and extremities, elongation of the teeth, an aversion to sunlight (which indeed aggravates tissue damage), and—quite understandably—erratic or psychotic behavior. Reportedly, many cases of congenital porphyria have been uncovered in areas of Sweden and

Switzerland, which might indicate a possible explanation as to why those nations were the source of many historical reports of werewolves.

Supernatural accounts of lycanthropy still surface from time to time. According to *The Fortean Times*, a 1976 broadcast of the BBC news program *Nationwide* covered numerous British werewolf sightings linked to the discovery of a pair of Celtic stone heads in a Hexham family's garden.

German folklore scholar D. L. Ashliman documents an event as recently as 1988, during which several guards at the Morbach munitions installation outside Wittlich, West Germany, witnessed a seven- to eight-foot tall wolflike biped leap over a twelve-foot-high fence to escape. The creature's appearance eerily corresponded with the extinguishing of the "eternal flame" at a local shrine to the last lycanthrope killed in Germany. According to legend, if the flame goes out, the werewolf will return. No further sightings were reported.

At the end of 1999, according to the Associated Press, an exorcism was performed in China on a twenty-one-year-old woman named Ying-Ying who was believed to be possessed by the spirit of a dead cat. She had not spoken or behaved like a human being since the age of nine, during which time she had lived like a cat, walking on all fours, meowing, purring, scratching, and eating like a feline. The exorcism was reportedly successful.

With the turn of the new millennium, could such things *still* be possible?

primals in popular culture

DOUBT AS TO THE REALITY of werewolves and their kin has not slowed the steady flow of pop-cultural lycanthropes. Though they have never approached the popularity of vampires as the pop bogeymen of choice, werewolves have enjoyed a long and healthy moonlit romp across countless pages and screens. In accordance with the cultural attitudes discussed above, the image of the lycanthrope has evolved somewhat over time. In early literary incarnations, werewolves were traditionally evil supernatural monsters; in contemporary tales, the werewolf is more often an innocent who becomes the victim of the transformative curse, struggling to keep his sanity, protect those dear to him, and aching for redemption and release by any means.

Mythic beliefs in shapeshifters and animal-people predates literature, rooted in half-forgotten folk tales, oral storytelling traditions, and many cultural artifacts and documents. The elder gods and deities of Greek and Roman mythology often assumed the shape of animals to traffic (and sometimes mate) with mortals. The origins of those tales are almost untraceable. Furthermore, the themes and images assume new meanings for each successive generation. For instance, Circe changed Odysseus's men to pigs in Homer's *The Odyssey* (a text whose origins remain lost to antiquity; the current standard text dates back to at least 400 B.C., with evidence indicating the first written transcription may have existed as far back as 700 B.C.). Nearly three thousand years later, the same man-to-pig imagery has become a political metaphor in the climax of George Orwell's parable *Animal Farm* (1946) or as the punchline to Coke Sam and Bruce Arntson's satiric feature film *Existo* (1999).

The earliest recorded accounts of werewolves appear in Greek and Roman myths and literature. In Ovid's *Metamorphoses*, a man named Lycaeon dared to serve human flesh to a group of visiting deities; as punishment, he was changed into a wolf. Petronius wrote of a werewolf in the *Satyricon*.

Aesop's Fables, popular fairy tales, folk tales, and nursery rhymes offered their own menageries of talking animals and beast-people. The ravenous wolves of "Little Red Riding Hood" and "The Three Little Pigs" offered chilling childhood variations on the theme, as did the cursed prince who became a beast, returning to his mortal form only after knowing the love of a woman, in "Beauty and the Beast." Those were committed to print by many transcribers and authors, their origins in oral folk tales difficult to trace.

The venerable *Mother Goose Tales* by Charles Perrault was first published in France in 1697, with its first English translation appearing in 1729. Perrault's "Petit Chaperon Rouge" (Little Red Riding Hood) has no earlier recorded historical precedent, though it traveled well and became the German "Rotkappchen," which Jacob and Wilhelm Grimm subsequently transcribed from local storytellers and published in 1812. Gabrielle Suzanne, Madame Le Prince de Beaumont, and others are credited with variations and adaptations throughout history; the older the version, however, the more primal and savage the monster and its appetite.

Horror scholar Brian J. Frost traces the roots of lycanthropy in European fiction to thirteenth-century author Marie de France's romantic novel *Lay of the Bisclavaret* and the medieval French romance *William and the Werewolf* (first translated into English in 1350). Thereafter, the werewolf most frequently pops up in nonfiction texts until the advent of the early nineteenth-century Gothic movement.

The sixteenth-century occultist Theophrastus Paracelsus wrote of the two spirits in man, one human, the other bestial, and his conviction that persons dominated by the animal spirit would behave as animals. After death such a person would dwell in the afterlife as an animal, and, if consumed by his cravings, might return to the mortal realm as a werewolf. Sprenger and Kramer's infamous witch-finder's bible, the *Malleus Maleficarum* ("Hammer of the Witches"), featured a passage on lycanthropy, referring to "William of Paris [who] tells of a certain man who thought that he was turned into a wolf...," followed by the hearsay history of the case.

Gothic novels of the nineteenth century seized on such beliefs as grist for their imaginative writings. Though the most sophisticated Gothic novelists rarely introduced the theme, others gave the bloodthirsty brutes center stage, as in Weber's *Wolf: or, The Tribunal of Blood* (1806) and G. W. M. Reynolds's popular serialized novel, *Wagner, The Wehr-Wolf* (1846), which ended its Faustian lycanthropy tale after seventy-seven episodes.

Alexandre Dumas, renowned Continental author of the adventure classic *The Three Musketeers*, authored *The Wolf-Leader* (1857), in which an eighteenth-century peasant makes a pact with the devil in hopes of elevating his social status. Frustrated and rejected at every turn, he ultimately uses up his wishes and Satan claims him, changing him into a werewolf.

The most bracingly modern variation on the werewolf theme was Robert Louis Stevenson's classic *The Strange Case of Dr. Jekyll and Mr. Hyde* (1886), which brought a fresh psychological, scientific, and moral spin to the venerable archetype, anticipating Jungian and Freudian interpretations of lycanthropy by over two decades.

Stevenson introduced a calculated, chemically induced separation of the dual natures of man, splitting the kindly Dr. Jekyll from the sadistic, bestial Mr. Hyde. Hyde, it should be noted, was very specifically *not* a wolf-man. At first, the savage Hyde persona reverts to Jekyll's original self once

the chemical runs its course, leaving Jekyll to agonize over his alter ego's crimes, much like the cursed innocents of lycanthropic lore. However, Jekyll's continuing self-medicated indulgence of the Hyde persona turns the tables, necessitating the use of the elixir to change back to Jekyll, culminating in suicide when the threat of capture and lack of the transformative drug takes its toll.

Written even as the horrific unsolved Jack the Ripper murders rocked London, Stevenson's tale embodied many of its era's cultural ills, including prostitution and drug abuse. It also echoed a number of Victorian era dualities: the cruel class divisions between the aristocracy and the poor, and the former's predation of the latter for its own amusement; the hypocritical sexual mores, repressing intimate relations in the home while covertly fueling the prostitution of women and children. Thus, Stevenson succinctly adapted ancient lycanthropic beliefs to his contemporary landscape with terrifying immediacy, urgency, and conviction, contributing to the genre an archetype as powerful as Shelley's *Frankenstein* and Stoker's *Dracula*.

One year later, Stevenson wrote a more traditional lycanthropy novelette, "Ollala," a similarly modern narrative in that it reads like a case history of its peculiar insanity.

Whereas Stevenson dissected Britain's inner demons, Rudyard Kipling's "The Mark of the Beast" (1891) wrestled with the Empire's imperialistic legacy. The tale involved a British officer in India whose drunken desecration of a religious temple prompts a leper priest to "infect" him with the soul of a beast, manifesting itself as a rabies-like malady, inducing increasingly animalistic behavior until his mates force the leper to lift his curse.

Another tale of an Englishman in India confronted by the bestial product of soul-migration was Sidney Warwick and Arthur Applier's "A Vendetta of the Jungle," in which a woman is devoured by a tiger only to have her soul enter the cat's body. The American master of the macabre Ambrose Bierce offered his own variation on the theme in his classic short story "The Eyes of the Panther" (1893).

Perhaps the greatest of all female lycanthropes was the femme fatale of Clemence Housman's "The Were-wolf" (1896), which was also arguably the first classic werewolf novel. Science fiction, horror, and fantasy scholar and anthologist Sam Moskowitz declared Housman's achievement "the single greatest work of fiction on the theme of lycanthropy," and it remains a powerful reading experience.

Western society was still reeling from the devastating impact of Darwin's recently published *Origin of Species* when celebrated author H. G. Wells unleashed his short novel "The Island of Dr. Moreau" (1896). Many were outraged by the novel's merciless marriage of vivisectionist surgery and Darwinian theory. It is a subversive horror tale further charged with an unsettling subtext critical of exploitative imperialist and missionary attitudes toward Third World cultures.

Moreau's remote island was inhabited by a menagerie of beast-men. The hero discovers these creatures are the products of the good doctor's radical attempts to surgically transform experimental animal subjects into "evolved" beast-men. Like Stevenson, Wells introduced a horrifying and utterly modern reinvention of the animal-man archetype, custom-designed to address the turn-of-the-century's qualms about the new sciences, the attendant theological issues, and profound questions about man's origins and nature the clash of the two belief systems raised.

With the turn of the century, the Edwardian era continued to produce its share of neo-Gothic werewolf tales. H. H. Munro's (better known by his nom de plume "Saki") wry "Gabriel Ernest" (1910) was a perverse anecdote, noteworthy for featuring the first of many teenage lycanthropes, an amoral feral child who preys on unwary innocents and the ignorance of adults. American master of the supernatural short story Algernon Blackwood wrote many imaginative werewolf tales such as "The Camp of the Dog" (1908).

Rooted in similar psychological convictions was Frank Norris's *Vandover and the Brute* (1910), the most intimate and naturalistic handling of the theme since Stevenson's "Ollala." Norris, best known for his novel *McTeague*, abandoned the traditional supernatural or pseudo-science trappings to portray the utter degradation of the human spirit. The novel unflinchingly traces its protagonist's descent into madness as the man imagines himself a wolf while he runs about on all fours and bays at the moon. It is a remarkable anticipation of Freud's "Wolf-Man."

In the pulp magazines, Darwin's theories spawned a procession of evolutionary primals. *Pearson's Magazine* published Wardon Allan Curtis's wonderfully absurd "The Monster of Lake Lametrie" (1899), in which a man's brain was crudely transplanted into the skull of a living Elasmosaurus.

The first of at least four silent film adaptations of "Beauty and the Beast" emerged from France in 1899. The first "Big Bad Wolf" hit the screen in a French adaptation of *Little Red Riding Hood* (1901); ten more threatened Red before the coming of sound, not counting the many animated cartoons. The first genuine lycanthropy film, *The Cat that Was Changed into a Woman* (1910), was derived from an Aesop fable and introduced the screen's first feline shapeshifter. In 1913, a French production of Wells' "The Island of Dr. Moreau" appeared under the title *L'île d'Epouvante*.

Thereafter, inspired by the ongoing success of its many stage adaptations, Stevenson's *The Strange Case of Dr. Jekyll and Mr. Hyde* offered the richest vein of silent film adaptation variations, yielding over a dozen versions before the silent era ended. John Barrymore starred in the definitive silent era version of *Dr. Jekyll and Mr. Hyde* (Famous Players, 1920), trumping producer Louis B. Mayer's updated version set in New York City and starring Sheldon Lewis.

British and American authors explored fresh variations in the magazine, pulp, and novel markets. English author David Garnett's self-explanatory *Lady into Fox* (1922) foreshadowed "The Fox Woman" by Abraham Merritt.

The emergence in 1923 of the popular American pulp magazine *Weird Tales* led its native authors to dominate the genre, and shapeshifter tales flourished as never before. Seabury Quinn, among the most popular of the *Weird Tales* scribes, made his debut with a werewolf tale, "The Phantom Farmhouse" (1923), one of the first slices of Americana lycanthropy. Quinn's most popular creation, the psychic sleuth Jules de Grandin, debuted in 1925, and often dealt with vampires and werewolves. *Weird Tales'* premier werewolf auteur was H. Warner Munn, who penned an ongoing series of interlocked narratives featuring a thousand-year-old warlock dubbed "The Master." Science fiction author Jack Williamson's novelette fusion of lycanthropic horror and science fantasy "Wolves of Darkness" originally appeared in *Strange Tales* (1932).

In Hollywood, Paramount mounted the most distinguished of the early sound horrors, Rouben Mamoulian's masterful *Dr. Jekyll and Mr. Hyde* (1931), which remains the best of all its cinematic adaptations. Fredric March earned the Academy Award for Best Actor for his portrayal of the doomed doctor.

Portions of the transformation scenes were created with uninterrupted single takes, using color filters, that gradually revealed makeup effects prepared with corresponding coloration, leading audiences to believe they had seen March's complete transformation onscreen; when Hyde emerged in full regalia, the illusion was complete. With precious little variation, the technique wasn't improved upon until the makeup technology revolution of the early 1980s.

Paramount also produced the gruesome and downbeat *Island of Lost Souls* (1933). Charles Laughton starred as the saturnine Dr. Moreau in this genuinely chilling adaptation of H. G. Wells's controversial novella. Bela Lugosi lent impressive support in his role as the wolflike Sayer of the Law, whose awe and fear of Moreau and "The House of Pain" from whence he came was palpable. Lugosi's recitation of the Law ("Are we not men?") later became an anthem for the 1980s mutant rock band Devo. Moreau's wolf-men, however, were *not* werewolves.

The first known sound lycanthrope film was adapted from German novelist Alfred Machard's *Der Schwarze Mann*, which was translated and retitled *The Wolf Man (The Were-Wolf)* in 1925, and subsequently filmed in Germany as *Le Loup-Garou* (1932).

Guy Endore wrote the era's most popular werewolf novel, *The Werewolf of Paris* (1933). American author Endore based his narrative on the case history of twenty-five-year-old French military officer Sergeant-Major Francis Bertrand, who was captured in Paris in March 1849, and subsequently tried and convicted of grave-robbing and cannibalism. In his defense, Bertrand argued at his trial that he had "surrendered to an irresistible impulse," and became a wolf before committing his crimes; after desecrating the bodies, he would seek shelter and there lie in a trance until he was again himself. Endore adhered to Bertrand's claims, touching on traditional superstitions. The novel was an international success, and MGM snapped up the film rights.

Eager to beat MGM to the plate, Universal rushed production on the first American sound lycanthropy thriller, *Werewolf of London* (1935). The werewolf lore invented for the original screenplay was cumbersome: seeking a rare, elusive Tibetan flower that blooms only at midnight, a botanist (Henry Hull) is bitten by an Asian werewolf (Warner Oland, in fine form and soon to be the definitive Charlie Chan). He returns to London with the bloom and the blight, changing into a rather well-dressed werewolf with the coming of the full moon. Oland follows Hull to London, where they both die tussling over the Tibetan blossom they each require (but only one can have) to cure their affliction.

Universal's next attempt struck pay dirt, and makeup master Jack Pierce created the "look" for all movie werewolves to follow. *The Wolf Man* (1941) starred Lon Chaney Jr. as the archetypal cinematic werewolf Larry Talbot. Bitten by a Gypsy lycanthrope (played by Bela Lugosi), Talbot was cursed to transform and seek human flesh with every full moon. *The Wolf Man,* somberly crafted by screenwriter Curt Siodmak and director George Waggner, remains the definitive werewolf movie. Willing to endure Pierce's painstaking makeup applications, Chaney made the role of earnest, earthy, tormented Larry Talbot his own.

"Even a man who is pure in heart, and says his prayers by night, may become a wolf when the wolf's bane blooms, and the moon is full and bright...." That bit of verse was wholly invented by Siodmak and delivered by the elder Gypsy played by Maria Ouspenska. Indicative of the film's enduring stature is the fact that Siodmak's distillation of various lycanthropy lore (including the necessary use of silver to slay the shapeshifter) and that bit of verse were indelibly etched on the imagination of subsequent generations, who considered any cinematic deviation from this litany borderline heresy, in much the same way that many people still adhere to some of the vampire lore Bram Stoker invented for *Dracula*.

Though the climax freed Talbot of the curse, beaten to death with a silver-crowned cane by his father (Claude Rains), he was resurrected for four more outings. Grave robbers removed the wolfsbane from Talbot's corpse, prompting *Frankenstein Meets the Wolf Man* (1943), which earned big bucks and drove poor Larry to join the Universal monster-mashes *House of Frankenstein* (1944) and *House of Dracula* (1945), seeking and, in the latter, finding a cure (a bone-softening fungus!) for his condition. Alas, the cure didn't last long. Talbot finally found eternal peace by saving Bud and Lou from the evil designs of Dracula (Bela Lugosi in his only return to the role that made him famous) in *Abbott and Costello Meet Frankenstein* (1948). Chaney's Wolf Man returned to menace Abbott and Costello one more time as TV's first lycanthrope, guest-starring on a 1950 episode of the live broadcast *Colgate Comedy Hour*.

Meanwhile, MGM mounted their top-drawer version of *Dr. Jekyll and Mr. Hyde* (1941) starring Spencer Tracy, whose Hyde was realized with very little makeup, relying almost entirely on his performance.

But the most vivid and terrifying human-to-beast transformation of the 1940s appeared in a cartoon: Walt Disney's *Pinocchio* (1940) traumatized a generation of children when Pleasure Island claimed Pinocchio's playmate Lampwick, changing him into a braying donkey onscreen to be used as slave labor.

The Return of the Vampire (Columbia, 1944) acknowledged the existence of World War II, placing Bela Lugosi's Draculalike vampire and Matt Willis's groveling werewolf lackey in the European war theater. The German blitz-bombing of London disinterred Lugosi's vampire.

The only real innovation brought to the genre completely eschewed the "look" popularized by *The Wolf Man*—essentially by showing nothing at all—and added an erotic charge to the shapeshifter mystique with *Cat People* (RKO, 1942). Together, producer Val Lewton and director Jacques Tourneur fashioned a compellingly ambiguous tale of a young woman (Simone Simon) who believes her Serbian heritage and curse causes her to change into a murderous cat when she is angered or sexually aroused.

With its contemporary setting and calculated refusal to cater to the title's sensationalistic promise, *Cat People* ushered in a new approach to cinematic horror. The studio, however, felt it necessary to insert a single shot of an actual panther, compromising the doubt Lewton and Tourneur so carefully nurtured. Lewton produced two films with titles suggesting further explorations of the theme: *The Leopard Man* (RKO, 1943), and *The Curse of the Cat People* (RKO, 1944), but neither involved shapeshifters.

Though producers rallied to imitate Lewton's accomplishments, none had the wit or finesse to understand, much less embrace, the new aesthetic. Universal countered with Larry Talbot's return in the monster fests and its own beast-woman: Paula Dupree, played by the exotic

Acquanetta in the first two installments, *Captive Wild Woman* (1943) and *Jungle Woman* (1944). Vicki Lane was the sorry ape-girl in the final chapter, *Jungle Captive* (1945).

And there were wolf-women: Columbia's *Cry of the Werewolf* (1944) starred Nina Foch, who delivered a striking performance as the cursed Gypsy queen. June Lockhart was the *She-Wolf of London* (Universal, 1946), a faked female lycanthrope.

Another faux Universal werewolf plagued the Canadian wilderness until Sherlock Holmes (Basil Rathbone) unveiled the all-too-human scoundrel in *The Scarlet Claw* (1944). Meanwhile, Republic Studios spat out its masculine *Cat People* knockoff, *The Catman of Paris* (1946). Even cheaper was *The Creeper* (Reliance, 1948), starring Onslow Stevens.

However, the most alluringly feline of all cinematic lycanthropes was indeed a cat-man from Paris, Jean Marais's Beast from *Beauty and the Beast* (1946), a classic fantasy film impeccably crafted in war-torn France by Jean Cocteau, one of Europe's premier artists. He realized the beloved fairy tale with timeless clarity, poetry, and vision.

In the 1940s the genre found fertile soil in the burgeoning comic-book industry. Publishers had begun to gravitate toward horror even as the previous decade came to a close. In *Detective Comics* #31 and #32 (1939), the fifth and sixth appearances of Batman, the Dark Knight Detective battled a mysterious vampire called the Monk. Infiltrating the villain's Hungarian castle, Batman was forced to battle and destroy ferocious werewolves left as guardians by the vampire.

Gilberton Publishing's Classics Comics and Classics Illustrated series adapted Stevenson's *Dr. Jekyll and Mr. Hyde* with crude vigor in 1943 (followed by *Frankenstein*, various Poe adaptations, and others).

Legendary comics artist Wally Wood lent a hand to yet another full-length comic adaptation of *Dr. Jekyll and Mr. Hyde* (*A Star Presentation Magazine* #3, Fox Features, May 1950) before beginning his tenure with the most beloved *and* infamous of all pre-Code horror comics publishers, EC Comics, illustrating stories for *Tales from the Crypt*, *Vault of Horror*, and *Haunt of Fear*.

The EC Comics line featured many tales of werewolves and shapeshifters, as did their countless competitors. They embraced all aspects of the literary and cinematic lycanthropes: wolfmen, cat-women, leopard-men, bat-men, and all manner of shapeshifters and animal-humanoids populated the explosion of horror titles rushing out of every publishing house.

EC's debut horror comic, *The Crypt of Terror* #17 (1950; picking up its numbering from an earlier potpourri of non-horror titles, and soon to be retitled *Tales from the Crypt*) featured a werewolf cover and the story "Curse of the Full Moon." The lycanthropes delineated by fellow EC artist Jack Davis in later issues were far more bloodthirsty and animalistic than any prior movie makeup creations. Davis's lycanthropes were foaming, rabid savages.

The notorious Kefauver hearings targeting horror comics and the subsequent adoption of the Comics Code in October 1954 brought the horror cycle to an end. The code specifically forbade the depiction of "werewolfism" in comic books, and for almost a decade, they were purged from the newsstands.

In effect, they had already been banished from movie screens. Abbott and Costello may have hammered in the last nail in the coffin of the Universal monster series, but the killing blow had been delivered with the real-life atrocities of World War II.

Variations on Stevenson's venerable *Dr. Jekyll and Mr. Hyde* and Wells' "The Island of Dr. Moreau" dominated the screens during the science fiction monster boom of the 1950s. In fact, Stevenson's creation ushered in that new science-horror era as the butt of Bud and Lou's buffoonery in *Abbott and Costello Meet Dr. Jekyll and Mr. Hyde* (Universal, 1953, in which Costello himself turned into a rotund Hyde), the Hyde-less tedium of *The Son of Dr. Jekyll* (Columbia, 1951), and Edgar Ulmer's *Daughter of Dr. Jekyll* (Allied Artists, 1957), which sported its own ersatz Mr. Hyde.

Atom-age authority figures spread new lycanthropic infestations with their deliberate misuse of modern science. The bottom-of-the-double-bill feature *The Werewolf* (Columbia, 1956) was a grim sleeper, chronicling the pitiless manhunt for a tormented modern lycanthrope, a hapless accident victim "rescued" by suspect surgical experimentation performed upon him while he was unconscious. Robert Clarke produced and starred as *The Hideous Sun Demon* (Pacific, 1959), an inversion of the traditional nocturnal shapeshifting lore in which a scientific accident and exposure to the sun's rays turns its hapless innocent into a homicidal lizard-man.

I Was a Teenage Werewolf (AIP, 1957) made a fortune at the box office as teens flocked by the carload to the first film ever to proclaim its allegiance to their generation by using the term "teenage" in its title. The combo—monsters and juvenile delinquents—was irresistible, and the film itself made good on its promise by pitting a miserable, misunderstood high school misfit (future TV star Michael Landon) against an unyielding adult community.

Meanwhile, fantasy and science fiction authors offered richer variations. Anthony Boucher's *The Compleat Werewolf* (1942) and Jane Rice's "The Refugee" (1943) broke fresh ground, whereas James Blish's lively novella "There Shall Be No Darkness" (1950) followed tradition, setting its werewolf tale in a Scottish castle. *Weird Tales* veteran August Derleth worked a werewolf into one of his Sherlock Holmes homages featuring sleuth Solar Pons, "The Adventure of the Tottenham Werewolf" (1951), and fellow vet Clark Ashton Smith penned the satirical "A Prophecy of Monsters" (1954). Joseph Payne Brennan's "The Hunt" (1958) was an elegantly simple lycanthropy tale, and among the best.

THE FLY

But the freshest take on the theme appeared in the pages of the *Magazine of Fantasy and Science Fiction*. Bruce Elliott's fascinating "Wolves Don't Cry" (1954) told the tale of a "were-man," a wolf cursed with periodic transformations into the form of a man.

Far more influential was George Langelaan's potent sci-fi story "The Fly," first published in *Playboy* (June 1957) to much acclaim, winning the magazine's Best Fiction Award. Franz Kafka's existential horror novel *Metamorphosis* (1912) had established the man-to-insect archetype for the twentieth century, but Langelaan's spin spoke the language of the post–World War II era. Twentieth Century Fox snapped up the rights and scored a smash hit with *The Fly* (1958).

In Langelaan's story a scientist (Al—who later changed his name to David—Hedison) recklessly fuses his atoms with the molecular structure of a fly during an experimental transmission of matter, emerging with the insect's head, "hand," a degenerative mental condition, and an appetite for sugar. He opts for suicide, coaxing his wife to crush the insect head and hand in a press, and his opposite—a pathetic insect with a pasty hairless and toothless human head and hand also created in the incident—dies horribly in a spider's web in one of the era's most sickening finales. Its cry of "Help meeeeeee!" has become an iconic pop-cultural sound bite, popping up to this day in songs, music videos, and even Spike Lee's recent film *Summer of Sam* (Miramax, 1999).

RETURN OF THE FLY

The Fly's success led to sequels and imitations, prompting the scientific shapeshifters to move down the evolutionary ladder to mix and match with the invertebrates. The original scientist's son survived a similar transformation in *Return of the Fly* (1959). Eager to correct the family curse, his heirs went on to create a relatively shapeless clutch of atomic mismatches in *The Curse of the Fly* (1965). Two decades later, David Cronenberg explored the possibilities with more conviction in his moving, horrifying remake *The Fly* (Twentieth Century Fox, 1986), bolstered by Jeff Goldblum's remarkable central performance as the scientist Seth Brundle. Brundle-fly's son (Harley Cross as a child, Eric Stoltz as a teen) was unwillingly dragged into resurrecting dad's experiments in *The Fly II* (Twentieth Century Fox, 1989).

Bookending the entire Fly family album was a clutch of imitators, led by Roger Corman's knockoff *The Wasp Woman* (Filmgroup, 1960). True to form, Corman mounted a low-budget remake in 1996 to cash in on the ongoing popularity of Cronenberg's film in the video market, though he spent enough to craft a far more convincing insect-woman.

Other 1950s Atom-Agers were inspired by Wells's "The Island of Dr. Moreau." *The Return of the Fly* was originally double-billed with *The Alligator People* (Twentieth Century Fox, 1959), a nicely mounted and played tale of covert primitive genetics experiments in the bayou.

For 1950s Hollywood, box office receipts plummeted as once-faithful audiences stayed home to watch their TV sets. The studios gradually realized the financial opportunities in selling or leasing their film backlogs to television.

When Universal offered its "Shock Theater" package for broadcast, a whole new generation enjoyed *Frankenstein*, *Dracula*, and, of course, *The Wolf Man*. The increasing popularity of these resurrected classics among young late-show viewers gave birth to a new breed of newsstand magazine, heralded by the successful debut of *Famous Monsters of Filmland* (Warren, 1958). The revival of interest in the classic 1930s and '40s monster movies inspired some producers to craft their own remakes, with the most influential emerging from England.

Most popular of all were those that emerged from the British Hammer Films, who finally tackled the werewolf legend with characteristic vigor and blazing Technicolor (a first, apart from the animated cartoon werewolves). *The Curse of the Werewolf* (Hammer, 1961) heralded itself as an adaptation of Guy Endore's *The Werewolf of Paris*, though it was set in medieval Spain. Folklore new to the screen was introduced as the infant lycanthrope's baptism is spoiled by the inexplicable boiling of the holy waters.

Despite the box office success of Hammer's effort, there were few creditable successors or contemporaries. Hammer toyed with female shapeshifters in *The Gorgon* (1964), featuring Barbara Shelley turning into a mythical Medusa, and *The Reptile* (1966), but they never again dealt with lycanthropy.

Hammer's take on Jekyll and Hyde was *The Two Faces of Dr. Jekyll* (aka *House of Fright*, 1960), in which scruffy Jekyll turns into dapper, sadistic ladies' man Hyde (both Paul Massie). Jerry Lewis went them one better with Hyde-as-lounge-lizard Buddy Love in *The Nutty Professor* (Paramount, 1963). Amicus, Hammer's primary U.K. competitor in the 1960s, featured a female werewolf in the first of the five stories that comprised its popular compendium feature, *Dr. Terror's House of Horrors* (1965).

The first stop-motion puppet werewolf and Mr. Hyde joined the *Mad Monster Party* (Embassy, 1967) on the kiddie-matinee circuit, from Arthur Rankin and Jules Bass, producer of the popular holiday TV special *Rudolph the Red-Nosed Reindeer*. Almost three decades later, Tim Burton and Henry Selick would include a werewolf in their affectionate stop-motion puppet ode to the Rankin-Bass tradition, *The Nightmare Before Christmas* (1993).

The magic was spent. By the time director Oliver Drake trotted out his amateurish mummy-vs.-"jackal man" epic set in Las Vegas, *The Mummy and the Curse of the Jackals* (1969), the monster schtick and Vegas glitz seemed mummified. The genre had reached a dead end in more than one medium.

There were precious few original werewolf novels during this period, though science fiction author Clifford Simak's *The Werewolf Principle* (1967) stands out with its hyperadaptable hero shapeshifting at will. Philip José Farmer's scandalous *The Image of the Beast* (1968) found the Los Angeles Police Department investigating a cult of sexually active vampires, werewolves, and shapeshifters feeding on the human race, sprouting bizarre sexual organs, and shooting their own porn "snuff" films. Nothing else approached Farmer's excess or Simak's fresh variation, though Vercors's *Sylva* (1963) offered a were-vixen, a fox who changed into a woman.

Though werewolves had been explicitly banned from Code-approved comics, a few stray mongrels managed to slip through the bars from time to time. In the pages of their respective DC comic-book adventures, screen comedians Bob Hope and Jerry Lewis occasionally tangled with an ersatz, somewhat cuddly wolfman (dubbed "Dog-Boy"), and *Superman's Pal Jimmy Olsen* became a none-too-threatening Universal-style teen "Wolf Man of Metropolis" (*Jimmy Olsen* #44, DC Comics, 1960).

DC's titles always boasted the most outlandish transformations and transformative superheroes, including the shapeshifter Metamorpho and the Jekyll and Hyde–inspired villain Eclipso, who would change from mild-mannered scientist into super-villain during eclipses, which occurred with alarming frequency (debuting in *House of Secrets* #61, 1963).

Congorilla was an ongoing backup series in *Adventure Comics* (#270–281, 1959–61) in which jungle explorer Congo Bill would "swap bodies" with a mysterious golden gorilla, utilizing its strength and power while its simian mind languished in Bill's human shell. An update of that series was published in 1999 as the miniseries *Congo Bill*.

DC often indulged in variations on the theme. An installment of writer Robert Kanigher's popular 1960s War That Time Forgot series pitted soldiers against dinosaurs in the pages of *Star-Spangled War Stories*, and boasted a shapeshifter who transformed into a ravenous Tyrannosaurus rex in a story titled "My Buddy Was a Killer Dinosaur!" In time, even Superman (transformed in one adventure into an ant-headed superbeing by Red Kryponite) and Batman changed into a variety of weird creatures, the latter battle the ultimate shapeshifter, Clayface (beginning in *Detective Comics* #298, 1961).

As noted earlier (see Vampires), two comic-book publishers—Dell and Gilberton—had never signed with the Comics Code Authority, and thus were free to exploit the early 1960s horror boom. Gilberton rushed their *Classics Illustrated* adaptation *Dr. Jekyll and Mr. Hyde* into multiple printings with a new painted cover, while Dell topped them by licensing the Universal Monsters from their parent studio. Thus, *The Wolfman* hit the comic racks in 1962, though the adaptation had little to do with the classic film. Nevertheless, the licensed horror comics were a great success for Dell, prompting them to later create a batch of superhero-monster spin-offs, including *The Werewolf* (1966).

The black-and-white horror comic magazines *Creepy* and *Eerie* featured many fine werewolf yarns crafted by editor-writer Archie Goodwin for veteran EC Comics artists including Jack Davis and Reed Crandall. Goodwin also wrote werewolf tales illustrated by such comics legends as Steve Ditko (cocreator of *Spider-Man*), Neal Adams, and master fantasy artist Frank Frazetta. Frazetta's last comics story of the era was "Werewolf!" in *Creepy* #1 (1964), and its massive African werewolf was one of the most genuinely frightening lupine creatures in comics history.

The atomic age of shapeshifters in comics and movies spawned the definitive shapeshifter superhero, *The Hulk* (debuted May 1962). The Hulk was an inspired fusion of superhero and SF-horror archetypes, and Marvel Comics' straightforward nuclear-era updating of *Dr. Jekyll and Mr. Hyde* was safe enough to pass muster with the Code. Surviving exposure to a deadly bomb test (á la the film *The Amazing Colossal Man*, AIP, 1957), mild-mannered genius Bruce Banner changes uncontrollably into the Frankenstein monster–like Hulk when aroused or angered.

Writer-editor Stan Lee and artist Jack Kirby created the Hulk, though many others followed in their footsteps. Lee and Ditko also created a reptilian variation on the theme, the Lizard, as a villain for *The Amazing Spider-Man* (beginning with #6, August 1963) and Mr. Hyde himself would periodically lock horns with other Marvel heroes (tangling first with Thor in *Journey into Mystery* #99–100, December 1963–January 1964). However, none of them registered in the pop imagination with the impact of the Hulk.

The Incredible Hulk enjoyed wider popularity from 1978 to 1982 as a CBS-TV series and quartet of TV movies (the first two on CBS in 1987, the last two on NBC in 1988 and 1989) starring Bill Bixby as Banner and Lou Ferrigno as his green alter ego.

In one memorable episode a werewolf stalked the submarine corridors of the Seaview on Irwin

Allen's *Voyage to the Bottom of the Sea* (ABC-TV, 1964). Television was wary, though, of werewolves and shapeshifters, partially because the effects were too costly.

Since television also had to avoid overtly horrific material, producers simply shied away from the genre. Little Eddie Munster (Butch Patrick) was the feral-looking son of a vampire mom and Frankensteinian dad on *The Munsters* (CBS, 1964–66), but he was more of a suburban wolf-lad than lycanthrope, and just as safe as the comedy cameo werewolves in shows like *The Monkees* (NBC, 1966–68), *The Sonny and Cher Comedy Hour* (CBS, 1971–77), *Get Smart* (NBC and CBS, 1965–70), and so on.

Dark Shadows (ABC-TV) brought old-fashioned lycanthropy to the afternoon soap opera arena in 1969 during one of its lengthy flashbacks to a colonial Collingswood plagued by witches, vampires, and a werewolf. But by that time, the most devout *Dark Shadows* fans—American teens—had already left home to let their own hair grow long, experiment with recreational drugs, and find their way in a brave new world.

With the countercultural youth movement of the 1960s, a new generation of cartoonists revitalized the comics medium by establishing their own publishing venues. Many of the new comics—called "comix" by their creators and fans—emerged from the eclectic underground newspapers that sprang up from coast to coast. In 1968 New York City's most prominent underground paper, *The East Village Other*, spun off a tabloid dedicated solely to the new comix titled *Gothic Blimp Works*, providing a periodical venue for Trina Robbins's cat-woman character in *Panthea*. Half woman, half lion, the alluring *Panthea* offered a fresh female take on the lycanthrope and jungle-adventure genres, turning the stereotypes on their ears while laying bedrock for the feminist "wimmen's comix" movement of the early 1970s.

The only male underground comix artist to consistently improve upon the archetypes provided by precursors like Jack Davis and Frank Frazetta was Richard Corben, who launched his career in fanzines and underground comix with crude but vigorous efforts like the werewolf tale "Dead Hill" (1969). Corben continued to play with and expand upon the werewolf archetype with a series of inventive stories in both underground comix and the Warren newsstand comic magazines *Creepy, Eerie*, and *Vampirella*. The best of Corben's lycanthropy stories were later collected in *Werewolf* (Catalan, 1984).

There were other notable comix shapeshifters. Tim Boxell's explicit adaptation of Philip Jose Farmer's revisionist 1968 novel *The Image of the Beast* (Last Gasp, 1973) wed alien werewolves, vampires, and graphic sex and gore with excessive glee. Armando and Joana Zegri's playful *The Legend of the Wolfman* (Wolfman Comix, 1976–81) brought a feel-good "spirit of the night" lycanthrope into the Age of Aquarius. The Warren line of newsstand horror magazines also offered many engaging lycanthropy comic stories, prominent among them "Night of the Jackass!" The complete series was collected in *Eerie* #115, and briefly revived by Harris Comics in the 1990s as *Hyde-25*. Warren also introduced Pantha, a panther-woman, in its *Vampirella* magazine, and that character was also resurrected by Harris Comics in the 1990s.

Warren/Harris's Pantha is not to be confused with a DC Comics character of the same name, however. DC's version was a panther woman who was a member of the superhero group the Teen Titans. Another member of the Titans was Changeling (aka Beast Boy), who has the ability to turn himself into any species of animal and first appeared as a member of DC's *The Doom Patrol* in #99 in 1965. Interestingly, his powers are almost exactly the same as those of Jana, one of the Wonder Twins, superheroes who were members of TV's DC Comics–based cartoon *Superfriends* from 1973 to 1975.

In mainstream four-color comics, the revision of the restrictive Comics Code lifted its specific ban on "werewolfism." In 1973 DC's new horror title *Swamp Thing* featured a startling, spindly-legged breed of Old World werewolves drawn by Berni Wrightson, and forever changed the archetype. In 1974 *Detective Comics* #455 featured a potent Batman-werewolf yarn, and Jack Kirby's cursed man-to-demon shapeshifter hero Jason Blood met his match in the Old World lycanthrope, similarly cursed by an ancient bestial alter ego, "The Howler," in *The Demon* #6 (DC, 1973).

By then Batman had already confronted a shapeshifter peculiarly attuned to his image and origins. With the reinvigoration of the Batman series in the wake of its TV-inspired "camp" period and the arrival of artist Neal Adams, the stories and art had become leaner and meaner. Adams and writer Frank Robbins collaborated on an inspired tale in which the Dark Knight met the Man-Bat, an unfortunate scientist whose experiments transformed him into an animalistic creature that both mirrored and made literal the most primal aspects of the Batman. Man-Bat debuted in *Detective Comics* #400 in June 1970. In subsequent appearances, the Man-Bat's still-human wife willingly changes her form to become the She-Bat, eventually earning her own short-lived series of stories (beginning in *Detective* #424, 1972).

The Man-Bat continued to appear now and again, eventually starring in his own one-shot, a miniseries, and an aborted monthly; the character may have inspired the drive-in movie *The Bat People* (aka *It Lives by Night*, AIP, 1974).

Meanwhile, Marvel Comics responded to the revision of the Code and the horror movie boom with a flood of monster comic titles. Marvel's sleek, slavering *Werewolf by Night* was tested in *Marvel Spotlight* #2 (February 1972) and proved popular enough to earn its own title in September that same year. A quartet of writers—including *Tomb of Dracula*'s author Marv Wolfman ("At last! A werewolf written by a Wolfman!" the credits cried)—kept the book on track, but it was Mike Ploog's artwork that brought life to the deft melding of the Larry Talbot and *Teenage Werewolf* archetypes.

The main character of *Werewolf by Night*, Jack Russell, differed from the classic wolfman in that he changed three times a month, during the full moon and on the nights before and after. That change allowed for stories to unfold at a more natural pace.

Marvel's own knockoff, *Man-Wolf* (debuting in *Creatures on the Loose* #30, 1974), had none of the virtues of *Werewolf by Night*. Marvel also bred its own cat-woman, as *Tigra the Were-Woman* debuted in *Marvel Chillers* #3 in 1976. Tigra went on to become a member of Marvel's flagship superhero team the Avengers, but has not been a prominent character in some years.

Oddest of all 1970s werewolf comics was Neal Adams's lavishly illustrated comic adaptation of (and packaged with) the Peter Pan record album *The Story of Dracula, Frankenstein, and the Wolfman* (1975), which brought the trio of traditional monsters together in an energetic free-for-all.

Marvel also boasted a plethora of other animal-based heroes and villains, including Stegron

the Dinosaur Man, who debuted in *Marvel Team-Up* #19, and the X-Men villain Sauron, essentially a human pterodactyl. The late '60s had already given the world the Knights of Wundagore when in *The Mighty Thor* #134, the High Evolutionary (whose name is self-explanatory) had become Marvel's own version of Dr. Moreau by accelerating the evolution of various animals and turning them into warriors for his cause.

Restrictions on broadcast television standards began to loosen, opening the door for traditional monsters to hit the airwaves in less diluted form. Made-for-TV horror movies had begun with Jean Renoir's French teleplay, *Le Testament du Doctor Cordelier* (1959), and Michael Rennie had played the dual role when restrictions were tight in Gore Vidal's adaptation for CBS-TV's anthology program *Climax!* (1955). *Dark Shadows* creator Dan Curtis produced the best-ever made-for-TV adaptation of *The Strange Case of Dr. Jekyll and Mr. Hyde* (ABC, 1968) starring Jack Palance as Jekyll and Hyde. Kirk Douglas subsequently starred in a made-for-TV musical adaptation of Stevenson's classic (NBC, 1973), and others followed. The musical *Jekyll and Hyde* is currently running on Broadway.

TV also made an attempt at the "wild child" story, with the short-lived 1977–78 ABC series *Lucan*. Two decades later, actress-director-producer Jodie Foster would take on the wild-child story herself, in the much more highbrow form of *Nell* (1994), a motion picture directed by Michael Apted and also starring Liam Neeson and Natasha Richardson.

The first original prime-time TV werewolf horror movie was *Moon of the Wolf* (ABC, 1972), based on Leslie H. Whitten's slice of Southern Gothic novel and starring Bradford Dillman as the Louisiana lycanthrope. Director Curtis Harrington brought a stylish period atmosphere to veteran novelist Robert Bloch's teleplay *The Cat Creature* (ABC, 1973), which involved an Egyptian curse and a mummy cat-woman. In 1974 Dan Curtis reunited with Richard Matheson for *Scream of the Wolf* (ABC, 1974), in which Clint Walker was a fake werewolf, stalking human prey to relieve the tedium of his retirement from big-game hunting. But those TV monsters paled alongside their big-screen brethren, who were spilling blood and baring breasts with reckless abandon.

In an endearing and surprisingly enduring wedding of the Universal monster archetype with the 1970s European explosion of horrific sex and gore, Spain's Paul Naschy starred as the tormented lycanthrope Count Waldemar Daninsky in a lively series of low-budget howlers beginning with *La Marca del Hombre-lobo* (1968). The film, cut by almost half, was released in the United States as *Frankenstein's Bloody Terror*. In 1996 Naschy mounted a belated comeback vehicle, *Licantropo: El Asesino de la Luna Llena* (*Werewolf: The Full Moon Killer*), but by then Waldemar Daninsky had long since become an anachronism.

The vital 1970s lycanthropes came into contact with timely pop stars, politics, and countercultural elements. A political correspondent (Dean Stockwell), bitten while on the Eastern European beat, returned stateside to become *Werewolf of Washington* (Millco, 1973), dying only after the curse was passed to the president. Rock stars Harry Nilsson and Ringo Starr pranced with a hippie werewolf in *Son of Dracula* (1974), hairier-than-usual biker gangs revved their engines through *Werewolves on Wheels* (1971), and a well-groomed lycanthrope appeared in *The Boy Who Cried Werewolf* (1973).

Lycanthropy wasn't restricted to Anglo-Saxons, either. Black big-game hunter Calvin Lockhart

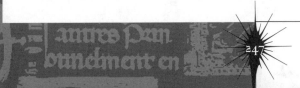

staged a "whodunit" parlor mystery to ferret out a werewolf in *The Beast Must Die* (Amicus, 1974), and Bernie Casey starred as *Dr. Black & Mr. Hyde* (1976), turning into an evil albino Hyde. The conservatives reasserted their claim on the genre with *The Shaggy D.A.* (Disney, 1976), in which the shapeshifting teen hero of *The Shaggy Dog* (1959) had grown up to become the first lycanthrope lawyer, played by Dean Jones. Now *that's* scary!

Wells's "The Island of Dr. Moreau" (AIP) was remade yet again in 1977 with Burt Lancaster. This version of Moreau undoes the premise of Wells's novel when he devolves Michael York into a beast-man to join his brood of "manimals." *Manimal* was also the title of a very short-lived 1983 NBC-TV series about a detective who could take the form of any animal.

In the 1970s Stevenson's *Dr. Jekyll and Mr. Hyde* spawned its share of reinterpretations. Notable for the presence of Christopher Lee was *I, Monster* (Amicus, 1971), with Lee as the Jekyll-surrogate Dr. Marlowe, who gives way to his gruff alter ego, Blake. *Dr. Jekyll and Sister Hyde* (Hammer, 1971), informed later gender-bender variations like Jeremy Scott's novel *Doctor Jekyll and Miss Hyde* (1983) and parodies such as the 1995 film *Dr. Jekyll and Ms. Hyde*.

Far more adventurous was Polish director Walerian Borowczyk's *Bloodlust: The Strange Case of Dr. Jekyll and Miss Osbourne* (1981), starring Udo Kier as Jekyll, who periodically submerges himself in a bathtub full of his solution to emerge as the monstrous Hyde (Gérard Zalcberg). The run expired with a chuckle, *Dr. Heckyl and Mr. Hype* (1980), in which Oliver Reed camped it up in the title role.

Released in 1982, *Jekyll and Hyde: Together Again* emphasized drug abuse humor, which *Edge of Sanity* (1989) took even further, with *Psycho*'s Anthony Perkins in one of his final roles, wallowing in sex, mayhem, and twitchy scenery-chewing.

Werewolves, shapeshifters, and primals became far more vital cinematic creations during the revolution in makeup, special effects, and puppetry of the early 1980s. In 1980 and '81 alone, while radio airwaves coincidentally reverberated with Warren Zevon's ballsy rock tune "Werewolves of London," a veritable renaissance in makeup wizardry from young practitioners like Rick Baker and Rob Bottin attracted international audiences to revisionist horror films like *The Howling* (Embassy, 1981) and *An American Werewolf in London* (Universal, 1980). Thanks to a brace of new technologies, cinematic shapeshifters appeared to change before viewers' very eyes, stretching bone, tendons, and skin to impossible extremes.

An American Werewolf in London was the story of an American tourist who runs afoul of a werewolf on the British moors and must deal with the horrible consequences. Rick Baker won a special Academy Award for the film's eye-popping transformation sequence. Director John Landis flaunted Baker's accomplishment by staging the change in a fully lit room and offset the traditional horrors with disorienting bits of black comedy.

For *The Howling*, based on Gary Brandner's 1979 novel, Bottin enhanced his jaw-dropping makeup miracles with all the sidelighting, shadows, slobber, and smoke director Joe Dante would indulge. Dante, Bottin, and screenplay writer John Sayles had grown up with Shock Theater, *Famous Monsters*, cartoons, comics, and comix, and they collectively brought a vigorous energy and sly, self-referential wit to the project that made *American Werewolf* seem square by comparison.

The Howling is peppered with the names of werewolf movie actors, directors, and characters, and brimming with clips from its precursors and onscreen nods to icons such as beatnik Allen Ginsberg's poem "Howl." Dante and Sayles used these common reference points with the audience to spice the brew, framed by its television news and "reality TV" opening and closing set pieces.

Makeup master Dick Smith anticipated the new age with his own shapeshifter, the scientist (William Hurt) who reverts to his primal form through reckless experiments with drugs, sensory deprivation, and reversion techniques in Ken Russell's adaptation of Paddy Chayefsky's novel *Altered States* (Warner Brothers, 1980).

Edward Levy's 1981 novel *The Beast Within* portrayed a child's struggle with lycanthropy, a story that metamorphosed into the bizarre human-cicadae of the film adaptation, *The Beast Within* (MGM/UA, 1982). Bottin topped them all with the ultimate cinematic alien shapeshifter in John Carpenter's critically lambasted *The Thing* (Universal, 1982), a genuinely terrifying paranoid classic far truer to John W. Campbell Jr.'s source story "Who Goes There?" (1938) than Howard Hawks's 1951 film version.

Director Paul Schrader revamped the revered *Cat People* (1982) to meet the new "seeing is believing" aesthetic, drowning the suggestive shadows of the Lewton original in overt incestuous sexual angst, flashes of nudity and splashes of gore.

Rick Baker transformed singer Michael Jackson into a were-cat for the state-of-the-art music video *Thriller* (1984). The video altered the music video form forever, bringing a previously unrealized cinematic potential to MTV. Directed by noted filmmaker John Landis, it was, in a sense, a minimovie, a first for music video, and even inspired a "making of" documentary.

This brief renaissance culminated in Neil Jordan's inventive *The Company of Wolves* (1985), a self-aware and genre-savvy art-house meditation on all things lycanthropic.

Amid this heady stew, the screen adaptation of Peter Straub's landmark novel *Ghost Story* (1979; filmed by Universal, 1981) unfortunately eschewed the novel's central conceit of an ultimate shapeshifter—the Manitou of North American Indian legend that Straub proposes is the source of many legendary beings, including werewolves and vampires. Straub's malignant "ghost" Eva Galli is a seemingly immortal femme fatale who meets her end in the diminished form of a stinging, but easily crushed, wasp.

The cinematic lycanthrope revival coincided with a fresh dose of werewolf novels and comic books. The novels included Robert Stallman's Book of the Beast trilogy *The Orphan* (1980), *The Captive* (1981), and *The Beast* (1982); *Abel/Baker/Charlie* (1984) by John Maxim, featuring rampaging physical manifestations of the protagonist's id and ego; Kit Reed's wry *Blood Fever* (1982, penned under the sly nom de plume "Shelley Hyde"); Thomas Tessier's excellent mesh of supernatural and Freudian lycanthropy elements, *The Nightwalker* (1979); and Bill Pronzini's anthology, *Werewolf!* (1979), which collected old and new short stories. Prolific Maine author Rick Hautala kicked off his impressive run of novels with *Moondeath* (1980), chronicling a lycanthrope's reign of terror over fictional Cooper Falls, New Hampshire.

Berni Wrightson illustrated the first edition of horror master Stephen King's "Cycle of the Werewolf" (1983), which was later adapted to film as *Silver Bullet*. Also in 1983, author Chelsea Quinn Yarbro, known more for her vampire novels, released her novel *The Godforsaken*.

The most original werewolf variation of the decade was Whitley Strieber's debut novel *The Wolfen* (1980), which abandoned the shapeshifter myths to propose a pack of highly intelligent über-wolves coexisting with, and feeding upon, mankind in contemporary New York City. The film version of *Wolfen* (1981) proved to be a surprisingly intelligent and earnest adaptation.

WHITLEY STRIEBER

PHOTO BY BETH GWINN

U.K. writer Alan Moore, Wrightson's successor on the comic book *Saga of the Swamp Thing,* crafted a feminist parable in which a put-upon Maine housewife's menstrual cycle and a full moon gives vent to her bottled-up anger via lycanthropy (#40, DC Comics, 1984). Those sober, serious efforts shared the newsstands with sillier stuff: *Weird War Tales* #93 (DC Comics, 1980) featured the origin of the Creature Commandos, a trio of GI monsters including lycanthropic Oklahoma farmboy Warren Griffith.

Actor Bruce Payne's arrogant British manner made him a choice villain in a number of films, including the made-for-cable TV hybrid horror film *Full Eclipse* (HBO, 1993), mixing a black hero (Mario Van Peebles), a rogue band of vigilante cops, Hong Kong–style action sequences, and science fiction werewolves for thrills and chills. There were other super-science shapeshifters: in the Italian *Metamorphosis* (Imperial, 1990) the guinea-pig scientist uncontrollably regresses into a rather stupid-looking "dinosaur man," while *Metalbeast* (1994) presented a more lethal science fiction/cyborg variation, the first genetically bred biomechanical lycanthrope.

Romance fueled the lover's triangle between beauty Sherilyn Fenn, a werewolf beast, and his evil twin brother (Malcolm Jamieson in a dual role) in Charles Band's surprisingly effective *Meridian* (1990). *Meridian* complements the quirky romance of Clive Barker's Midian, the legendary dwelling place of monsters in his novella "Cabal," which Barker filmed as *Nightbreed* (1990). Barker's breed were a pretty weird bunch, counting shapeshifters among their ranks, as were the hairless, incestuous were-cat/zombies who suck the life force out of virgins in Mick Garris's *Sleepwalkers* (1992), from Stephen King's uneven first original screenplay.

The weirdest and scariest shapeshifters ever to torment a teen hero, however, were the sluglike "shunters" who consider adopted son Billy Warlock beneath their kind, and thus suitable only as food, in Brian Yuzna's one-of-a-kind *Society* (1989).

There were also the humanoid rodent mutations of *Nutriaman: The Copasaw Creature* (aka *Terror in the Swamp*, 1985), and let's not forget the boy-to-rodent and witches-into-rodents transformations in Nicolas Roeg and Jim Henson's adaptation of Roald Dahl's *The Witches* (1990).

A new generation of teenage werewolves marked their territory toward the end of the cycle. Larry Cohen had anticipated the shift with *Full Moon High* (1981), in which a teen football star (Adam Arkin) was bitten by a Romanian werewolf and never aged.

Big box office returns rewarded Michael J. Fox's star turn as the hirsute high school basketball hero *Teen Wolf* (1985), which yielded the lesser *Teen Wolf Too* (1987) and a Saturday morning cartoon show (CBS, 1986–89). The inevitable Disney sequel *Return of the Shaggy Dog* (1987) came soon after, and Michael Landon playfully re-created his classic *Teenage Werewolf* role for a single Halloween episode of his popular "angel" fantasy TV series *Highway to Heaven* (NBC, 1987). Stephen King soon reinforced the actor's claim to the teen werewolf throne by making Landon's image from *I Was a Teenage Werewolf* one of the waking visions that terrified the preteen cast of the TV-movie adaptation of King's novel *It* (ABC, 1990).

And still the teens came: Stephen Geoffreys was teen misfit Evil Ernie, transformed by a vampire's kiss and pathetically kicking off in werewolf form in *Fright Night* (1985). Corey Haim played a preteen wheelchair-bound werewolf-hunter in *Silver Bullet* (1985), adapted by Stephen King from his novella "Cycle of the Werewolf." The teenage heroes of *Waxwork* (1988) were threatened by a bunny-eared werewolf (John Rhys-Davies) in one of the exhibits-come-to-life; in *Waxwork II: Lost in Time* (1992), they are confronted by an animated Jekyll and Hyde diorama. Director Fred Dekker mounted an affectionate homage to the Universal monster classics for his teen monster-hunters, *The Monster Squad* (1987).

With the 1990s came a massive torrent of horror and suspense stories for young adults and teens. With the advent of such series as R. L. Stine's Goosebumps (for younger readers) and Fear Street (for young adults), and the success of Christopher Pike and other novelists writing for that age group, horror stories achieved enormous popularity with a new generation. A number of the new young-adult horror books, of course, concerned werewolves and other shapeshifters.

In 1996 K. A. Applegate's stunningly successful YA book series *Animorphs* made its debut. The series revolves around five kids who, in the first book, *The Invasion*, encountered an alien called an Andalite. Dying, it revealed to the kids that a race of evil aliens called Yeercks were trying to take over the universe. In order to combat the Yeercks, the Andalite gifted the five children with the power to transform themselves—or *morph*—into any animal they wished.

At least fifty books have been published in the series, not including the various spin-off book titles, including *Animorphs Megamorphs* and others. *The Animorphs* television series debuted in 1998, and a stream of merchandise, including action figures and board games, followed in its wake.

Blood and Chocolate (1997) by Annette Curtis Klause was a teen werewolf romance—a sub-genre that had already spawned a number of adult novels—that scored with readers and critics alike. *Party of Five* and *Time of Your Life* star Jennifer Love Hewitt optioned film rights to the book.

Nickelodeon's *One Hundred Deeds for Eddie McDowd* picked up the legacy left behind by Disney's *Shaggy Dog* and others. In the kids' series, a bully is transformed into a dog until he performs one hundred good deeds, and is adopted as a pet by a kid he had previously bullied.

Charles Band's opportunistic low-budget film *Shapeshifter* (1999) also went after the teen audience. The targeted readers and viewers had grown up on a fresh batch of Saturday morning and syndicated monster cartoons, including reruns of the teenage *Fangface* (ABC, 1978–79), who was joined in later episodes by the baby werewolf Fangpuss, and the NBC series *Gravedale High* with a teen werewolf. Universal produced its own monster cartoon series *Monster Force* (syndicated, 1994), featuring their animated revamp of the "official" Wolfman.

Hanna-Barbera cranked out *Drak Pack* (CBS, 1980–82), the two-hour special "Scooby and the Reluctant Werewolf" (1989), and *Wake, Rattle, and Roll* (syndicated, 1990–91), which offered an episode titled "Monster Tails." Werewolves also popped up in individual episodes of Hanna-Barbera's *The New Fred and Barney Show*, *Road Rovers*, *The Completely Mental Misadventures of Ed Grimley*, and others. One twist on the theme was 1985's syndicated TV cartoon *Thundercats*, which featured humanoid cats as warriors on an earthlike planet.

True to form, Matt Groening's popular animated TV series *The Simpsons* sent up the whole genre in one of its classic Halloween compendium episodes (1999) in which the Simpsons' goody-two-shoes neighbor Flanders turns into a werewolf ("Arrrgh—didley!").

Aspiring to more adult concerns, Jack Nicholson starred in the prestige werewolf yarn *Wolf* (1994). Similar adult aspirations informed the revamp of Stevenson's *Dr. Jekyll and Mr. Hyde* drawn from Valerie Martin's novel *Mary Reilly* (1991, filmed 1995), which retold the venerable tale from the point of view of Jekyll's maid, played by Julia Roberts.

The 1990s hunger for definitive revamps also yielded the *The Island of Dr. Moreau* (1996), starring Marlon Brando as the most eccentric Moreau of them all.

The first cinematic werewolves created with computer-generated effects shambled out of Silicon Valley late for the party, beaten to the punch by the eye-popping high-tech science fiction cyborg-shapeshifter effects of *Terminator 2* (1991). Eric Red's moody *Bad Moon* (1996) had Michael Paré shapeshift in an ungainly blur of CGI distortion, while the greater screen time afforded the CGI lycanthropes of *An American Werewolf in Paris* (1997) only confirmed their very un-scary cartoonish design.

The best use of morphing and CGI techniques in the genre appear now and again on *The X-Files* (see below) and *Buffy the Vampire Slayer*. As yet, filmmakers in the 1990s have not mobilized visionary skills comparable to those of their effects technicians, and the genre seems once again in need of a creative jolt similar to that which reinvigorated the field in the early 1980s.

Comic-book authors and cartoonists continue to push the envelope in new directions. DC Comics' short-lived *Scare Tactics* took the questionable plot of a rock 'n' roll band comprised of monsters—including a werewolf—and managed to eke a compelling story out of it.

ROBERT R. McCAMMON

Writer Alan Moore and artist Kevin O'Neill brought Dr. Jekyll and Mr. Hyde back to join *The League of Extraordinary Gentlemen* (Wildstorm/DC, 1999), a turn-of-the-century collective of fiction's best and brightest. Jekyll and Hyde, Jules Verne's Captain Nemo, H. G. Wells's Invisible Man, Mina Harker from Stoker's *Dracula*, and H. Rider Haggard's Allan Quartermain pitch their combined abilities against Sax Rohmer's Fu Manchu, with Hyde depicted as a towering eight-foot monster.

The last dozen or so years of the twentieth century provided a number of interesting examples of the werewolf novel, some of them quite excellent. A pair of wonderful historical werewolf tales were published in 1989. In S. P. Somtow's *Moon Dance*, the author pits werewolves of Austrian nobility who have emigrated to the late-nineteenth-century American West against Native American werewolves of the Lakota Sioux. Equally fascinating that year was bestselling author Robert R. McCammon's *The Wolf's Hour*, a World War II espionage novel in which a master spy pitting himself against the Nazis is also a werewolf.

A trio of notable books appeared in 1991. Whitley Strieber released *The Wild*, about an average family man who follows a primitive urge and runs off to the wilderness to become a werewolf. Peter Rubie's *Werewolf* revolved around British authorities attempting to solve savage murders during the World War II Nazi blitz on London. Perhaps most original that year was Brian Hodge's inventive *Nightlife*, which used the Los Angeles drug trade and the native peoples of the Venezuelan rain forest in the crafting of a tale about a mystical, primitive hallucinogen that causes some humans to transform into ravening, primal beasts.

NANCY A. COLLINS

PHOTO BY BETH GWINN

In the waning days of the briefly hip, gory subcategory of horror termed "splatterpunk," some of its practitioners offered their own version of the classic werewolf. In their novel *Animals* (1993), John Skipp and Craig Spector offered a lycanthropy myth that posited that all humans had the beast within them, and only needed it to be drawn out. That same year, Nancy A. Collins, then best known for her vampire novels, released *Wild Blood*. Two years later, Collins followed with *Walking Wolf: A Weird Western* that, like Somtow's *Moon Dance*, featured Native American werewolves.

Though there have been a number of short-story anthologies focusing on lycanthropy, one of the most interesting was *Otherwere* (1996), in which the tales ran the gamut of various wereanimals but kept away from the wolf variety.

Perhaps television will provide a vehicle for more adventurous explorations of the theme, as networks have demonstrated an unusual affinity with the primals genre. After all, Fox launched a new era in television when it introduced a fourth network with the debut of their two-hour made-for-TV movie *Werewolf* (1987). In the pilot, one-eyed Old World werewolf Skorzeny (grizzled Chuck Connors) put the bite on yet another hapless teen hero (John J. York), whose palm was thereafter branded with a pentagram and who changed whenever he got angry. Fox's spin-off series found the youth seeking Skorzeny (and vice versa) and a cure and, of course, tangling with other werewolves. It was also the first television series to open each week with a disclaimer, stating the program might be too intense for younger viewers. Though the series was short-lived (1987–88), its impact cannot be overstated.

Since then the Fox network has played its part in keeping the faith. Even in its first season, *The*

X-Files boasted its share of shapeshifters. The program's original shapeshifters have been compelling and frightening, and in the case of both the sickening hair-and-fingernail fetishist of "Irresistible" (1995) and the gargoyle-like serial-killer of "Grotesque" (1996), their fleeting transformations may or may not have been the product of their victims' fear and imaginations. The enigmatic shapeshifting alien factions on the show have become central to the complex conspiracy thread that runs throughout the entire series.

In 1998 novelist Alice Borchardt, sister of bestselling author Anne Rice, began a series of werewolf novels set in eighth-century Rome with *The Silver Wolf*, followed in 1999 by *Night of the Wolf*. Werewolves continue to appear in novels, comics, movies, and on television as we begin the twenty-first century. They are a staple of popular culture, as evidenced by the 1998 United States postage stamp series of classic Universal monsters, which of course included *The Wolf Man*.

A new moon is rising for the werewolves of old, promising fresh blood in the new millennium.

SNAKE AND FISH PEOPLE

THE SERPENTINE DEMONS (also see Demons) and amphibious humanoid swimming team of *Buffy* have their own peculiar cold-blooded forefathers and mothers. Male serpent beings much like *Buffy*'s Machida have been fixtures of many cultural myths, legends, and contemporary horror fiction, comics, and films. Like Machida, the Greek serpent-god Erechthonios was portrayed as a snake-man whose lower half was serpentine, much like the Chinese god Foki.

Snake-women have a surprisingly resonant niche in folklore. From India to China and Hong Kong, Eastern myth and lore is populated by a plethora of snake-women interacting with humanity, and their kind have become fixtures of Asian supernatural fiction, theater, and fantasy films.

In film Rosemary Theby was an Indian dancing girl cursed to become a ten-foot constrictor, only to change back to her original form two thousand years later to take her revenge in *The Reincarnation of Karma* (1912). Another Indian girl transformed into a snake to bite the man who shot her in *The Vampire* (1913), one of the first British horror films ever made, followed by *Hebe the Snake Woman* (1915). *Cult of the Cobra* (1955) starred Faith Domergue as a high priestess who journeyed to America, changing into a cobra to kill the U.S. GIs who photographed a forbidden ritual.

Snake Woman (1961) concerned a turn-of-the-century doctor whose injections of snake venom into his pregnant wife turned their daughter into a shapeshifter. Hammer Films revamped the premise for John Gilling's atmospheric *The Reptile* (1966).

Amphibious humanoids are familiar primals, too. The mythical Sirens lured sailors to their deaths on rocky shores, metamorphosing eventually into equally alluring but less threatening mermaid forms. The Greek deity Poseidon (Neptune in Roman myth) was one of the Titans, among the most powerful and primal of the elder gods, and as ruler of the oceans was often depicted with fishlike attributes, such as a merman's tail. Hans Christian Andersen's fairy tale "The Little Mermaid" told the tragic story of a mermaid who abandoned her fish form for love of a mortal and paid the ultimate price. Twentieth-century variations on the theme such as *Miranda* (1948), *Mr. Peabody and the Mermaid* (1948), *Splash* (1984), and Walt Disney's cartoon feature adaptation *The Little Mermaid* (1989) avoided such tragic consequences, favoring light romance and happy endings.

More original was John Lamb's oddball *Mermaids of Tiburon* (1962), in which a marine biologist (George Rowe) found a treasure trove of pearls guarded by genuine mermaids.

More frightening hybrids had an indelible impact on contemporary horror fiction. Writer H. P. Lovecraft's loathing for seafood perhaps informed his unnerving strain of amphibious humanoids that first surfaced in his formative short story "Dagon" (1919), in which a man escaping from a German sea raider during World War I washed up on a section of ocean floor raised by an earthquake. He discovered carvings of outsize fishmen, and in due time a living specimen rose from the sea.

Lovecraft's subsequent creation of his renowned Cthulhu Mythos (see Demons) was rooted in similar invented ancient oceanic horrors, harbingers of a return of a race of aquatic elder beings eager to regain dominion over the planet. Lovecraft's "The Shadow over Innsmouth" (1926) proposed a beachhead in the titular decaying Massachusetts seaport village inhabited by hideous, scaly half-humans.

Other bizarre amphibious mermen (played by dwarfs in froglike suits) were discovered in the ocean's depths in MGM's lavish adaptation of Jules Verne's *The Mysterious Island* (1929), though Verne's Nemo had never confronted such beings in the original novels.

Such cataclysmic culture clashes were rare in the genre. More often, amphibious throwbacks secreted themselves away or languished in remote bayous, lakes, and lagoons. The definitive pop-cultural "fish man" remains the Gillman, who was introduced in *Creature from the Black Lagoon* (Universal, 1954), originally in 3-D. Actually, the Gillman made his public debut during an Abbott and Costello skit on *The Colgate Comedy Hour* (1954), crashing through a wall to promote Universal's upcoming feature. Producer William Alland conceived the monster, but director Jack Arnold and studio makeup man Bud Westmore and his team of designers brought the creature to vivid life. To this day, its remarkable design has never been bettered.

The creature was a hit, making his way from his home in the backwaters of the Amazon to wreak havoc in sunny Florida in *Revenge of the Creature* (1955) and suffer an ignoble post–burn therapy surgical conversion to a flayed, air-breathing, gill-less shadow of his former self in *The Creature Walks Among Us* (1956). Alas, the Gillman was last shown dressed like a prisoner, bleeding from bullet wounds and staggering toward the sea, most likely to drown.

The Alligator People (1959; see Primals) were mutations with none of the Gillman's grace or iconic stature, much like the fish men of science fiction drive-in curios like *Destination Inner Space* (1966), the Cornish specimens in the Vincent Price vehicle *War Gods of the Deep* (AIP, 1965; aka *City Under the Sea*), the dead resurrected as fish monster-men of *The Horror of Party Beach* (1964; see Walking Dead), and the completely bogus fish-man (Jon Hall) of *The Beach Girls and the Monster* (aka *Monster from the Surf*, 1965).

Russia's *The Amphibian Man* (1962) appeared monstrous before assuming a more acceptably handsome human appearance, though keeping his gills. But Don Knotts *de*-evolved, transforming completely from fish-loving milquetoast to animated talking fish in order to save the day for the Allies in World War II by knocking out Axis subs in *The Incredible Mr. Limpet* (Warner Brothers,1964). A remake of that movie is currently in production.

Science fiction has also explored underwater races and civilizations on other planets. Both *Buck Rogers* (1929–67) and *Flash Gordon* (1934–present) tangled with extraterrestrial humanoid fish-men in their comic-strip adventures, establishing the pattern for decades to follow. The most lavish amphibious humanoid culture ever brought to the screen recently graced George Lucas's *Star Wars Episode 1: The Phantom Menace* (1999).

Buffy the Vampire Slayer

GHOSTS

GILES: "Many times [a] spirit is plagued by all manner of unworldly troubles. But, being dead, it has no way to make its peace. Growing ever more confused, ever more angry..."

BUFFY: "So—it's like a regular teenager. Only dead."

—"I ONLY HAVE EYES FOR YOU"

IN A WAY, GHOSTS ARE THE SIMPLEST of all of the "monsters" we have seen on *Buffy the Vampire Slayer*. This could be attributed to the fact that the series has presented so few such spirits. Or it may merely be this: the lore regarding ghosts is voluminous and diverse, but the core, defining factors as to what makes a ghost are relatively consistent.

Humans die. Some cultures believe that their souls, or spirits, live on after death. Ghosts, then, are the souls of the dead whose spirits do not move on to another plane of existence. Instead they linger here, tied to their old homes or families or familiar haunts—the origin of that particular usage of the word.

Yet beyond those basic facets of ghostly lore are a near infinite variety of permutations. Some ghosts are malevolent, some benevolent. Some are destructive (such as the familiar poltergeists), some helpful. Some are quite self-aware, and others are mindless wanderers. Some can possess physical objects or living beings, much in the way demons are purported to do, others cannot even make themselves visible.

In all of those examples, however, the basic nature of the ghost remains constant. This is also true of the presentation of ghosts thus far in the universe of *Buffy the Vampire Slayer*, though we have few other details.

From the one episode that is most specifically about the traditional ghost, "I Only Have Eyes for You" (season two), the spirits are able to manifest themselves, to temporarily alter their surroundings (or at least create the illusion of such alteration), and to possess human bodies. In that case (see below), the spirits were trapped in an endless cycle, repeating the events that led to their deaths. Like many ghosts of legend and folklore, the spirits were unable to move beyond the earthly plane because they had unfinished business that had to be resolved first.

Some ghosts, like those in season four's "Pangs," have unfinished business that takes the form of vengeance upon the living for some wrong, whether real or imagined.

> **HUS:** "You can't stop me."
> **BUFFY:** "You're very wrong about that."
> **HUS:** "I am vengeance. I am my people's cry. They call for Hus, the avenging spirit, to carve out justice."
> **BUFFY:** "They tell you to start an ear collection?" **—"PANGS"**

There is little general discussion of ghosts on the series, though the subject does come up in season one's "Out of Mind, Out of Sight," which featured an invisible girl initially thought to be a ghost. In a portion of the script that was cut because of length, the Watcher, Rupert Giles, relates his single previous experience with a ghost.

> "...in Dartmoor. A murdered countess, very beautiful. She used to float along the foothills, moaning the most piteous..."
> —GILES, IN "OUT OF MIND, OUT OF SIGHT"

In a portion of the episode that made the final broadcast cut, he goes on to elaborate, sharing some of his knowledge on the subject.

> "From what I've read, having a ghost pass through you is a singular experience. It's a cold, amorphous feeling, makes your hair stand on end."
> —GILES, IN "OUT OF MIND, OUT OF SIGHT"

The rarity of ghosts on the series should in no way be construed as a lack of interest on the part of its writers and producers. Given the title of the series, and the nature of vampires in Joss Whedon's mythology, it is only natural that the majority of the monsters are vamps and demons.

The Influences

OF THE SHOW'S WRITERS, supervising producer Marti Noxon has the greatest affinity for ghost stories. She grew up with a difficult family situation and found that the themes of repentance and second chances found in many movies about hauntings echoed her own concerns.

"I look back at the stories I'd written before I started [to work on *Buffy*], and I [realize that I] was constantly telling the story of my family and my fears and didn't even realize it. Three of the four screenplays I wrote before I started working on *Buffy* were about ghosts; people who had died and were trying to right the wrongs they had done while they were alive in order to set free the people who were suffering for their own ills."

When it comes to the pop-culture influences that have affected the way she imagines ghosts, two films immediately come to mind.

"*Poltergeist* is one of my favorite movies of all time. It's one of the scariest," Noxon states of the 1982 Tobe Hooper–directed gem. "I think it's a very influential movie, with a lot of core issues that writers don't even realize they rip off all the time. Not only that, but it's really deeply felt, a very emotional movie. The reason I love the movie so much is the story between the mother and the daughter. And it holds up. It still looks really good."

Another of her favorites is British writer-director Anthony Minghella's 1991 directorial debut, *Truly, Madly, Deeply*.

"It's one of the most influential movies for me," Noxon says. "It's about a woman who has lost her husband but can't move on. She's grieving, it's been a year or two, but everything she does is wrapped up in her dead husband.

"One day, suddenly, he shows up again. He's dead, but he's in their house and they can relate to each other like he's still alive. He's cold to the touch, but he can warm up beneath the blankets. You even get the indication that they go to bed together. At first they're both incredibly joyful, but slowly but surely he starts to be a real pain in the butt. He's always hanging out, but then his ghost friends show up and they're always watching movies on the VCR while she's trying to work. He can't ever leave the house. His friends are annoying and always there. He's constantly playing an instrument.

"Meanwhile, she's met a suitor who's the best guy and perfect for her, but she's not ready. The payoff of the movie is that she finally realizes it isn't going to work. It's not good for either of them and she asks him [the husband] to go. The denouement is that she realizes that that was why he was there the whole time, to set her free. It's a huge sacrifice, and he still loves her.

"Ghost stories are pretty much ground zero for me," Noxon concludes. "I think people's relationship with death and with loss informs all great stories."

A profound sentiment, and one that is especially true about *Buffy the Vampire Slayer* . . . and not merely the episodes involving ghosts.

The Ghosts

THOUGH FEW AND FAR BETWEEN, the ghosts we've seen on *Buffy* have been quite interesting, with each representation differing from the last.

SID

"I hunt demons. Yeah, you wouldn't know it to look at me. Let's just say there was me, there was a really mean demon, there was a curse, and then next thing I know I'm not me anymore. I'm sitting on some guy's knee with his hand up the back of my shirt."
—SID, IN "THE PUPPET SHOW"

EPISODE: "The Puppet Show," season one

KEY RELATIONSHIPS: Sid was killed and cursed by a group of demons called the Seven so that his spirit was trapped within a ventriloquist's dummy.

UNIQUE ATTRIBUTES: Sid was able to move through the world inconspicuously enough that he managed to kill all seven of those demons over the course of many decades.

MOST MONSTROUS MOMENT: His horny dummy shtick.

CURRENT STATUS: Having destroyed the last of the Seven, Sid's soul was released from the dummy and was able to move on to its final reward.

In horror films and television programs, there is a grand tradition involving ventriloquist's dummies come to life. In "The Puppet Show," *Buffy* added a wonderful twist

to that classic conceit. The episode concerns a series of murders at the school during which organs are harvested from the victims. Eventually, Giles establishes that a group of demons called the Brotherhood of Seven are responsible (see Demons).

At first they interrogate likely suspects. Soon, though, they come to believe that the culprit is Sid, a wooden dummy belonging to a student ventriloquist who plans to perform in the school talent show. A wild assumption under normal circumstances . . . but these are hardly normal circumstances.

Sid *is* alive, but is neither a demon nor a murderer.

He's a ghost. In life, he was a demon-hunter. At some point in his travels, he ran afoul of the Brotherhood of Seven, was killed, and as the result of a curse his spirit was trapped within the wooden dummy. Only when all seven have been killed can his spirit move on. In the "Puppet Show," Sid finally achieves that goal, and it appears that his soul does pass from this world at last.

Or does it?

Many *Buffy* fans on the Internet have expressed interest in Sid, and they're not alone in that. Dean Batali and Rob Des Hotel—now writers for *That '70s Show*—penned "The Puppet Show" script, and they'd love to see Sid return.

"There's no proof that Sid is dead," Batali notes. "That's my favorite episode that we wrote. We originally pitched a crazy guy with a dummy, like the movie *Magic* [1978, from the novel by William Goldman]. But Joss said he'd always wanted to do a movie in which the dummy is good. That was a phenomenal twist because nobody saw it coming. I remember the Internet [buzz] that night. Beforehand, people said, 'Oh, I saw the description in *TV Guide,* and it's gonna be really stupid because the dummy is always evil.' Then the same people wrote back and said, 'I was fooled!'"

Batali also notes that there was more to Sid than made it into the episode.

"We had to write a whole back story for Sid that never aired. At one time, we had a two-page scene [revealing how he was trapped in the dummy]. He was a cop on the east side of Boston and he was going after this guy he thought was a serial killer but turned out to be a demon. Sid chased him into a magic shop and there was a big shoot-out and he got killed or something like that. We had a complete history for Sid before he became a dummy."

He also confirms that "there was talk of bringing Sid back at one point, just for fun."

Rob Des Hotel is equally enamored of the character. "I just want to say, I've

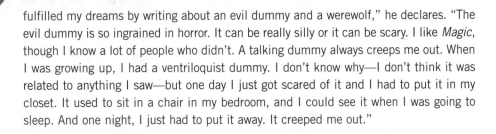

fulfilled my dreams by writing about an evil dummy and a werewolf," he declares. "The evil dummy is so ingrained in horror. It can be really silly or it can be scary. I like *Magic*, though I know a lot of people who didn't. A talking dummy always creeps me out. When I was growing up, I had a ventriloquist dummy. I don't know why—I don't think it was related to anything I saw—but one day I just got scared of it and I had to put it in my closet. It used to sit in a chair in my bedroom, and I could see it when I was going to sleep. And one night, I just had to put it away. It creeped me out."

WILLOW ROSENBERG (AS A GHOST)

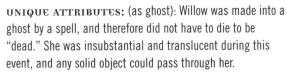

GILES: "Okay, then, let's review. At sundown, everyone became what they were masquerading as—"
WILLOW: "Right. Xander was a soldier and Buffy was an eighteenth-century girl."
GILES (staring at her rocker babe outfit): "And—your costume?"
WILLOW: "I'm a ghost."
GILES: "Yes, but a ghost of *what*, exactly?"   **—"HALLOWEEN"**

EPISODE (as ghost): "Halloween," season two

KEY RELATIONSHIPS: See "Magic Users"

UNIQUE ATTRIBUTES: (as ghost): Willow was made into a ghost by a spell, and therefore did not have to die to be "dead." She was insubstantial and translucent during this event, and any solid object could pass through her.

CURRENT STATUS: Willow has since, of course, reverted to a flesh-and-blood human.

When chaos worshiper Ethan Rayne first came to Sunnydale (in season two's "Halloween"), he played a nasty little trick on the town's population. Ethan opened a costume store and put a spell on the costumes so that on Halloween night, those who bought their costumes from his store would magically be turned into whatever their costume represented.

On Halloween night, Willow Rosenberg, uncomfortable in the hot rocker outfit she tried on, put her reliable new ghost costume on over the "babe" outfit. When the spell took effect, she fell down dead, and her spirit, still in the hot outfit, rose up out of her "dead" body. For the duration of that episode, Willow Rosenberg was a ghost, passing through objects and people, unable to touch anything (though she did catch the eye of a guitarist named Oz).

When Giles forced Ethan to reverse the spell, Willow became flesh and blood again.

JAMES STANLEY AND GRACE NEWMAN

WILLOW: "It says here that a student murdered a teacher on the night of the Sadie Hawkins dance. The rumor was that they were having an affair and she tried to break it off. After he killed her, he went into the music room and shot himself."

XANDER: "Ladies and Gentlemen—we have a poltergeist." —"I ONLY HAVE EYES FOR YOU"

EPISODE: "I Only Have Eyes For You," season two

KEY RELATIONSHIPS: James was a Sunnydale High student in 1955 and Grace was his teacher. They became romantically involved, and when she tried to break it off, he killed her and then himself.

UNIQUE ATTRIBUTES: James's guilt trapped his and Grace's spirits in the school, doomed to relive their last moments. As poltergeists they had various abilities, including creating horrifying physical manifestations of ectoplasmic energy such as snakes and wasps, moving physical objects, and possessing living humans.

MOST MONSTROUS MOMENT: Trapped in the cycle of past events, James's spirit caused a school janitor to murder a Sunnydale teacher.

CURRENT STATUS: The cycle broken by Buffy and Angel's intervention, James's and Grace's spirits have gone on to their final reward.

Featured in the second-season episode "I Only Have Eyes for You," James and Grace are identified by Giles as poltergeists. The word comes from the German, meaning "noisy ghost." This brand of spooks is often destructive, wreaking havoc upon the place they haunt.

James Stanley, a student at Sunnydale High in 1955, fell in love with a teacher named Grace Newman. Against every rule and moral tenet, she loved him in return and they began an affair. But Grace knew their relationship was wrong and eventually wanted to end it. On the night of the annual Sadie Hawkins dance, when female students traditionally asked the boys they liked to be their dates, she tried to tell James that it was over.

His reaction was tragic and fatal. Panicked and desperate, he was driven to violence by the prospect of losing his love. James held a gun on her, trying to force her to talk to him. The gun accidentally discharged, and Grace was killed. Overcome with guilt, he killed himself as well.

In the spring of 1998, with the Sadie Hawkins dance just around the corner, the area of the school where the tragedy occurred in 1955 began to manifest signs that it was haunted. Individuals who passed through that corridor were suddenly possessed by the spirits of the dead lovers and forced to reenact their tragic last moments. A male student nearly killed a female student before Buffy intervened. Later, however, with Buffy not around, a janitor forced to play the role of James shot and killed a teacher named Miss Frank, fatally put in the role of Grace.

There were other manifestations as well—moving objects, ghost-writing (in the case of a teacher who was surprised to discover the profanity his traitorous arm had scrawled on the blackboard without his being aware of it), and even the decaying arm of a corpse lunging from Xander Harris's locker and trying to drag him in. The poltergeists also managed to manifest physical illusions, like a cafeteria full of snakes and a swarm of wasps. As usual, Buffy and her friends turned to the Watcher, Rupert Giles, for answers.

> GILES: "Fascinating. It sounds like paranormal phenomena."
> WILLOW: "A ghost? Cool!"
> XANDER: "Oh, no, not cool. This was no wimpy chain-rattler. This was more like—'I'm dead as hell and I'm not gonna take it anymore.'"
> GILES: "Exactly. Despite the Xander-speak, that's an accurate definition of a poltergeist."
> XANDER: "I defined something? Accurately? Check me out. Guess I'm done with the book learning!"
> BUFFY: "So we've got some bad boo on our hands?"
> GILES: "Well... A poltergeist is extremely disruptive—and what you described certainly fits the bill."
> WILLOW: "What can we do? Is there any way to stop it?"
> GILES: "The only tried and true way is to figure out what unresolved issues keep the spirit here—and resolve them."
> BUFFY: "Great. So now we're Dr. Laura for the deceased."
> GILES: "Only if we can find out who this spirit is. Or...was." **—"I ONLY HAVE EYES FOR YOU"**

Eventually, Buffy and company concluded that the poltergeists were James Stanley and Grace Newman, whose spirits were in turmoil out of his need for forgiveness. The spirits had tried to communicate with Buffy to draw attention to their plight, to bring closure to their long years of haunting. Their efforts included moving a 1955 yearbook to draw attention to the event that precipitated the tragedy. Giles had been convinced that the ghost was that of his murdered love, Jenny Calendar, and his hope that this was so blinded him from the truth for some time.

In order to attempt to communicate with James, whose guilt had trapped both his and Grace's spirits on this plane, Buffy allowed herself to be possessed by him. Unbeknownst to her, however, Angel (in his evil incarnation) was also nearby. He entered the school, determined to destroy her, only to be possessed by Grace's spirit. The scenario that led to their deaths played out again, this time with the gender reversed, and Buffy, as James, shot Angel, as Grace. But this time the drama did not end there. Since Angel was a vampire and did not die from the gunshot, the cycle of violence they had been trapped in was broken. Grace and James could confront each other, Grace could forgive him, and both spirits could move on to their final reward.

Buffy found herself kissing Angel just as the spirits abandoned them. Her heart was wrenched by this tiny moment in which she was given a taste of what it would be like to have him back and not evil. For his part, Angel was revolted but confused by the events and retreated, postponing his planned attack on the Slayer for another day.

It is interesting to note that in the fourth season the series presented a second poltergeist episode, "Where the Wild Things Are," that posited a very different type of poltergeist. In that episode, the poltergeists weren't the spirits of dead children at all—and therefore not really ghosts. Instead, they were the trace energy left behind by the psychological terror suffered by children who had once lived there, as well as their sublimated sexual feelings. Though James and Grace were also defined as poltergeists, the two varieties are clearly very different.

HUS

XANDER: "I hate this guy."

WILLOW: "He's only doing what was done to him."

XANDER: "I didn't give him syphilis!"

GILES: "But you freed his spirit, and after a century of unrest he saw you as one of his oppressors."

XANDER: "So he rises up and infects the first guy he sees? That's no fair."

WILLOW: "Like you've never woken up cranky." —"PANGS"

EPISODE: "Pangs," season four

KEY RELATIONSHIPS: Hus was a being created from the combined spirits of Chumash tribespeople who had been horribly killed in Sunnydale.

UNIQUE ATTRIBUTES: Hus had the ability to create weapons and even warriors using some form of mystical energy and to command those magical constructs into battle. He also had the ability to change his form, taking on various animal forms including crows, a coyote, and a bear.

MOST MONSTROUS MOMENT: Hus murdered a museum curator while stealing an ancient Chumash knife.

CURRENT STATUS: Unknown. Hus was defeated, but—even though the truth of what happened to the Chumash is out—there was no real indication that the anger of the spirits had subsided.

Season four's Thanksgiving episode, "Pangs," brought an interesting twist on the series' representation of ghosts. Construction on a new University of California at Sunnydale Cultural Partnership Center—ironically meant to foster intercultural understanding—led workers to accidentally break into the ruins of an eighteenth-century mission, where members of the Chumash Native American tribe were unjustly executed. Finally freed, the spirits of the dead Chumash combined together into a single "spirit of vengeance" called Hus, who struck back at those now residing upon the native soil of the Chumash.

Hus killed a museum curator while stealing a Chumash stone knife, a weapon of his long-dead tribe. He also proved himself capable of taking on the forms of various animals. As a warrior, Hus's instinct was to strike at his enemy's most powerful warrior. In this case, that was Buffy. To aid him, the spirit of vengeance called up an army of ghost warriors that were apparently not actual ghosts but magical constructs of some sort.

The conflict spurred a funny, spirited, and thought-provoking debate about the American Thanksgiving holiday among the series' main characters, with Willow quite vocal on one side, Giles on the other, and Spike offering his own hilariously politically incorrect third opinion. Angel, who had already left Sunnydale for L.A., appeared in this episode, aiding Buffy against Hus and his warriors without her knowing about it.

Despite the qualms felt by all involved, Hus was destroyed at the episode's conclusion. Buffy realized that only the stolen Chumash knife could destroy him, and she used it against him. Early in the episode it was noted that a new site for the cultural center would have to be found while archaeologists studied the old mission. It is not clear if that will allow the spirits that composed Hus to rest in peace.

The nature of spirits

GHOSTS AND GHOST STORIES have existed since before the written word. Defined as disembodied spirits of the dead, ghosts are an integral part of the belief in life after death. Although no one has ever been able scientifically to prove or disprove the existence of the soul or life after death, belief in both persists.

Nearly every culture on earth has held a belief in some form of an afterlife, and each has had individuals who claim to communicate with the spirits. In those cultures where ancestors are revered, as in many Native American tribes for example, spirits are believed to dwell among the living. Therefore, visions of ghosts are commonplace and even welcome. In fact, spirits are invoked for advice and for support of those still living, and the shaman, who has the ability to call upon these spirits, is a well-respected member of the community. In many Western cultures, however, where the soul is believed to pass on to another plane of existence, ghosts are considered unnatural and feared. Those who claim to be able to communicate with ghosts are frequently looked upon with suspicion and considered frauds (until one needs to *get rid* of a ghost!).

Whereas ideas about the afterlife—and what mortal behavioral requirements allow entry—are different from culture to culture, ghostly themes are fairly universal. Some spirits are kind and some malevolent, but nearly all are treated with a certain level of respect and dread. Special feasts honoring the dead have been a tradition since ancient times, as the living seek to venerate those who have passed while also imploring them not to return. Throughout the ages good spirits have been called upon to foretell the future, give advice, and console the living; evil spirits have been kept at bay through the use of amulets, charms, and rituals.

Ghosts manifest themselves for a variety of reasons. Some return to seek revenge, some to right a wrong, some to obtain a decent burial. In legend, myth, and fiction (and many believe, in reality), spirits have returned to impart information, console the bereaved, warn of impending death or danger, or even provide a service. Some of these apparitions simply do not understand that they are dead, while others remain emotionally attached to certain places and are therefore unable to pass to the next plane of existence.

Such spectral figures may appear once or many times. They may appear at any time of the day or night, but they are generally confined to a specific area, such as a house, a cemetery, an old battlefield, or a deserted road. Ghosts may manifest themselves as sounds, odors, an unexplained touch, or the sense of a presence. They may be well defined or blurred and indistinct. They may be solid, casting a shadow or a reflection in a mirror, or wispy. Their movements may be jerky and stiff or graceful. They may communicate verbally, wordlessly, or not at all.

Ancient ghost stories

THE DEAD HAVE EXISTED beside the living since ancient times, and like the living, have been prone to all manner of behavior, for good or ill. The Assyrians believed in the *ekimmu*, the spirit of any man who died an unpleasant or violent death.

The *keres* were ancient Greek spirits who escaped from the jars containing their mortal remains and made a general nuisance of themselves.

The early Romans had three classes of ghosts: *lares*, *larvae,* and *lemures*. The *lares* were spirits of the dead, generally ancestors, who lived with the household and offered protection in return for food. The *larvae* were evil spirits, of which the *lemures* were a type. The *lemures* were the spirits of those who left no heirs or those who died prematurely and were doomed to haunt the earth until the end of their normal lifespan.

Among some Native American tribes, *kachinas* were the spirits of dead ancestors. These spirits resided in what are now the San Francisco Mountains and acted as intermediaries between their living relatives and the gods. According to Hopi tradition, *kachinas* become clouds and bring the rain. Although generally playful and beneficial, the *kachinas'* behavior was also occasionally malevolent.

The Rise of Christianity

MOST EARLY BELIEFS about spirits held that they were either relatively harmless mischief makers or actually helpful. As Christianity evolved, however, the notion of ghosts changed. Early Catholics believed in purgatory, where souls newly freed of their fleshly bonds were cleansed while awaiting entry to heaven. The specters of Christian belief were generally reputed to appear as pale, sad people, often brandishing the marks of their suffering and reminding those still living to obey the church so as not to suffer a similar fate.

One of the most vital aspects of Christian doctrine is the belief in the Holy Trinity as an explanation of the nature of God. The Trinity is composed of God, the Father (the infinite, eternal power that Christians believe created the universe); God, the Son (Jesus Christ, a human man born of a virgin mother and invested with the grace and divine nature of God, making him *both* man and God simultaneously); and the Holy Spirit (also frequently referred to by Christian clergy as the Holy Ghost; the divine essence of God that had been merged with the flesh of Jesus, freed of its corporeal shell upon the crucifixion of Christ).

Closer examination of the Holy Spirit reveals more a manifestation of God's divine power rather than anything so mundane as a ghost. However, the Gospels—Bible stories about Christ, his disciples, and the Holy Spirit—very clearly portray the third member of the Trinity as the ghost of Jesus. It is likely the Gospels were written in such a way so that the average Christian of the day would be able to understand such a fundamental piece of Christian theology.

As many Protestant churches began to splinter off from Roman Catholicism, each developed its own separate doctrine. Protestants did not generally believe in purgatory. The leaders of the Protestant churches held that ghosts were illusions that could be caused by angels, but were more likely the work of demons and therefore evil.

The Formation of the familiar myth

EVERY GEOGRAPHICAL REGION in the world has its own indigenous "true" ghost stories, legends, and lore rooted in its respective local history, ancient and current. They provide rich veins of folklore and reported haunts, which many authors have gathered and published. For our purposes, however, we will only mention the shared or most common forms of these ghosts and hauntings.

Ghosts have taken many forms in Western culture. The "radiant boys," most prominent in Europe and England as early as the ninth and tenth centuries, were the specters of children who had been murdered by their mothers and the "gray ladies" are ghosts of women who died violently while pining away for love.

The Weeping Woman—*La Llorona*—is a Mexican ghost, though she has been spotted throughout the American Southwest and as far away as the Philippines. This tortured soul wanders the night in tears, desperately searching for her murdered child. She has been a fixture of Mexican lore, fiction, and films, including the first major Mexican horror film, *The Crying Woman* (1933) and later efforts like *The Curse of the Crying Woman* (1961).

Visions of spectral travelers have been reported throughout history, across the world. Often spotted on back roads and in deserted way stations, ghostly travelers have also appeared on trains, planes, and in cars, usually the vehicle in which they died. Such apparitions have also been said to offer assistance or direction to living travelers in distress or to ask for directions themselves. Phantom hitchhikers are reputed to stand by the roadside until a ride is offered, then to enter the vehicle and converse with the driver, only to disappear just before arriving at their stated destination.

Probably the two most famous phantom vehicles are Abraham Lincoln's funeral train and the Flying Dutchman. In 1865, after Lincoln's assassination, his body was transported from Washington, D.C., to his hometown of Springfield, Illinois, by train. Those who have lived along the rail line claim that the black-draped train still passes slowly by on the anniversary of the president's death.

The Flying Dutchman is an ancient sailing ship whose sightings are said to augur disaster. Although many legends surround the ghostly vessel, the central tale is almost constant—that of a stubborn captain whose actions caused the ship to sink during a storm. As a result, the captain and crew have been doomed to sail the seas for eternity.

Ghosts are also said to manifest themselves as deathbed visions, not only in the West but in Eastern cultures, as well. Many deathbed visions share a common characteristic, that of a glowing being dressed in white or a bright light in which the presence of someone familiar is felt. The being or presence is usually a close relative who has already passed, but some have described what they believe to be angels or core religious figures, including Christ, Krishna, Yama, etc. Deathbed visions usually come to those who are suffering a gradual death and are believed to help ease the way into the next life.

There are a great many stories of apparitions appearing to the living, usually to offer reassurance that the deceased visitor's spirit is happy in the afterlife. Other tales relate incidents in which specters have supposedly communicated vital information to the living.

Of course, no discussion of ghosts would be complete without making mention of poltergeists—those pesky, noisy spirits that seem to delight in wreaking havoc. Poltergeists are rarely visual apparitions, but they are annoying, cruel, and destructive. Best known for throwing stones and starting fires, these spirits have also been the cause of odd odors, unexplained sounds, levitation of objects, and destruction of property. Lore regarding poltergeists varies. Some believe them to be angry ghosts or spirits who have simply lost their way. Others claim they are not really ghosts at all, preferring to blame such mischievous destructive activity on witchcraft or demons. In a more modern twist, some parapsychologists (who study strange, supposedly supernatural phenomena) suggest that poltergeist activity can be attributed to the subconscious psychic energy of those still living.

from Myth to fiction

THE EARLIEST WRITTEN GHOST STORIES appeared in classic Greek and Roman literature in which ghosts generally offered advice, repaid debts, found murderers, or begged for a proper burial. The Roman poet Ovid wrote of the specter of Remus returning from the dead to name his assassin in 43 B.C.

The most notable classical ghost story is Odysseus's encounter with the spirits of the underworld in Homer's *The Odyssey*, circa 9 B.C. (also see Walking Dead). Homer's ghosts were restless and noisy but generally harmless. However, this concept of spirits changed over time. In 4 B.C., Socrates called ghosts helpful but also threatening, and Plato warned others to stay away from graves where one might encounter a spirit's manifestation. About the same time Seneca, a Roman philosopher and dramatist, wrote ghosts into his plays as narrators, usually in the prologue but occasionally as part of the continuing narrative as well.

The first written account of a haunted house came from Pliny the Younger in 1 B.C. In a letter to a friend, he wrote about Athenodorus of Athens, who bought a rundown house rumored to be haunted and cursed.

Also in 1 B.C. the Greek philosopher Plutarch wrote in his *Life of Cimon* that the Chaeronea baths were haunted. A violent man named Damon had been murdered in the baths, and his spirit was believed to haunt them. His presence was made known through loud moans and other noises that became so disturbing to neighbors that the baths were permanently sealed.

The earliest known record of poltergeist activity appeared in Germany in A.D. 858 in the chronicle *Annales Fuldenses*. The article describes how an "evil spirit" threw rocks at a farmhouse on the Rhine, caused fires, and berated the farmer for his alleged sins.

William Shakespeare featured ghosts in his classic plays. *Richard III* (1594) includes several ghosts, all of whom were murdered by King Richard. Julius Caesar's ghost visits his assassin, Marcus Brutus, on two separate evenings, his presence heralded by a flickering candle, in *Julius Caesar* (1599). In *Hamlet* (1601), the title character's father appears as a ghost to implore Hamlet to seek revenge for his murder.

Macbeth, written in 1606, contains the most frightening ghost in all of Shakespeare's dramas: the ghost of the murdered Banquo is a truly horrifying specter as he returns silently to haunt Macbeth during a dinner party. Only Macbeth can see him and must continue with the party as though nothing were wrong.

Nineteenth-century ghost tales set the stage for the enduring image of the phantom in the modern horror story—that of a threatening, tormented, and tormenting spirit. In 1819 and 1820, Washington Irving published a series of short stories in a collection titled *The Sketchbook of*

Geoffrey Crayon, which contained one of the most famous American ghost stories ever written, "The Legend of Sleepy Hollow," about a headless horseman terrorizing travelers on a deserted New England thoroughfare.

There have been numerous film adaptations of "The Legend of Sleepy Hollow," beginning in 1958 with a terrific animated version from Disney. In 1980 Jeff Goldblum and Meg Foster starred in a made-for-TV version for NBC. Tim Burton's breathtaking *Sleepy Hollow*, (see Magic Users) was released in 1999 by Paramount, with a fresh perspective on that popular story.

Famed nineteenth-century British author Charles Dickens believed the ghost story was especially appropriate at Christmastime. In 1843 he wrote the first of several Christmas ghost stories, "A Christmas Carol," which has been called by many his most enduring and best-loved story. This tale of redemption presents a quartet of ghostly apparitions who visit Ebenezer Scrooge at Christmastime to convince him to change his miserly ways.

There have been numerous adaptations of "A Christmas Carol" on stage, film, and television. The first talking motion picture was a British version filmed in 1938, although some feel the best movie adaptation to date is the 1951 British feature starring Alastair Sim as Scrooge. In 1970 Cinema Center released a musical adaptation of Dickens's story called *Scrooge,* with Albert Finney as the title character and Sir Alec Guinness portraying Jacob Marley. The following year, ABC broadcast British animator Richard Williams's ambitious half-hour animated version of *A Christmas Carol*, with none other than Alastair Sim providing the voice for Scrooge.

Paramount's *Scrooged* (1988) starred Bill Murray as a mean-spirited television executive in a comedic update of the story. George C. Scott tried his hand at the role in a handsomely mounted American television production by Hallmark/CBS in 1984. Even the Muppets got in on the act with their own version in 1992. Patrick Stewart (*Star Trek: The Next Generation*) thrilled audiences for several years with his annual reading of the story on the Broadway stage before playing Scrooge in a well-received TNT made-for-cable version in 1999.

Irish author J. S. Le Fanu was one of the most influential horror writers of the nineteenth century and a key figure in the development of the modern ghost story. Le Fanu published several volumes of his work, beginning with *Ghost Stories and Tales of Mystery* (1851) and ending with *In a Glass Darkly* (1872), a year before his death. However, it was not until 1923, when a collection of his stories (*Madame Crowl's Ghost and Other Tales of Mystery*) was published, that he finally received the recognition he deserved.

Guy de Maupassant is widely considered the greatest French practitioner of the short-story form. During the 1880s he penned several short tales, which featured ghosts, such as "La Petite Roque" (1885) and "La Morte" (1887).

The Nobel Prize–winning British author Rudyard Kipling wrote several ghost stories set in India, all between 1885 and 1891 (with the exception of "They" in 1905 about the ghosts of children). His first short story, "The Phantom Rickshaw," was written in 1885 and published in 1888 as part of a compilation titled *The Phantom Rickshaw and Other Tales*.

The late nineteenth century to early twentieth century is considered the golden age of the ghost story because of the quality of those that were written. The economic uncertainty of the time created an atmosphere conducive to fright and suspense. Additionally, the development of the short story and novella provided an ideal vehicle for sustaining the emotional intensity of a true ghost story, without the subplots needed to fill the length of a novel.

Henry James saw his classic novella "The Turn of the Screw," published in 1898 at the height of the golden age. A young governess, who also narrates the tale, is hired to care for two orphaned children, Flora and Miles, at an English country estate owned by the children's uncle. The governess soon senses two spirits haunting the premises. She believes the two to be the ghosts of a past chauffeur and her own predecessor.

In 1961, Twentieth Century Fox produced a film adaptation of "The Turn of the Screw," called *The Innocents*. With a screenplay by Truman Capote and William Archibald, directed by Jack Clayton and starring Deborah Kerr and Michael Redgrave, this film carries a reputation as one of the best ghost stories ever filmed. *The Turn of the Screw* was also made into a two-part television movie in 1974 and was filmed again in 1992 and 1999.

THE INNOCENTS

In 1904 British author and scholar M. R. James released his first collection, *Ghost Stories of an Antiquarian*. A great admirer of J. S. Le Fanu, James shares his status as one of the architects of the modern ghost story. James is credited with some of the most technically perfect ghost stories ever written. His last volume, *Collected Ghost Stories*, first published in 1931, is still in print today.

Pulitzer Prize–winning American author Edith Wharton also wrote several fine ghost stories between 1904 and 1937, mostly as a tactic to overcome her own fear of ghosts and the supernatural. Her most chilling effort, "Afterward" (1910), is about a young woman whose marriage is threatened by a ghost, although the ghost's presence isn't realized until "afterward." The narrative also contains a superb haunted-library scene.

Other great American and British authors who wrote ghostly tales include Arthur Machen, Ambrose Bierce, Nathaniel Hawthorne, and Algernon Blackwood, whose short story "The Willows" (1907), though concerned more with evil spirits than human souls, is widely considered a classic of the form.

French magician George Méliès incorporated many ghosts into his short films, beginning with *The Bewitched Inn* (1897). *Summoning the Spirits* (1899) introduced the first film medium conducting a séance, which he promptly parodied in *Up-to-Date Spiritualism* (1900) and his later *A Spiritualistic Meeting* (1906). From Sweden, director Victor Sjöström's *The Phantom Carriage* (1921) is among the earliest masterpieces of the horror cinema.

In the 1921 silent feature *The Haunted Castle*, the great German Impressionist filmmaker F. W. Murnau crafted a tale of a nobleman who invites a group of guests to his castle for a hunt.

It is one of the finest early examples of the Gothic horror film, which would later be explored by such directors as Francis Ford Coppola (*Dementia 13*, 1963) and Ken Russell (*Gothic*, 1986).

The earliest Japanese ghost films were produced during the silent era. Kenji Mizoguchi's lost film *The Passion of a Woman Teacher* (1926) introduced the classic vengeful female ghosts of legend and myth to cinema, driving the lovers responsible for her suicide to their own deaths. Only the most elegant and austere of the genre were exported to Western countries, among them Mizoguchi's own *Ugetsu* (1953), which is still considered by many to be among the finest films ever made.

The Ghost Walks, directed by Frank R. Strayer in 1934, was one of many films to exploit the genre's archetypal formula of people trapped on a dark and stormy night in an eerie old mansion. In that picture, individuals who claim to see ghosts roaming the halls are later found murdered.

Topper (MGM/UA, 1937), the famously popular ghost comedy adapted from the Thorne Smith novel, starred Cary Grant and Constance Bennett. In the film, a fun-loving couple who are killed in a car crash must perform a good deed before being allowed entry to the afterlife. The film spawned two sequels, *Topper Takes a Trip* (1939) and *Topper Returns* (1941). It was also the inspiration for a 1950s television series starring Leo G. Carroll as Topper and a 1979 made-for-TV movie starring Kate Jackson (*Charlie's Angels*).

The horror comics of the 1940s, *Eerie*, *Adventures into the Unknown*—and the EC Comics of the early 1950s, *Haunt of Fear*, *Tales from the Crypt*, *Vault of Horror*—often contained stories about ghosts and hauntings. Since 1940 ghostly characters not only have been supporting characters and villains in comic-book titles but supported titles of their own.

The most interesting and enduring of those characters in any of the established superhero universes is DC's the Spectre, who made his first appearance in 1940 in *More Fun Comics* #52. Hard-boiled police detective Jim Corrigan was kidnapped and killed by crime boss "Gat" Benson, but the dead detective's angry spirit was returned to Earth. There he continued with Jim Corrigan's life while battling evil in all its forms as the green-cloaked grim visage of death called the Spectre.

The Spectre was one of the founding members of the Justice Society of America, the first superhero team in comics. When the JSA first appeared in *All Star Comics* #3 (1940), the Spectre was part of the team that also included Wonder Woman, Dr. Fate, Starman, Dr. Midnite, the Atom, Sandman, and Hawkman. The Spectre continued to appear in *More Fun Comics* until issue #101, published in 1945. Another comic-book ghost hero, Uncle Sam, first appeared in *National Comics* #1–3 (Quality Comics Group, 1940). Uncle Sam appeared in his own series, *Uncle Sam Quarterly*, which ran for eight issues beginning in 1941. Uncle Sam continued to appear in various comics as part of a superhero team called the Freedom Force. The Freedom Force received its own series in 1976 that ran for fifteen issues. The last time the spirit of freedom was seen was in a beautifully painted two-issue miniseries from DC Comics in 1997.

In 1940, Universal Pictures released the Bob Hope comedy *The Ghost Breakers*. Based on a play by Paul Dickey and Charles W. Goddard, the wildly funny film served as the inspiration for future outings from Abbott and Costello and spawned a remake starring Dean Martin and Jerry Lewis (*Scared Stiff*, Paramount, 1953).

In 1941 Noel Coward wrote and produced *Blithe Spirit* for both the London and New York stage. The story concerns a wealthy British couple who hold a séance and call up the spirit of the

husband's first wife. Unfortunately she refuses to leave and ends up killing the second wife in an attempt to bring her husband to the afterlife. Both wives then haunt the husband until the medium at last sends them back to the spirit world. The 1945 film version starred Rex Harrison as the husband and Margaret Rutherford in a delightful reprise of her stage portrayal as the medium, Madame Arcati. *Blithe Spirit* received an Academy Award for special effects.

Comedy legends Bud Abbott and Lou Costello teamed up to make the 1941 comedy *Hold That Ghost* for Universal, though the specter in that film turned out to be a fake. A far more interesting Abbott and Costello ghost yarn is the 1946 Universal feature *The Time of Their Lives*. The film opens during the American Revolutionary War with Costello and his girlfriend (Marjorie Reynolds) being wrongly shot as spies and cursed to haunt the land until someone can prove them innocent. The story jumps forward to 1946, where Abbott plays the descendant of the scoundrel responsible for the whole mess, who attempts to help the spirits prove their innocence. A wonderful little film, it is unique in that it relies not at all on the duo's vaudevillian past.

Many other popular screen comedy teams took their shot at the ghostly formula. The East Side Kids (later known as the Bowery Boys) tangled with Nazis, fake ghosts, apparently real zombies, and Bela Lugosi in *Spooks Run Wild* (1941) and *Bowery at Midnight* (1942). *Ghost Crazy* (aka *Crazy Knights,* 1944) pitted its phony ghosts against Monogram's dire comedy trio Billy Gilbert, "Slapsie Maxie" Rosenbloom, and Shemp Howard (later of the Three Stooges). Musical comedian Kay Kyser teamed with Boris Karloff, Peter Lorre, and Bela Lugosi in *You'll Find Out* (1940) in yet another bogus haunted-house burlesque. Ole Olsen and Chick Johnson starred as *Ghost Catchers* (1944) in the zaniest of the crop, featuring Jack Norton's drunken tap-dancing ghost and a welcome final act in which genuine ghosts unveil the fake ghosts.

Hit Comics #25 (Quality Comics, 1942) introduced Kid Eternity. Christopher "The Kid" Freeman was a young sailor aboard a ship during World War II when it was viciously attacked by a German U-boat and sunk. As he approaches the Gates of Eternity, he is told he should still have seventy-five years left. To make up for the error, the Kid is allowed to inhabit his old body and is given special powers. *Kid Eternity* made a return to comics with a DC/Vertigo miniseries in 1991 and a regular monthly title in 1993 that lasted only sixteen issues. In 1999 Kid Eternity was slain by the evil Mordru the Dark Lord in the first issue of the relaunched *Justice Society of America*.

The year 1942 was a good year for ghosts in comic books. First appearing in *Flash Comics* #29 from National Periodical Publications, the Ghost Patrol consisted of three former members of the French Foreign Legion who returned from the dead to battle Nazi aggression during World War II. After the war, the three ghosts became crime fighters, appearing in *Flash Comics* through issue #104 in 1949. That same year the Grim Ghost was introduced in *Sensation Comics* #1, also from National Periodical Publications. First appearing in *Crack Comics* #27 in 1943, Captain Triumph was Quality Comics Group's answer to D.C.'s Spectre.

The 1940s were also a golden age for ghost stories on the silver screen. In 1944 Paramount Pictures released *The Uninvited,* an eerie, classically suspenseful treatment of ghosts haunting the living. Director Lewis Allen tried to rekindle his success with *The Unseen* (1945), in which *Uninvited* star Gail Russell was again plagued by a haunting. Despite a script co-authored by famed mystery novelist Raymond Chandler, the film did not live up to its predecessor's success.

That same year brought *The Canterville Ghost* (MGM/UA, 1944), loosely based on a short story by Oscar Wilde and starring Charles Laughton and Robert Young. A young man walled up by his father to die for cowardice on the battlefield in the seventeenth century is doomed to be a ghost until a descendant performs a heroic act in his name. This version updates the original plot to include the Nazi threat. Two made-for-TV versions have modernized the story even further. A 1986 adaptation starred Sir John Gielgud and the 1996 Hallmark/CBS version starred Patrick Stewart as the ghost and Neve Campbell as an American teenager who befriends and tries to help him.

The British horror classic *Dead of Night* (Ealing Studios, 1945) is an exceptional ghost anthology, and arguably among the most influential horror films ever released. The film's main characters gather in the drawing room of a Gothic mansion to recount several frightening incidents. The stories involve a phantom hearse, the ghost of a murdered child, a haunted mirror, a ghost on a golf course, and a ventriloquist. Each builds in intensity with a finale that brings the characters full circle to a twist ending that has since become somewhat clichéd: surprise! They're all ghosts themselves.

The magical romance *The Ghost and Mrs. Muir* was released in 1947 by Twentieth Century Fox and starred Rex Harrison and Gene Tierney. Based on the 1945 novel by R. A. Dick, the film is about a lonely widow who moves into a house by the sea that also happens to be haunted by the spirit of a crusty old sea captain. The two collaborate on a bestseller and, of course, fall in love. This charming, beautifully made film also served as the inspiration for a short-lived television series with Edward Mulhare and Hope Lange in the title roles.

In comic books, 1947 was marked by the appearance of the first ghostly comic villain, the Gentleman Ghost, in National Periodical Publication's *Flash Comics* #88.

The "friendly ghost," Casper, made his first appearance in a Paramount/Famous Funnies animated short in 1945. The lonely spirit searched for a playmate throughout his adventures in the afterlife, a theme that continued through his fifty-five theatrical shorts and into a regular television series in 1950, and then a new, younger-skewing version in the 1960s. Casper was the studio's second most successful character, after Popeye.

In 1949, St. John Publishing Co. was the first to produce Casper comics. The initial attempt at a comic book was canceled after only five issues. In 1952, however, Harvey Publishing obtained the rights to Casper in an effort to break into the children's comic-book business. A whole cast of supporting characters was introduced, including Wendy the Good Little Witch, Hot Stuff, Nightmare the Ghost Horse, the Ghostly Trio, and Spooky the Tuff Little Ghost. Casper became so popular in the comics that he appeared in a number of Harvey titles such as *Casper and Friends*, *Casper and Nightmare*, *Casper's Strange Ghost Stories,* and *Casper and the Ghostly Trio*. Casper's popularity spurred other companies to action and spawned such titles as Charlton Comics' *Timmy the Timid Little Ghost* in 1956.

The 1995 big-screen version of *Casper* (Universal) is a combination of live action, provided by Bill Pullman and Christina Ricci, and high-tech animation. It spawned several direct-to-video follow-ups, including *Casper and Wendy*. The Friendly Little Ghost remains a popular star of comic books, movies, and television.

The notorious pre-Code horror comics had their share of ghosts. *Classics Comics,* aka *Classics Illustrated,* adapted many ghostly tales, including Shakespeare's *Hamlet* and Nathaniel Hawthorne's *The House of the Seven Gables.*

By 1950, the western had become quite popular in comic books. That year, Compix/Magazine Entertainment struck a new formula by combining the western motif with a ghost story. The Ghost Rider first appeared in A-1 Comics #27, though he wasn't actually a ghost. Rather, this western hero was schoolteacher Carter Slade, who rode the frontier serving the cause of justice. Over the series' fourteen issues, more supernatural elements were added, making it unclear whether the Ghost Rider was a man or a ghost. In 1967 Marvel Comics resurrected the Ghost Rider in its own series in which Carter Slade was murdered and his brother, Marshall Lincoln Slade, carried on the legend. That series lasted six issues, downplaying the ghostly, supernatural elements. The western Ghost Rider also made some appearances in several Marvel comics throughout the 1980s in the guise of Hamilton Slade, Lincoln's grandson. (Though he is now called the Phantom Rider to avoid confusion with a more modern Marvel Comics character of the same name.)

The one-shot *Spook Comics* (Bailey Pub., 1946) was the first all-ghost title, and pulp publisher Street & Smith soon brought *Ghost Breakers* (two issues, 1948) to the newsstand.

The tamer ACG titles like *Adventures into the Unknown* and *Forbidden Worlds* featured at least one ghost per issue, and other publishers cranked out *Amazing Ghost Stories* (St. John, three issues, 1954–55), *Ghost Comics* (Fiction House, eleven issues, 1951–54), *Spook* (seven issues, Star Pub., 1953–54), and others. The uncredited author of the one-shot *The Dead Who Walk* (Realistic, 1952) crafted a surprisingly effective modern ghost tale. Unlike more gruesome horror comic staples, ghosts remained conceptually and visually inoffensive enough to survive the 1954 purge and subsequent reign of the Code. Though DC Comics' *House of Mystery* and *House of Secrets* quickly evolved into fantasy and science fiction, competing publishers who had survived the purge kept the faith with new titles like *This Magazine Is Haunted* (Charlton, 1951–54, revived 1957–58) and others.

Even in the world of comic books, however, not everyone believed in ghosts. In 1951 *Star Spangled Comics* #122 (National Periodical Publications) introduced Dr. Terence Thirteen, Ghostbreaker, a debunker of ghostly phenomena. Dr. Thirteen earned a living investigating paranormal phenomena and traveled the globe trying to prove that ghosts and spirits do not exist.

Cheap to evoke and tame enough to offend no one, ghosts quickly made the leap to the new home entertainment invader—television. Early TV horror programs like *Lights Out!* (NBC, 1949) and *Inner Sanctum* (1951) were radio spin-offs and relied heavily on ghosts and comfortably off-camera haunts. This tepid breed faded with NBC's short-lived *Great Ghost Tales* (1961). Their big-screen counterparts, however, were becoming more aggressive.

In England, director Vernon Sewell clung tenaciously to a single ghost story throughout his career. His debut feature, *The Medium* (1934), told the tale of an inexplicable haunting dealt with by a psychic medium. Sewell remade the story as *Latin Quarter* (1945), *The Ghosts of Berkeley Square* (1947), aboard his own yacht as *Ghost Ship* (1953), and finally got it right with the effectively chilling *House of Mystery* (1961). Better still is the opening weird tale, "In the Picture," from the anthology film *Three Cases of Murder* (1954). In that segment, an artist and a number of other spirits live on in the painting of a house that literally absorbs viewers, allowing the painter to continue perfecting his art at the cost of each fresh victim's life.

American exploitation films toyed with ghosts. *The Screaming Skull* (Allied Artists, 1958) had a husband contriving to drive his wife insane with faked screaming skulls, until a bevy of genuine

crying craniums drives him over the edge. The teen horror movie craze yielded *Ghost of Dragstrip Hollow* and *The Headless Ghost* (both AIP, 1959). Director Ed Wood Jr. completed his tale of fake mediums and real ghosts, *Night of the Ghouls* (1959), only to let it languish unseen for twenty years, because he couldn't pay the final film processing fee.

In 1958 Allied Artists released William Castle's classic feature *The House on Haunted Hill*. Castle was the master of the form; many of his horror films were released with an in-theater gimmick meant to terrify audiences. *House on Haunted Hill* stars Vincent Price as an eccentric millionaire who invites five people to stay overnight in his house, which has been the scene of several murders. Whoever is able to spend the whole night on Haunted Hill will earn $10,000. Theaters showing the feature were specially rigged so that at a particular point in the story, an illuminated skeleton would fly over the heads of the audience, seemingly right from the screen. A 1999 Warner Brothers remake upped the bounty to one million dollars and moved the action from a mansion to an abandoned asylum.

Shirley Jackson's extraordinary novella "The Haunting of Hill House" has unnerved readers since its initial publication in 1959. A tale of subtle psychological terror, it has earned worldwide respect as one of the significant haunted-house stories of the age.

In a rare surprise, the film version of this classic novel is equally frightening. Directed with subtle precision by Robert Wise, *The Haunting* (MGM/UA, 1963) is among the best supernatural thrillers ever made. While the viewer helplessly watches Julie Harris (as Eleanor) wend her way through a psychological minefield, the real horror is left to the audience's imagination as the story unfolds. Wise brilliantly makes the foreboding structure a fifth character of the piece and photographs it in an effectively oppressive fashion. Unfortunately, a 1999 Dreamworks remake with Lili Taylor and Liam Neeson was so laden with special effects that audiences missed the subtle terror that made the 1963 version—and the original novella—so terrifying.

The legendary macabre anthology series *The Twilight Zone* made its debut on CBS in 1959. The venerated series, hosted by Rod Serling, was loaded with tales of the supernatural and science fiction, and managed to produce some of the best ghost stories ever broadcast on television—many with famous cast members—but never more so than in the year 1961.

"Long Distance Call" featured young Bill Mumy (*Lost in Space*) receiving calls on a toy phone from his deceased grandmother. In "A Game of Pool," Jack Klugman played a pool shark who faces off against the ghost of another legendary player (Jonathan Winters). That same year, "The Passersby" featured a parade of Civil War specters. Finally, the episode "Death's Head Revisited" was a landmark for television, as it featured the ghosts of Jews murdered at Nazi concentration camps haunting a former Nazi officer for his role in the Holocaust. Serling wrote both that episode and 1963's harrowing "He's Alive," in which a young Dennis Hopper portrays a neo-Nazi leader being coached by the ghost of Adolf Hitler.

Veteran director Jacques Tourneur (*Cat People*; see Primals) helmed one of the series' most understated ghost stories, "Night Call," from a script by Richard Matheson, in which an invalid spinster receives phone calls from a long-dead lover. The premise of another Matheson-scripted episode, "Little Girl Lost," may have inspired the ghost feature *Poltergeist* (see below).

Those are a mere handful of the ghost stories from *The Twilight Zone*. Over the years, numerous other horror TV anthology series have included ghost stories among their plotlines, including *Alfred Hitchcock Presents* (CBS, 1955–64), *One Step Beyond* (ABC, 1959), *Way Out* (CBS, 1961), *Thriller!*

(NBC, 1960–62), *Dark Shadows* (ABC, 1966–69), *Journey to the Unknown* (ABC, 1968), *Ghost Story* (NBC, 1972), *Night Gallery* (also hosted by Serling, NBC, 1970–73), the syndicated *Friday the 13th* (1987–1990), and the Showtime original series for cable, *Poltergeist: The Legacy* (1996–present).

DC's 1961 war comic *G.I. Combat* #87 presented an interesting twist on the ghost story. During World War II, the ghost of Alexander the Great assigned the ghost of Civil War General Jeb Stuart to act as guardian for the M3 tank commanded by the general's namesake, Lt. Jeb Stuart. The spectral general was not pleased, as the tank crew was made up of Northerners, but Lieutenant Stuart, who could see the general's ghost, obliged the guardian spirit by flying the Confederate flag on the tank's antenna. From that time, it came to be known as the Haunted Tank.

Dell Publishing and Gold Key were the most aggressive of all the early 1960s comics publishers when it came to ghosts. They licensed popular TV series like *The Twilight Zone* and *Boris Karloff's Thriller* (quickly retitled *Boris Karloff's Tales of Mystery*) into lucrative and long-lasting comics series, along with Gold Key's *Ripley's Believe It or Not! True Ghost Stories* (94 issues, 1965–80) and the later *Grimm's Ghost Stories* (60 issues, 1972–82). Best of all was Dell's pair of 1962 horror comic one-shots, *Tales from the Tomb* and *Ghost Stories*, both boasting strong scripts from *Little Lulu*'s John Stanley. *Ghost Stories* proved popular enough to launch a series that lasted into the 1970s (37 issues, 1962–73). *Classics Illustrated* also offered their own one-shot true ghost story comic in their popular *The World Around Us* educational series, *The Illustrated Story of Ghosts* (Gilberton, 1960). Charlton Comics launched their own ghost titles including *Ghostly Tales* (169 issues, 1966–84), *Ghost Manor* (77 issues, 1968–84), *The Many Ghosts of Dr. Graves* (75 issues, 1967–82), and others. Only after the Code was revised in 1969 would DC follow suit with *Ghosts* (112 issues, 1971–82) and the like.

The year 1962 brought the release of a singularly chilling motion picture experience. *Carnival of Souls* (Harcourt) is a relatively obscure cult favorite that resurfaced in 1989 with missing footage restored by director Herk Harvey. An eerie psychological thriller, it centers on a woman who survives a car crash into a river and is then plagued by a white-faced phantom.

Riccardo Freda's *The Ghost* (1963) was a key Italian horror film of the decade. Set in Scotland in 1919, the film stars horror-movie queen Barbara Steele and Peter Baldwin as an adulterous couple who plot to murder the woman's husband. Their plan backfires when the husband returns to drive them to madness and death. *Castle of Terror* (aka *Castle of Blood*, 1964) is another fine Italian ghost story starring the omnipresent Steele.

Italian horror maestro Mario Bava directed the best ghost stories of the cycle. *Black Sabbath* (1963) was an anthology film; the first episode, "A Drop of Water," adapted a Chekhov story of a woman haunted by the spirit of a dead medium into a remarkable play of sound, color, and suspense that still packs a punch. *What!* (1965) is set in a nineteenth-century castle haunted by the ghost of a murdered count who was also sadistic and chauvinistic. *Kill, Baby...Kill!* (1966) was re-released in the 1970s as *Curse of the Living Dead*, part of the popular drive-in triple bill known as Orgy of the Living Dead. Bava closed the decade with the stylish, perverse *A Hatchet for the Honeymoon* (1969).

1965 brought us NBC-TV's short-lived series *My Mother the Car*, starring Jerry Van Dyke as a lawyer who gets in a decrepit 1928 Porter to try it out, and turns on the radio only to have his mother, who died seventeen years earlier, talk to him from the speakers.

In Robert Aldrich's *Hush...Hush, Sweet Charlotte* (Twentieth Century Fox 1964), an apparent haunting drives Bette Davis to commit mayhem and murder way down South. Grand Guignol follow-up to the same team's blockbuster *What Ever Happened to Baby Jane?* (Seven Arts-Associates, 1962). Drive-ins favored Bert I. Gordon's *Tormented* (Sinister, 1960), memorable only for its seaweed-smothered ghost haunting a lighthouse.

The artiest drive-in pic of the era was *Spirits of the Dead* (1968), a European Poe-pourri collecting three adaptations from Edgar Allan's classic short stories. The best drive-in ghost movie of the decade was *The Skull* (Amicus, 1965), stylishly visualized by director Freddie Francis (cinematographer of the ghost classic *The Innocents*) from Robert Bloch's famed short story in which the skull of the Marquis de Sade kills anyone foolish enough to possess it. Amicus also offered a vengeful grand piano, animated by the spirit of the pianist's possessive mother, in their omnibus film *Torture Garden* (1967).

In Japan, ghost films remained the most popular of all horror films. Only one, the elegant anthology feature *Kwaidan* (1964), garnered much attention in the United States, though it was a box-office failure in its home country. Far more popular in Japan was less formal, more flamboyant fare like *The Ghost of the Hunchback* and its follow-up *Ghost of the One-Eyed Man* (both 1965), *Illusion of Blood* (1966, from the frequently adapted kabuki play *Ghost of Yotsuya,* 1825), *Curse of the Blood* (1968), *The Snow Woman* (1968), the poetic *The Bride from Hades* (1968), and many others. *Kuroneko* (1968) enjoyed some popularity in the United States, with its somersaulting vengeful female ghosts and black cat familiars. The most ambitious of the era's Japanese ghost movies was *The Hundred Ghost Stories* (1969). The ravishing anthology featured the most delirious procession of ghost monsters ever seen at that time, including a spectral woman who strangles her murderer husband with her elongated serpentine neck, a one-eyed "umbrella ghost" with a whiplike tongue, and a climactic frenzied horde of ectoplasmic creatures.

The Spectre made his return to the DC Comics universe in 1966–67. First appearing in *Showcase Comics* #60, 61, and 64, the character began an evolution that would continue into the twenty-first century. That same year, American Comics Group tried its own hand with a Spectre-like series by introducing Nemesis. First appearing in *Adventures into the Unknown* #154, Nemesis was a federal agent assassinated for standing up to organized crime. Nemesis returned to Earth with a host of ghostly powers including flight, invisibility, and super strength, which made him nearly invulnerable.

DC Comics seemed to be the leader in the creation of comics featuring ghostly characters. In 1967 *Strange Adventures* #205 introduced Boston Brand, trapeze artist extraordinaire, who was murdered and returned to fight evil as the ghostly Deadman.

In the fall of 1969 CBS aired the first *Scooby-Doo, Where Are You?* cartoon in its Saturday morning lineup. The series followed four teenage detectives (the Scooby Gang) and their Great Dane, Scooby-Doo, as they traveled the country solving bizarre mysteries often involving alleged ghosts, although most of the time the climax revealed the culprits were actually flesh-and-blood criminals.

Scooby-Doo enjoyed widespread popularity from the time of its premiere. Scooby-Doo changed networks in 1976, jumping to ABC to star in the *Scooby Doo/Dynomutt Hour.* In 1977 the first two-hour Saturday morning cartoon in history appeared as *Scooby's All-Star-Laff-A-Lympics.* In 1979 Scooby's nephew Scrappy-Doo joined the cast. As of this writing, *Scooby-Doo* continues to enjoy success through reruns on the Cartoon Network and direct-to-video features including *Scooby-Doo on Zombie Island* (1998) and *Scooby-Doo and the Witch's Ghost* (1999). A live-action movie version has long been rumored to be in the works.

In 1970, three years after Marvel's failed revival of *Ghost Rider*, DC tried its hand at the Western/ghost combination. El Diablo first appeared in *All Star Western* #2 as bank clerk Lazarus Lane.

The ghostly western was not relegated only to comic books. *High Plains Drifter* (Malpaso/Universal, 1972) starred Clint Eastwood—who also directed—as a mysterious gunslinger who is hired to protect a town from a group of desperadoes. Some time earlier, the desperadoes had murdered Jim Duncan, the town's lone lawman. The film's ending strongly suggests that Eastwood's character was the ghost of Jim Duncan. A dozen years later, the actor-director made *Pale Rider*, a very similar film, though bereft of ghostly implications.

Following the basic structure of *High Plains Drifter* was the Brat Pack teen road-revenge ghost movie, *The Wraith* (Lightning, 1986), with Charlie Sheen as a speed-racing avenger. A later variation on the theme was the TNT original film *Purgatory* (1999), returning to the western setting in a town that wasn't what it seemed to be as outlaws Eric Roberts, Randy Quaid, and Donnie Wahlberg faced off with gunless sheriff Sam Shepard. (Hint: He didn't need a gun.)

The most evocative low-budget ghost film of its period was John Hancock's *Let's Scare Jessica to Death* (Paramount, 1971), which remains a classic of its kind. This genuinely eerie film focuses on insecure, unstable Jessica (Zohra Lampert), whose attempt to find peace and sanity living on a country farm is shattered by the odd, scarred townsfolk and the intrusion of a squatter (Mariclare Costello), who Jessica suspects is a vampiric ghost. The startling moment when Costello submerges in a lake wearing a bathing suit only to surface in a Victorian wedding gown is one of the ghost genre's most potent chills.

The Possession of Joel Delaney (ITC, 1972) is a jarring shocker in which wealthy New Yorker Shirley MacLaine is tortured as her brother (Perry King) becomes the vessel for the spirit of a homicidal youth.

One of the eeriest films ever made is Nicolas Roeg's seductive, devastating psychic thriller *Don't Look Now* (Casey/Eldorado, 1973). Based on Daphne du Maurier's novella, the film follows Donald Sutherland and Julie Christie as they seek shelter in Venice from the pain of their daughter's death, only to catch fleeting glimpses of a scarlet-frocked figure that may or may not be their child's ghost.

In 1971 came Richard Matheson's classic novel *Hell House*. Regarded as the Mount Everest of haunted houses, Belasco House had been empty for more than twenty years after having stood witness to scenes of unimaginable horror and depravity wrought by its former resident, Emerick Belasco. Two previous expeditions to investigate its secrets met disaster, with most of the participants destroyed by murder, suicide, or insanity. As the novel begins, four strangers arrive at the forbidding mansion, fiercely determined to probe Belasco House for the ultimate secrets of life and death. Matheson wrote the screenplay for the film adaptation, *The Legend of Hell House* (Twentieth Century Fox, 1973).

Also published in 1971 was Thomas Tryon's bestselling novel *The Other*. The delightfully suspenseful story takes place in 1935 on a Connecticut farm where several recent deaths have shaken up a family. Told from the viewpoint of ten-year-old twins, one reserved and dour, the other more normal, the novel is heavy with religious symbolism and focuses on the abnormal relationship between the two boys. Tryon also wrote the screenplay for the 1972 Twentieth Century Fox film by the same name. A faithful adaptation, the movie retains many of the book's shocking moments as well as its layered ending.

Ghosts were standard fare in made-for-TV horror movies, which had to depend upon less graphic and more atmospheric implied terrors lest they offend network censors or prime-time audiences. The ghosts of a downed B-52 haunted the sands of the Libyan desert in *Sole Survivor* (CBS, 1970). Barbara Stanwyck braved *The House That Would Not Die* (ABC, 1970). Patty Duke and David McCallum were tormented by possession and a tinkling music box in *She Waits* (CBS, 1971). And long-haired hippie ghost Jan-Michael Vincent fell in love with Bonnie Bedelia in the shot-on-videotape romance *Sandcastles* (CBS, 1972). The best of these was Steven Spielberg's tale of poltergeist activity and demonic possession *Something Evil* (CBS, 1972). But British television topped them all with Nigel Kneale's potent tale of scientists unraveling an ancient haunt only to unleash far older and more lethal elemental forces in *The Stone Tape* (BBC, 1972).

Marvel resurrected Ghost Rider in 1972, abandoning the white-garbed Western gunfighter for a far more contemporary version. With the popularity of stuntman Evel Knievel, it seemed only natural that the new Ghost Rider introduced in *Marvel Spotlight* #5 was stunt motorcyclist Johnny Blaze, who made a deal with the devil to save the life of his terminally ill foster father.

The Spectre returned to the DC Universe in the early 1970s in *Adventure Comics* #431–40, where Jim Corrigan worked as a police detective while the Spectre acted as judge, jury, and executioner.

PETER STRAUB

PHOTO BY BETH GWINN

Peter Straub, master of the modern literary ghost theme, wrote *Julia* in 1975. The story begins with the title character separating from her husband after a near breakdown following the death of her daughter. She moves to a new home in London but finds herself haunted by the malicious spirit of a little girl. She initially mistakes the apparition for that of her recently deceased daughter, but soon realizes it is the spirit of another youngster with her own insidious agenda. The novel was adapted to the big screen in a 1976 British-Canadian production called *The Haunting of Julia*, starring Mia Farrow.

Jay Anson's *The Amityville Horror* was released in 1977 and quickly became a bestseller. The novel was a terrifying documentation of the 1975 case of poltergeist activity that supposedly occurred in a house in suburban Long Island. The house had been the site of gruesome murders when a twenty-three-year-old man killed his entire family. A family bought the house, ignoring the superstitions surrounding it. Twenty-eight days later, they fled from the house, claiming they had been terrorized by evil spirits. The family reported ghostly apparitions, clouds of flies, windowpanes that broke spontaneously, unexplained temperature changes, levitations, green slime, putrid odors, and moving objects. The book inspired the 1979 American International Pictures feature by the same name starring James Brolin and Margot Kidder, which frequently deviates from the book, increasing the confusion around what is fact and what is fiction.

The success of the film spawned a makeshift series, including prequel *Amityville II: The Possession* (1982) and *Amityville 3-D* (1983, which was indeed in 3-D in its original release). A slew of direct-to-video and made-for-television offerings (1989, 1990, 1992, 1993, and 1996) exemplified the law of diminishing returns.

Dan Curtis's *Burnt Offerings* (PEA, 1976) found a completely dysfunctional family—dad Oliver Reed, mom Karen Black, grandma Bette Davis, and annoying tyke Lee Montgomery—caretaking a haunted house and an unseen old mother in the attic. Dead gangsters possessed the living in *J. D.'s Revenge* (1976) and Curtis Harrington's *Ruby* (Dimension/Krantz, 1977), and again in *Retribution* (Virgin, 1987). Reincarnation was depicted as a destructive form of ghostly possession in American International's *The Reincarnation of Peter Proud* (1975) and Robert Wise's *Audrey Rose* (United Artists, 1977). A possessed car terrorized the countryside in *The Car* (1977), and others popped up in the anthology film *Nightmares* (MCA, 1983) and New Zealand's *Dark of the Night* (Live, 1985). A Nazi ship snuffed its crew, including Richard Crenna, in *Death Ship* (Embassy, 1980). However, Crenna survived the haunted-house antics of *The Evil* (Embassy, 1978), while fellow TV exile Doug McClure suffered worse in the made-in-Japan film *The House Where Evil Dwells* (MGM/UA, 1982).

James Herbert's somber novel *The Survivor* was filmed in 1981, telling the tale of a pilot (Robert Powell) seeking justice after he is killed by a terrorist's bombing of his plane. The best exploitation ghost movie of the period came from Italy; Mario Bava's final effort was *Shock* (1977), a mesmerizing feature about a woman driven to insanity and suicide by the ghost of her dead husband. The American distributor released the film as *Beyond the Door II*, a faux sequel to *The Exorcist* rip-off *Beyond the Door*. Under any name, it effectively scared audiences. *The Nesting* (1981) also scored with its tale of a haunted brothel dominated by a gravel-voiced spectral madame played by Gloria Grahame in her final film role.

The Shining (1977) is one of the great literary masterpieces of modern horror, and without a doubt the finest haunted-house story since Shirley Jackson's *The Haunting of Hill House*. In Stephen King's frightening tale a recovering alcoholic with a penchant for violence, Jack Torrance, takes a position as caretaker in an empty ski lodge in Colorado, accompanied by his wife, Wendy, and their young son. The Overlook Hotel, with its long history, is as majestic and beautiful as it is mysterious and hostile. Cut off from the rest of civilization by winter's most brutal elements, the hotel weaves its malevolent spell over Jack. He begins to see the ghosts in the hotel as his comrades in arms and the alliance threatens the survival of his family. His psychic son, Danny, sees the hotel for what it really is, and fights the hotel's malignancy.

Stanley Kubrick brought the novel to the screen in a 1980 Warner Brothers release. Kubrick shifted the emphasis from the supernatural elements of the novel to a man's descent into madness brought on by the exacerbation of his inner demons in an intensely isolated environment.

Stephen King scripted a new adaptation as a 1997 ABC television miniseries. Although it was a more direct translation from page to screen, it still stopped short of achieving the sheer fright of the novel. Perhaps that is one ghost story best left on the printed page, the horror left to the terrified reader's imagination.

Though many do not think of them as such, ghosts also populate George Lucas's original Star Wars trilogy, beginning with the spirit of Jedi Master Obi-Wan Kenobi in *Star Wars* (Fox, 1977). The ghosts of Yoda and Darth Vader (aka Anakin Skywalker) were added to the series' spiritual roster in the subsequent films, *The Empire Strikes Back* (1980) and *Return of the Jedi* (1983). The three watch over Luke Skywalker, the Jedi who is their student (and Vader's son).

Also in 1977 came another ghostly tale from Peter Straub. *If You Could See Me Now* is a tale of vengeance from beyond the grave.

In 1979 Straub's *Ghost Story* saw print for the first time. In this most famous of his ghostly novels, the main characters are a group of old men who call themselves the "Chowder Society" and who gather monthly to tell spooky stories. Buried within the dynamics of this group of old cronies is the secret of the death of a woman many years before—a woman who was actually a shapeshifting, supernatural beast. When this spirit creature returns to seek vengeance, these men must face their deed and fight for their lives and the lives of their neighbors. The film version (Universal, 1981) collected some of the greatest older actors of the time—Douglas Fairbanks Jr., Fred Astaire, Melvyn Douglas, and John Houseman—to play the members of the Chowder Society.

Director Peter Medak's film *The Changeling* was released in 1980. George C. Scott starred as a recently widowed musician who moves into a new home inhabited by the spirit of a young boy who had been dead some seventy years. A favorite among film buffs, it deserves its reputation as one of the great cinematic ghost stories.

In 1982 special effects finally caught up with the ghost story, thanks to producer Steven Spielberg, director Tobe Hooper (*The Texas Chainsaw Massacre*), and their MGM/UA film *Poltergeist*. The movie earned a place in both film history and pop culture with a visual feast of spectral apparitions and a tightly plotted, well-acted tale of angry ghosts in suburban California. The film was a huge success and spawned two theatrical sequels, *Poltergeist II: The Other Side* (1986) and *Poltergeist III* (1988).

In 1983 Stephen King released his novel *Christine*, about a haunted 1958 Plymouth Fury. Trailblazing horror director John Carpenter (*Halloween, The Fog)* helmed the film version, which was released the same year by Columbia Pictures.

That year brought another interestingly twisted variation on the cinematic ghost story from Twentieth Century Fox. *The Entity* was adapted by Frank De Felitta from his book, itself based on actual events that occurred in Los Angeles during the 1970s. A widowed mother (Barbara Hershey) claims to have been raped by an invisible force that is haunting her house. The spirit is never seen clearly in the film, a device that keeps up the tension level.

The biggest ghostly hit of the 1980s was *Ghostbusters* (Columbia, 1984), a spectral comedy directed by Ivan Reitman and starring Bill Murray, Dan Aykroyd, and Sigourney Weaver. The offbeat tale successfully balanced eye-popping special effects with great low-key performances from Murray and the rest of the cast. Aykroyd, who co-wrote and co-produced the film, revealed that it was inspired by 1940s comedies such as *Ghost Breakers*.

No other ghost-related film has had the pop-cultural impact of *Ghostbusters*. It was the number one box-office draw of 1984, with more than $130 million earned, beating the second Indiana Jones film by more than $20 million to become the fifth highest-grossing film of all time (as of that year). A 1989 sequel, *Ghostbusters II*, also racked up decent box office.

Primary among a new breed of ghost comedies from Hong Kong is Sammo Hung's (CBS's *Martial Law*) exhilarating *Encounters of the Spooky Kind* (1980). The giddy blend of Eastern ghost lore, martial-arts action, and over-the-top slapstick gags spawned many imitations, such as *Till Death Do Us Scare* (1982), *Kung Fu from Beyond the Grave* (1982), and others. There were plenty of serious ghost horrors, too, including *Obsessed* (1983), *Possessed* (1983), and the influential *A Chinese Ghost Story* (1987), a ravishing romantic fantasy that remains one of the most beautiful and entertaining ghost films ever made. *A Chinese Ghost Story Part II* (1990), *A Chinese Ghost Story III* (1991), *Ghost Legend, Ghostly Love* (1991), and others followed; many of these Hong Kong efforts reached Western audiences later in the 1990s, influencing many United States and United Kingdom productions.

American ghost comedies still had their following. The most successful of the post-*Ghostbusters* breed was New World's *House* (1986) which proved popular enough to spawn three sequels: *House II: The Second Story* (1987), *House III* (retitled *The Horror Show*, 1989), and *House IV: Home Deadly Home* (1992). Gene Wilder directed, co-wrote, and co-starred with his wife Gilda Radner and frequent cohort Dom DeLuise in *Haunted Honeymoon* (1986), an affectionate evocation of the 1940s ghost comedies.

Meanwhile, the enduring *Poltergeist* and *Amityville Horror* series spawned their share of imitators, including the Italian gorefest *Ghosthouse* (1987), Wings Hauser terrorizing with tools as *The Carpenter* (1989), Wings Hauser again, terrorized by *The Wind* (1987), the cheat ghosts of *Bad Dreams* (1988), the genuine spooks haunting *The Sleeping Car* (1990), and others. A brief flurry of haunted prison movies inexplicably emerged at once, including *Force of Darkness* (1986), *Death House* (1987), *Slaughterhouse Rock* (1988), *Death Row Diner* (1988), and *The Chair* (1989). The best of the bunch was action-director Renny Harlin's debut feature *Prison* (Empire, 1988), introducing Viggo Mortensen as the protagonist intent on busting out of the big house. There were more ghost Westerns, too, including *Ghost Town* and *Ghostriders* (both 1988). Phillip Badger's romantic *The Forgotten One* (1990) was a fine change of pace, but cable TV offered one of the best ghost films of the cycle, *Gotham* (Cannon/Warner Brothers, 1988), with Tommy Lee Jones in top form as a hard-boiled private dick who falls for a ghost (Virginia Madsen).

In 1987 the Spectre resurfaced once more as the star of his own comics series, with reduced powers and a new mission: to prevent people from killing others and to avenge the unjustly slain in ways fitting the crimes. This left plenty of room for some creative Spectre-caused deaths but none with the visceral impact of the 1973 appearances.

1988 saw the release of two excellent ghostly films. The first, *Lady in White* (New Century Films), was a wonderful old-fashioned ghost story. The second film was director Tim Burton's oddball hit *Beetlejuice* (Geffen Pictures, 1988). The film is a comic journey into the afterlife as a recently deceased couple (Geena Davis and Alec Baldwin) try to save their New England farmhouse from the bizarre renovations wrought by the new owners, an obnoxious New York couple. Davis and Baldwin are forced to enlist the help of bio-exorcist "Beetlejuice," the "ghost with the most," to drive the humans out. Michael Keaton is wonderfully sleazy in a mostly improvised role and his performance, combined with Burton's fertile directorial imagination, make this a very memorable movie.

Chucky, the plastic boy doll animated by the soul of a malicious serial killer (Brad Dourif) also made his debut in 1988, in Tom Holland's *Child's Play*. The film was disowned by its original production studio (MGM-UA professed they had qualms over the content of the film), and the property was picked up by Universal and nurtured into a profitable series and minor licensing and merchandising franchise through *Child's Play 2* (1990) and *3* (1991).

The character languished until director Ronnie Yu chose *Bride of Chucky* (1998) as his second American feature, infusing it with the inventive energy and bawdy excess of his stylish Hong Kong masterpieces.

In 1989 Universal Studios released a pair of ghostly tales that tugged at filmgoers' heartstrings. *Field of Dreams*, written and directed by Phil Alden Robinson and adapted from the novel *Shoeless Joe,* by W. P. Kinsella, is a sentimental favorite among many filmgoers.

Steven Spielberg's *Always* is an updated version of a 1943 film, *A Guy Named Joe*. Holly Hunter plays a woman whose boyfriend (Richard Dreyfuss) is killed in a plane crash. Dreyfuss is given the opportunity by angel Audrey Hepburn (in her last film role) to return to earth and guide a young pilot in his career and his budding relationship with Hunter.

Novelist Rick Hautala's *Winter Wake* was also published in 1989, the first in an impressive run of eerie, atmospheric ghost stories—including *Dead Voices* (1989), *Cold Whisper* (1991), and *Ghost Light* (1993)—that centered on families plagued by spectral visitors.

R. L. STINE

PHOTO BY BETH GWINN

R. L. Stine created the first of his many horror series specifically for young adults and children in 1989. The Fear Street series, beginning with *The New Girl* (about a young girl who returns from the grave to wreak havoc on the lives of fellow high school students), featured several ghostly tales for the young-adult audience.

Welcome to Dead House, the first of more than sixty Goosebumps titles, was published in 1992, about two children who move to a new house in a new town, only to find both haunted. *Goosebumps* was also produced as a TV series for the Fox Network beginning in 1995 and its success has spawned yet another Stine creation for children, *Ghosts of Fear Street* (#1 *Hide and Shriek* was published in 1995).

Marvel Comics gave *Ghost Rider* another shot in 1990, this time as teenager Dan Ketch, now possessed by the spirit of vengeance. Dan was transformed into a leather-clad, chain-swinging, flaming-skulled creature of retribution whenever an evil act was committed. This take on the Ghost Rider was hugely successful, running almost through the entire decade before cancellation.

Paramount Pictures' hugely successful 1990 release *Ghost* is an enjoyable mix of romance, thriller, and fantasy, directed by Jerry Zucker. Whoopi Goldberg earned an Academy Award for her portrayal of a medium who discovers ghosts are real.

Candyman (Propaganda Pictures, 1992), based on Clive Barker's story "The Forbidden," is an eerie psychological thriller about a murderous spirit seeking revenge on a society that persecuted and murdered him. As helmed by Bernard Rose (director of the chill-inducing *Paperhouse*, a marvelously eerie ghostly tale in its own right), the film is filled with unusual touches that intensify the suspense and make the film a cut above the usual fare. The 1995 sequel *Candyman: Farewell to the Flesh* had slick production values and the 1999 *Candyman: Day of the Dead* was a direct-to-video release.

The Spectre returned from the afterlife yet again in 1992. This take on the ghostly avenger took the best parts of the previous stories and melded them together with an entirely fresh concept. The series did what no other had done before—it defined what the Spectre truly was: the wrath of God, the biblical power sent to smite those who displeased the Almighty. This Spectre was probably the most powerful being in the DC Universe, and it became harder for the ghost of Jim Corrigan to contain that power. The series ran until 1998 and ended as Jim Corrigan was finally allowed to rest in peace and the wrath of God returned to heaven . . . for a time.

In 1993 hard-boiled mystery novelist James Lee Burke took a bit of a detour with *In the Electric Mist with Confederate Dead*. Though the book did star Burke's best-known character, Dave Robicheaux, it also featured the ghost of a Confederate army general. William Hjortsberg's 1995 novel *Nevermore*, which featured Arthur Conan Doyle and Harry Houdini as characters, also included the ghost of Edgar Allan Poe in a supporting role.

Dark Horse Comics brought us perhaps the sexiest take on a ghostly character with its introduction of Ghost in *Comics' Greatest Worlds* #3 in 1993. Clad in flowing white cape, hood, and bustier, and wielding twin Colt .45s, *Ghost* believed that she was in fact the restless spirit of a reporter murdered by organized crime when she proved too good an investigator. Ghost received her own monthly series in 1995.

The film *Heart and Souls* (Columbia Pictures, 1993) starred Robert Downey Jr., Alfre Woodard, and Charles Grodin in a tale of four San Franciscans who die in a bus accident in 1959. Their spirits become inescapably linked to a child born at the exact moment of their death.

On television in 1993, Chris Carter's *The X-Files* premiered on Fox TV, telling stories not only of extraterrestrial encounters but of paranormal encounters as well. Heading into its seventh year, *The X-Files* has featured several episodes of a ghostly nature, not the least of which includes Agent Dana Scully's sighting of her father minutes after his death halfway through the first season, in "Beyond the Sea." During their years together, Agent Fox Mulder and his partner, Scully, have also investigated poltergeist activity in an office complex ("Shadows"), the possession of a little girl by the vengeful spirit of a murdered police officer ("Born Again"), and a house haunted by the ghosts of Ed Asner and Lily Tomlin in "How the Ghosts Stole Christmas."

A vastly underrated movie offering was director Peter Jackson's *The Frighteners* (Universal, 1996). A fabulous mix of drama and comedy, the film starred Michael J. Fox as a "ghostbuster" who is actually a con man. His partners in the con? The ghosts themselves.

Novelist J. K. Rowling's 1997 *Harry Potter and the Sorcerer's Stone* tells the story of ten-year-old Harry's adventures while studying sorcery at the Hogwarts School of Witchcraft and Wizardry. Among the school's colorful characters are a number of ghostly beings including Professor Binns, Nearly Headless Nick, Moaning Myrtle, the Bloody Baron, Peeves the Poltergeist, the Fat Lady, and the Fat Friar.

The most prominent recent ghost story in novel form was Stephen King's *Bag of Bones* (1998). Subtitled "a haunted love story," the book featured a multitude of ghosts, which plague bestselling author Mike Noonan after the untimely death of his wife, Johanna. Though the haunting begins innocently enough, the story ends with Noonan and his wife's ghost trapped in a struggle between the vengeful spirit of a murdered turn-of-the-century blues singer and the sinister specters of the town fathers who did her in a hundred years earlier.

In the DC Comics 1999 miniseries *Day of Judgment*, a rogue angel of heaven named Azmodel takes control of the wrath of God to become a villainous version of the Spectre. In an epic story line involving all of the supernatural and superpowered characters in the DC Universe, Azmodel was eventually defeated as the ghost of former Green Lantern Hal Jordan is allowed to bond with God's wrath and become the new Spectre, the most recent incarnation of the Spectre is scheduled to receive his own monthly series in 2000.

The year 1999 saw the arrival of two stunning films featuring ghosts. Artisan's *Stir of Echoes*, directed by David Koepp and starring Kevin Bacon, was adapted from Richard Matheson's 1958 novel of the same name.

Hollywood Pictures' *The Sixth Sense,* starring Bruce Willis and eleven-year-old Haley Joel Osment, was the second highest-grossing film of 1999 and nominated for several Academy Awards. Osment plays Cole, a boy whose odd behavior stems from scary dreams that experts have been unable to decipher. As a last resort, child psychologist Willis steps in, essentially the only person who stands between the boy and an institution. Willis finally realizes the boy can communicate with the dead and helps him understand the spirits are seeking his help in finding closure to their lives so they might rest in peace. Writer-director M. Night Shyamalan takes the calculated risk of stockpiling his conventional shocks, so that when he unleashes them late in the game, they act upon characters for whom the viewer has affection. It pays off, thanks to Osment, the rest of the movie's fine cast, and the mood set by the atmospheric photography. The classic twist ending had audiences raving, but it was not the first time that particular twist had been used.

In the world of entertainment, the success of *The Sixth Sense* has spawned a search by producers and publishers for quality ghost stories. Already ghosts are being drawn into the new century with the premiere of the NBC/Dreamworks supernatural drama *The Others*. Debuting in February 2000, the series is about a group of people, each able to communicate with the other side in a different way, who come together in an attempt to help others as well as help themselves. Undoubtedly this is but one of many more stories about ghosts to come.

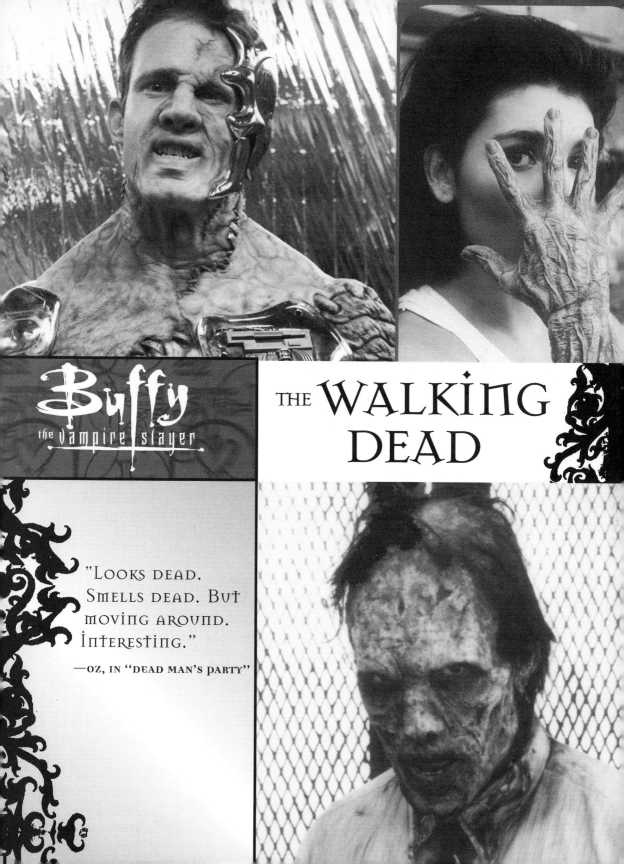

Buffy the Vampire Slayer

THE WALKING DEAD

"LOOKS DEAD. SMELLS DEAD. BUT MOVING AROUND. INTERESTING."

—OZ, IN "DEAD MAN'S PARTY"

ZOMBIES. REANIMATED CORPSES. Call them what you will, the walking dead have become as familiar an element of the horror story as ghosts and werewolves. In the plethora of pop-culture examples, there are a multitude of varieties of zombies and ways in which one can be created. In the end, however, all of those resurrections can be attributed to one of two main factors: magic, or science.

Magical reanimation of the dead can take almost any form, utilizing whatever kind of magic the writer can imagine. Scientific reanimation has appeared in the guise of a passing comet or satellite in such films as *Night of the Living Dead* and *Night of the Comet*, as a gas or serum in *Return of the Living Dead* and *Re-Animator*, and, most notably, as lightning drawn down from the heavens by a mad scientist in the many permutations of Mary Shelley's 1816 novel *Frankenstein*.

On *Buffy the Vampire Slayer*, the presentation of zombies runs the gamut. The Frankenstein template has been used twice, with Daryl Epps of "Some Assembly Required" and season four's villainous patchwork demon, Adam.

Other appearances of the walking dead on the series owe their greatest debt to George Romero's Living Dead trilogy, as have most film and TV zombies since the release of the first film in the series, 1968's *Night of the Living Dead*. In these films, a satellite returning to earth emits strange radiation that causes the dead to rise from their graves and feast on the living.

Though most of the zombies on Buffy have been reanimated through magical means, Romero's influence is keenly felt, particularly in the third season's "Dead Man's Party."

As for mythology, what do we know about the walking dead in the Buffyverse? Some are animated by science and some by magic. Some are relatively mindless, while some retain the personalities they had in life—for better or worse. Joss Whedon and company have left the phenomenon wide open for interpretation, creating the potential for innumerable stories yet to be told. It should be noted, of course, that *Buffy*'s vampires are corpses that have been reanimated by the presence of a demon residing within the dead human body. That makes them demons *and* walking dead, a unique hybrid that cannot be defined as merely one or the other.

the influences

"FOR ME, IT'S ALL ROMERO. *Night of the Living Dead*, the trilogy," reveals Joss Whedon of his thought process when it comes to zombies. "They're dead; they eat the flesh of the living. It's simple, it's horrifying, it gets it done."

However, Whedon's admiration of Romero's work did not prevent him from making his own "rules" when it came to the presentation of zombies. In season two's "Some Assembly

Required," when the bodies of recently deceased girls began to disappear from the cemetery and it was thought that someone might be raising them up as zombies, Xander was concerned about them eating his flesh. Giles specifically told him that "zombies don't eat the flesh of the living." That was definitely Whedon's intention.

"We don't have them eating the flesh of the living, 'cause quite frankly, eeeew," he says with a chuckle. "But that is the look and style of movement we go for."

Buffy's creator doesn't want to be tied down to that interpretation, however, not even with his no-eating-the-living rule.

"Early on, one of the first [episode ideas] I had was a guy raising zombies and having to explain that they don't eat the flesh of the living; that they got a bad rap 'cause of the damn movies," Whedon notes, adding that in his mind, there are all different types of zombie. On *Buffy*, he notes, "Zombie is a relative term."

The series' makeup master, Todd McIntosh, also has a love of zombies and is well aware of the Romero connection.

"Zombies are a perennial favorite, aren't they?" McIntosh jokes. "Hollywood is so steeped in Romero's movies now. When those films came out, they completely changed our view of what zombies are about. To my mind, it's all linked with *Fangoria* magazine. *Fangoria* and zombie movies and gushing blood and eating brains and the big comedy sweeps in those movies all blend together as one cultural path.

"Then there are the previous generation of zombie movies. There's a wonderful Peter Cushing Hammer film where he's in India and his son is introduced to a cannibalism cult and is kept locked in the attic. They kill guests and feed them to him. That was before the explosion of brain-eating zombie stuff.

"Also, there was an episode of *Kolchak: the Night Stalker* that explored the voodoo connection. That was an interesting variation," he adds, recalling a particular scene in which intrepid investigator Carl Kolchak is forced to climb into the back of a hearse in a junkyard, pack salt into the sleeping zombie's mouth, and then sew its lips together.

For visual purposes, McIntosh notes, "Buffy has to fight, but it would be very interesting to have some things like that that she has to do—things that are more mentally squeamish. But with voodoo, you're talking about an active, living religion, and you have to be very careful [not to offend]."

the walking dead

DARYL epps

"You're going to feel a little pinch, maybe a little discomfort around the neck area. But when you wake up, you'll have the body of a seventeen-year-old. In fact…you'll have the body of several."
—ERIC, EXPLAINING TO CORDELIA THAT SHE IS TO BE REANIMATED AS DARYL'S BRIDE,
IN "SOME ASSEMBLY REQUIRED"

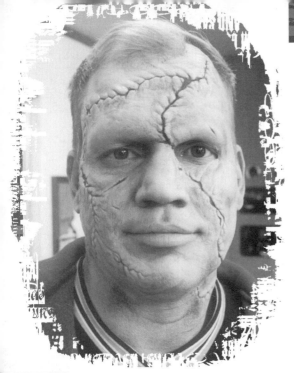

EPISODE: "Some Assembly Required," season two

KEY RELATIONSHIPS: Killed in a rock-climbing accident, Daryl was brought back to life by his younger brother, Chris, and Chris' friend Eric, who then attempted to build Daryl a girlfriend.

UNIQUE ATTRIBUTES: Daryl had been an all-star football player before his death.

MOST MONSTROUS MOMENT: He was willing to have Eric kill Cordelia in order to put her head on the monstrous patchwork woman they were creating as his mate.

CURRENT STATUS: Daryl was inside a building when it burned down, destroying his body and killing him for the second time.

Daryl Epps was a star football player at Sunnydale High before his young life ended tragically in a rock-climbing accident in 1996. A short time later, as revealed in season two's "Some Assembly Required," Daryl was patched together and brought back to life Frankenstein-style by his younger brother, **Chris,** and Chris's friend **Eric Gittleson.** He was a horrid sight, his wounds from the climbing accident and his sickly pallor making him look monstrous.

With his mother in seemingly eternal mourning upstairs (and ignoring Chris), the new Daryl remained hidden away in the basement. His loneliness overwhelmed him, and he begged Chris and Eric to make him a female companion. They went about salvaging parts from recently dead teens, but they found that human brains atrophied when embalmed, so they needed a fresh brain. Very fresh.

> **WILLOW:** "A couple days and [the heads] are useless. They're gonna need something really fresh. Buffy, you don't think they'd…"
> **BUFFY:** "I think anyone who cuts dead girls into pieces does not get the benefit of any doubt." —**"SOME ASSEMBLY REQUIRED"**

Eric was willing to kill to get it, but Chris did not want to be a murderer. Eric showed photos of several girls from school to Daryl, and he chose Cordelia Chase, whom he had dated when he was still alive.

At first Buffy and the others had no idea Daryl had been brought back to life. The stolen cadavers were found with parts missing and expertly cut away, but nobody knew why. Buffy, Willow, Xander, and Giles determined that only a few Sunnydale students would be well versed enough in physiology to make those cuts, and they searched the lockers of those few. In Chris Epps' locker, they found anatomy books, and in Eric's, an image of a patchwork woman pasted together from cut-up bits of different photos. It was then that they realized the two were intending to "build" a woman.

Only when she confronted Chris did Buffy realize that Daryl had already been brought back from the dead. Eric abducted Cordelia, and he and Daryl planned to kill her and attach her head to the female body they were building. When Buffy intervened, disrupting their experiments in the school's old science building and saving Cordelia, a fire broke out. Rather than leave his partially constructed mate to burn alone, Daryl went into the flames after it and was also destroyed in the blaze. It must be presumed that Chris and Eric faced some charges in relation to the grave robbing, and that Eric may have faced charges for assaulting and abducting Cordelia.

AMPATA GUTIERREZ, AKA INCA MUMMY GIRL

GILES: "These are definitely boys' clothes. Why would a girl pack these?"
BUFFY: "How about this one. What kind of girl travels with a mummified corpse…and doesn't even pack lipstick?"
—"INCA MUMMY GIRL"

EPISODE: "Inca Mummy Girl," season two

KEY RELATIONSHIPS: Ampata was romantically involved with Xander. While in Sunnydale, she lived with Joyce and Buffy Summers.

UNIQUE ATTRIBUTES: She was a five-hundred-year-old mummy who was able to appear young by sucking the life force from living humans.

MOST MONSTROUS MOMENT: She was willing to kill Xander, whom she professed to love, in order to live.

CURRENT STATUS: Buffy destroyed Ampata at the end of "Inca Mummy Girl."

In season two's "Inca Mummy Girl," Buffy and her friends went on a field trip to the local museum. There, a Sunnydale High School student named **Rodney Munson** ventured a bit too close to an oddly well-preserved Incan mummy. When he tried to steal a valuable-looking ancient seal from her withered hands, the mummy came to life and killed Rodney, sucking the life from him. The seal had been keeping her in

that state for five hundred years, but now that she had absorbed his life force, she appeared to be a beautiful young woman.

Research revealed that half a millennium earlier, the Incan girl was sacrificed to the gods. Now she woke up in Southern California. On the run, the mummy came upon a foreign exchange student named **Ampata Gutierrez** at the Sunnydale bus terminal, killed him, and took his place. Coincidentally, Ampata was to stay at Buffy's house during the exchange period.

Ampata continued her masquerade, attending Sunnydale High in the place of the dead exchange student whose name she had stolen. She was taken aback when Giles—who was investigating Rodney's disappearance—asked her to translate what had been written on the seal that had once kept her trapped. She purposely translated it incorrectly, telling Giles that she thought it implied that an image on the seal represented the mummy's bodyguard, though it really was the image of a guard who was supposed to prevent her from ever coming back to life.

Xander was immediately attracted to Ampata, and offered to show her around the school. The two grew fond of each other, and he asked her to attend a dance celebrating world cultures with him. She agreed.

During that time she was pursued by a member of the same sect that had sacrificed her five hundred years before. He was there to stop her from killing and to force her to return to her mummified state. She sucked the life from him just as she had from Rodney Munson.

While the others were at the world culture dance, Giles and Buffy heard about the mummified guard and realized that Ampata had translated incorrectly. They wondered if she had done so on purpose and investigated her belongings at Buffy's. In the trunks there they found the "boy clothes" belonging to the *real* Ampata, and his corpse as well.

At the dance, the mummy was beginning to wither again and needed to suck someone's life force to stay alive and young. She did not

want to kill Xander and so instead drew another Sunnydale student, **Jonathan Levenson,** backstage with her. Pretending she wanted to kiss him, she was about to suck his life out when Xander interrupted. Ampata fled to the museum. When Buffy, Xander, and the others caught up to her, Ampata attacked Willow. Xander told her that if she was going to "kiss" anyone, it should be him. He forced her to choose between killing him and dying herself. Though she had come to care for him greatly, she chose to attack him and try to suck his life force. Buffy intervened in the nick of time. The Slayer kicked the withering mummy across the room. Already quite desiccated, she exploded in a cloud of dust.

Buffy felt a great deal of kinship with this tragic soul, someone else who was chosen by her people for a job she did not want, but she was not about to allow that empathy to endanger her friends.

THE DEAD MAN'S PARTY

OZ: "I think the dead man's party has moved upstairs."
GILES: "It makes sense. It's the mask in Joyce's bedroom they're after."
CORDELIA: "Mask? They're here to exfoliate?"
                                              —"DEAD MAN'S PARTY"

EPISODE: "Dead Man's Party," season three

KEY RELATIONSHIPS: The zombies in "Dead Man's Party" were brought to life by a mask through which the demon Ovu Mobani could focus its power. Among the resurrected dead was a woman named Pat, a friend of Joyce Summers.

UNIQUE ATTRIBUTES: For some of them, like the zombie cat, the most unique attribute was their smell!

MOST MONSTROUS MOMENT: The zombies killed Pat.

CURRENT STATUS: When Buffy defeated Ovu Mobani, the zombies were destroyed.

In the second episode of season three, "Dead Man's Party," Joyce Summers brought home from her gallery a Nigerian tribal mask she believed was nothing more than primitive art. Actually, however, it held the power of a zombie demon called **Ovu Mobani** ("the evil eye"). Its power resurrected an entire army of deceased, shambling, decaying Sunnydale residents. The first of the zombies to come to Buffy's attention, mainly due to its smell (and in an apparent nod to Stephen King's *Pet Sematary*) was a dead cat that ran into the Summerses' home when the door was opened. The mask was acting as a beacon, drawing the

dead to it. If one of them should put on the mask, it would become the living embodiment of Ovu Mobani, and the demon would walk the earth.

In the midst of Buffy's welcome home party (after she had run away to Los Angeles at the end of the previous season), zombies crashed into the house, killing anyone they could, including Joyce Summers's friend **Pat.** As chaos ensued, Pat came back to life, made her way to Joyce's bedroom, and donned the mask, becoming Ovu Mobani. The demon (in Pat's body) could shoot paralyzing rays from its eyes.

Buffy battled Ovu Mobani, and Giles informed her that to defeat it she had to destroy its eyes. The Slayer drove a garden spade into the zombie-demon's eyes, and Pat was vaporized in a flash of burning light, as were the other zombies that had been raised.

The mask was absorbed into the earth, and that was that for the undead legions of Ovu Mobani.

For now.

JACK O'TOOLE AND FRIENDS

GILES: "What are you doing here?"
XANDER: "We've been raising...some heck. Listen, if you guys need help—"
GILES: "Thank you, but the best thing you can do right now is keep yourself out of trouble."
XANDER: "Not much chance of that..."
    GILES: "There's something different about this menace. In the air, I can feel it. The stench of death."
    XANDER: "I think that's Bob."   **—"THE ZEPPO"**

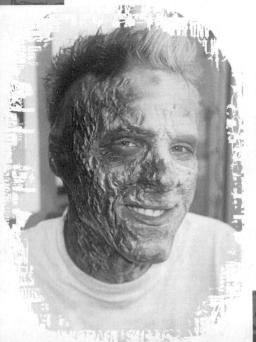

EPISODE: "The Zeppo," season three

KEY RELATIONSHIPS: Jack, Dickie, Parker, and Bob were best buds.

UNIQUE ATTRIBUTES: Unlike the shambling zombies of "Dead Man's Party," these guys retained their memories and personalities. Apparently a different kind of magic was at work here.

MOST MONSTROUS MOMENT: They tried to blow up Sunnydale High (and they watch *Walker, Texas Ranger*).

CURRENT STATUS: They were all killed (again) by the end of "The Zeppo," each in a different way.

"The Zeppo" focused on Xander Harris, who was concerned that he might be seen as (or might actually *be*) the weak link in the Scooby Gang.

CORDELIA: "It must be hard when all your friends have, like, superpowers. Slayers and werewolves and witches and vampires and you're like this little nothing. You must feel like…like Jimmy Olsen."   —**"THE ZEPPO"**

Attempting to be cooler, he borrowed his uncle's car, changed his attitude, and hooked up with the shallow but attractive **Lysette.** While out with Lysette he had a fender bender with Jack O'Toole, a bullying local guy who was none too pleased (even though the car he was in was one he was in the process of stealing).

Jack threatened Xander and was prepared to beat him bloody (and perhaps even stab him) when a police officer approached them. Xander told the cop nothing was going on, that everything was all right. After the man had left, Jack was impressed that Xander hadn't narced on him, and latched onto him.

Xander, taken aback but also pleased to be befriended by such a tough guy, went along for the ride. Or, rather, drove. Since he had a car at his disposal, Jack made him the "wheel man." Together the two guys and Lysette went to pick up several of Jack's other friends. Those friends, unfortunately, turned out to be dead.

Using a ceremony of dark magic, Jack raised Bob, who had been shot in the head eight months before while robbing a liquor store. (Jack would have raised him earlier, but he had to wait for the stars to align.) Lysette ran away screaming. Second to be raised was Dickie, who appeared to have been burned to death. Finally, there was Parker, who had been thrown off a bridge by a gang called the **Jackals.**

Xander reluctantly drove them around town as they decided what to do first to celebrate their return. He had been afraid to try to leave, but when they broke into a hardware store he knew he had to. The zombie crew decided that Xander felt left out because he was still alive, and they were determined to kill him. It was then that Jack revealed that he himself had been shot in a drive-by three weeks earlier. His "grandpappy" had used dark magic to resurrect him. He had not been dead more than ten minutes before he was brought back to life, which explained why he looked so much more alive than the others and was able to pretend that he was still alive, even going to school.

Now that the boys were all back together, they wanted to party, catch up on *Walker, Texas Ranger,* and blow up Sunnydale High School, not necessarily in that order.

Xander knew he had to stop them. Unfortunately, he felt quite distant from Buffy and the others at that point. Throughout the episode it was revealed that another threat had arisen in Sunnydale, something on the apocalyptic level, and that the Hellmouth might open. Though he offered his help, Xander was brushed off by his friends, who

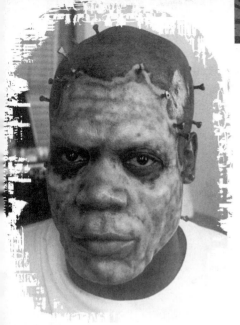

did not seem to need his help or even notice that he was not around. He had said he had plans, after all, and when they saw him with Jack and the other zombies, he had pretended that everything was all right. Obviously everything was not all right. Xander knew they had bigger things to deal with, however, and determined to handle the zombies on his own.

While in the car, Xander grabbed Parker and pulled him part of the way in through the window, then drove away, dragging the zombie with him. He pumped Parker for information, but while asking how he could defuse the bomb (the "cake" they were baking to blow up the school), he drove too close to a street sign and the zombie was decapitated.

In the climax of the episode, while the others fought to keep the demons from the Hellmouth from escaping and the apocalypse from coming, Xander was mere feet away, fighting the zombies who wanted to blow up the school. Bob was crushed by a soda machine that had been toppled by his skirmish with Xander. Dickie was eaten by demons from the Hellmouth. Xander faced off against Jack over the bomb in the boiler room, where he delayed the zombie so that Jack was forced to defuse the bomb himself to avoid being destroyed. Xander left the furious zombie there, but when Jack went to leave, he opened the wrong door. It was a full moon, and Oz had turned into a werewolf. The gang—dealing with the opened Hellmouth in the library—had put him into a room off the boiler room, and when Jack opened the door, Oz (in werewolf form) tore him apart.

ADAM

ADAM: "I am a kinetically redundant, bio-mechanical demonoid. Designed by Maggie Walsh. She called me Adam, and I called her Mother."

DR. ANGLEMAN: "Adam. Maggie would want you to stand down."

ADAM: "Yes. But I seem to have a design flaw."

DR. ANGLEMAN: "Oh God . . ."

ADAM: "In addition to organic material, I'm equipped with GP2D11 infrared detectors, 140 MWS, mirospec 4000 sensors, a harmonic decelerator plus DC serv. . . ."

BUFFY: "She pieced you together out of parts of other demons."

ADAM: "And man. And machine. Which tells me what I am but not who I am. . . ."

—"GOODBYE, IOWA"

FIRST APPEARANCE: "The I in Team," season four

OTHER EPISODES: season four: "Goodbye Iowa," "Who Are You," "Superstar," "New Moon Rising," "The Yoko Factor," and "Primevil"

KEY RELATIONSHIPS: Adam was created by Maggie Walsh, felt a certain kinship with Maggie's protégé Riley Finn, and led a group of demons and vampires in an attack on the Initiative. He also briefly allied himself with Spike.

UNIQUE ATTRIBUTES: Adam was a unique creation, patched together by Maggie Walsh and Dr. Angleman out of various parts of man, demon, and machine. He was powered by a uranium core.

MOST MONSTROUS MOMENT: Adam murdered a small child simply to study human biology.

CURRENT STATUS: Buffy, infused with the energy of her friends, killed Adam in "Primevil."

The Initiative was a federal government operation set up to capture and study supernatural beings, aka Hostile Sub-Terrestrials (or HSTs) in order to find ways to neutralize the threat they represent. However, the program's director, Maggie Walsh, had a second agenda. Along with one of the Initiative's scientists, Dr. Angleman, Maggie worked in room 314 to create a monster of her own.

The word among the monster community in Sunnydale was that horrible things were happening at the Initiative's headquarters, particularly in Room 314. Thanks to comments made by the sorcerer Ethan Rayne, Giles grew suspicious and passed those suspicions on to Buffy. Likewise, Buffy's inquiries made her boyfriend, Initiative agent **Riley Finn,** equally curious. Before they could discover more, however, the recently completed project rose up like many classic monsters in popular culture to destroy its creator. Adam, as he was called, killed Maggie Walsh at the end of the fourth season's "The I in Team." Using the bone spear that he could make jut from his arm—really the arm of a Polgara demon Angleman had given him as part of his work patching together the ultimate monster—he skewered Maggie . . . calling her "Mommy."

In the next episode, "Goodbye Iowa," the newly escaped, cybernetically enhanced Adam made his first non-Initiative kill—a small boy—to learn more about the inner workings of a human being. Buffy and the others believed that Maggie had set the Polgara demon after the Slayer, and it killed the boy instead. They were unaware of the Polgara's death, or of Adam's existence. Dr. Angleman allowed Initiative commandos to believe the Polgara was still alive and had been responsible for Maggie's murder. To find out the truth, Buffy and Xander broke into the Initiative. They came face-to-face with Riley and Dr. Angleman and, eventually, with Adam.

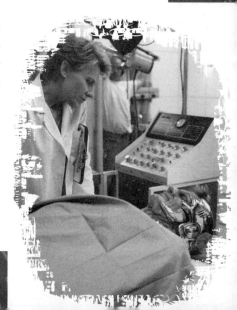

> "I've been thinking . . . about the world. I wanted to see it. Learn it. I saw the inside of that boy, and it was beautiful, but it didn't tell me about the world. It just made me feel. So now I want to know about me. Why I feel. What I am. So I came home."   —ADAM, IN "GOODBYE IOWA"

Adam had broken into the Initiative to get information on himself and many other things. He had bypassed security and come into possession of certain records on disk, which he placed into the hard drive in his chest to scan. When Adam learned that Riley had been drugged, manipulated, and shaped by Maggie, he began to see Riley as a sort of brother to him. Adam revealed that he had discovered what Maggie's long-term plan was. Before he could continue, however, (and before the audience could learn more) the situation grew violent. Adam killed Dr. Angleman, injured Riley, and fought Buffy, giving her a sound beating before escaping.

> **"I could barely fight him. It sounded like Maggie designed him to be the ultimate warrior. He's smart, and fast . . . he gave the commando guys the slip, no problem."**
> —BUFFY, IN "GOODBYE IOWA"

In "This Year's Girl," Buffy and friends were surprised to discover a demon that had been murdered and torn open by Adam.

> **BUFFY:** "He's studying biology. Humans, demons, whatever he can get his hands on and tear apart."
> **WILLOW:** "Learning what makes things work."
> **XANDER:** "I really don't want to be around for the final exam." —"THIS YEAR'S GIRL"

In the following episode, "Who Are You?" Adam not only analyzed the status of vampires in the world, but found that he felt a certain kinship with them and actually befriended several, including **Boone**.

> **ADAM:** "Vampires are a paradox."
> **BOONE:** "Okay, we're a paradox, that's cool . . ."
> **ADAM:** "Demon in a human body. You're a hybrid. Natural and unnatural. You walk in both worlds, and belong to neither. I can relate. Come. We've got a lot to talk about."
> —"WHO ARE YOU"

In that same episode, speaking to Boone and other vampires he had gathered around him, Adam began to explain his grand plan and purpose.

> **ADAM:** "I have been blessed. I have a gift that no man has, no demon has ever had. I know why I'm here. I was created to kill, to extinguish life wherever I find it, and I have accepted that responsibility. You have lived in fear and desperation because you didn't have that gift. But it's time to face your fear."
> **BOONE:** "Tell us what to do."
> **ADAM:** "You are here to be my first. To let them know I'm coming. I am the end of all life, of all magic. I'm the war between man and demon, the war that no one can win."
> —"WHO ARE YOU"

In "Superstar," the episode in which nebbishy Jonathan Levenson performed a spell that made him the best at everything, changing the world in the process, it was revealed that Adam's power source is "a small reservoir of uranium 235." That meant that not only did Adam not need to eat, but that he could go on operating "essentially forever." Also, in order to kill him they would have to destroy him completely. Even decapitation would not kill him. Interestingly, Adam was also the only being fully aware that the world had changed (Buffy sensed it as well, but not so clearly). When speaking with one of his vampire acolytes, **Jape**, he explained why.

> **"I'm aware. I know every molecule of myself and everything around me. No one—no human, no demon has ever been as awake and alive as I am. You're all shadows."**
> **—ADAM, IN "SUPERSTAR"**

In "Where the Wild Things Are," Buffy and Riley fought a vampire and a demon at the opening of the episode, and the two were obviously allied with one another, something very rare.

> **"As a rule, demons have no empathy for species other than their own. In fact, most consider vampires abominations—mixing with human blood and all."**
> **—GILES, IN "WHERE THE WILD THINGS ARE"**

Or, as Buffy put it, "Demons hate vamps. They're like stripes and polka dots. Major clashing." Buffy and Riley suspected that Adam was behind it, and Giles concurred. Even then, however, they had no idea what Adam was planning, what he had determined his purpose to be. In "New Moon Rising," Adam approached Spike (who tried to whale on him and failed) and offered to remove the chip in Spike's head in exchange for Spike's help against the Slayer. He revealed to Spike that he intended to create a race of beings like himself. In order to do that, he commanded his vampire and demon followers to allow themselves to be captured by the Initiative, filling that facility to greater than capacity, a fact Riley noted when the gang discussed the decline in recent demon attacks. When it came time to execute his plan, Adam released all those creatures in the Initiative's holding cells, creating a battle between humans and demons that he hoped would result in lots of both sorts of corpses, which he could use for raw materials. He also resurrected Maggie Walsh, Dr. Angleman, and Forrest (who died in "The Yoko Factor"), utilizing his own technology to help him subdue and control Riley, though they were all later dispatched by Riley. With Spike's help he attempted to separate the Slayer from her friends in "The Yoko Factor," but he failed. After performing a spell that merged the life energy of Giles, Willow, and Xander with her own, Buffy was able to defeat and kill Adam in "Primevil."

definitions

THE WALKING DEAD stand apart from ghosts in that they are corporeal, flesh-and-blood creatures, not specters and apparitions. Technically, vampires in the Buffyverse are also resurrected dead, but they are a unique species because a demon is occupying the body, and thus are traditionally depicted as being far more intelligent, self-aware, and crafty than the generally mindless rank of the walking dead. Vampires, like ghosts, are also characterized by their own particular rules of creation, behavior, and destruction.

As referenced in the following pages, the walking dead are reanimated corpses, zombies, or Frankensteinian creations stitched together from pieces of the dead, wandering skeletons, or living body parts. Unlike ghosts, they are quite real to the touch; in fact, some of them will take a nasty bite out of you if you get too close. Unlike vampires, they do not "live" (unlive?) forever; in most lore, their flesh continues to decay, and eventually there isn't enough tissue left to walk around. Also unlike vampires, they do not drink blood. Depending upon which of the walking dead one is discussing, their dietary requirements are either nonexistent or meatier than the exclusively liquid diet vampires require.

The dead and resurrected dead in mythology

AS H. P. LOVECRAFT NOTED IN HIS ESSAY "Supernatural Horror in Literature," the archetypal tales of the walking dead, "[the] shade which appears and demands the burial of its bones," and others "were taken from the earliest oral sources, and form part of mankind's permanent heritage." The promise and dread inherent in the concept of the resurrected dead is as old as storytelling itself and probably older, stirring in mankind's most primal dreams and nightmares.

In Greek, Roman, Nordic, and other legends, intrepid heroes or forlorn lovers sometimes visited the land of the dead to speak to or attempt to rescue the dearly departed from the cold bowels of the afterworld. In Greek mythology, the souls of the dead left their bodies and thereafter dwelled in the afterworld, later referred to as the underworld. It was believed that the souls of the departed were pale, insubstantial shadows of their former selves, lacking courage or intelligence. Only a select few carried on their afterlives as they had their lives: Minos judged souls after his demise, Orion was still a hunter, and Hercules remained a hero capable of feats of strength and courage, an immortal living forever on Mount Olympus.

The afterworld was more than either a limbo or hell; it was a place of judgment and justice, where Hades (ruler of the underworld) and three sons of Zeus (Aeacus, Minos, and Rhadamanthys) judged all who entered. Thanatos (Death) and Hypnos (Sleep) dwelled there; at the gates stood Cerberus, the multiheaded watchdog. The subterranean rivers Acheron, Lethe, and the Styx flowed through the underworld. To cross the Acheron into the underworld itself, one had to deal with the ferryman, Charon. If the newly arrived dead did not have a gold coin for Charon, they were refused passage and forever damned to wander the deserted shore without refuge. This is where the practice of putting a coin in the mouth of the dead came from.

Still-living Greek heroes sometimes entered the underworld to interact with dead souls; they were vital precursors to the walking dead tales of today. Grief-stricken when his wife, the nymph Eurydice, succumbed to snakebite, Orpheus journeyed into the underworld, soothing Cerberus and eventually charming Hades and Persephone, who allowed him to reclaim Eurydice under the condition he did not look at her during their journey out of the underworld. Before reaching the gates, Orpheus imprudently looked back, and she was forever reclaimed by the realm of the dead. The tragic tale of Orpheus was told and retold in many forms and media, and remains among the most evocative tales of love, longing, and the world of the dead. Jean Cocteau's poetic modern cinematic interpretation, *Orpheus* (1949), redefined the myth for the twentieth century. The lively, inventive, romantic teenage horror/fantasy *Highway to Hell* (1991) retold the tale in bracingly contemporary terms and featured the coolest Cerberus and Charon yet committed to film.

The greatest of all the Greek heroes, Hercules, was ordered to fetch Cerberus from his post at the gates of the underworld as his final labor for his rival Eurytheus, the ruler of Greece.

Mario Bava's colorful *Hercules in the Haunted World* (Woolner Brothers, 1961) sent Hercules and Theseus to Hades to obtain a golden apple necessary to rescue his beloved Dianira, who was under the spell of the evil Lyco (Christopher Lee).

Hercules also journeyed to the kingdom of Hades in an episode of the syndicated cartoon series *The Mighty Hercules* (1963–64), as well as the animated Walt Disney feature *Hercules* (1998, with James Woods voicing Hades), though the ranks of the dead were depicted tastefully or kept off-screen altogether. The most faithful of the numerous comic-book adaptations and revamps was artist Sam Glanzman's pet project, *Hercules*, which yielded thirteen issues and one black-and-white magazine (Charlton Comics, 1967–68). Sam Raimi and Robert Tapert's popular *Hercules: The Legendary Journeys* TV series (1995–present) has occasionally tapped into the Greek myths of the afterworld and the walking dead, as has its popular spin-off series *Xena: The Warrior Princess*.

According to myth, the resurrected dead also threatened the Greek hero Jason during his quest for the Golden Fleece aboard the ship *Argo*.

Building on the lively sword fight between the legendary Arabian hero Sinbad and a living skeleton in his classic fantasy film *The 7th Voyage of Sinbad* (1958), special-effects maestro Ray Harryhausen brought the living-dead warriors to vivid life in his film adaptation of the legend, *Jason and the Argonauts* (1963). Harryhausen's murderous sword-wielding reanimated skeletons made an indelible impression on a generation of young filmgoers, including director Sam Raimi, who affectionately emulated Harryhausen's effects for sequences in the film *Army of Darkness* (1992; see below). Harryhausen's later adaptation of Greek mythology *Clash of the Titans* (1981) sent Perseus (Harry Hamlin) to a faux underworld, paying a skeletal Charon for passage and slaying a stop-motion animated Cerberus.

In Nordic mythology, the underworld was ruled by Hela, one of the three monstrous children sired by the witch Angerboda and the evil Loki, who was forever conspiring against the Norse gods. Hela had the form of a woman, with the appearance of life on one side of her body, while the other

half was that of a corpse. Judged as evil as her parents by Odin the All-Father, Hela was cast forever out of sight of the gods into the underworld of Niflheim, where she assumed power over all nine realms of the underworld from the hall of Elvidnir.

Every world mythology had its vision of the afterlife and its respective realms of the dead and tales of the walking dead. The most renowned of them remains the Egyptian myths, thanks to the still-standing monumental pyramids and the unique burial tradition of mummification, which preserved the bodies of the dead into modern times.

εgyptian cults of the Dead and Mummies

THE EGYPTIAN CULTURE remains a testimonial to the pervasive human hunger for eternal life, and the worship of the dead and life after death. The pharoahs of Egypt were honored by burial within the vast subterranean chambers of the pyramids, where their bodies were embalmed, wrapped in bandages, steeped in preservative chemical baths, and interred in nearly airtight sarcophagi.

The discovery of these remarkably preserved ancient monarchs captured the imagination of the public throughout the Victorian era, yielding at least two genre landmarks, Jane Webb's novel *The Mummy* (1827) and Theophile Gautier's short story "The Mummy's Foot" (aka "Princess Hermonthis," 1840). In America, Edgar Allan Poe crafted the satirical "Some Words with a Mummy" (1845) parodying the craze for all things Egyptian with his droll tale of a revived mummy who criticizes the modern world.

Sir Arthur Conan Doyle's short story "The Ring of Thoth" (1890) portrayed a man's obsession with transcending life and death to be reunited with "his" mummified Egyptian princess, Atma. Doyle's "Lot No. 249" (1892) was adapted almost a century later for British television's *Conan Doyle* (1967) and updated for the anthology feature *Tales from the Darkside: The Movie* (1990).

Bram Stoker's novel *The Jewel of the Seven Stars* (1903) further popularized the combination of reincarnation and mummies with its elaborate tale of a five-thousand-year-old Egyptian queen resurrected in turn-of-the-century London through the occult power of a jewel. Stoker's novel was adapted to film three times, faithfully in director Seth Holt's final feature, *Blood from the Mummy's Tomb* (1971), and less so in the gory Charlton Heston vehicle *The Awakening* (1980) and the direct-to-video *Bram Stoker's The Mummy* (1998).

The first living mummies of the cinema appeared in Georges Méliès' *Robbing Cleopatra's Tomb* (1899) and the playful short film *The Monster* (1903). Walter Booth's *The Haunted Curiosity Shop* (1902) was a similar fantasy drawn in part from Gautier's "The Mummy's Foot."

The first proper mummy movie was Gerard Bourgeois's *La Momie du Roi* (aka *The Mummy of the King of Ramsee*, 1909), also produced in France. Edwin Thanhouser's *The Mummy* (1911) followed, along with *When Soul Meets Soul* (1912), *The Vengeance of Egypt* (1912), *The Egyptian Mummy* (1913), *The Undying Flame* (1917), and Ernst Lubitsch's *The Eyes of the Mummy* (1918). Burton Stevenson's novel *A King in Babylon* (1917) based its romantic horror tale of mummies and reincarnation in a film being shot in Egypt, during which the actors were overwhelmed by memories of shared pasts and prior lives.

The publicity attending Howard Carter's 1922 discovery of the 3,300-year-old tomb of the child-king Tutankhamun and his royal treasures sent shock waves around the globe. Out of those discoveries arose tales of ancient curses awaiting those who desecrated such sacred monuments and graves, and the unique horror archetype of the walking-dead mummy, reawakened to protect or seek revenge.

Belief in the curse of the mummy's tomb was rooted in a real event: The sponsor of the King Tutankhamun expedition, Lord Carnarvon, succumbed to an insect bite in April 1923, months after the opening of Tut's tomb. According to some reports, the cause of Carnarvon's death was never detected. The press seized on this event, exaggerating its import to eventually report the death of twenty-two others participating in the expedition prior to 1929. Other sources maintain those were false reports; many of the expedition members did live well into the 1960s.

The furor provided the premise of many a horror film thereafter. One of the reporters covering the news was John L. Balderston, who subsequently wrote for theater and film, including the screenplay of the definitive "pharoah's curse" film, *The Mummy* (1932; see below). Other authors could not wait to capitalize on "Tutmania" and the purported curse. Sax Rohmer rushed his play *Secret Egypt* to the stage in 1923 and his novel *Brood of the Witch Queen* to the publishers (1924), beating Agatha Christie to the punch with her play *Akhnaton* and the Hercule Poirot story "The Adventure of the Egyptian Tomb" (1924), concerning a false curse.

Karl Freund's motion picture *The Mummy* (Universal, 1932) remains the classic of the form, a somber, hypnotic horror film derived from Conan Doyle's "The Ring of Thoth." Boris Karloff endured one of Jack Pierce's most painstaking makeup jobs (eight hours per session) to star as Im-Ho-Tep, the titular fiend who rose from his sarcophagus as a foolish archaeologist read aloud from the life-giving Scroll of Thoth.

Karloff briefly returned to his native England to play another crazed Egyptologist seeking eternal life at any cost in *The Ghoul* (1933), considered a "lost film" until the discovery of a tattered print in the early 1970s. Karloff's likeness remains the primary one associated with the Universal Monster *Mummy* merchandise, as reflected by the 1998 U.S. postage stamps featuring the classic monsters.

The Mummy's Hand (1940) was the first and liveliest of what quickly became a profitable low-budget series for Universal. *The Mummy's Hand* featured cowboy star Tom Tyler (in his only horror role) as the Egyptian Prince Kharis, who lost his tongue and was mummified alive for the crime of stealing sacred tana leaves to resurrect his deceased love Princess Ananka.

Lon Chaney Jr. appeared as Kharis in *The Mummy's Tomb* (1942). After a little over an hour of mayhem, Kharis was torched, only to return in *The Mummy's Ghost* (1943). In *Ghost*, Kharis got the girl, sinking into quicksand during the climax with his aging princess firmly in his arms.

Their bodies were fished out of the Louisiana bayous (!) in *The Mummy's Curse* (1944), allowing the resurrected Ananka to regain her youth, only to wizen again moments before Kharis pulled a monastery ceiling down on their heads one last time.

The horror pulp magazines took the theme seriously, publishing many tales of reanimated mummies and Egyptian occultism. Prominent among them were Robert Bloch's "The Eyes of the Mummy" (1938), Tartleton Fiske's "Beetles" (1938), Donald A. Wollheim's "Bones" (1940), and Seabury Quinn's "The Man in Crescent Terrace" (1946).

In the late 1940s and the early 1950s, four-color mummies stalked through garishly colored pulp pages of titles like *The Beyond, The Unseen, Chamber of Chills*, and many others. The host of *Beware Terror Tales* (Fawcett, 1952–53) was a mummy as well.

The most amusing of all the pre-Code comic mummy stories emerged from the esteemed EC line: the story "Lower Berth!" from *Tales from the Crypt* #33 (1952), in which a circus freak-show attraction, Myrna the Mummy, became a mommy after falling in love with Enoch, the pickled two-headed man in the sideshow. Their hideous squalling offspring grew up to be the EC Comics host, the CryptKeeper!

Drive-in and grindhouse screens offered fresh venues for the theme. The low-budget *Pharoah's Curse* (1957) ballyhooed "A Blood-Lusting Mummy that Kills for a Cat Goddess!" A petrified victim of Pompeii's volcanic cataclysm came to life in another drive-in variation on the mummy theme in *Curse of the Faceless Man* (1958).

Even better was Hammer Films' *The Mummy* (1959), starring Christopher Lee as a rather athletic Kharis on a search-and-destroy mission against the desecrators of the tombs. Hammer later produced *The Curse of the Mummy's Tomb* (1964) and *The Mummy's Shroud* (1967), reshuffling elements of the formula. Best of all was the previously noted *Blood from the Mummy's Tomb* (1971), a disjointed (due to the death of director Seth Holt during production) but effective adaptation of Stoker's *Jewel of the Seven Stars*.

In 1962 the unexpected success of the Aurora Monster Model kits prompted Dell Comics to license the Universal Monsters for a series of one-shot comics. Dell's *The Mummy* featured a mummy that looked like Kharis but shot death rays from his good eye. Aurora later sold a drag-racing Kharis model, the Mummy's Chariot.

Starved Egyptologists had to satisfy themselves on the small screen with Lon Chaney Jr.'s brief mummy appearance on the *Route 66* episode "Lizard's Leg and Owlet's Wing." Best was Curtis Harrington's made-for-TV chiller *The Cat Creature* (1973; see Primals), a cat-woman tale with Egyptian occult themes and a memorable conclusion in which the femme-feline mummy was attacked and reduced to rags by a roomful of housecats.

Meanwhile, publisher James Warren and editor Forrest J. Ackerman began including short black-and-white horror comics in the pages of *Famous Monsters of Filmland*'s companion title, *Monster World* (1964–66), including adaptations of Universal's *The Mummy* and *The Mummy's Hand*. The success of these led Warren to launch all-comics horror 'zines *Creepy, Eerie*, and *Vampirella*.

As noted previously, underground cartoonists rose to prominence later in the decade. Jack Jackson's "The Intruder" in the underground horror comix title *Skull* #1 (1970) remains one of the most chilling mummy stories ever presented in the comics medium. Comix artist Richard Corben brought his distinctive art and flair for horror-comedy to the genre in his full-color story "Terror Tomb" for Warren's *Creepy* #61 (April 1974), in which the despoilers of the tomb of Khartuka were punished in an unusual manner.

Unfettered at last by revisions to the Comics Code, which permitted horror comics to return to the newsstand, Marvel Comics followed suit with a far more straightforward reinterpretation of the mummy menace for the Living Mummy in *Supernatural Thrillers* #7–15 (1974–75).

On the big screen, mummies figured in *The Curse of the Jackal* (1969) and *The Spanish Assignment Terror* (aka *Dracula vs. Frankenstein*, 1969). Beefy horror star Paul Naschy later played the burliest mummy in movies in *The Mummy's Revenge* (1973).

The eruption of the Italian zombie "gore" films in the wake of the international success of George Romero's *Dawn of the Dead* (1979; see below) inevitably rubbed off on the mummy genre. The American-Italian co-production *Dawn of the Mummy* (1981) stuck to the traditional by-the-numbers formula with a few notable alterations like graphic disembowelment close-ups.

Fred Dekker's lively *The Monster Squad* (1987) warmly paid homage to Universal-style monsters, including a lethal but convincingly fragile mummy (Michael MacKay). The fact that the film failed to find its target audience indicated how distant the "famous monsters," including Dracula, Frankenstein's monster, and the Creature from the Black Lagoon, had become.

Literary horror had not completely abandoned the archetype, however. Edward D. Hoch's "The Weekend Magus" (1980) offered an original tall-tabloid-tale of a mummy and a mummified Scottish sea serpent, spun with wry wit. Novelist John Curlovich, writing as Michael Paine, penned a wonderfully eerie entry into the subgenre with 1988's *Cities of the Dead*. Anne Rice's novel *The Mummy, or Ramses the Damned* (1989) sought to reinvigorate the archetype with Rice's steamy blend of horror, history, and eroticism.

The 1990s closed with a surprising revival, spearheaded by Universal Studio's own remake, *The Mummy* (1999). Writer-director Stephen Sommers (*Rudyard Kipling's The Jungle Book*, 1994; *Deep Rising,* 1998) revamped elements of Universal's Im-Ho-Tep and Kharis films into a lively comedy-adventure. This Imhotep (Arnold Vosloo) was depicted as an almost elemental being capable of manifesting himself out of sand. Owing as much to the action serials and popular Indiana Jones films (and featuring its own reckless adventurer played by Brendan Fraser) as any mummy film or tale, Sommers's *The Mummy* was essentially a horror movie for audiences frightened of real horror movies. Clearly, the director judged the tenor of his target audience correctly, for *The Mummy* scored big at the box office and on video; a sequel is currently in the works.

Australian director Russell Mulcahy (of *Highlander* fame) directed the original *Tale of the Mummy* (aka *Talos the Mummy*, 1999), but the most original variation on the theme was Michael Almereyda's *The Eternal* (1999), featuring the mummified remains of a two-thousand-year-old Irish druid witch tended by Christopher Walken. *The Eternal*'s mummy was drawn from the famed "bog people," whose bodies were remarkably preserved for thousands of years by the odd composition of the Irish bogs.

science and resurrection: frankenstein and body parts

NO SINGLE "MONSTER" ARCHETYPE has been as popular, pervasive, and relevant to real-life science as the one commonly—and wrongly—referred to by its fictional creator's name. Frankenstein was the name of the doctor, not the monster, and they both owed their conception to an imaginative teenage girl named Mary Wollstonecraft Godwin Shelley (1797–1851).

History notes that *Frankenstein* the novel was conceived by Shelley one June evening in 1816 on the shores of Lake Geneva, Switzerland. In the company of Mary's half-sister Claire Clairemont, Mary's companion British poet Percy Bysshe Shelley, and their neighbors Lord Byron and Dr. John Polidori (see Vampires), it was decided that an interesting way to pass the time might be for each of them to write a Gothic tale.

"It was a dark and stormy night," as the time-honored line goes, when Mary found herself unable to sleep, overwhelmed by visions of a "pale student of unhallowed arts kneeling beside the thing he had put together" (quoted from Shelley's introduction to the 1831 edition of her novel). Seized by the ramifications of her vision, and the inherent blasphemy of "any human endeavor to mock the stupendous mechanism of the Creator of the world" (again quoting Shelley's intro), she wrote the first draft of *Frankenstein, or The Modern Prometheus* (the subtitle was a reference to the mythical Prometheus, whom the gods had punished for bringing man the gift of fire).

Mary expanded her effort, and it was published sans her name in 1818. The novel was a success, and Shelley proudly signed her name to all subsequent editions. The events surrounding the conception of the novel alone have yielded speculative short stories, novels, and at least three films to date (Ken Russell's *Gothic*, 1986; Ivan Passer's *Haunted Summer*, 1988; and *Rowing with the Wind*, 1988). Shelley also appeared as a character in the opening of *The Bride of Frankenstein* (1935), played by Elsa Lanchester, and in Roger Corman's adaptation of Brian Aldiss's 1975 novel *Frankenstein Unbound* (1990), portrayed by Bridget Fonda.

The most obvious and oft-cited precursor to Frankenstein was the Jewish folk legend of the golem, a clay man brought to life by Rabbi Judah Loew ben Bezalel to save the Jews of the Prague ghetto from persecution and banishment. Though the golem was not a resurrected dead being per se, it remains the primary influence on the Frankenstein tale, and attention must be given to this venerable archetype. The golem was animated using magical runes carved into the giant's forehead or, in other versions of the legend, into a Star of David worn by the clay being. The creature saved the village and went on a rampage until the mystic runes were scraped from his brow (or the star was pulled from his neck).

Gustav Meyrink's novel *Der Golem* (1914) was just one of many transcriptions of the legend. The golem became the first classic movie monster, thanks to a trio of German silent versions of the legend, all starring Paul Wegener, as the clay giant, and his wife Lyda Salmonova. They are *Der Golem* (1914), *Der Golem un die Tanzerin* (1917), and the definitive screen version, *Der Golem* (1920), which had a profound impact on all horror films that followed, including Universal's entire Frankenstein series. The giant's rampage was stopped by the innocent intervention of a little girl who pulls the mystic amulet from the golem's neck. The image of a giant brought to his knees by a little girl would resonate throughout the genre. The golem subsequently appeared in many short stories, novels, comic books, films, and television shows, most recently in the *X-Files* episode "Kaddish" (1997).

Less than five years after the original publication of Shelley's *Frankenstein,* there were five London stage productions playing to audiences. *Presumption! Or, the Fate of Frankenstein* (1823) was the most successful. *Frankenstein* quickly established a new genre of fiction as well, with honorable entries from authors like Ambrose Bierce ("Moxon's Master," 1893) and others.

Frankenstein was first adapted to film by the Thomas Edison Film Company in 1910. The first feature-length adaptation was *Life Without Soul* (1915), starring British stage actor Percy Darrell Standing as the monster, followed by an Italian adaptation starring producer Umberto Guarracino as *Il Mostro di Frankenstein* (1920).

Throughout the silent era, variations on the theme thrived. Georges Méliès founded the odd but still popular "animated body parts" subgenre in shorts, including *The Phrenologist and the Lively Skull* (1901) and the celebrated *The Man with the Rubber Head* (1902, in which Méliès himself played a scientist inflating and deflating a chattering duplicate of his own head until it burst).

The science fiction, horror, and mystery pulps brimmed over with tales of Frankenstein-like experiments and monsters. H. P. Lovecraft's serialized succession of six Herbert West: Re-Animator stories (1921–22) were among his first published works, and were the source for the most faithful of all Lovecraft film adaptations, director Stuart Gordon's debut "splatter" masterpiece *Re-Animator* (1985). Lovecraft's pen pal Clark Ashton Smith outdid his mentor's gory tale with "The Colossus of Ylourgne," in which multiple corpses were distilled into a titanic undead being that goes on a rampage.

Director James Whale's *Frankenstein* (1931) was a major hit, salvaging Universal's sagging fortunes, making Boris Karloff a star, and ensuring makeup master Jack Pierce's version of Frankenstein's monster as the definitive version of the creature in the public imagination. It was the enduring popularity of Whale's *Frankenstein* that led to the popular mistake of assigning the scientist's name to the monster. Whale, Karloff, and Pierce's vision of the Frankenstein monster—with his squared-off skull, scars, heavy-lidded eyes, and electricity-conducting "bolts" jutting from his neck—became one of the genre's greatest icons, populating countless ads, animated cartoons, storybooks, comic books, TV shows, movies, and cereal.

Universal produced a popular series of films featuring their version of the monster. Jack Pierce stayed on board for the bulk of the series, but James Whale helmed only the first sequel, *The Bride of Frankenstein* (1935), which didn't match its predecessor's box-office success but went on to be revered as one of the greatest horror films ever made. In the 1990s, the film's enduring legacy and that of its eccentric director were immortalized in a number of biographies, biographical novels like Christopher Bram's *Father of Frankenstein* (1995), and Bill Condon's biographical film *Gods and Monsters* (1998).

Karloff wore the monster's makeup for one more film, the stylish *Son of Frankenstein* (1939), before abandoning the role. "There was not much left in the monster to be developed," Karloff later admitted. Universal felt otherwise, headlining the monster in an ever-waning series. The initial entries, *The Ghost of Frankenstein* (1941) and *Frankenstein Meets the Wolfman* (1943; see Primals), were ingenious and entertaining enough sequels.

The monster (Glenn Strange) suffered diminishing roles in the more-is-less monsterfests *The House of Frankenstein* (1944), *The House of Dracula* (1945), and the satiric *Abbott and Costello Meet Frankenstein* (1948). For all intents and purposes, the Universal Frankenstein's monster was dead.

Comic books plastered Frankenstein's monster and pastiches of his likeness across their covers and pages whenever possible. The first monster comic-book series was Dick Briefer's *Frankenstein*, which began as a feature in *Prize Comics* (in most issues from #7–68, Prize Publications, 1941–48). *Classics Illustrated* debuted their faithful adaptation of *Frankenstein* in December 1945 and kept it in print (with revised and improved cover illustrations) well into the 1970s. Frankenstein-like mad scientists and monsters were frequent villains in superhero comics, including "The True Story of Frankenstein" Batman and Robin adventure in *Detective Comics* #135 (1948). Frankenstein's monster was a frequent guest star in every horror comic book publisher's lineup. Marvel Comics' early

incarnation, Atlas, published more Frankenstein's monster comic stories than any other comics company, beginning with Captain America's confrontation with "The Curse of Frankenstein" in *USA Comics* #13 (1944).

EC got in on the act with "Monster Maker" (*The Haunt of Fear* #17, 1950), illustrated by "Ghastly" Graham Ingles, who drew EC's first true Frankenstein's monster tale "The Monster in the Ice" (*The Vault of Horror* #22, 1951). Ingles also illustrated EC's final Frankenstein story, "Ashes to Ashes" (*The Vault of Horror* #40, 1954), in which Frankenstein's descendants nurtured a perfect embryonic female being from generation to generation.

In 1952 Lon Chaney Jr. played the monster in a live-broadcast adaptation of Shelley's novel on the science-fiction series *Tales of Tomorrow* (ABC). The prior year, Chaney had appeared as the monster on *The Colgate Comedy Hour with Abbott and Costello*.

Bela Lugosi spouted now-immortal dialogue by Alex Gordon and director Ed Wood Jr. while trying to create yet another master race in *Bride of the Monster* (1954). Boris Karloff played both scientist and (in a single close-up) his own creation in the bizarre atomic-age artifact *Frankenstein 1970* (1958), which was also the first CinemaScope Frankenstein feature.

With teenagers the primary audience for most of the era's horror films, it should come as no surprise that teen Frankenstein's monsters soon followed. Herman Cohen's follow-up to his wildly successful *I Was a Teenage Werewolf* (1957, see Primals) was, naturally, *I Was a Teenage Frankenstein* (1957).

Britain's Hammer Films studio spun profits from surprise hits like *The Quatermass Experiment* (1955) into their most ambitious production to date, the first color, feature-length adaptation of Shelley's novel, under the title *The Curse of Frankenstein* (1957). With Universal's trademarked version of Frankenstein's monster under strict legal protection, screenplay writer Jimmy Sangster and director Terence Fisher brought their focus back to Dr. Frankenstein himself (played by Peter Cushing), and maintained that focus throughout the next decade and a half.

The movie broke international box-office records and heralded a bloody new breed of horror. Peter Cushing's cool, calm, almost reptilian Dr. Frankenstein added an utterly modern amoral tone to the proceedings that was sustained throughout Hammer's subsequent Frankenstein films, creating a remarkable series that coincidentally charted the waxing and waning of the studio, director Fisher, and star Cushing. The series included *The Revenge of Frankenstein* (1958) and *The Evil of Frankenstein* (1964), but the presence of the Universal prototype—now legally accessible to Hammer—hardly made up for the lost ground. Fortunately, Cushing was still on board. Terence Fisher was brought back to direct *Frankenstein Created Woman* (1966). *Frankenstein Must Be Destroyed* (1969) pushed Cushing's role to fiendish new extremes. Cushing appeared in a cameo as the doctor in the Sammy Davis Jr.–Peter Lawford vehicle *One More Time* (1970) before rejoining Terence Fisher for their last hurrah, *Frankenstein and the Monster from Hell* (1973).

Kids were a prime target for Frankenstein merchandise during the 1960s monster boom. Aurora launched their popular line of monster model kits with a black plastic replica of Frankenstein's monster striding over a grave, suitable for painting, and they later offered the outsize, moveable Big Frankie. Frankenstein Soaky toys made the monster a perfect bath companion, and Frankenberry breakfast cereal made the monster the perfect way to start the day.

Gold Key Comics published *The Little Monsters* (1964–78), featuring an entire cartoon Frankenstein monster-like family who were popular enough to warrant coloring books and other merchandising items. Hal Seegar's *Milton the Monster* (1966) was a kindly cartoon Frankenstein's monster, and Hanna-Barbera's Saturday morning lineup included *Frankenstein Jr. and The Impossibles* (1966–67). Rankin-Bass's theatrical stop-motion animation feature *Mad Monster Party?* (1966) featured parodies of the classic monsters designed by EC and *Mad* artist extraordinaire Jack Davis, whose remarkable "Six-Foot Frankenstein" poster adorned many a bedroom wall in that era.

Universal was already trading on its venerable Frankenstein's monster trademark with Fred Gwynne's loveable Herman Munster, patriarch of prime-time TV's *The Munsters* (1964–66) and the cinematic spin-off feature, *Munster, Go Home!* (1966).

Dell Comics' line of licensed Universal Monsters comics started with *Frankenstein* (1962), a crude update set in contemporary America. Warren's black-and-white horror comic magazines *Creepy* and *Eerie* published numerous Frankenstein-inspired stories, including the EC-like birth of horror host Uncle Creepy himself in "Monster Rally!" (*Creepy* #4, 1966).

The monster appeared in Marvel's *The X-Men* #14 (1968) and *The Silver Surfer* #7 (1969) and arguably provided visual inspiration for *The Incredible Hulk* (see Primals).

The Beatles' animated feature *Yellow Submarine* (1968) featured a Frankenstein cartoon cameo, and Ringo Starr played second fiddle to Harry Nilsson and Freddie Jones's Baron Frankenstein in the murky rock musical *Son of Dracula* (1973).

The most celebrated countercultural Frankenstein spin-off was Richard O'Brien's crafty stage musical *The Rocky Horror Picture Show*, which was filmed in 1975 and went on to become a midnight movie phenomenon, turbocharged by Tim Curry's "sweet transvestite" Dr. Frank N. Furter. Jim Sharmon, the Australian director of the cult film, made only one other Frankensteinian feature, *Summer of Secrets* (1976), starring the remarkable Arthur Dignam as a scientist who resurrects his dead wife with brain surgery.

The square-afroed *Blackenstein* (1972) was the first Vietnam vet monster (Joe DeSue), gnawing on its female victims' vitals until L.A.P.D. canines tore him to pieces. The liberated *Lady Frankenstein* (1972) wanted to bed down with her monster.

The exquisite Spanish drama *The Spirit of the Beehive* (1973) offered a moving, marvelous meditation on the theme with its delicate fantasy about a Castillian child (Ana Torrent) whose life was forever changed after she sees a local showing of James Whale's *Frankenstein*, exploring the very real power of the film that sparked so many dire imitations.

There were numerous Frankenstein parodies, too. The best of these was undoubtedly Mel Brooks' inspired *Young Frankenstein* (1974), a loving homage to and send-up of the classic Universal horrors co-scripted by his star Gene Wilder, with co-star Peter Boyle (of TV's *Everybody Loves Raymond*) as the monster.

TV produced a number of worthwhile *Frankenstein* adaptations, starting with the British Thames Television version (1968) scripted by Robert Muller and starring Ian Holm as both creator and creation. Christopher Isherwood's compelling (if mistitled) *Frankenstein: The True Story* (NBC, 1973) was a lavish two-part production rivaling the best of the cinematic adaptations. Other TV Frankensteins included *The Henderson Monster* (1980) and Robert Vaughn as *Doctor Franken* (1980).

With the 1970 relaxing of the Comics Code specifying Shelley's novel as a model of the new decorum, DC Comics briefly indulged writer Marv Wolfman and artist Michael Kaluta's backup series "The Spawn of Frankenstein" in *The Phantom Stranger* #23–30. Mike Ploog beautifully illustrated "The Brain of Frankenstein" in Warren's *Eerie* #40 (1972), the warm-up for Ploog's striking run on Marvel Comics' *The Monster of Frankenstein* #1–6 (1973). The series continued with John Buscema's art as *The Frankenstein Monster* for another dozen issues (1973-75). Marvel added the monster to the inevitable team-up *The Legion of Monsters* (one-shot black-and-white magazine, 1975) and published their own Mary Shelley adaptation in *Marvel Classics Comics* #20 (1977).

Science-fiction writers took up the challenge and crafted far more compelling variations on Shelley's creation. Harry Harrison's "At Last, the True Story of Frankenstein" (1965) played on the hucksterism explicit in the countless Frankenstein rip-offs with his tale of a descendant of Frankenstein eking out a living with the sideshow exhibition of the monster. Science-fiction author and historian Brian Aldiss, who declared Shelley's novel the first true work of science fiction, crafted a fresh, inventive reevaluation of the mythos in his expansive novel *Frankenstein Unbound* (1975), which thrust creator and monster into a speculative future. Roger Corman produced and directed an uneven film version in 1990.

Clive Barker and the Dog Company brought their own revisionist *Frankenstein in Love; Or, The Life of Death* (1982) to the stage, directed by Malcolm Edwards.

Legitimacy and ambition were the bane of more recent attempts to create the "definitive" Frankenstein in any given media. One of the most infamous and expensive Broadway botches was the 1981 stage production of *Frankenstein*, which was only performed once before folding. Franc Roddam's film *The Bride* (1985) was undone by weaker elements.

There were two more made-for-TV stabs at "definitive" adaptations, the 1984 British TV version starring Robert Powell and David Warner as Frankenstein and his monster and writer-director David Wickes' 1993 version with Patrick Bergin and Randy Quaid in the respective roles. Kenneth Branagh's *Mary Shelley's Frankenstein* (1994) aimed high and offered a top-drawer cast led by Robert De Niro's memorable monster, but was seriously compromised by the screenplay's omission of key story points.

Action movies embraced Frankensteinian science in *Silent Rage* (1982), *The Vindicator* (1984), *Class of 1999* (1990), and *Universal Soldier* (1992, plus three sequels, 1998–99). Marvel Comics anticipated the trend with their own futuristic variation on the theme, "Deathlok the Demolisher." Introduced in *Astonishing Tales* #25, (1974), Deathlok starred in two self-titled, failed monthly series in the 1990s.

The definitive pop-cultural icon for this science fiction variation was Paul Verhoeven's *RoboCop* (1987), which built upon the streamlined model of James Cameron's *The Terminator* (1984) and spawned two less-successful sequels, a TV series, a cartoon show, and a line of action figures.

In the wake of such wall-to-wall carpets of action and violence, the resurrection of the dead and construction of artificial humans seemed old hat, as demonstrated by harmless diversions like Ivan Passer's *Creator* (1985), Simon Wincer's *D.A.R.Y.L.* (1985), and teen deviations like John Hughes's *Weird Science* (1985), Wes Craven's *Deadly Friend* (1986), and *Not Quite Human* (1987) and its sequels (1989, 1992). Barret Oliver, who played the artificial boy of *D.A.R.Y.L.,* restored life to his roadkill pet dog Sparky in Tim Burton's marvelous short film *Frankenweenie* (1984).

Even better was Burton's fairy-tale Frankenstein *Edward Scissorhands* (1990), starring Johnny Depp as the desperately lonely, displaced artificial boy with blades for fingers. After that, Disney was eager to indulge Burton's pet projects one more time, producing the stop-motion animation extravaganza *Tim Burton's Nightmare Before Christmas* (1993), with its inspired Dr. Frankenstein and Bride of Frankenstein surrogates, Dr. Finkelstein and Sally.

Director Stuart Gordon and producer Brian Yuzna's *Re-Animator* (1985) maintained the specifics and tenor of H. P. Lovecraft's pulp potboiler, but went to extremes pushing the envelope in its calculatedly outrageous mix of horror, humor, and gore. Yuzna tried to recapture lightning in a bottle with the sequel *Bride of Re-Animator* (1990). The underrated but erratic horror-action-comedy *Dead Heat* (1988) pushed the envelope in its own way.

Teen Frankenstein's monsters and zombies reigned anew in the 1990s. Roger Avary's *Mr. Stitch* (1995) was a compelling rethinking of the theme. *Zombie High* (1988) transcended its two-bit title to plop Virginia Madsen into an exclusive high school where the teachers survived multiple generations by tinkering with the brains (and assuming the identities) of their students.

Finally, it should be noted that Frankensteinian science also informed the disturbing strain of horror in which severed or transplanted body parts possess lives of their own. Maurice Renard's novel *Les Mains d'Orlac* (1920), the tale of a pianist who loses his hands in an accident and fears the murderer's hands grafted in their place have their own homicidal will, was filmed as *The Hands of Orlac* (1924 and 1960), *Mad Love* (1933), and *Hands of a Stranger* (1962).

Robert Florey's *The Beast with Five Fingers* (1947) adapted the short story by William Fryer Harvey, pitting mad Peter Lorre against the animated severed hand of his nightmares. It subsequently informed art films like Luis Bunuel's *The Exterminating Angel* (1962), drive-in fodder like *The Crawling Hand* (1963) and *Demonoid* (1979), "serious" horror films like Oliver Stone's *The Hand* (1981, adapted from Marc Brandel's novel *The Lizard's Tail*), gleeful gorefests like Sam Raimi's *The Evil Dead II: Dead By Dawn* (1987) and *Severed Ties* (1991), and black comedies like *Idle Hands* (1999, see below).

Eric Red's *Body Parts* (1991) gamely tried to encompass the entire resurrected-body-pieces genre in its script, which updated Renard's *Hands of Orlac*. Clive Barker brilliantly lent unlikely substance to the imagery in his excellent short story "The Body Politic" (1984), which was turned into an episode of Mick Garris's made-for-TV omnibus feature *Quicksilver Highway* (1998).

In 1999, the *Buffy* spin-off *Angel* presented its episode "I Fall to Pieces," in which a woman was stalked by a man capable of sending his body parts off on various and separate errands. These included using his floating eyeballs as ersatz remote cameras with which to spy on her.

Lazarus and the Christian Belief in the Resurrection

THE BIBLICAL IMPORTANCE of ancient Egypt in the Old Testament anticipated the vital role resurrection would play in the New Testament. Its assertion that Jesus Christ was the son of God who died for the collective sins of mankind, was buried, and rose bodily from the dead to join his Father in heaven is the basis of Christian belief. Of course, the Bible itself has undergone many revisions, translations, and editions, each prompting countless interpretations, often at odds with one another.

By all accounts, however, Jesus raised Lazarus from the dead in one of his many miracles. The New Testament's book of John 11:1–44 tells how Lazarus of Bethany died. When Jesus and his disciples arrived, they were greeted outside the village by Lazarus's sister Martha, and "found that he had been in the tomb four days already." Jesus promised Martha "Thy brother shall rise again," and she affirmed her belief and devotions to Christ and the Lord. Thereafter, Jesus went to Lazarus's tomb, ordered the stone at the mouth of the cave be rolled back, and entered.

Speaking first to his Father in heaven, Jesus thanked him for hearing his voice, and asked that the gathered crowd "may believe that thou didst send me." John 11: 43–44 concludes, "And when he had thus spoken, he cried with a loud voice, Lazarus, come forth. He that was dead came forth." Thus, Lazarus was resurrected from the dead, further alarming the Pharisees and chief priests who ultimately conspired against Jesus to cause his own crucifixion, death, and resurrection into glory.

With the Bible as the ultimate source, the life, death, and resurrection of Jesus Christ has inspired many hymns, songs, stories, novels, comic books, films, and television programs portraying those events as truth. There are far too many cinematic interpretations of the New Testament that include Lazarus's resurrection from the dead and Christ's own death and resurrection to discuss here. Primary among them are D. W. Griffith's *Intolerance* (1917), Cecil B. DeMille's *The King of Kings* (1927; remade by Nicholas Ray in 1961) and *Ben-Hur* (1925, 1959), *The Lawton Story* (aka *The Prince of Peace*, 1949), *Quo Vadis* (1951), *The Robe* (1953), *Day of Triumph* (1954), *The Big Fisherman* (1959), *The Greatest Story Ever Told* (1965), Pier Paolo Pasolini's *The Gospel According to St. Matthew* (1966), the made-for-TV *Jesus of Nazareth* (1977), *Jesus* (1979), and others. There was also a flurry of musical reinterpretations of the New Testament produced in the 1970s, the most famous of these being Andrew Lloyd Webber's *Jesus Christ Superstar* (1970, filmed in 1973), along with *Godspell* (1970, filmed in 1973) and Johnny Cash's *The Gospel Road* (1973).

EC Comics' science fiction comics title *Weird Science* #13 (1952) offered "He Walked Among Us" and proposed an alien world where a visitor from space named Jerome Kraft insinuated himself into the culture, and his uses of medical technology to heal were interpreted as miracles. By proposing a science fiction reinterpretation of the New Testament in which the Messiah was a visiting alien, it proved an audacious precursor to Gore Vidal's *Messiah* (1954), Michael Moorcock's *Behold the Man* (1966/69), and others. More controversial still were Hugh Schonfield's *The Passover Plot* (1969, filmed in 1976), Nikos Kazantzakis's *The Last Temptation of Christ* (1970, filmed by Martin Scorsese in 1988), the made-for-TV *The Day Christ Died* (1980), and others, some of which proposed the death and resurrection never occurred or were faked miracles.

Such speculative fictions and satires usually provoked condemnation and protests from devout Christians who consider such fiction blasphemous in nature. The Christian belief in Jesus Christ's miraculous revival of the dead Lazarus and his own bodily resurrection from the dead remain a constant wellspring for interpretation, controversy, skepticism, and devotion.

The Walking Dead in Western Literature and Pop Culture

GREEK AUTHOR PHLEGON'S "Philinnion and Machates" involved a corpse-bride, a tale later related by Proclus and the inspiration for Goethe's "The Bride of Corinth" and Washington Irving's "The German Student." There were countless tales of the walking and wandering dead in oral lore, stories, fables, and songs, few of which are still known or read today. Medieval ballads were filled with ghosts and the walking dead, including the ghost of Sir Gawain and the fiendish tomb-dweller that confronted Sir Galahad. But many of those were ghosts, not corporeal beings, and hence not relevant here (see Ghosts).

An animated corpse visited a bedside in Matthew Lewis's seminal gothic novel *The Monk* (1796). Edgar Allan Poe (1809–49) made more extensive use of such revenants: Poe's resurrected dead were neither ghosts nor walking dead per se, but some other incarnation of "undeath" reflecting the dreadful obsessions of his calculating, calmly mad narrators. "The Facts in the Case of M. Valdemar" (1840) features the most corporeal of his undead characters. Poe's justifiably celebrated *Tales of the Grotesque and Arabesque* (1840) more often showcased chilling reincarnates like "Ligeia" and "Morella," the life-draining "Oval Portrait," or the pestilent death-incarnate figure that intrudes upon "The Masque of the Red Death." Poe's stories and poems have been adapted to stage, comics, and film literally hundreds of times, prominent among these Roger Corman's 1960s revisionist adaptations of Poe starring Vincent Price.

Robert Louis Stevenson's "The Body Snatcher" (1881, first published in 1884) was drawn from the true crimes of the notorious grave robbers Burke and Hare, who profited from providing cadavers for surgeons and medical students. Val Lewton produced an excellent film version in 1945 that improved on Stevenson's text and showcased one of Boris Karloff's finest performances as the body-snatcher Gray.

Few walking dead were more frightening than the never-glimpsed resurrected corpse knocking at the door during the climax of humorist William Wymark Jacobs's "The Monkey's Paw" (1902), one of the most frequently reprinted of all horror tales. An elderly couple wish upon the titular magical monkey's paw to bring their son, who was crushed to death in an industrial accident, back to life; as a knock is heard at the front door, the father (who did not initially believe in the paw's power) feverishly wishes his son back to the grave. The tale has been adapted to stage, film, and television many times.

An eleventh-century folktale of a traveling monk and his somnambulist slave inspired the celebrated German expressionist nightmare film *The Cabinet of Dr. Caligari* (1919). Whether he was undead or merely comatose, Cesar the somnambulist (Conrad Veidt) was the screen's first zombie, influencing every horror film to follow.

Abel Gance's World War I melodrama *J'Accuse!* (1919) included a feverish nightmare in which the war's dead rose from the battlefields to march against the living. Gance mobilized a battalion of French soldiers on leave from the trench wars to stage this and other battle scenes for the film; thereafter, they were returned to the front to certain death.

Predating the film was poet Robert Service's nightmarish masterpiece "March of the Dead." First published in 1907 in *The Spell of the Yukon* (aka *Songs of a Sourdough*), the poem's marching rhythm begins with the glorious return of a war's victorious soldiers, only to have the sky turn dark as the corpses of those not fortunate enough to survive the battle return to march through the streets. It remains one of the most chilling pieces of poetry ever published.

F. Brooke Warren's stage play *The Face at the Window* was filmed many times (1919, 1920, 1932, and Tod Slaughter's classic 1939 version), and featured a murder victim revived from the dead just long enough to identify his killer.

The pulp magazines of the era published many tales of the walking dead, such as H. P. Lovecraft's "The Outsider" (1920), "In The Vault" (1925), and "Cool Air" (1926), Clark Ashton Smith's "The Empire of the Necromancers," and A. Hyatt Verrill's potboiler "The Plague of the Living Corpses" (*Amazing Stories, 1927*).

zombie jamboree

W. B. SEABROOK'S *THE MAGIC ISLAND* (1929) claimed to be "a living history of the Voodoo rites set down by a man who has drunk the sacrificial blood." Seabrook introduced the word *zombie* to the public with his lurid, supposedly factual accounts of Haiti's voodoo cults and processions of living dead men damned to do the bidding of their masters. The book was a bestseller, and public curiosity about such strange and terrifying creatures was aroused. Kenneth Webb's play *Zombie* (1931) was the first theatrical production to cash in on Seabrook's revelations, but it was only the beginning. The Halperin Brothers' crude, dreamlike *White Zombie* (1932) starring Bela Lugosi was the first zombie film.

Zombies proliferated in the pulps, radio plays, and movies of the day. The pulps offered stories like August Derleth and Marok Schorer's voodoo tale "The House in the Magnolias" (1932), Robert E. Howard's "Pigeons from Hell" (1938), Thorp McClusky's "While Zombies Walked" (1939), and others. The motion picture *Voodo* (yes, that's how it was spelled; 1933) was actually set and filmed in Haiti, while *Ouanga* (aka *Love Wanga* and *Crime of Voodoo*, 1936) was filmed in the West Indies. Voodoo in America's deep south was featured in *Chloe* (1934), and *Drums O' Voodoo* (1934).

Boris Karloff capitalized on his rocket to fame as the monster in the Universal Frankenstein series by playing a procession of vengeful walking dead and scientists experimenting with bringing the dead back to life. Michael Curtiz's *The Walking Dead* (1936) established the pattern. *The Man They Could Not Hang* (1939) was the first and best of a quintet of such films Karloff made at Columbia, starring Karloff as a wrongfully executed scientist resurrected by his assistant. Karloff was the kindly *Man with Nine Lives* (1940), revived from his own crude ice chamber to tinker with those he blamed for his failure before his deep-freeze rest.

Victor Halperin's own successor to *White Zombie* was *Revolt of the Zombies* (1936), which proposed the existence of an army of undead Cambodian soldiers.

Abel Gance had already used such imagery in *J'Accuse!*. Appalled at the possibility of another European war, Gance prepared a monumental remake of his silent epic. Gance's heroic research scientist hero (Victor Francen) actually raised an army of all those slain in war and sent them marching against the living. The climactic montage of the ranks of the dead (many of them horribly maimed living survivors of World War I, known in France as *la Union des Gueles Cassées*) remains a genuinely awesome, harrowing sequence.

J'Accuse! (1938) barely played screens in France before authorities seeking favor with Hitler effectively banned it, as Nazi Germany already had. It enjoyed few play dates in England, and in the United States, the distributor trimmed Gance's epic down and retitled it *That They May Live*, unsuccessfully marketing it as an important subtitled "art" picture before pushing it into the exploitation grind-house circuit as an out-and-out horror film. Gance's masterpiece malingered in obscurity until being restored to its complete form and reissued in 1991. It is among the most powerful and important films of its genre.

The serials had their wartime walking dead menaces, too: the evil master spy Zarnoff (Irving Pichel) was resurrected after his execution and menaced *Dick Tracy's G-Men* (1939) through fifteen chapters of the serial. The true-crime radio program *Gang Busters* inspired a completely fictional thirteen-chapter Universal serial of the same name (1942) in which scientist and crime lord Ralph Morgan (the Wizard of Oz himself!) brought a ring of executed criminals back to life.

Mad scientist Lionel Atwill saw to it that electrocution only made Lon Chaney Jr.'s *Man-Made Monster* (1941) into the lethal equivalent of a walking electric chair. A decade and a half later, Chaney re-created the role for *The Indestructible Man* (1956). In *The Mad Doctor of Market Street* (1942), Atwill was at it again. Mad doctor George Zucco turned David Bruce into *The Mad Ghoul* (1943), forced to cut out still-living human hearts necessary to sustain his withered zombie state.

Zucco was back in *The Voodoo Man* (1944), with John Carradine and Bela Lugosi in tow. Carradine had already had his turn in *Revenge of the Zombies* (1943). Republic's *Valley of the Zombies* (1946) brought the 1940s zombie cycle to a close with Ian Keith as an undead undertaker who needed fresh blood to complete the stolen formula that kept him ticking.

Jacques Tourneur's haunting, poetic *I Walked with a Zombie* (1943) was based on an article about Haitian voodoo by Inez Wallace, and was accurately summarized by producer Val Lewton at the time of its production as "Jane Eyre in the West Indies."

Pioneer underground filmmaker Maya Deren was the only director of note to actually travel to Haiti and film authentic voodoo rituals she eventually participated in, an experience that profoundly affected her and yielded a remarkable book, *The Divine Horsemen: The Living Gods of Haiti* (1953).

The only zombie to register as an ongoing character from countless World War II–era adventure, jungle, and superhero comic books was Solomon Grundy. A pasty-skinned giant created when plant matter congealed over a human skeleton, Grundy took on a life of its own in Paul Reinman's "Green Lantern" episode of *All-American Comics* #61 (1944). Grundy went on to battle other superheroes to the present day, including Superman. Inspired by Theodore Sturgeon's pulp story "It" (1940), Grundy and his contemporary, the Heap (introduced in *Airboy Comics* #4, with his origin story in #9, both 1946) kicked off a strangely enduring comic-book walking dead permutation in which vegetation was the resurrecting agent.

The archetype inexplicably flowered anew twenty-five years later with DC's *Swamp Thing* (introduced in *House of Secrets* #92, 1971), Marvel's *Man-Thing* (debuting in the black-and-white zine *Savage Tales* #1, 1971), and Skywald's revival of *The Heap* as a four-color one-shot (1971) and ongoing series in their black-and-white horror magazine line (debuting in *Psycho* #2, 1971), and continuing off and on to the present.

The first periodical horror comic title was ACG's *Adventures into the Unknown* (1948–67), which immediately embraced the walking-dead theme. Atlas (soon to be better known as Marvel) Comics took and maintained their lead, publishing more than a dozen horror titles under their imprint, with the living dead as frequent cover and story stars. By the time the horror comics boom of 1951–54 began, the walking dead had assumed an iconic power on the newsstand. Bill Everett's "I, Zombie" in *Menace* #6 (Atlas/Marvel, 1953) was a prime specimen, competently written and beautifully illustrated. Almost two decades later, it would provide the inspiration for Marvel's *Tales of the Zombie* series (see below).

One-shots like *Horror from the Tomb* (Premiere, 1954), *City of the Living Dead*, and *The Dead Who Walk* (both from Avon, 1952) focused exclusively on walking dead and zombie stories. The last hurrah of the pre-Code horror comics was "Born in the Grave" in *Dark Mysteries* #19 (1954), a tale of a zombie child born of two corpses buried together.

EC's first horror story was "Zombie Terror" in *Moon Girl* #5 (1948), an unspectacular precursor of the glorious excesses to follow. The Comics Code Authority in October 1954 specifically banned any further use of the walking dead.

The science fiction cycle of the 1950s dressed up plenty of tried and true walking-dead traditions with pseudoscience. *Donovan's Brain* author Curt Siodmak concocted *Creature with the Atom Brain* (1955)

Voodoo Island (1957) had Boris Karloff using the juices of carnivorous plants to create zombies. That same year, the inevitable *Teenage Zombies* hit drive-ins.

Ed Wood Jr.'s now-beloved *Plan 9 from Outer Space* (1959) ostensibly concerned an incompetent trio of aliens mounting the titular "Plan 9" invasion coup, involving the revival of corpses Tor Johnson, TV horror host Vampira, and a dentist pretending to be a resurrected Bela Lugosi (Lugosi died prior to production, after filming only two scenes). Reviled upon its release and promptly relegated to late-night television, *Plan 9* was itself brought back from the dead and revered as "The Worst Film Ever Made" by the early 1970s, marking a pronounced change in popular tastes.

Edward L. Cahn's *Invisible Invaders* (1959) was just as awful, but much less fun.

Jack Pierce created the makeup for the *Giant from the Unknown* (1957), a golem-like Spanish conquistador (pro boxer Buddy Baer) revived from the dead by a bolt of lightning, much like the caveman, Tyrannosaurus rex, and apatosaurus of *Dinosaurus!* (1960). Countless prehistoric men and monsters have come back from the dead in stories, comic books, and films. That is an additional avenue of investigation that could spawn a book of its own.

British zombies made their mark, too. Terence Fisher directed the unusual science fiction zombie shocker *The Earth Dies Screaming* (1964) in which robotic alien invaders reduced the local populace to blind zombies. Writer-director John Gilling crafted Hammer's *Plague of the Zombies* (1965), in which the dead of a small Cornwall village were stolen from their graves to provide cheap labor at the local squire's tin-mine operation.

Del Tenney's low-budget black-and-white grind-house feature *Curse of the Living Corpse* (1964) played a successful double bill with Tenney's *Horror of Party Beach* (Twentieth Century Fox, 1964), whose ridiculous amphibious monsters were the first of the ecological walking dead. The film made lots of money and boasted dreadful surf-rock songs such as "The Monster Stomp," a "Death Certificate" gimmick for theater patrons, and a photographic monster comic magazine from Warren Publishing.

The short-lived TV series *Thriller* (1960–62) presented some effective adaptations and original stories featuring the living dead. John Newland directed an excellent adaptation of Robert E. Howard's chilling zombie tale "Pigeons from Hell" (1961). Robert Florey's eerie "The Incredible Dr. Markesan" (1962) was adapted from a short story by August Derleth and Mark Schorer, starring series host Boris Karloff as a deceased scientist.

Warren Publishing had bypassed the Comics Code with *Creepy*, *Eerie*, and *Vampirella* in the mid-1960s. Archie Goodwin edited and scripted the early issues, crafting many excellent tales. After his departure, the Warren line continued to showcase fine zombie stories like Tom Sutton's "It!" (*Creepy* #53, 1973).

George Romero's *Night of the Living Dead* (1968) marked a new age in modern horror with its genuinely apocalyptic vision of contemporary America overrun in a single evening by a mindless, hungry onslaught of the walking dead. Filmed in Pittsburgh by a ragtag team of commercial and industrial filmmakers eager to produced their first feature, *Night of the Living Dead* was a remarkably polished effort that plucked the nerves of a decade plagued by political assassinations, civil unrest, the Vietnam War, race riots, and student revolution.

Its stark black-and-white cinematography and urgent narrative gave the horrific scenario a documentary-like credibility that lent stunning force to its subversive undermining of audience expectations. The hero was black, the heroine a near-comatose basket case, the patriarch an opportunistic

HORROR OF PARTY BEACH

coward, the menacing hordes easily cut down as individuals but implacable and unstoppable en masse. The comfortable genre formulas were violated at every turn: the teenage couple is reduced to meat for the ghouls, the daughter becomes a zombie, and—horror of horrors—the hero dies at dawn, mistaken for a zombie by a rescue-and-cleanup crew of gun-toting rednecks. Looking back, it is almost impossible to communicate the impact *Night of the Living Dead* had on audiences seeing it for the first time in the Age of Aquarius.

Night of the Living Dead also introduced cannibalism to the genre. Diet had never been substantially addressed in zombie lore, except to cite what should not be fed to the walking dead. In *The Magic Island*, W. B. Seabrook specified "...zombies must never be permitted to taste salt or meat" (page 96).

Romero's living dead ate living flesh out of base instinct, seeming to require the sustenance. In the extended laboratory sequences in *Day of the Dead* (1985), Romero allowed his mad scientist (Richard Liberty) to analyze the craving, determining that the undead had no need for sustenance, they simply craved flesh. There were predecessors: almost all of H. P. Lovecraft's Herbert West: Re-Animator stories (1921–22) found West's mindless reanimates reverting to cannibalism.

Such dietary extremes were still rare enough (no pun intended) that Hammer considered cannibalism a novel shock to spice up *The Revenge of Frankenstein* (1958). Herschell Gordon Lewis's *Blood Feast* (1963) enhanced its status as the first color "gore" film with cannibalism, too, and yet the explicit scenes of cannibalism in *Night of the Living Dead* were revelatory horrors, forever redefining the genre.

The cult success of *Night of the Living Dead* inspired an interesting variety of low-budget chillers including the extraordinary *Let's Scare Jessica to Death* (1971; see Ghosts), *Children Shouldn't Play with Dead Things* (1972), *Messiah of Evil* (1973), the suspenseful *House of the Seven Corpses* (1974), and others. The EC horror comics Romero cited as an influence on *Night* were also brought to the big screen in the Amicus omnibus feature *Tales from the Crypt* (1971).

Bob Clark's excellent *Dead of Night* (aka *Deathdream*, 1973) evoked "The Monkey's Paw" with its grim tale of a dead American soldier resurrected by his mother's desperate wish that her son come back home. Return home he does, as a walking corpse stinking of decay and in dire need of regular "fixes" of blood, heroin-style.

The cult success of Romero's film also inspired cartoonists. The walking dead were a volatile symbol to many of the underground comix scene. That generation of artists was full of righteous, countercultural anger and the walking dead of the undergrounds indulged an unspeakable array of dietary, carnal, and political appetites. Like the hungry dead of George Romero's *Night of the Living Dead*, these zombies had teeth, and they went for the jugular every time.

Richard Corben's "Lame Lem's Love" (*Skull* #2, 1970) was a slice of Southern swamp-Gothic, in which the sex and violence were more aggressive than ever seen in an American horror comic.

Italian walking-dead tales like *Death Smiles on a Murderer* (1972) and Spanish zombie films like *Horror Rises from the Tomb* (1972) paved the way for a far more aggressive, angry breed brought into sharp focus by the international impact of Romero's *Night of the Living Dead*. Jorge Grau's chilling Spanish-British co-production *Don't Open the Window* (aka *The Living Dead at Manchester Morgue*, 1974) was the first to incorporate and expand upon Romero's example.

Amando de Ossorio's *Tombs of the Blind Dead* (1971) featured the skeletal, robed Knights Templar riding their undead steeds in slow motion in search of victims to suck dry. Though the narrative was inconsequential, the knights themselves were inspired living-dead horrors. The film proved successful enough to prompt de Ossorio to make three more entries, *Return of the Evil Dead* (1973), *Horror of the Zombies* (1974), and *Night of the Seagulls* (1975).

Freddie Francis's offbeat *The Creeping Flesh* (1972) starred Peter Cushing and Christopher Lee as rival Victorian scientists at odds over a prehistoric skeleton that grows flesh where the bone is exposed to moisture. Lee and Cushing also co-starred in *Horror Express* (1972) as rival scientists aboard a train stalked by a resurrected prehistoric humanoid possessed by an alien presence. Stranger still was William Castle's final film, *Shanks* (1974). The film marked the very odd cultural collaboration of Castle—the self-proclaimed king of gimmick horror—and France's national treasure, the mime Marcel Marceau, playing a mute puppeteer who may or may not be capable of resurrecting the dead.

Sugar Hill (1974) meshed blaxploitation, gangsters, and silver-eyed zombies, though it was bettered by the blaxploitation-gangster-possession walking dead revenge tale *J.D.'s Revenge* (1976).

Dan Curtis produced and directed *The Norliss Tapes* (1973)—an imitation of his own *The Night Stalker*—working from a script by William F. Nolan. Curtis Harrington's TV movie *The Dead Don't Die* (1974) was an entertaining evocation of the 1940s hard-boiled detective capers.

Chicago gangsters were also the target of an undead creature in the classic and harrowing *Kolchak: The Night Stalker* (1974–75) episode "The Zombie." Rod Serling's *Night Gallery* (1970–73) broadcast numerous episodes featuring living corpses, including Richard Matheson's "The Funeral" (1970) and an adaptation of H. P. Lovecraft's "Cool Air" (1971).

DC editor Joe Orlando took advantage of the 1970 revision of the Comics Code to shift such tepid mystery titles as *House of Mystery* and *House of Secrets* into horrific territory. Orlando plunged the DC anthology titles into an energetic run of fine horror stories, with the living dead frequently involved. Marvel Comics followed suit with their own four-color anthology titles including *Chamber of Darkness, Supernatural Thrillers*, and others, and a boom in monster comics like *Tomb of Dracula* (see Vampires), which often featured the walking dead. Supernatural heroes were in vogue as well, including Brother Voodoo (*Strange Tales* #169–173, 1973–74). Unlike DC, Marvel launched a series of black-and-white horror magazines, among them *Tales of the Zombie* (ten issues, 1973–75). The first issue opened with a reprint of Bill Everett's pre-Code story "I, Zombie" (from *Menace* #5, 1953), using it as an origin tale of sorts for the new zombie adventures that followed.

The film *Shock Waves* (1977) reintroduced the notion of Nazis building an undead master race, with scarred Third Reich refugee Peter Cushing touting the threat of the unstoppable Toden Corp as pasty blond Aryan zombies stumbling up from the surf off the coast of Florida. Many more Nazi zombies followed. These included Joel Reed's *Night of the Zombies* (1981, not to be confused with Bruno Mattei's 1980 film of the same name) and an eruption of European entries, such as *Zombie Lake* (1980) and *Oasis of the Zombies* (1981). Also notable were the zombies of Robert R. McCammon's 1980 novel *The Night Boat*, a crew of undead manning a sunken Nazi U-boat.

George Romero's *Dawn of the Dead* (1979) devastatingly extended *Night of the Living Dead*'s premise and apocalyptic narrative. *Dawn* brought the horrors of the original into the harsh light of day. An uneasy quartet of civilians and paramilitary SWAT-team members purges an abandoned shopping mall of its walking dead. Romero's storytelling and attention to character was impeccable, but his calculated pacing of the relentlessly graphic mayhem (compliments of makeup maestro Tom Savini) was literally breathtaking, shifting from horror to hilarity to tedium only to set up the climactic frenzy with masterful precision. Nothing like it had ever been seen before, establishing a new extreme for the genre. Released unrated at a time when independent distributors could capitalize on such a novelty, *Dawn* initiated a fresh horror cycle.

Dawn of the Dead was co-produced by Italy's master of horror, Dario Argento. Released in a slightly different version in Italy under the title *Zombi*, the film was an immediate sensation, opening the floodgates for a torrent of Italian productions like Lucio Fulci's misleadingly titled *Zombi 2*, which we will hereafter refer to by its American release title, *Zombie* (1979).

Zombie was a hit too, and Fulci continued to cultivate his peculiar strain of gore-drenched, cannibalistic, walking dead cinema with *Gates of Hell* (1980), the nightmarish *The Beyond* (1981), and the gripping *House by the Cemetery* (1982).

Romero and author Stephen King soon offered their own affectionate send-up of the genre and specifically the pre-Code horror comics they had been weaned on, inventing their own fictional horror comic for the anthology feature film *Creepshow* (1982). Two of the stories, "Father's Day" and "Something to Tide You Over," were pastiches of the pre-Code walking-dead revenge tradition, playfully staged with exaggerated multicolor lighting schemes and stylized performances. In an elegant turnabout worthy of the EC formula they tethered to, *Creepshow* was adapted as a trade paperback horror comic book, illustrated by Berni Wrightson.

A genuinely creepy back-from-the-dead tale was the centerpiece of John Carpenter's wonderfully atmospheric 1980 creeper *The Fog*, a story more reminiscent of classic horror novels than films.

Walking-dead horror fiction reflected and expanded upon the post–George Romero landscape, with Romero himself contributing an introspective psychological horror story to the anthology *Modern Masters of Horror* (1981). T. E. D. Klein's editorial tenure on *Twilight Zone* magazine (1981–89) shepherded many fine living-dead entries, setting the tone for the decade. Individual stories stand out—"Nightcrawlers" (1984) by Robert McCammon, filmed by William Friedkin for *The New Twilight Zone* (1985); "Where There's a Will" by Richard Matheson and his son Richard Christian Matheson—as did the anthologies themselves.

Novelist and short story author Charles L. Grant further distinguished himself as one of the genre's premiere anthologists, and his top-drawer modern horror collections *Nightmares* (1979), *Horrors* (1981), *Terrors* (1982), *Fears* (1983), and others showcased many prime walking-dead tales. James Russo, co-author of the screenplay for *Night of the Living Dead*, novelized *Night* in 1973 and continued as a novelist and occasional filmmaker. His walking-dead novels include the sequel *Return of the Living Dead* (two versions, 1978 and 1985) and *Voodoo Dawn* (1980). George Romero and Susanna Sparrow's novelization of *Dawn of the Dead* (1979) ushered in a torrent of walking-dead novels, with Thomas H. Block's *Mayday* (1979), John R. Maxim's *Platforms* (1980), and Brian Moore's *Cold Heaven* (1983) providing the cream of the crop. Director Nicolas Roeg subsequently filmed *Cold Heaven* in 1992.

There were a number of worthy walking-dead films produced during the early 1980s horror boom: *Dead and Buried* (1980), *One Dark Night* (1982), and Sam Raimi's *The Evil Dead* (1983), which carried on the tradition of Romero's made-in-Pittsburgh achievements. Raimi and company shot their film with precious little money, endless invention, and manic abandon in a remote Tennessee backwoods cabin. A group of college students reawaken an ancient evil with their discovery of the forbidden Book of the Dead, and they succumb one by one to possession and resurrection from the dead over the course of a single evening until only one (Bruce Campbell) remains.

Raimi virtually remade his original for the sequel *Evil Dead 2: Dead by Dawn* (1987). Raimi and Campbell picked up the ball one more time with *Army of Darkness* (1992), an even bawdier finale in which Campbell takes on an army of "Deadites" led by his own living-dead doppelganger (also played by Campbell).

With the emergence of music videos as a fresh medium popularized with MTV's early-1980s rise to prominence, zombie imagery quickly established a new beachhead. Although the expected ghoulish walking-dead imagery characterized "shock rock" acts from Alice Cooper and Ozzy Osbourne to Marilyn Manson and Rob Zombie, the continuing popular acceptance of even the most extreme Romero-esque zombie homages was apparent among the most mainstream pop performers. John Landis directed the extended music video accompanying Michael Jackson's *Thriller* (1983), which was the best-selling pop album of all time. Tapping into Jackson's affection for horror movies, Landis and Jackson staged an elaborate zombie dance number with makeup by Rick Baker. Many others followed, continuing up to the recent Backstreet Boys' video "Everybody Backstreet's Back" (1998), featuring zombies, vampires, and Backstreet Boys Nick Carter as a mummy, Brian Littrell as a werewolf, and Kevin Richardson as a scaly Mr. Hyde.

Romero wrapped up his living-dead trilogy with the grim *Day of the Dead* (1985), an intelligent, introspective distillation of the apocalypse scaled down from his original script by budgetary and time restraints.

The film's moral focus was absolute, and Tom Savini's makeup effects and Romero's orchestration of the violence were more convincing than ever before. Unfortunately, distribution practices had changed, locking out unrated films and making it impossible to approach the guerrilla success *Dawn of the Dead* had enjoyed a decade earlier. Furthermore, *Day of the Dead* was forced to go toe-to-toe with the broader parody of Dan O'Bannon's *Return of the Living Dead* (1985), a non-contestable title awarded via John Russo's previously published sequel novel (which the film ignored) and the partners' long-standing agreement that each of them could formulate a sequel, with Russo retaining propriety over use of the term "living dead." *Return* was clever and kinetic, a worthy effort and revisionist parody. Sadly, however, its release blocked Romero's chance at any reasonable distribution of his unrated conclusion. It was the end in more ways than one.

Audiences and theater owners were far more comfortable with *Return*'s R-rated splatter-slapstick horror-comedy than Romero's vision of hell-on-earth. *Return of the Living Dead* worked on its own terms, proposing that *Night of the Living Dead* was based on an actual localized event caused by a toxic-waste spill. *Return* was a success, spawning two sequels. The second, *Return of the Living Dead 3* (1993) was an excellent, extremely gory downbeat horror-romance directed by Brian Yuzna.

Stephen King's novel *Pet Sematary* (1983) was the tale of a mystic "power spot" capable of raising the dead who were buried there, hidden deep in the Maine forests beyond a local pet graveyard. The novel provided a vehicle for King to explore a parent's most profound fear—the loss of a child—and addressed the question of what might result if the parent were tempted with the possibility that they might be able to bring a dead child back to life. It was W. W. Jacobs's "The Monkey's Paw" writ large and given an urgency only the loss of a very young child could create.

Clive Barker's *Books of Blood* (1984) marked a new beginning for horror. Barker's transformative, transgressive breed of horror was razor sharp and outrageous. Barker's novella "The Hellbound Heart" (1985) provided the source material for his directorial debut *Hellraiser* (1984; see also Demons). The film included the most convincingly character-driven, sexually motivated resurrection of the dead in cinema history. The painfully slow, organic reconstruction of the dead was central to the narrative and harrowing emotional impact of *Hellraiser*. *Hellbound: Hellraiser II* (1988) was the result of other hands apparently working under Barker's tacit approval.

The mid-1980s horror revival was characterized in comics mostly by newsstand titles like *Moon Knight* (Marvel, 25 issues, 1980–85) and *Saga of the Swamp Thing* (DC Comics,

1981–96), which straddled the horror and vigilante superhero genres. *Moon Knight* was another vigilante superhero in the mold of the Spectre and Deadman (see Ghosts).

Relaunched to exploit the Wes Craven movie adaptation (1981), *Swamp Thing* stayed truer to its genre roots with the debut of British writer Alan Moore on the title (with #20, 1983). Moore reintroduced the series' undead villain, Anton Arcane, and in an extended story arc (#25–31, 1984) portrayed Arcane's possession of the husband of his niece Abigail, using an entourage of fly-blown zombies to achieve his ends. This explicit walking-dead imagery (and the implicit incest angle of the possession subplot) raised the hackles of the Comics Code Authority, who denied *Swamp Thing* #29 the Code seal of approval, setting in motion a chain of events that would have long-standing effects on the comic-book industry.

Though the 1970 Code revisions had relaxed the ban on depictions of the walking dead, it was felt that the zombies in this particular story were too explicitly detailed and their roles too unsavory. Undaunted, DC published the issue uncut and thereafter ceased submitting *Swamp Thing* to the Code for approval, establishing their "Sophisticated Suspense" imprint, which was subsequently transformed into their Vertigo Comics imprint for mature readers. Moore scripted one more lively walking-dead two-parter (#41–42), a slavery-retribution voodoo tale set in a Louisiana plantation home serving as the set for a Mandingo-like film production.

Such imaginary voodoo horrors paled in comparison to the grim reality of life in modern Haiti and the truth behind the zombie mythos. A man named Clairvius Narcisse was pronounced dead at Haiti's Albert Schweitzer Hospital on May 2, 1962. Two veteran physicians signed his death certificate, his wife Marie Narcisse verified the identity of the body, and two days later Clairvius Narcisse was buried. Almost twenty years later, in 1980, a very dazed and confused Clairvius Narcisse stumbled into his family home. The Narcisse case marked the first internationally recognized, medically documented evidence of the actual existence of "zombies," breaking through the plantation-era legacy and police-state enforced obfuscation of poor or no records of births and deaths. Within zombie lore, there was even a term for Narcisse's condition: he was a Zombi savanne, that rare specimen who returns to a normal existence (as opposed to the spirit Zombi astral, the physical Zombi cadavre, and the working stiff Zombi jardin).

It was this reality that Harvard ethnobotanist Wade Davis plunged into when he initiated the Zombie Project in 1982. Working with a diverse team of professionals in the sciences, arts, and theology, the project initiated the first actual investigation of the existence, use, and origin of "zombies" and medical potential of the herbs rumored to induce the zombie state. The Project eventually discovered that the poisonous tetrodotoxin was the essential ingredient of the "zombie powder" actually used by voodoo priests to create and sustain the semblance of death. Davis published his observations as *The Serpent and the Rainbow* (1985). Screenwriters Richard Maxwell and A. R. Simoun and director Wes Craven extrapolated Davis's scientific travelogue into the harrowing film adaptation in 1987.

The stark contrast between the exotic allure of Haiti and the fearful political reality of its cruel government and impoverished people was also evoked in the *X-Files* episode "Fresh Bones" (1995).

Upscale Hollywood voodoo exercises like *The Serpent and the Rainbow, Angel Heart* (1987; see Demons), and the Santeria chiller *The Believers* (1987) spawned a brief flurry of voodoo and zombie pics like *Voodoo Black Exorcist* (1989), *Headhunter* (1989), and others. *Voodoo Dawn* (1989), co-written by *Night of the Living Dead* co-creator John Russo from his own novel, featured an early performance from actress Gina Gershon.

Tom Savini's 1990 remake of Romero's *Night of the Living Dead* (1990) was surprisingly effective. Having already cut his teeth directing episodes of TV's *Tales from the Darkside,* Savini's debut helming a feature demonstrated consummate skill and assurance. The remake was prompted by the need for Romero, Russo, and their associates to reclaim legal ownership over the title.

Wes Craven's attempt to spawn another horror franchise featured *Shocker* (1989), an electrocuted serial killer (Mitch Pileggi, who would later play the role of Skinner on *The X-Files*) who willed himself back to life to stalk his son, using electricity as his vehicle. A similar resurrected killer graced *The First Power* (1990). Even the *Friday the 13th* slasher franchise veered into walking-dead turf, making the almost-unkillable arise from the dead as a truly unkillable homicidal zombie in *Friday the 13th, Part VI: Jason Lives* (1985) and three subsequent sequels. More zombies popped up in *The Dead Pit* (1989), *John Carpenter's Prince of Darkness* (1987), *The Vineyard* (1989), and *Demon Wind* (1990).

Mainstream novelists like Rick Hautala found mileage in the walking-dead genre in *Moon Walker* (1989), which mobilized an army of undead potato-picking workers in Maine. The bad-boy "splatterpunk" movement rattled its saber in the horror field, yielding one self-ballyhooing anthology, *Splatterpunks* (1989), and John Skipp and Craig Spector's definitive living-dead anthology *Book of the Dead* (1989), sanctified by George Romero's foreword and packed with an exceptional cutting-edge collective of original walking-dead stories by punks and veterans alike, including Stephen King, Robert R. McCammon, Joe R. Lansdale, and Ramsey Campbell. Douglas E. Winter's contribution, the extraordinary "Less than Zombie," abandoned the usual genre trappings to present an unflinching snapshot of the "real" walking dead, a remorseless pack of street punks who kill their own.

JOHN SKIPP AND CRAIG SPECTOR

PHOTO BY BETH GWINN

Another entry in *Book of the Dead*, Philip Nutman's terse CIA special ops versus zombies tale "Wet Work," spawned Nutman's apocalyptic novel *Wet Work* (1993). Skipp and Spector were back with more to offer in *Still Dead: Book of the Dead 2* (1992).

The wry horror of Tiziano Sclavi's Italian comics series *Dylan Dog* (1986–present) achieved breakthrough bestseller status in its native country, with more than three hundred thousand copies sold each month, spawning an annual *Dylan Dog* horror film festival and Michele Soavi's marvelous film adaptation of Sclavi's Dylan Dog novel *Dellamorte Dellamore*, released in the United States as *Cemetery Man* (1995).

The cable TV series *Tales from the Crypt* (1989–94) was at its best when adapting its episodes from the EC pre-Code library of stories. It spawned action figures, juvenile novelizations, two cartoon spin-offs (*Tales from the Cryptkeeper* and *Secrets of the Cryptkeeper's Haunted*

House), and two feature films to date, *Demon Knight* (1995; see Demons) and *Bordello of Blood* (1996).

One of the co-producers (and occasional directors) of *Tales from the Crypt* was Robert Zemeckis (of *Back to the Future* fame), who subsequently embraced the new CGI special-effects technology to realize the outrageous, cartoony mutilations of the mainstream Hollywood comedy *Death Becomes Her* (1992).

Fangoria magazine's direct-to-video *I, Zombie* (1999) was the best of the teen zombie offerings, a surprisingly somber and effective gem relating the nitty-gritty details of a young man's awakening to the grim realities of being a zombie.

Rodman Flender's *Idle Hands* (1999) offered the screen's first slacker zombies and the most hilarious reason ever stated for the reanimation of the dead. His hand possessed by a demon, teen pothead Anton (Devon Sawa) unwillingly killed his two best friends (*Buffy*'s own Seth Green and Elden Henson), who returned as the undead. When asked why they're back, they described their encounter with "this big, bright white light at the end of a long tunnel . . . and uncool music, like Enya." The slackers shrugged off the afterlife: "Ah, we figured . . . it was really far."

James O'Barr's *The Crow* (Caliber/Tundra/Kitchen Sink, 1981, 1989–92) was a modern variation on the Spectre and Deadman (see Ghosts), a murder victim risen from the grave to avenge his death and that of his beloved wife, though unlike the Spectre or Deadman, Eric Draven was resurrected as a corporeal being. O'Barr's evocative blend of Gothic romanticism and vigilante action struck a nerve, earning a growing cult readership and movie deal in a remarkably short period of time. Martial arts expert Brandon Lee delivered a potent, brooding performance as the lead in director Alex Proyas's faithful film adaptation *The Crow* (1993), but Lee's tragic death during the filming (an on-set accident involving a prop handgun) almost scuttled the production.

Lee's death (inexorably linked to that of his father, Bruce Lee, in 1971) perversely anchored the tragedy and despair inherent in O'Barr's original narrative and art. The film was successful enough to prompt a pair of sequels. Boasting style but lacking Lee's galvanizing presence, *Crow 2: City of Angels* (1996) bombed at the box office, and its failed merchandising scheme precipitated the demise of the *Crow* comics series' publisher, Kitchen Sink Press. The *Crow* franchise came back from the dead, yielding the current *Crow* TV series (1999–present) and a third film, as yet unreleased as of this writing. Todd McFarlane's *Spawn* comic-book series (1992–present) emulated the multiple-media crossover success with its demonic variation on the same theme (see Demons).

The always-apocalyptic post-Romero zombie landscape was also littered with miscellaneous comic-book series dedicated to the exploits of the flesh-eating undead. Artist Vincent Locke made his mark with his detailed pen-and-ink renditions of *Deadworld*, an independent horror series that outlived the demise of its first publisher (#1–8, Arrow, 1987–88) to survive into the 1990s (#10–present, Caliber, 1989–present).

Deadworld's relative success sparked a brief flurry of similarly gory zombie comics, including Del Stone Jr. and David Dorman's one-shot *Roadkill: A Chronicle of the Deadworld* (1993) and the chaotic *Zombie Wars* (FantaCo, 1991–92) from *Teenage Mutant Ninja Turtles* co-creator Kevin Eastman. This ragtag cycle culminated in the umbrella title *Zombie World* from Dark Horse Comics (1997–present).

Video games have had as profound an impact on the walking-dead genre as Romero's seminal *Living Dead* trilogy once did. Earlier horror video games like *Night Trap* (1992) had interlaced interactive game scenarios with sometimes explicit filmed gore sequences, raising parent and authoritarian outrage. Indeed, the original edition of *Night Trap* was pulled from the market to be supplanted with a tamer version. *Resident Evil* (1996) made a plethora of walking dead and mutants the focus of the action, and quickly became a blockbuster success.

Two sequels followed, *Resident Evil 2* (1998) and *Resident Evil 3: Nemesis* (1999), with *Resident Evil: Gun Survivor,* the first version designed to be played with a light-gun, slated for release in 2000. A series of novels based on the game debuted in 1998.

The impact of those games on other media is already evident. Director David Parker's debut direct-to-video feature *The Dead Hate the Living* (2000) patterned the look of its zombies after those in *Resident Evil.*

With *Resident Evil: Code Veronica* and many other walking dead horror-action games due in 2000, and the recent announcement of a third volume in the *Book of the Dead* fiction anthology series, there appears to be no shortage of fresh "dead meat" in the very near future.

The enduring legacy of literature, comics, movies, songs, and the foothold established by the walking-dead genre in the still-emerging interactive game technologies demonstrates its lasting grip on our imaginations, and its adaptability to each generation's needs and nightmares.

Buffy
the Vampire Slayer

BOGEYMEN

RILEY: "What's a Slayer?"

FORREST: "Slayer? Thrash band. Anvil-heavy guitar rock with delusions of Black Sabbath."

RILEY: "No. A girl. With powers."

FORREST: "Oh. The Slayer. Oh, yeah, man. I've heard of the Slayer."

RILEY: "Fill me in."

FORREST: "Well, the way I got it figured, Slayer's like some kind of Bogeyman for the Sub-Terrestrials. Something they tell their little spawn to get them to eat their vegetables and clean up their slime pits."

RILEY: "You're telling me she doesn't exist."

FORREST: "Oh, wait a sec. Am I bursting somebody's bubble here? Maybe this is a bad time to tell you about Lara Croft. And the Easter bunny." —"DOOMED"

BE GOOD, OR THE BOGEYMAN WILL GET YOU. It is not politically correct anymore, but once upon a time, parents said such things to their children on a regular basis. According to legend, a bogeyman was a kind of hobgoblin, or mythical monster that abducted and murdered naughty children. But not all folklore about bogeymen indicates that the preyed-upon children must be naughty. In some cases, the victims are not only children, but entire regions.

Folklore and fable are filled with stories about mysterious individuals who lurk in the shadows and mists of a city or village and prey upon its citizens. But how does one define a bogeyman in the universe of *Buffy*, when the vast majority of monsters who aren't vampires or werewolves are considered demons? The answer: very loosely.

With der Kindestod, it's actually quite simple to make the required connection to classify it as a bogeyman. First, it is never identified as a demon, but it is an ancient, nonhuman creature that preys on children. A Germanic legend invented for the series, der Kindestod not only behaves like a classic bogeyman, he looks like one as well.

Beyond that, however, the bogeymen of the Buffyverse are defined by one fundamental element: Their look, their presentation, and the manner in which they move and behave are all modeled upon the eeriest elements from fairy tales.

the influences

IT IS INTERESTING TO NOTE that when asked what he fears, Whedon invariably comes back to two interconnected themes. First, people scare him. *Terrify* is actually the word he uses. Beyond that, his childhood fears revolved around the humanlike supernatural predators most commonly associated with fairy tales. Bogeymen, really.

"The things that terrify me [as an adult] are people," he notes. But he adds that creatures like der Kindestod are "based on a 'this creeped me out as a kid' thing. The guys with weird flesh over their eyes in [season three's] 'Amends' were designed as some sort of creepy, kind of *Jacob's Ladder*-y thing. A deformed human is scarier than a big reptile with fangs."

He adds that with most of the monsters on the series, "We've been having more fun than fear. At the end of the day, they're just slimy things for

Buffy to kill." But there are exceptions. At the time of this interview, Whedon was preparing to direct his script for the landmark fourth-season episode "Hush," which featured half an hour without dialogue and some of the scariest villains ever to appear on television, the Gentlemen. For Whedon, they represented a purposeful step away from monsters that are "more fun than fear," and a step toward the things that frightened him as a child.

"I'm about to design a new batch for an episode I'm doing," he said at the time. "I want to get back to that creepy sort of silent-movie *Nosferatu* kind of fear. *Nosferatu* is definitely big. I loved that movie when I was a kid. That guy resonates with me as both creepy and hypnotic. So I'm looking at designing some things that are, again, a little bit more fairy tale, childhood creepy, instead of just big, brawny stuntmen with scales."

The Bogeymen

THE UGLY MAN

BUFFY: "I'm glad you showed up. You see, I'm having a really bad day."
THE UGLY MAN: "Lucky Nineteen."
BUFFY: "Scary. I'll tell you something though. There's a lot scarier things out there than you. And now, I'm one of them."
    —AFTER BUFFY'S NIGHTMARE OF BECOMING A VAMPIRE HAS COME TRUE, IN "NIGHTMARES"

EPISODE: "Nightmares," season one

KEY RELATIONSHIPS: The Ugly Man was spawned from the comatose dreams of young Billy Palmer, based on his fear of his kiddie league baseball coach.

UNIQUE ATTRIBUTES: The Ugly Man was a creature made wholly out of Billy's dreams, but he was solid and could hurt or kill living humans.

MOST MONSTROUS MOMENT: The Ugly Man beat a girl named Laura for smoking in school.

CURRENT STATUS: When Billy awakened from his coma, the Ugly Man disappeared.

Like many bogeymen of folklore and fiction, the Ugly Man was a creature manifested out of the unconscious mind of a child. In the creature's single appearance in the season one episode "Nightmares," it existed only as a construct of the imagination of young Billy Palmer.

Billy had been the victim of a beating; later it was revealed he was beaten by his **Kiddie League baseball coach,** who attacked the boy as punishment for botching a critical play. The boy was in a coma subsequent to the attack, and during that time the Ugly Man—a being created by his mind based on the template of the violent coach—manifested itself in the real world. In fact, the script described the Ugly Man this way:

> "Look up bogeyman in the dictionary, you'll see his picture. His face is hideous, distorted; he wears a strange, stunted cap on his head; he has a flap of skin that runs over his dreadful lips, one eye is torn and shredded, and where his right arm should be is a big old club." —PRODUCTION NOTE FROM "NIGHTMARES" SCRIPT

The boy's nightmares, including the Ugly Man, began to alter reality in the town, touching upon other Sunnydale citizens and making their own nightmares come true. A student named Wendell was attacked by spiders. Xander found himself naked in class. Giles could no longer read any of the five languages he was normally fluent in. Buffy's father, Hank, appeared (or at least the nightmare version of him did) to tell Buffy that it was her fault her parents' marriage had broken up.

A girl named Laura was beaten up by the Ugly Man for breaking rules about smoking in school. The Ugly Man said "Lucky Nineteen," a phrase he returned to time and again. It turned out that nineteen was Billy Palmer's jersey number, and that the coach had often called him "Lucky Nineteen."

Billy's unconscious mind astrally projected itself into this nightmare version of reality, and was thus on the run from the Ugly Man. His dreamscape spilled out of his mind and merged with the nightmares he had managed to bring to life from the others. The terrifying clown of Xander's nightmares and Willow's stage fright were all made real. Worst of all, Buffy's fear of the Master becoming free became reality. When the Master hurled her into a grave and buried her alive, only to have her emerge from the grave later as a vampire, two more of Buffy's worst fears were realized.

Billy's astral form sought out Buffy for her help. Giles realized that they needed to wake Billy. They all went to the hospital, where they looked on as Buffy had her final battle with the Ugly Man. Buffy defeated the Ugly Man with Billy's astral form observing, and she inspired him to wake up and confront his fears, just as they had all been forced to do. Billy woke up and everything returned to normal. Shortly thereafter, the Kiddie League coach who had beaten Billy showed up; when he said the phrase "Lucky Nineteen," he unintentionally revealed his crime. Billy confirmed it. Giles and Xander apprehended him, and the man was subsequently arrested.

With that revelation, it seems unlikely that the Ugly Man could ever return.

DER KINDESTOD

RYAN: "He comes at night. The grown-ups don't see him. He was with Tina. He'll come back for us."

BUFFY: "Who?"

RYAN: "Death."   —**"KILLED BY DEATH"**

EPISODE: "Killed by Death," season two

UNIQUE ATTRIBUTES: Der Kindestod was only visible to children, madmen, and the feverishly ill.

MOST MONSTROUS MOMENT: It spent its life killing children. They were *all* monstrous moments.

CURRENT STATUS: Buffy snapped the monster's neck at the end of "Killed by Death."

In season two's "Killed by Death," Buffy was hospitalized after injuries sustained in a battle against the then-evil Angel combined with a terrible flu to sideline her from Slaying duties. During her stay in the hospital, she discovered that something was preying on the kids in the pediatrics ward. A child had died, and Buffy, in a feverish state, thought she had seen the monster who caused it. That along with experiences she had had as a child (see below), made her believe other children in the ward when they told her about the monster that was coming for them.

Research ensued, and soon enough, Buffy and friends realized they were dealing with der Kindestod. Dressed like an "eighteenth-century undertaker," with flesh like white clay and rows of needle-sharp teeth, the creature was lurking in the corridors of the hospital attacking children.

The main difficulty in fighting the monster was that der Kindestod was only visible to children, madmen, and people with extremely high, hallucinatory-level fevers.

> "It's called 'Der Kindestod.'...The name means 'Child Death.' This book says that he feeds off children by sucking the life out of them. Blech. Anyway, afterwards, it looks like they died because they were sick." —**CORDELIA, IN "KILLED BY DEATH"**

Der Kindestod hovered over its victims, usually pinning them to their beds, and its eyes protruded from its head, elongating and becoming probiscises through which it sucked the life force from them. When Buffy was a small child, der Kindestod killed her cousin Celia in a hospital while Buffy watched. Celia screamed for help but, while she could see her killer, Buffy saw nothing but her cousin dying mysteriously and violently and could do nothing about it.

Buffy recovered from her flu, but when they realized that it was her fever that had allowed her to see der Kindestod, she intentionally ingested a virus so that she would get a fever again. Thanks to that high fever, Buffy was able see the monster again, and their conflict resulted in its death when she broke its neck.

"I'm actually a really big fan of the Kindestod," Joss Whedon says. "The Kindestod scared people more than any monster we had made [up to that point]. Very specifically, he was designed that way. I drew a picture of him. I can't stress how bad [the drawing] was, but I had a very specific thing in mind for him.

"A lot of our demons are built in the fantasy mode. They're not scary; they're just kind of cool looking. [With der Kindestod] I wanted to get into that real childhood Grimms' fairy tale fear, and so I designed a guy in the classic mode with the beak nose and the dark hat and the big scary old man kind of monster. A lot of people just wigged."

The episode featuring der Kindestod went through a multitude of versions before finally making it to the screen. "Killed by Death" writers Rob Des Hotel and Dean Batali remember the process quite well.

"This episode was actually based on the idea of a day care center," Batali notes. "The first draft had Buffy and the gang doing community service at an orphanage, which conveniently also housed elderly people. It was an experiment to combine elderly people with children because it was healthy interaction for both of them. Joss thought old people were creepy. We had pitched a lot of ideas about evil children. To me, it's one of the great 'lost' Buffy episodes because I really liked the script.

"Every time one of the children was to be adopted, the prospective parents would die. The children were seen getting together in a circle, and you thought they were doing the killing, and the old people were very nice and in danger. In the end, it was discovered that it was the old people doing the killing in order to keep the children around. They were going to steal the life out of the children or something; it was very complicated. There were cats involved in it, too. The old people actually turned into panthers. It was horribly complicated.

"Anyway, it didn't work, so we changed it to a hospital. Buffy was sharing a room with this old woman who seemed innocent and lovely but in the middle of the night she was turning into the Kindestod and going and sucking the life out of the children. There was an interesting scene when the Kindestod is climbing up the side of the building and turns into the old woman, then slips in through the window and crawls into bed. But it got even more complicated because she was invisible as the Kindestod but visible as the old woman.

"It just didn't make sense. How you could see her now, and not then? Some of that carried over into the final version, where you couldn't see the Kindestod unless you were a child or had a really high fever. Our problem was that it was a monster that had three steps. It was an old woman who turns into a monster who is then invisible. We got rid of the old woman [aspect of the story]."

His writing partner Des Hotel notes that there were even more complications leading up to the creation of the finished episode.

"Der Kindestod really came out of sheer desperation to find the appropriate monster to be roaming the hospital," Des Hotel says. "It was originally an old woman, but there was no way to make that not be about aging. The part we liked was that kids are in the hospital, and Buffy does not like hospitals. The reason kids don't like hospitals is that death creeps around, so we thought, what if death is really creeping around? I'm not familiar with any specific lore like it, though I'm sure it exists."

As to the monster's method of killing his victims, that also came from the myriad versions of the story that ended up resolving themselves into a frightening and coherent hour of television.

"Part of where his method of killing came from is that when the killer was intended to be an eighty-five-year-old woman, she used a cat idol to summon all these cats, and using the cats' power, she could take the youth from these kids. The idea was that you had to smash the cat idol to destroy her power. We all discussed the folklore about cats doing that thing, where they sit on your chest and suck your life out."

Batali and Des Hotel also recall that there was some debate as to whether or not der Kindestod was a solo act, or part of a race of such creatures. But Joss Whedon has the final word on that theory.

"What's scary about the Kindestod is that there's just one," Whedon insists. "When you say 'race' you get into science fiction. That's not to say there couldn't be another. But you don't think, 'The bogeyman and his bogeyman clan are coming.' You think of the bogeyman, that thing that embodies my fear. To say there's a race of them makes it less scary, as opposed to saying there's a thing that wants to hurt me and I'm a child. We wanted something . . . scary, on the level of childhood fantasy."

THE GENTLEMEN

"Who are the Gentlemen? They are fairy-tale monsters. What do they want? Hearts. They come to a town....They steal all the voices, so no one can scream. They need seven. They have at least two. In the tales, no sword can kill them. But the princess screamed once and they all died." —FROM VOICELESS GILES'S SLIDE-SHOW PRESENTATION, IN "HUSH"

EPISODE: "Hush," season four

UNIQUE ATTRIBUTES: The Gentlemen floated above the air instead of walking and had monstrous footmen to do their bidding. The sound of a human voice could kill them. They used magic to gather human voices to prevent that outcome.

MOST MONSTROUS MOMENT: Their modus operandi included the tearing out of human hearts.

CURRENT STATUS: Buffy's scream made their heads explode—literally—at the end of "Hush."

In the groundbreaking season four episode "Hush"—more than half of which transpired without any spoken dialogue whatsoever—Buffy had a prophetic dream warning of danger to come. In the dream, a small girl holding a carved wooden box in her hands chanted a children's rhyme in a singsong voice:

"Can't even shout. Can't even cry. The Gentlemen are coming by. Looking in windows, knocking on doors . . . they need to take seven and they might take yours. Can't call to mom. Can't say a word. You're gonna die screaming but you won't be heard."
—SPIRIT GIRL, IN "HUSH"

The eerie, childlike song and the dream prophesied the coming of "the Gentlemen," horrible, bogeymen-type creatures who would arrive in a town and magically collect the voices of the population in a box. They needed people to be silent so that when they attacked in their effort to harvest seven human hearts, no one could scream. Silence was required because the sound of a human scream could kill them.

Once Giles had done his research, he set up a kind of slide show to clue in Buffy and the others. "They are fairy-tale monsters," he revealed through pictures. "In the tales, no sword can kill them, but the princess screamed once and they all died."

The Gentlemen were horrid, pale-faced creatures dressed in long black garments who floated in the air rather than walking. Their faces were etched with permanent grins, and they never spoke. Also, they had monstrous servants, their footmen, who aided them in their search for victims whose hearts they could steal.

By the episode's end, with the aid of new love Riley Finn, Buffy battled the Gentlemen, destroyed the magical box—returning the stolen voices of the people of Sunnydale—and then she screamed. The sound of her voice caused the Gentlemen's heads to explode.

There is no way to know if the group of Gentlemen who came to Sunnydale were the only ones.

What Lurks Beneath the Bed

IN A WAY, every being described in this book is a bogeyman, or boogeyman, embodying otherwise nameless fears and dread. The term *bogeyman* is often an all-encompassing one. The all-devouring wolf of "Little Red Riding Hood" (see Primals), the troll beneath the bridge that threatened the three Billy Goats Gruff, the cannibal witch of "Hansel and Gretel," today's alien abductors who can pass through walls and steal sleeping "specimens" from their beds. Those are bogeymen, one and all, as were real-life child killers like King Herod and Gilles de Rais. But can any of them really lay claim to being *the* bogeyman?

In the distant past, Death was a bogeyman, come to claim all mortals at the end of their days; but the skull-faced, cloaked, grim reaper figure is Death itself, much more than a mere bogeyman. Death's sibling, Sleep, was also considered a bogeyman in some cultures (see discussion of the Sandman, below). At one time, Father Christmas, the benevolent fellow we now call Santa Claus, was a bogeyman whose omnipotent powers and terrible cravings terrified children. Once named, however, those creatures of the night ceased to be "bogeymen" in all but the general sense of the word. For once otherwise named and identified, none of them are *the* bogeyman.

The name *bogeyman* is still commonly used as a sort of catchall moniker for any unwelcome haunt or visitor who cannot be otherwise identified. It is usually associated with otherwise-nameless creatures hungry for human flesh, specifically that of children—hence, the enduring use of the term to frighten children into behaving or going to bed, and the necessity of keeping a night-light on for the traumatized youngsters. Even using that somewhat narrower definition, we would necessarily have to include fairy-tale ogres, trolls, goblins, ghouls, changelings, faerie-folk, werewolves, demons, fictional cannibals from Jack's beanstalk giant to Hannibal Lecter, and real-life cannibals from Sawney Beane to Jeffrey Dahmer. This chapter would thus be longer than any other in this book. We must dig deeper and ask ourselves: Who or what *is* the bogeyman?

Bogeyman Legend and Lore

SOME FOLKLORISTS, PSYCHOLOGISTS, and researchers argue that the bogeyman's identity as it is now popularly understood emerged with the rise of children's literature, beginning with the publication of *Mother Goose Rhymes* in 1697. Clearly, bogeyman lore predates such printed literature and emerged from a venerable oral tradition of myths and legends. The bogeyman became something fairly specific throughout the twentieth century.

The term has its roots in Celtic and European faerie lore, where bogies, bogeys, and bogles dwelled. The word is also associated with the term *bug,* which originally meant "devil." In *Abbey Lubbers, Banshees, and Bogarts* (1979), Katharine Briggs described bogies and their kin— "bogles, bug-a-boos, and bogey-beasts"—as "a whole class of mischievous, frightening, and dangerous creatures whose delight it is to torment man." Related faerie folk at times fit this definition: consider the diminuative brownies, a species of hobgoblin known in the Scottish Lowlands and much of England, who sprouted elongated, pointy noses to become boggarts when they indulged in particularly malicious mischief. Bogies and bogles belonged to the Scots' fabled Unseelie Court, elevating them to a higher level of nocturnal malice.

Bogies and their kind occasionally gathered to frighten people, but most of them were considered solitary creatures. As evidenced in tales recorded by Briggs such as "The Bogie's Field," in which a crafty farmer's turn of a phrase cleverly outwitted a bogie laying claim to a field he wished to farm, bogies could be tricked, but they were also feared and could bedevil a person to an early grave.

In time bogies were identified with specific names, forms, and behavior. The Scots called them *bogles,* and they were believed to torment only wicked persons and protect those in need of shelter or care. Bauchan or bogans were mischievous beings that were believed to aid humans they liked. The Cornish spriggans were bogies who were believed to protect faerie folk, rushing to confront anyone foolhardy enough to try and capture, insult, or steal from their masters. The grotesque, savage spriggans were said to be the ghosts of giants slain by the invading Britons.

Many shapeshifting bogie-beasts inhabited regional lore of the United Kingdom. The Shock was indigenous to Suffolk, and believed to resemble a horse, donkey, calf, an oversized canine, or a spectral funeral procession. Though the shock could assume the form of a dog, the Skriker of Lancashire and Yorkshire, the Barguest, the North Country's Padfoot, the Hedley Kow, and the free-roaming fairy blackdogs were more often described as specifically canine bogie-beasts.

With their flaming red eyes, sharp teeth, horns, and long tails, these creatures were widely feared; some of them, like the Barguest, were considered a kind of banshee (the Celtic prophet of death), and it was very unlucky to see one. Other wild fairy beasts like the "grant" and wild fairy horses like the Each Uisge of the Highlands were also considered bogie-beasts.

There were many other nursery bogies specifically designed to keep children in line in the outdoors, such as Jack-up-the-Orchut, the Gooseberry Wife, Lazy Laurence, Melsh Dick, and Churnmilk Peg. Others kept little tykes away from pools of water, where Jenny Greenteeth, Nelly Longarms, and Grindylow waited (or waded) to snatch unwary children into the deep.

There were also Tom Poker, Old Scratty, Mumpker, Tankerabogus, and Tom Dockin in the British Isles. Author Marina Warner cites Switzerland's Child-Guzzler, Germany's Erlking, and France's malignant Le Grand Lustucru, Pere Fouettard, and Monsieur and Madame Croquemitaine, all of whom likewise preyed on wayward chidren.

The nursery goblin Raw-Head-and-Bloody-Bones, aka Tommy Rawhead, malingered in pits or dark cupboards waiting for humans. Novelist Clive Barker later fleshed out this bogeyman and gave him a more regal legacy to craft one of the most terrifying of all contemporary monster stories,

"Rawhead Rex" (1984). Despite the timely updating of the theme, Barker's primordial brute still preferred children's flesh.

The Nursery Bogeyman

ISABELLA DE MORELOOSE'S AUTOBIOGRAPHICAL MEMOIRS (1695) referred to childhood tales of "bugbears" and "bogeymen." In 1697, *Mother Goose Rhymes* and fairy tales transcribed by Charles Perrault from the oral tradition saw print. By the time of famed artist Francisco de Goya's celebrated graphic album *Los Caprichos* (1793–98), the moniker of "bugbear" or "bogeyman" was common enough to provide the foundation of his third plate, "Que viene el Coco" ("Here's the Bugbear," or "Here Comes the Bogeyman"). In this illustration, Goya pictured a cowled adult frightening two cowering children, huddled and crying alongside an adult woman, who gazes up at the figure with a strangely bemused expression.

The bogeyman figure used to terrify children into preferred behavior was just a precursor of the devils, demons, witches, and ogres adults feared as well. Spain's "El Coco" was also pictured as a black devil, an image that (like Italy's catchall bogeyman moniker *l'omo negro*) later assumed racist connotations, though such figures still haunted the most terrifying sequences in Walt Disney's cartoon feature *Pinocchio* (1940), herding wayward children into seduction, transformation, subjugation, and slavery on Pleasure Island.

Common fears of the dark, of sleep, of death, of being consumed were always associated with the amorphous bogeyman. In *No Go the Bogeyman*, Marina Warner excavates a rhyme from Brittany that is still sung, concluding with the image of "the great Lustucru who is passing... carrying off in his knapsack all the little children who aren't asleep."

From Folklore to Fiction

THE MYTHICAL "SANDMAN" who brings sleep and dreams was often portrayed in folklore as a threatening bogeyman, associating sleep with death—which often was the case before twentieth-century medicine and parenting practices minimized the common catastrophe of crib death. In Greek mythology, Thanatos (Death) dwelled in the Underworld with his brother Hypnos (Sleep) and Hypnos's son Morpheus (Dreams). Even today, popular culture occasionally embraces those venerable beliefs with evocative power. The original comic-book character named the Sandman, who debuted in 1939 (in *Adventure Comics* #40 and *New York World's Fair* comics, both from National Periodicals) was a vigilante hero, revised (in *Adventure Comics* #72–91) by writer Joe Simon and Jack Kirby to become an otherworldly superhero who watched over and protected all who sleep, and kept the dream realm free of villains and monsters.

NEIL GAIMAN

Neil Gaiman's sophisticated revamp *The Sandman* (DC Comics, 1989–97) knowingly incorporated many world mythologies and fantasies into its elaborate tapestry, from the Arabian Nights to Shakespeare's *A Midsummer Night's Dream*, with the enigmatic Morpheus at its center.

It was not always thus. In setting the stage for his tale "The Sand-Man" (1817, first published in 1855), German author Ernst Theodor Amadeus Hoffmann evoked the traditional Sandman of nursery lore, describing the Sandman as a real creature, "a wicked man, who comes to little children when they won't go to bed and throws handfuls of sand into their eyes, so that they jump out of their heads all bloody; and he puts them into a bag and takes them to the half moon as food for his little ones; and they sit there in the nest and have hooked beaks like owls, and they pick naughty little boys' and girls' eyes out with them."

Hoffmann's classic story impressed Sigmund Freud, who drew much from the tale for his famous essay "The Uncanny." Freud found in Hoffmann's terrifying loss-of-eyes imagery a metaphor for castration fears. As with the bogeymen Lustucru, the fearful early incarnations of Santa Claus, and others, the Sandman's bag was an essential prop, used to carry away its bloody booty. The loss of one's eyes, of the power of sight; the loss of one's genitals, of one's potency; the loss of one's voice, as in the *Buffy the Vampire Slayer* episode "Hush"—all embody aspects of the dread of sleep, that most vulnerable state of being when we might fall prey to dreams, nightmares, or the bogeyman.

Paul Berry's eerie British stop-motion animated short *The Sandman* (1991) offered a remarkable meditation on childhood fears of bedtime and sleep. In some fantasies, the Sandman is still portrayed as *a* bogeyman —but the Sandman, in all his permutations, is no longer *the* bogeyman, if ever he was considered such.

Children's lullabies and storybooks used their imaginary bogeymen to discourage specific behaviors frowned upon by parents and caregivers. There are many examples we could give, but one will suffice. Samuel Clemens, aka Mark Twain, published a "freely translated" edition of Dr. Heinrich Hoffmann's children's rhyme book *Struwwelpeter* (*Slovenly Peter*, 1845), which included "The Story of Little Suck-a-Thumb." This short rhyme (accompanied in Twain's edition with four crude, vivid illustrations) depicted the fate of little Conrad, whose mother warned him not to suck his thumb while she was away. "The great tall tailor always comes/To little boys that suck their thumbs...He takes his great sharp scissors out/And cuts their thumbs clean off—and then/You know, they never grow again." Sure enough, Conrad dismissed his mother's stern warning and "the great, long, red-legged scissor-man" sheared his thumbs off. Though intended by both Hoffman and Twain as satire, Freud's castration anxieties were never delineated with more chilling clarity.

Countless storybook, rhyme, and lullaby bogeymen served similar disciplinary ends. With the turn of the cenury, the archetype still held sway, as demonstrated by Victorian cartoonist and painter Richard "Dicky" Doyle's illustration "The Bogeyman" (1890), depicting a lanky stick-limbed grotesque carting off a ragged batch of children, one dangling from his hand, the others limp in the basket slung over his shoulder. That same year, a music-hall song titled "The Bogey Man" was published. In the next half-cenury, the bogeyman's role would shift dramatically.

twentieth-century schizoid bogeyman

FROM ITS BEGINNINGS, cinema brought a variety of bogeymen to the screen, beginning with Georges Méliès's uncharacteristically grim short *In the Bogie Man's Cave* (1907), in which the titular Bogie Man was shown chopping apart a little boy and devouring him. Later fantasy films were careful not to similarly traumatize younger viewers with their bogeymen.

Gradually, the pop-cultural bogeyman began to assume a more benevolent and complex relationship with its audience, who found more to relate to than to fear in the mythic figure. Throughout John Stanley's script and art tenure on the comic-book series *Marge's Little Lulu* (Dell/Gold Key, 1947–70), the never-shown bogeyman was a scary outsider lurking in the eternal darkness of a neighbor's basement. *Little Lulu* firmly placed its bogeyman amid the small-town American neighborhoods its readers lived in, affirming its existence in a recognizable contemporary world.

Whereas the bogeymen of lullabies and bedtime tales had once been wielded by parents to keep their kids in line, the tables had turned. In the once despised and now revered pre-Code horror comics, contemporary imaginary bogeymen began to offer succor against unfair, abusive authority figures. In the EC comic story "Grounds...for Horror!" (*Tales from the Crypt* #29, April 1952), the brutal stepfather (who is a butcher by profession) of a boy named Artie sadistically capitalized on the child's fear of the dark by shutting him in an unlit closet at the slightest provocation. In time, Artie seemed to deal with the abuse by interacting and talking to an invisible being he called Hozir, which lived in the dark closet. Artie insisted, however, that Hozir was real and wanted to punish the stepfather.

In the end, mother came home to find Artie sobbing in a locked closet and the stepfather literally reduced to mincemeat on his butcher's table.

With Maurice Sendak's *Where the Wild Things Are* (1963), bogeymen became once and for all time viable alter egos for children. Despite their fierce demeanors, claws, horns, and bellowing, Sendak's "wild things" were really metaphors for wild impulses of the main character, a boy named Max, and as such could of course be tamed by the child himself. Max's never-shown mother calls him a "wild thing" when he wears his wolf suit and pretends to attack and bite. Thus, Max's tale empowered the young reader and dissipated any fears raised by the early pages of the book.

Max's successors included Calvin of Bill Watterson's comic strip *Calvin and Hobbes*, whose own ambivalent relations with the bogeymen living under his bed provided chuckles and insight into the archetype's current status quo in the era of books like Anne Sayre Wiseman's *Nightmare Help: A Guide for Parents and Teachers* (1986). As in *Little Lulu*, the bogeymen are a "fact" of Calvin's life, however savvy (or clueless) his parents may be. Raymond Briggs's *Fungus the Bogeyman* (1977) extended the association, playing to children's affection for gross body humor.

More traditional bogeymen haunted two episodes of *the Real Ghostbusters* cartoon series (ABC, 1986–88, based on the popular feature film *Ghostbusters*, 1984; see Ghosts), both scripted by Michael Reaves: "The Boogie Man Cometh" (1986) and the sequel, "The Bogeyman Is Back" (1987; the altered spelling is from the series).

Live-action films embraced the new bogeyman aesthetic. *Monster in the Closet* (Troma, 1986) was a gory black comedy parodying the archetype, one of the few such bogeyman comedies not specifically targeted to young audiences.

The surprise sleeper box office popularity of Tim Burton's farcical feature *Beetlejuice* (1988, see Ghosts) marked the rising popularity of suitable-for-all-ages black comedies. The Disney Channel anticipated the *Beetlejuice* theme with the made-for-cable *Mr. Boogedy* (1986) and *Bride of Boogedy* (1987), both written by Michael Janover, directed by Oz Scott, and starring Howard Witt as Mr. Boogedy, the benevolent haunt of a practical-joke-loving suburban family. Disney later broadcast the similar *Don't Look Under the Bed* (1999). Disney also bankrolled directly on Tim Burton's name to produce *Tim Burton's The Nightmare Before Christmas* (1993), an expansive stop-motion animated puppet feature presented as a fantasy musical-operetta composed by frequent Burton collaborator Danny Elfman, which introduced the villainous Oogie Boogie, a boisterous Cab Calloway–inspired bogeyman depicted as a canvas-bag being animated by venomous insects.

Though *Little Monsters* (1989) was dismissed by many as a *Beetlejuice* knockoff, it succinctly redefined the role the bogeyman had come to assume for latch-key children growing up with dwindling middle-class comforts, high divorce rates, and broken homes. Too often left to their own devices, children began to see the bogeyman as a suitable playmate.

In the wake of Raymond Briggs's *Fungus* and the *Fungus the Bogeyman Plop-Up Book* and the theatrical success of *Beetlejuice*, cartoons like *Beetlejuice* (CBS, 1989–91) and *The Ren and Stimpy Show* (MTV/Nickelodeon, 1991–94) reveled in gross-out humor. Once the snot-and-puke barrier had been broken, animated cartoons were free to indulge in the new, friendly bogeyman-as-alter-ego archetype with Briggs-like abandon. Australia-based Danger Productions produced the stop-motion animated series *Bump in the Night* (ABC, 1994–96) featuring a menagerie of bogeys living under beds, in cupboards, and even toilets.

The same TV season introduced Klasky Csupo Inc's cartoon series *Aaahh!!! Real Monsters* (Nickelodeon, 1994–96), in which a class of student monsters and bogeys at Monster Academy learned how to scare their victims.

By the 1990s, the bogeyman was no longer an unwelcome bedroom invader but a merchandisable mass market commodity—a far cry from the fearful monsters once used to scare children into proper daytime and bedtime behavior.

Bogeymen with Blades and Teeth

THOUGH VERY YOUNG CHILDREN found an increasing sense of camaraderie with the traditional bogeymen figures once used to frighten them, not all the contemporary bogeymen were so comforting. Far more distressing were the bogeymen haunting Ken Bruce's cartoon short *Lullaby* (1991), a maim-the-tot anecdote malicious enough to place in *Spike & Mike's Sick & Twisted Festival of Animation Volume 1* (1993). Richard Donner's *Radio Flyer* (1992) and other films plucked similar nerves in the midst of naturalist stories of domestic abuse. None did so as eloquently as David Cronenberg's *The Brood* (1979), an elaborate exploration of the ravages and legacy of misplaced parental rage in which the now-adult victim of such abuse (Samantha Eggar) biologically manifested her own anger as a brood of murderous mutant children.

Stephen King has explored the contemporary family-related guises of the bogeyman archetype more frequently and fluently than any modern writer. King's novels *'Salem's Lot* (1975), *The Shining* (1977), and *Cujo* (1981) overtly incorporated childhood terrors of barely seen horrors. In *'Salem's Lot*, it is the specter of a hanging man and the moment of recognition when a priest realizes the vampire's face is that of his closet-lurking childhood bogeyman "Mr. Flip." In *Cujo*, a child's fear of a slavering bogey-beast in the closet manifests itself with murderous intent as the rabid St. Bernard Cujo (remember, Scottish and Celtic bogey-beasts usually manifest themselves as monstrous dogs).

King explored the theme concisely very early in his career with the short story "The Boogeyman" (originally published in *Cavalier*, March 1973; reprinted in *Night Shift*, 1978), a tale told by an oddly insensitive, aloof, and abrasive father to his psychiatrist Dr. Harper. Lester Billings had lost all three of his children to "crib death." Billings related his growing belief that the bogeyman was the culprit, chronicling each child's terror of their room's closet and his own belief that by leaving their closet doors open, he allowed the bogeyman access to them. Even as we assume Billings was the killer, he returns to Harper's office to find the closet door opening wide, where the bogeyman waits, whispering "so nice" as it emerges with "its Dr. Harper mask in one rotted, spade-claw hand."

The apparent affirmation of the creature's existence in the final line settles nothing, given Billings's mental condition. In *Stephen King: The Art of Darkness* (1984), Douglas E. Winter declared "The Boogeyman" to be an "important key to all of Stephen King's horror fiction."

King's novel *The Shining* expanded upon the father-as-bogeyman theme (as did its 1980 film adaptation by Stanley Kubrick and the 1997 TV version). In one particularly vivid passage, the psychic child Danny realized that the force haunting the Overlook Hotel had overtaken his father: ". . . it was coming for him. It was hiding behind Daddy's face, it was imitating Daddy's voice, it was wearing Daddy's clothes. But it was not his daddy."

King subsequently explored this theme to its nightmarish conclusions in the ambitious, epic-length novel *It* (1986).

To date, all of King's works cited above have been filmed, including New York University School undergraduate student Jeffrey C. Schiro's adaptation, *The Boogeyman* (1995). *Stephen King's IT* was produced as a two-part TV movie (1990), and it consolidated the novel's considerable strengths (particularly in its first half, detailing the harrowing childhoods of its collective cast of characters). Another Stephen King bogeyman popped up in the final episode of the anthology film *Cat's Eye* (1985), in which the nominal feline hero of the film rescued little Drew Barrymore from an unexplained miniature troll-like creature that emerged from the baseboard in her bedroom to steal her breath as she slept.

While King's bogeymen traded primarily on familiar lore brought into a modern context, there were other, more brutal extensions of the themes already in existence and far more on the way. Some were spawned by the underground horror comix of the late 1960s and early 1970s, which were ushered in by *Bogeyman Comics* (three issues, 1969–70), the brainchild of San Francisco comix guru Gary Arlington. The titular "Bogeyman" was the host of this debut horror comix series, a hollow-eyed, howling apparition who occasionally appeared in the stories themselves, true to the

tradition of the pre-Code EC comics that inspired the title. *Bogeyman* #1 also embraced the archetype through the raw, primitive art of its solo writer-artist Rory Hayes.

Hayes remained the prime contributor as more polished underground cartoonists contributed to subsequent issues until the planned *Bogeyman* #4 was delayed and finally published as *Laugh in the Dark* (1971). Hayes's Bogeyman host made one more appearance in *Skull Comics* #1 (1970).

Almost a decade later a new breed of contemporary bogeyman appeared, intent on inspiring genuine terror in older children and young adults. Michael Myers, the masked "Shape" of the *Halloween* film series (1978–98), was the first of these coming-of-age bogeymen, a potent new incarnation rooted in contemporary urban legends calculated to tap teenage fears.

JOHN CARPENTER

John Carpenter's *Halloween* seemed to emerge from the woodwork, dauntingly simple in design and elegantly straightforward in its execution. Borrowing elements from Bob Clark's psycho-killer gem *Black Christmas* (aka *Stranger in the House*, 1974) and drawing in part from the urban legend about a baby-sitter trapped in a house with a killer making phone calls to her from upstairs, *Halloween* quietly debuted in October 1978 with little fanfare. It quickly snowballed into one of the most profitable independent films in cinema history.

The action opened on Halloween night 1963, where six-year-old Michael Myers (Will Sandin) inexplicably stabbed his teenage sister to death. Fifteen years later, Michael escaped from an asylum and returned to his hometown on Halloween. Wearing a nondescript mask (actually an unpainted William Shatner *Star Trek* mask!), he stalked baby-sitter Laurie Strode (Jamie Lee Curtis), killing her circle of friends before coming after her and her young charges. Later in the film series Laurie was revealed to be Michael's other sister.

Michael Myers, referred to in the credits as the Shape, was presented as a mute, implacable predator throughout. Eschewing the comforting revisionist bogeymen of post-Sendak children's literature and media, *Halloween* refuted any potential identification with its bogeyman, wryly introduced as a more chilling childhood alter ego: unlike Sendak's Max, Carpenter's preadolescent "wild thing" butchered his sister.

After Laurie blinded and repeatedly stabbed the Shape, Dr. Sam Loomis (Donald Pleasence) emptied his revolver into the killer, driving him over a second-story balcony to his apparent death—only to have him disappear into the night. Shaken, Laurie stammered, "Was that the bogeyman?" to which Loomis replied, "As a matter of fact, it was." Carpenter closed with a montage of the shadowy interior of the house and the dark streets of the town itself, accompanied by the sound of Michael's breathing. He was simply gone, as if merged with the night: opaque, implacable, and seemingly unkillable.

Halloween II (1981) was of interest for its repetitive use of the venerable Pat Ballard tune "Mr. Sandman," overtly linking Michael Myers's faceless, murderous nightcomer with E. T. A.

Hoffmann's eye-plucking Sandman. The third installment in the series was strangely unrelated to the previous or subsequent films.

By 1981, movie screens were already swarming with all manner of homegrown Michael Myers wannabes. Many of them based their respective stalkers and killers on invented regional bogeymen such as the "Cropsy Horror" of *The Burning* (1981). In time, those urban legend–inspired psychopaths culminated in savvy, self-aware, revisionist slasher films such as *Scream* (1996).

Paramount's *Friday the 13th* series (1980–93)—featuring the hockey-masked killer Jason— was the most pervasive and profitable *Halloween*-inspired series of them all. In *Friday the 13th Part 2* (1981), Jason had assumed center stage; he held that position in all but one film, where his murderous legacy was mimicked by a fake "Jason" (in *Friday the 13th Part V: A New Beginning*, 1985). With the next episode (*Part VI*), Jason rose from his grave to join the ranks of the resurrected dead (see The Walking Dead), extending his cinematic reign for three more installments. As of this writing, a tenth film in the series had just been announced.

Despite the wishes of *Halloween*'s creators, Michael Myers resumed his bogeyman role (and Donald Pleasence returned as Dr. Loomis) in the wake of Jason's waning series for *Halloween 4: The Return of Michael Myers* (1988), this time stalking his unfortunate little niece (Danielle Harris). Two more meandering sequels followed (1989 and 1995) until Jamie Lee Curtis took on Michael one last time in *Halloween H2O* (1998).

The most potent modern pop-culture variation on the Sandman bogeyman archetype remains Wes Craven's creation Freddy Krueger. The immolated child murderer who plagued the nightmares of teenagers in the *Nightmare on Elm Street* film series (1984–94) was certainly a modern-day bogeyman, able to manifest himself physically in order to kill his victims, asleep or awake (though sleep remained his preferred vehicle throughout the series).

Tellingly, Freddy's mercurial shapeshifting abilities were designed to reflect and embody the very specific phobias of his victims. Thus, Craven's Krueger embodied *all* the bogeymen ever known, though it is important to note that he is never referred to as such. Craven contributed to the script of *A Nightmare on Elm Street 3: The Dream Warriors* (1987) and returned for *Wes Craven's New Nightmare* (1994), which provided a compelling final act to the series.

The *Nightmare* series habitually indulged in special-effects set pieces, gore, music-video diversions, and groan-inducing wisecracks. Despite Craven's triumphant return to the series, New Line still could not resist having Freddy's gloved hand make a cameo appearance at the end of *Jason Goes to Hell: The Final Friday* (1993), establishing the precedent for a long-awaited (but as yet unfilmed) wrestling match between corporate Hollywood's two most profitable bogeymen.

Whereas once parents had used the bogeyman to frighten their children into acceptable behavior, modern parents now fought corporate America to keep such images away from their offspring. But even without the movies, the restraint that had once applied to network television had all but disappeared, and thus quite disturbing bogeymen could be found on the small screen as well.

David Lynch and Mark Frost collaborated on the enigmatic, dreamlike TV series *Twin Peaks* (1990–91), which for a time captured a cult audience with the mystery of who in the sleepy Northwest town of Twin Peaks might have killed teenage ingenue Laura Palmer (Sheryl Lee). The series' convoluted mystery and engaging semi-satire of soap opera melodramatics soon gave way to Lynch's peculiar brand of mysticism, hinging the solution to its central mystery on an increasingly elusive stream of premonitions, dreams, and waking visions of a parallel realm. This eerie curtained world of "the Red Lodge" was inhabited by a backward-speaking dwarf, doppelgangers, and a murderous spirit presence named Bob (Frank Silva), an ancient evil that had possessed Laura's father, Leland (Ray Wise) since childhood, driving him to incest, sadism, and murder. Bob was a startling incarnation of the bogeyman archetype, a long-haired, denim-jacketed vagrant first seen hunkered down at the foot of Laura's bed. Bob was later seen gazing out from a mirror Leland stared into, and at the point of claiming another victim, Leland seemed to become Bob.

At another critical point, Bob was associated with the sudden appearance of an owl, recalling E. T. A. Hoffmann's predatory Sandman and implying shapeshifting abilities. Echoing and amplifying Stephen King's association of the bogeyman myth with domestic abuse, infanticide, and murderous alter egos, Lynch continued to explore the back story of Twin Peaks, Bob, the Red Lodge, and the perverse relationship between father Leland and daughter Laura in the feature film "prequel" *Twin Peaks: Fire Walk with Me* (1992). Though critics and audiences abandoned the series, *Twin Peaks* continues to attract a strong cult following and ongoing critical reassessment of its accomplishments. It remains the most compelling reinvention of the bogeyman archetype to date, though it will certainly not be the last.

As we enter the new millennium, the bogeyman is sure to take on new and fascinating permutations.

Marcie Ross
"Have a nice summer."

Buffy the Vampire Slayer

INVISIBLE PEOPLE

XANDER: "Well, that was a buncha laughs. Look, Buff, we're all tired and a little on edge. Maybe Willow's overreacting. I'm sure part of it's 'cause of how you've been pushing away girl lately. But now's not the time to let that stuff tear us apart. What I'm saying is, I'm still with you. Right by your side, all the—"

BUFFY (eyes darting around): "Xander?!"

XANDER: "Funny. Nice to see you haven't lost your sense of inappropriate humor."

—AFTER XANDER IS RENDERED INVISIBLE, IN "FEAR, ITSELF"

ARE INVISIBLE PEOPLE NECESSARILY MONSTERS? Of course not. It would have been more accurate, perhaps, to include the sole permanently invisible person from *Buffy the Vampire Slayer* under the category Human Monsters. However, given the special ability that makes them more—or less—than human (the definition of *monster* in this book), we felt that individuals with such an odd condition or power ought to be represented with their own category. A major factor in the decision was this: like the vampire, the werewolf, the zombie, the ghost, and the witch, the invisible person is an archetypal pop-culture "monster."

In the mythos of *Buffy*, we have solid information on only one invisible person, Marcie Ross (see below). Buffy, Giles, and the others believe Marcie's transformation was caused by proximity to the Hellmouth. However, in the end of the episode with Marcie ("Out of Mind, Out of Sight"), it is revealed that people turning invisible is not nearly as uncommon as we were led to believe. Apparently there are a lot of invisible people, and most of them have been co-opted to work for the American government as spies and assassins.

> **"Greek myths talk about cloaks of invisibility, but they're usually just for the gods. . . . Research boy comes through with the knowledge."**
> **—XANDER, IN "OUT OF MIND, OUT OF SIGHT"**

Marcie's invisibility drove her somewhat mad, making a shy high school girl angry and brutal enough to commit murder. Though we don't have enough information to determine if there are heroic invisible people in the *Buffy* universe, the number of invisible people with Marcie at the end of that episode seems to imply that many have had the same behavioral changes due to their condition.

The Invisible People

MARCIE ROSS

BUFFY: "Okay, this is my problem. I touched the thing. It didn't go through me, it bumped into me. And it wasn't cold."

XANDER: "So this means, what—that we're talking about an invisible person?"

BUFFY: "A girl. She spoke. Said Harmony deserved what she got."

GILES: "A girl on campus with the power to turn invisible."

XANDER: "Man, that is so cool. I'd give anything to be able to turn invisible. (off their looks) Well, I wouldn't be beating people up. I'd use my power to protect the girls' locker room."

—"OUT OF MIND, OUT OF SIGHT"

EPISODE: "Out of Mind, Out of Sight," season one

KEY RELATIONSHIPS: None. That was the problem.

UNIQUE ATTRIBUTES: Through some combination of quantum physics and supernatural influence, the fact that Marcie was completely ignored by other people at Sunnydale High turned her invisible.

MOST MONSTROUS MOMENT: Marcie would have mutilated Cordelia if Buffy had not stopped her.

CURRENT STATUS: Federal operatives from a covert intelligence agency took Marcie into custody and forced her to become an invisible assassin. Her current whereabouts are, of course, unknown.

At Sunnydale High School, Marcie was a nobody. Even when she could look in the mirror and see her face, she was invisible to everyone around her. When she raised her hand, the teacher didn't see her. When she tried to connect with other students—breaking through her shyness—they didn't even notice she was there.

The situation continued to grow worse, until one day Marcie began to literally fade out of reality. She was still there; flesh and blood, a human being. But she had become truly invisible, and started to violently lash out at those who she blamed for her condition, the most popular kids in school. Marcie attacked baseball player **Mitch Fargo** with his own baseball bat, then spray painted LOOK on his locker. Then she pushed Harmony Kendall down the stairs. Harmony's best friend, and Mitch's girlfriend, was Cordelia Chase, the most popular girl in school. She was an obvious next target.

At first Buffy, Giles, and the others considered the possibility that a ghost might be responsible for the attacks, but Buffy had been bumped into by the invisible girl, and Giles confirmed that ghosts were not solid. Searching the school for some clue, Buffy heard eerie flute music coming from an empty music room.

When Willow searched the Internet for a list of missing kids, they discovered that the most recent one was Marcie Ross, a Sunnydale student none of them knew, but who had played flute in the school band. Buffy investigated, and above the music room, she found the place where Marcie had been hiding, along with her yearbook. Everyone who had signed her yearbook wrote, "Have a nice summer," which the Scooby Gang knew meant that none of the signers had actually known Marcie.

Rupert Giles, the Watcher, theorized that the supernatural influences of the nearby Hellmouth might have skewed reality enough to cause Marcie's condition, but

that was never verified. In fact, the true culprit was quantum mechanics. Eventually, Giles realized that because Marcie was *perceived* as invisible, she *became* invisible. In a line cut from "Out of Mind, Out of Sight" before broadcast, due to length, Giles conjectured, "reality is shaped, even created, by our perception of it."

Driven insane by her condition, Marcie tried to kill Buffy when confronted, and also tried to asphyxiate a teacher, **Ms. Miller,** who had ignored her. Cordelia, who would later become a reluctant part of Buffy's circle of friends, saved the teacher's life, only to see the word LISTEN chalked onto the board by an invisible hand.

Buffy and her friends took it upon themselves to keep Cordelia, about to be crowned May Queen, safe, but Marcie was determined to have her revenge. She played her flute to lure Giles, Willow, and Xander into the boiler room in the school's basement, then slipped out and locked them in—with gas leaking from a broken main. Angel eventually saved them.

Meanwhile, she managed to get the drop on Buffy and Cordelia, knocking them out. They woke to find themselves tied up, her prisoners and faced with the final message: LEARN. Marcie was determined to destroy the thing she thought separated her from Cordelia: Cordy's beauty. She was going to mutilate Cordelia's face.

CORDELIA: "What have you done to my face?"
MARCIE: "Your face. That's what it's all about, isn't it? Your beautiful face. That's what makes you shine just a little bit brighter than the rest of us. We all want what you have. To be noticed. To be remembered. To be seen."
CORDELIA: "What are you doing?"
MARCIE: "I'm fulfilling your fondest wish. I'm gonna give you a face no one will ever forget."
—**"OUT OF MIND, OUT OF SIGHT"**

Buffy managed to stop Marcie from mutilating or killing Cordelia—a moment that was the turning point in the popular girl's relationship to Buffy and her friends. Unfortunately, the Slayer was prevented from helping Marcie further by FBI agents **Doyle** and **Manetti,** who had been trailing Marcie and now took her

into custody, meeting Buffy's inquiries about the commonness of invisibility with silence.

Marcie was taken to an FBI facility and put into a classroom with other invisible people. The teacher asked them to open the textbook in front of them, and it was revealed that they were studying assassination and infiltration.

Marcie Ross's current whereabouts are unknown.

But, then, that's the whole point, isn't it?

XANDER HARRIS (AS AN INVISIBLE PERSON)

"I'd offer my opinion, but you jerks aren't going to hear it anyway. Not that 'didn't go to college boy' is worth listening to."   **—XANDER, IN "FEAR, ITSELF"**

EPISODE (as Invisible Person): "Fear, Itself," season four

UNIQUE ATTRIBUTES (as Invisible Person): None of Xander's friends could see or hear him.

CURRENT STATUS: Xander's "invisibility" was only temporary. He remains one of the Slayer's closest friends and a loyal member of the Scooby Gang.

On Halloween night 1999, Xander attended a Halloween party at the Alpha Delta fraternity house on the UC Sunnydale campus with his girlfriend, Anya, and their friends, including Buffy, Willow, and Oz. Xander had been finding it difficult to adjust to the new status quo in their lives: his friends from high school had all gone on to college, but he had decided not to do so, and was instead living in his parents' basement. Students at UC Sunnydale considered him a "townie." Those things had begun to make him feel as though he was no longer an important part of their circle of friends.

In preparing for the party, a fraternity brother had inadvertently drawn a real magic circle on the floor that would summon Gachnar, a Fear Demon, if the spell were completed (see Demons). When Oz cut himself while setting up musical equipment and bled in the circle, the influence of Gachnar began to take over the house. Halloween decorations came to life. At the party that night, the individual fears of those in the house—including the Scooby Gang—began to manifest themselves in reality. Willow could not control her magic. Oz could not control his transformation into a werewolf and nearly hurt Willow, then ran from her, illustrating a fear they *both* had (and one that would become reality two episodes later).

Xander became invisible, at least to his friends. They could not see or hear him, and thought he had wandered off. He panicked and grew frustrated with the confirmation of the fears that had built up in him since the others began to attend college.

When they all came together again, the effects of those fear manifestations wore off, and Xander became visible to his friends again. Willow discovered the book from which the student who had originally drawn the magic circle had gotten the spell, and they realized what they were up against. Buffy inadvertently completed the spell, calling Gachnar to the earthly plane, but the demon turned out to be only a few inches tall. Its presence made them realize how small and petty many of their fears were.

invisible people in folklore and popular culture

the origins

THE CONCEPT OF INVISIBILITY has been part of the human experience since time began. We've all felt invisible at times—when our hard work at school or the office goes unrewarded or when we wave to an acquaintance across the street and receive no acknowledgment. Invisibility is often forced on individuals, for it is the very nature of humanity to ignore that which we find unpleasant or uncomfortable. The homeless, disabled, and disfigured have always constituted the most invisible segments of the population. Certain religious and tribal customs involve shunning, casting out, or excommunicating those who have somehow violated the moral mandates of the group. These people then become invisible to the group at large, ineligible for benefits as simple as social contact.

The idea of invisibility has sparked creative minds since the earliest writings of the ancient Greeks. Throughout popular culture, myths, and folklore, characters have become invisible through the use of hats, cloaks, rings, and serums, and have used this power for numerous purposes ranging from spying on one's neighbors to stealing hidden treasure and even fighting crime.

In Greek mythology Hades was absolute master of the underworld, the infernal regions where, separated from their bodies, the souls of those who had completed their earthly existence took refuge. Although Hades left the underworld only twice (to abduct his wife, Persephone, and to seek treatment for a wound inflicted by Hercules), he was in possession of a helmet of invisibility.

Although it doesn't appear that Hades used the helmet himself, he did lend it out on two occasions. Hermes used it during a war against destructive giants to slay their leader, Hippolytus. Young Perseus also wore the helmet to defeat the dreaded Gorgon. By rendering himself invisible, he was able to approach the snake-headed monster unseen and cut off her head.

Fairies have always been a prominent part of folklore throughout Europe, particularly in the British Isles. Generally appearing as tiny, humanlike beings with wings, fairies have the power to shapeshift and make themselves invisible at will. Their behavior is notoriously unpredictable and frequently mischevious.

French fairies (fees) are predominantly female and also have the ability to become invisible and to change their shape. The fees are generally good, but as with all fairies, they are very unpredictable. In Norwegian folklore, the huldrefolk are invisible fairies who live in another dimension behind a veil of invisible vapor.

The Rosicrucians were a secret sect whose roots date back to fifteenth-century Germany and who flourished throughout the fifteenth and sixteenth centuries, practicing healing, occultism, and alchemy. One of the Rosicrucians' beliefs was that it was possible to be rendered invisible through the reawakening of dormant abilities that we all possess. Through special metaphysical and occult teachings, the secret society believed that anyone could become invisible if he or she so desired.

The formation of the familiar Myth

THE BROTHERS GRIMM published three volumes of fairy tales between 1812 and 1822. At least one of thOse tales, "The Twelve Dancing Princesses," featured a cloak of invisibility. A king discovered each morning that his twelve daughters had danced holes in their shoes during the night. He decreed that any man who could determine where his daughters spent their nights would be allowed to marry one and become the next king. One day a poor, wounded soldier received an invisible cloak in exchange for helping an old woman. The soldier presented himself to the king and that night sat with the twelve princesses. He pretended to be asleep and when the princesses left their room by a secret exit, he donned the cloak and followed. He spent the next three nights dancing in an underground castle with the princesses and their dates, always being sure to arrive home ahead of them. He made his report to the king, was granted the eldest princess's hand in marriage, and lived happily ever after.

From Myth to Fiction

PERHAPS THE MOST FAMOUS bit of fiction involving invisibility is H. G. Wells' 1897 novel *The Invisible Man*. This terrifying story concerns obscure scientist Hawley Griffin, who invents a formula that will render the skin, bone, and blood invisible. The scientist uses himself as a guinea pig and achieves invisibility with a single injection. Unfortunately, he is unable to reverse the process, and the same formula that made him invisible slowly drives him murderously insane as he desperately searches for a cure.

Another infamous fictional character, the Shadow, was introduced to readers of pulp fiction in the spring of 1931 by publishers Street and Smith. Created by Walter B. Gibson—a newspaperman and magician—the Shadow was a mysterious crime fighter who used hypnotic powers to make himself invisible and defeat such colorful villains as the Condor, Shi Wan Khan, and the Wizard of Crime. Although the pulp magazine adventures were popular throughout the 1930s and 1940s, the Shadow received most of his notoriety through radio dramas in the 1930s.

In 1933 Universal Pictures released the movie version of Wells' *The Invisible Man,* a very faithful adaptation. Directed by the great James Whale (*Bride of Frankenstein*), the film made a star of Claude Rains, even though in the role of scientist Jack Griffin, he was either wrapped in bandages or invisible throughout most of the action. One of Universal's monster classics, the invisibility effects are really quite amazing and stand up to the scrutiny of today's movie audiences used to high-tech effects.

Fantasy grand master J. R. R. Tolkien wrote his classic tale *The Hobbit* in 1937, following the adventures of Bilbo Baggins and his quest for lost treasure under the guidance of Gandalf the wizard (see Magic Users). In one particular escapade, Bilbo comes upon a small metal ring that renders its wearer invisible. Three times the Ring saves Bilbo and his companions and eventually helps him save the day and end their quest.

In 1940 Universal released a sequel, *The Invisible Man Returns,* starring horror great Vincent Price as Jack Griffin's brother, who has been wrongly accused of murder. He uses Jack's serum to render himself invisible and escapes prison to track down the real killer before the drug coursing through his veins drives him insane. Although not as eerily effective as the original, it's still a very entertaining addition to the Universal horror stables. Universal continued its series with the release of *The Invisible Man's Revenge* in 1944.

In 1948 Universal Pictures released the classic *Abbott and Costello Meet Frankenstein*. This spine-tingling comedy had the comic duo battling all manner of supernatural creatures as Dracula tries to transfer Costello's brain into the Frankenstein monster's head. After a battle royale with both of those monsters, and the Wolf Man as well, Bud and Lou manage to reach a rowboat and hurry away from the castle, only to find themselves accompanied by a cigar-smoking, Vincent Price–voiced invisible man in the hilarious final scene.

Universal released *Abbott and Costello Meet the Invisible Man* in 1951. In this outing the comedy team play private investigators who are hired by a prizefighter to clear him of a murder charge. To hide from the police (a familiar Universal theme), the prizefighter injects himself with a serum that causes invisibility. The fun really starts when Costello gets into the ring and appears to knock out the champ.

In 1954 and 1955, Tolkien published *The Lord of the Rings,* with *The Fellowship of the Ring* trilogy that continues the adventures of the hobbits in Middle-earth. As the trilogy opens, Bilbo Baggins has passed the Ring down to his nephew, Frodo. Gandalf the wizard visits Frodo and tells him he must destroy it before it can be taken by the evil Sauron. The trilogy follows Frodo's adventures as he heads for Mount Doom to drop the Ring into the fires of a great volcano.

Also in 1955 DC Comics' *Detective Comics* #225 introduced readers to J'onn J'onzz, the Martian Manhunter. Accidentally transported to earth by a scientist attempting to communicate with Mars, J'onzz possessed certain powers including super strength, shapeshifting, telepathy, the ability to fly, and the ability to render himself invisible. Now trapped on earth, J'onn joined forces with other heroes of the age. Along with Superman, Batman, Green Lantern, and Wonder Woman, J'onn was a founding member of the Justice League of America, whose first adventure appeared in DC's *Brave and the Bold* #28 in 1960.

The cult-favorite 1956 MGM film *Forbidden Planet*, scripted by Cyril Hume, was inspired by Shakespeare's *The Tempest*. In 2200 a spaceship from Earth lands on the planet Altair II and is attacked by an invisible monster whose silhouette is visible only when it touches the ship's outer force field. It is revealed in the course of the film that a scientist is conducting experiments with alien technology that has caused his id to take on a bestial life all its own and to go on a rampage.

Republic Pictures' 1958 *Fiend Without a Face* introduced movie audiences to a new and terrifying invisible threat. In this monster flick a scientist accidentally creates one of the more memorable and disturbing of the 1950s movie monsters. The creatures are invisible for a large portion of the film, but that doesn't prevent them from wreaking havoc on a Canadian Air Force base and sucking the brains out of their victims. The monsters, revealed at the end of the movie with a blast of radiation, resemble hideous throbbing brains with tentacle-like spinal cords for tails.

The year 1957 also saw the release of MGM's *The Invisible Boy,* about a young genius who reassembles a previously destroyed robot (Robbie the Robot, a character that had previously appeared in *Forbidden Planet*). The robot is so thankful that he turns the boy invisible, then falls under the control of a power-hungry monster computer, UNIVAC, as the boy, still invisible, frantically tries to prevent the mad machine from taking over the world. It is a refreshing take on the invisible man theme with some wonderful comedic moments and special effects.

C. S. Lewis' series of novels, the Chronicles of Narnia, was published throughout the 1950s. The third book, *The Voyage of the Dawn Treader,* continues the adventures of Edmund and Lucy Pevensie in the fictional land of Narnia. In one tale, they land on an island populated by invisible creatures, servants of a great wizard who cast a spell of invisibility on themselves to hide their ugliness.

Comic books continued the invisible theme throughout the 1960s, beginning with the introduction of the Invisible Kid as a member of the futuristic Legion of Superheroes in DC's *Action Comics* #267 (1960).

In 1961 comic book legends Stan Lee and Jack Kirby created the most famous invisible character in the history of comic books when the Invisible Girl made her first appearance in Marvel Comics' *Fantastic Four* #1. Susan Storm was part of a team testing an experimental starship when cosmic rays mutated their bodies and Susan gained the power to create force fields around herself and others, as well as the ability to render herself invisible. She took on the code name Invisible Girl, and the foursome formed the team of adventurers known as the Fantastic Four.

Sue Storm was briefly turned into a villain by the villainous Psycho Man during a fight in *Fantastic Four* #285. Wielding enormous power, she called herself Malice until her teammates were able to restore her true personality. It was following this misadventure that she realized how powerful she actually was. As a result of that coming of age, she changed her code name to the Invisible Woman.

DC Comics' *Showcase* #23 (1963) featured Hal Jordan as the Green Lantern, dealing with a truly awesome threat. Through a bizarre type of mind over matter a soft-spoken scientist called forth from his own subconscious an entity called the Invisible Destroyer. Feeding on radiation, the monster attempts to detonate an atomic bomb off the coast of California but is destroyed by the Green Lantern and his power ring.

The popular ABC-TV prime-time cartoon *Jonny Quest* ran from 1964 to 1965. The episode "The Invisible Monster" featured a creature composed of pure electrical energy, brought to life by Dr. Isaiah Norman in an experiment gone horribly wrong.

The first issue of Tower Comics' *T.H.U.N.D.E.R. Agents* (1965) introduced an android named Noman. Noman has the brain signature of Professor Dunn, a brilliant scientist who, on the verge of death, agrees to transfer his brain pattern to the android's body so he might continue his work for T.H.U.N.D.E.R. Able to transfer his consciousness to other android bodies hidden around the world, Noman also has a cloak that can impart total invisibility with the flick of a switch.

The Hanna-Barbera cartoon *Space Ghost* ran on CBS from 1966 to 1968. Created by Alex Toth, Space Ghost was an intergalactic police officer based on Ghost Planet. Dressed in a white bodysuit with black hood and yellow cape, the crimefighter's power came from his red utility belt and wristbands. Able to fly, teleport, and survive under water and in space, Space Ghost could also render himself invisible. His ship, the *Phantom Cruiser,* was endowed with many secret weapons, including the power to become invisible. Space Ghost can now be seen hosting *Space*

Ghost Coast to Coast, a comedy talk show mixing animation and live-action guests that still runs on the Cartoon Network.

Kurt Russell was one of the many actors to be part of the Walt Disney family of teen stars. *Now You See Him, Now You Don't* (1972) was a sequel to Disney's 1970 hit *The Computer Wore Tennis Shoes* and starred Russell as a college student who accidentally discovers a formula for invisibility.

The third episode of ABC-TV's *Kolchak: The Night Stalker* series (1974), titled "They Have Been, They Are, They Will Be . . . ," had intrepid reporter of the bizarre Carl Kolchak involved with a menace revealed to be an invisible alien that stopped on Earth to repair its craft and feed on the bone marrow of warm-blooded animals. NBC-TV returned to the classic formula in 1975 with the short-lived series *The Invisible Man*. David McCallum (*The Man from U.N.C.L.E.*) starred as invisible scientist Daniel Westin.

A new Invisible Kid—Jacques Foccart of Earth—joined the Legion in *The Legion of Super-Heroes Annual* #1 (DC Comics, 1982) and still serves as a member of its Espionage Squad.

The Greek legend of Perseus and Andromeda was brought to the screen in 1981 with United Artists/MGM's *Clash of the Titans*. In the film, as in the legend, Perseus uses a magical helmet that confers invisibility upon him, and aids him not only in winning the hand of his lady love, Andromeda, but also in capturing the winged horse, Pegasus. The film features fabulous creatures of myth created by legendary special effects wizard Ray Harryhausen.

H. F. Saint's 1982 novel *Memoirs of an Invisible Man* was about a man who becomes invisible following a nuclear accident in a secret, American government research facility. The book focuses on the day-to-day difficulties of being invisible as the character tries to stay one step ahead of an unnamed U.S. government agency that wants to "study" him. The novel served as the basis for the 1992 Warner Brothers picture of the same name directed by John Carpenter and starring Chevy Chase.

A new twist was put on the invisibility theme with *Predator* (Twentieth Century Fox, 1987), directed by John McTiernan and starring Arnold Schwarzenegger. A team of government mercenaries on a rescue mission in Central America run into an intergalactic big-game hunter looking for human trophies. The Predator uses advanced alien technology to render itself invisible so that it can effectively stalk and hunt its prey.

The success of *Predator* led to the 1990 sequel *Predator 2*, starring Danny Glover and Gary Busey (and minus Schwarzenegger). Glover plays a tough Los Angeles cop who pits his skills against the invisible aliens hunting the mean streets of L.A. during a heat wave.

Sleepwalkers (Columbia/TriStar 1992), which boasts an original screenplay by horror master Stephen King, is the story of two shapeshifting monsters, mother and son, who have assimilated themselves into normal society while feeding off the souls of virgins. In addition to being shapeshifters, the strange, hairless catlike creatures also have the ability to make themselves and objects invisible.

Universal Studios brought the famous pulp magazine crimefighter and old radio sensation the Shadow to the big screen in the eponymous feature in 1994. Alec Baldwin played Lamont Cranston, a wealthy playboy who, as the Shadow, has the ability to cloud men's minds so they cannot see him. In this adventure the Shadow must defeat the villainous Shi Wan Khan, a descendant of Genghis Khan, who has similar mind-clouding abilities and wants to take over the world using a pre–World War II nuclear bomb.

Writer Jeff Mariotte and artist John Cassaday's comic-book masterpiece of the Old West, *Desperadoes* (Homage Comics, 1997) tells the story of four outlaws in pursuit of a serial killer terrorizing the New Mexico territory in 1879. The killer, Leander Peik, is not a run-of-the-mill psychopath—he has the nasty tendency to target innocent women with half-breed children. Peik murders the children, removes their skins, and bathes in their blood. By doing this, he gains amazing strength and the power to become invisible to his enemies.

Also in 1997, America's Best Comics began to publish one of the most unusual titles in some time, *The League of Extraordinary Gentlemen,* written by comics legend Alan Moore (*Watchmen*) and illustrated by Kevin O'Neill. It is a superhero team book, but with a difference. Rather than the usual gaudily clad musclemen, this comic presents a team made up of famous characters from Victorian literature, such as Wilhelmina Murray (Jonathan Harker's fiancée from *Dracula*), Captain Nemo (from *20,000 Leagues Under the Sea*), Alan Quartermain (from *King Solomon's Mines*), Dr. Jekyll and Mr. Hyde, and Hawley Griffin, the scientist from H. G. Wells' *The Invisible Man*.

The cloak of invisibility returned to children's literature in J. K. Rowling's extraordinarily popular *Harry Potter and the Sorcerer's Stone* (1998). Young wizard-in-training Harry Potter receives the gray cloak as a Christmas gift, which comes in quite handy during his many adventures.

Universal's 1999 movie *Mystery Men* was based on comic-book characters created by Bob Burden, which made their first appearance in *Flaming Carrot* #16 and #17, published by Aardvark-Vanheim in 1987. The story centers around a group of misfit superheroes, among them Invisible Boy, amusingly played by Nickelodeon's Kel Mitchell. After years of being overlooked and ignored, he has developed the ability to become invisible . . . but only when no one's looking.

The power of invisibility will be carried on into the twenty-first century. *The Hollow Man*, currently in production in Hollywood, is directed by Paul Verhoeven of *Total Recall* and *Starship Troopers* fame and stars Kevin Bacon and Elisabeth Shue. As of this writing, the script appears to follow the usual invisible formula, i.e., a scientist discovers way to make people invisible and tests it on himself.

More promising may be the Sci-Fi Channel's upcoming new series, *Invisible Man*. Scheduled for a June 2000 premiere, the series will star Vincent Ventresca as a thief recruited for a secret government experiment that will turn him . . . well, *you* know.

Buffy the Vampire Slayer

FAITH AND THE HUMAN MONSTER

JOYCE: "Faith, why do you think she's like that?"

FAITH: "Oh, you know, she's a nut job."

JOYCE: "I just don't understand what could drive a person to that kind of behavior."

FAITH: "How do you know she got drove? Maybe she just likes being that way."

—AFTER FAITH HAS SWITCHED BODIES WITH BUFFY, IN "WHO ARE YOU"

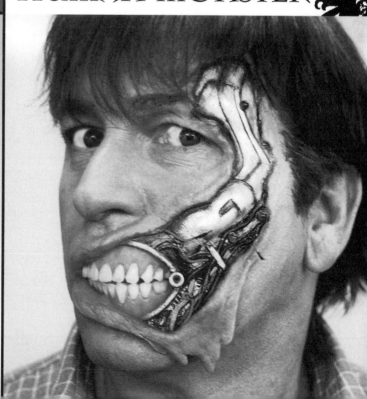

VAMPIRES, ZOMBIES, WEREWOLVES . . . those are monsters. It has always been simple for human society to take a step back, look at those hideous mythical creatures, and label them as such. As master horror novelist Stephen King once put it, "I'm okay, you're okay, but ughh, look at that!"

Over the course of this massive undertaking, however, we have been forced to create our own parameters for the definition of the word *monster.* Within the Magic Users chapter, for instance, we have included characters like Willow Rosenberg and Amy Madison, who are noble and good. Certainly, they are not monstrous in the same way that vampires and werewolves are.

But they *are* more than human. They have powers beyond humanity's understanding. Many people would find such a thing frightening, even monstrous. In the past, scientific advancements a large portion of the population could not understand might have been considered magical or evil. Even in modern times, such scientific "magic" as cloning gives humanity a pause and *some* a shudder.

Thus under the heading of "the human monster" we could include Willow, Amy, Tara, and other magic users. By extension, our definition also encompasses the Slayer. As we stated at the outset, based on those parameters Buffy herself readily fits the bill. She is far more than human, with abilities beyond what our species is capable of, or even has the capacity to understand.

For that matter, the same would be true of Kendra.

Or Faith.

TARA: "You're like, cool monster fighter."
WILLOW: "Well, technically, Faith's not a monster, and as for fighting? I'd be lucky if I
bruise her fist with my face."   —**"THIS YEAR'S GIRL"**

Witches, Slayers, sorcerers—all are both human and, by our definition, monsters. Yet there are enough monstrosities to examine in human society without including even the faintest trace of the supernatural.

True human monsters are, sadly, all around us. We see them each night on the news. We read about them in our history books and mourn the victims of their atrocities. Jeffrey Dahmer. Jack the Ripper. Adolf Hitler. Yet human monstrosity is not limited to murder and rape. The word *monster* applies to molesters and abusers, drug-trade predators, the heartless and shallow, and even the bitter, belittling monsters that exist in all walks of life. There are so many people whose behavior is unnatural or inhuman that we need go no further to find our monsters. We don't really need vampires or werewolves.

Or do we?

In a world where such real, visceral horrors are so disturbingly commonplace, the horrors on the screen or page may be more comforting than terrifying. We can close the book. We can turn off the television when the show is over. We have *control*. But in the real world, the show is never over. Nothing is more disturbing or more monstrous than that.

The brilliance of *Buffy the Vampire Slayer* is not its ingenious mythology, wonderful as it may be. Rather, it is the way the menacing creatures of legend mirror the monsters that mere human beings must face each day. Despite its plethora of ghosts and ghouls and things that go bump in the night, the series has also had its share of real human monsters.

Some examples to consider:

+ Buffy's old friend **Billy Fordham** in "Lie to Me." Dying of a brain tumor, he purposefully betrayed her, attempting to help Spike capture her in exchange for eternal life.

+ The **Kiddie League baseball coach** of "Nightmares." So brutal and shallow was the man that he beat twelve-year-old Billy Palmer into a coma simply because he blamed the boy for the loss of a baseball game.

+ **Ted Buchanan,** the mad scientist (from "Ted") who built a psychotically conservative robot to replace himself when his own death seemed imminent.

+ **Frawley, Frederick,** and **Hans,** the human assassins who participated in Slayerfest '98 ("Homecoming") and were willing to kill high school girls for money.

+ **Tucker,** the Sunnydale High student who sicced **Hellhounds** on the school prom out of nothing but spite. ("The Prom")

+ **Coach Marin** and **Nurse Greenleigh** of "Go Fish." Echoing "Nightmares," they endangered the lives of the members of the swim team in hopes of improving the team's chances. Later, Coach Marin turned to murder to protect himself.

+ **The lunch lady** in "Earshot." Over time, she became so fed up with her lot in life that she attempted to put rat poison in the cafeteria food at Sunnydale High.

+ "The Pack." Before they were possessed by primal spirits, **Kyle, Tor, Rhonda,** and **Heidi** were already mean-spirited bullies.

+ The demon-worshiping fraternity brothers in "Reptile Boy," who were willing to sacrifice the lives of others for their own material gain.

+ Modern-day Frankenstein **Eric Gittleson** in "Some Assembly Required," who helped resurrect a friend's dead brother and was later willing to kill to create a "bride" for monstrous Daryl Epps.

At least Chris Epps refused to do more than rob graves, a heinous act in itself.

✦ **Pete Clarner,** the jealous boyfriend whose insecurity led him to create a serum that altered him physically and emotionally, and made him not merely jealous, but abusive and, later, homicidal. ("Beauty and the Beasts")

✦ **Gwendolyn Post,** the evil, power-hungry ex-Watcher of "Revelations," bent on acquiring the magic inherent in the demonic Glove of Myhnegon and willing to kill to get it.

✦ **Maggie Walsh,** the director of the Initiative, who used her position to conduct secret experiments on demons and other creatures, created the hybrid demon named Adam, chemically enhanced her operatives without their knowledge, and was willing to kill to keep her activities a secret. (Though she did, eventually, get her due.)

✦ **Jack,** the bitter bartender of "Beer Bad," who was tired of being condescended to by smug college students, so he served them a specially brewed beer that reverted them to cavemen.

People. Just people. The simplicity of that fact is in many ways more disturbing than any supernatural creature could be. And the simpler the evil, the more insidious.

"I've always been afraid of witches," says *Buffy* creator Joss Whedon. "Scary old ladies. The seminal movie that scared the shit out of me was *Horror Hotel*, and it's not monsters. It's just people in cowls and foggy old graveyards, chanting. For me, that's just the scariest anything needs to be. People are scarier than creatures every time out of the gate. Creatures are fun."

Co-producer Jane Espenson agrees. She reflects upon "Earshot," an episode she wrote, which included both the homicidal lunch lady and suicidal geek Jonathan.

"You have the human monster [represented by] the lunch lady, but in Jonathan's behavior, too. Bringing a gun to school, whether he was going to shoot everyone else or himself, was an act of terrible anger and aggression. Both of those things are human monstrosities."

To David Greenwalt, the epitome of the human monster on Buffy is Ted Buchanan, from the second season episode "Ted." *Wait a minute*, you'll say. *Ted was a robot!* True, but the robot was built to replicate exactly the original Ted Buchanan, a mad scientist whose machine self went on to murder the human Ted's wife and three others after the scientist passed on.

"Buffy behaves a little bit like a snotty adolescent to Mom's new boyfriend, who seems perfectly nice," says Greenwalt, who co-wrote the episode with Joss Whedon. "But she's actually right about him. What's scary about Ted is his very blandness; his almost religious, 'everything's going to be okay, I'm in control, Daddy's home' [attitude]. The soft and sweet side of him is what is so scary; that *other* people don't see that this is a monster. There are a million families in America like that, where Mom and Dad look so good on the outside and go to church on Sunday, but you get inside that house and it's . . . terrifying, because Dad is an abusive totalitarian."

Greenwalt also notes that while working on the episode "We definitely looked at the movie *The Stepfather*." That 1987 thriller, which starred Terry O'Quinn in the brutal title role, offers a harrowing example of the human monster in a serial killer who keeps marrying single mothers in search of the perfect family, only to slaughter them upon becoming disappointed.

Yet that is only one among millions of examples of the human monster that could be drawn from history, folklore, legend, and popular culture. Any attempt to trace such representations would reach back beyond the Old Testament of the Bible and forward to include every newscast, and the vast majority of popular entertainment today.

Sad to say, there are far too many human monsters.

However, it would be a grave error to paint such real people and fictional characters as black and white or one-dimensional. For there is another major difference between real human monstrosities and supernatural or mythical ones.

Abnormal brain chemistry may account for certain psychopathic and sociopathic behavior, but most human monsters are not born that way; they are made into what they are by circumstance, by experience and example. Some are merely people who are lost in their lives, and are eventually surprised to find that they have become monsters. That does not mean that such individuals are not still to be reviled for their actions, but nor does it mean we can ignore the circumstances that transformed them.

On *Buffy the Vampire Slayer*, there is no better example of such a tragic transformation than Faith. Though she is also a supernatural being and thus, by our definition, a "monster," we will deal here with her more as a monster on the human level.

FAITH

FIRST APPEARANCE: "Faith, Hope, and Trick," season three

OTHER EPISODES: season three: "Beauty and the Beasts," "Homecoming," "Revelations," "Amends," "The Zeppo," "Bad Girls," "Consequences," "Doppelgangland," "Enemies," "Choices," "Graduation Day, Parts One and Two"; season four: "This Year's Girl" and "Who Are You"

KEY RELATIONSHIPS: Faith kept emotionally distant from the Slayer's circle, but Giles (and later, Wesley) served as her interim Watcher. She was close to Buffy for a while, but ultimately betrayed her. Angel tried in vain to get through to Faith, when they were both in Sunnydale. While working for the evil Mayor, Faith developed a surrogate father-daughter relationship with him. Though Faith did not really date while in Sunnydale, she did have a one-night stand with Xander.

UNIQUE ATTRIBUTES: Faith is an activated Slayer, giving her increased strength, agility, and stamina. She is a well-trained fighter and has the ability to heal rapidly. Though Faith has not revealed any prophetic dreams as of yet, we can assume that as a Slayer, she may develop this talent (as Buffy has demonstrated).

MOST MONSTROUS MOMENT: During patrol with Buffy, Faith accidentally murdered a human, the deputy mayor…and didn't feel remorse.

CURRENT STATUS: After leaving Sunnydale, Faith was last seen in jail in Los Angeles.

One of the basic tenets of *Buffy*'s mythology dictates that when one Slayer dies, another is called. In the first-season finale "Prophecy Girl," Buffy died by drowning, albeit briefly, before being given CPR by Xander and resuscitated. Despite the short-lived nature of her demise, the mystical forces that call a Slayer were set in motion.

GILES: "It seems, that somehow, another Slayer has been sent to Sunnydale."
WILLOW: "Is that even possible? I mean, two Slayers at the same time?"
GILES: "Not that I know of. The new Slayer is only called after the previous Slayer has died—Good lord…You *were* dead, Buffy."
BUFFY: "I was only gone for a minute."

GILES: "Clearly, it doesn't matter how long you were gone. You were physically dead, causing the activation of the next Slayer."

KENDRA: "She...died?"

BUFFY: "Just a *little*."

—"WHAT'S MY LINE? PART TWO"

As a result a second Slayer, Kendra, came to Sunnydale during the series's second season, only to be abruptly dispatched by Drusilla in that season's two-part finale, "Becoming."

Upon Kendra's death, yet another Slayer was activated.

Her name is Faith.

The early months of her time as a Slayer are still shrouded in mystery. Her accent indicates that Faith is from the Boston area, where she lived a miserable existence with her alcoholic mother. During her first appearance in season three's "Faith, Hope, and Trick," certain things were revealed. In her brief time as Slayer she was apparently drawn to Missouri with her Watcher to face Kakistos, a very old vampire who was preying on a community there.

During the conflict, Kakistos horribly murdered Faith's Watcher.

BUFFY: "He killed [your Watcher], didn't he."

FAITH: "They don't have a word for what he did to her."   —"FAITH, HOPE, AND TRICK"

She struck Kakistos in the face with an ax before fleeing for Sunnydale to hook up with Buffy, whom her deceased Watcher had told her about. Upon her arrival, however, she did not give a true account of what had happened, perhaps embarrassed by her actions. Eventually, of course, the truth was revealed, and with Buffy's encouragement, Faith found the courage to fight and destroy Kakistos (see Vampires).

For a time, all seemed well. Faith had no interest in attending Sunnydale High School, but the Watchers Council allowed her to stay in Sunnydale with Rupert Giles operating as Watcher for both Slayers. It quickly became apparent that Faith was Buffy's polar opposite, outrageous and visceral enough to make Buffy seem conservative by comparison. Yet somehow the girls began to get along, developing an almost sisterly camaraderie and competitiveness.

But Faith could not compete. Sunnydale was Buffy's town. Giles was Buffy's Watcher. Buffy had a home and a mother and friends and a boyfriend, and Faith had none of those things. Still, she managed to sublimate her envy and loneliness for a time.

Then came the turning-point episode "Revelations," in which Faith discovered that Buffy had been hiding Angel's return from the demon dimensions from everyone. In the same episode, Gwendolyn Post arrived to take up duties as Faith's Watcher, only to have it revealed that she was not sent for Faith at all, but had come for her own sinister purpose (as previously noted).

Twice in one episode this tragic figure, who met every disappointment with bluster and bravado to hide her real feelings, felt betrayed by people she trusted.

Faith seduced Xander in "The Zeppo," an act that may have been a way for her to try to get some of what Buffy has for herself, and to feel less lonely. Buffy attempted to reach out to her, and the two Slayers seemed to be growing close once more. Faith's wildcat attitudes had even begun to influence Buffy by the "Bad Girls" episode, which also introduced Wesley Wyndam-Pryce, the new Watcher appointed by the Council to take charge of both girls.

When Faith accidentally killed a human being, Allan Finch (the deputy mayor of the demonic mayor of Sunnydale), and showed no remorse over it, her life was altered forever. She had taken a step into the darkness that she would find it nearly impossible to reverse. Faith betrayed Buffy by lying to Giles, telling him that Buffy had killed the man.

Buffy made many attempts to reconcile with Faith, hoping that she would be able to make the other Slayer realize the horror of what she had done. But Faith had already begun a slide into a life of evil that Buffy could not stop. In the very next episode, "Consequences," Faith offered her services to the Mayor, who had been preparing for a century for an Ascension during which he would become a pure demon the likes of which were rarely seen on earth (see Demons).

In "Enemies," Faith and the Mayor hatched a plan to steal Angel's soul again so that he would destroy Buffy. First, Faith attempted to seduce him, knowing that sex would be a catalyst to him losing his soul. When he rebuffed her advances, the Mayor called upon a nonhuman, supernatural shaman from another realm to rob Angel of his soul. Faith splashed Angel with blood, the Shaman chanted, and Angel appeared to become the evil Angelus once again.

Soon it was revealed that though Angel seemed evil, it was only a ploy he, Buffy, and Giles had concocted to get Faith to reveal the Mayor's plans and her own duplicity. Giles knew the Shaman, and the being owed him a favor from a previous interaction; the Shaman conspired with them to fake Angel's metamorphosis.

From that point on Buffy and Faith were enemies indeed, though Buffy still wanted to find a way to rehabilitate her.

Throughout her relationship with the Mayor, Faith managed to get some of what she was missing in her life. He quickly became a father figure to her, even speaking to her in Ward Cleaver-esque paternal tones.

> **MAYOR:** "We'll keep your old place, in case you need to see your friends there. But from now on—"
> [Faith has run to the bed, is jumping up and down on it.]
> **MAYOR:** "Shoes! Shoes!"
> [She jumps off, landing in front of him.]
> **FAITH:** "Thanks, Sugardaddy—"
> **MAYOR:** "Oh! Faith. I don't find that sort of thing amusing. I'm a family man. Now. Let's kill your little friend."`   —**"DOPPELGANGLAND"**

He even gave her gifts, including a new apartment and a hunting knife she cherished. This not only assuaged her feelings of loneliness, but inspired in her a desperate loyalty, despite the man's evil nature. As far as Faith could tell, the Mayor was the only one who cared about her. She would not betray him.

In "Choices," an unrepentant Faith caught Willow breaking into the Mayor's office in an attempt to discover more about his planned Ascension. Willow was held captive, but was later traded back to Buffy and her friends for the Box of Gavrok, which the Mayor needed for his Ascension. In the ensuing battle with both the Mayor and the creatures of the box, Faith was forced to leave her precious knife behind.

As the Mayor's Ascension approached with the two-part season finale "Graduation Day," he was desperate to find a way to draw Buffy's attention away from that event, and

had Faith poison Angel. The only antidote was for Angel to drink the blood of a Slayer. Finally, Buffy gave up hope of redeeming Faith and went hunting for her, planning to "feed" her to Angel. Buffy was winning the fight, and stabbed the villainous Slayer with her own knife, but a badly wounded Faith escaped. Faith lapsed into a coma and was hospitalized, and Buffy was forced to give her own blood to Angel. She ended up in the hospital not far from her former friend. With Buffy unconscious and Faith comatose, the two Slayers somehow touched minds. Buffy found a changed Faith. "It's my head. Lotta new stuff," as Faith put it. For her part, Faith gave Buffy some of her strength so that she might carry on the fight against the Mayor, as well as the key to his destruction.

> "You wanna know the deal? Human weakness. It never goes away. Even his."
> —FAITH, IN BUFFY'S DREAM, IN "GRADUATION DAY, PART TWO"

At last, the lonely, tragic girl had found a kind of redemption.

Subsequent to the Mayor's defeat, the comatose Faith was hospitalized in Sunnydale. In the fourth-season episode "This Year's Girl," she awoke from that coma.

Buffy the Vampire Slayer's executive story editor Douglas Petrie—who wrote "This Year's Girl" and three of the previous Faith-related episodes ("Revelations," "Bad Girls," and "Enemies")—was happy to have another chance to work with the character.

"I connected with Faith early on. I love that character. She's totally tragic," Petrie says. "The whole key to Faith is that she's in pain. If you took that away, she would be a monster. But she's so lonely and so desperate, and all her toughness comes out of trying to cover that. That's what real monsters are made of. No one thinks they're really a monster.

"I wrote three episodes with Faith last year. You've always got a carrot you can dangle in front of her. Mrs. Post is the mother she never had. Buffy and her friends

are the best friends she never had. The Mayor is the dad she never had. So she's always looking for a family and always coming up short and making these horrible choices, and it drove her insane. Plus I think she was missing a couple of screws to begin with. 'If you don't love me, you will fear me,' is kind of her m.o. She's not a stable girl, but a fun one.

"Her name is wildly ironic. She's the most faithless character we've got. She doesn't trust herself, or anyone around her. We try to do that with a lot of our monsters. It's much more fun if you look at it from their point of view."

In "This Year's Girl," after waking from her coma, Faith found Sunnydale drastically changed. The Mayor, her mentor, father figure, and benefactor, was dead. Angel was living in Los Angeles. Buffy was in a relationship with Riley. Reeling, Faith found herself on the run from both the police (for the murder of the mayoral aide she killed in "Bad Girls") and operatives of the Watchers Council. Then she discovered that the Mayor had left her a contingency plan in the event of his defeat and demise— a device called a Katra, which would switch her mind and spirit with Buffy's, placing the two Slayers in each other's bodies.

Faith implemented the body switch. In Faith's body, Buffy was arrested by the police and then taken into custody by the Council operatives. During that time, Faith (in Buffy's body) impersonated her. While at first she was her usual, cruel self, now that she was actually seeing the world with Buffy's eyes, she slowly began to see herself differently. Buffy's mother and friends loved her, and thought Faith a dangerous, even evil, psychopath. As Buffy, Faith had sex with Riley, who professed his love to her while believing she was Buffy.

All of those things worked on Faith's mind, disturbing her own certainty that she was evil. She used Joyce Summers's credit card to buy herself a plane ticket out of the country. While at the airport (in the second installment of this two-part story, "Who Are You"), however, she saw a news report about hostages being held in a church by people she knew were vampires.

Something had happened to Faith. She planned to leave, but somehow, she found herself drawn to that church. Now that she had been living Buffy's life, she felt somehow driven to heroic deeds that accompanied that persona. Faith herself did not seem to understand what she was doing. It soon became clearer, however. Buffy had escaped from the custody of the Council operatives. But when Buffy arrived at the church (still wearing Faith's body), Faith seemed to lose track of her own identity. The lines between them, at least in Faith's mind, began to blur.

"You think I'm afraid of you? You're nothing!" Faith screamed at Buffy, and by extension, at herself. "You're disgusting! A useless, murdering bitch!"

Buffy quickly used the new Katra that Willow and Tara had magically created to return the Slayers to their rightful bodies. Faith pushed Buffy away and fled, her mind in turmoil. She had seen herself with the eyes of others, and in living Buffy's life, had seen what she might have had if things were different.

Shortly thereafter she went to Los Angeles (in two episodes of *Angel*, "Five by Five" and "Sanctuary") where she attempted to begin a new life in typical brutal fashion. Soon she was engaged by the shady law firm Wolfram and Hart to kill Angel, and gleefully accepted the assignment. When the moment came, however, she found herself unable to kill him. Angel reasoned with her, forced her to look inward at her own intentions, and Faith crumbled into his arms in tears, redeemed at last.

The last shot of "Sanctuary" is of Faith, calmly sitting in an L.A. jail cell, having surrendered to the police.

As evidenced by the remarkable story of damnation and redemption that Faith has suffered through, human monsters can change. Some can break the cycle of their own cruel and even evil behavior. But that is no simple task. After all that she has done, Faith's redemption is by no means complete. Nor are the issues that drove her to her monstrous behavior resolved.

Though we have extended the definition of *monster* for the purposes of this book to include beings created or influenced by the supernatural, in the end, we return to the simpler definition. As a vampire, Angel is a monster. As a werewolf, so is Oz. As the Slayer, Faith has abilities that are superhuman. Monsters.

But true monstrosity is, in the end, defined by human behavior. *Buffy the Vampire Slayer* has shown, time and again, that monsters can find their redemption.

Ya gotta have Faith.